ARCHAEOLOGICAL INVESTIGATIONS IN THE LOWER MOTAGUA VALLEY, IZABAL, GUATEMALA: A STUDY IN MONUMENTAL SITE FUNCTION AND INTERACTION

University Museum Monograph 80

QUIRIGUA REPORTS
Robert J. Sharer, General Editor
VOLUME III

ARCHAEOLOGICAL INVESTIGATIONS IN THE LOWER MOTAGUA VALLEY, IZABAL, GUATEMALA: A STUDY IN MONUMENTAL SITE FUNCTION AND INTERACTION

Edward Mark Schortman

THE
UNIVERSITY
MUSEUM
of Archaeology and Anthropology

Published by

THE UNIVERSITY MUSEUM
University of Pennsylvania
Philadelphia
1993

Design, editing, production
  Publications, The University Museum

Printing
  Science Press
  Ephrata, Pennsylvania

Library of Congress Cataloging-in-Publication Data
Schortman, Edward M.
    Archaeological investigations in the lower Motagua Valley, Izabal,
Guatemala: a study in monumental site function and interaction /
Edward Mark Schortman.
        p.   cm.—(Quirigua reports; v. 3)   (University Museum
monograph; 80)
    Revision of thesis (Ph. D.)—University of Pennsylvania, 1982.
    Includes bibliographical references (p.   ) and index.
    ISBN 0-924171-19-7
    1. Quiriguá Site (Guatemala)   2. Mayas—Architecture.   3. Mayas—
Land tenure.   4. Mayas—City planning.   5. Land settlement
patterns—Guatemala—Izabal (Dept.)   6. Archaeological surveying—
Guatemala—Izabal (Dept.)   7. Izabal (Guatemala: Dept.)—
Antiquities.   I. Title.   II. Series.   III. Series: University
Museum monograph; 80.
    F1435.1.Q8Q57   vol. 3
    972.81'31—dc20   92-44440
                                                               CIP

Table of Contents

List of Figures

List of Tables

Preface

This report on the investigations of the Quirigua Archaeological Project (QAP) within the lower Motagua valley (LMV) northeast of the site of Quirigua was originally written as the author's dissertation for the Anthropology Department of the University of Pennsylvania. The writing of that dissertation concluded in late 1982, with the inevitable result that many of my original interpretations and conclusions now seem embarrassingly dated. In preparing this monograph for publication in the Quirigua Reports (QR) series I have, therefore, rewritten and updated most of my earlier chapters. The data sections (Chaps. 2-4) remain pretty much as written in 1979-82 with only some minor changes in organization. The only significant modification in these sections involves the simplification of all artifact descriptions in Chap. 4. More detailed accounts are to appear in QR 6 where accounts of all LMV artifact patterns, including data from Quirigua and its environs, will be synthesized. The interpretive chapters (Chaps. 5-9) have undergone more serious revision. This is especially true for Chap. 8, which has been completely rewritten for this monograph. The reader is referred to my original dissertation (1984) if s/he wishes access to data or views not included here.

Needless to say, the work reported herein could not have been accomplished without the considerable support of many individuals and institutions. Funding was generously provided by The University Museum of the University of Pennsylvania (especially the Francis Boyer Fund), the National Geographic Society, the Tikal Association, the National Science Foundation (BNS 7624189), Mr. Landon T. Clay, and Dr. John M. Kershishian. Conduct of the work in Guatemala was inestimably advanced by the help of Patricia A. Urban, my valued colleague and wife. Pat Urban's help in all phases of the investigation, from survey through analysis, was invaluable and literally made a difficult task not only possible but enjoyable. Julie Benyo, Andrea Gerstle, and Beth Collea helped considerably with survey and excavation, and Mary Bullard patiently and consistently saw to the organization of all laboratory tasks. Robert Sharer, my thesis advisor, friend, and director of the QAP, provided considerable moral and logistical support during the conduct of the work in both Guatemala and the United States. He also helped analyze the LMV ceramics and has played a major role in editing and seeing this volume through to publication. Wendy Ashmore, director of investigations in the immediate Quirigua hinterland and my valued colleague, also provided many helpful and stimulating suggestions which have improved the logic of the arguments presented herein. David and Rebecca Sedat were responsible for the efficient running of the QAP and made my stays in the field pleasant and enjoyable. Ms. Laurie Tiede is largely responsible for pushing and prodding my intractable prose into publishable form. I am very grateful for the intelligence she has brought to this work. Dr. Luis Lujan Muñoz, former Director of IDAEH (Instituto de Antropología e Historia), provided important assistance in Guatemala, while Mr. Roy C. Wells and Sr. Carlos Chute of BANDEGUA (Del Monte Corporation), and Srs. Raúl Calderón and Francisco Fernández provided us with both permission to excavate on their lands and logistical support during the work. I owe a tremendous debt of thanks to all of these individuals as well as to the people of Las Quebradas, Choco, and Playitas who worked with me throughout the research period. I remain, of course, solely responsible for all errors of fact and interpretation contained within the following pages.

I

Introduction

This study reports on the data collected and analyzed during three field seasons (1977-79) of research in the lower Motagua valley (LMV), Izabal, Guatemala. The report also provides an interpretation of these data, phrased as series of hypotheses covering chronology, intrasite activity patterning, regional interaction, and interregional interaction. The chronological hypotheses deal with the periods of occupation at the recorded LMV sites, while those on intrasite activity patterning tentatively reconstruct site functions (identifications of past activities and their spatial distribution). Regional interaction concerns the nature of the contact among contemporary LMV sites, including Quirigua, and the discussion of interregional interaction considers how these centers were integrated within communication networks extending beyond the valley and including distant populations. A summary of these hypotheses is given at the end of the report (Chap. 9), along with a brief synopsis of the evidence and assumptions on which they are based. The models have not been tested; rather they are intended both to provide an interpretive summary of the patterns observed in the collected data and to furnish a framework to guide further study in the LMV.

GENERAL BACKGROUND: THE QUIRIGUA ARCHAEOLOGICAL PROJECT

The research described here was carried out as part of the Quirigua Archaeological Project (QAP; see Quirigua Reports Vols. 1, 7, and 8—hereafter QR 1, 7, 8). The lower valley encompasses an area of roughly 2000 km² bounded on the northwest, southeast, and southwest by the high rugged peaks of the Sierra de las Minas and Sierra de Espiritu Santo ranges (see Fig. 1). The northeastern boundary is the Caribbean coast. This broad tropical lowland zone falls within the area traditionally defined as the southeastern Maya lowlands (e.g., Thompson 1970). Within the LMV unquestionably the most widely known archaeological site is Quirigua, and it was here that the University of Pennsylvania initiated a long-term research project (1974-79). The goals of this program were three: to evaluate and expand existing knowledge concerning the history of occupation of Quirigua itself; to place that site in its immediate cultural context; and to provide information on the occupational history of the entire LMV (see QR 1). Following from these goals there was a threefold division of research responsibilities within the QAP. Attempting to satisfy the first objective, the site-core program focused on investigations within the monumental center of Quirigua as defined by the current limits of the archaeological park (Jones 1977; Jones et al. 1983; Sharer 1990; Sharer et al. 1979). Here a very detailed sequence of occupation and construction was revealed, the major activities practiced at the site through time were defined, and the outlines of a dynastic history drawn (ibid.). The site-periphery program under Wendy Ashmore concentrated on establishing the immediate cultural context of Quirigua by focusing its research within a 5-km radius of that site (Ashmore 1977, 1981b, 1984; Sharer et al. 1979). This work has led to the redefinition of the spatial and temporal boundaries of Quirigua and, in conjunction with the site-core work, to a better understanding of the range of activities carried out at this major center (ibid.). Finally, the LMV (or wider valley) program was designed to furnish a regional perspective—aimed at prehistoric reconstruction within the 1800-km² area extending from the Caribbean coast to the limits of the site-periphery research zone.

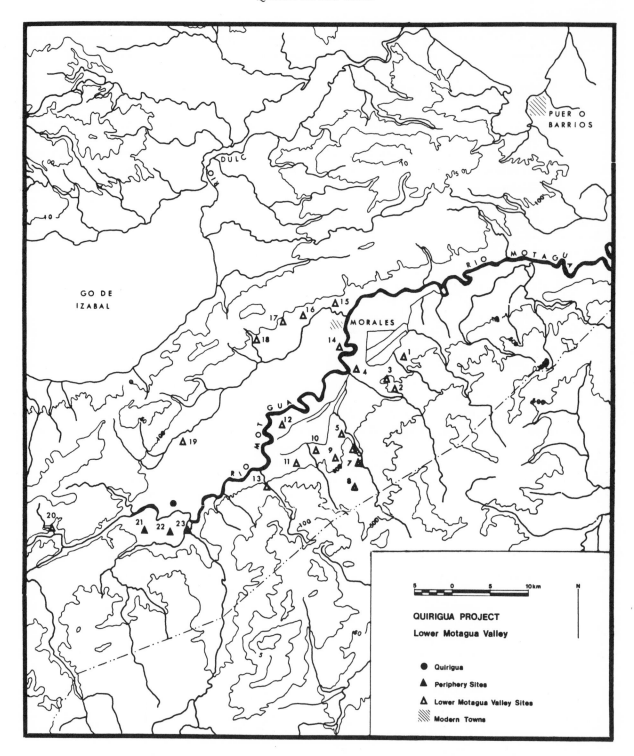

Figure 1.   Map of the Lower Motagua Valley.

ARCHAEOLOGICAL BACKGROUND:
THE LOWER MOTAGUA VALLEY

Prior to the work of the QAP, research in the LMV was devoted primarily to investigations in the site core of Quirigua itself (Hewett 1911, 1912, 1916; Morley 1935, 1937-38). Investigations concerned with the nature and distribution of settlement beyond Quirigua were more superficial. Within what is currently defined as the site-periphery area, Hewett conducted a brief survey and excavation program among "hundreds of lesser mounds" on the first river terrace north of Quirigua (Hewett 1912: 165-171).

Farther to the northeast, within the wider valley, archaeological research has been long-lived if sparse. Karl Sapper located and partially mapped the site of Las Quebradas and noted the site of Juyama prior to the beginning of this century (Sapper 1895). Gustav Strömsvik (1936) found and briefly reported on the large site of Comanche Farm, while Heinrich Berlin (1952) carried out a very cursory reconnaissance and mapping program at the centers of Playitas and Arapahoe Viejo. Ricketson and Blom (1940) summarized the results of some of these earlier surveys, but added no new observations. As a result, prior to 1960, only five major centers were known within the wider-valley survey area.

The next major survey effort within the wider valley was carried out by Timothy Nowak of Harvard University. From 1972 to 1975 Nowak conducted an extensive reconnaissance of the LMV with some limited test excavations at a few selected sites (Nowak 1973a, 1973b, 1975). During 1972 and 1973 he worked independently; from 1974 to 1975 he operated under the auspices of and with funding provided by the QAP. This preliminary survey indicated both a density of settlement and a complexity of site configuration beyond that which had been originally reported. Unfortunately, after Nowak ceased his research in 1975 no notes or information on his work, save for that embodied in his preliminary reports (1973a, 1973b, 1975), was provided to the QAP. The artifacts recovered by Nowak from surface collections and excavations were eventually housed in the QAP laboratory, but their provenience data were largely lacking (see App. I for a more detailed summary of Nowak's lower-valley work). Thus, on the basis of the information available in 1975 little could be said about the appearance or period of occupation of any of the sites located by Nowak.

In 1977 the LMV program was reactivated under the direction of the present author. With the help of Patricia Urban, this effort extended over three seasons (1977-79). The general goal of furnishing information on the prehistory of the research area remained the same as it had been under Nowak's direction. In addition, several more specific objectives were defined by Schortman in 1977. First, to relocate and record in detail sites already noted by Nowak, but for which there was insufficient information. Second, to expand investigations beyond those areas intensively studied by Nowak, ultimately providing a total foot survey of the research area. Third, to test several models developed prior to the 1977 season, dealing with the determinants of site location. Evaluation of these hypotheses required a thorough and extensive survey of the LMV (Schortman 1976). Fourth, limited test-pitting of a sample of sites to determine the ages of the recorded loci. The satisfaction of these specific objectives would have met the general goal of providing detailed information on the prehistory of the research zone.

Several problems developed during the 1977 season, however, which severely limited the achievement of these aims. First and foremost was the size of the sites discovered. It turned out that Nowak's original reports did not provide an accurate record of the extent of the centers found by his survey. For example, Nowak had originally indicated that Las Quebradas contained just over 70 structures, but our survey located 295. Because of the inadequacy of Nowak's reports, and the large size of the recorded sites, what was initially intended to have been a rapid program of relocating and recording prehistoric loci quickly became a prolonged task of basic mapping and description.

The second problem involved restrictions on time and money. Only three seasons had been set aside for the work, supported by a limited amount of research funds. Due in part to continuing inflation in the United States and Guatemala, the work force available to the LMV program shrank considerably: we employed ten to 14 men in 1978, six in 1979. The conjunction of these factors led to a radical reformulation of the research goals.

The new objectives were drawn up at the end of the 1977 field season. Because of the inadequacy of Nowak's site descriptions, our first aim was to locate accurately and record in detail those centers which had already appeared in Nowak's reports. Second, the program of excavations at particular loci had to be expanded to ensure that a reasonable number of structures at these centers were tested. Accordingly, fewer individual sites could be excavated than had been originally planned. Third, all work was concentrated within that portion of the valley where Nowak had recorded the greatest site density. This is an area of roughly 180 km² bounded on the northwest and southeast by the Rio Motagua and the Sierra de Espiritu Santo respectively, and on the northeast and southwest by the Rios Quebrada Grande and Tepemechines (see Fig. 1). It was in this zone that the rechecking of Nowak's earlier findings began, and as it constituted a well-defined segment of the larger valley, we decided to focus our energies here. Any hope of trying to survey the entire valley had to be abandoned as all available effort was devoted to recording adequately the very large sites within these 180 km².

Thus the results of Nowak's original reconnaissance stand as the best available inventory of sites within most of the wider valley (see Nowak 1973a and 1973b for a statement of the restrictions on his survey work). As noted in the conclusion of this report (Chap. 9), future work in the LMV should be devoted to expanding the survey beyond the area described herein.

Finally, we could not record the full range of settlement types within the newly reconstituted survey area. Rather, those centers with monumental architecture became the research focus. Monumental architecture is here defined as construction which, impressionistically, would have required formal architectural skills in design, a mass of labor in construction, and access to an amount of building material beyond that needed for simple domestic construction (R. Adams 1981). Practically, monumental constructions are defined as large architectural complexes composed of

several structures with an average height of 1.5 m or higher. Sites without such constructions were recorded as found but were not actively sought. The rationale for this restriction was threefold. First, we had begun our checking of Nowak's reports at these larger centers, leaving little time to survey adequately the remainder of the scaled-down research zone. Second, we believed that the study of the largest LMV sites would provide categories of data similar to those recovered from Quirigua and the monumental site-periphery loci: i.e., monumental architecture, site planning, and associated artifacts. Concentration on the monumental wider-valley centers would facilitate comparisons with the largest body of QAP data, that associated with monumental construction (in the site-periphery area only one nonmonumental site was excavated, while two monumental centers were tested (Ashmore 1981b). Third, it was assumed that the largest LMV centers grew by accretion. Consequently the most massive sites should preserve the longest chronological sequences. For the amount of time and energy available, monumental loci simply appeared to hold the greatest potential for providing the maximum amount of information. The results of these changes were a serious reduction of the area covered, a restriction of the types of sites sought, and the adoption of an opportunistic survey and excavation strategy. All of this means that the data collected are not necessarily representative of broader LMV patterns, nor does this report contain information pertaining to all aspects of the wider-valley settlement system. Nonetheless the material collected retains some significance. These data furnish information on the prehistory of the LMV which was not previously available (Chaps. 2-4). Further, the material presented herein can be treated as the empirical base out of which interpretations can be inductively generated (Chaps. 4-9), though additional work is required to test them.

ARCHAEOLOGICAL BACKGROUND: ADJACENT AREAS

Areas surrounding Quirigua and the LMV have also been the focus of earlier archaeological work. To the north, c. 20 km from Quirigua, Barbara Voorhies (1969) completed a survey along the shores of Lake Izabal, defining a very dispersed settlement pattern which apparently contains no sites comparable in size and complexity to those noted in the LMV. Approximately 100 km to the west of Quirigua, in the middle Motagua valley, the Carnegie Institution of Washington carried out a brief survey and excavation program

centered on the site of Guayatan near the present town of San Agustin Acasaguastlan (Kidder 1935; Smith and Kidder 1943). The result of this work was the recognition of a fairly dense and socially stratified population in the middle Motagua valley at some point in the Classic period. Research in the middle Motagua has more recently been continued by Gary Walters (1980). Copan, a major Lowland Maya site c. 60 km south of Quirigua in western Honduras, has been the focus of intermittent study for almost a hundred years. Again, the emphasis of the early research was primarily on recording the extensive glyphic inscriptions of this site, and secondarily on clearing structures for reconstruction and test-pitting to establish a ceramic sequence (Gordon 1896; Morley 1920; Trik 1939; Longyear 1952). Recently, in 1976 and 1977, Gordon R. Willey of Harvard University conducted a broad-based survey and excavation program within the Copan valley (Leventhal, Demarest, and Willey 1987; Willey and Leventhal 1979). This program was continued and enlarged in projects directed by Claude Baudez (1983), William Sanders (Sanders and Webster 1983; Sanders 1986; Webster and Gonlin 1988), and, most recently, William Fash (1983, 1988). Approximately 90 km northeast of Quirigua, in northwestern Honduras, the Naco Valley Project conducted a program of excavation and settlement-pattern studies (Henderson 1975; Henderson et al. 1979; Urban 1986b; Urban et al. 1988, 1989). The recent work of the La Entrada Archaeological Project in the valley of the same name c. 22.5 km to the southeast in Honduras has also produced significant data relevant to this report (Nakamura 1985, 1987; Nakamura et al. 1986, 1991). The result of this and similar archaeological work conducted farther afield in Honduras and El Salvador has been to increase our knowledge of a few select sites or zones within what can be defined as the southeastern Maya lowlands, while leaving a great many gaps between these points (see Urban and Schortman 1987). Such a mosaic is inevitable in any region in which research is still in its early stages. As noted above, it was partly to aid in this "filling-in" process that the QAP, and specifically the LMV program, were initiated.

Very little ethnographic or ethnohistoric material is available for the LMV. One of the reasons for this dearth is the rapid depopulation of the area beginning at the end of the Late Classic period (c. AD 1000). While there is some evidence of population within the LMV in the 16th century, the number of people involved appears to be considerably less than was the case for the Late Classic, and there is no suggestion of any center of power within the area (Ashmore 1981b: 344-347). Population dropped even further during the 17th-19th centuries (ibid.: 348-353). Today, the population of the valley is primarily Ladino: immigrants who have entered the region over the past 100-150 years (ibid.: 353). As a result, there are no known indigenous groups within the lower valley whose history can be traced, even tentatively, back into the local prehistoric era.

Traditional Maya communities exist in areas adjacent to the LMV. To the south, near the town of Chiquimula, Wisdom (1940) has provided an ethnography of the Chorti Maya. The Chorti have undoubtedly changed considerably as a result of Spanish contact and domination. Even if this was not the case, however, it remains uncertain whether this culture group inhabited the LMV prior to the Spanish Conquest (Thompson 1970). The ethnohistoric study of Pokomam peoples at the time of the Conquest has only peripheral bearing on this report, as it has been proposed that Pokomam distribution extended only as far north as the town of San Agustin Acasaguastlan, in the middle Motagua valley (Miles 1957).

In conclusion, it does not seem possible to establish direct continuity between any known traditional people and the group(s) who inhabited the LMV in the prehistoric past. Yet both Miles's Pokomam and Wisdom's Chorti materials provide a general background of possible patterns of behavior which may be useful in the interpretation of the prehistoric data. Nevertheless, a direct archaeological link cannot be established between the primary period of LMV occupation (AD 700-850) and any present occupation. It is therefore not possible to apply specific interpretive models directly derived from ethnographic or ethnohistoric research to the study reported here.

ENVIRONMENTAL BACKGROUND

The Rio Motagua originates in the highlands of Guatemala and extends for roughly 350 km before emptying into the Caribbean near the modern city of Puerto Barrios. Over this distance the Motagua passes through a number of different environments, from the high, cool mountains of El Quiche near its headwaters, to the arid hills of the middle Motagua in the Department of Zacapa, to the hot, moist lowlands of the lower valley in the Department of Izabal. Only a brief overview of the physical features that characterize this last area, the LMV, is possible given the paucity of information on the subject. This discussion will cover geology, hydrography, weather and climate, soils, and flora and fauna.

GEOLOGY

The LMV lies within the physiographic province of "Old Antillia," which includes northern Central America and the islands of the Greater Antilles (West and Augelli 1976: fig. 2.1, 31). Within this area of rugged mountain ranges, the LMV forms part of a continental plate boundary that extends from the Valley of Chiapas in Mexico out into the Caribbean, where it becomes the "Bartlett Deep" (ibid.: 32). The Motagua valley escarpments contain Paleozoic to Cenozoic metamorphic rocks in the form of schists, gneisses, and granites (West 1964b: fig. 4), as well as rhyolites, marble, and sandstone (at least in the southwestern part of the valley) and gold deposits in a few restricted zones. The valley floor itself is buried beneath a deep mantle of alluvial soils deposited by the Rio Motagua and its tributaries.

The research area is also in a zone of "general earthquake activity" (West and Augelli 1976: fig. 2.11). It is situated along the Motagua Fault, whose last major slippage, on February 4, 1976, caused considerable damage both within the valley and throughout Guatemala (Bevan and Sharer 1983).

HYDROGRAPHY

As the Rio Motagua enters the lower valley, it widens to between 60 and 200 m, reduces its velocity, and takes on a meandering course (Tamayo and West 1964: 96). The channel depth here is between 2 and 5 m (ibid.). In addition, at least 16 major tributaries, most flowing from the Sierra de Espiritu Santo range to the south, enter the Motagua in its lower course. These streams appear to be perennial (see Fig. 1).

The Rio Motagua carries a load of suspended material ranging from fine silts through sands and gravels to large rounded cobbles. Before construction of modern levees, most flooding occurred during the period from October to November, depositing silt that resulted in the buildup of wide, fertile natural levees (Tamayo and West 1964: 96). The tributaries that have been examined by the author—the Rio San Francisco on the north and the Rios Juyama, Chinamito, Bobos, and Quebrada Grande on the south—carry a considerable volume of water in the drier months of January to April; presumably this flow is even greater during the wetter part of the year. Most of these smaller streams also transport a wide range of load sizes, from silts to cobbles, along the portions near the hills where they were examined.

WEATHER AND CLIMATE

The LMV is situated within the Tierra Caliente of Central America, where diurnal temperatures range from 85-90° F. during the day to 70-75° F. at night (West and Augelli 1976: 36, 38). The mean annual temperature does not vary more than 5 to 10° F. (ibid.). Specifically, the valley is in the Tropical Rainforest zone, Koeppen's Af (ibid.: fig. 2.19) or Afw' (Escoto 1964: fig. 14). This is an area of high temperatures and rainfall throughout the year with some lessening of precipitation in the months of January through April (West and Augelli 1976: 45; Escoto 1964: 213; Whetten 1974: table 1). Rainfall generally reaches or exceeds 2000 mm per year (ibid.). Specific records indicate that during 1953-57, the mean annual rainfall was 1815 mm for the immediate Quirigua area (ibid.).

SOILS

In general, the LMV is characterized by three major soil types. On the broad floodplain of the Motagua and its tributaries is a deep deposit of azonal alluvial soils introduced by these watercourses when they periodically overflow their banks (Stevens 1964: fig. 7). As noted earlier, this area of prime agricultural land is rich in minerals and plant nutrients (West 1964a: 376; West and Augelli 1976: 48), especially along the natural river levees and other slightly higher areas not subject to intermittent waterlogging (ibid.). In the latter areas, where drainage is poor, gleization occurs, resulting in dark gray to yellow and gray mottled soils which may be heavily leached and acidic (Stevens 1964: 287, 300). These hydromorphic soils would have been of only limited use to prehistoric agriculturists, as they lack abundant supplies of the necessary nutrients and minerals and are very sticky and hard to work (ibid.). Waterlogged soils and areas of standing water have been observed at the sites of Choco, Las Quebradas, Playitas, Quebrada Grande, and Comanche Farm. It is not known whether this condition also obtained in the past or is due to changes in local drainage conditions subsequent to the abandonment of these sites.

To the south, on the flanks of the Espiritu Santo hills, are zonal red and yellow podzolic-lateritic soils (ibid.: fig. 7). The northern hills, the Sierra de las Minas, are characterized by zonal reddish brown and yellowish brown lateritic soils (ibid.). Brown calcareous lithosols are also found on the northern valley margins (ibid.). These soil groups are generally considered to be less fertile farmland because they have been leached of many minerals and nutrients and lose their productivity rapidly once the forest cover is removed (ibid.: 282-284, 299; West 1964a: 376). Erosion is classed as slight on the valley flats and moderate on the hill slopes (Stevens 1964: fig. 9).

Undoubtedly, a complete soil survey of the research zone would result in a more detailed picture of local edaphic conditions. The general description of the region would probably remain the same, however: an area of very fertile agricultural lands on the higher areas of the floodplain with zones of lesser fertility to be found in lower-lying swampy areas, and along the hills. All the sources agree that the region could have supported a considerable population prehistorically (West 1964a: 376; West and Augelli 1976: 48).

Today it is difficult to gauge directly the fertility of this land for the growing of aboriginal crops, as most of the floodplain has been preempted by the commercial cultivation of bananas. Agronomists from the banana plantation system, BANDEGUA, indicate that the floodplain is an excellent area for raising this crop. High precipitation and humidity, however, have frustrated their efforts to introduce other commercial floras, such as pineapples, and produce them on a large scale (M. Olevsky, pers. comm. 1979).

FLORA AND FAUNA

The LMV is in the Tropical Rainforest zone (Wagner 1964: fig. 1), an area originally characterized by a dense growth of multiple stories of large broadleaf evergreen trees. These trees form a closed upper canopy denying sunlight to the forest floor (ibid.: 230). The result is a lush and varied overgrowth, consisting of such trees as the giant ceiba, mahogany, American fig, rubber tree, and palm, and a relatively sparse undergrowth (West 1964a: 375). Large vines and clinging epiphytes are also common (West and Augelli 1976: 46).

The Neotropical fauna that occupies this zone consists of a profusion of different species of birds, among them parrots, toucans, macaws, and parakeets, as well as a rather limited range and number of mammals (ibid.: 382-383). Terrestrial mammals, such as the agouti, tapir, brocket deer, peccary, and rabbit, are less numerous than their arboreal counterparts, the monkey, squirrel, kinkajou, and opossum (ibid.: 381-382). Carnivores found in this zone include jaguars, ocelots, margays, and jaguarundis (ibid.: 382). River fish are reported to be numerous and varied in this region as well (ibid.: 376).

As of 1977-79 much of the tropical rainforest and its dependent fauna had disappeared from the surveyed portions of the valley. This is due in large part to the incursions of banana plantations in the area beginning in the early part of this century (F. Adams 1914) and continuing to the present day. It is ironic that perhaps the best-preserved section of tropical habitat is currently growing on the protected archaeological site of Quirigua. Within this relic stand of tropical forest such tropical life forms as the toucan and peccary can still be found.

SUMMARY

It is impossible to say how much the LMV environment has changed from the period of primary occupation (c. AD 700-850) to the present. As noted above, the nature of the vegetation has been modified by commercial agricultural practices. Today, most of the valley flats are either planted in bananas or covered in dense grass for cattle pastures; unused portions are covered in tangles of secondary growth. Nonetheless, it seems likely that the basic structure of the physical setting briefly outlined above has been stable over the 1100 years since the investigated sites were abandoned. As a result, it is assumed within this work that the environmental setting described above is applicable to the Terminal Late Classic period.

ORGANIZATION OF THE REPORT

As noted earlier in the chapter, the purpose of this report is to present both data and some working hypotheses as to what these data mean behaviorally. In archaeology, any body of data may be approached in two principal ways. The material remains of the past can be used to test one or more previously developed hypotheses, by means of a series of derived predictions which should be satisfied if the theoretical construct is correct (the Hypothetico-Deductive approach: see Hempel 1966; Binford 1968). Alternatively, the collected data can be examined for patterns, and a hypothesis or series of hypotheses developed as a means of interpreting those patterns (the Inductive approach: see Binford 1968). In this second method, which is followed here, the data serve as the basis for generating hypotheses that can be evaluated only in the course of subsequent research. Clearly these approaches are not mutually exclusive; inductive research is usually guided by theoretical considerations, and hypotheses themselves are frequently first developed inductively and later tested deductively. Nonetheless, each of these analytical schemes has a different set of goals; the results and their manner of presentation will differ accordingly. The data collected by this project and those gathered by Nowak for which provenience information was available were examined for patterns which, in turn, were accounted for by a series of currently untested hypotheses. In conformance with this approach, the collected data are described first and in some detail to provide the reader with as clear an idea as possible of the empirical basis of all the subsequent interpretations.

The first part of the report is divided into three chapters: Survey, Excavation, and Architecture and Site Planning (Chaps. 2-4). Chapter 2 contains accounts of all located sites as they were seen on the surface, with emphasis on three topics: location and setting, current status, and site description.

Chapter 3 discusses in detail the excavations undertaken at the three large sites of Choco, Las Quebradas, and Playitas. The rationale for choosing these centers for excavation is outlined here and the overall excavation strategy and goals are discussed. The nature and amount of material recovered, and the sequence of natural and cultural events associated with each excavated structure are also presented. What is known of Nowak's excavations at the sites of Playitas and Juyama is reported, using the same format, in App. I.

The final data section, Chap. 4, synthesizes the material patterns derived from an analysis of the survey and excavation data at two levels: architecture and site planning. For reasons of economy, the descriptions of portable remains (artifacts) appear in the volume devoted to the QAP artifacts (QR 6), although chronological and functional conclusions derived from these data are used here. Two caveats are warranted. First, because of the opportunistic manner in which the data were collected, any noted material patterns must be treated as hypotheses whose validity is subject to further testing. Second, the patterns noted are, by and large, restricted to a segment of the total valley settlement system, that is, to those sites with monumental architecture located within a limited portion of the valley. As will be noted in Chap. 4, the consistency of the recovered material gives some confidence that ultimately the observed patterns will be validated for all sites with monumental architecture in the LMV.

The interpretive portion of the report (Chaps. 5-9) presents a series of hypotheses to account for the patterns noted in the data. The assumptions and data underlying these hypotheses are made as clear as possible in order to facilitate their further evaluation and testing. Each interpretive chapter builds on the arguments presented in the preceding chapter so that all sections are interrelated, as well as being arranged in order of increasing speculation.

II

Survey

INTRODUCTION

The primary goal of the survey portion of the LMV program was to locate and record sites containing monumental architecture in the lower valley east of the limits of the Wider Periphery Survey Zone (Ashmore 1981b). Because of the large size of this area, c. 1800 km², and given the limitations of resources and time, it became necessary to restrict the survey to a segment of the lower valley in order to gain coherent results. The segment chosen was the area south of the Rio Motagua bounded on the northeast by the Rio Quebrada Grande, on the southwest by the Rio Tepemechines, and on the southeast by the high hills of the Sierra de Espiritu Santo. The choice of this area was based primarily on the relatively large number of sizable centers it contained, as indicated by Nowak's 1972-75 survey. This same work revealed an apparent absence of major sites in other parts of the LMV.

A total of nine sites with monumental architecture and 12 without such constructions were recorded by the LMV program. Recording procedures varied somewhat by site and are discussed in the summaries that follow. In general, given our research focus (Chap. 1), more effort was devoted to recording large centers with monumental constructions than to their nonmonumental counterparts. Extensive notes were taken on these nine large sites and instrument-assisted maps were made of at least portions of them. Following general practices for the Maya lowlands (e.g., Carr and Hazard 1961), all mapped buildings were rectified and drawn at a scale of 1:1000. The remaining 12 settlements were recorded primarily through notes, only occasionally being mapped where time permitted and/or some facet of their organization required. Surface collections, almost invariably small, were made wherever possible. As noted earlier, this situation is hardly ideal. Ultimately, a more thorough survey should be carried out within the 180-km² study zone and the LMV at large to better document settlement form, distribution, and variation.

In the following section, each site or site zone is described under three major headings: Location and Setting, Current Status, and Site Description. The sites of Cruce de Morales, Monterey, Finca America, and Puente de Virginia are grouped together because of their similarity in setting, current status, and overall form and appearance. Furthermore, all of them were only cursorily examined.

In order to facilitate the descriptions and avoid redundancy, a glossary of commonly used terms follows.

GLOSSARY OF SURVEY TERMS

Site: Any spatial clustering of evidence of prehistoric occupation, ranging from artifact scatters to visible architecture. *Locus* and *settlement* are used interchangeably with *site*.

Site zone: Areas of multiple, separable but still closely spaced architectural and/or artifactual aggregations, grouped into a single macro-unit for descriptive purposes. This does not imply that the aggregations are all contemporary.

Plaza: A space defined on two or more sides by construction. Access is through the corners, at least three of which are left open.

Quadrangle: A monumental structure group composed of four substructures that completely surround an enclosed space. Access to the central space is restricted by construction, i.e., at least two corners are sealed. *Court complex* is used synonymously with *quadrangle* throughout this report. Abbreviated Quad.

Closed court: The central space contained within the quadrangle and to which access is restricted by the surrounding buildings. *Court* is also used as a synonym.

Group: Any aggregate of two or more constructions organized around a central space (plaza or court). Within site zones (Playitas, Las Quebradas, and Quebrada Grande) the component loci are given group

9

designations; *group* here is capitalized and followed by a Roman numeral, e.g., Group I, II, and so forth, or preceded by a direction, e.g., East Group.

Platform: A raised substructure which may or may not have supported additional construction on its summit. Abbreviated PL in figure labels, Plat. in text.

Operation: All collecting and recording activities within the QAP were divided into subsets geared to the investigation of the research universe. Major divisions were designated operations which, in turn, could be subdivided into more specific studies, suboperations (Op. and Subop. or SUB-OP). Each recorded site within the LMV for which we have excavated or surface collections was given an Op. number (e.g., Op. 20). Distinct investigations conducted within these loci, whether surface collections of particular areas or excavations of individual platforms, were then given Subop. designations, indicated by a letter following the Op. number, e.g., Subop. 20A, 20B, 20C.

Lots: Collection units made within particular suboperations, numbered sequentially as they were defined in the course of fieldwork.

Main group: The largest construction aggregate, determined by structure size and/or complexity, within a site or segment of a site zone (a designated Group). *Principal group* is also used in this sense. Both terms can apply to plaza or quadrangle units.

Structure: Any evidence, elevated above current ground surface or not, for the existence of a prehistoric building which still retains some of its integrity; i.e., it is sufficiently well preserved to reconstruct its overall form. Abbreviated STR in figure labels, Str. in text.

Step-terrace: A mode of construction commonly employed in the LMV to raise monumental-sized substructures. Unless otherwise noted, it consists of long, low, narrow steps with risers built of unfaced stones, usually cobbles, and runners constructed of flat-laid schist slabs. The latter deeply underlie the next ascending riser. This has the advantage of providing a stable base for each riser, which, in turn, effectively counterbalances the supporting treads and creates a closely integrated contruction system. These terraces commonly step up in short increments to the structure's summit and tend to run the length of the construction on at least one side.

Slabs: Long thin stones, usually of schist, commonly employed as terrace treads.

Cobbles: River-worn, rounded stones with no evidence of artificial modification.

Chunks: Unmodified angular stones (synonym: *rubble*).

Pebbles: Small, usually rounded stones often employed as chinking stones in LMV walls.

Monument: A large stone ascertained, because of its location and/or evidence of human modification, to have been the focus of aboriginal activity. Abbreviated M in figure labels, Mon. in text.

Rock concentration: A moderately dense concentration of stones and, at times, artifacts that suggests the former presence of a now-destroyed construction. Abbreviated R.C.

PLAYITAS SITE ZONE (Locus 200, Op. 20)

LOCATION AND SETTING

General Location: The Playitas Site Zone (see Fig. 1) is 4.2 km northeast of Choco (Locus 212) and c. 9.4 km southwest of the Las Quebradas Site Zone (Locus 205).

Topography: This zone is situated primarily on the flat floodplain of the Rio Chinamito at the point where the river issues from the Espiritu Santo mountains to the southeast. The few scattered structures that compose Group III in the far southeastern portion of the locus are the only exception: they are situated on small level areas in the first foothills of the Espiritu Santo range. Group II, while on the floodplain, is on a low (c. 1-1.5 m high) rise above the plain's level.

With the exception of some slight evidence of occupation in the hills to the northeast of the river, the meandering course of the Rio Chinamito forms the northeast boundary of the zone. In fact, no structure has been recorded more than 2.1 km west of the river's current course (see Fig. 2; 2a in text, 2b in map pocket).

Resources: During the three dry seasons in which this area was visited (1977, 1978, and 1979) the Chinamito carried a considerable volume of water as it flowed adjacent to the zone. The level of the river below its banks varied from c. 2.2 m in the south near Group II to c. 3.5 m east of Group IV, dropping roughly 1.3 m over a 1.85-km straight-line distance. The Chinamito maintains a fairly constant width of 9 m

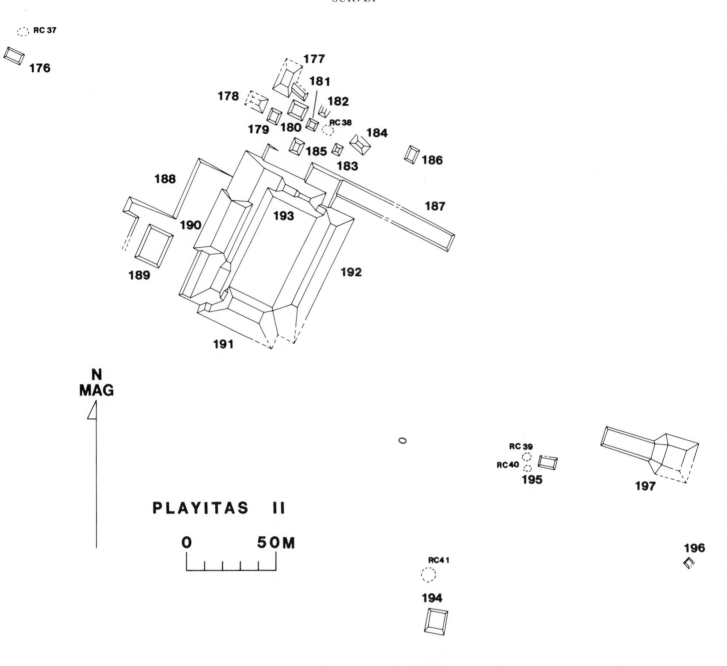

Figure 2a.   Map of Group II, Playitas.

over this distance. As a result, both the modern inhabitants and their aboriginal counterparts would have had easy access to an excellent year-round source of water.

The Chinamito also serves as a ready source of the ubiquitous LMV building stone, the river-worn cobble. Such cobbles were plentiful in the river in 1977-79, especially in the southern part of the zone, where the Rio Chinamito was depositing the heavier portions of its load after leaving the mountains. To the north, the prevalence of these cobbles decreased until east of Group IV no cobbles were noted. No natural source was found for the schist slabs, some of them quite large, that were also used in construction at

Playitas. It is presumed that schist could have been obtained in the adjacent hills. These slabs were probably quarried but appear to have been little modified after removal from the source.

The land on which the zone lies appears to be potentially productive. With the broad floodplains of the Rios Motagua and Chinamito extending all around, there is no apparent limit to available farmland. The location of commercial banana orchards within 2 km to the northwest confirms local soil fertility.

The pass cut by the Rio Chinamito and its tributaries extends into the mountains to the southeast of the zone, across the Guatemalan boundary into the northern La Florida valley, Honduras. A modern trail follows this river and one of its southwestern tributaries past the modern *aldea* (village) of Mojanales to the border, where another extensive trail system begins on the Honduran side. This latter system extends southeastward toward the Rio Chamelecon, whose valley in turn provides a major artery running toward the Caribbean coast of Honduras. Major Late Classic centers are situated on the Honduran side of the *sierra* along this route, including Techin and Nueva Suyapa in the northern La Florida valley (Nakamura 1987). The Honduran trails also lead southwestward to the Late Classic center of El Paraiso (Yde 1938; Vlcek and Fash 1986) and, eventually, to the major site of Copan, both in Honduras. As a result, the route passing through Mojanales to the southeast ties into a very broad system of trails linking numerous important prehistoric centers.

The Rio Chinamito, like the Rio Bobos to the north, cuts one of the few passes through the hills separating Guatemala from Honduras and provides at least topographic support for the existence of an important aboriginal communication route in this area. The position of the aforementioned centers of Techin and Nueva Suyapa along the corridor supports its prehistoric significance. If, as seems likely, contacts to the southeast were prehistorically important, then those passes which afforded a relatively easy route for such communication would have been of strategic value. Playitas' location along one such route, where the Chinamito first leaves the confines of the Espiritu Santo mountains, would have allowed it to control any commerce that flowed through that pass.

CURRENT STATUS

Mechanized plowing was the single greatest cause of site destruction, especially in 1979, when much of Group V was plowed in preparation for planting grass seed in the northern part of the zone. In this group, plowing extended as far as the river on the east and to 250 m west, 375 m south, and 200 m north of the main group. The result was that most of the structures surrounding the principal group in Group V, in particular those below 1 m high, were plowed over with consequent destruction of their summits and flanks. While the general sizes and orientations of most of these structures could still be discerned in 1979, soon after the plowing was finished, there was little doubt that much construction has been seriously disturbed. The furrows cut by the metal disks were 0.35-0.7 m deep. At this depth, as excavations at Playitas illustrate (see Chap. 3), considerable damage may have been done to at least the upper levels of occupation and construction. In all, 73 structures were noted as damaged by this activity. In addition to plowing, the digging of agricultural canals, especially in Groups I and V, also resulted in the destruction of at least portions of structures.

Natural agents, especially tree roots, had also disturbed construction in this zone. Whereas plowing affected primarily the lower structures, tree growth was concentrated on the taller constructions, those 3-8 m high, and usually on summits, where the damage was most severe. The main groups of Groups I and V were particularly affected. Here, as elsewhere in the valley, the large palms had insinuated their broad root systems into the interstices of construction, dislodging many stones.

There were several more specific disturbances. Structures 200-76, -71, -123, and -116 in Group I had been penetrated by a 5- to 7-m-wide cut associated with a now-abandoned banana tramline. Also, to the south and east of Group I the land was covered throughout the period of study by standing water. Possibly this swampy condition which engulfed Str. 200-72, -84, and -105/125 was the result of recent modifications in the area that had disrupted drainage. Roadwork in the southern part of the zone sheared off the southeast corner of Str. 200-192 and -191, which formed the eastern and southern sides of the Group II principal group. Structure 200-197 to the east of this aggregate had also lost its southeast corner, while Str. 200-187 to the north had been bisected by road construction. Also in Group II, Str. 200-177 and -178 had been truncated, though the cause of this damage was not immediately discernible.

Group III is situated in the midst of modern

habitations on the southwest side of the Chinamito, and it is likely that at least some prehistoric remains have been obliterated.

Looting did not appear to have been a major problem at Playitas, and only two instances of this activity were noted in 1979. In the far northwestern portion of the zone, Str. 200-3 in Group IV had been cut by a 0.7-m-wide by 5.2-m-long trench. This excavation bisected the western flank of the platform and extended to its summit. The other area of looting was in the northwestern corner of Group II, where a small excavation no more than 1 m deep was found. Little damage was apparent.

In total, 92 constructions were either damaged or largely destroyed within the Playitas Site Zone as of 1979.

Ownership: BANDEGUA.

SITE DESCRIPTION

Previous Work: The first recorded visit to Playitas was by Berlin (1952), attracted by reports of large, carved-stone tenoned heads. During his survey a transit map was made of the Group I main group. Berlin concentrated his short description of Playitas on a discussion of the tenoned heads that purportedly came from this aggregate and noted very little of the general plan and architecture of the site (ibid.: 41-42). He did, however, record the presence of stone slabs, some still *in situ*, in the structures of Group I's central closed court (ibid.: 41). Nowak (1973b: fig. 4) relocated this complex in 1972 and remapped the principal group and several of the surrounding structures originally recorded by Berlin (ibid.). No description of the locus appeared at that time or subsequently. In 1973 or 1974 he returned to Playitas and mapped the principal group and its immediately adjoining structures in Group II (Nowak 1975: fig. 1). At some point during this period he also carried out a test-pitting program in the Playitas area. Three of his test excavations were relocated by the LMV program: two within the Group II main-group closed court and another between Str. 200-180 and -181, 32 m north of that plaza (ibid.: 16-17, figs. 2-4). Only a very brief report on this work exists (see App. I).

Recording: The Playitas Site Zone was mapped over the course of two seasons (1977 and 1979). In 1977 Nowak's map of the Group II principal court was field-checked; although altered in some of its details, it was not greatly modified. Also at this time, structures east of the Group II main group were mapped with a tripod-mounted Brunton pocket transit and a 30-m tape. Both Nowak's and Berlin's maps of the Group I main group were judged to be sufficiently inaccurate to warrant redrawing them entirely. In 1979 Groups I, IV, and V were mapped using a transit, and Groups I, II, IV, and V were all tied together on a single map. While the clearing carried out by BANDEGUA in 1979 helped us immensely, some additional removal of vegetation remained to be carried out in Groups I and V. The bases and summits of structures were cleared to determine their overall dimensions and the presence of any superstructures. Paths were also cut through the major plazas in search of monuments. In all, 47 person-days were invested in clearing structures for mapping. Group III was not transit-mapped and was recorded solely by notes.

Description: The Playitas Site Zone was the largest unit recorded in the LMV program. In all, the mapped portion of this zone measures 2.805 km northwest-southeast by 0.92 km northeast-southwest. If Group III is also included, the length of the zone is increased to 3.455 km northwest-southeast. Within this total area, 212 individual structures and 42 rock concentrations were recorded. The breakdown of these constructions by height is given in Table III.1.

Except for Group III the general pattern of structure arrangement is a main group containing a quadrangle. This unit occurs both as a single element, as in Groups II, IV, and V, and as part of a larger configuration consisting of several adjoining quadrangles, as in Group I (see Fig. 2). Scattered around these main groups are numerous smaller constructions. Some of these humbler structures are arranged into orthogonally organized plazas, while others occur singly or in irregular groups in which the component structures do not share a common orientation. Another general pattern of site morphology can be seen in Fig. 2; at least three separate clusters of structures are found focused on the main groups of Groups I, II, and V, and another more dispersed agglomeration lies to the north surrounding the smaller Group IV main group. Structures are concentrated in the areas immediately surrounding their principal groups and then diminish rapidly beyond. This can be seen most clearly between Groups I and V.

The major problem for the definition of designated Groups (distinct site-zone segments) is apparent in those areas where no true gaps in structure distribution exist. In attempting to solve this dilemma, two methods are employed. The simplest approach is to draw a line connecting the midpoints of the quadrangles in each aggregation and then draw a boundary perpendicular to these connecting lines at a point midway between their origins. This is the principle behind the construction of Thiessen polygons, used by geographers and archaeologists to define regions where other clear-cut criteria of identification are absent (Haggett 1965: 247-248; Hodder and Orton 1976: 59-60, 78-80). This technique is probably adequate for the establishment of approximate boundaries between adjacent major groups with surrounding clusters of structures, especially since it is fairly certain that no other major groups exist that would cause serious revisions in the lines drawn. The Group limits resulting from this process do not bisect structures; in only one case do they actually cut through a group (Str. 200-44 and -48). The structures of this latter aggregate would be included with Group IV in computations as the majority of the structures fall on that side of the boundary (Haggett 1965: 247-248). The fact that the boundaries do not intersect structures or groups is testimony to the general paucity of construction away from the principal groups.

Another approach is to draw the Group limits as detailed above and then measure the distances between those structures or groups that fall on or near boundaries with other structures or groups further in toward the principal groups. Structures would be included with one Group or another depending on the affiliation of their "nearest neighbor." Measurements would be taken from, and to, the center of a group or structure. The assumption in this case is that those structures located on the boundary should be included with the Group whose representative is closest to them, thus allowing for continuous distributions and softening the arbitrariness of the limits. In reality, this procedure introduces little change from the previous results; the only area affected is that between Groups I and IV, where three structures and a rock concentration formerly classed with Group I now pass to Group IV (Str. 200-49/51 and R.C. 200-5). All figures for the number of structures per Group have been established on the basis of this second approach.

Group II in the far southern portion of the zone, therefore, consists of 22 structures and five rock concentrations scattered over an area roughly 145 m northeast-southwest by at least 180 m northwest-southeast (Str. 200-176/197, R.C. 37-41). The Group is divided into three parts by dry arroyos that run roughly northeast-southwest toward the Rio Chinamito on the west and east sides of the principal group. The effect of these natural features is to isolate the main group and its immediately adjacent construction from two much smaller aggregates, one to the east (Str. 200-194/197, R.C. 39-41) and the other to the west (Str. 200-176, R.C. 37).

Four of the structures (Str. 200-190/193) composing Group II are of monumental proportions and enclose on all sides a court that measures 54.5 m northeast-southwest by 27.5 m northwest-southeast. The surface of the plaza is at approximately the same level as the ground surface on the north, and becomes increasingly higher than ground surface on the east, west, and south, as the ground falls off gradually to the southwest. At maximum, the plaza is 2.5 m above ground level on the south.

The structures north and west of the principal group tend to be aligned with respect to the large constructions of that unit, though this is far from universally true. No clear groups appear in this area, though this lack may be less a product of aboriginal design than a result of modern destruction.

Still in the immediate area of the principal group, the rather extensive terrace system (Str. 200-188) built into the walls of the 1.5- to 2-m-deep arroyo west of this monumental complex is unusual for a valley site. The use to which these terraces were put is unknown, though it is possible that their primary function was to retard erosion. At Las Quebradas similar terraces seem to have been used to enhance architecture, but this was not the case here. Structure 200-187, which extends 69 m east from a northern projection of Str. 200-193, is also unusual. This low construction is unique in known LMV centers.

Group V, 1 km northwest of Group II, consists of 56 structures and 30 rock concentrations within an area 785 m northwest-southeast by 412.5 m northeast-southwest. While structure densities follow the generally observed pattern in dropping off markedly to the southeast and northeast, this is not the case to the northwest and southwest: here, although the frequency of construction does decrease, there is no true gap or break in the presence of structures. Group V is divided into two portions by a 0.75- to 1-m-deep dry streambed. By far the vast majority of its structures are situated north of this course, though several structure groups are found south of it as well.

The principal group is a quadrangle (Str. 200-164/

167). The ground on which this quadrangle is built gradually drops off from the northeast toward the south and southwest. The court surface at its northeast corner is at about the same level as ground surface, while it is c. 0.45 m above ground surface at the northwest corner, and considerably above the surrounding terrain at the southwest and southeast corners (c. 1 m and 0.85 m respectively). The northeast corner of the court is closed by a wall 3.5 m wide by 0.5 m high: all the remaining corners restrict access by virtue of their height above ground surface. The area of the enclosed court is 59 m east-west by 53 m north-south (measured across the center).

Another unusual feature associated with this group is the sloping, ramplike surface that extends to the west from the main group's southwest corner (Str. 200-167A). The recent plowing of this feature may account for the way its margins diverge to the west. This "ramp," which provided a point of formalized access to the quadrangle, is unique in known LMV centers.

As can be seen in Fig. 2b, there is a general lack of orthogonality in structure arrangements both within and surrounding the Group V main group. Among the smaller structures, some of this seeming irregularity may be attributable to the intensity of recent plowing. This is not the case for the principal group, whose structures were too high to have suffered this fate.

Another feature that distinguishes Group V is the way in which the smaller constructions cluster to the west of Str. 200-167. While several groups of two or three platforms are found to the south and northwest of the quadrangle, by far the majority of the structures are concentrated into two irregular, poorly defined aggregations numbering nine structures and five rock concentrations (for the southeastern one, Str. 200-148/156, R.C. 28-32), and 15 structures and seven rock concentrations (for the southwestern one, Str. 200-130/144, R.C. 12-18). Also in this area is a low-lying, long, narrow platform, Str. 200-157, whose west end fades into a natural rise. Given its location, it is tempting to see this feature as an isolated remnant of what might have been a walkway that once extended west-northwest from the "ramp" built into the main group.

Group I contains 78 structures and two rock concentrations within an area 562 m east-west by 604 m north-south. The principal group in this zone consists of three contiguous quadrangles which together cover an area of 16,210 m². The central closed court is 70.5 m east-west by 50 m north-south, while the smaller south closed court is 44.25 m east-west by 14.75 m north-south. The somewhat less massive northeast closed court measures 31 m east-west by 36.5 m north-south. The main group is dominated by Str. 200-77, which faces onto both the central and the south closed courts and rises to a height of c. 7.5 m. It was on the summit of this construction that the sculpted tenoned heads recorded by Berlin (1952: 41-42) were found. In the case of both the central and the south closed courts, the corners are obstructed by construction, while in the northeast closed court the northwest corner was left open, although access to the court is narrowly defined by the 4-m gap between Str. 200-72 and -84.

The main group is orthogonally arranged. Beyond this aggregation, structures, especially the larger ones in the immediate vicinity of these monumental constructions, generally share the alignment of the principal group. Individual structure groups are, nevertheless, hard to define within the immediate area of the main group. As Fig. 2 shows, in moving away from the principal group toward the northeast, even the general trend toward orthogonality is lost and groups become more irregular in their organization.

Group IV consists of 51 structures and five rock concentrations located within an area roughly 657 m northeast-southwest by 797.5 m northwest-southeast. A point that is immediately obvious upon examining Fig. 2b is the very dispersed nature of this Group and yet the fairly strong tendency for most of the component structures to be arranged into orthogonal groups. The structures of the main group, the smallest such element noted in the site zone (Str. 200-21/24), enclose a court no more than 19 m northwest-southeast by 31.5 m northeast-southwest. In contrast to Groups I and V, the smaller structures composing this Group are not concentrated in the immediate vicinity of the principal group but are spread out more evenly over the landscape in aggregates of two to eight constructions (three or four being the most common). Single structures are relatively rare here. Each of these groups is physically dominated by one large structure.

Group III is the smallest of the five aggregations constituting the Playitas Site Zone. Five structures (Str. 200-198/202) are known to belong to this cluster, ranging in height from 0.75 to 2 m and arranged orthogonally around a small plaza. In addition to this aggregation, which in no way approaches in size or complexity any of the Group I, II, IV, or V main groups, there is some slight evidence of prehistoric occupation to the northeast across the Chinamito. Here four increasingly higher small plateaus immediately south of the floodplain support a very restricted area of flat land, roughly 10 m² on each rise. One possible structure is located on each, averaging 0.25-0.5 m high and 4 m long by 2.25 m wide. None of these level surfaces supports more than one structure. None has artifactual material on its surface or stones from construction. In fact, the only cultural material recovered from this area is two small fragments of obsidian from the surface of the path leading up the hillside. As there is no indication that modern activities might be responsible for these low rises, it remains possible that they represent the foci of ancient occupation. Nevertheless these possible structures are not included in platform counts for the center. The area in the foothills immediately to the southwest of these possible structures is completely covered by the BANDEGUA town of Bobos. If any structures were located here they have been destroyed, as modern construction is dense and extensive.

Several general statements pertaining to visible architecture can be made for the zone. First, the larger substructures, especially those which make up the principal groups, are most commonly built up using the step-terrace technique, as inferred from several extant wall lines. These narrow terraces appear to run the full length of the structure faces and are not restricted to specific portions of them. On those monumental substructures in which no wall lines are visible on the surface, the presence of this technique is suggested by large numbers of cobbles and slabs found as surface debris. In the several structures of this size that have been cut by modern activities, e.g., Str. 200-76 and -79, the fill consists of a hard-compacted orange earth. An exception to this system of long, low, and narrow step-terraces is the wide schist-slab terrace running all the way around the interior of the central closed court of Group I's main group. This broad terrace is found between half and a third of the way up the sides of Str. 200-76/79 in this quadrangle (see Fig. 2). Also of interest here is a line of schist slabs, protruding just above ground surface, located on the court side at the base of Str. 200-78. Both of these features, broad slab terraces and basal-projecting slab lines, are also found at Choco (Locus

212). Structures 200-76 and -79 in Group I also show evidence of broad slab terraces on their noncourt-facing sides (see Fig. 2b).

The summits of monumental structures are usually too heavily disturbed by root action for the nature of their superstructures to be determined. On Str. 200-23 in the Group IV main group, however, five square concentrations of tightly packed river cobbles were noted flush with summit level. These features, similar to those from the East and West Groups of Las Quebradas, are spaced regularly at 3- to 5-m intervals on the summit and are presumably associated with superstructure construction. As at Las Quebradas, their appearance here suggests that they might have been bases for now-destroyed pillars. Also located on this summit is a set of cobblestone lines on the eastern edge. These features appear to enclose a room c. 2.5 by 5 m, though excavations did not clearly confirm this interpretation (see Chap. 3). A similar line of cobbles was also noted on the summit of Str. 200-167 in the Group IV main group. All of these stone lines had no elevation when found and may well have functioned as foundations for perishable upper constructions. The lack of considerable quantities of tumbled stones on the structures in question suggests that other, more perishable material was used in superstructure construction.

The smaller structures around the main groups, those below 1 m high, are more variable in the amount of stone debris associated with them. Several in Group IV have no visible stones at all, while the majority have at least a few river cobbles. Stone slabs are only infrequently found on the humbler platforms, indicating that they were probably built not in the step-terrace style, but rather of low cobble walls with only an incidental use of stone slabs. (See Chap. 3 for a description of a low structure excavated in Group IV, Str. 200-16.) *Bajareque* fragments found in several of the surface lots collected from the lower, plowed platforms in Group V suggest that this material was used in the construction of superstructures.

Earth construction unfaced by stones was recognized at two locales in the zone. The ramp associated with the Group V main group, though plowed, is devoid of stones, suggesting that it was built solely of earth. In the Group IV main group, the eastward projection of Str. 200-23 and the far northern end of Str. 200-24 have no stones whatsoever on their surfaces. Again, earthen construction is suggested (the

TABLE 2.1

SURFACE COLLECTIONS

Lot #	Contents	Depositional Significance	Provenience
20A/40	3 pcs. obsidian	Surface	General surface, Group II (Nowak collection)
20A/41	3 pcs. obsidian	Surface	General surface, Playitas Zone (Nowak collection)
20A/60	4 figurine frags.; stone carvings	Surface and Rio Chinamito	Private collection from Playitas Zone
20B/1	171 sherds; 4 censer frags.; 1 *bajareque* frag.	Surface, plowed structures	Str. 200-156 W of Group V main group
20B/2	103 sherds; 8 pcs. obsidian; 3 *bajareque* frags.	Surface, plowed structures	S of Str. 200-158/159, Group V
20B/3	18 sherds; 1 *bajareque* frag.	Surface, plowed structures	N of Group V main group, around Str. 200-127
20B/4	12 sherds	Backdirt of looted structure; mixed surface and fill	Str. 200-3, Group IV
20B/5	8 sherds; 9 censer frags.	Surface, plowed structures	NW of Group V main group around Str. 200-128/129
20B/6	56 sherds	Surface, plowed structures	Found around R.C. 19-22, Group V
20B/7	27 sherds; 1 *bajareque* frag.	Surface, plowed structures	Between Str. 200-68/114 in Group V
20B/8	Lost	Surface	General area of Str. 200-3, Group IV

north end of Str. 200-24 was investigated by a small excavation, Op. 20I, and is discussed in Chap. 3).

Finally, while most of the main group courts show no evidence on the surface of having been paved, the Group V principal court's surface is covered with a jumbled, though continuous, layer of small white quartzlike cobbles. This layer is similar in appearance to the layer of white stones found in the central closed court in the Las Quebradas West Group. These stones occur over most of the court though they are more obvious in the center.

Special Features:

A series of stone tenoned sculptures, which had apparently been used as architectural ornaments, were found both on the summit of Str. 200-77 in the Group I main group and at the base around all four of its sides by Berlin (1952: 41-42, figs. 4-5). The sculptural repertoire included renditions of human heads, masks, upper bodies (human), human arms and legs, and assorted architectural ornaments. Berlin's analysis led him to see definite stylistic similarities between this material and that located at other Maya sites, in particular Copan and Quirigua.

Alluviation: Given the location of Playitas on the floodplain of the Rio Chinamito, it is probable that some of the lower structures are lost to view under river-deposited silts. Excavations in Groups I and IV suggest that as much as 0.5-0.6 m of silt has been deposited in this area since abandonment.

Surface Collections: The surface collections made at Playitas in 1977 and 1979 (excluding a private collection, Lot 20A/60) comprise 395 sherds, 13 censer fragments, 14 pieces of obsidian, and six fragments of *bajareque* (wattle and daub). The majority (six) of these lots came from the plowed area of Group V, especially among the smaller structures. In addition to this material two lots were collected by Nowak and were available for analysis; the precise provenience of these collections is not known (see Table 2.1).

Excavations: Seventeen excavations were carried out in the Playitas Zone in 1979 by the LMV program. Thirteen of these took place in Group IV, four in Group I. Beyond this work, it is known that Nowak dug at least three test pits in the area of Group II (see App. I). Group V was not investigated by either Nowak or this project (see Chap. 3).

LAS QUEBRADAS SITE ZONE (Locus 205, Op. 24)

LOCATION AND SETTING

General Location: The Las Quebradas Site Zone is 4.4 km south-southwest of the Quebrada Grande Site Zone (Locus 206), c. 9.4 km northeast of the Playitas Site Zone (Locus 200), and c. 4.3 km southeast of the Bobos Site Zone (Locus 209). (See Fig. 1.)

Topography: The three principal Groups of the Las Quebradas Site Zone occupy the relatively flat summit of a high bluff overlooking the Rio Bobos floodplain to the south and west. This bluff, which rises c. 14 m above the valley flats and constitutes a section of the first low foothills of the Espiritu Santo mountains, is part of the same ridge system that extends northwest and supports Locus 230. The summit of this ridge is divided into three topographic sectors. The West and East Groups each occupy a relatively flat space on the east-west-oriented bluff's summit and are connected by a much narrower neck of land. The Northwest Group, on the other hand, is separated from the West and East Groups by a ravine oriented northeast-southwest. This ravine varies in depth from c. 12 m on the west to 7 m on the east. The Southeast Group is located on a lower bluff, c. 4-5 m above the Rio Bobos floodplain, and roughly 800-900 m east-southeast of the East Group. Structures in the Southeast Group are immediately adjacent to the bluff's edge.

Resources: The Las Quebradas Zone is well provided with both water and building stones. As noted above, the Rio Bobos, a large tributary of the Rio Motagua, carries water year-round and is only 1.1 km to the south and west of the site zone. In addition, numerous tributaries of the Bobos carry a moderate amount of water even in the dry season and run fairly close to the zone: Pablo Crique skirts the base of the Las Quebradas bluff on the south and west, and an unnamed stream flows in the above-noted ravine that cuts through the site. Beyond these water sources, there are also two springs, one in the side of the bluff just below Str. 205-109 and the other in the base of the ridge at the level of the current rail line below Str. 205-26 and -27 (Fig. 3; in map pocket).

Sources of construction stone are equally close at hand. The beds of the Rio Bobos and, to a lesser extent, its small tributaries contain quantities of well-worn cobbles, a very commonly used stone in all Las Quebradas construction. In addition to these sources, a very rich deposit of cobbles some 1 km southwest of the site was being mined in 1978 by BANDEGUA. The area south and west of the locus on the floodplain was also littered in 1978 with large heaps of cobbles, apparently produced by modern dredging activities in the Bobos and its tributaries (see below). No sources of the stone slabs used at Las Quebradas were found. It is presumed that, given the large numbers used, they must have been procured in the adjacent Espiritu Santo mountains.

The agricultural potential of the land surrounding the site appears to be quite high, although because of modern patterns of ownership much of that land is not planted in subsistence crops. The flat broad floodplain of the Rio Bobos seems to be rejuvenated each year with flood-deposited silts. Continual cropping thus may have been a possibility in the past. The ridge top occupied by the site is also planted, although use of this area seems to entail a period of fallowing after each harvest: the East Group was cultivated for *milpa* (mixed planting of corn, beans, and squash) in June 1977 and had not been replanted as of January 1979.

Two further factors are also of potential aboriginal importance in the Las Quebradas area. First, the Rio Bobos cuts through the Espiritu Santo mountains to the southeast, extending well over the border into Honduras. In fact, the headwaters of the Bobos and the Rio Chiquila in Honduras are located only 2.7 km apart in the same highland valley. The latter river is a tributary of the Rio Chamelecon, whose broad valley currently provides one of the major communication channels to both the Ulua valley and the Caribbean coast to the north, and to the interior of Honduras and ultimately to Copan to the southwest. While current maps show a dense network of trails associated with the Rio Chiquila and extending down to the Chamelecon, no modern trails were found along the Rio Bobos in 1977 and 1979. A map defining landholding boundaries in the Las Quebradas area prior to 1926, however, clearly shows a "road to Honduras" that followed the Bobos or one of its tributaries to the southeast. This use of the Bobos as a pass over the Espiritu Santo range confirms the potential usefulness of that route implied by the local topography. A large Late Classic center, Tras Cerros, has recently been reported in the high mountains near the headwaters of the Bobos on the Honduran side of the frontier. The location of such a massive site along the putative Bobos/Chiquila communication corridor points to the pre-Hispanic significance of this route (Nakamura

1987). The Las Quebradas Zone, therefore, situated at the point where the Rio Bobos issues from the Espiritu Santo mountains, would have been in a strategic location to profit from any commerce that moved along this route. The Rios Bobos and Chiquila would have provided an important link between Las Quebradas and a variety of locales in what is today Honduras. This link is all the more crucial as the Bobos provided one of the two known passages across the Espiritu Santo range (the other being the Rio Chinamito near Playitas).

A second feature of potential importance is the presence of gold in placer deposits in the rivers around Las Quebradas. On maps printed at the turn of the century, in fact, Las Quebredas was called "Quebradas de Oro" because of the richness of the gold deposits in its streams. Placer mining operations using mechanical dredges were carried out in and around the Bobos during the early decades of this century. Presumably, as most of the gold was being carried in the Bobos and its tributaries, the actual techniques involved in its procurement could have been quite simple and within the reach of aboriginal technology. Despite the potential ease of acquisition, there is no evidence that the prehistoric occupants of the zone actually exploited this resource.

CURRENT STATUS

The principal agents of destruction at Locus 205 are road building, house construction, and looting, along with such natural agents as root action and erosion. Looting has been mercifully light at Las Quebradas and is concentrated primarily in the East and West Groups. In the former aggregation, a short, deep trench has been sunk into the summit of Str. 205-262, while an extensive series of illicit pits appears in the southern part of the Group in the area designated Str. 205-270. In the West Group, our team noted that a 3- to 4-m-long trench had recently been dug into the west side of Str. 205-16. A 0.5-m-deep pit was also found dug against the south side of Mon. 1 in the central court. Road building had inflicted damage on a total of 17 structures located in the East, West, and Northwest Groups. Eleven constructions had been disturbed in this way in the East Group (Str. 205-199, -204, -205, -217, -237/239, -244, -246, -247, and -260), five in the West Group (Str. 205-23/25, -37, and -38), and one in the Northwest Group (Str. 205-135). All of these roads had been built to facilitate the movement of cattle, and required the bulldozing of paths c. 3-5 m wide. While several structures lost as much as a third

to a half of their total lengths in the process, most of the larger structures, at least, had been avoided or lost only a corner. The incorporation of pre-Hispanic features into modern house complexes has also resulted in localized damage to construction. The three structures in the East Group (Str. 205-191/193) that were used in this fashion in 1978 had each suffered severe damage, especially on their summits. In the Northwest Group, modern occupation increased in intensity near its northeastern margin and it appeared that five to ten structures, all under 1 m high, were destroyed in this area simply through modern reuse.

Cattle operations in the northeastern part of the East Group, involving the construction of pens and weighing stations, resulted in the destruction of several small structures, leaving behind only rock scatters (R.C. 3, 4, and 9). The gold-mining operations, involving dredging watercourses with large steam shovels, damaged portions of the Southeast Group. While this activity had little effect on the ridge-top structures in the East, West, and Northwest Groups, it did damage platforms located much closer to the floodplain, cutting off the southern edge of the Southeast Group and truncating Str. 205-274 and -275.

Erosion is a problem in the East, West, and Southeast Groups, where seven, eight, and three structures, respectively, have been damaged by this process. All of these constructions are found along the edge of the ridge and are slowly decomposing as the cliff faces erode. Finally, the shallow and extensive root systems of palm trees have dislodged construction stones at many of the larger structures. This damage is especially pronounced on the summits of monumental substructures where these trees are most prevalent.

Ownership: The East, West, and Southeast Groups of the Las Quebradas Site Zone were owned by the Fabrica de Madera Las Quebradas, a plywood-producing firm with a factory in the Las Quebradas *aldea*. The Northwest Group fell within the *aldea* of Los Cerritos and was in private hands. The precise owner(s) was not determined.

SITE DESCRIPTION

Previous Work: Of all the major centers in the LMV, with the exception of Quirigua, Las Quebradas was probably the earliest to be located and described. Karl Sapper (1895, 1897) found this site in the early 1890s. In addition to locating it on his map of archaeological sites in Guatemala, he provided a brief report of his discovery, illustrated with a map of part of the center (ibid.). While it is difficult to say with certainty which portion of the site Sapper actually saw and recorded, it appears that most of his work was concentrated in the area of the West Group, where he encountered the major quadrangle that dominates this aggregation. After Sapper's work, Las Quebradas did not reappear in the literature for some 40 years, until Ricketson and Blom's (1940) account, apparently based on Sapper's earlier work. In 1972 Nowak visited Las Quebradas and produced a map of the East and West Groups showing a total of 70 structures (1973b: fig. 3).

Recording: The West, East, and Northwest Groups were mapped, using a transit, over the course of nine weeks in 1978, during which time excavations were also carried out. The Southeast Group was recorded primarily by notes and a sketch map of the structures using a hand-held Brunton pocket transit and paced distances. In all, c. 20 days were spent mapping and 100 person-days in clearing. Because of the size of the site and the denseness of the vegetation covering most of it, structures were cleared at their bases to determine overall dimensions, along their summits to locate superstructures, and in an axial line up their flanks to locate any unusual features such as broad terraces. If such features came to light in the axial clearing, then the appropriate face of the structure was fully cleaned of vegetation; otherwise the structure was not exposed further. Limitations of time and resources determined this spot-clearing approach. In areas of the site that were too thoroughly overgrown to investigate easily, teams of workers cleared lines of sight to locate and then defoliate smaller structure groups. In this way all of the site zone was examined.

The two unmapped structures shown in the East Group (see Fig. 3) were found in deep vegetation after clearing operations had terminated. Although they could not be mapped, their location was recorded. All structure heights in the West, East, and Northwest Groups were derived from instrument measurements, while the heights of construction in the Southeast Group were estimated by eye. The one exception to this was the Str. 205-110/112 cluster in the West Group, which was mapped with a tripod-mounted Brunton pocket transit and a 30-m tape. Platform heights here were estimated.

Description: In total area, the mapped portion of Las Quebradas—the East, West, and Northwest Groups—includes 275 structures, ten rock concentrations, which probably represent destroyed constructions, and two recorded but unmapped structures, all within an area 1.21 km east-west by 0.76 km north-

south. With the addition of the Southeast Group, the Las Quebradas Zone swells to 295 buildings, including rock concentrations, in an area roughly 2 km east-west by 1 km north-south. Construction is not evenly distributed over this zone, however. Most aboriginal occupation is concentrated in the area around the West and Northwest Groups on the ridge top overlooking the Rio Bobos. To the southeast, toward the higher hills of the Espiritu Santo range, occupation thins out rapidly. This is especially curious as there are no obvious topographic features to distinguish the southeastern bluffs from those supporting the major groups to the northwest. In fact, only c. 600 m southeast of the East Group is a ridge c. 12-14 m above the Bobos floodplain whose summit contains a wide expanse of flat land without aboriginal construction. This is the area that supports most of the modern housing of Las Quebradas *aldea*. While it is possible that recent construction resulted in the obliteration of prehistoric remains here, it seems unlikely that this destruction would have been so complete as to leave no sign of an earlier occupation. It is of further interest that the one group located outside of the major ridge-top occupation, the Southeast Group, is situated not atop this southeastern bluff, but at its base, 30-40 m to the south. The avoidance of this ridge as a locus for prehistoric construction remains unexplained.

The Las Quebradas East and West Groups, with no clear natural dividing line between them, are defined in much the same manner as the Playitas groups. The Northwest Group is separated from the rest by the deep ravine noted earlier. The Southeast Group is defined by its isolated position vis-à-vis the remainder of the center.

The East Group is the area of most intensive building activity, with 124 recorded structures and eight rock concentrations spread over an area 493 m east-west by 598 m north-south (see Fig. 3). This is the largest of the Groups in the Las Quebradas Zone. In a general sense, the distribution of structures here follows a common pattern: a series of monumental quadrangles (three in this case) constituting an architectural focus surrounded by other, smaller structures scattered either singly or in small groups. Outside of this rather general resemblance to other LMV Groups, the East Group has certain features that mark it as distinct, even within the Las Quebradas Zone. The size of the structures surrounding the major courts is one of these aspects (see Table III.2). The average height of the structures that encompass the three principal quadrangles is 4.88 m. Only the structures in Group I of Playitas even approach these in height. The platforms in the environs of these quadrangles also reach considerable heights, as for example do Str. 205-205, -199, and -230, respectively 5, 5, and 3.85 m high. The average height of all structures in the East Group is 1.32 m. By contrast, the areas of the two completely enclosed major courts in this Group are quite small: the west court measures 37.5 m², while the east court is 24 m north-south by 9 m east-west. The large plaza to the south encompasses an area 88.5 m east-west by 60 m north-south, and possesses a configuration known from only one other group in the survey area, the Las Quebradas West Group. Here, while the northeast plaza corner is closed by construction, the southeast remains open, albeit narrowly defined by Str. 205-261 and -262, and the entire western side possesses no structures. This latter face, however, is not without artificial modification: a 6.75-to 7.3-m-high terrace (Str. 205-264) was constructed on it, possibly to create and surely to maintain the steep face of the drop-off. While the west side of the plaza is open, therefore, access to the plaza from this side is not direct. The east court is also unusual in that it is raised c. 4.1 m above the surrounding ground level. This small "acropolis" is the most inaccessible area of the entire zone, with entry to it obtained only by scaling the steep western face of Str. 205-256, a structure which itself faces into a court completely enclosed by high construction. In all, the area covered by these three adjacent monumental units is 158 m north-south by 132 m east-west.

Many of the structures surrounding the main group are arranged in aggregations in which principles of orthogonality and the apparent desire to take advantage of natural contours vie for supremacy. In those areas of the East Group where the land is relatively flat, the arrangement of structures tends to be orthogonal. To the north, where the land drops off rapidly into the northeast-southwest ravine (quebrada), the structures take advantage of the ridge edge to enhance their apparent heights (Str. 205-165, -167, -168, -170, -172) and are built into the sloping south face of the bluff. Here, despite the presence of a precipitous drop, the structures are arranged at very close to right angles to each other. Structure size, in addition to the nature of the terrain, also affects orthogonality in that constructions c. 1 m high or higher tend to be located in orthogonally arranged groups, while those below that height are more likely

to be scattered individually or integrated into irregular aggregates.

Also in the area of Str. 205-156, -157, -160, -163, and -175 is found some evidence of low (c. 0.5 m high) terracing, which provides relatively small areas of flat terrain. Despite the drop-off to the north and south, however, there was surprisingly little effort invested in terracing these slopes to make more land usable. Outside of the small amount of terracing seen in the area of Str. 205-155/175, most of this activity resulted in the enhanced appearance of architectural groups, e.g., the high terrace built along the west side of the large plaza in the main group (Str. 205-264). Structures in general were not built in low-lying, potentially swampy areas, e.g., the southeastern portion of the East Group.

The three contiguous monumental units of the principal group are oriented c. N 2° 30′ E. The alignments of other constructions vary considerably.

The West Group consists of 112 structures and one rock concentration located within an area 404.5 m east-west by 295.5 m north-south. The breakdown by height of the structures composing this aggregation is given in Table III.2.

The West Group, like its eastern counterpart, is dominated by a main group that consists of three adjoining monumental units, two of which are quadrangles with their corners closed by construction and one of which has at least two corners unobstructed. Around this complex are scattered a series of smaller groups, some of which are orthogonally arranged and others of which are not. In general, the structures composing the West Group are somewhat lower than those in the East Group. The average height of the structures defining the main group is 2.17 m, while the average height for all the structures in the West Group is 1.03 m. The areas of the major courts/plazas in the West Group are as follows: the north court measures c. 24.5 m northeast-southwest by 45.5 m northwest-southeast; the south court is almost square, 53.5 m north-south by 54.5 m east-west; and the south plaza measures 35 m north-south by 55 m east-west. The total area covered by the three contiguous courts/plazas is c. 108.5 m east-west by 180 m north-south.

The structures surrounding the main group follow some of the same organizational patterns seen in the East Group. In particular, a tendency toward orthogonality is noted among structures more than 1 m high located on relatively flat terrain, e.g., Str. 205-23/25 west of the central court. Smaller structures diverge strongly from the orthogonal in their organization, whether occupying flat land (Str. 205-47/49) or built into the southern hill slope (e.g., Str. 205-100/107). In general, however, most of the platforms in the West Group are oriented orthogonally within individual groupings and follow the overall orientation of the Group as represented by the main group, c. N 10° 0′ W. This tendency toward mutual alignment is more pronounced than that noted in the East Group and may be due in large part to the West Group's control of more flat ridge top than is available in the east. It should also be noted that the principal plazas of the East and West Groups do not share a common orientation.

As can be seen in Fig. 3, construction surrounding the West Group major quadrangles is densest in the immediate area of these units and tends to drop off, both in density and in the size of the structures involved, away from them. As in the east, low, swampy areas were avoided for construction, e.g., east of Str. 205-79.

An interesting feature not recorded at other loci in the LMV is the long, rather sinuous construction composed of Str. 205-30 and -31, along the southern bluff edge. At first thought to be a modern feature, i.e., debris piled up from bulldozing, this feature proved on closer examination to have a regular outline; moreover, there is no evidence of bulldozing in the vicinity.

Terracing in the West Group, while it does occur, is limited in its preserved extent. Short, low (c. 0.5 m high) terraces of river cobbles extend from several structures, e.g., Str. 205-26 and -27, and in one case, a c. 1-m-high terrace functions as a substructure for another platform, Str. 205-44. As in the east, extensive terracing to create areas of flat land is absent, and terraces seem to have been employed primarily to enhance existing structures and to slow erosion around them.

Finally, the south plaza in the west main group is unusual in that it proved to be a mirror image, albeit on a smaller scale, of the plaza in the east main group. As with its eastern counterpart, two corners of the plaza are closed or restricted by construction, while one side, the east in this case, is devoid of structures. This open side, however, is defined by a c. 0.4-m-high stone-faced terrace so that access to the plaza from the east is not direct. Monumental plazas such as those found in the East and West Groups are uncommon in Motagua valley centers, and the fact that the two located here face each other marks Las Quebradas as unique architecturally within the region.

The Northwest Group consists of 41 structures and

one rock concentration within an area 513 m northeast-southwest by 197 m northwest-southeast. All but seven of these structures are low (c. 0.5-1 m high) platforms arranged in small groups of three to five structures (see Table III.2 for height breakdown by structure). The seven exceptions completely enclose a court that measures 52.5 m east-west by 35 m north-south and constitute the main group dominating this aggregation. Unlike its counterparts in the East and West Groups, this architectural focus has only one closed court and not several contiguous units.

In general, the Northwest Group structures are smaller and more dispersed than those noted in the other major aggregations in the zone. There does not appear to be any appreciable clustering of smaller constructions in the immediate area of the principal group; rather they tend to be evenly dispersed around it. The average height of the main group's structures is 2.01 m, while the average structure height for the entire Northwest Group is 0.85 m.

Despite these differences in size, the principle of orthogonality in structure arrangement holds here as in the East and West Groups. Perhaps in part because of the relatively wide expanse of flat terrain available in this area, the structures in each individual group are orthogonally arranged. There does not seem to have been any attempt to orient the different structure aggregates with respect to each other, however, and an overall Group orientation is lacking. Also, as has been noted before, very small structures in a group often show different alignments from the larger platforms composing that cluster.

Low, potentially swampy areas were avoided in locating construction, e.g., the area between Str. 205-122/125 and Str. 205-128/130. Construction is largely limited to higher, better-drained terrain.

The only unusual features are related to the plan of the principal group. First, there is a very low platform extending into the middle of the court. This 0.29-m-high structure, Str. 205-121, is unique among known centers in the LMV. Second, the southern and western constructions surrounding the court function as platforms that support smaller structures, a feature recorded at Quebrada Grande (Groups I and III) and in the West Group in the Las Quebradas Site Zone, but unknown elsewhere at LMV sites. Finally, the principal court is closed on its north side by a combination of platform construction and a faced natural rise (Str. 205-120). The eastern third of the north closing construction consists of a natural rise faced on its court side by a series of low, narrow terraces in the typical LMV step-terrace style. This use of natural contours

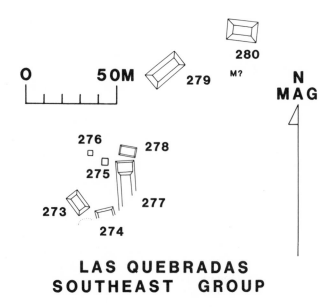

Figure 4.   Map of the SE Group, Las Quebradas.

to complete quadrangles is very uncommon in the survey zone.

The Southeast Group consists of eight structures spread over an area c. 100 m northeast-southwest by 75 m northwest-southeast. This is the smallest of all the Las Quebradas Groups examined, and as an inspection of Fig. 4 will show, it does not contain a main group defined by monumental construction. The average height of structures here is even lower than in the Northwest Group. In overall appearance, the Southeast Group resembles one of the larger outlying aggregations that surround the monumental foci of other Groups. Four of the eight structures are arranged into one more or less orthogonal plaza, one structure on each of the four sides, with all of the plaza corners open and free of construction. The largest structures in the Group (Str. 205-279/280), however, are to be found northeast of this plaza, where they do not form part of any recognizable grouping.

On the basis of surface indications, the monumental structures at Las Quebradas are built in the step-terrace technique. These low, narrow terraces could be seen in several cases facing the sides of large platforms.

Other architectural features were also noted on the surface of these massive constructions. On the summits of Str. 205-256, -257, -259, -14, and -15, lines of unfaced river cobbles were found flush with the surface. These features may well have functioned as

foundations for perishable superstructures—a general absence of tumbled stone suggests that the superstructures were not built primarily of this material. In addition, on six platforms (Str. 205-41 and -253/256) there are small, 1- to 2-m-square quadrilateral stone features. These squares are built of closely packed river cobbles, currently even with the summit surface, and occur singly, in pairs, and in regularly spaced lines across structure summits. One of these squares was excavated on Str. 205-41 and is discussed in Chap. 3. While these elements were obviously used in superstructure construction, it is difficult to determine their precise function. They do, however, look like pillar bases and might have served to support columns of either stone or perishable materials (see Chap. 3).

In general, on the basis of the surface survey alone, the primary building stones used in monumental construction are the naturally shaped river cobble and schist slab. Only a very few stones show any evidence of having been intentionally cut and shaped, and none of these are still *in situ*. In all places where larger structures have been cut, the fill is a very hard-compacted reddish orange clay. This is the same type of earth that forms the surface of the bluff.

Smaller structures, those below 1 m in height, lack any evidence of the step-terrace technique and generally have cobbles, but no stone slabs, on their surfaces. Clear wall lines were not recorded on these humbler constructions. In the Southeast Group, even on the taller structures, slabs are rare or absent, leaving open the possibility that the architecture here is different from that in the rest of the zone. The fill exposed in the smaller structures is the same type of hard reddish orange clay noted above.

In several cases, in particular Str. 205-85 and -206, a platform was found whose sides are step-terraced and yet whose summit is of earth and bears no trace of stones. No purely earthen platforms were recorded in this locus. Several constructions in the East Group have one or two small, narrow projections extending from one of their faces (e.g., Str. 205-247 and -261). These features are built of cobbles, and are usually no more than 0.2-0.4 m high and 3-5.5 m long by 2-3.5 m wide. They appear too small to have functioned as platforms supporting residences and their use(s) remains unknown. Finally, on several of the monumental constructions, especially in the East Group, a broad terrace is clearly visible on one flank of a platform. These terraces are built of long schist slabs and are distinct from the narrow step-terraces, which are usually no more than 0.35-0.4 m wide and high (see Str. 205-261).

None of the courts in the East and Northwest main groups shows any evidence of a paved surface. In the West Group, however, a surface concentration of small white round cobbles was found covering an area roughly 19.5 m north-south by 23.5 m east-west in the central court. The area in which these cobbles are found is not raised above the general court level, the rest of which shows no sign of having been paved. The association of this feature with Mon. 1, which stands at almost the exact center of its southern edge, suggests that these white cobbles served as a surface related to the use of that monument (see Chap. 3).

Special Features:

Seven uncarved monuments were found in the fully enclosed courts of the East, West, and Northwest main groups. Some of these monuments (Mon. 4-7) show no evidence of any artificial modification, and in these cases their designations as monuments are based on their location, size, and mutual alignments.

Monument 1: The single monument found in the West Group is a column of hard gray crystalline stone placed in the approximate center of the south court. When found, this massive stone was broken, with the butt end still in the ground and the severed portion of the shaft lying close by to the south. The total reconstructed length of Mon. 1 above ground surface is c. 2.83 m, while the roughly oval cross-section measures c. 0.63 m wide by 0.46 m thick. The two broad faces of this column are not flattened but are convexly curved. The top is ragged and ill shaped. The area around the monument was excavated (Op. 24B) and is described in Chap. 3.

Monument 2: A pecked stone sphere made of a hard gray crystalline stone similar to that of Mon. 1, located almost exactly in the center of the main group court in the Northwest Group. This stone measures 0.51 m in diameter and does not seem to protrude far below the surface. The area around Mon. 2 was excavated in 1978 (Op. 24L) and the results are reported in Chap. 3.

Monument 3: Located 18 m east of Mon. 2, within the same court. Monuments 2 and 3 approximately bisect the court on an east-west line. Monument 3 is another pecked stone sphere made of the same material as Mon. 2. The only difference between the two is that Mon. 3 is smaller, with a diameter of 0.34 m.

Monument 4: A large, flat, unmodified slab 1.05 m east-west by 1.34 m north-south, located in the center of the small east court in the East Group. When found, Mon. 4 was lying flat and was more or less flush with the surface of this court. A trench was excavated on the east and west sides of Mon. 4 in 1978 (Op. 24P) and is discussed in Chap. 3.

Monument 5: A round, unmodified white quartz boulder 1 m in diameter and located in almost the exact center of the west court of the East Group's main group. This stone does not appear to have protruded far below ground surface. A small pit was placed against the north side of Mon. 5 in 1978 (Op. 24Q) and is discussed in Chap. 3.

Monument 6: Located 13 m north of Mon. 5 along the north-south axis of the west court, Mon. 6 is essentially identical to the central quartz boulder.

Monument 7: Located 15 m south of Mon. 5 along the north-south axis of the west court, Mon. 7 is essentially identical to Mon. 5 and 6.

Monument 8 (?): A possible large stone monument was also found c. 11 m S 16° 0' E from the southwest corner of Str. 205-280 in the Southeast Group. This stone is c. 2.5 m long, 0.8 m wide at its widest point, and oriented S 26° 0' W. At the time it was found in 1979, one end protruded 0.32 m above ground surface while the rest sloped down to below surface level. The stone is a fine-grained quartzlike material with many small shiny mica inclusions. It does not appear to have been modified artificially to produce its roughly columnar shape. The location of the "monument" out in the open and not within an enclosed court is quite unusual for the LMV. This fact, coupled with the location no more than 40 m to the north of a steep natural rise from which natural boulders might have derived, urges a certain amount of caution in our calling this stone a monument.

Alluviation: The location of the Las Quebradas structures on bluffs overlooking the Rio Bobos precludes the burial of prehistoric features by alluvial deposits. This is confirmed by excavations in the East, West, and Northwest Groups revealing minimal natural overburden.

Surface Collections: Eighteen surface lots containing 418 sherds, two *incensario* fragments, 316 pieces of chipped stone, four *bajareque* fragments, one ground stone fragment, and one figurine fragment were obtained from the Las Quebradas Zone in 1977-79. Of these collections, seven are from the East Group, eight

TABLE 2.2

SURFACE COLLECTIONS

Lot #	Contents	Depositional Significance	Provenience
24A/1	30 pcs. obsidian	General surface (Nowak collection)	W Group
24A/2	20 sherds; 7 pcs. obsidian	Mixed surface and buried material	Postholes, E Group, c. 37 m W of Str. 205-165
24A/3	4 sherds; 2 pcs. obsidian	Mixed surface and buried material	Postholes, E Group, c. 35 m W of Str. 205-166/172
24A/4	9 pcs. obsidian; 1 pc. chert; 1 *bajareque* frag.	Surface	Corner junction of Str. 205-1 and -2, W Group
24A/5	2 sherds; 89 pcs. obsidian	Surface	Path along SE margin of E Group leading to Las Quebradas *aldea*
24A/6	2 pcs. obsidian	Surface	NW Group among smaller str.
24A/7	19 sherds	Mixed surface and burial material	Tree-root hole, summit of Str. 205-25
24A/8	5 sherds; 6 pcs. obsidian	Surface	SE margin of W Group near Str. 205-108 and -109
24A/9	1 metate frag.	?	Donated from Las Quebradas area
24A/10	4 pcs. obsidian	Surface	North of E and W courts, main group, E Group
24A/11	9 sherds; 71 pcs. obsidian	Surface	East of Str. 205-199, -194, -205, and -217, E Group
24A/12	19 pcs. obsidian	Surface	From cattle corral E of Str. 205-227 and -228, E Group
24A/13	1 sherd; 19 pcs. obsidian	Mixed surface and fill(?) material	Surface of Str. 205-223, disturbed by cattle corral, E Group
24A/14	100 sherds; 7 pcs. obsidian	Mixed surface and fill material	Tractor cut through str. W of central court, W Group
24A/15	136 sherds; 17 pcs. obsidian; 1 *bajareque* frag.	Mixed surface and fill material	Tractor cut through Str. 205-24 and -25, W Group
24A/16	27 sherds; 23 pcs. obsidian; 1 *bajareque* frag.	Mixed surface and fill material	Tractor cut through Str. 205-38, W Group
24A/17	37 sherds; 1 censer frag.; 1 figurine frag.; 2 pcs. obsidian	Mixed surface and fill material	Tractor debris pile W of N court, W Group
24A/18	57 sherds; 1 censer frag.; 8 pcs. obsidian; 1 *bajareque* frag.	Mixed surface and buried material	Mining operation cut below Str. 205-275, SE Group

from the West Group, one from the Northwest Group, one from the Southeast Group, and one is a donated find (24A/9) from the general Las Quebradas area (see Table 2.2).

Excavations: Seventeen excavations were carried out in the Las Quebradas Site Zone in 1978: eight in the West Group, three in the Northwest Group, and six in the East Group. These are described in Chap. 3.

QUEBRADA GRANDE (Locus 206, Op. 41)

LOCATION AND SETTING

General Location: Quebrada Grande is c. 4.4 km northeast of the Las Quebradas Site Zone (Locus 205) and c. 6.7 km northeast of the Bobos Site Zone (Locus 209; see Fig. 1).

Topography: The four groups composing this archaeological zone extend through the *aldea* of the same name in a rough north-south line for a distance of c. 640 m on the broad, flat floodplain of the Rio Quebrada Grande, a southern tributary of the Rio Motagua. The foothills of the Espiritu Santo mountains begin 1.25 km to the southeast of the site.

Resources: The present residents and their aboriginal predecessors were well supplied with water both from the Rio Quebrada Grande, which flows 0.83 km to the southwest of the zone, and—more conveniently—from its many tributaries that run through the modern *aldea* and within roughly 100 m of all four of the prehistoric Groups. Even during the dry season when the zone was visited (early to mid-March 1978 and 1979), both the Quebrada Grande and its tributaries carried a considerable volume of water. Building materials, in particular the ubiquitous river cobble, are also available in these streambeds. It should be noted, however, that the cobbles here are somewhat smaller than those found in other rivers, such as the Rio Chinamito, and the principal stream load in the Quebrada Grande and its affluents is a fine gray sand. The relatively small size of cobbles deposited in the area of the Quebrada Grande Site Zone may be due to its distance from the foothills of the Espiritu Santo mountains. Even so, the sources of building stones would not have been too distant from the site zone. The source of the schist slabs used in construction at Quebrada Grande is unknown, although it most probably lies in the same hills to the southeast.

The land surrounding the site zone was reported by local informants to be very rich agriculturally, though much of it in 1978 and 1979 was used as pasture and only small plots were devoted to *milpa* cultivation.

No modern trails extend southward from the *aldea* toward Honduras, and the Rio Quebrada Grande itself appears to run only a relatively short distance in that direction into the Espiritu Santo range. As a result, it does not provide a likely ancient route. The only modern trail of any importance passing through this zone runs north-northeast from Las Quebradas to Las Conchas on the Rio Animas to the northeast of Quebrada Grande. This route is part of a broader network linking the *aldeas* on the southern edge of the valley with each other and with the town of Morales, the municipal center. No prehistoric significance could be safely imputed to this route.

Quebrada Grande, like Choco and Comanche Farm, is situated well out onto the floodplain, near a major banana orchard (c. 1.7 km to the southeast). This association with an area of commercial farming combined with the reputedly good soils in the vicinity of the site suggests that Quebrada Grande's size and presumed importance may have owed more to control of good agricultural land than to any profit made from trade. Further consideration of the factors affecting the location of this site is reserved for discussion in Chap. 7.

CURRENT STATUS

The most commonly seen form of disturbance in the site zone is stone robbing. All of the Groups that could be examined in any detail (Groups I-III) have suffered from this problem. In Group I most of the smaller structures surrounding the main group are denuded of stone, as is the northeast corner of the main group itself, where modern construction is concentrated. In Group II, the general lack of visible stones in the main group indicates stone robbing in the past, and in Group III, the areas surrounding modern houses are largely devoid of stone. In addition, some damage has been done by hoeing for *milpa* and by shallow pitting associated with the use of modern constructions. The latter type of destruction is most obvious in the more heavily settled Group III main group, and the smaller structures surrounding the Group I principal group.

Root action may have caused some damage at the

site, though this appears to have been relatively slight. The most extensive natural agent of destruction is a small tributary of the Rio Quebrada Grande, c. 4 m wide and 1 m deep, which has cut away the eastern third of Str. 206-12 in the Group II main group (see Fig. 6). No evidence of purposeful looting was recorded.

Ownership: Group I was owned by Sr. Juan Ramon Sandoval-Ramirez in 1979. Ownership of the remainder of the zone was not determined.

SITE DESCRIPTION

Previous Work: Nowak located a site near the Quebrada Grande *aldea* on his valley map (1973b: fig. 2) but included neither a site map nor any description of its features. As noted elsewhere, Nowak called this site "Los Cerritos" after the BANDEGUA banana plantation near which it lies. The name has been changed here because the site actually lies within the *aldea* of Quebrada Grande, and another site, northwest of Las Quebradas, was found in 1978 within the *aldea* of Los Cerritos.

Recording: Because of time and money limitations in 1978 and 1979, the remote location of the Quebrada Grande Site Zone, and the nature of the covering vegetation, most of this locus was recorded solely by notes. Sketch maps, made by using a handheld Brunton pocket transit to determine the structure orientations, and pacing to define their basal dimensions, were drawn for the Group I and II main groups. The Group III main group was mapped in 1978 with a Brunton pocket transit mounted on a tripod, and a 30-m tape. Group IV was too densely overgrown in both 1978 and 1979 to be even sketchmapped. All structure heights were estimated in the field by eye. Attention in both seasons was concentrated on recording large monumental units and the smaller structures immediately surrounding them. While some effort was devoted to examining the wider area around these foci, it is very likely that some structures were missed. In all, one day in 1978 and one in 1979 were devoted to recording this locus, while four days with a crew of 12 Guatemalan laborers were spent in 1978 clearing the structures in preparation for recording.

Description: In all, 49 structures and three platforms, scattered over a span of 640 m north-south, were identified in the Quebrada Grande Site Zone. Those structures may be divided into four more or less distinct Groups. Each of these consists of a main group of orthogonally arranged monumental architecture, which surrounds on all sides an enclosed court and which, in turn, is surrounded by a series of smaller structures found either singly or in small groups. The main groups vary in complexity from simple single-quadrangle arrangements, e.g., Groups II and III, to more complex units involving adjoining quadrangles, e.g., Group I (see Figs. 5-7; see Table III.3 for a breakdown of structures by height).

In more specific terms, Group I consists of 18 structures within an area roughly 180 m north-south by 250 m east-west (Str. 206-1/10 and Plat. 1 mapped; see Fig. 5). About half of these constructions are monumental structures arranged orthogonally around two adjoining courts, which they enclose on all four sides. Despite the general similarity in form of these linked quadrangles to those noted in other LMV centers, there are some striking differences as well. First, the Group I monumental structures are oriented S 84° 0′ W as opposed to the more typical north-south alignments of the other valley examples. The general form of the constituent courts is also somewhat different. The east court is surrounded on all sides by construction, with the corners closed by construction including a narrow wall which seals the southwest corner. The level of this court appears to have been lower than the surrounding ground surface. The west side of the east court is bounded by a massive platform (Plat. 1) unique among all known LMV sites, which stands 5.5 m high and measures roughly 55 m east-west by 58 m north-south at its base. This platform provides a foundation for five structures which together define a second plaza on its summit. The northwest, southwest, and northeast corners of this plaza are left open, though access is still restricted by the height of the supporting substructure, while the southeast corner is closed by a 0.75-m-high narrow wall connecting Str. 206-6 and -7.

Extending 55 m to the north from the northwest corner of the supporting platform is Str. 206-4, which at an orientation of N 6° 0′ E is aligned at a slightly different angle from the rest of the group.

The areas of the two major courts are 40 m east-west by 39.5 m north-south for the west raised plaza and 66.5 m east-west by 54 m north-south for the east court.

To the east and northeast of these ten structures are eight additional, lower constructions, three of which

27

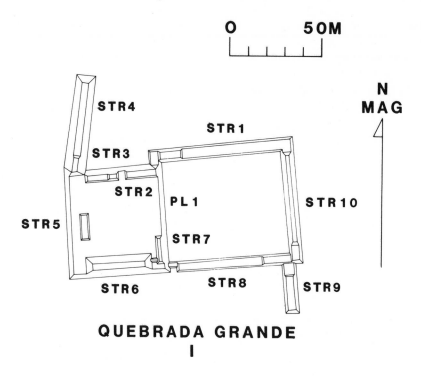

Figure 5. Map of Group I, Quebrada Grande.

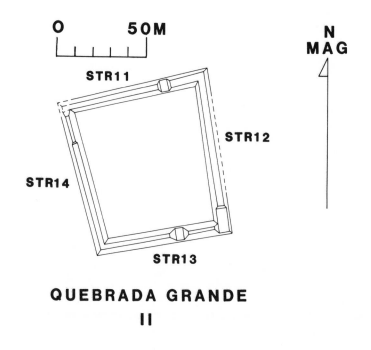

Figure 6. Map of Group II, Quebrada Grande.

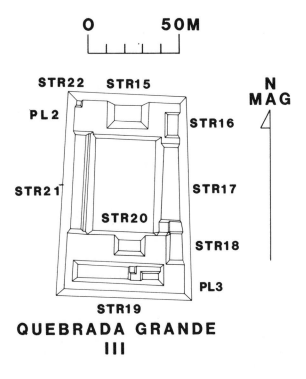

O   50M

STR22   STR15   N
                         MAG
PL2

                  STR16

STR21   STR17

        STR20   STR18

                  PL3

        STR19

QUEBRADA GRANDE
III

Figure 7. Map of Group III, Quebrada Grande.

are arranged into an orthogonal plaza group. This latter plaza is situated on a natural rise 85-90 m S 77° 0' E of Str. 206-9 and is surrounded on all but the western side by construction. The corners providing access to this plaza are left open. The remaining structures appear to have been scattered singly. All of these surrounding structures are 1-2 m high.

Group II, c. 200 m S 7° 0' E from Group I, consists of nine structures scattered over an area 160 m north-south by 100 m east-west. The Group could be divided into two parts: a main group (Str. 206-11/14) composed of a single court enclosed on four sides by monumental construction, and a slightly smaller aggregate located c. 90 m to the northwest, about equidistant between the principal Group I and II court complexes.

The main group's four structures range in height from 1.75 to 4.5 m with most between 3.5 and 4.5 m high: they are orthogonally arranged and oriented between S 9° 0' E and S 10° 30' E (see Fig. 6). All of the court's corners are closed: the northeast, southeast, and southwest by construction, and the northwest by a natural rise into which Str. 206-11 and -14 are built. The only obvious points of access are in Str. 206-11 and -13, in both of which structure summit heights dip

to within 0.4 m of the court level. The court measures 70 m north-south by 64 m east-west and appears to be at approximately the same level as ground surface to the south.

The cluster of smaller structures northwest of the main group consists of four constructions orthogonally arranged around a court, which they enclose on all four sides. The southwest and southeast corners of this court are closed by low constructions, which connect adjacent structures, while the northeast and northwest corners are left open. The structures range in height from 1 to 4 m, with three of them falling between 2 and 4 m. The general orientation of the plaza is N 12° 0' W. In addition to the four structures delimiting the above court, a fifth construction (c. 1 m high) was found north of and connected by a low saddle to the northwest corner of the northern structure of the quadrangle. This entire aggregation of five structures is situated atop a c. 3.5-m-high natural rise reinforced on the north with cobble terracing. This is the same rise into which the Group II main group has been built.

Group III (Fig. 7) is 410 m S 10° 0' W of Group II; its main group is composed of eight structures orthogonally arranged around and fully enclosing a court that measures 49.5 m north-south by 33 m east-west and is oriented N 3° 30' E to N 1° 0' W. The arrangement of structures in this court complex (Str. 206-15/22 and Plat. 2 and 3) is somewhat different from the arrangements found at other sites. In particular, the southern portion of the main group consists of a 36-m-wide platform (Plat. 3) that stands 3 m high on the south and supports two structures (Str. 206-19 and -20) facing each other across a distance of 3.75 m. In addition, two low structures are situated on the northwest and northeast corners of Plat. 2 (Str. 206-22 and -16 respectively). This latter structural arrangement has been recorded elsewhere only at Las Quebradas in the West and Northwest Groups. The level of the enclosed court appears to be approximately the same as that of the surrounding ground surface.

Beyond the main group, four smaller structures were noted. Three of these humbler constructions are arranged into an irregular group roughly 60 m north of the main group, while one is located by itself c. 40 m north of the main group. All four of these structures are between 1 and 1.5 m high. In all, Group III contains 12 structures within an area 108 m north-south by 70 m east-west.

TABLE 2.3

SURFACE COLLECTIONS

Lot #	Contents	Depositional Significance	Provenience
41A/1	5 sherds; 1 pc. obsidian	Surface	Group III main group
41A/2	2 sherds	Surface	Small group, roughly 1 km SW of Group III
41A/3	5 sherds; 26 pcs. obsidian	Surface	Area of road at turnoff to *aldea* of Quebrada Grande

Group IV is 90 m south-southeast from Group III and seems to conform to the general pattern noted at other Quebrada Grande Groups, with a court surrounded on all four sides by structures and the corners closed by construction. A difference here may be that the structures which define the main group court are relatively low: the west structure is roughly 1 m high while the south structure steps up to 1.5-2 m. No difference is noted in elevation between the court level and the surrounding ground surface. The main group is oriented roughly N 34° 0′ W. In heavy vegetation southwest of this main group, four low structures were reported by local informants. Unfortunately, because of the ground cover, these reports were not verified in 1978 or 1979. If these four structures are taken into account, Group IV contains a total of eight structures.

Beyond these Groups, two additional structures, one c. 2 m and the other c. 1 m high, were found on the south bank of the Rio Quebrada Grande roughly 1 km southwest of Group III. River action in this area had led to the partial destruction of the larger structure and may have resulted in the obliteration of others.

The step-terrace technique appears to have been favored in the construction of monumental structures within the zone. This contention is based on the recognition of several extant wall lines at both Groups I and III, and the fact that cobbles and slabs are the most common form of building debris scattered on the surface of large constructions in Groups I, III, and IV. The Group II monumental structures are devoid of stones, and while their height suggests that the step-terrace approach was probably employed here as well, there is no clear evidence to support this view. A variant of the step-terrace approach was found on the artificially faced hill slope in Group II (see above). Here, unfaced river cobbles are set into the north hill flank and arranged into short step-terraces constructed without the use of stone slabs.

The summit of Str. 206-17 in the Group III main group has evidence of cobble alignments set flush with its surface. In addition to these lines, several squares of close-packed cobbles also flush with the summit surface are set on top of this structure at regular intervals of c. 3.5 m. These features are reminiscent of the cobble squares found at Las Quebradas, Mojanales, and Playitas on the tops of monumental constructions. Presumably, both the cobble lines and stone squares functioned in superstructure construction, with the former acting as foundations for perishable walls, and the latter as pillar bases for stone or perishable columns (see Chap. 3). Unfortunately, the summits of most monumental structures at Quebrada Grande are so badly disturbed that the nature of their superstructures could not be determined on the basis of surface remains.

The smaller structures found around the main groups were largely devoid of stones when investigated in 1978 and 1979, so little can be said of the nature of their construction.

Alluviation: The possibility exists, as with all floodplain sites, that the deposition of river silts during floods by the nearby Rio Quebrada Grande might have obscured lower structures completely, and visible structures to an unknown degree.

Surface Collections: Twelve sherds and 27 pieces of obsidian were recovered from the surface of the Quebrada Grande Zone (Lots 41A/1-3; see Table 2.3). In addition to this rather paltry collection, a realistically modeled hollow human ceramic head found in the area of Group I was examined. This head is c. 12.6 cm high, to the break at the neck, and c. 9.1 cm wide. The paste is tan with few inclusions and quite hard, while the surface is smoothed but not polished. The figure wears a cap with modeled spikes that comes down just above the eyes, and the mouth is open. In the back of the head, just below the top of the cap, is a hole c. 1 cm in diameter, which provides a second means of access into the interior of the head. Residents of the Group I area reported finding a ground stone artifact, either a mano or a metate, in the same general area. They could recall finding nothing else in the Quebrada Grande Zone over the various years in which they have lived there.

Excavations: None.

CHOCO (Locus 212, Op. 21)

LOCATION AND SETTING

General Location: Choco is situated on the commercial *finca* (farm) of the same name, c. 5.6 km southeast of the Comanche Farm Site Zone (Locus 210), c. 4.2 km southwest of the Playitas Site Zone (Locus 200), and 3.1 km northeast of Arapahoe Viejo (Locus 216; see Fig. 1).

Topography: Locus 212 sits on the broad, flat floodplain of the Rio Encantado, a tributary of the Rio Motagua, and is c. 1 km north of the foothills of the Espiritu Santo mountains (see Fig. 1).

Resources: Choco is well situated with respect to several natural resources, especially water. The Rio Encantado is a broad, fast-flowing stream, even in the dry season, running 0.8 km to the west of the site. It is possible that this river, which was canalized by BANDE-GUA c. 1.6 km northwest of the locus, may once have run even closer to the site.

The Encantado is also a source of river cobbles similar to many of those employed in building at the site. Other stones used in construction, in particular the large slabs and chunks of granitelike stone comparable to those noted at Locus 210, are not evident in the observed sections of the floodplain. The foothills of the Espiritu Santo mountains, however, might well have been the source for these stones.

The area around the site appears rich in agricultural potential, though much of it was used in 1978 for the production of oil palm and as cattle pasture. Subsistence (maize) farming was limited to areas immediately surrounding modern houses, and toward the foothills to the south where cash cropping and cattle raising did not provide competition.

A special feature noted at Choco in 1978 was the presence of a small cacao grove c. 0.4 km south-southwest of the main group. It has been proposed that Quirigua controlled rich cacao lands in the Late Classic and that this crop might have contributed to the importance of the site (Sharer 1990). The discovery of cacao trees here and on the first bench north of the site of Quirigua adds a certain plausibility to the argument for elite control of this valuable crop in the Late Classic (see Chap. 7 for a fuller discussion of this topic).

Unlike the Rios Bobos and Chinamito, the Encantado does not appear to have provided a viable passage across the Espiritu Santo range toward Honduras. No evidence for the existence of such a route existed in 1978, and the topographic situation would seem to argue most strongly against it (see Fig. 1).

CURRENT STATUS

Informants reported that in the recent past more structures were visible at the site, and that at least some had been lost over the years to mechanized plowing. No direct evidence to support this claim was noted. Another cause of disturbance is the presence of a series of drainage canals c. 1-1.5 m deep. While it appeared that only three of these channels had actually cut extant structures (Str. 212-58, -34, and -3; Fig. 8; in map pocket), it is possible that some subsurface features were also disturbed by the ditches.

The major cause of disturbance, however, is the large oil palm trees which grow in considerable numbers over many of the structures. The extensive, albeit shallow, root systems of these palms are responsible for dislodging many stones from at least the terminal construction levels, especially on the summits of the larger structures. In these areas, no clear superstructure lines remain and the surface is littered with debris dislodged by the trees.

Evidence for looting is limited to Str. 212-1, -3, and -4, which show signs of having been cut by short, shallow trenches.

Ownership: Sr. Francisco Rosale.

SITE DESCRIPTION

Previous Work: Arlen Chase (pers. comm. 1977) reports that, while assisting Nowak in 1974, he visited the site of Choco and made a sketch map of the main group (Str. 212-1/7). No other reference to this site is known.

Recording: Choco was recorded over the course of two field seasons. The first visit was made in April 1977, at which time the overall extent of the locus was assessed, notes were taken, and a map was made of a structure group located in the northern part of the site (Str. 212-73/76) with a tripod-mounted Brunton pocket transit and a 30-m tape. Because of this center's size and apparent importance, investigations were continued in late March 1978, at which time three and one-half weeks were devoted to additional efforts to define the limits of occupation, transit-mapping of the located structures, and test excavations in and around several of the component constructions. Some eight days with a crew of four to eight men were spent clearing vegetation in preparation for mapping.

The area around all of the mapped structures was examined for further evidence of prehistoric habitation, with special attention being paid to the backdirt and banks of the numerous canals. No further evidence of occupation was noted in any of these ditches. In addition, a further 100-125 m was examined to the north, south, and west of the mapped limits. This brief reconnaissance resulted in the location of a four-structure group c. 125 m north of Str. 212-73/76. A sketch map was made of this group but was not incorporated into the map shown as Fig. 8. The investigations to the south and west encountered a light scattering of structures, none higher than 2 m, which could not be mapped because of time restrictions. Another site over 1 km to the south, apparently located where the Rio Encantado issues from the foothills, was also reported by local informants but not visited. The primary obstacle to the Choco survey was the dense overgrowth immediately east of the main group which allowed only limited reconnaissance in this direction. Despite informants' reports of additional structures in this area, including possibly one large construction, this sector remains unexplored. As a result, Fig. 8 presents a conservative picture of Choco's size.

Description: The Choco locus consists of 84 structures covering an area 697 m north-south by 500 m east-west. The breakdown of structures by height is presented in Table III.4. The site is dominated by a group of seven monumental structures arranged orthogonally around the four sides of two adjacent courts oriented roughly S 19° 15′ W and N 83° 30′ W.

Both of these courts are completely enclosed by construction. The south court constitutes the largest enclosed space located to date in the LMV, measuring 82 m north-south by 65 m east-west. The north court is somewhat smaller: 23 m north-south by 40 m east-west. Both courts are raised 0.75-1.05 m above the surrounding ground surface. Around this group (Str. 212-1/7) are scattered a series of isolated structures and small groups, some of which are orthogonally arranged (e.g., Str. 212-44/46 and -66/69) and others are not (e.g., Str. 212-31/42). There is no strong tendency for these outliers to be aligned in accordance with the orientations of the main group. The high incidence of isolated constructions may be due to the aforementioned effects of plowing and subsequent structure destruction. The small aggregations found around the main group also tend to possess one structure somewhat larger than the other constructions in the group: a pattern that also characterizes the main group, where Str. 212-1 and -4 are much higher than any of the other components.

In general, outside of the area immediately north and east of the main group, structure density at Choco is quite low.

Every structure but the lowest, c. 0.5-1 m high, shows some signs of having been built using the step-terrace technique. Stone slabs, river cobbles, and rough granitelike rubble abound on all of the larger structures. Despite the damage to the summits of many constructions, some terrace lines were noted on the lower slopes of several structures. These narrow terraces appear to extend the entire length of the structures. The size of the stones involved varies considerably: most of the rubble and cobbles measure c. 0.2 by 0.18 m, though some are as large as 0.46 by 0.26 m. The larger stone slabs are 2 by 2 m. The smaller structures usually have no stones on their surface, or alternatively, a light scattering of rubble and cobbles. No extant wall lines were noted on these humbler constructions.

In addition to such general features there are several other aspects of visible architecture that are more restricted in their distribution at Choco. First, on the summit of Str. 212-76 a sizable concentration of schist slabs was noted, apparently tumbled from their original positions. The slabs are reminiscent, in their location and density, of similar concentrations recorded on the surface at Locus 210, in particular Str. 210-6 and -8. As was postulated for Locus 210, these slabs may have served as a foundation for a superstructure. Another feature at Choco is the preva-

TABLE 2.4

SURFACE COLLECTIONS

Lot #	Contents	Depositional Significance	Provenience
21A/1	1 metate frag.	Surface	Surface, main group
21A/2	1 sherd	Surface	Surface, general

lence, on the tallest structures (Strs. 212-1 and -4), of broad terraces constructed of large stone slabs. Each of these structures has two c. 2-m-wide terraces on its side facing into the south court and one on the opposite side. Similar to this is an unusual feature of Str. 212-7, the platform closing off the north side of the north court. This structure has a terrace on the south, protruding just above ground level, composed of horizontally laid long, thick stone slabs, measuring c. 2 m long by 1.75 m wide. This terrace is visible for almost the entire length of the southern face of Str. 212-7 and stops c. 4 m east of the northwest interior corner formed by Str. 212-7 and -6. This type of feature is known from only one other locality, the Group I main group in the Playitas Site Zone, where it is found on Str. 200-78. Interestingly enough, this is the only other LMV Group in which the very broad upper slab terraces similar to those seen on Str. 212-1 and -4 are also found (Str. 200-76/79).

Prepared masonry is rare in the valley outside of Quirigua, but cut and faced blocks were found on the surface of Str. 212-1. These blocks, situated on the northern upper slopes of this platform above the second broad terrace, have been largely disturbed by root action. A line of three on the west may be *in situ*, however. The cut blocks measure 2 m long by 1 m thick and are concentrated on the east and west sides of the center line. While masonry found at both Choco and other centers could have been either artificially faced or merely selected for its naturally smoothed surfaces, these blocks are surely modified. This surface evidence suggests that Choco is architecturally somewhat distinct from its comparably sized neighbors, a suspicion borne out by excavation (see Chap. 3).

Alluviation: Given Choco's location on the floodplain of the Encantado, it is very possible that at least some small structures have been buried by river-deposited silt. Excavations suggest that construction outside of the main group may have been buried by as much as 0.4-0.6 m of silt. While such deposits could obscure smaller constructions, no evidence of their former presence was forthcoming in any of the old ditches that cross-cut this locus.

Surface Collections: The only artifacts recovered from the Choco surface are one sherd (Lot 21A/2) and a single basalt metate fragment from the general area of the principal group (Lot 21A/1). A collection of three sherds which a local informant recovered from the Rio Encantado contains two fragments of a common LMV utilitarian type, and one rather enigmatic piece with a hollow, hourglass shape, similar to a "pot-stand." This object stands 0.14 m high and is red slipped on both interior and exterior.

Excavations: Thirteen excavations were carried out in 1978 and are reported in Chap. 3.

COMANCHE FARM SITE ZONE (Locus 210, Op. 23)

LOCATION AND SETTING

General Location: The Comanche Farm Site Zone is c. 7.9 km northwest of the Playitas Site Zone (Locus 200), c. 5.6 km northwest of Choco (Locus 212), and 1.7 km south and east of the Rio Motagua (see Fig. 1).

Topography: The Groups composing this zone are situated on the broad, flat to rolling floodplain of the Rio Motagua, c. 5.5 km north of the foothills of the Espiritu Santo mountains.

Resources: No natural resources or special features of aboriginal value were readily apparent in the immediate area of this locus in 1977. It is possible, however, that shifts in the course of the Rio Motagua over the years, and recent efforts by BANDEGUA to canalize natural rivers, have greatly altered the Precolumbian setting. First, with respect to the Motagua, recent investigations in the area surrounding Quirigua strongly suggest that the Late Classic channel of this river ran much closer to the center than is now the case (Ashmore 1981b). This offers the possibility that the Motagua might once have flowed closer to the site of Comanche Farm as well. A major BANDEGUA canal which carried a considerable volume of water even in the dry season ran c. 1 km south of the site zone in 1977. If, as has been the case in other places on BANDEGUA land, the canal represents the capture and channeling of a previously natural stream, then this river might have originally flowed closer to Comanche Farm. Unfortunately, the resolution of these possibilities would require deep and extensive excavations in and around Comanche Farm to recover data on river-channel deposits and shifts. Even if no rivers flowed adjacent to Locus 210, fresh water might still have been obtained by means of shallow wells similar to those reported by Ricketson from the Aztec Farm area (1935), and more recently by Ashmore from the immediate Quirigua periphery (Sharer et al. 1983; Ashmore 1984). Modern agricultural excavations in the zone indicate that even in the dry season the water table is quite high: c. 2-2.5 m below ground surface.

The close proximity of the zone to a center of intensive commercial banana cultivation, c. 1.15 km to the southeast in 1977, indicates that Locus 210 was situated on or close to good agricultural land. Interestingly enough, Comanche Farm is one of the few sites recorded in the LMV that are not located near an obvious source of building stones. As will be noted

later, even if the Motagua was considerably closer to the zone prehistorically, it does not appear that the stones used at the site, especially in the large Group I constructions, are those most typically found in that river.

CURRENT STATUS

Destruction of visible construction is due to both natural and cultural forces. Approximately 5.5 m of the western end of Str. 210-3 in Group II has been removed by construction of a drainage canal 0.6 m deep by 3 m wide (see Fig. 9). No cultural debris or evidence of construction was turned up by the other canals in this area, hence it is unlikely that much further damage has been wrought by these modern agricultural features in Group II. In Group III the principal agent of destruction is the cattle road that runs northeast-southwest across the northern part of the aggregation. A considerable segment of the north side of Str. 210-7 has been removed by the construction of this road, so that its original dimensions could no longer be reconstructed (see Fig. 10). The most heavily disturbed group, however, is Group I (see Fig. 11). Here a northwest-southeast canal c. 8 m wide cuts |through the southeast corner of the main group's south court, obscuring or destroying all information on the original appearance of this area. Another canal truncates the north side of Str. 210-14 in the north court of the main group. Furthermore, an aggregation of small structures c. 27.5 m west of the main group is damaged by a drainage channel which cuts

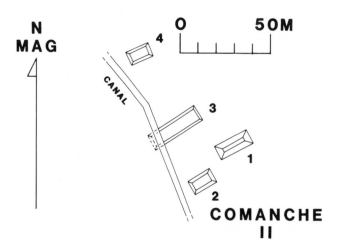

Figure 9.   Map of Group II, Comanche Farm.

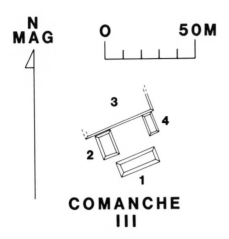

Figure 10.   Map of Group III, Comanche Farm.

southeast of the Group I main group, turned up any cultural debris.

In addition, palm trees with their extensive and shallow root systems have been responsible for dislodging a great many stones from construction, especially on the summits of the tall Group I structures.

Ownership: All of the Comanche Farm Zone lies within the BANDEGUA-owned Finca Lanquin.

SITE DESCRIPTION

Previous Work: The first description of the "Comanche Farm" site was provided by Strömsvik (1936) on the basis of a short visit he made in 1934 to what is here called Group I. Strömsvik described this group as consisting of a "Temple Plaza" that measured 65 m north-south by 50 m east-west and was surrounded completely by structures which he estimated to have been 7 m high (ibid.: 109). Strömsvik also noted cut stone blocks, some still *in situ*, ". . . in the manner of the early types of structures seen at Quirigua; a fairly smooth, rectangular face and a long, rough tapering, end tenoned into the wall" (ibid.). Most of the visible

through one of its number and buries the remainder under backdirt. More ditches, c. 1-1.25 m deep, are found south and southeast of Group I. While all of these are heavily overgrown only one, 40-110 m

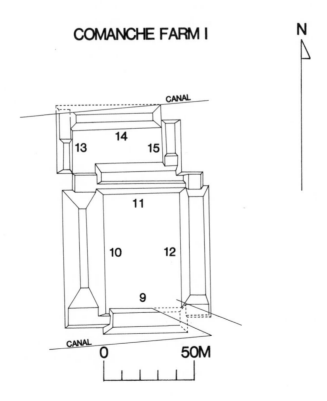

Figure 11.   Map of Group I, Comanche Farm.

stones, however, were river cobbles and chunks of sandstone, though some marble and "a number" of stone slabs were found which he interpreted as being "roof-stones" and capstones from collapsed corbel arches. Northwest of this "Temple Plaza" "a number of smaller mounds" were seen, though not reported in any detail. Strömsvik concluded his description by noting that 1-10 m of silt might have been deposited around the structures at the site (based on United Fruit Company estimates), and as a result not only were the visible structures taller than they appeared in 1934, but carved monuments might yet be preserved under this protective mantle (ibid.: 110). A sketch map was made of the main group and the other aggregations were visited.

Timothy Nowak also visited Group I, for it appeared on his map of the valley, though no description of the site was presented at that time (Nowak 1973b: fig. 2).

These earlier descriptions provided some information on the location and nature of Locus 210, but it was decided that more detailed data, in particular a map of the Group I main group, were required. As a result, "Comanche Farm" was relocated in April 1977 by the LMV survey program. While the general outlines of this site, especially Group I, conform to the description provided by Strömsvik, there are also some differences of interpretation.

Recording: The three located Groups in the Comanche Farm Zone that possessed visible architecture, Groups I, II, and III, were mapped in whole or in part with a tripod-mounted Brunton pocket transit and a 30-m tape. Group IV, a nonarchitectural unit, was recorded solely by notes. All structure heights given in Table III.5 are estimates arrived at by eye in the field. In the case of Groups II-IV, where the ground cover was light, 300-700 m around the visible

evidence of occupation was examined in search of additional cultural remains. Areas southeast and west of visible construction at Group I were covered to a distance of 300-500 m; terrain immediately to the north could not be examined because of the density of vegetation. Because of the size and complexity of the main group and limitations of time, the monumental quadrangle complex was mapped while the surrounding structures were only noted.

Description: The Comanche Farm Site Zone covers an area roughly 2.2 km northeast-southwest by 0.5 km northwest-southeast, and is dominated by the monumental construction of Group I in the far northeastern part of the zone. In addition to the 15 structures of Group I, two other architectural Groups (II and III) compose this zone, each with four structures, along with one nonarchitectural unit (Group IV), identified solely on the basis of a surface collection (Lot 22C/1), at the southwestern edge of the zone. The heights of the structures that make up this zone are given in Table III.5, while their distances from each other are summarized in Table 2.5.

Group II is a small aggregation of four structures, three of which (Str. 210-1/3) are orthogonally arranged around a plaza and one (Str. 210-4) is isolated c. 35.25 m to the northwest (see Fig. 9). A modern drainage canal occupied the west side of the plaza in 1977. The lack of cultural debris in the backdirt of this channel and our failure to locate any evidence of construction in its fairly clean walls suggest that this side of the plaza was originally left open. In all, the group extends over an area 50 m northeast-southwest by 85 m northwest-southeast.

Surface remains suggest that different styles of construction may have been employed in building Str. 210-1/4. Structure 210-1, the highest, and Str. 210-4 have no stones visible on their surfaces and may have

TABLE 2.5

COMANCHE FARM GROUP DISTRIBUTION

	Group I	Group II	Group III	Group IV
Group I	0	1.35 km NE	1.00 km NE	2.15 km NE
Group II	1.35 km SW	0	0.50 km SW	0.50 km NE
Group III	1.00 km SW	0.50 km NE	0	1.00 km NE
Group IV	2.15 km SW	0.50 km SW	1.00 km SW	0

*Distance and direction of those groups listed on the left margin from those enumerated in the upper row.

been constructed solely of the reddish brown earth found here. Structure 210-3, on the other hand, has a light surface covering of schist slabs, and Str. 210-2 has an equally light covering of rounded river cobbles. It appears, therefore, that there might have been two earthen platforms at Group II, and two that had at least a facing of uncut stones, cobbles, and slabs. Stone robbing cannot, however, be ruled out. No cut blocks were noted, nor was the common LMV pattern of step-terracing clearly in evidence.

Group III is one of the smallest groups recorded by this survey, covering an area no more than 39 m northwest-southeast by 41 m northeast-southwest (see Fig. 10). Here four relatively low structures are compactly and orthogonally organized around the four sides of a small plaza. All of the structures are lower on their plaza-facing sides, and indeed, the plaza surface seems to be raised slightly above ground surface on the west, south, and east. Whether this increased height is the result of artificial construction or, more likely, represents the use of a natural rise as a base for construction is unknown.

All of the structures in Group III are covered by moderately large river cobbles (averaging 0.28 by 0.4 m), suggesting the importance of this stone in construction. Schist slabs are relatively rare and only one was found protruding from Str. 210-8. The lowness of the structures and the general absence of stone slabs indicate that these platforms were probably built up using cobbles set into low, vertical walls similar to those revealed at other sites in excavation (see Str. 212-22, Chap. 3, for an example). No cut stone blocks were noted and there was no evidence for the existence of the step-terracing technique. Some pieces of *bajareque* were recovered from the surface of Str. 210-8, and though quite small, several did show evidence of having been flattened as in the forming of a wall or floor. These few fragments suggest that superstructures here were constructed of this material.

The focus of Group I is its main group (probably Strömsvik's "Temple Plaza") composed of two adjoining quadrangles oriented N 1° 0' W, sharing Str. 210-11, and defined by orthogonally arranged monumental construction (see Fig. 11). Of the two closed courts, the southern is the larger, measuring 61 m north-south by 47 m east-west, while the northern is 18 m north-south by 50 m east-west. As noted by Strömsvik (1936: 109), the level of the south court appears to be 0.5-0.75 m lower than the surrounding ground surface, while the north court may have been

raised the same distance above the 1977 ground level. The structures surrounding these courts are quite high, though not as uniformly tall as Strömsvik indicated (see Table III.5). The overall maximum size of the main group, measuring along the exterior lines, is 122 m north-south by 84.5 m east-west.

In addition to these contiguous court complexes, eight structures were also noted to the west. Seven of these platforms are found c. 27.5 m N 77° 0' W of the southwest corner of Str. 210-10. While canal-digging operations in this area did make it difficult to determine the exact size and orientation of these structures, they appear to have been grouped into a plaza arrangement. If the two best-preserved examples are at all representative, the structures here are roughly 20 m long and about 1 m high. In addition to this small group, one large isolated structure was found c. 50 m N 71° 30' W of Str. 210-14. This construction, Str. 210-16, oriented c. N 77° 0' E, is c. 5.5 m high and measures roughly 48 by 16.5 m at the base (the summit is c. 37 m long). Structure 210-16 had apparently been reused in recent times, as fragments of concrete, bricks, and iron rails (from old train lines) were found on the summit.

In all, the recorded portion of Group I consists of 15 structures covering, at maximum, 142 m north-south by 134.5 m east-west.

None of the faced and cut stone blocks described by Strömsvik were seen in 1977, nor was the presence of any sandstone or marble recorded. In fact, the principal building stones were a very hard, granitelike rock, usually in large, angular chunks, and the schist slabs so ubiquitous on monumental structures in the LMV. Some rhyolite fragments were also noted and river cobbles, so common in other sites, were relatively rare. One *in situ* wall, visible about one-third of the way up the north side of Str. 210-11, is a single course of the granite and rhyolite chunks, which take both rectangular and ellipsoidal shapes. Despite the tumbled nature of much of the visible construction, it appears from the association of sizable numbers of stone chunks and slabs on the larger structures that they were built in the step-terrace style. There is no evidence in the LMV outside of Quirigua for interpreting the many stone slabs found at these sites as roof- or capstones for corbeled vaults. The fill of Str. 210-9, as revealed by a canal cut on its south side, is reddish, hard-compacted clay enclosed by stone retaining walls, which unfortunately were much disturbed by the digging of the canal.

TABLE 2.6

SURFACE COLLECTIONS

Lot #	Contents	Depositional Significance	Provenience
22A/1	20 sherds	Surface	Str. 210-1, Group II
22B/1	4 sherds	Surface	Between Str. 210-7/8 and on Str. 210-8, Group III
22C/1	14 sherds	Below ground surface	Backdirt from cattle-watering hole, Group IV
22D/1	51 sherds	Surface	Summit of Str. 210-10
22D/2	3 sherds	Surface	Str. 210-16
22D/3	59 sherds; 2 figurine frags.	Mixed surface and fill	Canal cut through small str. W of Str. 210-10
22D/4	122 sherds; 2 censer frags.; 1 figurine frag.; 5 pcs. obsidian; 3 *bajareque* frags.	Mixed surfce and buried material	Canal cut SE of Group I main group

On Str. 210-14 and -16 and the small structure west of Str. 210-10 that was cut by the canal, schist slabs are by far the most common stones found on the surface. What these concentrations of slabs mean, outside of a possibly different construction technique for at least some Group I structures, is difficult to say. In the case of Str. 210-14, the location of most of these slabs on the summit may indicate their use in a superstructure, possibly as a foundation for a wall similar to that reported from the immediate Quirigua periphery (Str. 3C-5, Ashmore 1981b).

In addition to the visible architecture, a scatter of sherds and *bajareque* fragments was also found in the backdirt of a northwest-southeast BANDEGUA canal southeast of the main group. This overgrown channel was still fairly deep, c. 1.25 m in 1977, and contained running water. The distribution of sherds and *bajareque* pieces was limited to backdirt on the west side of the ditch and extended from 110 m to within 40 m of the main group (Lot 22D/4).

Group IV, c. 500 m southwest of Group II, provides the westernmost evidence of occupation found in the Comanche Farm Zone. This "Group" was defined solely on the basis of a surface collection of 14 sherds (Lot 22C/1) secured from the backdirt of a recently excavated cattle-watering hole. An examination of this excavation, which was dug at least 2.5 m into a reddish brown clay and was not overgrown, produced no evidence of any buried constructions that might have been associated with the recovered sherds. Examina-

tion of the surrounding fields also revealed no evidence on the surface of prehistoric construction. The only indication that there might have been structures in the area which have since been destroyed was supplied by a large number of river cobbles in the mud road immediately northwest of the watering hole. Their presence here suggests that a small group might have been destroyed to provide fill for the road. The possibility also exists, of course, that these stones were brought in from another locale for this purpose. In sum, while the cultural material found here indicates the existence of aboriginal occupation somewhere in the area, no firm evidence of associated construction was noted.

Alluviation: The question of the burial of construction by silt is still as open as it was in Strömsvik's day. That silt has been deposited by river floods in this area is not questioned; it is the amount of such deposits that is problematic. As a result, it is impossible to say whether and how many prehistoric features might have been obscured by flood deposits in the Comanche Farm Zone.

Surface Collections: The seven collections recovered from Comanche Farm comprise 273 sherds, two *incensario* fragments, five pieces of obsidian, three *bajareque* fragments, and three figurine pieces (see Table 2.6). Four of these lots are from Group I (22D/1-4) and one each from Groups II, III, and IV (Lots 22A/1, 22B/1, and 22C/1 respectively).

Excavations: None.

JUYAMA SITE ZONE (Locus 211, Op. 25)

LOCATION AND SETTING

General Location: The Juyama Site Zone is c. 4.75 km southwest of Arapahoe Viejo (Locus 216), and c. 13.5 km northeast of Quirigua (see Fig. 1).

Topography: Archaeological remains are not distributed evenly throughout this extensive zone, measuring c. 1.1 km east-west by 0.7 km north-south. Surface indications of aboriginal occupation are largely restricted to the tops of three more or less parallel ridges which extend northward from the cliffs of the massive Espiritu Santo range that mark the southern limits of the zone. The summits of these ridges slope gradually down from south to north, being 15-20 m high in the south and dropping to 3-5 m on their northern margins above the flat floodplain of the Rio Motagua. The latter river currently flows c. 1 km to the north. Separating these spurs are two fast-flowing tributaries of the Motagua, the larger of which, the Rio Juyama on the east, is c. 23 m wide and 1-1.5 m deep in the dry season. The second stream, which divides the central from the western spur, is only 4-5 m wide and c. 0.4 m deep at the same time of year. These two streams emerge from narrow chasms in the south and form wide floodplains at the northern ends of the spurs. The ridges supporting occupation slope down precipitously to the level of these intervening floodplains.

Resources: The aboriginal occupants of the Juyama Zone had easy access to a year-round source of water. Further, both of these streams possess a large number of rounded river cobbles in their beds. As cobbles appear to have been extensively used in construction here, both watercourses would have been a source of building stones. In addition, especially in the eastern portion of the zone, large stones are found scattered naturally in considerable numbers on the floodplain of the Rio Juyama, pointing to another potential source of construction material.

The floodplain of the two small streams and summits of the ridges are apparently too rocky to have provided good cropland. In fact, while much of this area was in private hands in 1979, relatively little of it was being farmed. On the other hand, the rich alluvial soils of the Motagua floodplain, immediately north of the zone, could have served as a close-by source of productive land. Also, east of the locus, toward the *aldea* of Juyama, more land was planted in maize, possibly indicating the presence of richer agricultural potential in this direction.

The Rio Juyama does not cut a pass across the Espiritu Santo mountains toward Honduras, and no modern trail extending in this direction was found. As a result, there are no strong topographic or modern-use grounds for assuming that Juyama was located on a major extravalley communication link during its period of prehistoric occupation.

CURRENT STATUS

Destruction of visible structures is most evident in the western portion of the zone, where approximately one-third of the extant buildings have been damaged by either looting or bulldozing. One group in this sector has been almost completely leveled by the latter activity. On the central and eastern ridges, however, very few disturbed structures were noted, though the denseness of the vegetation may well have obscured evidence of such damage.

Ownership: Private owners are currently unknown.

SITE DESCRIPTION

Previous Work: Previous work at Juyama, while taking place over c. 80 years, has been sporadic. Sapper (1895) was the first person to note Juyama's location, including the site on his general map of archaeological remains in the Maya area. Unfortunately, Sapper did not publish a description of Juyama. Ricketson and Blom (1940) in their catalogue of Mayan sites also included Juyama and located it on their map of the Maya area. This mention, with no further description, was probably based on Sapper's earlier note. Nowak visited Juyama in 1974 and not only recorded its location but also reported on a short excavation he undertook in the eastern portion of the locus (Nowak 1975), although he did not publish a report describing the site in general.

Recording: The remote location of Juyama and the density of enveloping vegetation precluded intensive investigations in 1979. The site was recorded primarily by notes and only two groups in the western portion of the locus were mapped, using a tripod-mounted Brunton pocket transit and 30-m tape. Informants reported the existence of several small structures, probably representing a continuation, in lower densities, of the known groups north, east, and west of the zone. Time did not permit testing these statements.

Description: In all, 110 structures were noted within the Juyama Zone. During the investigation of this locus several patterns of structure arrangement and location were observed. First, structures are arranged in groups of three to five, though some as large as 11 and a few isolated platforms were also recorded. In each of these groups one platform is larger than the rest and appears to dominate the smaller constructions scattered nearby. Second, in contrast to such hilltop sites as Las Quebradas and Arapahoe Viejo, where even groups of small structures tend to be orthogonally arranged, the irregular configurations of the Juyama aggregations are striking. Rarely are two consistently aligned platforms found in any of these groups. Finally, in the two cases—the western and central spurs—where the full breadth and length of the supporting ridges could be examined, structures tend to be concentrated along the edges of these ridges overlooking the adjacent streams and decrease in frequency away from this precipice. This is especially true on the western ridge, where no structures were noted more than 150-175 m west of the ridge edge. Also noted on the western and central spurs was the tendency to locate structures over the entire length of these spurs, even in the far southern portions, where they were found right up against the high cliffs of the Espiritu Santo mountains.

Turning to more specific features characteristic of different portions of the site, the west ridge supports 63 structures within an area roughly 700 m north-south by 750 m east-west. These buildings occur primarily in irregular groups of three to five, though isolated structures and one group containing eight platforms are also found. These groups are spaced c. 35-70 m apart. In general, the heights of these groups decrease toward the mountains in the south with most of the isolated structures being found up against the Espiritu Santo cliffs. Structure sizes range from 0.1 to 2.5 m, with most falling between 0.75 and 1 m. Figures 12 and 13 illustrate two aggregations from this part of the zone. Figure 12 represents a small group located on a low rise in the floodplain off the northern end of the western spur, while Fig. 13 is of a group atop that high spur. Neither of these clusters is strictly typical of all west spur groups. They convey some idea of Juyama structure arrangements (see Table III.6 for structure heights within these groups).

In contrast to the western portion of the zone with its numerous, relatively small groups, the central spur is dominated by two areas of monumental construction. Unfortunately, both of these clusters were densely

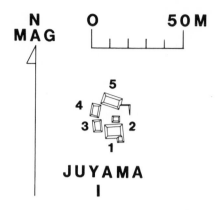

Figure 12.   Map of Group I, Juyama.

overgrown in 1979, so that while a sketch map was made of one (Fig. 14), the second, larger aggregate could not be directly observed. The structures on the middle ridge occupy a narrow, tapering area, roughly 300 m wide (east-west) on the south and 150 m wide on the north, and 450 m long (north-south). Within this area, 28 structures were identified, of which seven composed one of the largest observed Juyama groups (see Fig. 14). This aggregation is situated on a small segment of flat land high on the ridge top to the south, just at the point where the bluff joins the escarpments of the Espiritu Santo mountains. It is bounded on the west by a steep drop-off to a small *quebrada* (ravine). In this seemingly inaccessible location were found two massive constructions, the larger of which, Str. 211-11, is c. 8 m high and c. 46 by 27 m at its base, while the

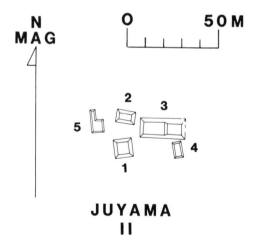

Figure 13.   Map of Group II, Juyama.

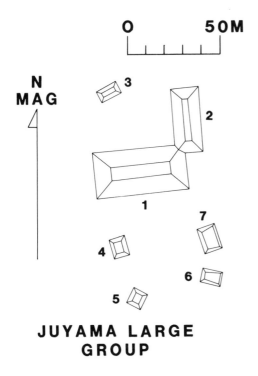

O   50M

N
MAG

3
2
1
7
4
6
5

**JUYAMA LARGE
GROUP**

Figure 14.   Map of the Large Group, Juyama.

second, Str. 211-12, is c. 7 m high. These two structures are oriented orthogonally and linked at their northeast and southwest corners respectively. Scattered around them are five smaller structures, c. 1.5-2 m high, which are neither organized into orthogonal groups nor oriented with respect to the major constructions. Several of these humbler platforms are built into the steeply rising hill slope that bounds the group on the south and east.

Approximately 80 m N 42° 0′ E of this group is another aggregation of four structures, all 0.75-1.25 m high, again situated on the high slopes of the central ridge. However, roughly 200 m north-northwest of the monumental group described above, a possibly even larger construction unit could be discerned within a dense morass of vegetation. An estimate of the exterior dimensions of this unit would be 150 m north-south by 75 m east-west. One of the largest visible structures may stand 9 m in height.

About 50 m north of this large group is another collection of seven structures in which heights range between 0.75 and 6 m. The structures here are not orthogonally arranged, but form a rough circle open on the east around the largest construction, which measures 26 by 8 m at its base and is oriented S 87° 0′

E. In addition to the aforementioned units, two additional groups of three low structures each are found east and northeast of the large monumental groups.

Finally, 19 structures were recorded in 1979 within an area roughly 150 m east-west by 225 m north-south in the far eastern part of the site. The structures noted in this sector are arranged into three groups, the largest of which contains 11 buildings. The platforms in this latter group stand to a maximum height of 1.5 m, with most falling between 0.75 and 1.25 m. Basal dimensions are fairly uniform, averaging 11.5 by 5.5 m. Constructions are not orthogonally arranged.

Approximately 75 m north of this group, immediately adjacent to the Rio Juyama, is an aggregation of four low (c. 0.5-1 m high), irregularly arranged structures. Roughly 85-90 m northeast of this last group and 10-15 m east of the Rio Juyama is the third recorded group in this sector, composed of four structures, the largest of which is c. 6 m high. This seems to be the group Nowak (1975) excavated in 1974. The group is not orthogonally arranged. On the basis of Nowak's map (ibid.) and subsequent observations, the largest structure is situated on the eastern edge of the aggregate and measures c. 27 m east-west by 38.25 m north-south at its base, with a c. 5.75-m-long projection extending from its north side. The other three structures are scattered around the larger one on the northwest and southwest and average c. 18.5 m long by 13 m wide in basal dimensions.

River cobbles and angular chunks are the predominant building stones found on structures throughout the site zone, while stone slabs are rare. Cut and faced blocks are totally absent, nor were *in situ* wall lines recorded on any of the structures in the locus. While it is fairly secure that the Juyama structures were built up by means of unfaced cobble-and-chunk walls, it is unclear exactly how these stones were employed in construction.

Alluviation: Nowak's excavations in the eastern part of the site indicated that up to 1.6 m of river-deposited silt may well have obscured a pre-Late Classic occupation in this sector (Nowak 1975). The proximity of the eastern ridge to the large Rio Juyama, no more than 5-7 m above it at its lowest point, may have made this part of the site especially susceptible to flooding. The height of the central and western ridges above the adjacent watercourse, however, precludes the loss of any structures in these areas to alluvial silts.

Surface Collections: Twenty-six sherds and nine

TABLE 2.7

SURFACE COLLECTIONS

Lot #	Contents	Depositional Significance	Provenience
25A/1	4 sherds; 4 pcs. obsidian	Disturbed structures	W ridge
25A/2	13 sherds; 5 pcs. obsidian	Disturbed structures	W ridge
25A/3	1 sherd	Disturbed structures	E ridge
25A/4	8 sherds	Disturbed structures	W ridge

pieces of obsidian were recovered from Juyama in 1979. Three of the surface lots defined at that time (25A/1, 2, and 4) were from disturbed structure groupings in the western part of the site, while one (25A/3) was from the eastern sector (see Table 2.7).

Excavations: No excavations were carried out here by the LMV program. Nowak's excavations in the eastern part of the site consisted of a 10-m-long, c. 2-m-deep face-back of a drainage canal c. 25 m northeast of the largest structure in the group noted above (Nowak 1975: 17-18, fig. 6). On the basis of Nowak's short report, it appears that he uncovered an Early Classic midden, buried by c. 1.6 m of river silts and gravels. Some fragments of possibly Preclassic material were also found, but in disturbed contexts. Nowak's important findings point to the existence of an earlier occupation in the LMV, predating the Late Classic and deeply buried by alluviation.

BOBOS SITE ZONE (Locus 209, Op. 33)

LOCATION AND SETTING

General Location: The Bobos Site Zone is 5.8 km northwest of the Las Quebradas Site Zone (Locus 205) and 9 km northeast of the Playitas Site Zone (Locus 200; see Fig. 1).

Topography: The Bobos Site Zone is situated on the flat, broad floodplain formed by the junction of the Rios Motagua and Bobos and is 200-300 m south of that confluence (see Fig. 1).

Resources: Water would have been readily available year-round from both the Bobos and Motagua rivers. Building stones, especially the ubiquitous river cobbles, are also commonly found in both rivers. The land around the site appears to be fruitful agriculturally. The location of the Bobos Zone, very near the point where the Rios Bobos and Motagua merged in 1979, puts it in a strategic position to control communication along the former watercourse toward the major center of Las Quebradas. If these two rivers joined at approximately the same point during the period of Bobos' prehistoric occupancy, then the residents of the Bobos groups might very well have been able to monitor interactions following the Rios Bobos and Motagua. The attraction of the route along the Rio Bobos lay not only in the presence of a major center,

Las Quebradas, along it, but also in the fact that one of the few passes providing access across the Espiritu Santo mountains toward Honduras is to be found to the south-southeast. A further discussion of the aboriginal importance of this route is presented in the section dealing with Las Quebradas (Locus 205).

CURRENT STATUS

Both Bobos Groups I and II appear to have suffered more from cultural than from natural forces. The Group I structures all lack stones on their surface, a condition local informants attribute to stone robbing by the current inhabitants. In Group II, because of the proximity to modern construction, the destruction is more pronounced. In addition to the lack of surface stones, the summits of Str. 209-10 and -11 have been flattened and heavily disturbed by modern activities; Str. 209-15 has been cut through perpendicular to its long axis from summit to base to facilitate drainage; and the southeast corner of Str. 209-13 and the northwest of Str. 209-14 have been truncated. Evidence of looting in the Bobos Zone was not recorded. The destructive effect of natural forces on the zone is apparently minimal.

Ownership: Unknown.

SITE DESCRIPTION

Previous Work: Nowak (1973a) located a site named "Bobos" on his general map of the valley without providing a description of that site. However, it is assumed that his site and the one recorded by this project are the same, based on their locations.

Recording: Both of the Bobos Groups were recorded, in addition to notes, by mapping with a tripod-mounted Brunton pocket transit and a 30-m tape. Besides the 15 mapped structures presented in Figs. 15 and 16, other constructions, scattered between the two aggregations, were recorded by notes alone.

Description: The 36 structures that constitute this zone are grouped into two orthogonally arranged complexes, with a series of low (c. 0.5-1.5 m high) constructions dispersed between them.

Group I, in the southern part of the zone, is composed of 15 structures, five of which are arranged orthogonally around a plaza, with the remaining ten situated singly in the area surrounding this plaza. The mapped section of the Group (see Fig. 15) covers an area roughly 165 m northeast-southwest by 85 m northwest-southeast; the total area covered by the Group is estimated at 200 m east-west by 162.5 m north-south. The heights of the component structures are presented in Table III.7. The plaza enclosed by Str. 209-4/8 is unobstructed by construction at all four corners and measures 57 m northeast-southwest by 54 m northwest-southeast. The plaza surface is 0.25-0.5 m above ground level on the west, north, and east. This elevation appears to have been the result of building Str. 209-5/8 on the edge of a natural rise, for the ground drops off perceptibly from the southwest, northwest, and northeast plaza corners. The plaza

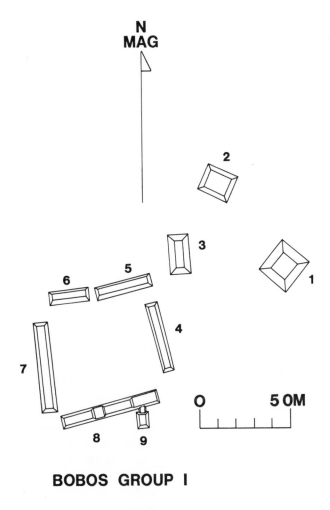

BOBOS GROUP I

Figure 15.   Map of Group I, Bobos.

43

and ground surfaces are at about the same elevation on the southeast. The location of the Group I plaza on a low rise may have facilitated drainage.

The structures enclosing the Group I plaza are extensive but do not attain great heights: the largest of the recorded platforms in Group I are situated to the northeast, where they form a nonorthogonally arranged group (Str. 209-1/3). Because no stones remain on the surface, it is very difficult to determine construction techniques.

Group II, c. 250 m north of Group I, is a compact cluster of six mapped structures (see Fig. 16, Str. 209-10/15) joined by connecting construction. Four of these buildings surround a small court on all sides. In addition to these there are a single, c. 1-m-high construction c. 25 m southeast of the southeast corner of Str. 209-15, and two low (c. 0.75 m high) platforms roughly 20 m west of Str. 209-13. The maximum area covered by the mapped structures is c. 106 m northwest-southeast by 105 m northeast-southwest. With the addition of the unmapped structures to the southeast and west, the Group extends roughly 124 m northwest-southeast by 125 m northeast-southwest. The area of the court enclosed by Str. 209-12/15 is 27.25 m northwest-southeast by 31 m northeast-

southwest. In contrast to the Group I plaza, all but two of the corners here are closed by construction, while the two that remain open are no wider than 1.25-3.5 m. Access to this court was therefore subject to stricter control.

There is more stone visible on the surface of these structures than elsewhere in the zone. River-worn cobbles and schist slabs are found, especially on the sides of Str. 209-10. The cobbles here are slightly more angular than those commonly found on LMV structures. Given the size of Str. 209-10 and the presence of these stones, it seems likely that this large platform was constructed in the step-terrace style of cobble risers and schist-slab runners. The same may very well have been the case for Str. 209-11, where similar stones are found on the surface. The absence of visible wall lines means that this must be verified by future work. Other construction techniques were probably employed at Group II. This is suggested by a channel bisecting Str. 209-15 that reveals a fill of fine-grained, light reddish brown clay mottled with gray toward the base, and an absence of stones either within the fill or acting as exterior retainers. While this situation may be attributable to stone robbing, it suggests the use of fully earthen platforms without stone facing walls. On the basis of informants' reports and the results of small modern excavations, the fill of Str. 209-10 and -12 is composed of the same fine light reddish brown clay.

Between these two Groups are several isolated structures which, though noted, were not mapped. The first of these structures recorded in 1979 was located in the far southern portion of the zone, c. 130 m south of Group I. This rectilinear structure stands c. 2.5 m high, is oriented S 59° 0' W, and measures roughly 18 m long by 13.5 m wide at its base. A narrow terrace was noted halfway up the structure on its north side.

Several other platforms were found in a rough group c. 150 m N 27° 0' W of Group I. The highest structure here stands c. 1.5 m high, is oriented N 83° 0' W, and measures 11.5 by 8 m at its base. It is possible that a low projection extends from this structure to the east, though the density of the vegetation at this point precluded further investigation. The remaining structures in this group range in height from 0.5 to 0.75 m. Other structures were seen scattered about the area between Groups I and II, approximately eight in all, but time did not permit their investigation. All are similar in terms of height and basal dimensions to those already noted. As with Group I,

BOBOS GROUP II

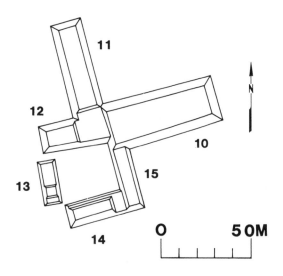

Figure 16.   Map of Group II, Bobos.

TABLE 2.8

SURFACE COLLECTIONS

Lot #	Contents	Depositional Significance	Provenience
33A/1 (Nowak collection)	4 sherds	Surface	Bobos Zone
33A/2	4 sherds	Surface	South of Str. 209-10, Group II

very few stones were found on the surface of the intervening buildings, though this absence may be attributable more to modern stone robbing than to aboriginal construction techniques.

Alluviation: The location of the Bobos Zone on the floodplains of both the Rios Motagua and Bobos raises the possibility that at least some low constructions may have been buried by river-deposited silts. Unfortunately, because of the lack of excavation, it is impossible to determine how large a role such deposits might have played in obscuring construction.

Surface Collections: One surface collection was made in the zone in 1979 (four sherds), and one small fragment of *bajareque* was recovered from the fill exposed by the cut through Str. 209-15. The people living on the site reported finding very few artifacts in the years they had lived there, with the exception of some scattered sherds from the summit of Str. 209-10. Nowak apparently made a collection off four sherds from this area, though their precise provenience is unknown (see Table 2.8).

Excavations: None.

MOJANALES (Locus 233, Op. 42)

LOCATION AND SETTING

General Location: Locus 233 is within the *aldea* of Mojanales c. 7.1 km southeast of Choco (Locus 212) and 7.5 km south-southeast of the Playitas Site Zone (Locus 200; see Fig. 1).

Topography: Mojanales is located in a small pocket valley cut by a tributary of the Rio Chinamito, c. 0.5 km north-south by 0.15 km east-west, at an elevation of 300 m, well within the high ranges of the Espiritu Santo mountains. The ground rises very sharply from the narrow flat valley floor on all sides. Both modern and ancient construction has eschewed location on the valley bottom: the prehistoric platforms are on 1- to 2-m-high rises above the river, while modern houses are by and large perched on the high escarpments overlooking the valley. This avoidance of low-lying areas probably results from the wetness of this area even in the dry season; the valley bottom may be waterlogged and swampy in the wet season (June-December).

Resources: Ready access to water for both modern and ancient inhabitants would have been provided by the small stream that runs through the valley before emptying into the Rio Chinamito c. 3.1 km to the north near Los Vitales (Locus 232). This channel presumably provides water year-round. The watercourse also contains cobbles of the size and shape noted on the surface of several of the Mojanales structures, suggesting that it served as a source of building stones. No natural source of the stone slabs, also found at this site, was noted, though it can safely be assumed that they were procured in the nearby hills. Good agricultural land does not seem plentiful in the valley, and the current residents concentrate their farming efforts on the steep hillsides.

Like Los Limones (Locus 231) and Los Vitales (Locus 232), Mojanales is situated on one of the major trail systems linking the railhead at Bobos with a series of small towns on both sides of the Guatemalan/Honduran border. Mojanales is on one of the few passes through the Espiritu Santo mountains between Honduras and Guatemala. If communication through this area was important aboriginally, then these passes would have been the most logical routes along which that contact could have been achieved. In this case, Mojanales would have been in a good position to profit from such interactions. As noted for Los Limones and Los Vitales, modern trade and movement through the pass is very brisk, especially on market day (Wednesday) at the Bobos railhead. Some of the residents interviewed have been on the Honduran side of the border and claim that Hondurans do, occasionally at least, come to trade in the Bobos market.

CURRENT STATUS

As of 1979, few if any of the structures composing Locus 233 appeared to have been disturbed by either looting or agricultural activities. The only damage sustained by any of the observed platforms came from natural causes, i.e., tree roots and erosion. The small stream had cut into the natural rises supporting aboriginal construction with the result that both Str. 233-2 and -6 had been damaged (Figs. 17 and 18). Tree roots, as always, have caused some disturbance to structure summits.

Ownership: Unknown.

SITE DESCRIPTION

Previous Work: None.

Recording: Because of the limitations of time imposed by the distance of this locus from Playitas (over three hours by horse from Bobos/Playitas), only seven structures were recorded in the valley. These platforms form two clusters, one of which, Group I with three structures, was mapped using a tripod-mounted Brunton pocket transit and a 30-m tape, while the second, Group II, was sketch-mapped (see Figs. 17 and 18). Close to half of Group II's total extent was obscured by vegetation so that the sketch map presented in Fig. 18 is only a partial representation of the aggregate. As with all sketch maps in this report, distances were paced and azimuths taken with a hand-held Brunton pocket transit. All structure heights were estimated by eye in the field (see Table III.8). It should be noted that informants reported the existence of additional structures "up in the hills" toward Honduras, though these were not visited owing to time limitations. The size of the structures that were located, in fact, strongly suggests that they were part of a larger site zone.

Description: Group I is located in the southeastern portion of the valley on a 1-m rise above the floodplain immediately northeast of the stream (see Fig. 17). The three structures composing this cluster, Str. 233-1/3, are arranged orthogonally around three sides of a

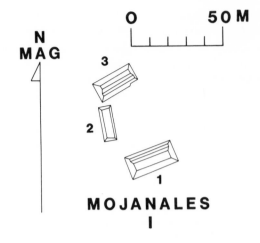

Figure 17.   Map of Group I, Mojonales.

plaza. The northeast flank is closed by a high steep rise into which Str. 233-3 has been built. The plaza thus enclosed measures 34 m northwest-southeast by 23 m northeast-southwest. The south and west plaza corners were left open, whereas access through the east corner was very narrowly defined by Str. 233-1 and the high hill face. Structure heights are given in Table III.8. In general, the range is between 0.5 and 2.75 m with two of the three over 2 m high.

Group II is c. 150 m northwest of Group I on top of a 2-m-high bluff above the valley floor, immediately west of the stream. Its four structures are more or less orthogonally arranged around the three visible sides (north, east, and south) of a plaza (see Fig. 18). In

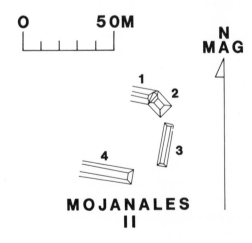

Figure 18.   Map of Group II, Mojonales.

general, the heights range from 1.4 to 5 m. Because of the dense vegetation in the western part of the cluster, it was not possible to determine the overall plan of the Group. It is known that at least the northeast and southeast corners of the plaza were left open. The only recorded case at Mojanales where two structures are linked by construction is in the northern part of the Group, where the two largest platforms, Str. 233-4 and -5, are joined by a 2.5-m-high saddle.

The larger structures at the site, all those except Str. 233-2, have river-worn cobbles and stone slabs on their surfaces. On the basis of this association of cobbles and slabs, the size of the structures involved, and the location of several possible wall lines in Group I, it would appear that the step-terrace technique was employed here. On the summit of Str. 233-1 square stone features were noted, similar in form and construction to those seen on structures at Las Quebradas and Playitas. These features at Mojanales are composed of fitted river cobbles now flush with the summit surface and spaced evenly along it. They measure c. 3 by 3 m. A line of cobbles was also found on the southwestern portion of Str. 233-3's summit, running parallel to the principal axis of the structure. Both of these features suggest that stone was used at least in the foundations of superstructures. Structure 233-2 has predominantly cobbles on its surface, though

some stone slabs are also present. While the step-terrace technique might have been employed here, it is rare to find this style associated with such low constructions. The fill exposed in both Str. 233-2 and -6, which have been cut by the stream, is of earth. The cobbles found at Locus 233 are not as well rounded as those found at other valley loci, and the slabs are relatively short and thick.

Special Features:

A petroglyph consisting of "hieroglyphs" cut into a natural rock face was reported to exist south of the Mojanales *aldea*. Unfortunately, the only person who knew the location of this feature, Sr. Venancio Estrada, could not be found and the carving was not investigated.

Alluviation: In both Groups the possibility exists that some low structures have been buried by flood-deposited silts.

Surface Collections: One sherd from the general surface of Locus 233 was found. One figurine head reported to have come from the Mojanales area was seen in a private collection in Bobos/Playitas. This was a human head, 0.09 m long and 0.09 m wide, hard-fired and solid with simple appliquéd mouth and eyes and a modeled nose.

Excavations: None.

ARAPAHOE VIEJO (Locus 216, Op. 28)

LOCATION AND SETTING

General Location: Locus 216 is c. 3 km southwest of Choco (Locus 212), c. 5.4 km southeast of the Comanche Farm Site Zone (Locus 210), and c. 7.1 km southwest of the Playitas Site Zone (Locus 200; see Fig. 1).

Topography: Arapahoe Viejo can be classed topographically with a group of similarly situated sites, including Juyama, Los Cerritos, and Las Quebradas, all of which are located in the low foothills of the Espiritu Santo range along the southern margin of the valley. Locus 216 is 80-90 m above the Rio Motagua floodplain, over which it holds a commanding view, and rests on a relatively flat terrace that slopes gradually down from south to north toward the valley floor. Immediately south, north, and northeast of this terrace the nature of the topography changes rapidly, rising quickly in the first direction to the first steep peaks of the Espiritu Santo mountains and falling off in the last two cases toward the Motagua.

Resources: Large, hard, fine-grained reddish brown boulders c. 3-4 m long are found in abundance in the southern part of the site and in the dry streambed that bounds the locus on the west. These stones are angular and have apparently not migrated a long distance from their original source. This type of stone is predominant on the surface of the structures at the site, indicating its extensive use in construction here. Similar stone could be seen in the exposed cliff faces of the Espiritu Santo range c. 300-400 m to the south.

In addition to building stones, the residents of Locus 216 would have been supplied with year-round water. Approximately 2.5 km to the west is the Rio Encantado, a southern tributary of the Rio Motagua which carries a large volume of water in the dry season. About 600 m to the southwest is a smaller, apparently perennial stream. As noted above, Locus 216 is bounded on the west by a c. 3-m-deep by 4.5-m-wide streambed, which was dry in March 1979. If this channel carried water when the site was aboriginally occupied, even if only in the wet season, this would have provided another very convenient water source. Nowak also reported the presence of a *quebrada* c. 69.7 m southeast of Str. 216-16, though he did not indicate whether it was a perennial or seasonal watercourse. This stream was not relocated in 1979.

The immediate area surrounding the site is very rocky, and the soil seems quite shallow. The agricultural potential of Arapahoe Viejo's environs thus was probably low. However, the fertile floodplain of the Rio Motagua, roughly 500-600 m to the north, could have provided abundant arable land for the aboriginal residents.

CURRENT STATUS

Structure 216-17, the largest construction at the site, has been heavily excavated on its western flank, leaving a large hole about as wide as the structure itself (Fig. 19). In general, however, destruction seems to be minimal at Arapahoe Viejo and even the ubiqui-

tous palm trees are largely absent. The considerable amounts of tumbled building stones so common at other loci are also not in evidence.

Ownership: Sr. Ramón Gableman.

SITE DESCRIPTION

Previous Work: Arapahoe Viejo was first discovered and reported by H. Berlin (1952: 42). His brief account gave a general idea of the location and nature of the site. Nowak relocated this locus and it appeared on his general map of the valley (Nowak 1973a). Nowak's map of the locus was not accompanied by a description (ibid.: fig. 5).

Recording: Arapahoe Viejo was mapped using a tripod-mounted Brunton pocket transit and a 30 m tape. All structure heights given in Table III.9 were estimated by eye in the field.

In addition to the mapped zone, which measures 270 m northwest-southeast by 170 m northeast-southwest, the area to the west was covered up to a

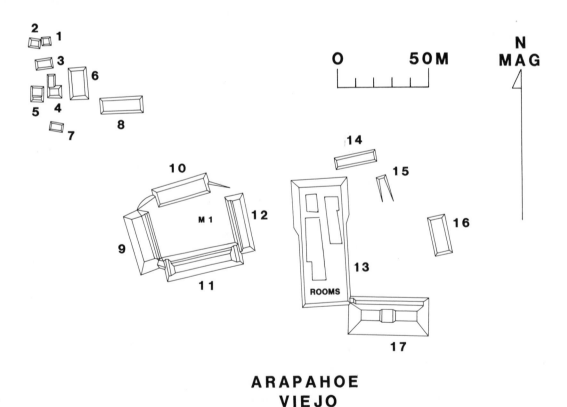

ARAPAHOE VIEJO

Figure 19. Map of Arapahoe Viejo.

distance of 600 m in search of additional evidence of aboriginal occupation, as were distances of c. 500 m to the north and 60-100 m to the east and south. Nothing was found to the west and south, but to the north, 35-40 m downslope from Str. 216-1 and -2, five structures no more than 1-1.5 m high were located; while to the northeast two structures were found c. 47 m from Str. 216-16. None of these constructions was examined in any detail, due to limitations of time and to the heavy growth of vegetation covering them.

Description: Arapahoe Viejo measures overall c. 310 m northwest-southeast by 220 m northeast-southwest and contains 24 visible structures (17 mapped; see Fig. 19). Because of the sloping nature of the terrain, structure heights vary, sometimes considerably, depending on the side used for a vantage point (see Table III.9). The unmapped structures are relatively low, 0.75-1.5 m high.

The 24 structures composing Locus 216 are organized into four assemblages: two monumental complexes surrounded by sizable architecture and two smaller plazas defined by more modest construction. Around these complexes are scattered individual structures which do not conform to any regular arrangements. Of the monumental foci, the one surrounded by Str. 216-9/12 is a quadrangle measuring 42 m north-south by 28 m east-west; only the northeast and northwest corners are free of construction. The major plaza is enclosed by Str. 216-13/17 and covers 71.3 m north-south by 46 m east-west; only the southwest corner is closed by construction. Of the two smaller plazas, that surrounded by Str. 216-6 and -8 measures 30 m east-west by 17.5 m north-south and is unobstructed by construction on its north and east sides. The small plaza noted in the deep overgrowth to the north does not appear to have been completely enclosed by construction. Within the context of each mapped plaza and quadrangle group there is a certain consistency in structure orientations; between groups there is variation in this regard. There is no clear single alignment for all platforms at the site.

The material used in construction is unmodified dark brown, fine-grained, hard stone which occurs naturally around the locus. Stone slabs, so common at other LMV sites, were not recorded here and neither were river cobbles or cut and faced blocks. On the basis of surface indications, therefore, the standard LMV step-terrace technique appears absent. It is possible, of course, that similar terraces were built of the locally available stone, similar to Str. 212-6 at Choco. Four of the six largest structures have a single 1- to 1.5-m-wide terrace on their court- or plaza-facing side (Str. 216-10/12 and -17). This kind of terrace was noted on several monumental structures at other valley sites. The small structures also have a surface covering of stone chunks. However, no wall lines are visible and the precise nature of small structure construction remains unknown. No surviving evidence was found to support Berlin's (1952: 42) contention that one of the structures was faced with well-cut stones forming a *talud* surmounted in turn by a low, vertical *tablero*.

Several other architectural features were recorded at Arapahoe Viejo. The most unusual of these is a series of "rooms" sunk into the summit of Str. 216-13. These three features are vertical-walled, roughly rectilinear, and between 1.5 and 2 m deep. They are slightly deeper on the north side than on the south. The walls consist of roughly coursed stone chunks with sparse mud mortar. Because of the amount of collapsed debris at the bottom of these depressions it was difficult to determine their original depths and the kind of flooring that may have existed. The regularity of these features, their sizes and nature of construction all suggest that they were an integral part of aboriginal construction. Their exact function could be determined only by excavation.

Artificial ground leveling by terracing is relatively uncommon at Arapahoe Viejo. One example of its use extends eastward from Str. 216-9. This 0.4-m-high feature represents an attempt to formalize a natural contour by means of a stone wall. There was no comparable attempt at formalization on the west side of the structure where another natural contour, 0.7 m high, is also found. The only other example of terracing is Str. 216-15, a 14-m-long by 5.8-m-wide construction with no elevation on its south side, extending from the line of a northeast-southwest natural rise c. 0.4 m high. Presumably the builders of Str. 216-15 took advantage of a natural rise to facilitate the construction of this platform.

Special Features:

Monument 1: An unadorned sphere with a diameter of 0.5 m, fashioned from the ubiquitous hard dark-brown local stone and located almost exactly in the center of the court defined by Str. 216-9/12. Within the valley, it bears a very close resemblance to Mon. 2 and 3 from the Northwest Group in the Las Quebradas Site Zone (Locus 205). The shape, size, and stone used are very similar in all these.

Alluviation: Because of the site's location high above the floodplain of the Rio Motagua, it is very unlikely that any structures were buried by river-deposited silts.

Surface Collections: One prismatic obsidian blade fragment was collected from this site by Nowak. No collections were made in 1979.

Excavations: None.

JUAN DE PAZ (LOCUS 207, OP. 47)

LOCATION AND SETTING

General Location: Juan de Paz is in the far southwestern portion of the survey zone, c. 17.1 km westsouthwest of Quirigua and 12.9 km west of Chapulco (see Fig. 1).

Topography: Locus 207 is built on a terrace that slopes gradually down to the south toward the Rio Motagua. This terrace stands 10-15 m above the Motagua and its margins are defined by relatively steep slopes.

Resources: Juan de Paz is well situated with respect to water from both the Motagua and the Rio Juan de Paz, c. 200 m west of the locus. Building stones, primarily cobbles, could also have been obtained from the Motagua. No sources of sandstone and schist, two other stones used in construction, were located in the immediate area. The fertile floodplain of the Rio Motagua at the base of the terrace, though somewhat narrow here, would have provided a productive zone for farming.

If, as has been claimed (e.g., Thompson 1966; Hammond 1972), the Motagua was a route of communication linking the Guatemalan highlands with the Caribbean coast, then Juan de Paz would have been favorably placed to profit from the traffic passing along it. The narrowness of the Motagua valley, here only c. 1.7 km wide at its maximum, would have put the occupants of Juan de Paz in a good position to control interactions along this route. The Atlantic Highway (CA-9), Guatemala's primary road link between the Caribbean and the highlands, currently bisects the locus, indicating the continued importance of this route and location even today.

CURRENT STATUS

Several structures have been disturbed by looters, though the worst destruction has been caused by bulldozing. Structure 207-71 in the southeastern part of the site has already lost approximately two-thirds of its total area (west, north, and east faces) to this activity, while several other platforms have been damaged to a lesser degree. It is possible that the Atlantic Highway, which passes c. 100 m north of the mapped portion of the locus, also caused the destruction of some structures when it was initially constructed.

Ownership: Sr. Valentin Cabrera.

SITE DESCRIPTION

Previous Work: Nowak noted the location of Juan de Paz on his overall map of the LMV (Nowak 1973b: fig. 2), though he provided no further information on it.

Recording: The site was mapped by surveyor's transit. Fortunately, owing to the absence of tall vegetation, clearing operations were largely unnecessary. Subsequent reports by Muller and Johnson, two State University of New York at Binghamton geology students, indicated that, in addition to the structures mapped, a smaller group was located 250-300 m to the north across the highway. Unfortunately demands on the time of all project members precluded following up this report. The subsequent discussion concerns itself solely with the buildings mapped in 1978. All structure heights were derived from instrument measurements (see Table III.10).

Description: Locus 207 consists of 81 structures concentrated in an area 186 m north-south by 233 m east-west.

Strictly defined plaza groups are uncommon at Juan de Paz, although considering the sizes of many of the structures involved, the degree of overall site-level orthogonality is rather remarkable. Such uniformity in alignment is not often seen outside the larger valley sites, nor is the degree of nucleation exhibited at Juan de Paz commonly found. Locus 207 is dominated by a large central plaza bounded on all sides by four mutually aligned structures (Str. 207- 31, -32, -32a, and -74). The area of this plaza is 54 m east-west by 29 m north-south and is delimited by four of the largest platforms at Juan de Paz. One of the other sizable structures at this site (Str. 207-3) is c. 40 m north of Str. 207-31, forming the northern end of a north-south alignment running from Str. 207-32 to -31 to -3. In short, the area from Str. 207-3 to -32, including the major plaza noted above, forms a spatial focus of Juan de Paz bisecting an otherwise dense concentration of small structures with a line of sizable constructions separated by large open spaces.

TABLE 2.9

SURFACE COLLECTIONS

Lot #	Contents	Depositional Significance	Provenience
47A/1 (Nowak collection)	34 sherds; 1 *bajareque* frag.	Surface	Juan de Paz area

A second recognizable plaza group is found in the eastern portion of the locus. Standing somewhat apart, this aggregate is composed of eight structures (Str. 207-64/71), seven of which surround the plaza on all sides but the south, while one (Str. 207-71) is located in the plaza's approximate center. The area thus defined measures some 47.5 m northeast-southwest by 40 m northwest-southeast.

The vast majority of the structures in the locus are covered with river cobbles and angular unfaced stone chunks. Given the prevalence of cobbles, the general paucity of stone slabs, and the low altitudes of most of the constructions involved, it would appear that the step-terrace style was not employed here. Rather, it seems likely that the structures were built up using low vertical cobble retaining walls, similar to those found among the humbler platforms excavated at Choco, Playitas, and Las Quebradas. This interpretation receives some confirmation from the cut faces of Str. 207-71. The fill exposed in truncated structures tends to be a hard-packed earth containing small stones with the latter sometimes concentrated at the base of the earthen fill. Exceptions to these general statements are found in the central area of the locus. Structures 207-32 and -32a are both faced with well-cut and smoothed sandstone blocks c. 0.5 m long by 0.33 m thick by 0.39 m deep, an *in situ* line of which was noted on the north side of the summit junction of these two structures. Another exception is Str. 207-3,

which has large sandstone and schist slabs protruding from its north face. These slabs measure 1.2-1.5 m long by 0.6 m wide by 0.12 m thick. It is interesting to note that the architectural exceptions at Juan de Paz pertain to the large central structures of the site, which are singled out not only by their size, but by the nature of their building material as well.

Despite the presence of monumental (1.5 m and higher) structures at Juan de Paz, their relative paucity and simple forms when compared to the previously mentioned centers led me to classify this locus as a nonmonumental site. According to the criteria of construction size and complexity, Juan de Paz was not a sociopolitical center on the level of Playitas or Quebrada Grande. The same argument applies to Oneida and other similar sites described in the following pages.

Alluviation: Given the position of Juan de Paz c. 10-15 m above the Rio Motagua, it is unlikely that portions of the site lie buried by flood-deposited silts.

Surface Collections: Sherds were noted on the surface in 1978, though because of their paucity and relative anonymity none were collected. Those seen were plain utilitarian body sherds. Nowak made a surface collection at the site that was analyzed in 1979. It consisted of 34 sherds and one fragment of *bajareque*, though it is unclear where on the locus this material was originally found (see Table 2.9).

Excavations: None.

ONEIDA (Locus 235, Op. 50)

LOCATION AND SETTING

General Location: Oneida is c. 11.7 km north of the Playitas Site Zone (Locus 200) and c. 3.75 km northwest of the Bobos Site Zone (Locus 219; see Fig. 1).

Topography: Locus 235 is on a terrace immediately west of the Rio Motagua. The Motagua is currently cutting a channel c. 10-15 m below the site of Oneida.

Resources: This locus is admirably located with respect to a year-round source of water from the Motagua, and from Salamon Crique to the west. Several dry (in April 1977) streambeds that extend through the locus might also provide at least a seasonal supply of water. The Rio Motagua carries a considerable number of potential building stones in the form of river cobbles, though, as noted below, it does not appear that these were extensively used in construction at the locus. The agricultural potential of the surrounding land appears to be good. Much of the terrain surrounding the Oneida site was planted in bananas during 1977, though presumably *milpa* could have been grown here as well. Oneida is adjacent to one of the potentially most important routes linking the Atlantic coast with the Guatemalan interior, the Rio Motagua. If this river functioned as a communication channel pre-Hispanically, and if it flowed near its present course at that time, then the aboriginal inhabitants of Oneida would have been in a strategic position to control such interactions. The supposition of the Motagua's pre-Hispanic importance seems reasonable in light of current evidence (Thompson 1966; Hammond 1972).

CURRENT STATUS

Oneida appears to have suffered relatively little destruction over the years. The houses—part of the *aldea* of Porvenir—that occupy the summits of several of the aboriginal structures in the northwestern part of the site have caused some localized destruction. In the far eastern portion of Oneida, the eastern face of one structure has been eroded by the Motagua. Other constructions located in this area have been completely destroyed by river action. No evidence of looting was noted.

Ownership: Unknown.

SITE DESCRIPTION

Previous Work: It is very probable that Nowak (1973a) visited this locus during his survey of the valley, as a site of Oneida appears on his valley map (ibid.). No published record of this visit currently exists, however, and no notes or plans from this survey are available.

Recording: Because of the broad extent covered by the locus and the wide dispersal of its structures, formal mapping was not feasible without the use of a transit. The expenditure of time required to record Oneida in this way was considered too great to be justified, given time and money constraints. Consequently, Oneida was recorded simply by notes.

Description: Locus 235 is composed of 50 recorded structures scattered singly and in irregular groups of three or four platforms over an area roughly 800 m east-west by 650-700 m north-south. The structures noted range in height from 0.5 to 3 m, with most falling between 0.5 and 1 m. The largest structures measure 60 m long by 11.5 m wide, though most are in the 8-by-4 to 18-by-14-m range. Groups of sizable constructions, i.e., 1.5-2 m high, tend to be arranged into orthogonal plaza complexes, while those consisting of smaller structures lack such regularity of alignment. The distances between individual structures or groups range from 75 to 350 m, with structure densities increasing gradually to the west away from the Motagua. The sizes of recorded platforms also increase in this direction.

In general, the overall plan of Oneida includes a series of at least three groups of large, orthogonally arranged platforms in the western portion of the locus within 250-300 m of Salamon Crique. These, in turn, are surrounded on the north, east, and possibly south by more irregularly arranged groups of smaller constructions. Despite this concentration of structures in the west, the locus must still be described as dispersed. None of the large groups at Oneida in any way approach the monumentality of the main groups at sites such as Las Quebradas and Playitas. The larger Oneida aggregates, in fact, more closely resemble outliers surrounding the massive Las Quebradas and Playitas quadrangles.

Few stones were found on the surface of any structure in Locus 235. Those stones that were seen were river cobbles and some slabs. In fact, on the basis of surface indications alone, many of the Oneida structures appear to have been built solely of earth. There is, of course, the possibility, given the site's proximity to a major modern settlement, that stones on the surface have long since been robbed for current construction. It is also possible that stone construction lies buried, as revealed in the excavation of Str. 212-22 at Choco (see Chap. 3). The Oneida structure cut by the Motagua, however, yielded a fill of reddish earth with no obvious stone facing walls. The larger structures in the western part of the locus have more surface stones. But, because of their proximity to modern houses and the disturbances wrought thereby, it is difficult to infer their mode of construction from surface remains alone. It seems possible that the smaller structures in this locus were built wholly or at least in part of earth, while the larger constructions to the west employed more stonework.

Alluviation: Given its location on a steep bank overlooking the Motagua, it seems unlikely that this locus was regularly inundated by floods or that its low structures were subject to burial by river silt.

Surface Collections: None.

Excavations: None.

TABLE 2.10

SURFACE COLLECTIONS

Lot #	Contents	Depositional Significance	Provenience
11A/2	2 manos; 1 obsidian tool, broken	Surface	Donated finds
11J/1	1 stone?; 69 sherds; 3 censers; 2 mano frags.; 1 metate frag.; 12 pcs. obsidian	Surface, plowed structures	Plaza surface
11J/2	22 sherds; 2 pcs. obsidian	Surface, plowed structure	Str. 052-1
11J/3	33 sherds; 8 pcs. obsidian	Surface	From area of preplowing probe that had uncovered sherd concentration

CRISTINA (Locus 052, Op. 11J)

LOCATION AND SETTING

General Location: Cristina is c. 8.3 km north-northeast of Quirigua and c. 13.1 km northwest of Juyama (Locus 211; see Fig. 1).

Topography: Locus 052 is built on the floodplain of the Rio San Francisco, raised somewhat above the valley floor as the land begins to rise toward the Sierra de las Minas to the northwest.

Resources: The Rio San Francisco, only c. 1.15 km north of Cristina, could have provided the inhabitants of this locus with a year-round supply of water. In addition, several *quebradas* that bound the locus on its north and east might represent courses of seasonal streams. The Rio San Francisco also carries a large number of river cobbles and thus could have been a source of these stones for construction. The agricultural potential of the land surrounding Locus 052 appears to be good; it was planted in a modern cash crop, tobacco, in 1976. There is no good evidence to suggest that Cristina was located along an aboriginally important communication route in the past.

CURRENT STATUS

Approximately two months before the Project's visit to this site, the land had been extensively plowed in preparation for planting tobacco, with the result that at least two structures had been completely obliterated and three of the remaining four had been plowed. These latter platforms were reduced in height by this activity and lost any clear alignment they once had. Structure 052-1, the tallest construction in the locus, was not plowed (Fig. 20).

Ownership: Philip Morris Tobacco Company.

SITE DESCRIPTION

Previous Work: None.

Recording: Cristina was investigated in February 1976. In addition to making surface collections and taking notes, the team mapped the four remaining structures using a tripod-mounted Brunton pocket transit and a 30-m tape (see Fig. 20).

Description: The locus consists of a single group of four structures arranged more or less orthogonally

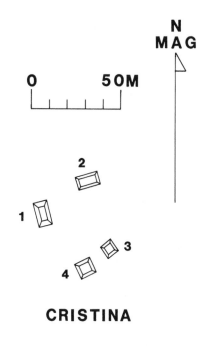

Figure 20.   Map of Cristina.

around all but the east side of a plaza. The total area covered by these constructions is 57.5 m north-south by 48 m east-west. The outline of a destroyed structure was found within 21 m west-northwest of Str. 052-3, although unfortunately its outlines were not clear enough to permit mapping. The location of the second reportedly destroyed structure could never be accurately ascertained.

Special Features:

To the northwest of Str. 052-2, a local informant reported locating "layer upon layer" of sherds in a small hole dug prior to plowing. Whether this probe had come upon a domestic midden could not be verified without further excavations, impossible given the state of plowing.

Alluviation: The location of Cristina close to the level of the Rio San Francisco floodplain suggests that some structures here were obscured by river-deposited silts.

Surface Collections: Three surface lots, 11J/1-3, were collected by the QAP at Cristina in 1976. These were not analyzed by the LMV survey program. In general, the density of surface remains thinned out rapidly beyond the immediate area of the plaza group, though isolated finds could still be made c. 50 m north of the structures. A final surface lot, 11A/2, consisting of several manos and the broken point of a bifacially worked obsidian artifact, was contributed by a local worker on the tobacco plantation. The exact provenience of these finds within the site is unknown.

Excavations: None.

LOS LIMONES (Locus 231, Op. 44)

LOCATION AND SETTING

General Location: The small site of Los Limones is c. 2.5 km south-southeast of the Playitas Site Zone (Locus 200), c. 2 km north-northwest of the site of Los Vitales (Locus 232), and c. 5 km north of Mojanales (Locus 233) in the *aldea* of the same name (see Fig. 1).

Topography: Locus 231 rests at an elevation of 200-250 m on the west bank of the Rio Chinamito in a small pocket valley formed by this river within the Espiritu Santo mountains. The valley itself is relatively small, only c. 200 m across at its widest point, and Los Limones is strictly bounded on the west, north, and south by the high cliffs of the Espiritu Santo range. It is limited on the east by the Rio Chinamito, which at this point runs against the steep precipice that defines the valley on this side. The ground on which the site is built slopes gradually down from west to east, to the Chinamito.

Resources: The close proximity of the Rio Chinamito, a fast-flowing, perennial stream, would have provided the aboriginal residents with an adequate supply of water year-round. Potential building stones, primarily waterworn cobbles, are plentiful in this streambed and would have been easily accessible to the prehistoric residents. Agricultural land is close by, as the structures are situated on one of the few relatively flat expanses in the area. Besides cultivation of the valley bottoms, hillside farming might have been carried out around the valley margins much as it was in 1979. As at Los Vitales and Mojanales, however, it should be noted that expanses of flat terrain are limited here, and good agricultural land might therefore have been at a premium.

Locus 231 is adjacent to one of the major trails leading south-southeast from the railhead at Bobos/Playitas through the mountains to Mojanales, and thence to Honduras (see Mojanales description, this chapter). This trail follows the route cut by the Rio Chinamito and one of its major tributaries, and while never very wide, might well have provided access through the mountains aboriginally. The site of Los Limones, like its modern successor, would have been in a strategic position to profit in some way from its location along this route. During the journey to Mojanales on the day of the Playitas market, it was noted that the Los Limones residents benefited from the traffic by selling foodstuffs to passersby, while being in a good position to purchase goods from these travelers, and by exchanging information with them.

CURRENT STATUS

The only modification to the land that was obvious during this brief survey was the building of a cattle enclosure in the western portion of the site. From the brief investigation of the locus, it appears that the structures have been little disturbed over the years.

Ownership: Unknown.

SITE DESCRIPTION

Previous Work: None.

Recording: The site was recorded solely on the basis of a rapid visual inspection: structures were counted and their heights estimated from the vantage point of horses along the trail. The reason for this limitation was lack of time.

Description: Los Limones consists of five structures scattered over roughly 200 m east-west from the Chinamito to the bordering hills. Structure heights range from 0.5 to 2.5 m, with most falling within the 1- to 1.5-m range. No clear plaza groupings were noted, though there is a concentration of three structures in the western part of the site, west of the extant trail. These constructions are c. 0.5, 1, and 1.5 m high, measure roughly 10-15 by 6-9 m at the base, and are not orthogonally arranged. To the east, almost on the bank of the Chinamito, are two additional structures, one of which, the largest at the site, is c. 2.5 m high, while the second, located to the northwest, rises c. 1.5 m. The central part of the site, where the vegetation is densest, might have contained several more buildings, though this was not verified.

On the basis of the three structures west of the modern trail that were examined at close range, the primary building material would seem to have been river-worn cobbles. No cut stone blocks were noted, nor were stone slabs much in evidence.

Alluviation: The location of this site so close to the level of the Rio Chinamito suggests that its lower eastern portion might have been at least partly obscured by flood-deposited silts.

Surface Collections: None.

Excavations: None.

LOS VITALES (Locus 232, Op. 45)

LOCATION AND SETTING

General Location: Situated on the same trail system as Los Limones (Locus 231), which is 2 km to the south-southeast, Los Vitales is c. 4.4 km south-southeast of the Playitas Site Zone (Locus 200) and 3.1 km north of Mojanales (Locus 233).

Topography: Los Vitales is situated at the point where the Quebrada Mojanal joins the Rio Chinamito in a small pocket valley c. 350 m east-west by 450 m north-south. The steep cliffs of the Espiritu Santo mountains define the valley on the north, south, east, and west, while the Chinamito, which runs against the high eastern cliffs, borders the site on the east. The Quebrada Mojanal divides the site, isolating two of the 11 structures south of it. The few flat areas available in the valley seem low-lying and prone to inundation during the rainy season: most modern and prehistoric constructions are either built into the encircling hills or located on low rises above the flat land.

Resources: The Rio Chinamito provides a year-round supply of water to the present residents and probably would have done so in the past. The Quebrada Mojanal also contains running water in the dry season. The Chinamito carries a large load of river-rounded cobbles, and this stone appears to have been used in construction at Locus 232. As with the other sites located in small valleys along this route, e.g., Los Limones, the location of good agricultural land might have been a problem. Farming of the valley slopes, especially with terracing, or the exploitation of small side valleys might have alleviated this concern. No good flat land for agriculture that was not threatened by periodic flooding was noted in the immediate site area.

If the trail that passes by the site was used aboriginally, then the residents of Los Vitales would have been in a position to profit from any commerce moving along it. The fact that the Chinamito and Quebrada Mojanal cut one of the few deep passages through the Espiritu Santo range into Honduras suggests that this route might have been attractive to prehistoric travelers. Brief observations made en route to Mojanales in March 1979 indicated that the present residents sold foodstuffs to passing traders, may have bought goods from these merchants, and certainly exchanged information with them.

CURRENT STATUS

Seven of the 11 structures are not significantly disturbed by recent activities. The remaining four, which are incorporated into modern house compounds, have been seriously disturbed, however. Damage here takes the form of a series of shallow excavations and the apparent removal of construction stones from their surfaces for use in modern buildings.

Ownership: Unknown.

SITE DESCRIPTION

Previous Work: None.

Recording: As with Los Limones, this site was recorded from horseback as we traveled to and from Mojanales. This method has its limitations, and the structures described are those found immediately adjacent to the current trail. No map was made and the description that follows is based solely on notes taken at the time. Again the primary limitation was time, in that the principal object of this reconnaissance was to visit Mojanales.

Description: The site of Los Vitales consists of 11 recorded structures extending over an area roughly 150 m north-south by 50-75 m east-west. These platforms range in size from 0.5 to 2.25 m high, though most are 1-1.1 m in height. Locus 232 consists of five individual terraces, each the size of a substructure platform, probably intended to support perishable upper construction. All of these terraces are built into the western boundary of this small valley. These structures are not organized orthogonally. They range in height from 0.75-1.5 m on their eastern faces to no elevation on the west where they join the hill face. In addition to these terraces, there are four constructions, just north of the confluence of the Rio Chinamito and the Quebrada Mojanal, arranged orthogonally around a small plaza bounded on all four sides by construction. This group is on a low rise above the valley flats and contains the largest recorded structure, standing c. 2.25 m high, which dominates the remaining constructions of about 1 m high. Two low (0.5-0.75 m high) structures are found south of the *quebrada* and are separated by 85 m from the plaza group.

Because of the rapidity of the survey and the amount of destruction suffered by the plaza group, it is difficult to determine the nature of the architecture. River-worn cobbles are the most common stone on the surface of structures, while stone slabs are rare and cut blocks entirely absent. In the few modern stone walls at the site, cobbles are again the predominant element, suggesting that they were the principal stones robbed from pre-Hispanic structures. Given the size of most of the structures and the absence of slabs, it is very unlikely that the step-terrace technique was employed in construction. Rather, based on the prevalence of cobbles, it seems likely that these structures were built up of low cobble retaining walls similar to those found in Str. 212-22 at Choco, and Str. 205-123 and -196 at Las Quebradas. The fill noted on four robbed structures is an orange earth.

Alluviation: Given the location of the plaza group and the five terraces above the level of the Rio Chinamito, it is not likely that any structures here have been significantly buried by river-deposited silts. The remaining two structures south of Quebrada Mojanal, closer to the river level, were more prone to periodic inundations and may have been buried to some extent by flood silts.

Surface Collections: None.

Excavations: None.

LOCUS 234 (no name; Op. 46)

LOCATION AND SETTING

General Location: Locus 234 is 2 km north of Mojanales (Locus 233), 5.5 km south-southeast of Playitas (Locus 200), and 1.1 km south-southeast of Los Vitales (Locus 232; see Fig. 1).

Topography: This site, situated on a small flat terrace on the west bank of the Quebrada Mojanal, is on the modern trail between Bobos, Playitas, and Mojanales. The size of this terrace is barely sufficient to support the structures, roughly 100 m northeast-southwest by 50 m northwest-southeast. The cliffs of the Espiritu Santo mountains closely define the area of the site on all sides save the east.

Resources: The Quebrada Mojanal is located close by Locus 234 and would have offered a perennial source of water and river-worn cobbles, the latter serving as building stones. Agricultural land is limited in the immediate area of the locus; more might have been found either on the adjacent hill slopes, which are rather steep, or c. 1 km to the south, where the valley widens out near the *aldea* of Mojanales.

As with Los Limones, Los Vitales, and Mojanales, Locus 234 is on a modern trail linking the *aldea* of Mojanales, and most probably others in Honduras, with the railhead at Bobos/Playitas. If this trail was in use aboriginally, and the fact that the Chinamito and Quebrada Mojanal afforded one of the few passes into

Honduras in the area seems to support this contention, then the residents of Locus 234 could have benefited from this association. In 1979 there was no modern habitation on this spot.

CURRENT STATUS

The structures seem little disturbed and the only construction of recent date in the area is a small cattle shed built close by on the same terrace.

Ownership: Unknown.

SITE DESCRIPTION

Previous Work: None.

Recording: Locus 234 is immediately adjacent to the aforementioned trail and was recorded from horse-back alone. Time did not permit a more thorough examination and the small size of the site and its close proximity to our vantage point did not recommend it.

Description: The site consists of two low (c. 0.5 m high) structures each no more than 12 by 8 m along its basal dimensions. They are arranged roughly parallel to, though not directly opposite, each other. No stones were visible on the surface; the dense grass cover might have masked any that were there.

Alluviation: The position of this site on a terrace above the Quebrada Mojanal suggests that it is not in serious danger of being flooded, hence the structures probably have not been obscured by river-deposited silts.

Surface Collections: None.

Excavations: None.

LA COROZA (Locus 208, Op. 43)

LOCATION AND SETTING

General Location: La Coroza is in the low foothills of the Espiritu Santo range c. 2.9 km southeast of Choco (Locus 212) and 3.3 km southwest of the Playitas Site Zone (Locus 200; see Fig. 1).

Topography: The site is located on relatively flat land at the northwestern end of a long narrow pocket valley extending back c. 750 m to the southeast. To the north the ground drops away quickly toward the flat floodplain of the Rio Motagua, while to the west and east are the high ridges of the Espiritu Santo mountains which flank this valley. The structures composing the site are on a natural rise c. 0.5 m above the surrounding flat terrain. Immediately to the north and east a small creekbed (dry in March 1979) roughly 1 m deep and not much wider winds around the locus.

Resources: The small stream channel that borders the site might have provided its aboriginal inhabitants with water, at least during the wet season. Small streams carrying water in March 1979, however, were relatively abundant within 1 km of the site to the northeast. The location and condition of the corn planted immediately southeast of Locus 208 indicate that good agricultural land is also to be found. Sources of potential building stones were not noted, though it is very possible that these exist either in rock outcrops in the Espiritu Santo mountains or in streambeds, especially along the larger rivers. The latter would have been the Rio Encantado, c. 2.7 km to the west, and the Rio Chinamito, c. 3.3 km to the north. Both of these carry large loads of river-worn cobbles, which are plentiful on the surface of the La Coroza platforms. There is no good basis, in terms of either modern use or topography, to suppose that La Coroza was positioned on an aboriginally important communication route.

CURRENT STATUS

All three of the investigated structures are disturbed to one extent or another. Two of these constructions, those in the northwestern part of the locus, have poorly preserved alignments due to a combination of tree root action and modern digging. The third structure, located in the area of densest overgrowth, has been recently looted, with a trench dug from the southern edge of the platform to its summit.

Ownership: Unknown.

SITE DESCRIPTION

Previous Work: None.

Recording: La Coroza was recorded solely by notes. The site was located during a more extensive survey of the area around the La Coroza *aldea*, prompted by reports of potentially early (Protoclassic/Early Classic) material's having been found in this area. As the location of any occupation predating the Late Classic had not been recorded by this project, we decided to investigate the reports from La Coroza.

TABLE 2.11

SURFACE COLLECTIONS

Lot #	Contents	Depositional Significance	Provenience
43A/1	25 sherds	Mixed fill and surface	From backdirt of looter's pit into str.

Description: The three structures at La Coroza are 0.5-1 m high and, in the case of the two cleared examples, measure 4.5 by 2.5 and 5.5 by 4.5 m. The third structure was too densely overgrown to measure, though it appeared no larger than the others. The structures are arranged into a small plaza group surrounded on three sides by construction and open to the south. The least damaged structure, which at 1 m high is also the tallest, closes off the north side of the plaza and is oriented roughly N 75° 0' W.

River-worn cobbles and small schist slabs were noted on the surface of the structures, cobbles being the predominant stone. No cut and faced stone blocks were recorded. The looted structure on the east side of the plaza also produced mostly cobbles in the backdirt and only a few slabs. Unfortunately, little information could be gleaned from examining the walls of the looter's trench, so extensive was the stone removal. The fill observed here was an orange-brown clay with few included stones. Given the size of the structures in this group and the prevalence of cobbles, it is likely that they were built up of low vertical cobble retaining walls which contained an earthen fill, similar to the humbler structures excavated at Choco, Las Quebradas, and Playitas.

Alluviation: Given the site's location, it is very unlikely that any La Coroza structures have been obscured by river-deposited silts.

Surface Collections: A single surface collection (Lot 43A/1) containing 25 sherds was made in 1979 from the backdirt of the aforementioned looter's trench. The material recovered was clearly classifiable as Late Classic and not Protoclassic/Early Classic in date (see Table 2.11).

Excavations: None.

COMMENTS

The search for indications of occupation prior to the Late Classic around the La Coroza *aldea* proved fruitless. This was attributable in part to the denseness of the natural and cultivated vegetation in the area. It was largely due to the latter problem that investigations in the La Coroza pocket valley had to be curtailed, though in terms of agricultural potential and access to water this small valley would be a likely location for more sites.

LOS CERRITOS SITE ZONE (Locus 230, Op. 40)

LOCATION AND SETTING

General Location: The two recorded structure clusters in the Los Cerritos Zone lie within the dispersed hamlet of that name, c. 1.7 km northwest of the Las Quebradas Site Zone (Locus 205) and c. 4.4 km southeast of the Bobos Site Zone (Locus 209; see Fig. 1).

Topography: Locus 230 occupies relatively flat areas atop a narrow northwest-southeast ridge, part of the same ridge system emanating from the Espiritu Santo range that supports the site of Las Quebradas. The terrain surrounding these groups is rugged, with frequent small and deep northeast-southwest ravines. The steepest precipice in the area, however, is the drop-off to the floodplain of the Rio Bobos, c. 75 m southwest of Group I and immediately south of Group II. This drop of 15 m does not pose an insurmountable obstacle to travel, and it is traversed by modern paths.

Resources: The site is well placed with respect to drinking water. The Rio Bobos, a tributary of the

Motagua, carries a considerable volume of water year-round and flows within c. 1.6 km of the zone. If, as seems to have been the case, river cobbles were employed on at least some structures, then a ready supply was available in the Bobos. The Rio Motagua, c. 5.2 km to the northwest, might have been another source of cobbles. Good agricultural land would have been available on the rich Bobos floodplain below the zone. Very little modern cultivation is evident on the ridge top; most of the summit is devoted to living quarters or raising domestic animals and chickens.

This zone is not in an obviously strategic position for the control of communication along an arguably prehistoric route. The broad floodplain of the Bobos, which provides easy access from the Rio Motagua to Las Quebradas, lies below the zone.

CURRENT STATUS

Of the two noted aggregations, Group I has suffered the more damage. Structures 230-1 and -2 have been excavated to obtain earth and stones for modern construction (Fig. 21). The result is the loss of the east end of Str. 230-1, and the southwest and southeast corners and most of the west face of Str. 230-2. In Group II the southwest corner of Str. 230-6 has also been truncated. There is some evidence, in the form of scattered stones and cultural debris, that at least one more structure may have existed in each aggregation and has since been destroyed (Fig. 22).

Ownership: Ownership of Group I is divided along a north-south line running across Str. 230-2 between Sr. Efraím Axsame on the west and Sr. Antonio Martínez Cacumen on the east. The owner of Group II was not determined.

SITE DESCRIPTION

Previous Work: Nowak recorded the presence of a site called "Los Cerritos" (1973a). The location of this site on his preliminary map makes it appear that it was named for the now-defunct BANDEGUA *finca* of the same name near which it was located, and was in actuality the site recorded here as Quebrada Grande (Locus 206). Because Quebrada Grande was found in 1978 and 1979 to be on land belonging to the *aldea* of Quebrada Grande, the QAP decided to reapply "Los Cerritos" to the material found within the *aldea* of that name located northwest of Las Quebradas. As far as could be determined, no one has ever recorded the structures in the Los Cerritos Zone as defined here.

Recording: The Locus 230 Groups were mapped, using a tripod-mounted Brunton pocket transit and a 30-m tape. All structure heights were estimated by eye in the field. The area around the mapped Groups was also covered to a distance of 70 m in search of additional evidence of prehistoric occupation.

Description: Group I (Fig. 21) consists of four extant structures, irregularly arranged, covering an area c. 35 m on a side. If the area of a possible destroyed structure in the southern part of the cluster is included, then the aggregation measures 50 m north-south. The heights of the component platforms are given in Table III.11. The area covered by the stone and artifact scatter in the southern part of the Group is 15 m north-south by 21 m east-west.

Group II (Fig. 22), 450 m northwest of Group I, consists of three extant structures, a low terrace, and a possible destroyed construction, irregularly arranged and measuring c. 50.25 m north-south by 69.5 m east-west. The area covered by the stone and artifact scatter that signals the presence of the destroyed construction in the eastern part of the Group measures c. 24 m north-south by 16.5 m east-west. Struc-

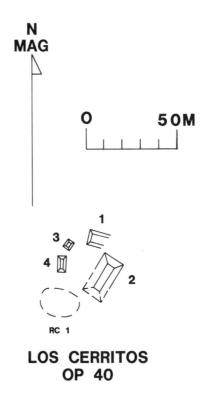

Figure 21. Map of Group I, Los Cerritos.

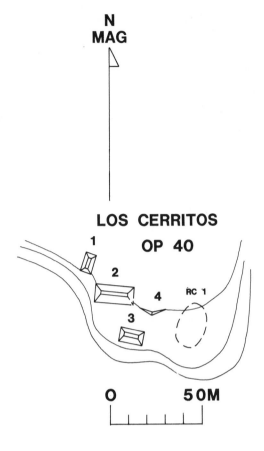

Figure 22.   Map of Group II, Los Cerritos.

stones. The general impression of the architecture, based on the prevalence of cobbles and excavations into similar-sized structures in the Las Quebradas Site Zone, is that the substructure platforms were probably built of a hard-packed earthen fill retained by low vertical walls made of cobbles. It is possible that some form of the step-terrace technique was employed in the larger structures, e.g., Str. 230-2.

Alluviation: The height of this zone above the Rio Bobos safely precludes the burial of structures by alluvial deposits.

Surface Collections: Three collections were made in the Los Cerritos Zone in 1978, two in Group I (40A/1 and 2) and one in Group II (40A/3). Lot 40A/1 derives from the cut made into Str. 230-1 and the path immediately adjacent to it, while Lot 40A/2 is from the debris concentration that marks the location of the destroyed structure. Lot 40A/3 comes from a comparable concentration of cultural debris in Group II. In all, these collections contain two sherds and 71 pieces of obsidian (see Table 2.12).

Excavations: None.

COMMENTS

It should be noted that, despite the location of both Locus 230 Groups over a kilometer distant from the Las Quebradas Site Zone, it is possible that they represent a continuation of residential occupation associated with the latter zone. Resolution of this question is difficult because the ridge top between Group I and the northern mapped limits of Las Quebradas is covered with either modern construction or dense vegetation. Under these conditions, it is impossible to determine whether the apparent drop in evidence of aboriginal occupation between the two areas is an accurate reflection of prehistoric conditions or merely an artifact of vegetation and modern destruction.

ture 230-8, the low terrace, marks an attempt to formalize, through stone construction, a short (c. 14.75 m east-west) segment of a natural rise. No further extension of this terrace was noted.

In both Groups, the predominant building stone on the surface is the river-worn cobble, while stone slabs are rare and faced blocks absent. The fill exposed in the cut structures, Str. 230-1, -2, and -6, is a hard-compacted, reddish orange earth with few included

TABLE 2.12

SURFACE COLLECTIONS

Lot #	Contents	Depositional Significance	Provenience
40A/1	2 sherds; 27 pcs. obsidian	Surface and in str. cut.	Str. 230-1
40A/2	38 pcs. obsidian	Surface	Destroyed str., Group I
40A/3	6 pcs. obsidian	Surface	Destroyed str., Group II

CRUCE DE MORALES, MONTEREY, FINCA AMERICA, PUENTE VIRGINIA
(Locus 201, Op. 47; Locus 202, Op. 48; Locus 203, Op. 49; Locus 204, Op. 26)

LOCATION AND SETTING

General Location: Cruce de Morales is 5.8 km north-northwest of Oneida (Locus 208) and 4.6 km east-northeast of Monterey (Locus 202) at the turnoff on the Atlantic Highway to the municipal center of Morales. Monterey is 2.95 km east-northeast of Finca America (Locus 203) and 6.5 km northeast of Oneida (Locus 208) between the 235- and 236-km markers on the Atlantic Highway, straddling both sides of that road. Finca America is 4.4 km northeast of Puente Virginia (Locus 204) and 8.3 km northwest of Oneida (Locus 208), adjacent to and northwest of the Atlantic Highway. Puente Virginia is 17.1 km northeast of Cristina (Locus 052) and 11.9 km north-northwest of the Comanche Farm Site Zone (Locus 210), immediately northwest of the Atlantic Highway.

Topography: All four of these loci occupy the first low bench rising c. 15 m to the north above the floodplain of the Rio Motagua. Each locus is on an area of flat to gently sloping land that ascends to the north toward the first steep cliffs of the Sierra de las Minas, no more than 150-250 m away.

Resources: Year-round sources of fresh water are readily available in the streams no more than 0.5 km from each locus. It is problematic whether stone was used in construction at any of these loci, though each of these watercourses carries a supply of river cobbles and would have been a convenient source of this material. The agricultural potential of the surrounding land is unknown, as it was all covered in low grass in 1977 and 1979. The fertile Motagua floodplain is close to all these loci, however. There is no compelling reason for believing that these sites were located adjacent to an aboriginal communication route.

CURRENT STATUS

Very little obvious disturbance of the structures was noted. The proximity of the Atlantic Highway (CA-9) to most of these sites suggests that some structures may have been lost during its construction, though such damage should have been localized. The fact that some of the structures of Puente Virginia were found amidst current *aldea* buildings and even formed the boundary of the soccer field here also indicates that a few constructions may have been obliterated as residences expanded. The fact that pre-Hispanic platforms are still to be found scattered among modern habitations strongly points out, however, that this destruction has not been systematic. The general lack of stones at many of these loci may well be attributable to stone robbing for current needs.

Ownership: Unknown.

SITE DESCRIPTION

Previous Work: Nowak (1973a) recorded the locations of these loci on his general map of the LMV. Unfortunately, no published report of his findings beyond this map currently exists, with the exception of one brief mention of an excavation he carried out at Puente Virginia (Nowak 1975: 18). The extent, exact location, and results of this work are unknown.

Recording: These four loci were inspected very rapidly to accomplish two goals: first, to locate them accurately; and second, to determine whether they were sufficiently large and complex to be classed with the monumental loci that form the focus of this study (see Chap. 1). Since this was not the case they, like Oneida (Locus 208), were not recorded in any detail. Plans to return and map several of them were postponed as all available time had to be invested in adequately recording the large centers further south. Recording was done solely in terms of notes and no sketch maps were made.

Description: All of these loci consist of roughly 20-50 structures of various sizes, the tallest 2-3 m high. While there does seem to be a tendency for the larger structures to form coherent groups, there is no evidence of the existence of large monumental court complexes such as dominate the sites of Choco, Comanche Farm, and Las Quebradas. Most of the visible structures stand c. 0.5-0.75 m high and are scattered without apparent plan throughout the site. As noted earlier, stones are rarely found on the surface of these loci, so it is not possible to determine the nature of the architecture.

Alluviation: The position of these loci on a relatively high eminence above the Rio Motagua floodplain suggests that they are not prone to inundation. Flooding from the several streams flowing nearby might have buried the very lowest constructions.

Surface Collections: None.

Excavations: None by the LMV program; some probing was done by Nowak at Puente Virginia, though its extent and results are unknown.

III

Excavation

INTRODUCTION

The excavations carried out by the LMV program were influenced by several considerations and limitations. Foremost among these were the extent of previous research in the area, site size, and restrictions on time and money. Because so little was known archaeologically about this region at the onset of research in 1977, we decided to concentrate on a restricted number of basic goals: 1) determination of the terminal period of occupation at the investigated sites; 2) reconstruction of the sequence of occupation at these sites; 3) analysis of the architecture of both monumental and small structures at major investigated centers; and 4) reconstruction of the activities carried out at the probed loci. Restrictions of time and money coupled with the substantial size of the located sites led to the use of an opportunistic excavation strategy. As a result, there is no way of evaluating how representative the data are of general LMV material patterns. The quantity of data recovered is also limited. Some 47 excavations were conducted at three sites: Playitas, Las Quebradas, and Choco.

To a certain extent, these concerns are reduced by the sheer redundancy of the recovered data. Excavation revealed very consistent patterns in methods of construction and ceramic assemblages (the latter relied on for dating). Nonetheless, any interpretation or generalizations based on this material must be phrased as hypotheses susceptible to further testing. This is especially true of activity reconstructions, which are severely hampered by the limited nature of the excavated data.

The three sites chosen for testing (Las Quebradas and Choco in 1978, and Playitas in 1979) were selected because their large sizes suggested that their residents played important roles in regional interactions. Any understanding of these loci would, therefore, provide some tentative insights into those dealings. Assuming that LMV sites grew through accretion, we also hoped that investigations in the largest examples would reveal a relatively long period of occupation on which a preliminary regional chronology could be developed. The information obtained from these massive centers would also be comparable to that unearthed at Quirigua and the Wider Periphery monumental foci (Jones et al. 1983). Such comparisons might provide insights into the total valley pattern of interaction on the elite level.

Finally, permission to excavate at Playtias, Las Quebradas, and Choco could be obtained and the necessary equipment moved to these locations on locally available transport. Centers such as Quebrada Grande and Juyama, while large, were logistically impossible to excavate in 1977-79. Once again, it is conceded that any attempt at understanding the full range of behaviors that characterized pre-Hispanic LMV populations must involve a systematic excavation program at the full range of located sites (see Chap. 9). Given the restrictions outlined earlier, however, the choice of Playitas, Las Quebradas, and Choco seemed warranted, as they promised to provide a maximum of information for the amount of effort that could be invested.

The same excavation plan was employed at each site. Trenches were placed axially, usually on the court/plaza-facing side of a monumental structure outside the limits of visible construction, and extending up onto its flanks. These probes were designed to uncover terminal levels of construction, penetrate structural fill to obtain sealed artifact deposits to date construction, and locate primary use-related deposits, such as caches or burials, to date structure occupation and reconstruct the activities associated with that occupation. Datable artifacts recovered from fill are in secondary context and provide only a general idea of the earliest time period in which the structure could have been built. The search for use-related primary deposits on the centerline of structures was based on precedents in the Maya area. In those cases where the axial line of a structure was severely disturbed, the trench was located slightly off center.

In three cases (Str. 200-23, 205-1, and 212-4) monumental structures were probed to a sufficient depth to determine whether or not buried construction existed. Unfortunately, the unstable nature of platform fill and facing construction, coupled with the heights of monumental structures, restricted the number of instances in which deep probes could be carried out.

At those sites with multiple quadrangle groups an attempt was made to test at least one monumental structure in each aggregate. An effort was also made to sample one structure in each court of multi-court quadrangles. In all, 11 monumental structures were probed in this fashion.

The backs or noncourt/plaza-facing sides of eight monumental structures were investigated, though rarely penetrated. The purpose of this work was threefold: to obtain an accurate measurement of the structure's width, to determine whether construction was the same on both court and noncourt sides, and to try to locate a midden, preferably stratified, associated with occupation. Where possible, these trenches were placed on the same line as the frontal axial probes.

Where superstructure features were visible on summits of monumental constructions, they were investigated through excavation. The goals here were to reveal something of the nature of monumental summit construction and to uncover artifacts in primary use-related contexts as a basis for activity inferences.

Six small structures were also tested to provide some balance to the picture of LMV material culture patterns as reconstructed from the large-structure excavations. The goals here were much the same as those outlined for their monumental counterparts: to date the period(s) of their construction and use, to reveal something of their architecture, and to uncover artifacts in sufficient numbers and appropriate contexts to allow activity inferences. Each of the six investigated structures was trenched axially up to the middle of the summit, and down to the base of construction. In two cases, Str. 212-22 and 205-196, the trench was carried all the way across the structure. Two humble platforms, Str. 212-22 and 200-16, were cleared for basal plan.

Special features were investigated as time allowed. Four monuments at Las Quebradas were excavated to determine their associated architecture and artifacts. Three test pits were dug to expose the extent of court surfacing at Choco, and two interior, closed court corners were dug to reveal the nature of corner closures (Choco and Group IV, Playitas). Also, a low construction connecting Str. 200-73 and -74 at Playitas was dug to expose its method of construction.

The following organization is employed in the data presentations. Each site is divided into its component Groups, where applicable, and probes in each aggregate are described separately. The structure was by and large the focus of investigation and hence serves here as the focus of description. The results of the excavation of each investigated structure are presented separately, beginning with the monumental and then moving to the smaller structures in the different individual Groups. In those cases where excavations were not structure-oriented they are described under a broader heading, e.g., the Choco south court, or the Str. 200-73/74 junction. Monument excavations are described separately at the beginning of the appropriate Group description.

A brief introductory section is provided for each structure which outlines the extent of the work carried out there, and any specific goals different from those outlined above. After this, a summary of the recovered excavated materials by general type (e.g., ceramics or obsidian), context (primary or secondary), and provenience is presented. The bulk of the description is in the Structural/Depositional Summary, which groups the uncovered elements into time spans (abbreviated T.S.) based on their period of deposition. Within each time span the cultural or natural significance of the included elements is explored, and arguments for their relative temporal position are advanced. Absolute chronological placement is reserved for Chap. 5. Time spans are numbered from latest to earliest; the larger the number, the earlier the span. In cases of superimposed construction, the latest phase takes the structure's number plus a "-1st" designation, while each successively earlier one is labeled with the next higher number: -2nd, -3rd, and so forth.

In addition to the work of this project reported herein, Nowak's excavations at Playitas Group II and Juyama are described in App. I. The same descriptive format is followed in App. I as is used in this chapter.

In order to aid the reader, a glossary of commonly used terms is provided here (additional terms are given in the introduction to Chap. 2).

Unit: Any uncovered element that functioned as part of construction. Abbreviated U in figure labels.

Feature: An uncovered element that has a cultural origin but is not demonstrably part of intact construction. Abbreviated F in figure labels, Feat. in text.

Stratum: A naturally deposited earth level or matrix. Abbreviated S in figure labels.

Midden: Cultural material deposited as the result of purposeful trash disposal. Abbreviated M in some figure labels.

Note that units, features, and strata are numbered independently in their own sequences for each structure. This sequence runs from bottom to top, earliest to latest, with the more recent elements having the higher numbers.

PLAYITAS

GROUP IV MAIN GROUP

STRUCTURE 200-23 (Figs. 23 and 24)

Structure 200-23 is a c. 1.77-m-high platform that closes the southern side of the Group IV major court. This structure was investigated in 1979 by means of three trenches, Op. 20C, D, and G. Operation 20C, 2.05 m east-west by 1.4 m north-south on the structure's summit, was initiated to expose the surface and interior features of a putative summit room discovered during survey. It was hoped that preserved within this construction would be a use-related primary deposit of artifacts, which would help date and identify the activities associated with Str. 200-23. Operations 20D and G, on the north and south faces respectively of Str. 200-23, were placed to reveal terminal-phase architecture, to measure the platform's original north-south basal width, to penetrate construction and obtain datable material from a sealed fill or primary context as an aid to dating the structure, and to search for a trash deposit associated with the final period of the structure's use. Operation 20D was a trench 1.5 m east-west by 4.1 m north-south which, in addition to exposing terminal-phase construction, was dug 1.4 m into structural fill to a maximum depth of 1.46 m below ground surface (see Fig. 24). Operation 20G was a trench 1.6 m east-west by 2.7 m north-south which exposed the basal levels of the terminal-phase construction but did not penetrate fill.

Excavation Lots: The Str. 200-23 excavations yielded 145 sherds, 46 censer fragments, four pieces of obsidian, one fragment of ground stone (metate), and 37 pieces of *bajareque*. This material was divided among five excavation lots, 20C/1-2, D/1-2, and G/1, three of which were from terminal occupation debris contexts (C/1, D/1, and G/1) and two were from construction fill (20C/2 and D/2) (see Table 3.1).

Time Span 4: The earliest period of activity uncovered in the Str. 200-23 area saw the deposition of the lower portions of Strata 1 and 4. The former is a fine-textured, reddish brown, highly micaceous clay

that runs below the bottom of the Unit 1 basal terraces on the north side of the structure by at least 0.03 m. Stratum 4 differs slightly from Stratum 1 in that it is an orange-brown fine-textured clay mottled increasingly with gray as the base of the excavation is approached. Also increasing with depth in Stratum 4 is the degree of compaction, though this is a gradual change with no marked discontinuities. Stratum 4 extends to a depth of at least 0.06 m below the base of the Unit 6 terraces on Str. 200-23's southern side. Unfortunately, no clear ground surface contemporary with the use of Str. 200-23 was noted on either side of the structure, so it is currently impossible to determine how much of Strata 1 and 4 was deposited prior to the final phase of construction. The small and uniform grain size of the clays in both strata points to their riverine origin; they were probably deposited as the result of floods by the nearby Rio Chinamito.

Because Units 1-3 and 6 (described below) are underlain by Strata 1 and 4, parts of these latter levels must have been deposited prior to this epoch of construction.

Time Span 3: The earliest evidence of construction uncovered is needed by Feat. 1, buried within the Unit 3 fill of Str. 200-23 (see Fig. 23). This is a 0.25-m-high pile of four exposed cobbles found only in the southwest corner of the trench at the base of excavation. These unfaced river cobbles are set in and surrounded by a distinctive hard-packed, greasy, gritty orange clay with some mica inclusions. Feature 1 could not be related to the latest level of construction (the Unit 1 step-terraces), nor does it appear to be a part of the surrounding earthen fill (Unit 3), a homogeneous clay largely devoid of stones. This feature is therefore interpreted as the remains of construction interior to Str. 200-23 (Units 1-6, see below); whether it actually predates Str. 200-23 by a considerable period of time or was integrated with it, serving as, for example, part of a fill-retaining wall, is uncertain. The fact that Feat. 1 is so low and amorphous and does not extend across the east-west width of Op. 20D suggests that it may well represent tumble from an earlier construction located further west.

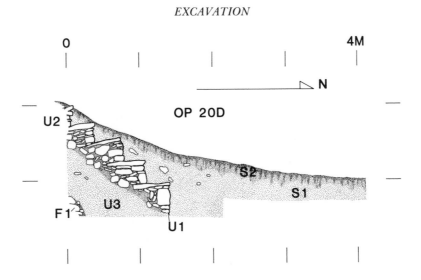

Figure 23.   Str. 200-23, Op 20D, Section.

Buried as it was within the clay fill of Unit 3, Feat. 1's deposition must have preceded the final building phase of Str. 200-23 (including the Unit 1 terraces). Feature 1 also sits 0.03 m below the bottom of Unit 1's basal terrace but 0.02 m above the base of excavation. Feature 1, therefore, must have been set in or onto Stratum 1, which it clearly postdates.

Time Span 2: The following period of activity saw the construction of Str. 200-23. On the north, court-facing side this entailed the laying of an earthen fill (Unit 3) to act as the foundation for a step-terrace system (Unit 1). The latter consists of a series of low narrow terraces, five of which were exposed in Op. 20D; their appearance and manner of construction are similar to those of other terrace systems recorded at Playitas (e.g., Str. 200-77 and -22) and other sites in the LMV. The low vertical walls are constructed of one or two courses of unmodified river cobbles, packed with chinking stones and set in a red clay mortar. These risers, in turn, support a series of horizontally laid stone slabs. These slabs, predominantly of schist, form the terrace treads and run back 0.29-0.35 m to and then under the next higher cobble riser, where they are counterweighted by the mass of the ascending terrace walls. Surface remains and the results of excavation in Op. 20F strongly indicate that the Unit 1 terraces originally ran the full length of the north face of Str. 200-23. The Unit 1 terraces rise a total of 1.42 m over a horizontal distance of 1.36 m and are oriented S 77° 0.5′ W.

Immediately underlying this terrace system is a sloping level, 0.3 m thick, of densely packed, horizontally laid river cobbles and pebbles set in a fine-textured, hard-compacted, greasy red clay matrix (Unit 2). This clay also underlies the stone level to a depth of 0.01-0.02 m in the east and west walls of Op.

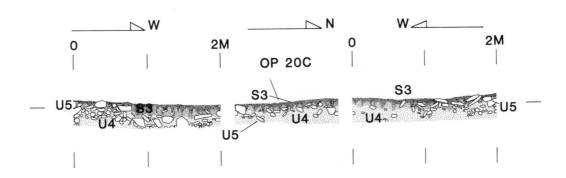

Figure 24.   Str. 200-13, Op 20C, Section.

65

TABLE 3.1

EXCAVATION SUMMARY

Lot #	Contents	Depositional Significance	Provenience
20C/1	45 sherds; 46 censer frags.; 1 pc. obsidian; 37 *bajareque* frags.	Terminal occupation debris (primary)	Within Unit 5
20C/2	6 sherds	Fill	Within Unit 4
20D/1	44 sherds; 2 pcs. obsidian	Terminal occupation debris (secondary)	Within Strata 1-2
20D/2	20 sherds; 1 pc. obsidian	Fill	Within Unit 2-3
20G/1	30 sherds; 1 metate frag.	Terminal occupation debris (secondary)	Within Strata 4-5

20D and to 0.15 m in the south. The stones within this fill tend to be stacked in columns 0.26-0.28 m high beneath the rear edges of the terrace slabs where these are overridden by the next higher terrace wall (see Fig. 23, second and third terraces). This practice provides support at one of the weakest points in the terrace construction: the area where the terrace slabs are counterweighted by the upper terrace walls.

Below Unit 2 is a fine-textured, reddish brown micaceous clay fill (Unit 3). This unit extends down to at least the base of construction and is homogeneous in composition, containing very few stones and only a small amount of cultural debris (Lot 20D/2).

The mode of construction of Str. 200-23 on the south side is very similar to that uncovered by Op. 20D on the north. Here Op. 20G revealed three step-terraces (Unit 6) constructed of 0.31- to 0.4-m-high vertical risers built with unmodified river cobbles, usually forming but a single horizontal course, and packed round with chinking stones and mud mortar. These low walls serve as supports for the terrace treads made of flat-laid stone slabs, primarily schist, which run 0.31-0.35 m back to and under the subsequent ascending terrace wall. As was the case on the north, surface remains indicate that the Unit 6 terraces originally ran the length of Str. 200-23's south face, with the possible exception of the east extension of that structure, where no surface stones were found. Above the excavated third terrace of Unit 6 are the remains of approximately four more step-terraces on the surface, all in bad states of repair. These terraces, in turn, appear to give way to a broader terrace at least 1 m wide (see Fig. 2). Within the excavated area, however, the three Unit 6 terraces rise a total of 1.04 m over a horizontal distance of 0.6 m and are oriented S 82° 0′ W.

The summit of Str. 200-23, as investigated by Op. 20C, produced only a few architectural features that can be identified as superstructure. All that was found here is a 0.22- to 0.26-m-thick level of pebbles and

TABLE 3.2

STRUCTURAL/DEPOSITIONAL SUMMARY TIME SPANS: 1-4

Time Span	Construction Stage	Activity	Features	Lots
1	—	Abandonment and burial of Str. 200-23-1st	Strata 1-5	20D/1, 20G/1
2	Str. 200-23	Construction and use of Str. 200-23-1st	Units 1-6	20C/1, 20C/2, 20D/2
3	—	Abandonment and collapse of possible buried str.	Feat. 1	—
4	—	Preoccupation deposition of natural soil levels	Lower portions, Strata 1 and 4	—

cobbles set in a fine-textured, reddish brown, micaceous clay matrix (Unit 5). This stone level is uneven at both its upper and lower margins (see Fig. 24). At several points, especially visible in the south excavation section, Unit 5 dips down into and below the base of excavation to an undetermined depth. At the point of this dip in the south wall is a surface of small stones, protruding from the base of excavation and extending only 1.4 m to the north at a width of 0.98-1.04 m east-west before it completely and rapidly disappears. As can be noted in Fig. 24, Unit 5 in the north trench wall does not penetrate the base of excavation. Unit 5 also contains a variable density of stones, ranging from the ones tightly packed in the eastern portion of Op. 20C to those more widely spaced on the west. This irregular level overlies a unit of fine-textured, reddish brown micaceous clay (Unit 4), very similar in appearance to, and probably a continuation of, the clay fill (Unit 3) that underlies Unit 2 in Op. 20D.

Attempts to locate the north and south walls of the presumed summit room met with little success: the large surface cobbles demarcating this feature have no depth in excavation. The regularity of these visible stone lines still suggests that they define a prehistoric feature. On the basis of the limited data, it appears that the investigated segment of the Str. 200-23 superstructure was built of perishable materials set on a low cobble footing. This conjecture is supported by the lack of large amounts of fallen stone construction debris in Op. 20C and G. The *bajareque* fragments found in Lot 20C/1 indicate that this material may have been the principal element used in summit wall construction. The pebble and cobble level of Unit 5 most likely represents a footing for a more formal floor, which would have served as the interior surface of this superstructure.

In general, the overall form of Str. 200-23 that emerges from Op. 20C, D, and G is of a 1.77-m-high and 13.15-m-wide substructure oriented S 77° 15′ W (north side) and S 82° 0′ W (south side). The superstructure has been built up by means of a series of long, low, and narrow step-terraces rising in short increments toward the summit. The step-terrace system of the north side appears to ascend without a break to the top of Str. 200-23, while on the south a single wider terrace marks a discontinuity within a system of otherwise narrow step-terraces. The summit of Str. 200-23 would appear to have been quite complex in its final form. Surface remains indicate the presence of five squares of packed cobbles aligned along the east-west axis of the structure. In excava-

tions at Las Quebradas (see below, this chapter, Str. 205-41), such features are interpreted as cobble bases for pillars built of perishable materials; they may have served the same purpose here. Also found on the summit are stone alignments initially interpreted as room outlines. When excavated, one of these "rooms" produced evidence that its walls were built of perishable material, probably *bajareque*, set on a low stone foundation and enclosing a floor underlain by a footing of pebbles and cobbles. The fill supporting all of this construction is a fine-textured, homogeneous micaceous clay, though some stone was employed immediately below the northern step-terrace system (Unit 2) to increase stability. Within Op. 20D it is fairly clear that the three included units are all part of the same building episode. Unit 3 underlies the stones of Units 1 and 2 (see Fig. 23). None of these elements could have functioned independently from the others. In Op. 20C, while Unit 5 clearly rests on Unit 4, both were probably deposited at or about the same point in time. Unit 4 is very similar in composition to the clay fill of Unit 3 exposed in Op. 20D and hence is probably part of the Str. 200-23 fill as well. While these relationships of units within specific trenches seem straightforward, no direct stratigraphic links have been established between the different operations. As a result, it is impossible to say securely whether Units 1-6 were all built at one time as part of a single coherent plan realized in the construction of Str. 200-23. What does appear to be certain is that all of the exposed units functioned as parts of a single structural entity during Str. 200-23's final phase of use. Also, it is very possible that Units 1-3 and 6 were laid down as part of the same building phase, as both employ the step-terrace construction style.

Lots 20C/2 and D/2 come from fill contexts (Units 4 and 3 respectively). Lot 20D/2 is associated with Unit 3 rather than Feat. 1 because few of the included items come from the area of the feature and nearly all were found in the overlying clay. Because of the close juxtaposition of Lots 20C/1 and 2 it is possible that some artifacts from the former worked their way down into the fill over time. Given the small and rather indeterminate appearance of Lot 20C/2, however, this does not pose a major problem. It is of course realized that while Lots 20C/2 and D/2 were deposited as part of the construction activities of T.S. 2, it is very probable that most of this material derived from earlier contexts elsewhere and was redeposited in construction fill.

Finally, Lot 20C/1 is included in T.S. 2 because it

was found intermixed with the stones of Unit 5. While the close proximity of Unit 5 to ground surface indicates the possibility of contamination from later deposits, this caveat is mitigated by several considerations. First, the included sherds are, in general, quite large with sharp, unworn edges. Second, a few of the sherds and most of the 46 censer fragments fit together, indicating that they are parts of ceramic items that have been broken in place. Both of these facts point to the breakage and loss of the Lot 20C/1 contents on the Unit 5 floor during the final phase of Str. 200-23's use with little later disturbance.

Time Span 1: After the abandonment of Str. 200-23, the exposed construction was buried by naturally deposited clays and silts. On the north, the lower four terraces of Unit 1 are buried at least in part by a fine-textured, reddish brown clay very similar in appearance to the fill of Unit 3 (Stratum 1). This earth level reaches a maximum thickness of 0.68 m immediately north of construction and continues down below the bottom of Unit 1's basal terrace, as noted earlier. Overlying Stratum 1 and burying portions of the fourth and fifth terraces of Unit 1 is Stratum 2. This upward-sloping soil level, between 0.07 and 0.13 m thick, consists of a fine-textured, greasy black clay with much included organic material and represents the humus horizon. Little stone debris was noted in either level.

On the south, Unit 6 is buried by the orange-brown, fine-textured clay of Stratum 4 described earlier. Like Stratum 1, Stratum 4 continues below the base of construction (see T.S. 4). Overlying this soil level is the humus horizon, Stratum 5, a fine-textured, dark gray-black clay that slopes up toward Str. 200-23 and runs at a thickness of 0.1-0.2 m. Very few stones are found in either Stratum 4 or 5.

Finally, above Unit 5 on the summit is a fine-textured, greasy, black to gray humus horizon (Stratum 3) very similar to Strata 2 and 5. This level varies in thickness between 0.08 and 0.14 m. As can be seen in Fig. 24, some of the stones of Unit 5 protrude into this level.

The fine texture and homogeneity of all these levels suggest that they are of riverine origin and were probably deposited as the result of floods by the nearby Rio Chinamito.

The stratigraphic position of Strata 1-5, overlying all of the exposed construction, clearly indicates that these soil levels were deposited after Str. 200-23 had been abandoned. As noted earlier, the lower portions of both Strata 1 and 4 may well have been set down in

T.S. 4, though exactly how much of the total depth of these levels is involved remains unknown.

Lots 20D/1 and G/1 derive from Strata 1-2 and 4-5 respectively. It should be noted, however, that even though this material was deposited in T.S. 1, it probably originated in T.S. 2 and was redeposited by postoccupation river floods. The small, homogeneous grain size of the strata in which these artifacts were found strongly suggests that the transporting floods were, by this point, moving with little velocity. As a result, the Lot 20D/1 and G/1 material was probably moved only a short distance from its original provenience, probably on Str. 200-23 itself. Both lots, therefore, most likely contain redeposited debris originally associated with the terminal occupation phase of Str. 200-23.

STRUCTURE 200-22 (Fig. 25)

Structure 200-22 closes off the north side of the Group IV main group and was investigated by two trenches in 1979: Op. 20E and H. The former was an excavation 1.6 m east-west by 2.5 m north-south, located in the approximate center of the south face of the platform. This trench was devoted to removing overburden from the final-phase construction, an operation that involved excavating down 0.9 m outside (south) of construction, and 0.2-0.6 m over it. Operation 20E was also carried down 0.1 m below the base of construction over an area extending c. 0.8 m south of construction. Operation 20H, on the northeast structure corner, measured 1.6 m east-west by 2.85 m north-south and had an extension 0.85 m east-west by 1.45 m north-south to the east. As with Op. 20E, no attempt was made to penetrate construction here and excavation was limited to removing the

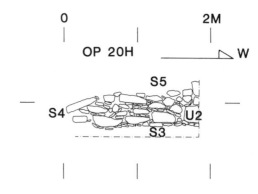

Figure 25.   Str. 200-22, Section.

overburden from terminal-phase architecture. Operation 20H was excavated down 0.6 m outside (north) of construction, and 0.15 m below it for a distance of c. 0.8 m north of the north Str. 200-22 wall. The goals of these trenches were three. First, to reconstruct Str. 200-22's terminal architecture; in particular, to see if the mode of construction on the court-facing south side was the same as that found on the north. Second, to gain some idea of the original north-south width of both Str. 200-22 and the court whose northern margin it defines. And third, to locate material in primary context associated with the final period of Str. 200-22's use. Such material could not only provide an insight into the types of activities carried out at this monumental construction, but also help in dating the final period of use. While both trenches were designed to accomplish these goals, it was especially hoped that Op. 20H, because of its location on the back (north)

side of the structure, would locate a midden deposit and thus satisfy the last excavation goal.

Excavation Lots: The nine lots defined for Op. 20E and H contain 779 sherds, 50 censer fragments, five figurine fragments, seven pieces of obsidian, and two *bajareque* fragments. Of these nine lots, two (20E/1-2) are from terminal occupation debris (primary) context; one (20E/3) represents terminal occupation debris (secondary) context; five derive from a trash deposit or midden associated with the terminal use of Str. 200-22 (20H/1-5); and one may contain items from a preconstruction level (20E/4; see Table 3.3).

Time Span 4: The first event identified in Op. 20E and H is the natural deposition of the lower portion of Strata 1 and 3. Stratum 1 in Op. 20E is a fine-textured, orange-brown clay with some mica inclusions. Stratum 3 in Op. 20H is a fine-textured gray clay with some orange and tan mottling, which decreases in

TABLE 3.3

EXCAVATION SUMMARY

Lot #	Contents	Depositional Significance	Provenience
20E/1	46 censer frags. (1 reconstructible ladle censer)	Terminal occupation debris (primary)	Within Stratum 1, 0.85 m S of Unit 1, 0.13 m above base of Unit 1
20E/2	46 sherds (44 from 1 vessel); 4 pcs. obsidian	Terminal occupation debris (primary)	Within Stratum 1, from level of 20E/1 to base of Unit 1
20E/3	51 sherds	Terminal occupation debris (secondary)	Within Strata 1-2, overlying Unit 1
20E/4	5 sherds	Preoccupation level (secondary?)	Within Stratum 1, from base of Unit 1 to 0.1 m below it
20H/1	260 sherds; 2 censer frags.; 3 figurine frags.	Terminal midden deposit (primary)	Within Stratum 4, 0.2-0.35 m below surface, from N trench wall to 1.4 m S; Midden 1
20H/2	47 sherds	Terminal midden deposit (primary)	Within Stratum 3, 0.35-0.58 m below surface, from N trench wall to 1.4 m S; Midden 1
20H/3	117 sherds; 1 figurine frag.; 2 *bajareque* frags.	Terminal midden deposit (primary)	Within Stratum 4, 0.2-0.35 m below surface, 0.8 m N of Unit 2; Midden 1
20H/4	224 sherds; 2 censer frags.; 1 figurine frag.; 2 pcs. obsidian	Terminal midden deposit (primary)	Within Stratum 3, 0.35-0.58 m below ground surface, from 0.8 m N of Unit 2; Midden 1
20H/5	29 sherds; 1 pc. obsidian	Terminal midden deposit (primary)	Within Strata 3 and 4, 0.2-0.58 m below ground surface in Op. 20H's E extension; Midden 1

Note: All depth measurements in Op. 20H were made from NW corner of Op. 20H.

TABLE 3.4

STRUCTURAL/DEPOSITIONAL SUMMARY TIME SPANS: 1-4

Time Span	Construction Stage	Activity	Features	Lots
1	—	Burial and abandonment of Str. 200-22	Strata 2, 4, 5, upper portion of Stratum 1, Feat. 1	20E/3
2	Str. 200-22	Use of Str. 200-22-1st	Midden 1, Strata 3/4 interface	20H/1-5, 20E/1-2
3	Str. 200-22	Construction of Str. 200-22-1st	Unit 1-2	—
4	—	Preconstruction deposition of natural strata	Stratum 3, lower 0.13 m of Stratum 1	20E/4?

prevalence where Stratum 3 underlies construction. As elsewhere at Playitas, no distinct flooring material caps the original ground surface.

The lower exposed portions of Strata 1 and 3 are included here for stratigraphic reasons. Both underlie basal construction units by at least 0.15 m, clearly indicating their temporal precedence *vis-à-vis* these units. Because no clear floor associated with the building of Str. 200-22 is located within or capping these strata, it is impossible to state precisely how much of them was deposited during this time span. The distribution of artifacts in Op. 20E and of architectural collapse in Op. 20H suggests that the exposed basal 0.13-0.23 m of these earth levels was laid down prior to the construction of Str. 200-22. Lot 20E/4 derives from Stratum 1 for c. 0.1 m below the base of Unit 1. It is possible that the few included artifacts were deposited during the next time period and pressed into this layer from above. Because there was no impermeable boundary to prevent this mixing, the assignment of 20E/4 to T.S. 4 remains equivocal.

Time Span 3: The next period of activity saw the construction of Str. 200-22. In contrast to Str. 200-23, Str. 200-22 is not constructed symmetrically on its court- and noncourt-facing sides. On the southern face (Op. 20E) the step-terrace principle was used (Unit 1). The four lowest step-terraces of Unit 1, set into Stratum 1, were exposed in Op. 20E, all in a fairly good state of preservation and constructed in much the same way as others noted at the site (e.g., Str. 200-23 and -77). Low vertical terrace walls stand 0.2-0.3 m high and are built of roughly coursed river cobbles packed round with small chinking stones and set in a mud mortar. These walls support the terrace treads, a surface of horizontally laid schist slabs run-

ning back 0.2-0.35 m to and then under the next ascending vertical terrace wall. In all, the four Unit 1 terraces rise 1.4 m over a horizontal distance of 0.9 m. Badly preserved fragments of additional terraces can be seen on the surface, above the four excavated examples, and there is no reason to doubt that this integrated facing once extended to the summit. Surface remains and excavations in Op. 20F also demonstrate that these low narrow terraces once continued unimpeded for the entire length of the south face of Str. 200-22. The orientation of the Unit 1 terraces is S 77° 15′ W, precisely parallel to the Unit 1 terraces of Str. 200-23 exposed on the southern side of the plaza (Op. 20D).

The exposed portions of the north and east basal walls of Str. 200-22 (Op. 20H) show a different mode of construction (see Fig. 26). Here a vertical wall

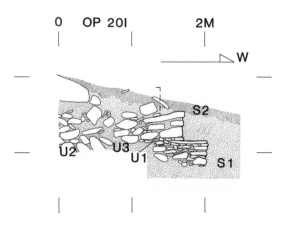

Figure 26. Str. 200-24, Section.

preserved to 0.4-0.58 m high is built of large unfaced river cobbles laid in three rough, horizontal courses, packed round with pebbles and set in a mud mortar (Unit 2). This wall, sunk into Stratum 3, is underlain by a thin level of chinking pebbles, 0.02-0.05 m thick, but is not capped by the stone slabs that form an integral part of almost all step-terrace constructions in the LMV. The north wall of Str. 200-22 (Unit 2) is oriented S 77° 15′ W. Unfortunately, time did not permit investigation of the junction of Units 1 and 2.

The inclusion of Units 1 and 2 in the same time period is based on the simple assumption that both were exposed during Str. 200-22's final period of use. The lack of an established stratigraphic link between them precludes determination of whether or not they were built at the same time.

Time Span 2: The ground surface exposed during the use of Str. 200-22 is difficult to determine. In Op. 20E, two lots, 20E/1 and 2, rested in Stratum 1 within 0.13 m above the base of Unit 1. Each of these contains almost exclusively the fragments of a nearly complete vessel, indicating that the objects were broken on an existing surface in this area and have subsequently suffered little dislocation. The stratigraphic position of this material points to the existence of an informal earthen court surface—somewhere within 0.13 m of the base of Unit 1—onto which debris from Str. 200-22 was deposited during or soon after its occupation. It also seems logical that part of Unit 1's basal terrace would be set into a preexisting earth level to increase its stability.

In Op. 20H, 0.23 m above the base of Unit 2, Stratum 3 gives way to another soil level, Stratum 4 (described below). Resting on this interface for a distance of 0.5 m to the north is a light scattering of stone architectural debris eroding from the neighboring structure (Feat. 1). These two pieces of evidence suggest that the ground surface into which the northeast corner of Str. 200-22 was set, and onto which its debris fell after abandonment, corresponds to a level 0.23 m above the base of construction (Unit 2).

The overall form of Str. 200-22 is a platform 11.05 m wide north-south, c. 1.12 m high, and oriented S 77° 15′ W. The basal construction employs at least two different styles. On the south, an apparent concern with mirroring the step-terrace system of the other four structures surrounding the Group IV main group has prevailed (Unit 1), while on the north and east a simple vertical wall functions as the basal construction element. This juxtaposition of different architectural techniques is noted elsewhere in Group

IV (see Str. 200-24) and in the LMV (see Str. 205-1-1st at Las Quebradas). No formal court surface could be found. Deposited over and apparently pressed into the ground surface recognized in Op. 20H was Midden 1, the trash deposit comprising Lots 20H/1-5. This element, which included artifacts—primarily sherds—exposed for a vertical depth of 0.38 m above and below the Strata 3/4 interface, was located throughout the trench and did not appear to decrease significantly in density with distance away from Unit 2. Artifact frequency did decrease toward the base of excavation. Midden 1 is interpreted as a terminal-phase deposit in undisturbed context for the following three reasons. First, the amount of material recovered here is far greater than that found elsewhere in the Group IV principal group. Second, the nature of the recovered ceramics, usually large and flat-lying sherds, indicates that the material was originally jettisoned in the area where it was found and was not dispersed and redeposited by natural forces. Third, the proximity of the artifacts to the noncourt-facing side of Str. 200-22 suggests that they represent trash thrown by the residents off the back of this structure. Midden 1's size, disposition of the sherds, and location indicate that it was associated with the final period of Str. 200-22's use. If, as seems likely, Midden 1 has been uncovered to its full depth, then its shallowness (0.38 m) points to a relatively short interval of accumulation.

Time Span 1: The final phase of activity involved the abandonment and partial burial of the platform. Evidence for abandonment is provided by Feat. 1, the aforementioned level of tumbled architectural debris lying on the Strata 3/4 interface in Op. 20H and extending north of Unit 2 for 0.5 m. This feature contains a light concentration of unmodified stones that derived originally from the adjacent construction. Very few tumbled stones were found in Op. 20E. On both the north and south sides the lower levels of construction are buried by naturally deposited clays. On the south (Op. 20E), Stratum 1, the fine-textured, orange-brown clay described earlier, buries the lower two terraces of Unit 1 to a depth of 0.6 m and is in turn overlain by a fine-textured, dark gray clay-humus horizon (Stratum 2). Both of these soil levels slope up toward construction (Unit 1).

On the north, Stratum 3 is overlain by Stratum 4, which contains Feat. 1 and is a fine-textured tan clay increasingly mottled to gray and orange as it approaches the Strata 3/4 interface. Stratum 4 buries Unit 2 by 0.05-0.1 m and is, in turn, overlain by a relatively thin (0.1 m thick) dark gray clay-humus horizon sloping up and over Unit 2. The fine, homogeneous texture of all these soils strongly suggests their deposition by river floods at the point where those inundations were no longer moving with great velocity and were carrying light loads.

Lot 20E/3 derives from Strata 1 and 2 above Unit 1 and must have been deposited during this same period. It is very probable, however, that the artifacts included in this lot were originally derived from the Str. 200-22 area in the preceding time span and were redeposited by natural forces in T.S. 1. As noted earlier, since the river floods which deposited Strata 1-2 were not moving with much velocity here, artifacts probably came from close by their final find-spot.

STRUCTURE 200-24 (Figs. 26 and 27)

Structure 200-24, a 1.81-m-high construction which closes the east side of the Group IV principal group, was examined by means of a single trench, Op. 20I, located on the building's northwest corner. This excavation consisted of two adjoining trenches, the one on the northwest 1.45 m north-south by 1.5 m east-west, and that on the northeast roughly 1.9 m north-south by 2.5 m east-west. The latter trench was irregular in shape and possessed a north extension 0.9 m north-south by 0.5 m east-west. The primary goal of Op. 20I was to locate the northwest corner of Str. 200-24. This objective relates to two broader aims. First, we wished to determine the internal dimensions of the main court and the nature of the construction to be found on the structures facing that central space. Second, it was noted during the mapping of the main group that the north end of this structure is devoid of stones, unlike its southern slopes; thus Op. 20I might determine if this indicates a change in construction styles.

Excavation Lots: The three excavation lots 20I/1-3 contain 138 sherds and three pieces of obsidian. Lots 20I/1-2 are from terminal occupation debris (secondary) contexts, while Lot 20I/3 is from fill (see Table 3.5).

Time Span 3: The first event recorded in Op. 20I is the deposition of the lower portion of Stratum 1, a fine-textured, reddish brown clay that both buries and underlies construction (see Fig. 26). As with the other excavations in the Group IV main group, no floor contemporary with the construction of Str. 200-24 was located, and thus it is not possible to say how much of Stratum 1 predates construction and how much of its depth was deposited subsequently. On the basis of present knowledge, at least the lowest exposed 0.16-0.2 m of this soil level, which clearly runs under Unit 1, must predate that building phase.

Time Span 2: The next period is defined by the construction of Str. 200-24, here represented by Units 1-3. Unit 1 is a step-terrace system of which four low, narrow terraces rising from west to east are exposed. The elements of this system are as follows: a series of 0.34-m-high vertical walls, built of coursed river cobbles and chinking stones set in a mud mortar, support the terrace treads, flat-laid schist slabs running back 0.32-0.33 m to and then under the next higher terrace wall. Immediately underlying these terraces is a dense packing, 0.28-0.31 m thick, of horizontally laid unmodified cobbles and pebbles set in a mud mortar. The base of this stone support system (included with Unit 1) steps up toward the east, paralleling the rise in the second terrace of Unit 1. At present it is impossible to say how much of the red-brown clay underlying Unit 1 was introduced as fill and how much is naturally deposited.

Unit 1 ends, as shown in Fig. 27, rather abruptly, stopping 0.25 m north of the southern trench wall. No clear corner was noted. To the south, it is likely that the Unit 1 terraces once continued for the length of the west face of Str. 200-24, although clear surface indications of this were not found. Above the third reconstructed Unit 1 terrace shown in Fig. 6, one more terrace is seen. The latter, constructed as were the lower three, terminates c. 0.15 m south of the north edge of Unit 1. The three most clearly exposed terraces are oriented S 12° 50' E and rise to a height of roughly 0.88 m over a horizontal distance of 0.92 m. Above the fourth terrace, no clear terracing was noted, indicating either a change in construction techniques or much poorer preservation in this area.

Unit 2, immediately east of Unit 1, is a mass of large river cobbles, each stone 0.07 by 0.19 to 0.2 by 0.24 m, packed with a fine-textured, red-brown clay. Unit 2 measures 0.42-0.5 m thick, taking the horizontally set stones to define its upper and lower boundaries. In horizontal extent, Unit 2 continues eastward into the excavation wall but does not proceed further to the north than the north end of Unit 1. While some of the stones in this unit appear to have been flat-laid, a great many have tumbled out to the north and several have collapsed to a level below that occupied by the lowest horizontal stones. Unit 2 appears to have functioned as a stone fill within Str. 200-24, though no clear evidence of the construction it once supported remains.

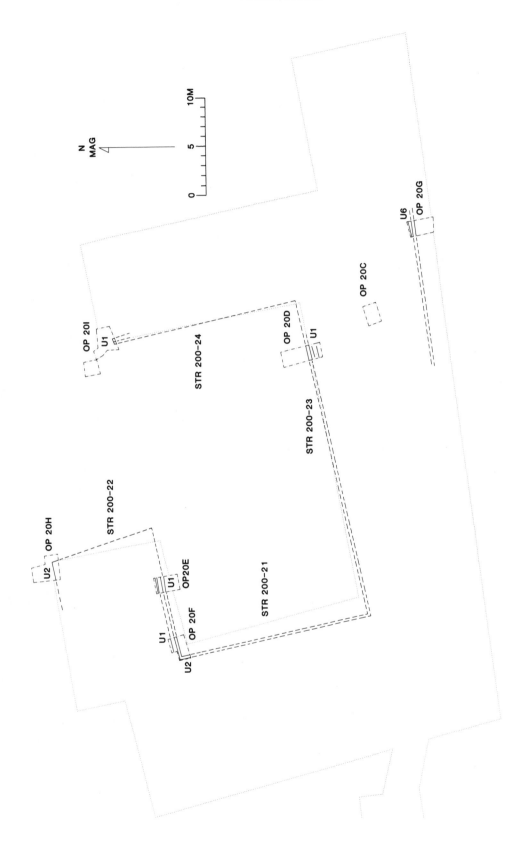

Figure 27.   Playitas Group IV Plan.

TABLE 3.5

EXCAVATION SUMMARY

Lot #	Contents	Depositional Significance	Provenience
20I/1	27 sherds	Terminal occupation debris (secondary)	Within Strata 1 and 2, NW Op. 20I pit
20I/2	63 sherds	Terminal occupation debris (secondary)	Within Stratum 2, NE Op. 20I pit, overlying construction (Unit 1)
20I/3	48 sherds; 3 pcs. obsidian	Fill	Within Unit 3, N of Unit 1, NE Op. 20I pit

North of Unit 2, proceeding for c. 1.6 m in that direction to the end of Str. 200-24, is Unit 3, composed of the same reddish brown, fine-textured clay largely devoid of stones that was described for Stratum 1. Unit 3 completely buries the north ends of Units 1 and 2 and rises to a level equivalent to the top of Str. 200-24 to the south. It seems implausible that this mass of earth was deposited by natural forces, since its alignment with, and exclusive location on the end of, Str. 200-24 is too close to be simply fortuitous. It does appear likely that Unit 3 was intentionally deposited very soon after the construction of Units 1 and 2. This point is suggested by the aforementioned northward tumble of stones from Unit 2, debris later buried by Unit 3. Units 1 and 2 terminate with no apparent effort to formalize their north ends.

These considerations indicate that Units 1 and 2 were built as integral parts of Str. 200-24 *but* were not meant to function as the northwest corner of that structure. At some point after the north exposed ends of Units 1 and 2 were laid down, construction ceased for a long enough period for the relatively loose fill of Unit 2 to begin to erode out, but not long enough for

the more thoroughly integrated stones of the Unit 1 terrace to do the same. Afterward, the earthen fill of Unit 3 was deposited, possibly to make a quick end to the work, which could no longer be finished with a continuation of the Unit 1 terraces; or perhaps as the fill for such construction, which was never completed.

The Unit 1 terraces clearly rest against the stone fill of Unit 2, providing good evidence that these elements were built at or about the same time. Lot 20I/3, from the Unit 3 fill, is included here. As these artifacts come from a fill deposit, however, it must be borne in mind that they were redeposited here from another context. The disposition of the tumbled Unit 2 stones indicates that Units 1 and 2 were raised above the ancient ground surface by a level of red-brown clay similar in composition to Stratum 1. Again, the problem remains how much of the clay beneath Units 1 and 2 is naturally deposited and how much is a cultural artifact. At present, it seems logical that the earth beneath the second and third terraces was at least partly brought in by human activity, as the tumbled Unit 2 stones fell to a level below the base of

TABLE 3.6

STRUCTURAL/DEPOSITIONAL SUMMARY TIME SPANS: 1-3

Time Span	Construction Stage	Activity	Features	Lots
1	—	Burial of Str. 200-24	Upper Stratum 1, Stratum 2	20I/1-2
2	Str. 200-24	Construction and use of Str. 200-24-1st	Unit 1-3, Stratum 1 below Unit 1	20I/3
3	—	Preconstruction deposition of natural soils	Lower Stratum 1, W of Unit 1	—

Unit 1. The clay beneath the basal step-terrace may have a natural origin.

Time Span 1: The final reconstructed period of activity involved the partial burial of Str. 200-24 by the upper portion of Stratum 1 and Stratum 2. The former soil level, described above, overlies portions of the lower three terraces of Unit 1 to a maximum depth of 0.32 m. Overlying Stratum 1 is the gray-black, greasy humus horizon of Stratum 2, 0.11-0.13 m thick, sloping up and over Str. 200-24 and burying Units 1-3. Both soil levels contain earth of such small homogeneous particle size that it seems likely they were deposited by low-velocity river floods.

The stratigraphic position of the upper portion of Stratum 1 and all of Stratum 2 indicates that these levels were deposited after Str. 200-24 had been built and abandoned. Although Lots 20I/1-2 derive from these levels, it is very likely that this material originally pertains to Str. 200-24's final phase of occupation and was redeposited by natural forces, i.e., river floods. Two lines of evidence support this contention. First, the matrix of Strata 1 and 2 indicates that this material was deposited by a river flood traveling with little force by this point. The included artifacts would, therefore, have derived from the immediate area. Second, the large size and the clean, unworn edges of the sherds from Lot 20I/2 suggest that this material came from nearby, most probably from Str. 200-24 itself.

NORTHWEST CORNER, GROUP IV MAIN GROUP (Fig. 27)

The northwest corner of the main group, formed by the juncture of Str. 200-22 and -21 on the north and west respectively, was investigated in 1979 by a single trench, Op. 20F. This excavation, 1.7 m north-south by 2.5 m east-west, was designed to determine how this corner had been closed, and to see if more sherds in primary context similar to those located in the adjacent Op. 20E (Lots 20E/1-2) could be found. Operation 20F involved the removal of overburden from terminal construction levels and excavating down to the base of final construction but not below it.

Excavation Lots: The six Op. 20F lots include 314 sherds, 14 censer fragments, ten pieces of obsidian, one metate and one mano fragment, five pieces of *bajareque*, and two figurine fragments. Of these collections, five contain terminal occupation debris, three from secondary (20F/1-2 and 5) and two from primary contexts (20F/3-4), and one was found in back-dirt (20F/6; see Table 3.7).

Time Span 2: The first period of activity recognized in Op. 20F is the construction of Units 1 and 2, the basal step-terraces of Str. 200-22 and -21 respectively. These two units were exposed for a horizontal distance of 2.05 m (Unit 1) and 1.05 m (Unit 2). Unit 1 represents a continuation of the three lowest terraces of Unit 1 exposed in Op. 20E, and both Unit 1 and the two exposed terraces of Unit 2 are built in a manner similar to that noted in Op. 20E. The vertical risers stand 0.35-0.4 m high and are constructed of horizontally coursed river cobbles (one or two courses) set on and packed round with chinking stones, all within a mud-mortar matrix. The cobbles employed range in size from 0.1 by 0.2 to 0.15 by 0.4 m.

Surmounting these low risers are the flat-laid schist slabs of the terrace treads. These slabs run back 0.25-0.4 m to and then under the next ascending terrace wall. As indicated by excavations in Op. 20E and surface remains, the low narrow terraces of Units 1 and 2 once continued for the entire lengths of their respective structures. Surface indications also suggest that these terraces continued further upslope toward the structure summits. However, due to postoccupation disturbance and collapse, and to the restricted nature of the excavations, it is not possible to say whether they once ascended all the way to the summit. The orientation of the Unit 1 terraces matches that of their counterparts in Op. 20E, S 77° 15′ W, while Unit 2 is aligned S 12° 30′ E, only 15′ divergent from a precise right angle. In all, the Unit 1 terraces rise c. 1.01 m over a horizontal distance of 0.65 m, while those in Unit 2 ascend 0.75 m over a 0.3-m distance.

Units 1 and 2 were laid down within the same time period, as indicated by their symmetry and the interdigitation of their elements. The intersection of the terrace surface and bases of Units 1 and 2 at the same level strongly implies that they were built together. With respect to their interdigitation, it is difficult to locate clear cases in which the stones of either Unit 1 or 2 run behind or abut those of the other. The slabs topping the lowest terrace do not display an obvious construction sequence, while one cobble of the basal Unit 1 terrace was found to run slightly behind its counterpart in Unit 2. On the second terrace, the slabs and cobble riser of Unit 1 were found, once again, to run slightly behind their opposite numbers in Unit 2. As a result of these observations, it appears that while Unit 1, and hence Str. 200-22, may have been built first, the construction of Unit 2 undoubtedly came soon afterward. Both elements were apparently part of the same integrated building effort.

TABLE 3.7

EXCAVATION SUMMARY

Lot #	Contents	Depositional Significance	Provenience
20F/1	109 sherds; 3 censer frags.; 1 pc. obsidian; 1 mano frag.	Terminal occupation debris (secondary)	Within Strata 1-2, over Unit 1 and 2
20F/2	43 sherds; 3 censer frags.; 4 pcs. obsidian; 5 *bajareque* frags.; 1 metate frag.	Terminal occupation debris (secondary)	Within Stratum 1, from below level of top of basal terrace of Unit 1 and 2 to base of construction
20F/3	13 sherds	Terminal occupation debris (primary)	Within Stratum 1
20F/4	28 sherds; 8 censer frags.	Terminal occupation debris (primary)	Resting on basal terrace of Unit 1 and 2
20F/5	119 sherds; 2 figurine frags.; 5 pcs. obsidian	Terminal occupation debris (secondary)	Same as 20F/2
20F/6	2 sherds	Questionable	Backdirt

The artifacts of Lot 20F/4 were found resting directly on the surface of the lowest Unit 1 and 2 terraces, buried by Stratum 1. This location, on construction and sealed by postabandonment deposits, implies that this lot contains debris lost during the final phase of occupation of Str. 200-22 and -21 and subsequently little disturbed. Lot 20F/3 is placed in this time period partly because the size of the included sherds and their unworn edges indicate that they have not been moved a considerable distance from their origin. It is probable, in fact, that Lot 20F/3 was deposited on the same informal earthen surface as were Lots 20E/1-2 and was, therefore, part of the same trash deposit as these latter lots.

Time Span 1: After the construction and use of these adjoining structures, they were abandoned and buried by naturally deposited soil levels. The first of these, Stratum 1, is a fine-textured, reddish brown clay containing some charcoal flecks and the majority of the cultural debris. Toward the base of Stratum 1, the lower 0.06-0.14 m exposed in Op. 20F, an increase in gray mottling was noted, though no clear soil change was evident. Artifacts were also found in the zone of gray mottling. This soil level buries both Units 1 and 2 down to their bases and was deposited over their exposed terraces. Stratum 2 is the ubiquitous gray-black, fine-textured humus horizon, which slopes up toward construction and overlies Stratum 1. Stratum 1 attains a maximum thickness of 0.8 m just south of the basal terrace of the two units, while Stratum 2 varies in thickness between 0.15 and 0.18 m. The uniformly small grain size of the clays in both strata indicates that this material was deposited by low-velocity river floods. The stratigraphic position of Strata 1 and 2 points to their deposition after the abandonment of the associated structures.

TABLE 3.8

STRUCTURAL/DEPOSITIONAL SUMMARY TIME SPANS: 1-2

Time Span	Construction Stage	Activity	Features	Lots
1	—	Burial of Str. 200-22 and -21	Strata 1 and 2	20F/1, 20F/2, 20F/5
2	Str. 200-22 and -21	Construction and use of Str. 200-22-1st and -21-1st	Unit 1-2	20F/3, 20F/4

Lot 20F/1 derives from above construction in Strata 1 and 2 and is therefore included in T.S. 1. Lots 20F/2 and 5 were recovered from Stratum 1, at depths equivalent to the top of Units 1 and 2's basal terraces down to the bottom of that construction. Because the deposition of Stratum 1 is assigned to this period, so are the included artifacts. For reasons noted elsewhere (see Str. 200-22/24) it is probable that the artifacts in Lots 20F/1-2 and 5 are redeposited terminal debris from Str. 200-21 and -22.

GROUP IV SMALL STRUCTURES

STRUCTURE 200-16 (Figs. 28 and 29)

Structure 200-16 protrudes 0.5 m above ground surface and closes the south side in a four-structure plaza cluster c. 234 m southwest of the Group IV principal group. This construction was investigated in 1979 by means of four trenches, Op. 20J-M. Three of these excavations were dug to determine the terminal basal plan of Str. 200-16: Op. 20K exposed the north wall and northwest corner of the basal construction, Op. 20L the west wall and southwest corner, and Op. 20M the southeast corner. These clearing operations involved the removal of overburden from the tops of the structure's walls, excavating down outside them between 0.75 and 0.88 m to expose their full heights, and, in all, the opening of a horizontal area of roughly 11.4 m². Operation 20J was a trench 1.6 m east-west by 4.7 m north-south along the approximate axis of the structure's north face and extending from 1.3 m north of construction to the center of the summit. In addition to the general excavation aims the purpose of this trench was both to reveal traces of terminal construction activity and, subsequently, to cut through them to determine whether any evidence of an earlier period of occupation was buried beneath. This trench was dug to a maximum depth of 1.06 m below ground surface.

Excavation Lots: The Str. 200-16 excavations produced 1226 sherds, 45 censer fragments, 32 pieces of obsidian, seven small *bajareque* fragments, six figurine fragments, and one metate fragment. This material has been divided into 12 excavation lots, all but two of which (Lots 20J/4-5) are from terminal occupation debris contexts. Lot 20J/4 is derived exclusively from construction fill, while the material in 20J/5 comes from a preconstruction level (see Table 3.9).

Time Span 5: The earliest level recognized in the Str. 200-16 excavations is Stratum 1. This layer,

devoid of any cultural material, is a tan, soft-compacted, fine-textured micaceous clay discovered at a depth of 0.77 m below the summit of Str. 200-16, and exposed to a thickness of 0.26 m. Also laid down around this time was a lower portion of Stratum 2, a light brown, fine-textured micaceous clay, underlying Str. 200-16's basal construction wherever it was exposed in Op. 20J-M (see Fig. 28). Strata 1 and 2 are distinguished by only slight differences in their color and consistency; they may represent a single soil unit with localized variations. The small grain size of the clays in these levels points to a riverine source, probably the nearby Rio Chinamito. There is no evidence that they were deposited by human activity.

The inclusion of Stratum 1 in this time span is based on its stratigraphic position below both construction (Units 1-3) and the earliest evidence of occupation uncovered in the Str. 200-16 area (Midden 1). Stratum 2 is also placed here because, as can be seen in Fig. 28, the lower exposed 0.1-0.2 m of this soil unit underlies Units 2 and 4. In addition, the base of Stratum 2 in Op. 20J is at the same elevation as the upper 0.08 m of Stratum 1.

Time Span 4: Capping Stratum 1 and protruding down into that level for a maximum depth of 0.22 m is Midden 1, representing the next phase of activity. Found at a depth of 0.78 m below the summit of Str. 200-16 and south of Unit 2 in Op. 20J, it consists of a highly compacted micaceous clay, with a somewhat darker tan color than that noted in either the underlying Stratum 1 or the overlying Unit 1 (see Fig. 28). Midden 1 varies in thickness between 0.04 and 0.22 m, maintains a relatively flat upper surface over its excavated extent, and slopes down at its base to the south roughly 0.18 m over an exposed horizontal distance of 0.86 m. It is distinguished by the large number of artifacts (Lot 20J/5) concentrated within its narrow confines: 173 sherds, 1 *incensario* fragment, three pieces of obsidian, and one fragment of *bajareque*. All the sherds were found lying flat, as though they had been pressed into an existing ground surface. Midden 1 must, therefore, represent occupation debris deposited prior to the construction of Str. 200-16. The shallowness of this midden indicates that the included items were deposited over a relatively short interval.

Also stratigraphically associated with this time period is Stratum 3, a light brown, fine-textured micaceous clay located 0.26 m below ground surface in the northern end of Op. 20J. This soil layer, which rests at the same level as Midden 1, is distinguished from its

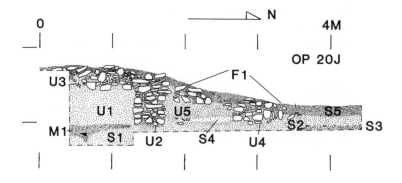

Figure 28.   Str. 200-16, Section.

surroundings (Stratum 2) not so much by its color and consistency but by the increased number of potsherds found within its narrow exposed limits (0.05-0.06 m thick). Although the artifact densities in Stratum 3 are not as great as those in Midden 1, the similarity in composition, elevation, and increased artifact densities in these entities suggests that they may represent the same preconstruction debris level, now separated by a horizontal gap of 2.34 m.

Time Span 3: The next time span involved the construction of Str. 200-16 (Units 1-3), set into the preexisting level of Stratum 2. The four retaining walls of this structure (Unit 2) are constructed of unmodified river cobbles laid in rough horizontal courses, chinked with small pebbles. All these stones are set in a core matrix of tan micaceous clay, forming

walls some 0.42 m thick (see Figs. 28 and 29). The size of the river cobbles generally falls within the range of 0.09 by 0.16 to 0.11 by 0.28 m. The larger cobbles tend to be near the base of the Unit 2 walls, especially at the exposed corners where they contribute to the stability of the structure. When excavated, these facings stood 0.41-0.6 m high; the best-preserved segment is along the north axial line (in Op. 20J), while the poorest is at the southwest corner (in Op. 20L). All of the exposed corners are tilted 0.08-0.11 m from the vertical.

The maximum dimensions of the basal construction uncovered in Op. 20J-M are 8.1 m east-west by 3.5 m north-south. While the form of the structure is quadrilateral, its sides are not precisely aligned with respect to each other: the north wall runs at S 83° 30' E and the south wall at S 81° 0' E, while the west wall is oriented S 9° 45' W and the east is a reconstructed S 15° 0' W.

The fill enclosed by Unit 2 is a moderately hard-compacted, tan, fine-textured, sterile micaceous clay (Unit 1). This unit buries Midden 1 and extends from the base of Unit 2 to within 0.15 m of the preserved top of that wall. Unit 1, 0.44 m thick, is capped in turn by a level of densely packed, small to medium-sized cobbles set in a tan, fine-textured micaceous clay (Unit 3). Unit 3, 0.24-0.31 m thick, was exposed only in Op. 20J and may be the remains of a foundation for a formal summit surface. The full horizontal extent of Unit 3 was not determined, although it was found throughout Op. 20J across the summit of Str. 200-16, a linear distance of roughly 2.2 m north-south. Unfortunately, no evidence indicative of the size or function of the superstructure that may have surmounted Str. 200-16 was found. The recovery of *bajareque* fragments from adjacent excavations points to a super-

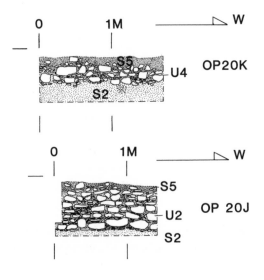

Figure 29.   Str. 200-16, Elevations.

TABLE 3.9

EXCAVATION SUMMARY

Lot #	Contents	Depositional Significance	Provenience
20J/1	156 sherds; 1 pc. obsidian; 1 *bajareque* frag.	Terminal occupation debris (secondary)	Within Strata 2, 3, 5, N of Unit 4
20J/2	25 sherds; 1 censer frag.; 2 pcs. obsidian	Terminal occupation debris (secondary)	Within Stratum 5, over and among stones of Unit 4
20J/3	30 sherds	Terminal occupation debris and fill	Within Stratum 5 and Unit 5, between Unit 4 and 2
20J/4	87 sherds; 2 pcs. obsidian; 1 *bajareque* frag.	Fill	Within Unit 5 in W extension of Op. 20J
20J/5	173 sherds; 1 censer frag.; 3 pcs. obsidian; 1 *bajareque* frag.	Preconstruction debris (primary)	Within Midden 1 at and below base of Unit 2
20K/1	260 sherds; 40 censer frags.; 9 pcs. of obsidian; 1 *bajareque* frag.	Terminal occupation debris (secondary)	Within Stratum 5, 0.15 m below ground surface
20K/2	125 sherds; 6 figurine frags.; 2 pcs. obsidian; 1 *bajareque* frag.	Terminal occupation debris (secondary)	Within Stratum 3, to base and N and W of Unit 2
20K/3	54 sherds; 7 pcs. obsidian; 1 metate fragment	Mixed terminal occupation debris (secondary)	Within Stratum 5 and Unit 5 and fill
20L/1	87 sherds; 1 pc. obsidian; 1 *bajareque* frag.	Terminal occupation debris (secondary)	Within Stratum 5, 0-0.15 m below ground surface
20L/2	81 sherds; 4 pcs. obsidian; 1 *bajareque* frag.	Terminal occupation debris (secondary)	Within Stratum 3, to base and W of Unit 2
20M/1	47 sherds; 3 censer frags.; 2 pcs. obsidian	Terminal occupation debris (secondary)	Within Stratum 5, 0-0.15 m below ground surface
20M/2	101 sherds	Terminal occupation debris (secondary)	Within Stratum 3, to S and E and to base of Unit 2

structure of this material, although its form remains unknown.

Also possibly associated with this period of activity is Stratum 4, exposed in Op. 20J as a level 0.02-0.06 m thick and 0.79 m long resting on Stratum 2, and composed of a compact, fine-textured, greasy, light orange clay with fewer mica inclusions than the underlying soil. The distinctive color of Stratum 4 sets it apart from other units and indicates that this material may have a cultural origin. It is very probable, given its location slightly above the base of Unit 2 (0.04 m), that it functioned as a living surface during the first period of Str. 200-16's use. No evidence of a similar stratum was located in Op. 20K-M. Alternatively, it is possible that Stratum 4 represents a shallow deposit of architectural debris, possibly decomposed *bajareque*, which was allowed to accumulate on a preexisting ground surface prior to further construc-

tion efforts. This interpretation does not contradict the previous contention that Stratum 4 indicates the location of a ground surface exposed during the use of Str. 200-16.

Structure 200-16's overall appearance during its initial phase of use was that of a roughly quadrilateral substructure of packed earthen fill enclosed on all sides by well-made cobble retaining walls at least 0.6 m high. Atop this platform was a packed cobble surface which probably supported a superstructure built of *bajareque*. To the north and slightly above the base of Unit 2, in the approximate center of the structure, is a distinctive soil level that may have served as formal flooring or represented a debris line deposited on a preexisting ground surface. Access to the summit of Str. 200-16 is problematic, as no evidence of steps was found.

The Unit 2 retaining walls, though exposed in four

TABLE 3.10

STRUCTURAL/DEPOSITIONAL SUMMARY TIME SPANS: 1-5

Time Span	Construction Stage	Activity	Features	Lots
1	—	Abandonment and burial of Str. 200-16	Stratum 5, upper portion of Stratum 2, Feat. 1	20J/1-3, 20K/1-2, 20L/1-2, 20M/1-2
2	Str. 200-16	Str. 200-16's modification and continued use	Unit 4 and 5	20J/4
3	Str. 200-16	Construction and use of Str. 200-16	Unit 1-3, Stratum 4	—
4	—	Preconstruction occupation and trash deposition	Midden 1, Stratum 3	20J/5
5	—	Preoccupation natural soil deposition	Stratum 1 and lower 0.1-0.2 m of Stratum 2	—

Note: Lot 20K/3 is from mixed contexts and is not discussed further here.

discontinuous segments, are interpreted as part of the same construction, based on three lines of evidence. First, in all exposures the Unit 2 walls are constructed in an identical fashion. Second, these walls intersect each other and are oriented so as to function as a single integrated structure. Finally, in each exposure Unit 2 is set into the same soil level (Stratum 2). The earthen fill (Unit 1) and the stone summit pavement (Unit 3) clearly belong to this construction, as they are enclosed by Unit 2 and overlie material associated with the previous time span (Midden 1; see Fig. 28). Stratum 4, the light orange clay fronting Unit 2 in Op. 20J, is also placed in this period on the basis of its stratigraphic position. Stratum 4 was found 0.04-0.05 m above the base of Unit 2, buried by the earthen fill of a later addition to Str. 200-16 (Unit 5). This level is bounded on its north edge by a stone retaining wall (Unit 4) associated with that later construction. Thus stratigraphy places the deposition of Stratum 4 prior to the construction activities of T.S. 2 (see below).

Time Span 2: At some point after the construction of Units 1-3, a low addition was made along the north face of the structure (Units 4-5). This addition is a wall (Unit 4) 0.22-0.3 m high, set into Stratum 2 and possibly truncating Stratum 4. Unit 4 runs roughly parallel to the north wall of Unit 2 (oriented S 81° 0' E) and is constructed of very roughly coursed river cobbles, 0.07 by 0.12 to 0.08 by 0.17 m, packed with chinking stones. In the two places where its interior construction is exposed, Op. 20J and K, Unit 4 has a core of small cobbles packed in a light brown, fine-

textured, micaceous clay matrix. These cobbles are not packed as tightly as in Unit 2 (see Figs. 28 and 29). Unit 4 is separated from Unit 2 by a horizontal distance of 0.85-1 m, while its base rests 0.04-0.06 m above that of Unit 2. Only the central and western portions of Unit 4 were exposed in 1979, although we presume, on grounds of symmetry, that this wall continues to the east as well. On the west, Unit 4 ends opposite the northwest corner of Unit 2 and does not turn a corner to the south; a western counterpart of this feature was not found in Op. 20K and L. The total reconstructed length of Unit 4 is 7.6 m.

The area between Units 4 and 2 is filled with a tan, fine-textured, micaceous clay (Unit 5), similar in appearance to Stratum 2, that buries both Strata 4 and 2. Although identical in color, texture, and type of inclusions, Stratum 2 and Unit 5 are differentiated on the basis of two indirect lines of evidence. First, in both Op. 20K and J, stone tumble derived from Str. 200-16 rests on a level equivalent to the top of Unit 4. This suggests that Unit 5 was already in position between Units 2 and 4 prior to the collapse of the former. Second, as can be seen in Fig. 28, the exterior face of Unit 2 is best preserved below a point equivalent in elevation to the top of Unit 4; above that level the wall stones show a greater tendency to fall out to the north. This implies that some sort of fill was piled up against the lower portion of Unit 2 and thereby acted to preserve it.

In this interpretation, therefore, Units 4 and 5 are integral parts of an earthen fill terrace 0.2-0.3 m high, fronted on the north by a low stone wall. The surface of this terrace was probably formed by the upper portion of the earthen fill, as no formal flooring was found. The north face of Unit 2 would have continued to protrude at least 0.3 m above the terrace surface. The Units 4-5 terrace is on the plaza-facing or north side of Str. 200-16.

Units 4 and 5 are additions to the original structure of Units 1-3. The principal evidence in favor of this assertion was revealed in Op. 20J and K, where the tan clay fill of the addition buried the lower 0.22-0.3 m of the Unit 2 north wall. The Unit 4 retaining wall is built on approximately the same ground level as is Unit 2, although Unit 4's base is 0.04-0.06 m higher than Unit 2's. Lot 20J/4 is defined for material found in the Unit 5 fill, although this debris was probably originally deposited elsewhere, being accidentally included in construction.

Time Span 1: After the construction of the northern terrace, Str. 200-16 was abandoned and buried by river silts. The unmodified river cobbles noted overlying Unit 5, as well as those found north of and adjacent to Unit 4, represent tumbled architectural debris (Feat. 1). In Op. 20J-M this stone collapse, which undoubtedly postdates occupation, rests largely within the uppermost soil level, Stratum 5, a gray-black, greasy, clay-humus horizon 0.12-0.15 m thick. Stratum 5 also buries the upper 0.11-0.15 m of Unit 4 and overrides the top of Unit 2. Some of the tumbled stones also protrude downward into Stratum 2. The architectural debris of Feat. 1 slopes away from Str. 200-16 for 1-1.4 m, with a decrease in stone density away from the structure. The upper portion of Stratum 2, which buries the basal 0.16 m of Unit 4 and the lower 0.3-0.38 m of Unit 2's exposed west, south, and east walls, was also deposited during this postoccupation period. The small, uniform grain size of both Strata 5 and 2 suggests deposition by periodic river floods.

Lots 20J/1-3, K/1-2, L/1-2, and M/1-2 are defined for these two soil units at or above the base of construction. In all probability this material was originally deposited during Str. 200-16's last phase of occupation (T.S. 2) and redeposited in T.S. 1 by natural forces, i.e., river floods (see Str. 200-23). Note that Lot 20K/3 is mixed, containing material from terminal debris and fill contexts.

STRUCTURE 200-17

Structure 200-17 is a c. 1.2-m-high structure that closes the eastern side of the plaza, the southern margin of which is defined by Str. 200-16. Investigation of Str. 200-17 was limited to two trenches, Op. 20N and O, in 1979. Operation 20N was a trench 1.8 m east-west by 1.2 m north-south, near the structure's southwest corner, while Op. 20O was an excavation 2.8 m north-south by 1.95 m east-west, on the northwest corner. Both were dug to a depth of 0.5-0.65 m below ground surface. The goals of these probes were the same as enumerated in the introduction to this chapter. Unfortunately, limitations of time, and the need to devote more effort to the excavations in Str. 200-16, required a reduction in work here. As a result, not as much information on architecture, dimensions, and the nature of associated artifacts was obtained for Str. 200-17 as was originally planned.

Excavation Lots: The five lots defined for the Str. 200-17 excavations contain 562 sherds, nine censer fragments, 30 pieces of obsidian, one piece of ground stone, and two figurine fragments. Four of these lots (20N/1-2 and O/1-2) are from terminal occupation debris contexts, while one (20N/3) comes from outside and beneath the level of exposed construction and may be the remains of a preconstruction occupation level (see Table 3.11).

Time Span 3: The sequence of deposition recognized in Op. 20N and O is similar to that described for the Str. 200-16 excavations. The initial period of activity saw the deposition of the lower portion of Stratum 1, a light brown, fine-textured, micaceous clay essentially identical in appearance to Stratum 2 in Op. 20J-M. Approximately 0.15 m of this stratum below the base of Unit 1 was revealed in Op. 20N, indicating that the earth layer served as the base on which Str. 200-17 was constructed. The small and uniform grain size of Stratum 1 suggests riverine material and this level was probably deposited by floods of the nearby Rio Chinamito.

The stratigraphic position of the lower portion of Stratum 1, running beneath the only evidence of construction exposed in Op. 20N and O (Unit 1), clearly places its deposition prior to that construction. Unfortunately, as was often the case at Playitas, no clear discontinuity in this stratum was observable to indicate the location of the ground level contemporary with Str. 200-17. It was therefore impossible to determine how much of Stratum 1 was deposited before construction, and how much afterward. Lot 20N/3 is defined for material found in Stratum 1 below and south of the base of Unit 1. The possibility exists, of course, that some material from above

TABLE 3.11

EXCAVATION SUMMARY

Lot #	Contents	Depositional Significance	Provenience
20N/1	58 sherds	Terminal occupation debris (secondary)	Within Stratum 2
20N/2	290 sherds; 5 censer frags.; 22 pcs. obsidian	Terminal occupation debris (secondary)	Within Stratum 1, to base of construction (Unit 1)
20N/3	20 sherds; 1 pc. obsidian	Preconstruction occupation debris (secondary?)	Within Stratum 1, below base of construction (Unit 1)
20O/1	78 sherds; 2 censer frags.	Terminal occupation debris (secondary)	Within Stratum 2
20O/2	116 sherds; 2 censer frags.; 2 figurine frags.; 7 pcs. obsidian; 1 mano frag.	Terminal occupation debris (secondary)	Within Stratum 1, to base of construction (Unit 1)

worked its way down to be mixed with this earlier deposit.

Time Span 2: Unit 1 was built after the deposition of the lower portion of Stratum 1. Unit 1, found in both Op. 20N and O, is a wall 0.25-0.35 m high constructed of unfaced river cobbles (c. 0.12 by 0.2 m) set in rough horizontal courses and packed round with small pebbles. Its base is not level, varying as much as 0.05 m over the exposed distance. Operation 20N uncovered the southern segment of Unit 1 and its southwest corner, while Op. 20O revealed its northern portion and northwest corner. In the former excavation, Unit 1 is oriented N 74° 30′ W; in Op. 20O it is aligned slightly differently, N 81° 30′ W. The reconstructed west wall, with a length of 13.9 m, runs S 12° 30′ W.

From the limited extent of Unit 1 exposed in 1979, it seems obvious that this low wall could not have functioned as the sole foundation for Str. 200-17.

Rather, it more likely served as a retaining wall for a low basal terrace that extended westward into the plaza. This low terrace probably is connected to an unrevealed higher construction to the east, much as Unit 4 of Str. 200-16 gives way to the higher Unit 2 wall on the south. As with Str. 200-16, no prepared plaza surface was noted extending to the west from this structure.

The two discontinuously exposed segments of Unit 1 are placed in this period, as they are presumed to have formed part of the same integrated construction. This presumption is based on their nearly identical construction and mutual alignment.

Time Span 1: The last recognized period of activity saw the abandonment of Str. 200-17, with subsequent architectural deterioration and burial by river-borne sediments. The collapse is represented by scattered stone debris (Feat. 1) found, primarily, sloping down

TABLE 3.12

STRUCTURAL/DEPOSITIONAL SUMMARY TIME SPANS: 1-3

Time Span	Construction Stage	Activity	Features	Lots
1	—	Abandonment and burial of Str. 200-17	Stratum 2, upper portion of Stratum 1, Feat. 1	20N/1-2, 20O/1-2
2	Str. 200-17	Construction and use of Str. 200-17	Unit 1	—
3	—	Preconstruction occupation	Lower portion of Stratum 1	20N/3

and away from Unit 1 within the uppermost soil level, Stratum 2, and the upper section of Stratum 1. The burial of exposed construction (Unit 1) is represented by both of these strata, the higher of which, Stratum 2, is the dark gray-black, fine-textured clay-humus level, which ranges in thickness between 0.1 and 0.15 m.

The stratigraphic position of Stratum 2 and the upper portion of Stratum 1, burying Unit 1, indicates that these two levels were deposited after the abandonment of Str. 200-17. The location of obviously tumbled architectural debris (Feat. 1) in these same strata further substantiates this interpretation. Lots 20N/1-2 and O/1-2 correspond to this time span, as they are defined for these soil levels. This does not necessarily mean that the included artifacts postdate the abandonment of the structure. Rather, it seems more likely that they were initially discarded during the final period of Str. 200-17's use and redeposited by the river floods responsible for Strata 1 and 2 (see Str. 200-23).

GROUP I MAIN GROUP

STRUCTURE 200-74 (Fig. 30)

Structure 200-74, 1.1-2 m high, is located along the east side of the northeast court of the Group I main group. This platform was investigated in 1979 by means of a single trench 1.45 m north-south by 3.4 m east-west, Op. 20P, dug into its west, court-facing side. In addition to exposing terminal construction, Op. 20P also extended 1.7 m into the fill of Str. 200-74 and 0.71 m below ground surface in front of the platform.

Excavation Lots: Operation 20P provided a meager 36 sherds from the three defined excavation lots. Of these, one (20P/1) is from a terminal debris context, one (20P/3) is from fill, and Lot 20P/2 comes from a mixed fill and terminal debris context. Unfortunately, Lot 20P/1 was stolen from the site before it could be analyzed. Like most of the material recovered from Op. 20P, Lot 20P/1 contains very few artifacts and all of the included sherds are very eroded (see Table 3.13).

Time Span 3: The first event revealed by Op. 20P is the deposition of Stratum 1, a tan, loosely compacted, sandy clay with some orange and gray mottling. This soil level, though exposed to a thickness of only 0.02-0.08 m, underlies subsequent construction (Unit 4) or is cut by it (Unit 1). The small, uniform grain size of this soil indicates that it was a riverine deposit, probably from the nearby Rio Chinamito. On the basis of this evidence it appears that Stratum 1 constituted the original surface on which later construction was built.

Time Span 2: The construction of Str. 200-74, involving Units 1-4, represents the next event exposed by Op. 20P. The first step in this activity was the laying down of a very hard-compacted, fine-textured, orange to tan clay mottled with darker orange and including some charcoal fragments (Unit 1). This clay clearly underlies the terrace construction of Unit 2 to a depth of at least 0.1-0.17 m and extends east to an undetermined point. The cultural origin of Unit 1 is suggested by its very close association with construction as well as its distinctive color, compactness, and charcoal inclusions, which collectively distinguish it from the natural strata located to the west (Strata 1-3). Unit 1 extends no further west than the western edge of the Unit 2 terraces, where it ends very abruptly (Fig. 30). The function of this deposit of hard-packed clay was probably as a foundation for the construction of Units 2-4, leveling the area where they were to be built.

Immediately surmounting Unit 1 are the four extant step-terraces of Unit 2. Though they were not well preserved when exposed, there is sufficient detail to reconstruct their original appearance. The risers stood 0.2-0.3 m high and supported a series of flat-laid, small (c. 0.2 m wide by 0.04 m thick) schist slabs, forming the terrace treads. These slabs ran back 0.24-0.3 m to and then under the next higher terrace wall. The rear portions of these slabs were counterweighted by superimposed cobble terrace risers and were underlain by a tightly packed, flat-laid cobble and chinking-stone layer all set in a hard-packed orange to tan clay similar to Unit 1 (all Unit 2). Those portions of the slab runners underlying the next step-terrace riser were supported by 0.2- to 0.84-m-high columns of unfaced river cobbles (Fig. 30), which must have greatly contributed to the stability of the structure. Below the level of stone fill immediately underlying the terraces (part of Unit 2) is a fill (Unit 3) of the same hard-packed orange to tan clay already described for Unit 1. It is very likely that Units 1 and 3 derive from the same source and were constructed at the same time. The only basis for separating them is their location on either side of the Unit 2 stone column supporting the fourth ascending step-terrace. Both served the same purpose, providing a footing for the exposed stone construction.

The four preserved Unit 2 terraces rise to a total height of 1.01 m over a horizontal distance of 0.88 m.

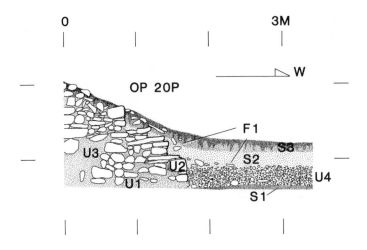

Figure 30.   Str. 200-74, Op 20P, Section.

That this terrace system once continued further upslope to the summit is suggested by both fragmentary surface remains and the cobble column (Fig. 30) at the far eastern edge of the trench. This column undoubtedly supported the rear edge of a slab in another step-terrace which has since been dislodged. Surface remains and the results of excavations in Op. 20P indicate that the exposed step-terraces continue for the entire length of the west face of Str. 200-74, at an orientation of roughly N 4° 30′ W.

Also associated with this construction activity is the laying down of Unit 4, a level 0.26-0.29 m thick of tightly packed pebbles and a few larger stones, all set in a hard-compacted tan clay matrix that overlies Stratum 1, abutting the lower 0.19 m of Unit 2's basal terrace. Unit 4 was deposited to raise the level of the plaza surface, at least in the immediate area fronting Str. 200-74, and to provide additional support to the basal terrace of Unit 2. This interpretation is supported by three lines of evidence. First, Unit 4's stony composition clearly sets it apart from the naturally deposited soil levels found above and below it (Strata 2 and 1). Second, the upper surface of Unit 4 is relatively flat and does not slope up to Str. 200-74 as would a natural soil stratum deposited after the latter's construction. Third, the upper portion of Unit 1 and the lower terraces of Unit 2 are buried by Unit 4, suggesting that all three elements were deposited at about the same time. Unit 2 rests directly on Unit 1 and was built over Unit 3 (Fig. 30). The deposition of Unit 4 acted to complement Units 1 and 2, and added to the stability of Str. 200-74.

The material recovered in Lot 20P/3 was deposited during T.S. 2. This material is included within Unit 3, though it most likely originally derived from earlier deposits and was redeposited here as part of construction fill.

Time Span 1: After the abandonment of Str. 200-74, the structure began to erode and collapse, and the lower four terraces of Unit 2 were buried by river-deposited silts. Stratum 2 covers Unit 4 to a depth of 0.17-0.26 m and is a fine-textured, moderately com-

TABLE 3.13

EXCAVATION SUMMARY

Lot #	Contents	Depositional Significance	Provenience
20P/1	Stolen	Terminal occupation debris (secondary)	Within Stratum 3
20P/2	34 sherds	Terminal occupation debris (secondary) mixed with fill	Within Strata 1 and 2 and Unit 3
20P/3	2 sherds	Fill	Within Unit 2

TABLE 3.14

STRUCTURAL/DEPOSITIONAL SUMMARY TIME SPANS: 1-3

Time Span	Construction Stage	Activity	Features	Lots
1	—	Abandonment and burial of structure 200-74	Strata 2-3, Feat. 1	20P/1
2	Str. 200-74	Construction and use of Str. 200-74	Units. 1-4	20P/3
3	—	Preconstruction natural soil deposition	Stratum 1	—

Note: Lot 20P/2 is from mixed terminal debris and fill contexts and is not considered further here.

pact tan clay. This soil level also runs over the lower three terraces of Unit 2. The humus horizon of Stratum 3, a black clayey level 0.12-0.19 m thick, caps Stratum 2 and the Unit 2 step-terraces. In both of these levels stone architectural debris (Feat. 1) is found, usually canted down to the west.

The stratigraphic position of Strata 2-3, overlying Units 2 and 4, indicates they were deposited after the construction and abandonment of Str. 200-74. The location of Feat. 1, the tumbled architectural debris derived from that structure, within these levels supports the contention that Str. 200-74 was already in the process of decay when the soil levels were deposited. Materials in Lot 20P/1 were found, at least in part, in these strata. Lot 20P/1 undoubtedly contains items originally deposited during the final phase of Str. 200-74's occupation and redeposited in Stratum 3, probably as the result of river flooding (see Str. 200-23). Lot 20P/2 is a mixed lot derived from the lower 0.11 m of Stratum 2 and Unit 4. This mixture of terminal debris and fill contexts presents a problem of interpretation.

NORTHEAST COURT, STRUCTURES 200-73/74 JUNCTION (Fig. 31)

The juncture of Str. 200-73 and -74, which closes off the east side of the northeast court, was examined by Op. 20Q, an extensive trench (3.3 m east-west by 4.85 m north-south) designed to locate the northwest corner of Str. 200-74 and its links to Str. 200-73 to the north. At many LMV sites, it was common to find several platforms linked by low, raised constructions termed "saddles," and this seemed to be the case between Str. 200-73 and -74. Up to that time, none of

these features had been excavated, and Op. 20Q was meant to remedy this situation.

Excavation Lots: Two excavation lots, 20Q/1 and 2, were recovered from Op. 20Q. Both are from terminal debris contexts. Lot 20Q/1, a very small collection of heavily eroded sherds, was stolen from the site prior to analysis. The material found in 20Q/2 comprises 22 sherds, one censer fragment, and two small pieces of *bajareque* (see Table 3.15).

Time Span 2: Because excavations were not carried below the base of construction, preconstruction events cannot be determined. The earliest documented period of activity saw the construction of Units 1-5. Unit 1, a series of step-terraces, three of which are sufficiently preserved to be recognizable, appears to be a continuation of the three lowest terraces of Unit 2 in Op. 20P. The basal terrace of Unit 1 stands to a preserved height of 0.31-0.35 m and is constructed of two rough courses of unmodified river cobbles packed with and underlain by a level of pebbles 0.01-0.03 m thick. This low vertical wall is surmounted by a series of horizontally laid schist slabs that, on the south and north, run back 0.28-0.3 m to and then under the next higher step-terrace. The Unit 1 basal terrace continues north across the full 4.7-m length of Op. 20Q, at an orientation of N 4° 30′ W, and appears to have been incorporated into the construction of both Str. 200-74 and -73. Extending back to the east of this terrace are the two higher steps of Unit 1. These are very similar in construction to their counterparts in Unit 2, Op. 20P, standing 0.24-0.25 m high, while the schist-slab treads run back c. 0.3 m to and under the next higher cobble wall. Though further step-terraces probably continued up to Str. 200-74's summit, the deterioration of the structure in this area has made

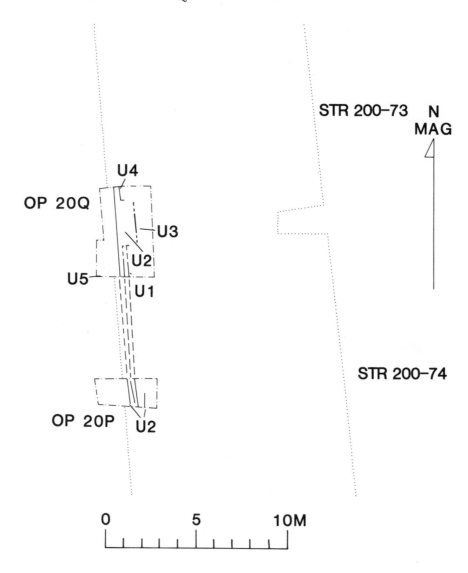

Figure 31.   Str. 200-73/74, Op 20Q, Plan.

their recognition impossible. Unlike the basal Unit 1 terrace, the upper two step-terraces continue north in Op. 20Q for a distance of only 0.85-0.95 m. No clear corner is formed by either of these two terraces, although, as noted below, it is quite likely that their northwest corner was in the immediate area of their extant north ends. The Unit 1 terraces rise 0.81 m over a horizontal distance of 0.55 m.

North of the Unit 1 terraces, and south of Unit 4, is a stone pavement (Unit 2). Resting on the same level as, and extending back from, the top of the Unit 1 basal terrace, this pavement consists of large, flat-laid, tightly packed, uncut stones 0.21 by 0.34 to 0.35 by

0.39 m, set in a fine clay matrix. To the east, this surface extends back for c. 1.15 m, at which point a 0.16-m cobble-faced step-up is encountered (Unit 3). The pavement topping this low rise (also Unit 3) is similar in appearance to Unit 2, though more disturbed by root action than the latter. The Unit 3 pavement was followed to the east for 0.91 m before the trench was terminated. Due to the poor state of preservation of Str. 200-74 and -73 in this area, it was impossible to determine the precise relationship between the Unit 3 pavement and the two flanking structures.

Returning to Unit 2, we noted during excavation

TABLE 3.15

EXCAVATION SUMMARY

Lot #	Contents	Depositional Significance	Provenience
20Q/1	Stolen	Terminal occupation debris (secondary)	Within Stratum 2
20Q/2	22 sherds; 1 censer frag.; 2 *bajareque* frags.	Terminal occupation debris (secondary)	Within Stratum 1

that this well-laid surface radically changes character within c. 0.66 m north of the north end of Unit 1's upper terraces. In particular, the stones in this limited area, 0.66 m north-south by 0.77 m east-west from the back of the Unit 1 basal terrace, are rounded cobbles, 0.07 by 0.07 to 0.1 by 0.15 m, and not the larger, flat stones found further north. In addition, more earth is visible between the stones here than in the rest of Unit 2. This change in the composition of the Unit 2 surface so close to the north end of Unit 1 suggests that this area actually contained a portion of the cobble fill that underlies the northwest corner of the Unit 1 terraces, and, with subsequent collapse, all that is left now is a "shadow" of those terraces. This interpretation is further supported by both the abrupt termination of the Unit 1 upper terraces immediately to the south and the fact that the stones found overlying this changed surface are horizontally laid, as though they served as fill for an overlying construction. The rocks noted above these flat-laid cobbles are invariably angled down to the north, indicating architectural tumble.

Defining the north edge of Unit 2 is a low step-terrace (Unit 4), which most likely represents the southwest corner of Str. 200-73. Unit 4 is a 0.25-m-high, roughly coursed, cobble and chinking-stone wall. This unit rests on the rear edge of the basal Unit 1 slab terrace and, in turn, supports a series of horizontally laid schist slabs. Preservation here is very poor, and it was not possible to determine whether these terraces once ascended to the summit, although it is likely that they did. Unit 4 is oriented N 4° 45′ W.

The last element associated with this period of construction is a level (Unit 5) of tightly packed pebbles, 0.01 m and less in diameter, set in a light brown, micaceous clay matrix which abuts the lower 0.21 m of the Unit 1 basal terrace on the west. Unit 5 is c. 0.25 m thick, has a level upper surface, and is restricted to the south wall of Op. 20Q, where it was exposed for a horizontal distance of 1.33 m east-west. This pebble and clay level closely resembles Unit 4 recognized in Op. 20P and apparently represents the latter's north edge.

The overall form of the Str. 200-73/74 junction obtained from the Op. 20Q excavations is as follows. Both Str. 200-73 and -74 are faced by low and narrow step-terraces, a very common technique found in almost all investigated LMV monumental structures. In this case, the upper terraces of the two structures are oriented close to N 4° 30′ W and terminate 2.4 m

TABLE 3.16

STRUCTURAL/DEPOSITIONAL SUMMARY TIME SPANS: 1-2

Time Span	Construction Stage	Activity	Features	Lots
1	—	Abandonment and burial of Str. 200-73 and -74	Stratum 2, upper portion of Stratum 1, Feat. 1	20Q/1-2
2	Str. 200-74	Construction of Str. 200-73 and use of Str. 200-74 and -73	Units 1-5	—

from each other. The basal terrace is shared by both platforms and serves to define the west margin of a formal stone floor (Units 2 and 3). This latter bi-level surface is the top of a low construction linking Str. 200-73 and -74 on their south and north sides respectively. West of these constructions the flooring, noted first in Op. 20P fronting Str. 200-74, seems to have ended slightly south of the northwest corner of that structure. Its place may well have been taken by an informal earthen surface which did not survive to be recognized. To the north of Unit 5 the matrix burying Unit 1 is a tan, slightly micaceous, fine-textured clay containing some stones (Stratum 1; see Stratum 2, Op. 20P, Str. 200-74). Since this level has buried all of the Unit 1 basal terrace, and no clear disjunction was found indicating the location of an informal court surface, it is not possible to determine how much of Stratum 1 was deposited before or after construction.

The fact that the Unit 1 basal terrace extends between Str. 200-73 and -74, serves as the western boundary of Units 2 and 3, and shows no discontinuity in its construction, strongly implies that all of these units were built and in use at the same time. With respect to Unit 5, its stratigraphic position, running up against the lower 0.21 m of Unit 1, clearly places its construction after the basal Unit 1 terrace. It thus seems likely that Units 1-5 were in use during the terminal occupation phase of Str. 200-73 and -74 and were probably contemporaneous constructions.

Time Span 1: Burying these units is the upper portion of Stratum 1, described above, itself overlain by a fine-textured, gray-black humus horizon (Stratum 2), 0.1-0.15 m thick. Included within both of these levels are stones derived from architectural collapse (Feat. 1), the density of which increases considerably toward modern ground surface. The fine and uniform grain size of these clays suggests that they were probably deposited by floods of the nearby Rio Chinamito.

While the lower portion of Stratum 1 is difficult to place chronologically, its upper portion, which buries the Unit 5 floor and the upper stones of the Unit 1 basal terrace, clearly postdates construction. Also deposited during the period following abandonment was Stratum 2, the humus horizon that obscures all excavated construction and Stratum 1. Feature 1, construction debris, must have been deposited after the adjacent structures were no longer occupied and being maintained. The material in Lot 20Q/1, found within Stratum 2, corresponds to this time span. It is very probable, however, that this material originated

during T.S. 2 in the area of Str. 200-73 and -74 and was redeposited in T.S. 3 by the river floods responsible for Stratum 2. Lot 20Q/2 comes from throughout Stratum 1. Depending on how Stratum 1 is interpreted, this could represent a mixture of terminal occupation debris, fill, and/or preconstruction material. As a result, Lot 20Q/2 is placed in the latest time span during which artifacts may have been deposited, with the realization that some mixing with earlier items is possible.

STRUCTURE 200-77 (Fig. 32)

Structure 200-77, the largest monumental construction (c. 7.4 m high) at the site of Playitas, was tested by means of two excavations, Op. 20R and S. The former was a small trench, 1.5 m east-west by 3 m north-south, on the north side of the structure. The goal here was to determine the nature of terminal-phase architecture, and to cut into architectural fill. We eventually excavated 1.08 m into the platform's hearting, reaching a maximum depth of 1.18 m below ground surface. Operation 20S was located on the south face of Str. 200-77 and measured 1.5 m east-west by 2 m north-south. This trench was dug to determine the nature of construction on this side of the structure, recover more cultural material from terminal debris contexts, and gain some idea of the platform's original north-south width. A problem that plagued work in both trenches was the constant seepage of water into the excavations. Even without consistent rain, this water remained at a fairly predictable level, equivalent to the top of the lowest exposed architectural unit. The seepage problem prevented deeper excavations.

Excavation Lots: A total of 753 sherds, 22 pieces of obsidian, and 14 pieces of *bajareque* were recovered from Op. 20R and S. This material was divided among four lots, 20R/1-3 and S/1, three of which (20R/1-2 and S/1) are from terminal debris contexts, while one (20R/3) is from fill (see Table 3.17).

Time Span 2: The first period of activity recognized in Op. 20R and S saw the construction of Str. 200-77 (Units 1-4 in Op. 20R and Units 5-7 in Op. 20S). Unit 1, a 0.13-m-high terrace fronting Str. 200-77 on its north side, extends 0.7 m north of the lowest step-terrace of Unit 2 (see below). It consists of a low, vertical pebble wall capped by a pavement of long schist slabs and cobbles extending for the total terrace width. Unit 1 does not continue under the next construction element (Unit 2), but rather abuts the base of that unit. Unit 2 is a system of four exposed

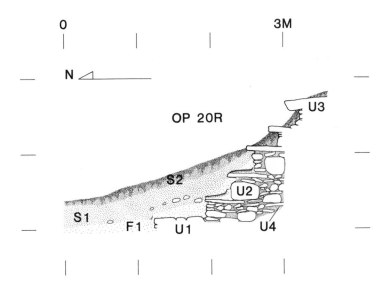

Figure 32. Str. 200-77, Section.

step-terraces with vertical walls 0.28-0.36 m high. These risers are built of unmodified river cobbles set in a rough horizontal course and packed with chinking stones. The Unit 2 walls are each surmounted by horizontally laid schist slabs which form the terrace treads. The latter extend back 0.36-0.43 m to and then under, for an additional 0.18-0.2 m, the next ascending terrace. All of the stones in this unit are set in a dense, hard-compacted, fine orange clay matrix. Surmounting the four exposed step-terraces of Unit 2, and sitting atop a 0.24-m-high cobble and chinking-stone wall, is the broad terrace of Unit 3. The construction of this element does not differ from the lower steps already described, but since it represents a break in the pattern of narrow terraces characteristic of Unit

2, it is designated a separate unit. Though not completely exposed, Unit 3 is at least 1 m wide and appears to have been surfaced by a series of very long, flat-laid schist slabs, some as much as 0.14 m thick. Above Unit 3, surface remains indicate that the low, narrow step-terraces of the type described for Unit 2 continue to the summit. Surface features also supply evidence that all of the recognized Str. 200-77 terraces continue for the length of the structure's north side. Unit 3 joins with similar broad terraces on the adjoining Str. 200-76 and -78 (Fig. 2). The lower, narrower terraces may do the same with their counterparts on these constructions. In all, Units 1-3 rise a total of 1.72 m over a horizontal distance of 2 m.

Underlying the Unit 2 terraces is a fill (Unit 4) of

TABLE 3.17

EXCAVATION SUMMARY

Lot #	Contents	Depositional Significance	Provenience
20R/1	656 sherds; 20 pcs. obsidian; 9 *bajareque* frags.	Terminal occupation debris (secondary)	Within Strata 1 and 2
20R/2	22 sherds	Terminal occupation debris (primary)	Within Feat. 1, overlying Units 1 and 2
20R/3	2 sherds; 1 pc. obsidian	Fill	Within Unit 4
20S/1	73 sherds; 1 pc. obsidian; 5 *bajareque* frags.	Terminal occupation debris (secondary)	Within Stratum 3

89

TABLE 3.18

STRUCTURAL/DEPOSITIONAL SUMMARY TIME SPANS: 1-2

Time Span	Construction Stage	Activity	Features	Lots
1	—	Abandonment and burial of Str. 200-77	Feat. 1-2, Strata 1-4	20R/1, 20S/1
2	Str. 200-77	Construction and use of Str. 200-77	Units 1-7	20R/2

tightly packed, horizontally set river cobbles and small slabs in a hard-compacted, fine-textured orange clay matrix. The aforementioned water seepage precluded our digging below the base of this fill unit.

In Op. 20S, the exposed construction is very similar to that described above. Unit 5 is the southern counterpart of Unit 1, a small 0.1-m-high stone wall, topped by a series of flat-laid schist slabs, which extends the width of the basal terrace. Rising above this unit are the four exposed step-terraces of Unit 6. These steps are 0.29-0.4 m high, composed of one or two courses of cobble and chinking stones topped by horizontally set schist slabs, which run 0.33-0.39 m back to and then under the next higher terrace. Above the fourth terrace is a similarly constructed 0.32-m-high stone wall, which supports a much broader (1.5 m wide) terrace surface (Unit 7). Above this terrace of long, horizontally laid schist slabs, the fragmentary remains of other narrow and low step-terraces proceed upslope to the summit. Surface remains also indicate that these and the other, lower, visible terraces of Units 6 and 7 continue the length of Str. 200-77's south face. Units 5-7 rise 1.81 m over a distance of 2.14 m.

The terrace surfaces exposed on the north and south sides of Str. 200-77 were originally covered with plaster, which has since eroded and collected at the base (Feat. 1 and 2 in Op. 20R and S respectively). Each of these features is a level 0.06-0.33 m thick of densely packed, very small and friable white plaster fragments, sloping down and over the lower two terraces of Units 2 and 6, over Units 1 and 5, and then down and away from construction. That plaster once covered all or most of the Str. 200-77 terraces is suggested by fragments of this material still adhering to the visible portions of the terraces above Unit 7, on the structure's south side.

The general form of Str. 200-77 as revealed by these two small excavations is a platform built of long, narrow, and regular step-terraces interrupted by symmetrically placed (north and south) broader terraces. The structure is oriented S 85° 30′ E and measures 32 m across its base north-south. All of the exposed construction was probably covered with white plaster during its final use—a feature unique, as far as is known, in the LMV outside of Quirigua and its immediate periphery.

The stratigraphic position of Units 1-4 in Op. 20R and Units 5-7 in Op. 20S clearly indicates that they were built as part of the same construction episode. The terraces of Unit 2 plainly support Unit 3 and overlie the fill of Unit 4 laid down for their support. While Unit 1 abuts the base of Unit 2 (see Fig. 32) and may have been placed after that terrace system, it still seems fairly clear that both were in use during the final use of Str. 200-77. Units 1 and 2 form parts of the same integrated construction. The same line of argument can be presented for the units exposed in Op. 20S. The issue of contemporaneity is more problematic in positing Units 1-4 *and* 5-7 within the same time span. No direct stratigraphic link can be established between these elements. As a result, only indirect lines of reasoning argue for their inclusion in T.S. 2. First, the form of construction exposed on the north and south is identical: a low, wide terrace giving way to four step-terraces, which in turn support a low but much broader terrace. This degree of symmetry implies the planning and building of those units as part of a single construction effort. Second, it seems logical, given the lack of overlying construction, to assume that even if the north and south sides of the structure were built at different times, they both would have ultimately been exposed and in use during the final phase of the structure's occupation.

The materials in Lots 20R/2-3 were deposited during this time span. Lot 20R/2 consists of items found resting directly on Units 1 and 2. This location, buried by Stratum 1 and Feat. 1 and atop construction, strongly implies that the material was discarded during Str. 200-77's occupation and prior to its abandonment. Lot 20R/3 consists of those few items deposited along with the Unit 4 fill. While this material reached its final location during the construction of Str. 200-77, at least some of these artifacts may have derived from earlier deposits.

Time Span 1: After the abandonment of Str. 200-77, during which time Feat. 1 and 2 were deposited, the lower flanks of the structure were buried by natural accumulations (Strata 1-4). The lowest of these strata, Stratum 1 in Op. 20R and Stratum 2 in 20S, are fine-textured gray clays with some included pebbles. These strata completely bury Feat. 1 and 2 and slope up toward construction, varying in thickness between 0.14 and 0.4 m. Capping these lowest soil levels are the humus horizons of Strata 3 and 4, on the north and south respectively; they are distinguished from Strata 1-2 by their slightly darker colors, dark gray to black. Strata 3 and 4 slope up and over construction and vary in thickness between 0.06 and 0.17 m. The small, uniform grain size of Strata 1-4 suggests their riverine origin and deposition.

The stratigraphic position of Feat. 1 and 2 and Strata 1-4 places them in the latest time span. Lots 20R/1 and S/1 belong to this period because their contents derive from these soil levels. All of this material probably originated further upslope, whence it was redeposited by natural forces (see Str. 200-23). This is especially true in the case of Lot 20R/1, the large size of which points to its original deposition in the immediate area, probably on the summit of Str. 200-77. In sum, the artifacts in Lots 20R/1 and S/1 most likely derive from the Str. 200-77 area during T.S. 2. After this period, as indicated by their provenience, they were redeposited in T.S. 1.

LAS QUEBRADAS

WEST GROUP

SOUTH COURT, MONUMENT 1 (Fig. 33)

Las Quebradas Mon. 1, located in the approximate center of the south court of the main group, was investigated in 1978 by means of a trench (Op. 24B) 2.36 m north-south by 1.44 m east-west, dug against the monument's north side. Operation 24B was carried down 0.7-0.8 m below ground surface to expose the monument's base. A shallow (0.11-0.16 m deep) looter's pit on the south side of the monument was also inspected and the disturbed artifacts collected (Lot 24B/1); no new excavations were initiated in this area, however. The goals of Op. 24B were to determine if Mon. 1 had been set into an artificial pavement or footing, to expose this rough slab to its full height, and to locate artifacts, hopefully in primary context, associated with the monument's use. Accomplishment of the latter goal would help to date the monument as well as provide evidence of the range of behaviors associated with it.

Excavation Lots: A total of 476 sherds, 260 censer fragments, 37 pieces of obsidian, and one figurine fragment were recovered from the eight excavation lots defined. Of these, three represent terminal occupation debris (24B/1, 2, and 5), one derives from architectural fill (24B/3), three from preconstruction levels (24B/4, 7, and 8), and one from mixed fill and preconstruction contexts (24B/6) (see Table 3.19).

Time Span 3: The first recognized event uncovered by Op. 24B is the natural deposition of Stratum 1, a hard-compacted, fine-textured orange-brown clay largely devoid of stones. The upper surface of the stratum is irregular, rising toward the south. The total thickness of this level was not determined, although it was exposed to a depth of 0.16-0.42 m. In general, the density of recovered artifacts decreases with increasing depth within Stratum 1, but there is no change in their frequency from north to south.

The stratigraphic position of Stratum 1, underlying Unit 1 and burying the lower 0.38 m of Mon. 1, indicates its deposition before both of these. Materials in Lots 24B/4, 7, and 8 were found within Stratum 1, apparently representing debris jettisoned prior to construction, during T.S. 2, most likely from occupation somewhere in the south court.

Time Span 2: The next event involved the setting of Mon. 1 and, shortly thereafter, the deposition of Unit 1. Monument 1 is a very roughly shaped, uncarved column with an oval to circular cross-section (see Chap. 2), fashioned out of a hard gray crystalline stone, broken in two when found. The butt section, 1.43 m high, 0.36 m thick by 0.59 m wide at maximum, was still set in the ground in 1978. This portion of the monument is roughly triangular, flaring out gradually toward the top, and tilting out of plumb to the south. The severed portion, found 0.19 m south of the butt, is 1.4 m long by 0.63 m wide and 0.46 m thick

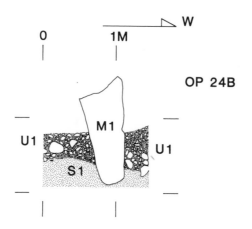

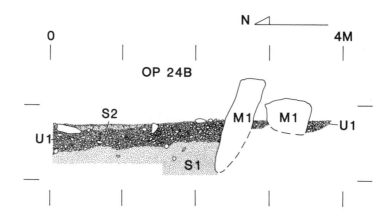

Figure 33.   Las Quebradas Op 24B, Section and Elevation.

(reconstructed). If no other fragments exist, the original height of Mon. 1 would have been c. 2.83 m.

Set against the butt of the monument to both the north and south is Unit 1, a level of tightly packed pebbles 0.28-0.32 m thick, with individual sizes ranging between 0.02 by 0.02 and 0.15 by 0.21 m. The matrix in which the stones are set changes somewhat with depth: the lower 0.1-0.14 m is a fine-textured, yellowish brown clay, while the upper 0.18 m is a dark gray clay-humus. It is very probable that, originally, all of the Unit 1 stones were set in the yellow-brown clay. The sizes of the stones decrease with depth and increase with proximity to Mon. 1. The larger stones placed around the base of the monument probably increased the latter's stability (see Fig. 33). In general, Unit 1 was artificially introduced on a preexisting ground surface (Stratum 1) both to support Mon. 1 and to provide a surrounding formalized surface.

Materials in Lots 24B/1-3 and 5 were found among the Unit 1 stones. Of these lots, 24B/1, 2, and 5 pertain to terminal occupation debris in primary context because of their location, condition on recovery, size, quantity, and type of material. All three lots are from the upper 0.16-0.25 m of Unit 1, indicating that the included artifacts would have been those deposited on the surface during use and pressed into it after abandonment. Many of the sherds, when found, were fairly large and were not appreciably

TABLE 3.19

EXCAVATION SUMMARY

Lot #	Contents	Depositional Significance	Provenience
24B/1	144 sherds; 138 censer frags.; 2 pcs. obsidian	Terminal occupation debris (primary)	In unit 1, upper 0.16 m, S of Mon. 1, looter's pit
24B/2	56 sherds; 11 censer frags.; 4 pcs. obsidian	Terminal occupation debris (primary)	In Unit 1, upper 0.2 m, N end Op. 24B to 0.86 m N of Mon. 1
24B/3	27 sherds; 11 pcs. obsidian	Fill	In Unit 1, lower 0.2 m, N end Op. 24B to 0.86 m N of Mon. 1
24B/4	13 sherds; 1 censer frag.; 1 figurine frag.	Preconstruction debris (secondary?)	In Stratum 1, N end Op. 24B to 0.86 m N of Mon. 1
24B/5	159 sherds; 95 censer frags.; 6 pcs. obsidian	Terminal occupation debris (primary)	In Unit 1, upper 0.23 m, from Mon. 1 to 0.86 m N
24B/6	63 sherds; 15 censer frags.; 6 pcs. obsidian	Mixed fill and preconstruction contexts	Lower 0.04-0.12 m of Unit 1 and upper 0.08-0.16 m of Stratum 1 from Mon. 1 to 0.86 m N
24B/7	11 sherds; 5 pcs. obsidian	Preconstruction debris (secondary)	In Stratum 1, 0.16-0.31 m in depth within this level
24B/8	3 sherds; 3 pcs. obsidian	Preconstruction debris (secondary)	In Stratum 1, 0.31 m to base of excavation in this level

eroded on their edges. This suggests that the material was not redeposited but was probably broken and dropped in the immediate vicinity. This supposition is further supported by the large size of the collections: 24B/1 with 284 items, 24B/2 with 71 objects, and 24B/5 with 260 fragments, which implies that these objects were not transported here by natural forces

after the abandonment of the south court. The Unit 1 fill of tightly packed, small to medium-sized stones, is not the sort of matrix in which large amounts of cultural material are typically found at LMV sites. (On the contrary, cultural debris is very sparse in stony fill, and those items found therein are usually small and heavily abraded.) This fact, again, indicates that the

TABLE 3.20

STRUCTURAL/DEPOSITIONAL SUMMARY TIME SPANS: 1-3

Time Span	Construction Stage	Activity	Features	Lots
1	—	Abandonment of south court	Stratum 2	—
2	South court	Setting and use of Mon. 1 and court	Unit 1, Mon. 1	24B/1-3, 5
3	—	Preconstruction natural soil deposition along with trash	Stratum 1	24B/4, 7, 8

Note: Lot 24B/6 derives from both fill (Unit 1) and preconstruction contexts and is not included, therefore, within a single time span.

artifacts in Lots 24B/1, 2, and 5 were not redeposited along with the stone fill of Unit 1, but were originally deposited on its surface. A fairly large proportion of the sherd content of these lots comes from *incensarios*, ceremonial incense burners whose use in association with a monument could be expected. All of these lines of evidence suggest that the three lots in question represent debris directly associated with, and deposited during, the final phase of Unit 1's use, and subsequently little disturbed from its original position. Furthermore, because the diagnostic artifacts recovered here fall within the ceramic period that characterizes the remainder of the site, it is presumed that the contents of these lots were deposited within T.S. 2 soon after Unit 1 and Mon. 1 were in position.

Lot 24B/3 is interpreted as material deposited along with the Unit 1 fill because it was found among the stones in the lower 0.18 m of Unit 1. It is also possible, however, that the 24B/3 artifacts are simply objects deposited on the Unit 1 surface which then worked their way down into that unit.

Time Span 1: After the abandonment of the south court, the 0.05- to 0.18-m-thick, dark gray, fine-textured humus horizon (Stratum 2) was formed. This level, as noted earlier, extends down into the upper portion of Unit 1 and is clearly defined overlying this unit for a distance of only 1.06 m in the southern portion of Op. 24B. Unit 1 otherwise extends up to the current ground surface and is not appreciably obscured by later soil deposits (see Fig. 33).

STRUCTURE 205-1 (Fig. 34)

Structure 205-1 was investigated in 1978 by means of two trenches, Op. 24C and D, near the medial lines of the west and east faces of the structure, respectively. The former was an excavation 1.25-1.45 m north-south by 9.12 m east-west, which began 3.9 m west of terminal-phase Str. 205-1 and extended eastward to the approximate center of the structure's summit. In addition to this major trench, Op. 24C had an extension which projected southward along the summit and measured 1.7-2.1 m east-west by 3.82 m north-south. Operation 24D was placed on approximately the same line as Op. 24C and measured 0.7-1.4 m north-south by 7.31 m east-west.

The Op. 24D excavation involved removing overburden which concealed the final construction phase, as well as probing beneath the base of that construction, a distance of 1.22 m overall below ground surface immediately east of the platform. Excavation was also carried 0.56 m into the fill of Str. 205-1-1st to be sure

that the east wall had, indeed, been encountered. This latter probe was dug to a depth of 1.64 m below ground surface. Excavation of Op. 24C removed 0.1-0.5 m of earth covering final-phase construction and extended 5.22 m into that construction. This probe was carried down to a maximum depth of 1.9-2.04 m below ground surface.

Excavation Lots: A total of 296 sherds, 18 censer fragments, 130 chipped stone artifact pieces, two *bajareque* fragments, one metate fragment, and one carbon sample were unearthed in both Op. 24C and D. In the former trench, 17 lots were defined: four are from occupation debris contexts (24C/1, 2, 9, and 14); 11 from fill (24C/3-8, 10-12, 16, and 17); one from a preconstruction level (24C/15); and one from a disturbed context (24C/13). In Op. 24D, three excavation lots related to Str. 205-1 were defined (24D/1, 2, and 4), all from terminal debris ontexts (see Table 3.21).

Time Span 5: The natural deposition of Strata 1 and 2, underlying exposed construction, marks the first period of activity exposed in Op. 24C and D. The lower of these two levels, Stratum 1, is a loose-compacted, very greasy, fine-textured dark brown clay containing some carbon flecks. It was exposed over a horizontal extent of only 0.88 m in the bottom of Op. 24C, sloping gradually upward to the east over this limited distance. Immediately above is Stratum 2, a relatively hard-compacted, fine-textured brown clay showing some orange mottling and containing a few pebbles and carbon flecks. It is 0.12-0.4 m thick and slopes up for a distance of 0.91 m toward the east. Further east in the deep probe made below Str. 205-1's summit (see Fig. 34), an identical soil level beneath several later stages of construction was found which might represent a continuation of Stratum 2 (see Unit 2, below).

On the east, Op. 24D encountered Stratum 3, which in color, consistency, and nature of inclusions is identical to Stratum 1. Based on this similarity and its stratigraphic position underlying all recognized construction, Stratum 3 is assigned to this preconstruction period and interpreted as a possible eastern extension of Stratum 1.

Both Strata 1 and 2 appear to represent the west side of a natural rise which ascended for some distance further east before dropping precipitously down to the level of Stratum 3. It was over this change in elevation that the subsequent constructions of Str. 205-1 were built. The difference in height between the east and west sides of the structure in its terminal

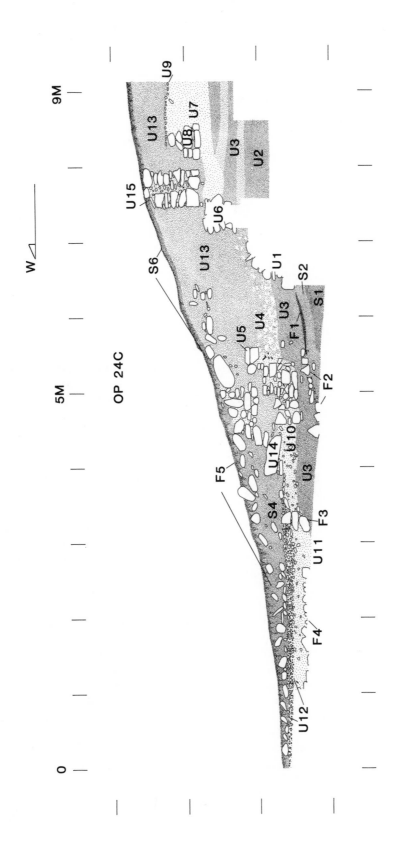

Figure 34a.   Str. 205-1, Section.

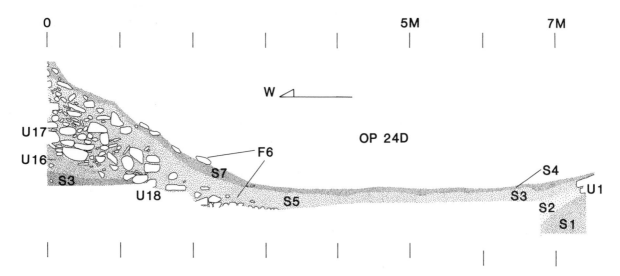

Figure 34b.   Str. 205-1, Section.

phase (1.9 m on the west and 2.52 m on the east) strongly suggests the presence of this natural rise. The east-west difference is currently 0.62 m and could have been the same in the past as well.

Time Span 4: Structure 205-1-3rd was built during T.S. 4. As uncovered in Op. 24C, this construction includes a low cobblestone wall (Unit 1) preserved to a height of 0.66 m, resting on Stratum 2, and aligned S 4° 15′ E. This wall is constructed almost exclusively of unmodified river cobbles with some chinking pebbles, set in a mud matrix. It rises vertically 0.49 m above a 0.15-m-wide basal step-out (see Fig. 34). In horizontal extent, Unit 1 runs north-south for 0.8 m across the width of Op. 24C, ceasing 0.55 m south of the north trench face. This termination of Unit 1 may result from postoccupation disturbance associated with later construction.

While Unit 1 was not cut through in 1978, a probe into the fill of Str. 205-1-3rd revealed a moderately compacted, fine-textured brown clay with some orange mottling, pebbles, and small carbon fragments (Unit 2). This fill was exposed to a depth of 0.31 m. The builders of Str. 205-1-3rd most likely took advantage of the aforementioned natural rise to facilitate their efforts and, as a result, the lower portion of Unit 2 may be a continuation of naturally deposited Stratum 2. It is therefore possible that not all of Unit 2 was actually laid down as a single fill deposit. These excavations revealed no sign of a formal summit floor for Str. 205-1-3rd; it may have had a simple tamped-earth surface.

Associated with the use of this structure is a lens 0.02-0.03 m thick of carbon-rich brown clay (Feat. 1), which slopes down from east to west for a distance of 0.82 m from a point 0.05 m east of and 0.02 m below the base of Unit 1. This level is found over the full width of Op. 24C and rests on Stratum 2. The high carbon content of Feat. 1, the presence of some cultural materials within it (Lot 24C/14), and its location sloping down and away from the base of Unit 1 strongly imply that it represents a level of debris washed from the west face of Str. 205-1-3rd that accumulated during the latter's use.

The east flank of Str. 205-1-3rd was not encountered in Op. 24D, so its east-west dimensions are unreconstructed. On the basis of what is known, this earliest of the Str. 205-1 constructions is a low platform faced on the west, at least in part, by a low stone retaining wall, and backed by a packed-earth fill. As noted above, the summit of this structure may have been surfaced by tamped earth; no sign of a superstructure was recorded.

Time Span 3: Following the abandonment of Str. 205-1-3rd, the next construction, Str. 205-1-2nd, was built. The first effort associated with this episode involved laying down a level of river cobbles and chunks set in a hard-compacted, orange clay matrix that includes carbon flecks and small pebbles (Feat. 2). At its eastern margin, Feat. 2 rests on top of Feat. 1 and thence slopes down to the west for a distance of 1.19 m into the base of excavation. The stones embedded in this feature form a very rough surface over the

TABLE 3.21

EXCAVATION SUMMARY

Lot #	Contents	Depositional Significance	Provenience
24C/1	20 sherds; 5 censer frags.; 1 pc. obsidian	Terminal occupation debris (secondary)	Within Strata 4 and 6, above construction
24C/2	50 sherds; 10 censer frags.; 8 pcs. obsidian	Terminal occupation debris (primary)	Atop Unit 12, buried by Feat. 5
24C/3	16 sherds; 29 pcs. obsidian	Fill	Within Unit 13, E of Unit 15
24C/4	19 sherds; 1 pc. flint; 3 pcs. obsidian; 1 pc. chalcedony	Fill	Within Unit 13, W of Unit 15 and E of Unit 14
24C/5	5 sherds; 3 pcs. obsidian	Fill	Within Unit 13, E of Unit 15 in Op. 24C's S extension
24C/6	16 sherds; 14 pcs. obsidian; 1 metate frag.	Fill	Within Unit 7, E of Unit 6
24C/7	9 sherds; 5 pcs. obsidian	Fill	Within Units 2 and 3, E of Unit 1
24C/8	13 sherds; 1 censer frag.; 10 pcs. obsidian	Fill	General, within Unit 13, between Units 4 and 5
24C/9	4 sherds; 1 pc. obsidian	Occupation debris (primary?)	Atop Unit 6, buried by Unit 13
24C/10	7 sherds; 4 pcs. obsidian	Fill	Within Unit 11, between Feat. 4 and 3
24C/11	12 sherds; 2 *bajareque* frags.	Fill	Within Unit 11, above Feat. 4
24C/12	20 sherds; 3 pcs. obsidian	Fill	Within Unit 10
24C/13	10 sherds; 12 pcs. obsidian	Disturbed by animal	Within Unit 3, burrow at S edge of Op. 24C
24C/14	34 sherds; 1 censer frag.; 9 pcs. obsidian; 1 carbon sample	Occupation debris (secondary)	Within Feat. 1
24C/15	5 sherds; 1 pc. obsidian	Preconstruction level?	Within Strata 1 and 2
24C/16	20 sherds; 11 pcs. obsidian	Fill	Within Unit 4
24C/17	6 sherds; 2 pcs. obsidian	Fill	Within Unit 15
24D/1	5 sherds; 1 censer frag.; 1 flint projectile point	Terminal occupation debris (secondary)	Within Strata 5 and 7 and Feat. 6
24D/2	10 sherds; 4 pcs. obsidian	Terminal occupation debris (secondary)	Within Strata 5 and 7, E of Str. 205-1 and W of 205-8
24D/4	15 sherds; 7 pcs. obsidian	Terminal occupation debris (secondary)	Within Strata 5 and 7 and Feat. 6, immediate area of Unit 18

1.25- to 1.45-m width of Op. 24C. The absence of both Strata 1 and 2 in this area indicates that Feat. 2 replaced these natural soil levels here. Feature 2 probably functioned as a footing for the stone steps of Unit 5, since it is restricted to the area immediately below this construction.

Soon after the deposition of Feat. 2, the builders introduced Unit 3, fill of moderately dense, fine-textured brown clay with some orange mottling and inclusions of carbon flecks and pebbles. Varying in thickness between 0.16 and 0.48 m, it was found on both the west and east sides of Unit 1. On the west Unit 3 extends 3.29 m from Unit 1 and buries not only Feat. 1 and 2 but also the lower 0.35 m of that earlier construction. As was the case with Stratum 2, which it resembles very closely, Unit 3 slopes gradually down

TABLE 3.22

STRUCTURAL/DEPOSITIONAL SUMMARY TIME SPANS: 1-5

Time Span	Construction Stage	Activity	Features	Lots
1	—	Abandonment and burial of Str. 205-1	Strata 4-7, Feat. 5-6	24C/1, 24D/1, 2, 4
2	Str. 205-1-1st	Construction and use of Str.205-1-1st	Units 11-18	24C/2-5, 8, 10, 11,17
3	Str. 205-1-2nd	Construction and use of Str. 205-1-2nd	Units 3-10, Feat. 2-4	24C/6, 9, 12, 16
4	Str. 205-1-3rd	Construction and use of Str. 205-1-3rd	Units 1-2, Feat. 1	24C/14
5	—	Preconstruction deposition of natural soil levels	Strata 1-3	24C/15

Note: Lots 24C/7 and 13 are either so thoroughly disturbed (24C/13) or from such a mixed context (24C/7) that they cannot be unambiguously placed within one time span.

toward the west. On the east, still within Op. 24C, Unit 3 was found overlying the almost identical fill of Str. 205-1-3rd (Unit 2). The dividing line between these two is indistinct but is defined as equal with the preserved top of Unit 1. Over its eastern exposed extent, Unit 3 contains two horizontal bands of slightly more orange-colored earth ranging in thickness between 0.08 and 0.12 m and separated from each other by 0.15-0.17 m. The upper portion of the eastern section of Unit 3, while more or less level, has a shallow depression where it intersects Unit 6 (see below). The meaning of this dip, which truncates the upper orange band of Unit 3, is presently unknown (see Fig. 34).

After the laying down of Unit 3, the three stone steps of Unit 5 were built. These steps, which rest in the uppermost portion of Unit 3, are constructed of river cobbles packed with chinking stones, all set in a hard clay matrix. They range in height from 0.2 to 0.38 m, with the lowest having the greatest preserved height, and rise, in total, 0.78 m over a horizontal distance of 1.03 m. All three steps run the width of Op. 24C (1 m north-south), and are oriented S 24° 0′ E. Immediately underlying the two lowest risers, the fill of Unit 5 consists of densely packed, horizontally laid cobbles, 0.04 by 0.07 to 0.12 by 0.2 m, set in the same hard clay matrix as the facing stones. This stone fill extends down 0.48 m to the base of the lowest step. Underlying the highest step to a depth of 0.33 m and extending back from it for 1.56 m to the east is

another fill element, Unit 4, of fine to moderately coarse, orange-brown clay with an increasing mottling to orange near its base. It serves as a backing to Unit 5 and overlies Unit 3 and the upper 0.33 m of Unit 1. If we accept the top of Unit 5 as the upper limit of this fill, Unit 4 is 0.39-0.47 m thick.

Unit 6, 1.52 m east of Unit 5 and resting 0.12 m above the top of the latter, is a wall 0.47 m high on the west and 0.4 m high on the east, built of river cobbles and small chinking stones set in a clay matrix, and aligned S 24° 0′ E. The absence of a clear floor sealing Unit 4 and connecting Units 5 and 6 makes the inclusion of Unit 6 in this construction stage problematic. Nonetheless, this unit probably functioned as a low step-up to a terrace leading east to the structure's summit.

While the lower 0.13 m of Unit 6 is buried on the east by the brown clay of Unit 3, the upper 0.27 m is backed by a different fill, Unit 7. This element, which buries Unit 3, is a very hard-compacted, gritty orange clay containing many pebbles and carbon flecks. Unit 7 was exposed for a horizontal extent of 1.56 m, over the western 1.01 m of which it maintains a relatively flat upper surface and ranges in thickness between 0.16 and 0.28 m. Unit 8 is on the eastern edge of this relatively even level, 0.53 m east and 0.02 m above the top of Unit 6. Unit 8, much like Unit 6 below it, is a low wall, 0.45 m high by 0.48 m thick, built of coursed cobbles with some chinking stones set in a clay matrix. The core of this wall is solid, flat-laid cobbles with very little earthen matrix. Unit 8 was exposed for a north-south extent of 4.6 m and is oriented S 12° 30' E. Immediately behind (east of) this wall, Unit 7 steps up to the level of the top of Unit 8 and reaches its maximum thickness of 0.6 m. Capping this fill unit and extending back for an exposed distance of 0.85 m from the top of Unit 8 is a level of flat-laid pebbles (Unit 9) 0.02-0.04 m thick, apparently the formal summit floor of Str. 205-1-2nd. The horizontal extent of this surfacing was difficult to determine: it was apparently limited in Op. 24C to the area between Unit 8 and the east excavation margin and from the north trench wall to a point 1.8 m south. It was not found west of Unit 8, nor was it clearly recognized in the Op. 24C southern summit extension.

In sum, Str. 205-1-2nd is a platform c. 1.88 m high on the west and oriented S 24° 0' E to S 12° 30' E, ascended on the west by a series of three stone steps (Unit 5). This stair gives way to an informal earthen surface (Unit 4) which leads east to a low stone step-up (Unit 6). This cobble wall is apparently backed by another earth floor above which stands the final ascending stone wall, Unit 8. This latter element demarcates the west edge of Str. 205-1-2nd's summit, which is surfaced, at least in part, by a thin pebble floor (Unit 9), underlain by a hard earthen fill (Unit 7). No trace of a superstructure was found.

Several additional elements might belong in this construction period. Feature 3 is a 0.39-m-high pile of unmodified river cobbles and a few pebbles set in a clay matrix 1.1 m west of Unit 5. It was found in the north trench wall of Op. 24C and extends only a limited distance south of that point (see Fig. 34). Although badly preserved on its southern edge, this feature may represent the stone retaining wall for a western terrace on the court-facing side of Str. 205-1-2nd, extending 1.42 m into that court. This possibility is suggested by the fact that Feat. 3 rests on the same fill (Unit 3) as the Unit 5 steps. Also, the top of Feat. 3 is 0.08 m below the top of the lowest Unit 5 step, a likely position if it represents the west edge of a terrace added onto Str. 205-1-2nd after Unit 5 was built. The fill unit backing Feat. 3, Unit 10, is a very hard-compacted, gritty orange clay with many included pebbles and carbon flecks, clearly distinct from underlying and overlying fills. Finally, the distinctiveness of this level and its clear association with Feat. 3, overriding Unit 3 and yet not found above the level of the top of the former element, support the existence of a western extension of Str. 205-1-2nd.

Feature 4 is a rough cobble surface that begins 0.48 m west of Feat. 3, at a level about equal to the base of that feature, and extends for 1.62 m into the western limits of Op. 24C. This surface is formed of more or less horizontally laid cobbles set on top of a clay matrix, 0.11 m above the base of Feat. 3. On the west it stands to a preserved height of 0.1 m. The many gaps in this surface and the irregular nature of its eastern edge, which does not form a clear north-south line over the width of Op. 24C, both create difficulties of interpretation. Feature 4 may be the remnant of a small platform that originally fronted Str. 205-1-2nd. Another viable alternative would see this surface as merely a debris level which fell from either Str. 205-1-2nd or some other undiscovered structure to the west. Regardless, the general absence of large stones either on the surface or in natural strata at Las Quebradas suggests that Feat. 4 has a cultural origin.

Feature 4 is placed in this time span because of its elevation and stratigraphic position. If Feat. 3 is associated with Str. 205-1-2nd, then Feat. 4 is at a depth consistent with a surface fronting that construction. Feature 4 is buried by Units 11 and 12, both within the next time span, clearly indicating that it was deposited before the terminal construction phase.

Lots 24C/6, 12, and 16 are from fill units associated with Str. 205-1-2nd: 24C/6 from Unit 7, 24C/12 from Unit 10, and 24C/16 from Unit 4. As with all fill units, it is probable that the included artifacts were deposited earlier elsewhere and redeposited as construction components of Str. 205-1-2nd. Lot 24C/9 consists of material found on the surface of Unit 6 and may represent debris deposited prior to the abandonment of the structure and associated with its use. Some mixing with fill material is, of course, possible.

Time Span 2: After the abandonment of Str. 205-1-2nd, a fill of hard-compacted orange clay (Unit 11), identical in appearance to Unit 10, was laid down west of Feat. 3. This hard clay covers Feat. 4 to a depth of 0.12-0.18 m and buries the basal 0.23 m of Feat. 3. Unit 11 served as the footing for a new court surface of tightly packed pebbles (average 0.02 m in diameter) set in a hard orange clay matrix (Unit 12). This level is 0.1-0.16 m thick and extends for an exposed distance of 3.9 m west of the lowest step of Str. 205-1-1st (Unit 14). Unit 12, with its relatively even upper surface, abuts and incorporates the upper cobbles of Feat. 3 and extends beyond that element for 0.5 m to the east. Unit 12 runs up to, but not under, the construction associated with the last recognized building episode, Str. 205-1-1st.

Rising above Unit 12 to the east is Unit 14, six

reconstructible steps which ascend 1.26 m over a horizontal distance of 2.4 m. The steps are built of river cobbles, usually laid in only one or two rough, horizontal courses, packed with chinking stones and set in an orange-red, gritty clay matrix. The best-preserved element of Unit 14, the basal tier, indicates that the cobbles composing the steps run back under the next riser without using additional slabs for treads. The lowest step possesses the largest cobbles, 0.2 by 0.27 to 0.17 by 0.38 m, with one measuring 0.53 m long. In the upper steps the facing cobbles average 0.06-0.12 m thick and 0.11-0.27 m long. The fifth reconstructed step is an exception to this, being constructed of very large (0.38 m long by 0.22 m thick) cobbles. Unfortunately, this step is so poorly preserved that its precise mode of construction cannot be ascertained. Step heights vary between 0.16 and 0.26 m, and the widths of the better-preserved lower three treads run 0.14-0.4 m, with the lowest step being the widest. Four of the six risers are set directly into the earthen fill of Unit 13. The two exceptions are the lowest riser, which rests on the hard orange clay of Unit 10, and the fourth step, which sits on a dense packing of horizontally laid cobbles c. 0.34 m thick. Owing to postabandonment disturbance in the south wall of the trench, only the lowest Unit 14 step presents a clear alignment of S 7° 0′ E, but the fragments of the other steps appear to conform to this orientation. Surface remains suggest that the Unit 14 steps continue for the full length of Str. 205-1-1st's west face, creating a series of long, low, and narrow terraces ascending to the summit. The result is a system like that produced by the more common step-terrace approach, but without the slab treads associated with the latter.

Unit 13 underlies Unit 14 and buries Units 4, 5, 6, and 10. This fill, very similar in composition to the earlier-deposited Unit 4 earth, is of a moderately gritty, hard-packed, orange-brown clay with very few pebble inclusions. This rather extensive unit, which ranges in thickness below the aforementioned steps from 0.08 to 0.3 m, serves not only as a foundation for the Unit 14 steps, but also as the surface that runs between the steps and the next major stone riser, Unit 15.

Unit 15, 1.09 m east of Unit 14, is a 0.77-m-high by 0.52-m-thick cobble and chinking-stone wall, which functions as the principal western retaining wall for Str. 205-1-1st's summit. This element is built of large, unmodified river cobbles set in horizontal courses, stabilized with small spalls and set in a hard clay matrix. In section, the facing cobbles on both the east and west sides extend 0.15-0.25 m into a core composed primarily of a hard clay with pebble inclusions. At its base three large cobbles make for a stable foundation. Unit 15 was exposed for a total horizontal distance of 5 m; it is much better preserved in the north than to the south and displays an alignment of S 11° 0′ E. Unit 15 rises slightly toward the center of its exposed north-south extent. The significance of this higher elevation is unknown. It may be merely an accident of preservation. A large amount of tumbled stone debris was found in the area of the rise, however, much more than was recovered elsewhere deriving from Unit 15. This increase in architectural collapse suggests that Unit 15 may have stood much higher here and could have been associated with a superstructure.

Underlying Unit 15 to a depth of 0.05-0.07 m is the orange-brown clay fill of Unit 13, which buries the earlier summit construction of Str. 205-1-2nd and extends eastward at a variable depth of 0.28-0.5 m to the limits of Op. 24C. While it seems likely that a summit flooring once existed, its proximity to the current ground surface has resulted in the loss of any trace of such a construction.

On the east, in Op. 24D, three elements were uncovered which probably belong to this construction stage. The first of these is Unit 16, a very hard-packed, orange-red, gritty clay with many pebbles, very closely resembling other fill units exposed in Op. 24C (Units 7, 10, and 11). It is an artificial fill laid atop the naturally deposited Stratum 3. Unit 16 slopes down rapidly from west to east, dropping 0.43 m over a distance of 0.86 m.

Set on this hard clay level is Unit 18, a poorly preserved vertical wall which marks the eastern limits of Str. 205-1-1st. Unit 18 is built of large (0.28-0.36 m long), horizontally laid river cobbles packed with some spalls, stacked vertically to form the wall's basal courses. Above these basal stones are other sizable unfaced rocks, most of which, however, are out of position and tumbled to the east. The Unit 18 stones are set in a hard clay matrix. Behind Unit 18 to the west is a densely packed fill of horizontally laid large cobbles, 0.11 by 0.23 to 0.09 by 0.2 m, and pebbles set in a clay matrix (Unit 17). Given the height to which Unit 17 rises and the distribution of Unit 18 stones, both *in situ* and tumbled, it would appear that Unit 18 once stood to a height of at least 0.7 m. There is no evidence that Unit 18 was terraced, and it probably reached this height in one step.

In sum, Str. 205-1-1st is 1.9 m high on the west and 2.52 m high on the east, 10.3 m wide, and oriented between S 7° 0′ E and S 11° 0′ E. On the side facing the south court, the structure is fronted for a distance of at least 3.9 m by a densely packed pebble surface (Unit 12) set above a hard clay fill (Unit 11). The western side of Str. 205-1-1st is faced by six narrow steps (Unit 14) that rise to a summit, delimited on the west by a high cobble and chinking-stone wall (Unit 15). Intervening between Units 14 and 15 and backing Unit 15 to the east is the orange-brown clay fill of Unit 13, which also acts as a foundation for Units 14 and 15. No trace of a superstructure, not even a paved floor, is found on top of Str. 205-1-1st. On the east, the structure is built up by means of a high cobble wall, which may have risen in one ascent to the summit level or have been part of a more complex terrace system, now largely destroyed. In contrast to the western side, where earthen fill was used almost exclusively, fill on the east seems to have been, in part, of flat-laid cobbles underlain by hard-packed clay (Units 16 and 17). The increased strain on construction caused by this attempt to build in high vertical increments using only unfaced stones may have led to a change in fill composition here. No formalized floor was discerned in this area leading east from Unit 18.

Because Op. 24C and D were never joined, no direct stratigraphic links were established between the eastern and western units. Units 11-15 on the one hand and Units 16-18 on the other are included as part of Str. 205-1-1st since they all represent construction that would have been exposed during the terminal period of Str. 205-1-1st's use; i.e., neither set is buried by later architecture. Thus it remains possible, if not likely, that the eastern and western sets of units were constructed at different times.

Lots 24C/3-5, 8, and 10-11 are all derived from earthen fill associated with Str. 205-1-1st and hence were deposited during T.S. 2. The same caveats noted earlier concerning the contemporaneity of artifacts found in fill with their associated construction pertain here. Lot 24C/17 was found in the stone and clay core of Unit 15 and was probably redeposited in T.S. 2. Finally, Lot 24C/2 consists of material recovered from the top of Unit 12, the western plaza surface. These artifacts, found directly on construction belonging to the final building phase, and buried beneath terminal architectural debris (Feat. 5), are interpreted as debris jettisoned during the use of Str. 205-1-1st that has suffered little subsequent disturbance.

Time Span 1: After the abandonment of Str. 205-1-1st, construction was partially buried by naturally deposited strata. On the west, in Op. 24C, the lower four steps of Unit 14 and all of Unit 12 are covered by Stratum 4, a fine-textured brown clay that reaches a maximum thickness of 0.49 m. Stratum 4's eastern counterpart is Stratum 5, a gritty brown clay exposed in Op. 24D. Both of these soil levels slope up markedly toward construction. Overlying them are the humus horizons of Strata 6 and 7, both of dark brown-black clay that varies in thickness between 0.05 and 0.1 m and caps construction.

Within all these postoccupation levels a relatively dense concentration of tumbled stone architectural debris was found. On the west, this collapse is represented by Feat. 5, while on the east it is seen in Feat. 6. The stones in both of these elements, usually large river cobbles, slant away from construction. In general, the density of tumbled debris decreases with increasing distance away from Str. 205-1-1st. On the west, the Feat. 5 stones lie immediately atop the stone surface of Unit 12, indicating that collapse began soon after abandonment, before significant soil deposition had taken place. On the east, Feat. 6 derives from the Unit 18 wall and the fill found behind it (Unit 17). On the west, the bad state of repair of most of the Unit 14 steps and the fact that the stones of Feat. 5 were found only west of this unit suggest that Feat. 5 represents the collapse of these steps.

It should be noted that there is little evidence of postabandonment occupation of Str. 205-1, and no reason to doubt that Strata 4-7 were naturally deposited.

Lots 24C/1 and D/1, 2, and 4, all derived from the aforementioned strata, represent T.S. 1. It seems probable that the items in these lots originally derived from the nearby area, probably from Str. 205-1-1st itself. This interpretation is based on both the proximity of Str. 205-1-1st and the association of these artifacts with the stone tumble interpreted as having come from the gradual collapse of the building. These four lots probably thus represent terminal Str. 205-1 occupation debris redeposited in the immediate area of the structure after abandonment.

STRUCTURE 205-41 (Figs. 35-38)

Structure 205-41, the c. 3.52-m-high construction which closes off the western side of the north court in the West Group's main group, was investigated in 1978 by means of three trenches (Op. 24E-G). Operation 24E was a trench 1.1-1.6 m north-south by 10.76 m east-west, set on the approximate axis of the

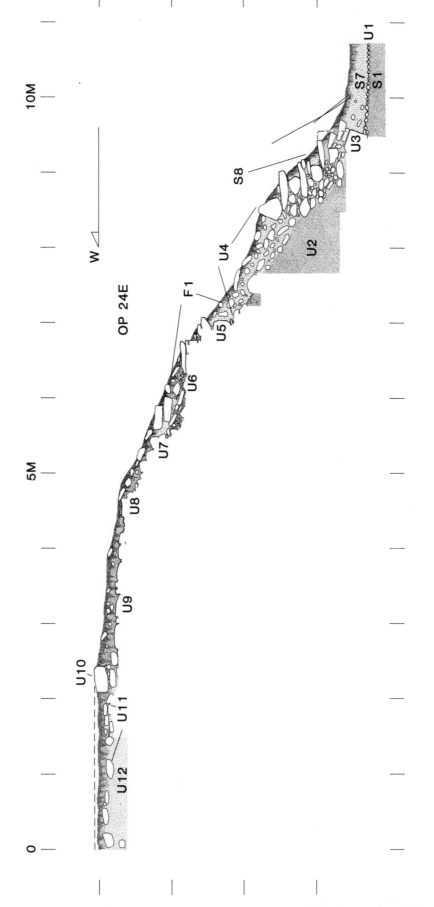

Figure 35. Str. 205-41, Op 24E, Section.

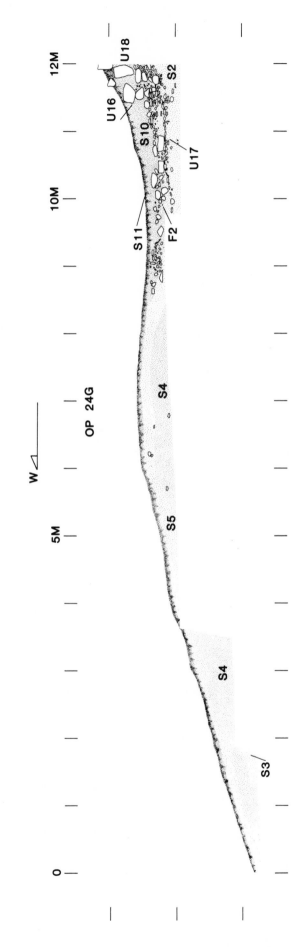

Figure 36. Str. 205-41, Op 24G, Section.

0   4M

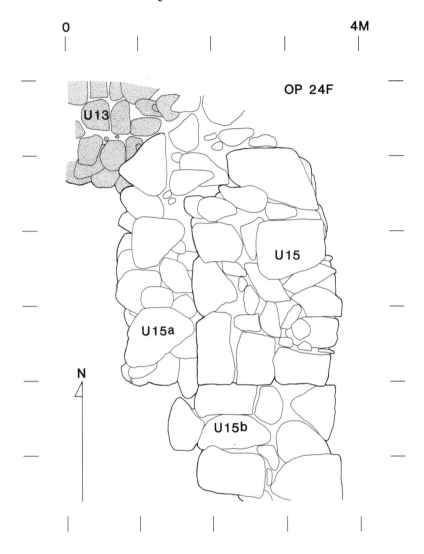

OP 24F

U13

U15

U15a

U15b

N

Figure 37a.   Str. 205-41, Plan.

structure's east face. As a result of the general project goals, Op. 24E was carried down 0.48 m in front of (east of) construction, for a distance of 1.8 m westward into architectural fill, and to a maximum depth of 1.4 m below ground surface in that unit.

Operation 24G was a trench 1.5 m north-south by 12 m east-west, dug against the west, noncourt-facing side of Str. 205-41 and bisecting Str. 205-49. The specific purpose of this excavation was both to expose terminal-phase architecture on the rear of the structure and to locate a trash deposit associated with its final period of use. Following from these and the more general project goals, Op. 24G was carried down to a maximum depth of 1.11 m below ground surface in the immediate area of Str. 205-41, although, by and

large, the depth of this excavation varied between 0.35 and 0.65 m. No attempt was made to penetrate construction fill. The trench was extended for a considerable distance to the west once it became clear that a rise in this area (formerly designated Str. 205-49) was part of an extensive midden associated with Str. 205-41.

Operation 24F was opened in order to investigate an architectural feature commonly found on the summits of the larger monumental structures at both Las Quebradas and the other valley sites: a roughly square element, flush with the summit surface, composed of tightly packed cobbles (see Chap. 2). The feature this excavation was designed to explore measures 2.05-2.15 m east-west by 3.1 m north-south.

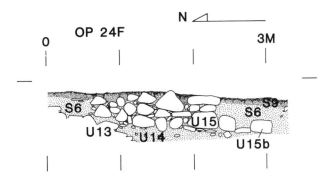

Figure 37b.   Str. 205-41, Section.

Excavation Lots: A total of 4435 sherds, 97 censer fragments, 155 pieces of obsidian, 72 *bajareque* pieces, five ground stone tool fragments, and 16 figurine fragments were collected from the 20 lots defined in Op. 24E-G. Of these, 13 are from terminal debris contexts, two are from fill, four derive from preoccupation levels, and one consists of material missed during excavations but retrieved from backdirt (see Table 3.23).

Time Span 4: The initial set of activities revealed in the Str. 205-41 area involved the deposition of Strata 1 and 2 on the east and west sides of the structure, respectively. Stratum 1, uncovered for a distance of 1.24 m east of construction, underlies Str. 205-41 (Unit 1, see below). Stratum 2, also found beneath exposed construction, is a fine-textured, densely packed, greasy, very dark reddish brown clay with very few inclusions, exposed for an east-west distance of 2.18 m. The large number of artifacts recovered from Stratum 2 (Lots 24G/3-4) is commensurate with the interpretation of this level as a terminal preconstruction occupation surface (the dark reddish brown color of Stratum 2 bolsters this interpretation, as this hue is documented in association with areas of eroded *bajareque*; see below, Unit 9). Stratum 1, on the other hand, with its relatively few included artifacts (Lots 24E/6-7), apparently represents a ground surface without the same intensity of occupation as its western counterpart. There is no reason to believe that either of these levels was deposited by other than natural forces. Neither stratum was exposed to its full depth: Stratum 1's exposed thickness is 0.22 m, while Stratum 2's is 0.1-0.19 m. Both also exhibit a fairly even upper surface, although Stratum 2 slopes down slightly to the west (Fig. 35).

Lots 24E/6-7 and G/3-4 derive from these two soil levels. The fact that Strata 1 and 2 are sealed by the Units 1 and 17 floors helps to minimize chances of possible mixing of material.

Time Span 3: Structure 205-41 is built on the aforementioned strata. As was the case with Str. 205-1-1st to the southeast, Str. 205-41 exhibits different construction styles on its eastern and western faces. On the east, the platform was built by means of a series of 11 (postulated) step-terraces divided into five separate units (Units 3-7) (see Fig. 35). Unit 3 consists of five terraces, each 0.28-0.3 m high and 0.24-0.35 m wide. Each riser has a single horizontal course of large, unmodified cobbles, packed with chinking pebbles and set into a clay mortar. Surmounting these low stone walls are flat-laid slabs, mostly of schist, which form the terrace treads. These slabs run back under the next ascending riser and are tenoned into the underlying fill. Excavation through the exterior face of Unit 3 revealed that these terraces are supported to a depth of 0.32-0.36 m by a level of densely packed cobbles and pebbles set in a hard clay matrix. This stone packing slopes upward to the west, following the ascending line of the Unit 3 terraces. Below this is a unit of hard-compacted, bright orange clay with many pebble inclusions, ranging in exposed thickness from 0.02 to 1.03 m (Unit 2). This clay level functions as the foundation for much of the Str. 205-41 construction (see Unit 12, below). Unit 3 rises a total of 1.58 m over a horizontal distance of 1.31 m and is oriented S 8° 30' E.

Above Unit 3, construction is very disturbed and the existence of a broad terrace (Unit 4) is hypothetically reconstructed. This break in the pattern of the lower narrow terraces is postulated because it is the most adequate way to link Unit 3 and the higher construction of Unit 5 (see Fig. 35). The incorporation of this broad terrace, which would have been 1.24 m wide and 0.3 m high, into an otherwise low and narrow

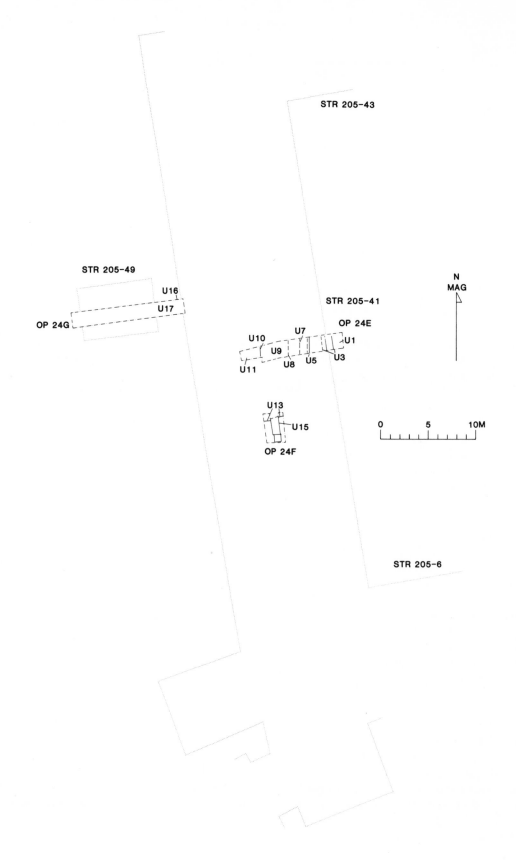

STR 205-43

STR 205-49

U16
U17
OP 24G

N
MAG

STR 205-41

OP 24E

U10   U7
U9   U1
U8 U5   U3
U11

U13
U15

OP 24F

0   5   10M

STR 205-6

Figure 38.   Str. 205-41, Plan.

TABLE 3.23

EXCAVATION SUMMARY

Lot #	Contents	Depositional Significance	Provenience
24E/1	Lost	Terminal occupation debris (secondary)	Within Stratum 7, E of Unit 3
24E/2	15 sherds; 3 pcs. obsidian	Terminal occupation debris (secondary)	Within Strata 7 and 8 and Feat. 1, above Units 1 and 3
24E/3	24 sherds; 2 censer frags.; 1 pc. obsidian	Terminal occupation debris (primary)	Resting directly on Unit 1, buried by Stratum 7
24E/4	29 sherds; 2 pcs. obsidian	Fill	Within Unit 2
24E/5	21 sherds; 4 pcs. obsidian	Terminal occupation debris (secondary)	Within Stratum 8, above units 5-7
24E/6	50 sherds	Preconstruction debris (secondary)	Within Stratum 1, 0.1 m below Unit 1
24E/7	5 sherds	Preconstruction debris (secondary)	Within Stratum 1, 0.1-0.23 m below Unit 1
24F/1	88 sherds; 7 censer frags.; 9 pcs. obsidian; 11 *bajareque* frags.	Terminal occupation debris (secondary)	Within Strata 6 and 9, above and around Unit 10
24F/2	64 sherds; 5 *bajareque* frags.	Fill	Within Unit 10
24G/1	67 sherds; 7 censer frags.; 1 pc. obsidian	Terminal occupation debris (secondary)	Within Stratum 10 and Feat. 2 immediately W of Unit 12 and above Unit 13
24G/2	688 sherds; 23 censer frags.; 2 figurine frags.; 10 pcs. obsidian; 3 metate frags.; 7 *bajareque* frags.	Terminal occupation debris (primary)	Directly atop Unit 13, buried by Feat. 2 and Stratum 10
24G/3	324 sherds; 8 censer frags.; 2 figurine frags.; 15 pcs. obsidian; 1 metate frag.; 4 *bajareque* frags.	Preconstruction occupation debris (primary)	Within Stratum 2, to 0.1 m below Unit 13
24G/4	284 sherds; 6 censer frags.	Preconstruction occupation debris (primary)	Within Stratum 2, 0.1-0.18 m below Unit 13
24G/5	193 sherds; 7 censer frags.; 10 pcs. obsidian	Terminal occupation debris (secondary)	Within Strata 10-11, W and above level of Unit 17, 1.4-2.4 m W of Unit 16
24G/6	419 sherds; 6 censer frags.; 2 figurine frags.; 3 pcs. obsidian; 1 *bajareque* frag.	Terminal occupation debris (secondary)	Within Strata 10-11, above Feat. 2, 2.6-3 m W of Unit 16
24G/7	246 sherds; 3 censer frags.; 2 figurine frags.; 9 pcs. obsidian	Terminal occupation debris (secondary)	Within Feat. 2, W of Unit 17, 1.4-3 m W of Unit 16
24G/8	1277 sherds; 18 censer frags.; 5 figurine frags.; 56 pcs. obsidian; 40 *bajareque* frags.	Terminal occupation debris (primary)	Within Strata 4-5 and 11, W of Feat. 2, 2.8-7.78 m W of Unit 16 (Midden 1)
24G/9	37 sherds; 12 pcs. obsidian; 1 mano frag.	Terminal occupation debris (primary)	Within Strata 3-5 and 11, 9.55-11.6 m W of Unit 16 (Midden 1)
24G/10	574 sherds; 10 censer frags.; 3 figurine frags.; 19 pcs. obsidian; 3 *bajareque* frags.	Terminal occupation debris (primary)	Within Strata 4-5 and 11, 7.78-9.55 m W of Unit 16 (Midden 1)
24G/11	30 sherds; 1 pc. obsidian; 1 *bajareque* frag.	None	Backdirt

Note: All *bajareque* counts include only those fragments which were large or interesting enough to save.

TABLE 3.24

STRUCTURAL/DEPOSITIONAL SUMMARY TIME SPANS: 1-4

Time Span	Construction Stage	Activity	Features	Lots
1	—	Abandonment and burial of Str. 205-41	Strata 6-11, Feat. 1-2	24E/1, 2, 5, 24F/1, 24G/1, 5-7
2	Str. 205-41	Use of Str. 205-41	Strata 3-5 (Midden 1)	24E/3, 24G/2, 8-10
3	Str. 205-41	Construction and modification of Str. 205-41	Units 1-18	24E/4, 24F/2
4	—	Preconstruction occupation debris	Strata 1-2	24E/6-7, 24G/3-4

step-terrace system has precedent as revealed in excavations at both Playitas (Str. 200-77) and Choco (Str. 212-4-2nd and -1st). The underlying fill of Unit 2 continues upslope beneath Unit 4 at the same angle as below Unit 3, although the close packing of horizontally laid stones found beneath the Unit 3 terraces is not in evidence here. Instead, the stones found in the Unit 4 area slant downward and are more dispersed.

Rising above Unit 4 are the two step-terraces of Unit 5, constructed in the same manner as Unit 3; they range in height from 0.28 to 0.45 m and the lower of the two is 0.3 m wide. In total, Unit 5 rises 0.73 m over a distance of 0.7 m. Extending back from Unit 5 is a broad surface, Unit 6. This terrace, 1.15 m wide, is built of flat-laid cobbles set in a clay matrix extending to the west from, and at the same level as, the stone slabs of the upper Unit 5 step.

The area between Unit 6 and the next recognizable architectural element (Unit 8) is severely disturbed and hence poorly understood. Presumably some form of step-terracing continued in this area, although no clear evidence of it was recovered. Based on the average heights and widths of the Units 3 and 5 terraces, three low narrow steps (Unit 7) are postulated to fill this void. These terraces would have risen 0.69 m over a horizontal distance of 0.86 m.

Unit 8 is a 0.15-m-high wall that rises above the putative Unit 7 and marks the eastern limit of the Str. 205-41 summit. This wall is built of unfaced river cobbles set in two rough horizontal courses, packed with pebbles and laid in a clay matrix. Unfortunately, tree-root activity on the summit has disrupted the north-south line of Unit 8, so that the wall is clearly preserved over only a portion of its total length and no clear orientation could be obtained.

In sum, Units 3-8 represent a step-terrace system, broken at intervals by two postulated broader surfaces, which rises 3.44 m over an east-west distance of 4.88 m to the summit of Str. 205-41. The orientation of this system, based on the two best-preserved components, Units 3 and 5, is between S 0° 30′ E and S 8° 30′ E. Surface indications are that these terraces run the entire length of the structure's east side and link up with their counterparts on the adjoining Str. 205-6 and -43 to form a court enclosed by a series of continuous, low, narrow terraces.

On the summit of Str. 205-41 in Op. 24E is a floor of flat-laid river cobbles and slabs, 0.11 by 0.12 to 0.25 by 0.35 m, set in a clay matrix (Unit 9). This surface extends westward from its original eastern limit (Unit 8) at a relatively even level for a distance of 1.99 m, at which point a 0.3-m-high step-up is encountered (Unit 10). This step-up, oriented S 2° 30′ E, is constructed of two horizontal courses of river cobbles, their interstices filled with pebbles, set in a clay matrix that rests on Unit 9. These cobbles extend for the entire 0.35-m width of this low rise. No construction core was noted in the center of Unit 10. To the west of this rise is a very uneven level of cobbles and small pebbles (Unit 11) which may represent the remains of a floor originally associated with Unit 10. When discovered in 1978, this level was most clearly represented within 0.73 m of Unit 10, after which the constituent stones became more dispersed. The surface of Unit 11 is 0.12 m below the top of Unit 10, while its base is 0.03-0.1 m above the bottom of the latter unit. Unit 11 is probably best interpreted as the remains of a stone foundation c. 0.2 m thick for a formal surface that ran back from the top of the Unit 10 step-up.

As can be seen in Fig. 35, Unit 11 rests on a very hard-compacted, bright orange clay with many pebble inclusions (Unit 12). This fill unit, exposed to a depth of 0.26-0.29 m, is very similar in composition to the hard clay fill underlying the lower Unit 3 step-terraces (Unit 2).

To the south, further evidence of Str. 205-41's summit construction was unearthed in Op. 24F. Here, a 0.48-m-high wall aligned c. S 77° 30' W was found (Unit 13). This wall is built of river cobbles, 0.12 by 0.2 to 0.2 by 0.2 m, set in a clay matrix and placed in a series of four steps 0.08-0.14 m high rising to the north (see Figs. 37 and 38). The widths of these low risers are 0.11-0.32 m, and their treads are not formalized by the use of stone slabs as with the Units 3 and 5 step-terraces. Rather, the cobbles forming the step faces also serve as tread surfaces. In all, Unit 13 rises to a height of 0.41 m over a horizontal distance of 1.15 m. No evidence of an occupation surface, formalized or otherwise, was noted south of Unit 13. It would appear that this low wall is the southern edge of a summit platform whose constituent parts to the north are preserved as Units 8-11 (exposed in Op. 24E). This interpretation, in the absence of an established stratigraphic link between the elements involved, is based on logic and elevations. The surfaces of Units 9 and 11 must have had a southern edge, and, as they were not found south of Unit 13, this latter unit may have functioned as their southern limit. Furthermore, the elevation of the exposed top of Unit 13 is only 0.13 m lower than that of the top of Unit 9, again supporting the proposed interpretation.

Built over the southern 0.49 m of Unit 13 is Unit 15, a later addition to the Str. 205-41 summit. This element does not rest directly on Unit 13 (Fig. 37), but is set onto a level of hard-compacted, reddish brown clay with many pebble inclusions (Unit 14). This fill unit, which underlies Unit 15 over its exposed north-south length, is similar in color and composition to the Units 2 and 12 clay fills exposed in Op. 24E. The uncovered thickness of Unit 14 is between 0.04 m and 0.19 m. Unit 15, itself, was originally a block of tightly packed cobbles 1.76 m north-south by 0.85 m east-west, the gaps between the stones filled with pebbles and a clay mortar. It stands 0.48-0.52 m high over most of its length, except where it steps up over Unit 13, where it is reduced to 0.29-0.32 m in height. Unit 15 is built of river cobbles set in roughly horizontal courses, with their flattest sides facing outward and with pebbles set into the interstices (Fig. 37). Its western and southern sides form very straight lines, so

much so that several of the stones might have been faced, especially those at the southwest corner. The eastern and northern sides are less clearly delimited. The top of Unit 15 is relatively flat, while its base slopes down very gradually to the south.

At some point after Unit 15 was built, two rough additions were made on the south and west (Units 15a and 15b respectively). Unit 15a is a level of large river cobbles, 0.22 by 0.49 to 0.3 by 0.36 m, extending 0.74 m south of Unit 15. This unit stands only one stone high, an average of 0.17-0.2 m, and is set on a level equivalent to the base of Unit 15 at this point (see Fig. 37). The Unit 14 clay fill that supports Unit 15 also runs under Unit 15a. In width, the latter element is coterminous with Unit 15 to the north. The stones employed in Unit 15a construction are much rougher than those delimiting the western and southern sides of Unit 15; as a result, Unit 15a's alignment is less clearly defined. The summit and base of Unit 15a slope down gradually from north to south.

On the west, Unit 15b extends 0.5-0.53 m from Unit 15. Unlike Unit 15a, the western addition stands to a preserved height of 0.48-0.52 m, roughly equivalent to Unit 15. Unit 15b is constructed of very roughly coursed river cobbles packed with chinking stones set in a clay matrix; it overrides Unit 13 to the same extent as does Unit 15, and is supported by the clay fill of Unit 14. The west-facing exterior wall of Unit 15b is not as well faced as its counterpart in Unit 15, and the stones used are much more irregular in shape.

In general, including both of its later additions, Unit 15 measures 1.52 m east-west by 2.47 m north-south and is oriented S 11° 0'E. Undoubtedly this complex of elements served as a base of an architectural feature which has since collapsed. Masonry construction seems unlikely given the lack of large numbers of obviously tumbled stones in the immediate vicinity. On the other hand, the sizable quantities of *bajareque* fragments found in Op. 24F suggest that this material might have been used in the summit construction for which Units 15-15b served as a foundation. It is likely that the Unit 15 complex was a stone base for a perishable pillar, now disappeared. Additional "pillar bases" may have been located across the summit of Str. 205-41, as part of the Str. 205-41 superstructure.

The western basal wall of Str. 205-41 (Unit 16) was revealed in Op. 24G, but because of postoccupation disturbance, it was not clearly defined (Fig. 36). Unit 16 consists of unmodified river cobbles (three remain in their original vertical alignment) underlain by a level of pebbles and schist slabs. The latter may have served as stabilizers for the upper wall construction. Unit 16 stands to a preserved height of 0.56 m and is 0.18-0.28 m thick. No evidence of a step-terrace system was noted here, and it is not clear how the west side of Str. 205-41 was constructed.

To the east stone fill, exposed for a horizontal distance of 0.32 m (Unit 18), consists of horizontally laid cobbles and pebbles in a clay matrix. Both Units 16 and 18 rest on the same dark reddish brown clay of Stratum 2. A second, vertical line of stones 0.36 m high was noted 0.07 m east of Unit 16 within this fill, serving as either a fill-retaining wall or the foundation for a now-destroyed higher construction.

Extending to the east and west of Str. 205-41 are two thin pebble surfaces, Units 1 and 17 respectively. Each of these is a single layer of pebbles 0.02-0.04 m thick. On the east, Unit 1 runs evenly over its exposed distance of 1.22 m and abuts the basal step-terrace of Unit 3. Unit 17 on the west proved more difficult to recognize, though it appears to run up to but not under the basal wall of Str. 205-41 (Unit 16). Unlike its eastern counterpart, Unit 17 is not level over its exposed extent but slopes down gradually to the west. Unit 17 also becomes less clearly defined and more uneven as it moves away from Unit 16, and it disappears entirely at c. 2.2 m west of the Str. 205-41 basal wall in Op. 24G.

Despite the lack of direct stratigraphic ties linking the units exposed in Op. 24E-G, all are included within the same construction stage since, with the partial exception of Units 13 and 15, no evidence was recovered to indicate that any of the exposed entities had been obscured by later construction. While it cannot be established that all of the uncovered units were built at the same time, it is clear that they were all in use during this time span, and functioned as integral parts of Str. 205-41.

On the summit, in Op. 24F, we have a clear case of multiple construction periods. Here Unit 13 is buried by the hard reddish brown fill of Unit 14, which in turn supports Unit 15. Obviously, Unit 13 was constructed before the modifications represented by Units 14-15 were initiated. Once built, Unit 15 itself was modified by small additions to its southern and western sides (Units 15a and b). The time elapsed between these different activities is unknown, although it does appear that the Units 14-15 complex is part of the same construction stage as Unit 13. Thus while a sequence of building activities is recognized here, their magnitude does not warrant the definition of a new construction stage.

Lots 24E/4 and G/2 were deposited during the construction of Str. 205-41. It is recognized, however, that this material was most probably redeposited from another source. There is, therefore, a difference in time between its period of use and the interval when it was incorporated into construction.

Time Span 2: Strata 3-5 were deposited after this period of building activity. Exposed in Op. 24G c. 2.68 m west of Unit 16, these three earth levels, because of the large numbers of artifacts they contained (Lots 24G/8-10), are interpreted as composing a midden (Midden 1) associated with the use of Str. 205-41. The lowest of the three earth levels, Stratum 3, was exposed to a depth of 0.16 m and a width of 0.52 m in the western portion of the trench. This level is a softly compacted, light red to orange greasy clay. Above it is Stratum 4, a very similar element differing only in its much more compact texture and slightly darker red color. This soil level extends in discontinuously exposed segments for a distance of 8.04 m, over which it rises 1.64 m from west to east. Its exposed thickness varies between 0.2 and 0.6 m. The uppermost of these three midden components, Stratum 5, resembles its lower counterparts and is distinguished from Stratum 4 only by its less firmly compacted texture. Stratum 5, exposed over a horizontal extent of 8.23 m, rises 1.8 m from west to east and is 0.05-0.22 m thick. Throughout all of these levels, very few stones are found. Together, Strata 3-5 form a low mound (the center of which was originally mapped as Str. 205-49) with a very gradual eastern rise and a more precipitous western slope. In fact, the midden was apparently deposited over a natural drop-off from east to west, though no clear trace of the original ground surface was located. It is also very likely that Strata 3-5 once formed parts of a single soil level, in which minor differentiations have developed as a result of postdepositional processes. In general, artifact densities within Midden 1 decrease toward the west, away from Str. 205-41, and with increasing depth, although sterile soil was not reached. This pattern suggests that the origin of the midden material is Str. 205-41. Structure 205-49, therefore, is now perceived as merely a mound of occupation debris and not a purposeful construction.

In summary, both the east and west sides of Str. 205-41 are flanked by a thin pebble surface. Rising above this floor on the east is a series of step-terraces, interspersed with two broader levels, that provide access to the summit. Summit construction appears to have been quite complex and is not fully understood. At least a part of this surface was paved with river cobbles (Unit 9). Unit 9 steps up to a slightly higher floor (Units 10 and 11) on the western summit edge in Op. 24E. Similarly, it is very probable that not all of the summit surface was paved: south of Unit 13 in Op. 24F no formalized surface was noted, and construction (Unit 15) rests directly on a clay level. Finally, at some point in the remodeling of Str. 205-41, cobble plinths that probably supported perishable pillars were added. The one excavated plinth was on the southern edge of the summit. How all of these elements were integrated into a single functioning superstructure remains unclear. What is obvious, however, is that the Str. 205-41 platform was erected to support a building that incorporated several different construction materials, including *bajareque*, river cobbles, and stone slabs. *Bajareque* probably played a large part in the summit construction, serving as the upper wall material set on stone foundations (large amounts of this material were in the Op. 24F summit excavation and in Midden 1 to the west).

The western flank of this substructure was probably constructed of a number of vertical cobble terraces of which only the lowest was recognized. Unfortunately, little is known of this side because of the poor state of preservation. During its final period of use, Str. 205-41 was 15.5 m wide, 3.52 m high, and oriented c. S 8° 30′ E.

While Str. 205-41 was in use, the trash resulting from its occupation was deposited off the back (west) in an extensive deposit (Midden 1). Strata 3-5, constituting Midden 1, are included in a single time span despite their vertically sequential position since the large numbers of artifacts recovered from these levels, Strata 4-5 especially, indicate that they were deposited at about the same time. The association of these levels and their artifacts with the use of Str. 205-41 is more difficult to establish and is based on several lines of indirect evidence. First, the artifacts increase markedly in density toward the structure, indicating that their original source was in this direction. Second, the exposed base of the deposit 2.6-8.8 m west of Unit 16 is at the same level as the Unit 17 floor. Finally, it is reasonable that the debris disposed of by the residents of this large platform would have been jettisoned off the back. It now appears that Str. 205-49 is not an actual platform but a rise formed as the result of midden accumulation.

Lots 24E/3 and G/2 are defined for materials found

directly atop the Units 1 and 17 floors respectively. Given this position, the included artifacts must have been deposited after the construction of these surfaces, and yet prior to the period of abandonment represented by the overlying Stratum 7 and Feat. 2. Lots 24G/8-10 were part of Midden 1 within Strata 3-5.

Time Span 1: Following this period of construction and use the structure was abandoned and no longer maintained. During this postabandonment period, Strata 6-11 were deposited along with Feat. 1 and 2. Stratum 7 is a fine-textured, orange-brown clay which buries the Unit 1 floor on the structure's east side to a depth of 0.14-0.28 m and slopes down from the west, where it covers portions of all the Unit 3 step-terraces. Stratum 7 was exposed over a horizontal distance of 2.08 m and does not continue upslope beyond the Unit 3 terraces. The counterpart to Stratum 7 on the west is Stratum 10, a medium-coarse, very dark brown clay. This soil level buries the lower 0.3 m of Unit 16 and continues east of that wall over the Unit 18 fill to a depth of 0.31 m. On the west, Stratum 10 overlies Feat. 2, the stone debris issuing from Str. 205-41, to depths of 0.02-0.28 m. On the summit, in Op. 24F, a hard-compacted, reddish brown clay with pebble inclusions, identical to the fill of Unit 14, buries the Unit 15 complex, extending from its base to just 0.09 m below its summit (Stratum 6). Stratum 6 also covers Unit 13 on the north to a depth of 0.12-0.24 m.

Features 1 and 2 were also deposited in T.S. 1. Both of these levels consist of tumbled stone debris from Str. 205-41. On the east, Feat. 1 is found in a deposit 0.36-0.48 m thick, sloping down over Units 4-8; very little debris was noted either on the summit or over Units 1-3. On the west, Feat. 2 is much more densely packed than Feat. 1. Here, a level 0.14-0.2 m thick, of cobbles and pebbles mixed with a fine-textured, greasy, dark reddish brown clay, rests on the Unit 17 floor. Most of these stones lie horizontally on this unit. Feature 2 extends for 2.83 m to the west of Unit 16. Stratum 6 may also have contained a tumbled debris level. This soil is a much deeper red than any of the other terminal strata uncovered in Op. 24E-G. Its unique coloration may be due to the large quantity of *bajareque* found around Unit 5—*bajareque* that may have stained this unit or may itself have been its principal component.

Capping these three levels are the ubiquitous humus horizons (Strata 8, 9, and 11), all three of dark brown to black clay. On the east, topping all construction, Stratum 8 extends upslope for the entire length

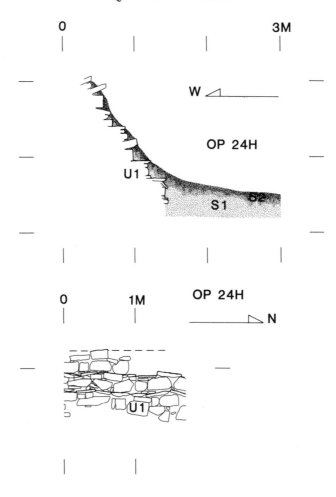

Figure 39.   Str. 205-14, Op 24H, Profile and Elevation.

of the trench, varying in thickness between 0.04 and 0.2 m. On the west, Stratum 11 also runs the entire 12-m length of Op. 24G, ranging between 0.03 and 0.13 m thick. Finally, on the summit in Op. 24F, Stratum 9, although not clearly defined, overlies both Stratum 6 and Unit 15 to a depth of 0.06-0.12 m.

Lots 24E/2 and 5, F/1, and G/1 and 5-7 are associated with these postabandonment strata and features. While this cultural material was deposited in T.S. 1, seemingly by the same natural forces that produced Strata 6-11, it probably originated in the preceding time spans. This interpretation is suggested by the large number of artifacts and their proximity to Str. 205-41.

SOUTH PLAZA, STRUCTURE 205-14 (Fig. 39)

Structure 205-14, the 4-m-high construction closing off the western side of the south plaza, was briefly investigated in 1978 by means of a single trench, Op. 24H. This excavation measured 1.6 m north-south by 2.6 m east-west, was placed on the approximate axis of the structure's east side, and was designed primarily to expose terminal construction levels. Surface remains suggested that the eastern terraces of this structure represented some of the best-preserved examples of the step-terrace mode of construction, which, although common at Las Quebradas, was rarely found in a good state of repair. Up to this time, only monumental structures facing closed courts had been investigated and it was felt that a plaza-oriented structure should be sampled. Operation 24H was carried down to a depth of 0.29-0.6 m below ground surface immediately east of construction, and the relatively shallow overburden was removed from the higher terraces. No attempt was made to obtain material from fill.

TABLE 3.25

EXCAVATION SUMMARY

Lot #	Contents	Depositional Significance	Provenience
23H/1	100 sherds; 13 pcs. obsidian	Terminal occupation debris and preconstruction debris, mixed	Within Stratum 1, E of Unit 1 from above and below base of Unit 1

Excavation Lots: One lot (24H/1) with a total of 100 sherds and 13 pieces of obsidian was recovered from the Op. 24H excavations, representing a mix of terminal occupation and preconstruction contexts (see Table 3.25).

Time Span 3: The first period of activity recognized in Op. 24H involved the deposition of the lower portion of Stratum 1, which underlies Unit 1 to an exposed depth of 0.1-0.3 m (see Fig. 39). This level of orange-brown clay, exposed for a horizontal extent of 1.56 m, continues to near the top of the basal Unit 1 terrace and contains no discontinuity that would mark an ancient ground surface contemporary with Str. 205-14. A few scattered pebbles, located just below and adjacent to the base of Str. 205-14, possibly representing outwash from the platform's erosion, suggest that this structure was built directly on the existing ground surface.

Lot 24H/1 includes some material gathered from Stratum 1 above the base of the lowest Unit 1 step. It was noted during excavation, however, that most of the recovered artifacts came from below the terrace, near the base of excavation. While some mixing is acknowledged, the contents of Lot 24H/1 for the most part thus correspond to the deposition of the lower portion of Stratum 1.

Time Span 2: After the natural deposition of the lower part of Stratum 1, Unit 1 was built. This construction has seven exposed step-terraces which rise 1.67 m over a 1.04-m horizontal distance. Each riser consists of a single horizontal course of unfaced river cobbles, 0.12 by 0.13 to 0.16 by 0.33 m, packed with chinking pebbles and set in a clay matrix. The risers serve to support the flat-laid stone slabs of the terrace treads which run back under the next ascending step. These terraces stand 0.2-0.33 m high, with most rising 0.2-0.24 m, and are 0.2-0.24 m wide (see Fig. 39). Terrace tops and bases are generally quite even, with the exception of the basal element, which slopes down from south to north. Above the highest terrace exposed, additional steps continue to the summit, similar in construction to those already described. Surface remains also suggest that the Unit 1 terraces ran the full length of Str. 205-14's east side.

Time Span 1: After the abandonment of this structure, the upper portion of Stratum 1, consisting of at least 0.3 m of matrix, and Stratum 2 were deposited. The latter is a dark brown humus horizon capping both Stratum 1 and, at least in part, the seven terraces of Unit 1.

TABLE 3.26

STRUCTURAL/DEPOSITIONAL SUMMARY TIME SPANS: 1-3

Time Span	Construction Stage	Activity	Features	Lots
1	—	Abandonment and burial of Str. 205-14	Upper Stratum 1 and Stratum 2	—
2	Str. 205-14	Construction and use of Str. 205-14	Unit 1	—
3	—	Preconstruction occupation	Lower Stratum 1	24H/1

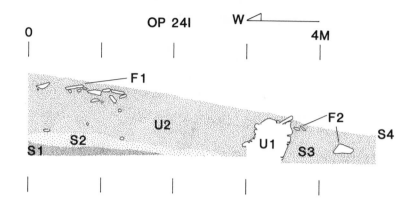

Figure 40.   Str. 205-88, Op 24I, Section.

STRUCTURE 205-88 (Fig. 40)

Structure 205-88, a 0.58-m-high construction 51 m east of Str. 205-1, was investigated in 1978 by Op. 24I, a trench 1.5 m north-south by 4.76 m east-west on the approximate axis of the structure's east side. This operation was begun 1.4 m east of the platform and was continued to its summit. Operation 24I penetrated 0.36-0.58 m below ground surface in front of the structure to locate its base, and was carried 3.1 m into construction fill in search of earlier building phases and sealed artifact deposits. Within this fill, excavations extended 0.63-1.08 m below ground surface (see Fig. 40).

Excavation Lots: Five excavation lots containing a total of 466 sherds, one figurine, three censer frag-

ments, and 80 pieces of obsidian are defined in Op. 24I. Of these lots, one is from a terminal occupation debris context (24I/1), two are from fill (24I/3-4), one comes from a possible preconstruction level (24I/2), and one is from a mixed fill and preconstruction context (24I/5; see Table 3.27).

Time Span 3: The first event recognized in Op. 24I was the deposition of Strata 1 and 2 and the lower 0.05-0.07 m of Stratum 3. Stratum 1 is a level of very dense, hard-packed, homogeneous brown clay with a thin scattering of pebbles on its surface, found beneath the fill of Str. 205-88. Stratum 1 is exposed for a horizontal distance of 1.9 m, over which it rises from the base of excavation 0.19 m from east to west. Above it is Stratum 2, a moderately dense, greasy, homoge-

TABLE 3.27

EXCAVATION SUMMARY

Lot #	Contents	Depositional Significance	Provenience
24I/1	110 sherds; 1 figurine frag.; 17 pcs. obsidian	Terminal occupation debris (secondary)	Within Strata 3 and 4 above base of Unit 1
24I/2	10 sherds	Preconstruction occupation debris (secondary)	Within Stratum 3 below base of Unit 1
24I/3	164 sherds; 1 censer frag.; 27 pcs. obsidian	Fill	Within Unit 2 and Stratum 4 from level equal to top of Unit 1 and above
24I/4	62 sherds; 11 pcs. obsidian	Fill	Within Unit 2, from level equal to top of Unit 1 to 0.2 m below that level
24I/5	120 sherds; 2 censer frags.; 25 pcs. obsidian	Fill and preconstruction debris (mixed)	Within Unit 2 and Strata 1-2 to base of excavation

TABLE 3.28

STRUCTURAL/DEPOSITIONAL SUMMARY TIME SPANS: 1-3

Time Span	Construction Stage	Activity	Features	Lots
1	—	Abandonment and burial of Str. 205-88	Upper part of Stratum 3, Stratum 4, Feat. 1-2	24I/1
2	Str. 205-88	Construction and use of Str. 205-88	Units 1-2	24I/3-4
3	—	Preconstruction occupation	Strata 1-2, lower part of Stratum 3	24I/2

Note: Lot 24I/5 represents a mix of material from both fill (Unit 2) and preconstruction (Strata 1-2) contexts and cannot, therefore, be placed in a single time span.

neous brown clay varying in thickness between 0.09 and 0.19 m. As with Stratum 1, this level rises 0.27-0.31 m above the base of excavation from east to west over its revealed extent of 2.66 m. Further to the east, beyond the eastern basal wall of Str. 205-88 (Unit 1) a brown clay level, less greasy but otherwise identical to Stratum 2, was uncovered (Stratum 3). This homogeneous layer underlies, in part, the earliest recognized construction to an exposed depth of 0.05-0.07 m. This stratigraphic position and the similarity in composition and texture between Strata 2 and 3 suggest that they were originally part of the same soil level before it was disturbed by the construction of Str. 205-88 (see Fig. 40). It is certain that Strata 1 and 2 and the lower portion of Stratum 3 have a natural origin, although they contain some cultural material (Lot 24I/2 and some of the objects in 24I/5) indicating that this area was occupied prior to the raising of Str. 205-88.

Lot 24I/2 corresponds to Stratum 3 below the level of Unit 1. Because of the lack of a barrier separating pre- and postconstruction deposits, however, some mixing of material is possible.

Time Span 2: After the deposition of these soil levels, Str. 205-88 was constructed, represented here by Units 1 and 2. Unit 1 is a low, 0.5-m-thick wall which stands to a preserved height of 0.42-0.5 m and retains the eastern side of Str. 205-88. This wall is built of large, unmodified river cobbles, c. 0.12 by 0.33 m, set in a clay matrix in three clear horizontal courses, packed with chinking stones to level the coursing. There is some chance that Unit 1 was capped by flat-laid schist slabs, several of which were found in tumbled positions. The larger and flatter river cobbles are employed on the exterior, eastern face of the wall while the interior is constructed of mostly smaller cobbles and pebbles (Fig. 40). When found, Unit 1 was slumping slightly to the east from its original, vertical position.

Backing Unit 1 on the west is the fill of Unit 2, a hard-compacted brown clay mottled with orange and yellow patches that contains some small, scattered charcoal and many pebbles. From west to east within Unit 2, its color changes from brown mottled with orange and yellow to light orange or yellow, probably representing a change in fill sources. Unit 2 is exposed to a depth of 0.62-0.76 m, buries Strata 1 and 2, and underlies Unit 1's west side by at least 0.13 m. Unit 2 also slopes up to the west to a maximum of 0.51 m above the preserved top of Unit 1, posing a problem as to the appearance of the summit of Str. 205-88. No floors or wall foundations were noted here; in light of that fact, two alternatives seem plausible. First, Unit 1 may have once stood sufficiently higher to contain the Unit 2 fill to its full height. Yet, with the exception of the aforementioned slabs, very little architectural debris was found east of Unit 1, and certainly not enough to account for the additional 0.51 m in height of that unit (see Feat. 2, below). Alternatively, Unit 2 may have been shaped so as to provide access to the summit, with Unit 1 remaining at its present uncovered height. Regardless of its access, the summit probably had an earthen floor.

In sum, it appears that Str. 205-88 has an earthen core and summit floor and is bounded on the east by a low stone retaining wall. Some scattered stones attest to the fact that the Str. 205-88 superstructure was built, in part, of stone, although the details of this construction remain obscure (see Feat. 1 below).

Materials in both Lots 24I/3 and 4 were recovered from Unit 2, but a few of the Lot 24I/3 artifacts come from Stratum 4, the overlying humus. While the artifacts found in the Unit 2 fill were deposited along with that earth during the construction of Str. 205-88, it is likely that many of them originally derive from earlier contexts. Lots 24I/3 and 4 contain redeposited items whose association with the date of construction and use of Str. 205-88 is tentative.

Time Span 1: After this period of construction, Stratum 4, the upper 0.27-0.48 m of Stratum 3, and Feat. 1-2 were deposited. As noted earlier, Stratum 3 is a homogeneous brown clay that extends from beneath the base of Unit 1 to 0.03-0.05 m below its top. Because no clear ground surface associated with the use of Str. 205-88 was located, it is impossible to determine just how much of this level was deposited prior to construction, and how much was laid down afterward. While the 0.05-0.07 m of this element that runs under Unit 1 was deposited before that wall was built, it is simply assumed that the remaining 0.23-0.48 m was laid down subsequently. Stratum 3 is exposed to a horizontal extent of 1.24 m. The other soil horizon in T.S. 1 is Stratum 4, the dark brown to black humus, which, though not clearly defined, runs over Stratum 3 and Units 1-2 to a depth of 0.04-0.06 m. Both Strata 3 and 4 are of natural origin.

Feature 1 consists of a scattering of stone slabs and cobbles near the center of the structure within the upper 0.13-0.19 m of Unit 2. These stones were not in place when found, and apparently represent tumble from Str. 205-88's superstructure. Feature 2 is a light scattering of cobbles and schist slabs extending east of Unit 1 for a distance of c. 0.92 m, representing architectural debris from Unit 1. As noted earlier, the low density of this debris implies that Unit 1 was never much taller than at present.

Lot 24I/1 comes from the upper portion of Stratum 3 and from Stratum 4 east of Unit 1. This material was probably originally deposited as occupation debris during the final period of Str. 205-88's use and, after

abandonment, was redeposited a short distance away by natural forces.

STRUCTURE 205-8 (Fig. 34)

Structure 205-8, the 0.5-m-high structure located c. 6 m east of Str. 205-1, was investigated by an eastern extension of Op. 24D that measured 0.7 m north-south by 3 m east-west. Operation 24D intersected the west side of Str. 205-8; its purpose was to locate a midden deposit associated with the final phase of use of either Str. 205-1 or -8. The failure to find such a deposit adjacent to Str. 205-1 led to the continuation of Op. 24D until it encountered the western basal wall of Str. 205-8. Once this unit had been uncovered no further horizontal clearing was carried out. Excavation was carried down no more than 0.75 m below ground surface, a depth of 0.53 m below the base of construction, to ensure that the full height of this unit had been exposed.

Excavation Lots: Only one lot, 24D/3 (four obsidian pieces), is associated with Str. 205-8, deriving from the far eastern sector of Op. 24D. This collection is described in Table 3.29.

Time Span 3: The first period of activity exposed in the Str. 205-8 area saw the deposition of Stratum 1, which underlies construction (Unit 1). This level is a densely packed brown clay with some pebbles, charcoal, and gritty inclusions. Stratum 1 slopes down to the west away from Str. 205-8, dropping 0.4 m over a horizontal distance of 0.61 m. Whether this steep gradient continues to the west, creating a deep depression between Str. 205-1 and -8, was not determined. At its maximum exposed thickness, Stratum 1 is 0.53 m deep. Stratum 1 appears to have been deposited naturally, though the few included carbon flecks may indicate the presence of human activity in the area at the time this level was laid down.

Time Span 2: The next phase of activity involved the construction of Unit 1, the western basal wall of Str. 205-8, and possibly the deposition of Stratum 2. Unit

TABLE 3.29

EXCAVATION SUMMARY

Lot #	Contents	Depositional Significance	Provenience
24D/3	4 pcs. obsidian	Terminal occupation debris (secondary)	Strata 3 and 4 W of Unit 1

TABLE 3.30

STRUCTURAL/DEPOSITIONAL SUMMARY TIME SPANS: 1-3

Time Span	Construction Stage	Activity	Features	Lots
1	—	Abandonment and burial of Str. 205-8	Strata 3 and 4	24D/3
2	Str. 205-8	Construction and use of Str. 205-8	Stratum 2	(?)
3	—	Preconstruction deposition of natural soil levels	Stratum 1	—

1 is constructed of unmodified river cobbles laid in two horizontal courses, packed with chinking stones, and set in a clay matrix. At the time of excavation, the lower stones of this wall were still in place though several of their higher counterparts had been dislodged and fallen to the west. The reconstructed height of Unit 1 is 0.19 m; it was insufficiently exposed horizontally for its orientation to be determined. Unit 1 rests on Stratum 1, although at least the lower 0.03 m of it is buried by Stratum 2. This latter layer, which seals Stratum 1, is a fine-textured, yellow-orange clay with some included pebbles. Stratum 2 is between 0.07 and 0.3 m thick; its upper surface slopes down to the west (0.14 m over 0.53 m horizontal distance), albeit more gradually than Stratum 1. It is possible that Stratum 2 was introduced artificially sometime during the construction of Str. 205-8 in an attempt to fill the depression noted above. Unfortunately, there is little evidence to confirm this view, and it is equally probable that Stratum 2 represents debris that eroded out of Str. 205-8 during and after its final period of use.

Time Span 1: Capping all of these elements are Strata 3 and 4. Stratum 3 is a gritty brown clay that marks the eastern continuation of Stratum 5 defined near Str. 205-1. This level slopes up to and buries Unit 1. The preserved thickness of Stratum 3 ranges between 0.14 and 0.16 m. Topping this level is the ubiquitous dark brown to black clay of the humus horizon (Stratum 4). Stratum 4 is 0.02-0.1 m thick and shows a tendency to thin out over construction (Unit 1). Both of these strata were undoubtedly deposited by natural means.

The four pieces of obsidian in Lot 24D/3 were redeposited by natural forces during T.S. 1 and probably originally derived from Str. 205-8 to the east, the closest known construction.

NORTHWEST GROUP

MAIN GROUP, PRINCIPAL COURT, MONUMENT 2 (Fig. 41)

Monument 2, a roughly pecked stone sphere located in the approximate center of the Northwest Group's main court, was investigated in 1978 by Op. 24L. This trench is divided into a northern and a southern part; the section on the south side of the monument measures 0.8 m east-west by 1.02 m north-south, while its northern counterpart is 0.8 m east-west by 2 m north-south. These trenches are separated by a 0.68-m baulk occupied by Mon. 2 itself, which was not excavated owing to the danger of displacing the sphere. The goals of this excavation were to determine the possible presence and nature of the platform or formalized surface into which Mon. 2 was set, and to recover artifacts associated with the monument's use as an aid to both dating this use and determining the kinds of activities associated with it. To accomplish these aims, Op. 24L was carried down 0.6-0.64 m on the south and 0.06-0.46 m on the north, well below the reconstructed base of Mon. 2 (see Fig. 41).

Excavation Lots: Only one lot, 24L/1, from the northern Op. 24L trench is defined in this excavation. Outside of a few extraneous examples, the majority of the recovered sherds derive from a very limited area at the northern edge of the trench, and are from a single *incensario* which apparently was deposited here

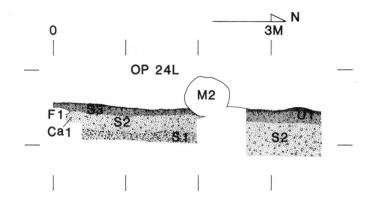

Figure 41. Las Quebradas Op 24L, Section.

in association with the use of Mon. 2 (Cache 1; see Table 3.31).

Time Span 4: The first period of activity recognized in Op. 24L involved the deposition of Strata 1 and 2. Stratum 1, found only on the north side of Op. 24L, is a hard-compacted, light orange clay containing a dense concentration of pebbles. This level is exposed over a north-south distance of 1.58 m and to a depth of 0.1-0.16 m. Its upper surface is relatively flat and is 0.2 m below the base of Mon. 2. Stratum 2 is found in both pits and is almost identical to Stratum 1 except that it is not as hard-compacted and contains fewer pebbles. On the north, Stratum 2 replaces Stratum 1 at the appropriate depth and shows a gradual increase in compactness and the density of pebble inclusions toward its base. This suggests that Strata 1 and 2 may represent a single soil level in which there is some variation in compactness and the amount of pebble inclusions from bottom to top and north to south. It appears that these strata are natural in origin, as similar, rocky orange soils are quite commonly found exposed on the surface of the Las Quebradas bluff.

Time Span 3: Unit 1 was laid down in the next period and Mon. 2 moved into position. Unit 1 is a level 0.16-0.21 m thick of densely packed pebbles 0.02

m and less in diameter, set in a clay matrix on the south side of Mon. 2. This clay matrix is a dark black humus exposed over a horizontal distance of 1.02 m; it seems to decrease slightly in pebble density toward Mon. 2 and does not continue north of the monument. The great increase in the density of pebbles over that found in the lower, naturally deposited Stratum 2, and the fact that the base of Unit 1 is only 0.08 m below the reconstructed bottom of Mon. 2, argue for this as an artificial surface associated with the use of Mon. 2. Whether the presence of Unit 1 solely on the south side of the monument is due to ritual significance associated with this direction, or simply an effort to level out the court's surface, remains unknown.

Monument 2, described in Chap. 2, is a roughly shaped stone sphere 0.51 m in diameter, fashioned from a coarse-grained gray stone. No carving was noted on its surface, nor is there any evidence that it was ever painted or plastered. Monument 2 is set directly on the Stratum 2 surface on the north, and is buried up to 0.2 m by Unit 1 on the north.

A final element associated with this period of activity is Feat. 1, represented by a single cobble c. 0.09 m thick, located 1.64 m north of Mon. 2 and immediately

TABLE 3.31

EXCAVATION SUMMARY

Lot #	Contents	Depositional Significance	Provenience
24L/1	74 sherds, 222 censer frags.	Offertory deposit to Mon. 2 (primary)	Within upper 0.14 m of Stratum 2, N trench, N of Mon. 2

TABLE 3.32

STRUCTURAL/DEPOSITIONAL SUMMARY TIME SPANS: 1-4

Time Span	Construction Stage	Activity	Features	Lots
1	—	Abandonment and burial of NW Group main court	Stratum 3	—
2	Main court	Use of M. 2 and main court	Cache 1	24L/1
3	Main court	Laying down of Unit 1 and Mon. 2	Unit 1, Mon. 2, Feat. 1	(?)
4	—	Preconstruction deposition of natural soil levels	Strata 1-2	—

north of Cache 2. This possibly defines the southern edge of Str. 205-121, a construction visible as a 0.29-m-high rise above the court's surface. This stone is roughly in line with the surface outline of this structure, and its base rests at the appropriate level, 0.04 m below the top of Stratum 2. Unfortunately, time did not permit the expansion of Op. 24L to test this hypothesis, thus the identification of Feat. 1 as part of Str. 205-121 remains conjectural.

Time Span 2: Also deposited at about this time was a broken *incensario*, many fragments of which were found concentrated within an area 0.27 m north-south by 0.13 m thick, 1.52 m north of Mon. 2 (Lot 24L/1 and Cache 1). The large number of sherds concentrated here, their proximity to Mon. 2, their location just below the ground surface associated with the sphere, and the fact that they are primarily of the same type, and most probably from the same item, indicate that the censer fragments are the remains of an offertory deposit related to activities around Mon. 2. This supposition is further supported by the large size of the recovered sherds, and their lack of edge erosion which points to their primary deposition.

The stratigraphic position of Cache 1 suggests that it was deposited during the period of Mon. 2's use. These censer sherds were located immediately below the earthen surface of Stratum 2 on which Mon. 2 is set. While these fragments could have been deposited at any time immediately before or after the placement of Mon. 2, it is probable that the elapsed time between these events was relatively short given the close proximity of the sherds to the Strata 2/3 interface.

In sum, Mon. 2 was a roughly hewn stone sphere c. 0.5 m in diameter, fronted on the south by a pebble pavement and on the north by an earthen surface. Also on the north, a censer was interred just beneath

the ground surface contemporary with the use of Mon. 2. Whether this cache was dedicatory to Mon. 2, or rather was associated with its use at some later period, remains unknown. Immediately north of this cache is Str. 205-121, a very low construction whose function and relationship to Mon. 2 remain unclear.

Time Span 1: Following the period of court use, Stratum 3 was deposited. This soil level is the dark black clay-humus horizon found quite commonly capping construction at Las Quebradas. Stratum 3 ranges in thickness from 0.06 to 0.13 m, overlies Feat. 1 by 0.06 m, and buries the base of Mon. 2 by up to 0.09 m. On the south, as noted earlier, the clay-humus is intermixed with the stones of Unit 1, and hence is not definable here as a separate level.

STRUCTURE 205-118 (FIG. 42)

Structure 205-118, the structure 3.9-7.28 m high that closes off the southern side of the Northwest Group's principal court, was investigated in 1978 by a single trench, Op. 24K. This excavation, dug into the northern face of the structure along its approximate axis, measures 1.5 m east-west by 3.23 m north-south, is dug down 0.33-0.58 m north of construction, and extends 1.46 m into architectural fill. The latter probe penetrates 1.42 m below ground surface to a point beneath the lowest exposed level of construction.

Excavation Lots: Ninety-two sherds were recovered from the four excavation lots defined in Op. 24K. Terminal occupation debris in both primary and secondary contexts accounts for the depositional significance of two of the lots, while the remainder are from fill (see Table 3.33).

Time Span 4: The first event for which evidence was found in Op. 24K was the natural deposition of

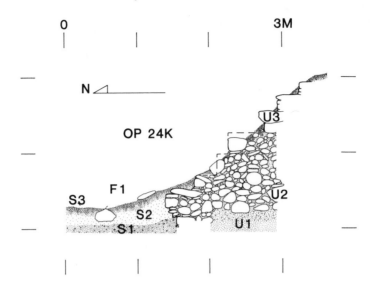

Figure 42.   Str. 205-118, Op 24K, Section.

Stratum 1. This soil level, exposed for a horizontal distance of 1.52 m and to a maximum depth of 0.2 m, is a hard-compacted, fine-textured reddish brown clay with numerous pebble inclusions, similar to Stratum 1 in Op. 24L. It runs up to, but not under, the construction associated with Str. 205-118 (see Fig. 42).

The stratigraphic position of Stratum 1, underlying postabandonment elements (Strata 2-3), indicates that this level was deposited prior to T.S. 1. The case for the temporal priority of Stratum 1 over Str. 205-118 (Units 1-3) relies on three lines of evidence. First, the upper 0.38 m of Unit 3's basal terrace has fallen onto the Strata 1/2 interface, while the lower 0.13 m of Unit 3, located below the interface, is still in place. This suggests that Unit 3 was sunk into Stratum 1. Second, debris associated with the use of Str. 205-118 (Lot 24K/2) was found resting atop Stratum 1. Finally, on the north, Stratum 1 extends down at least 0.08 m below the bottom of Unit 3.

Time Span 3: The next period saw the construction of Units 1-3, all associated with Str. 205-118's northern face. Unit 1, the first element to be deposited in this process, is a level of reddish brown clay, largely devoid of pebbles, which becomes increasingly hard-packed toward the bottom of its 0.24 to 0.3 exposed depth and increasingly gritty toward the top. Unit 1 also contains carbon flecks, most of which are concentrated in a horizontal level 0.09-0.12 m thick, 0.02-0.04 m below the base of the cobble fill of Unit 2 (see below). It is from this carbon-rich level that most of the artifacts in Lot 24K/4 come. We conclude that Unit 1 represents a fill, deposited probably to stabilize the northern construction of Str. 205-118 and set into either a prepared trench or a natural depression, and is not part of the natural soil (Stratum 1) exposed at about the same depth to the north. While Unit 1 is similar in color to Stratum 1, it does not contain the sizable numbers of pebbles that are characteristic of

TABLE 3.33

EXCAVATION SUMMARY

Lot #	Contents	Depositional Significance	Provenience
24K/1	20 sherds	Terminal occupation debris (secondary)	Within Strata 2-3
24K/2	50 sherds	Terminal occupation debris (primary)	Resting on Strata 1/2 interface
24K/3	6 sherds	Fill	Within Unit 2
24K/4	16 sherds	Fill	Within Unit 1 0.1-0.16 m below Unit 2

TABLE 3.34

STRUCTURAL/DEPOSITIONAL SUMMARY TIME SPANS: 1-4

Time Span	Construction Stage	Activity	Features	Lots
1	—	Abandonment and burial of Str. 205-118	Strata 2-3, Feat. 1	24K/1
2	Str. 205-118	Use of Str. 205-118	Strata 1/2 interface	24K/2
3	Str. 205-118	Construction of Str. 205-118	Units 1-3	24K/3-4
4	—	Preconstruction deposition of natural soil level	Stratum 1	—

Stratum 1. Also, Unit 1 contains carbon flecks and artifacts—which Stratum 1 lacks—thereby indicating its cultural origins.

Overlying Unit 1 is the densely packed cobble fill of Unit 2. These cobbles are horizontally laid throughout their 1.46-m north-south extent, and are set in a gritty reddish orange clay similar to that uncovered in Unit 1. Unit 2 covers Unit 1 at a fairly even level in the southern portion of the trench and drops down 0.2 m on the north, paralleling a similar downward extension of the structure's basal terrace (Unit 3).

Unit 2 was designed to serve as a firm foundation for the facing construction of Str. 205-118's north side, Unit 3. While it was not well preserved on recovery, Unit 3 consists of seven reconstructed step-terraces, which ultimately give way to a broader terrace (unexcavated). Each of the Unit 3 risers is built of roughly coursed river cobbles packed with chinking pebbles and set in a reddish brown clay. The number of cobble courses varies from one to two, although a single course is most common. Capping these risers are the flat stone slabs of the terrace treads, each of which runs back under the next ascending riser. In general, these terraces rise 0.16-0.28 m each and range in width between 0.17 and 0.3 m. The exceptions to this are the basal terrace, which is 0.51 m high, including 0.13 m sunk into the initially deposited Stratum 1 to firmly anchor construction; and the heavily disturbed terrace above the fourth step, which is slightly wider than the others, with a reconstructed width of 0.5 m. The lower riser of this terrace was still in place in 1978 and its position and that of the next higher step are certain (Fig. 42). A single broader terrace, c. 1.5 m wide, was noted above the seven terraces of Unit 3. Surface remains indicate that the Unit 3 step-terraces continue for the entire length of

Str. 205-118's north side. In sum, Unit 3 rises 1.91 m in height over a north-south distance of 1.68 m.

Time Span 2: No formal court surface was found north of Unit 3, although it is likely that the surface of Stratum 1 functioned as an informal floor during the use of Str. 205-118. The largest excavation lot recovered from Op. 24K (24K/2) is from the immediate area of the Strata 1/2 interface, suggesting that this level was exposed for the deposition of debris associated with the use of the neighboring structure.

Time Span 1: Stratum 2 was deposited after the abandonment of Str. 205-118, burying 0.3 m of Unit 3's basal terrace. This level, a loosely compacted, fine-textured tan to brown clay with few included pebbles, slopes up to Str. 205-118 and varies in thickness between 0.13 and 0.2 m. Immediately overlying Stratum 2 and also rising up to Str. 205-118 is Stratum 3. This dark black humus horizon obscures or buries all of Unit 3's terraces and is 0.08-0.11 m thick. Found within both earth levels, primarily north of Unit 3, is a light scattering of tumbled stone architectural debris (Feat. 1). All of the stones in Feat. 1 are of the same type found in construction: unfaced river cobbles and chunks.

Lot 24K/1, retrieved from Strata 2-3, contains artifacts probably derived from the nearby platform that were originally deposited during T.S. 2 and then redeposited, most likely by natural forces, after the period of this structure's use.

STRUCTURE 205-123 (Fig. 43)

Structure 205-123, a 0.43-m-high construction that closes off the west side of a small plaza 75 m east of the main group, was investigated in 1978 by Op. 24J. This trench measures 1.5 m north-south by 5.1 m east-west

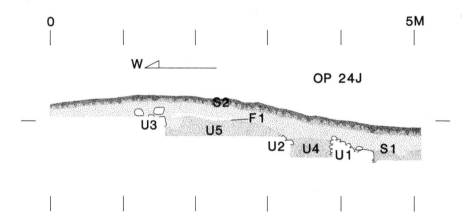

Figure 43.   Str. 205-123, Op 24J, Section.

and is placed against the east side of the structure along its approximate axis. Operation 24J was carried down 0.42-0.45 m below ground surface to the east of construction, and 0.39-0.6 m into architectural fill (see Fig. 43).

Excavation Lots: Five excavation lots containing 189 sherds, one censer, one figurine fragment, 19 pieces of obsidian, 58 *bajareque* fragments, and three ground stone fragments were recovered from Op. 24J. Three of these lots are from terminal occupation debris contexts (Lots 24J/1, 4, and 5), one is from fill (Lot 24J/2), and one is mixed, with material from both fill and terminal debris contexts (Lot 24J/3) (see Table 3.35).

Time Span 2: The first period of activity recognized in Op. 24J involved the construction of Str. 205-123 (preconstruction levels were not sampled at this locus). This structure is built primarily of earthen fill with a low stone foundation and retaining walls. On the east, the construction base is represented by a cobble and pebble wall 0.16-0.26 m high (Unit 1). This element consists, on the east, of a course of large cobbles (0.12-0.16 m thick and 0.2-0.3 m long) with naturally flattened faces on the exterior, resting on a level of pebbles that also fill the interstices between the irregular stones. This cobble course rises 0.17 m and its base slopes down gradually from north to south. From the top of these cobbles westward a slanting

TABLE 3.35

EXCAVATION SUMMARY

Lot #	Contents	Depositional Significance	Provenience
24J/1	91 sherds; 1 figurine frag.; 4 pcs. obsidian; 19 *bajareque* frags.; 1 metate frag.	Terminal occupation debris (secondary)	Within Strata 1-3, E of Unit 1
24J/2	12 sherds; 1 pc. obsidian	Fill	Within Unit 4
24J/3	52 sherds; 5 pcs. obsidian; 20 *bajareque* frags.	Mixed terminal occupation debris (secondary) and fill	Within Strata 2-3 and Unit 5, between Units 2 and 3
24J/4	27 sherds; 8 pcs. obsidian; 2 mano frags.	Terminal occupation debris (secondary)	Within Strata 2-3, W of Unit 3
24J/5	7 sherds; 1 censer frag.; 1 pc. obsidian; 19 *bajareque* frags.	Terminal occupation debris (secondary)	Within Feat. 1

TABLE 3.36

STRUCTURAL/DEPOSITIONAL SUMMARY TIME SPANS: 1-2

Time Span	Construction Stage	Activity	Features	Lots
1	—	Abandonment and burial of Str. 105-123	Strata 1-2, Feat. 1, 4, 5	24J/1
2	Str. 205-123	Construction and use of Str. 205-123	Units 1-5	24J/2

level of irregular small stones rises another 0.18 m and terminates in a vertical face (see Fig. 43). This western side of the Unit 1 wall, composed of pebbles and cobbles roughly set in a clay matrix, stands 0.25 m high with its base set 0.1 m above that of the wall's eastern face. In all, Unit 1 measures 0.59 m thick and is oriented S 15° 0′ W. It seems likely that Unit 1, although partially disintegrated when exposed, once possessed a second course of large cobbles on the east which would have brought this side up to the same height as the western portion. This would have given Unit 1 a reconstructed height of 0.35 m on the east and provided the first step-up onto Str. 205-123.

The 0.51 m² separating Units 1 and 2 is filled with a hard-packed, fine-textured reddish brown clay (Unit 4). While very little distinguishes this element from the overriding clay of Stratum 1, it is likely that this unit originally rose to the top of Unit 1. If so, Unit 4 would have been at least 0.28 m thick. The western portion of Unit 1 also rests on this clay level.

Unit 2 marks the western limit of Unit 4, with its base 0.12 m below the reconstructed top of this element. Unit 2, a wall 0.12-0.3 m high, is built of small unmodified cobbles, 0.06 by 0.11 to 0.04 by 0.06 m, placed in very rough horizontal courses and set in a clay matrix. The base of this narrow wall, no more than 0.15-0.18 m wide, is somewhat uneven, sloping down from north to south, and oriented S 6° 30′ W. Given the narrowness of this wall and the fact that its preserved top is even with that of Unit 1, it would seem that Unit 1 must have served as a foundation for a perishable upper wall. The recovery of considerable quantities of *bajareque* from the area east of Unit 2 (Lot 24J/1) indicates that this material was employed in the postulated construction.

For 1.6 m west of Unit 2 no trace of construction is found. If a link once existed between Unit 2 and the next definite architectural element (Unit 3), it must

have been built of earth. The upper surface of this putative earthen fill is suggested by the location of a clear postabandonment debris lens (Feat. 1), 0.2-0.26 m above the level of the preserved top of Unit 2. Assuming that this eroded debris has come to rest on a preexisting surface contemporary with the occupation of Str. 205-123, it seems likely that it marks the approximate level of Str. 205-123's upper terrace (see Fig. 43). The area defined within this reconstructed fill is also marked by a more densely packed clay than that which characterizes the overlying Stratum 1, again implying that an earthen fill unit backing the wall supported by Unit 2 can still be recognized here. As a result, Unit 5, the reconstructed fill element, is defined as a hard-compacted, fine-textured, reddish brown clay that rises 0.2 m above the top of Unit 2 and then runs 1.6 m back to and buries the lower 0.08 m of Unit 3.

Rising 0.17 m above the reconstructed top of Unit 5 is Unit 3, a low, 0.25-m-thick wall, oriented S 2° 45′ W and constructed of small unfaced cobbles, c. 0.1 by 0.15 m, set in a clay matrix. As with Unit 2, the narrowness of this element seems to preclude its ever having supported heavy masonry construction. It seems far more likely that it served as a foundation for a perishable wall. This interpretation is supported by the location of a level of collapsed *bajareque* fragments, some of which are smoothed on at least one side, immediately east of Unit 3 (Feat. 1). The fact that these fragments are concentrated near Unit 3 and decrease in density away from it suggests that they originally derived from Unit 3. The reddish brown clay ubiquitous throughout this excavation extends at the level of the top of Unit 3 for 1.33 m west to the end of Op. 24J. It is not clear whether this represents a continuation of the Unit 5 fill identified on the east.

As reconstructed here, Str. 205-123 has a low, broad eastern stone step-up which gives access to a 0.51-m-wide earthen surface, the first low, narrow terrace of this structure. Sunk just below this terrace level at its western edge is a stone foundation supporting a second riser, this time made of *bajareque*, which provides access to the next terrace. This latter surface is 1.6 m wide and, like its lower eastern counterpart, made of earth; it gives way in turn to a second stone foundation for more perishable construction. The summit of this structure was apparently surfaced with tamped earth. The platform stands to a total height on the east of 0.72 m and is oriented S 2° 45′ W to S 15° 0′ W.

Lot 24J/2 derives from construction fill (Unit 4). But this material may well have originated from an earlier source only to be redeposited here in T.S. 2.

Time Span 1: After a period of occupation, Str. 205-123 was abandoned and buried by naturally deposited clays, represented by Strata 1 and 2, which together obscure all of the aforementioned construction. Stratum 1 consists of a fine-textured reddish brown clay and differs from the fills of Units 4 and 5 only in that it is very loosely compacted. This difference may be attributable, in part, to disturbances by ant nests and roots. Stratum 1 east of construction does grade gradually downward into a more firmly compacted element. Stratum 1 is found throughout Op. 24J, reaches its greatest exposed depth (0.35 m) on the east, and buries construction to a depth of 0.04-0.24 m. Capping this level throughout its exposed extent is Stratum 2, the loosely compacted black humus horizon, varying in thickness between 0.05 and 0.11 m. Also associated with this period of abandonment is Feat. 1, a level distinguished by the concentration of *bajareque* fragments within its 0.04- to 0.06-m depth. This level is found c. 0.11 m above the base of Unit 3 and extends 1 m to the east. Feature 1

does not maintain a perfectly horizontal level throughout its extent, and exhibits a general downward slope to the east. It is not found continuously over the north-south width of the trench, but is most clearly represented in the south face of Op. 24J and absent from its northern counterpart. As already discussed, this lens would appear to have been a level of architectural debris.

Lots 24J/1, 4, and 5 are defined for Strata 1 and 2 and Feat. 1. It is very likely, however, that these artifacts were originally deposited as trash on the surface of Str. 205-123 and redeposited by presumably natural forces after abandonment.

EAST GROUP

EAST COURT, MONUMENT 4 (Fig. 44)

Monument 4, located in the approximate center of the east court, was investigated in 1978 by means of Op. 24P. This trench measures 1.5 m north-south by 4.16 m east-west and was carried down on the east and west sides of the monument to depths of 0.9-0.23 m and 0.39-0.42 m respectively. The purpose of this work was to determine whether Mon. 4 possesses an associated pavement, as do Mon. 1 and 2, and to sample any associated artifacts as indicators of ancient activity.

Excavation Lots: The four lots defined in Op. 24P contain 149 sherds and 64 censer fragments. Three of these collections come from terminal occupation debris contexts, while one, Lot 24P/1, is from fill (see Table 3.37).

Time Span 3: The first period of activity seen in Op. 24P involved the deposition of Unit 1, a hard-compacted pinkish orange clay with many pebble

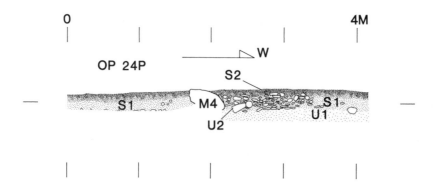

Figure 44.   Las Quebradas Op 24P, Section.

TABLE 3.37

EXCAVATION SUMMARY

Lot #	Contents	Depositional Significance	Provenience
24P/1	35 sherds; 19 censer frags.	Fill	Within Unit 2 and in Stratum 2 above Unit 2
24P/2	104 sherds; 21 censer frags.	Terminal occupation debris (secondary)	Within Strata 1 and 2, E of Mon. 4
24P/3	6 sherds; 19 censer frags.	Terminal occupation debris (secondary)	Within Strata 1 and 2, W of Unit 1
24P/4	4 sherds; 5 censer frags.	Terminal occupation debris (secondary)	Within Stratum 2, immediately over and around Mon. 4

inclusions, exposed to a depth of 0.13-0.15 m. Contrary to expectations, Unit 1 is not similar in composition to Unit 3 in Op. 24M, 2.6 m to the west, even though both share a similar elevation (the surface of Unit 1 is c. 0.08 m higher than the surface of Unit 3). Based on its stratigraphic position, elevation, and similarity to Units 1 and 2 in Op. 24M, it is likely that Unit 1 was deposited to build up and level the surface of the east court (see Str. 205-256, Op. 24M). It remains possible that Unit 1, with its relatively even upper surface, functioned as a court surface, although its dissimilarity in composition to the putative court surface fronting Str. 205-256 (Unit 3) remains unexplained.

As Op. 24P was not carried down to a sufficient depth east of Mon. 4, it is impossible to say whether Unit 1 continues in this area.

Time Span 2: After the deposition of Unit 1, Mon. 4 was set on its surface, and Unit 2 was constructed soon afterward. Monument 4, as is typical of East Group monuments, shows no evidence of having been shaped or modified in any way (see Survey, Chap. 2). It is a large (1.34 m north-south by 1.05 m east-west), rela-tively flat stone slab, at least 0.24 m thick. The monument rests on, and extends 0.02-0.03 m into, the surface of Unit 1. Unit 2, which fronts Mon. 4 on the west and buries the lower 0.22 m of that slab, is a surface built of tightly packed, horizontally laid small to medium-sized cobbles and slabs set in a clay matrix. Unit 2 rests on the Unit 1 surface, stands to a preserved height of 0.2 m, and is exposed for a horizontal extent of 1.2 m east-west. It is not clearly defined on its western edge and does not extend to the eastern side of the monument, where Stratum 1 is the exposed surface.

Lot 24P/1 derives predominantly from Unit 2. It is possible, however, that at least some of this material was originally deposited on Unit 2 during its use and subsequently worked its way into the stone fill. This possibility of mixing between terminal debris and fill contexts is suggested by the lack of an impermeable surface topping Unit 2. As a result, while Lot 24P/1 is defined as a fill deposit, it is recognized that not all of its included material may have been deposited as fill, but some may be related to the use of the court.

Time Span 1: After this building activity, and follow-

TABLE 3.38

STRUCTURAL/DEPOSITIONAL SUMMARY TIME SPANS: 1-3

Time Span	Construction Stage	Activity	Features	Lots
1	—	Abandonment and burial of east court	Strata 1-2	24P/2-4
2	East court 1	Construction of east court 1	Unit 2, Mon. 4	24P/1
3	East court 2	Construction and use of east court 2	Unit 1	—

TABLE 3.39

EXCAVATION SUMMARY

Lot #	Contents	Depositional Significance	Provenience
24Q/1	68 sherds; 5 censer frags.; 41 pcs. obsidian; 1 chipped stone flake; 5 *bajareque* frags.	Terminal occupation debris (secondary) (?)	Within Unit 1

ing the abandonment of the court, Strata 1-2 were deposited. Stratum 1, a fine-textured, loosely compacted brown clay 0.14-0.18 m thick, is identical in composition and relative elevation to Stratum 2 exposed in Op. 24M. Stratum 1 on the west overlies Units 1 and 2 to a depth of 0.15 m, while on the east it abuts the basal 0.1 m of Mon. 4. Given its stratigraphic position east of Mon. 4, it is likely that an undetermined portion of Stratum 1 was deposited in T.S. 2 and served as an earthen surface during the final occupancy of the court. Stratum 2 is a dark brown to black clay-humus horizon 0.08-0.1 m thick, which buries Stratum 1 to a depth of 0.05-0.07 m. The monument is only partially obscured by this level and remains visible on the surface.

Lots 24P/2-4 are defined for these strata. Most of this material originally derived from the immediate area, probably in T.S. 2, and was redeposited by natural forces in the subsequent period.

WEST COURT, MONUMENT 5

Monument 5, the central of the three monuments arranged in a north-south line within the west court, was briefly investigated in 1978 by means of a 1.5-m-square test pit (Op. 24Q) placed against its northern side. This was excavated to a depth of only c. 0.15-0.2 m, sufficient to expose the base of the monument, and was designed to uncover traces of architecture and

artifacts associated with the use of Mon. 5. Unfortunately, time limitations forced the cessation of work here before the trench could be completed.

Excavation Lots: One lot containing 68 sherds, five censer fragments, 42 pieces of chipped stone, and five *bajareque* fragments is defined in Op. 24Q (see Table 3.39).

Time Span 2: The first deposit revealed is Unit 1, a level of tightly packed, horizontally laid pebbles and small cobbles set in a clay matrix. This is exposed to a depth of 0.15-0.2 m throughout Op. 24Q, and buries the lower 0.15-0.2 m of Mon. 5. Unit 1 apparently functioned as a prepared surface into which Mon. 5 was set, although as excavations at Str. 205-256 (Op. 24N) show, this flooring does not extend throughout the west court and might very well have been limited to the monument's immediate environs. Monument 5 is a white, possibly quartzite, unmodified boulder 1 m in diameter.

Lot 24Q/1 was recovered from within Unit 1. All of the artifacts come from well up in Unit 1, within 0.15-0.2 m of its surface. There is no impermeable flooring on the unit that could have prevented the downward percolation of artifacts deposited on this pavement. These factors suggest that the artifacts in question were deposited during the period of use of Unit 1 and Mon. 5. Furthermore, it seems unlikely that so many artifacts would have derived from Unit 1's stone core, since this type of fill rarely contains

TABLE 3.40

STRUCTURAL/DEPOSITIONAL SUMMARY TIME SPANS: 1-2

Time Span	Construction Stage	Activity	Features	Lots
1	—	Abandonment and burial of west court	Stratum 1	—
2	West court	Construction and use of west court	Unit 1, Mon. 5	24Q/1

large amounts of cultural material (see, for example, Str. 205-256, Op. 24N).

Time Span 1: Following this period of activity, the court was abandoned and Stratum 1, a dark brown to black clay-humus horizon, was formed. This level buries Unit 1 and the lower portion of Mon. 5.

EAST AND WEST COURTS, STRUCTURE 205-256 (Fig. 45)

Structure 205-256, the c. 4-m-high structure shared by both the east and west courts, was probed in 1978 by two trenches, Op. 24M and N. The former is an excavation 1.5 m north-south by 3.91 m east-west into the east side of Str. 205-256 on its approximate axial line. Operation 24M extends onto Str. 205-256's summit and is sunk 0.78-0.9 m below ground surface east of construction to expose fully the basal levels of terminal construction. On the west, Op. 24N measures 1.5 m north-south by 3.86 m east-west and is slightly south of Str. 205-256's axial line. Excavation here extends 0.32-0.77 m below ground surface west of construction and advances 1.24 m eastward and 1.65 m below ground surface into construction fill. The latter probe into the structure was designed to locate sealed cultural deposits that would supplement the meager remains recovered from above construction.

Excavation Lots: The four lots (24M/1, N/1-3) defined in the Str. 205-256 excavations contain a total of 58 sherds, four censer fragments, and 37 pieces of obsidian. Of these collections, two are from terminal occupation debris contexts (24M/1 and N/1), one is from fill (24N/2), and one is from a preconstruction level (24N/3) (see Table 3.41).

Time Span 4: The first period of activity recognized in Op. 24M and N is the deposition of Stratum 1 on Str. 205-256's west side. This soil level is a fine-textured, reddish brown to orange-brown greasy clay with almost no inclusions. Stratum 1 rises from west to east over a distance of 2.43 m and reaches a maximum exposed thickness of 0.29 m in the eastern edge of the trench, where it underlies construction associated with Str. 205-256 (Units 8-10) (see Fig. 45). The available evidence indicates that Stratum 1 is a natural deposit and probably represents the west flank of the low rise on which Str. 205-256 is built. The fact that some cultural material (Lot 24N/3) was found in this level indicates human occupation in the area prior to this construction.

Time Span 3: Following the deposition of Stratum 1, the east court was raised, although it is uncertain how many construction phases are represented here. While time did not permit the deep probing of this court, the portion revealed in Op. 24M indicates that it is composed of fill. Unit 1, the lowest of the three levels exposed below the court surface, is a gritty, hard-compacted dark red clay with included pebbles up to 0.02 m in diameter. This unit slopes down gradually to the west under Str. 205-256 and is exposed to a depth of 0.04-0.09 m. Overlying Unit 1 is Unit 2, a hard-compacted, pinkish brown clay with many pebble inclusions (0.16-0.18 m thick). This element follows the same slope as Unit 1, eventually running under Str. 205-256. Unit 3, a fine-textured, hard-compacted orange to yellow clay with no included pebbles, caps this sequence and forms the court surface. It varies in thickness between 0.16 and 0.18 m over its exposed extent of 0.78 m. Unit 3 slopes down to the west and abuts the lower 0.18 m of Unit 4, an element of Str. 205-256.

Time Span 2: Following this period of court construction, Str. 205-256 was built. On the east, this platform consists of a series of four step-terraces (Unit 4) which provide access to a rough stone surface (Unit 5) and a low summit platform (Unit 6). The step-terraces are each composed of a riser 0.24-0.34 m high, built of roughly coursed, unmodified river cobbles packed with chinking pebbles and set in a clay matrix. These low vertical walls support horizontally laid stone slabs, which run back 0.26-0.32 m under the next ascending step and form the terrace treads. The one exception to this regular progression to the summit is the basal terrace, which stands to a height of 0.5 m. If we assume that Unit 3 functioned as the east court's surface during the use of Str. 205-256, then only the upper 0.28 m of this step would have been visible, the remaining 0.22 m having been buried within Unit 3. Surface indications suggest that the step-terraces of Unit 4 originally ran the length of Str. 205-256's east face. In general, Unit 4 is oriented S 9° 0' W and rises to a height of 1.03 m above court level over a horizontal distance of 0.78 m.

Resting 0.09 m above the top of the highest Unit 4 terrace, and extending 1.02 m to the west, is the Unit 5 summit surface, a series of flat-laid river cobbles and chunks set in a clay matrix and underlain, at least in the limited area exposed, by a fill of close-packed river cobbles (included within Unit 5). Unit 5 terminates on the west in an abrupt drop of at least 0.22 m and gives way to no clearly discernible continuing summit surface. Immediately to the south, however, in the south face of Op. 24M, a level 0.13-0.19 m thick of tightly

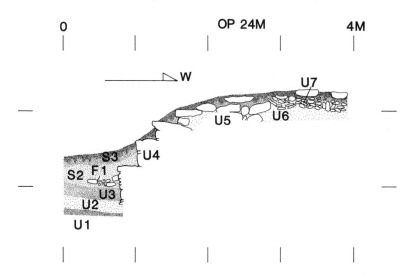

Figure 45a.   Str. 205-256, Section.

packed, horizontally laid small cobbles and slabs in a tan clay matrix was noted (Unit 7). The base of this unit is 0.05-0.1 m below the surface of Unit 5 while its top is 0.05-0.11 m above that level. In general, Unit 7 has a relatively even upper surface, although it does slope down gradually to the west. It does not extend any further north into Op. 24M than the south wall of that trench, and its uncovered face would appear to represent the northern end of this element. Unit 7 rests on a fill of medium- to fine-textured, light tan, gritty clay (Unit 6) exposed to a depth of 0.1-0.18 m. Unit 6 also buries the lower 0.18 m of Unit 5 and appears to be an earthen fill supporting summit construction (see Fig. 45).

In sum, the step-terraces of Unit 4 lead up from an earthen court level to a narrow stone landing (Unit 5) which, in turn, provides access to an earthen summit surface (Unit 6). On the south, sunk slightly into this earthen fill and rising above it, is a rough stone plinth represented by Unit 7. Surface remains suggest the presence of another such rise to the north just beyond the limits of the excavation.

The west face of Str. 205-256 is surfaced by another step-terrace system (Unit 9) consisting of 11 exposed terraces, each built of low cobble risers and stone slab treads. As in Unit 4, each riser supports a level of flat-laid stone slabs, some quite small (no more than 0.22 m long and 0.02-0.03 m thick), which run under the next ascending riser. The terraces each rise 0.12-0.24 m and are 0.22-0.3 m wide. There are, however, some exceptions to these uniformly low and narrow

terraces. The basal step is 0.3 m high and 0.39 m wide (reconstructed). It is also possible that the seventh and eighth terraces are 0.4 and 0.46 m wide respectively, although in both cases these widths are based on reconstructions from poorly preserved remnants.

The basal Unit 9 terrace rests on a level of stone slabs (Unit 10) roughly 0.38 m long that project 0.14 m beyond the front face of that construction. These slabs are identical to those employed in the Unit 9 terrace treads and are themselves underlain by a level of small cobbles. Unit 10 apparently functioned as a foundation for the step-terraces to minimize subsidence into the underlying clay (Stratum 1).

The Units 9 and 10 construction rises to a total preserved height of 2.96 m above the base of Unit 10, over a horizontal distance of 2.53 m. The terraces are oriented S 4° 0′ W and, to judge by fragmentary surface remains, run the entire length of Str. 205-256's west side. Surface indications also suggest that terraces similar to those seen in Unit 9 continue to the summit of Str. 205-256, although preservation in these higher levels is poorer than in the excavated basal portion.

Unit 9 is supported by a tightly packed level of river cobbles, slabs, and chunks (Unit 8). While most of these stones are horizontally laid, many, especially those closest to the exposed terraces, slant to the west. Unit 9 is heavily disturbed in this area, thus it is likely that this deviation from a flat-laid pattern is due to postabandonment destruction, especially by root action. The earthen matrix into which the Unit 8 stones

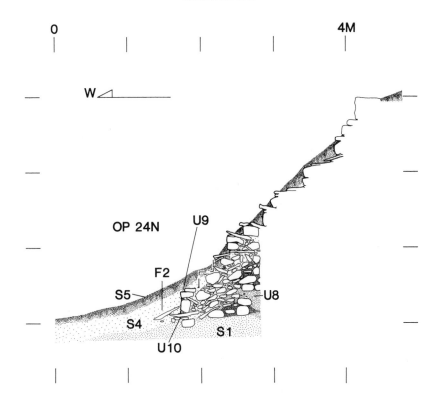

Figure 45b.   Str. 205-256, Section.

are set is variable, definable as several distinct pockets. Packed around the stones found under Unit 9 to a depth of 0.14-0.21 m is a fine-textured tan clay which slopes down rapidly from east to west, paralleling the stepping down of Unit 9. Beneath this level the Unit 8 stones are set in two different matrices. One, found in the middle and the base of the fill, is a greasy dark brown clay with included charcoal and small orange clay flecks. The upper pocket of this material is 0.16-0.33 m thick, while the lower pocket is no more than 0.09 m thick. The second soil matrix, also found in two discontinuous lenses, is a gritty, deep red clay. The upper pocket has a maximum thickness of 0.39 m, while the lower pocket is 0.02-0.18 m thick. All of these different clay matrices continue into the eastern excavation limit to an undetermined extent (see Fig. 45). These variegated clay lenses probably represent earth adhering to the Unit 8 cobbles when they were

TABLE 3.41

EXCAVATION SUMMARY

Lot #	Contents	Depositional Significance	Provenience
24M/1	6 sherds; 4 censer frags.	Terminal occupation debris (secondary)	Within Strata 2-3
24N/1	5 sherds; 27 pcs. obsidian	Terminal occupation debris (secondary)	Within Strata 4-5
24N/2	31 sherds; 4 pcs. obsidian	Fill	Within Unit 8
24N/3	16 sherds; 6 pcs. obsidian	Preconstruction occupation debris (secondary)	Within Stratum 1, beneath Units 8-10

TABLE 3.42

STRUCTURAL/DEPOSITIONAL SUMMARY TIME SPANS: 1-4

Time Span	Construction Stage	Activity	Features	Lots
1	—	Abandonment and burial of Str. 205-256	Strata 2-5, Feat. 1-2	24M/1, 24N/1
2	Str. 205-256	Construction and use of Str. 205-256	Units 4-10	24N/2
3	East court 1	Construction of east court	Units 1-3	—
4	—	Preconstruction occupation and soil deposition	Stratum 1	24N/3

originally deposited as fill and indicate that several sources were tapped for the construction of Str. 205-256.

In sum, Str. 205-256 is 1.54 m high on the east and c. 4 m high on the west, c. 10 m wide east-west, and oriented S 4° 0′ W to S 9° 0′ W. Both its east and west sides are mounted by a series of long, low, narrow step-terraces; on the east flank these terraces are set into an earthen fill associated with the raising of the elevated east court (Unit 3), while on the west they rest on a natural rise (Stratum 1). The Unit 10 slabs compensate for the inherent instability of this situation by providing a secure construction base. As noted earlier, summit construction includes rough, low stone plinths separated by a lower earthen surface (see above and Fig. 45). Because the east and west Str. 205-256 construction elements are not tied together by direct stratigraphic links, it is impossible to know if they were built at the same time. But, since none of these units were buried by later construction, they must have been exposed during the terminal phase of occupation and formed parts of a single functioning construction. Lot 24N/2 derives from the Unit 8 stone fill. It is very likely, however, that this material originated earlier in another area and was redeposited during construction.

Time Span 1: Following this phase of building and use, Str. 205-256 was abandoned and subsequently partially buried by naturally deposited earth levels. On the east, the first level deposited during this period is a very fine-textured, loosely compacted brown clay which slopes down from and buries the lower two terraces of Unit 4 (Stratum 2). This level is 0.12-0.4 m thick. On the west the comparable layer is Stratum 4, a fine-textured, loosely compacted tan clay

containing many roots. This level is 0.26-0.37 m thick and slopes over and down from the lowest three Unit 9 terraces. On both east and west these soil levels are capped by a dark brown to black humus horizon represented by Strata 3 and 5 respectively. Stratum 3 is 0.08-0.17 m thick and buries Units 4-7 completely or in part, while Stratum 5 is 0.05-0.1 m thick and obscures all but the two highest Unit 9 terraces. Also associated with this period are Feat. 1 and 2, scatterings of architectural debris found respectively in Op. 24M and N. Feature 1 is a fairly dense concentration of small to medium-sized stones extending 0.44 m east of the basal Unit 4 terrace. These stones are found solely within Stratum 2 and extend 0.1-0.16 m above the Unit 3/Stratum 2 interface. Apparently, this discrete collapse level fell onto the court soon after abandonment, since relatively little outwash has accumulated on the surface. On the west, Feat. 2 is a more dispersed scattering of fallen stones found primarily within Stratum 4 and sloping down and away from Unit 9. Lots are defined for Strata 2-3 (24M/1) and 4-5 (24N/1). While these locations point to their deposition after abandonment, it is likely that the included objects originated from Str. 205-256 during T.S. 2 and were subsequently dispersed to the nearby area, probably by erosional forces.

STRUCTURE 205-261 (Fig. 46)

Structure 205-261, the c. 6.5-m-high structure that closes the east side of the south plaza, was investigated in 1978 by means of Op. 24O. This trench, placed on the approximate axis of the structure's west face, measures 1.5 m north-south by 3.25 m east-west and reaches a maximum depth of 0.51 m below ground

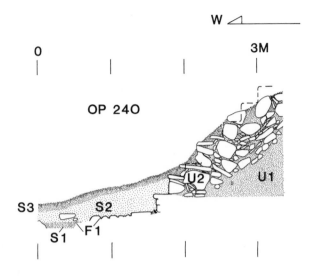

Figure 46.   Str. 205-261, Op 24O, Section.

surface west of construction. In addition to removing the overburden from terminal construction and clearing to the west, Op. 24O extends 1.58 m into architectural fill to a maximum depth of 1.39 m below ground surface.

Excavation Lots: Two lots containing 172 sherds, 18 censer fragments, 11 pieces of obsidian, one figurine fragment, and three pieces of *bajareque* are defined in Op. 24O. Of these lots, 24O/1 is from a terminal occupation debris context, while 24O/2 is from fill.

Time Span 3: The first event in the sequence of activity reflected in Op. 24O was the deposition of Stratum 1, a densely compacted, fine-textured orange clay exposed to a depth of 0.06-0.09 m. This naturally deposited stratum is revealed over a horizontal distance of 0.62 m in the western part of Op. 24O. Because it is found only in the western edge of Op. 24O and is not directly related to the exposed Str. 205-261 units, the inclusion of Stratum 1 within a

preconstruction time span is based on the indirect evidence of elevation. The bottom of the Str. 205-261 basal terrace (Unit 2) rests 0.12 m higher than the surface of Stratum 1, suggesting that Stratum 1 would run under, and hence predate, this construction.

Time Span 2: The next period of activity saw the construction of Str. 205-261, represented here by Units 1-2. Unit 2 is a series of five step-terraces underlain by a level of tightly packed cobbles 0.1-0.5 m thick. The upper exposed section of this element was heavily disturbed when uncovered (these step-terraces are reconstructed in Fig. 46). The terraces are built like those in Str. 205-256 and range between 0.22 and 0.3 m high by 0.22-0.23 m wide, based on the best-preserved examples. The Unit 2 step-terraces are oriented roughly S 2° 30′ W and rise to a reconstructed height of 1.66 m over a horizontal distance of 1.45 m. Surface remains indicate that these low,

TABLE 3.43

EXCAVATION SUMMARY

Lot #	Contents	Depositional Significance	Provenience
24O/1	97 sherds; 18 censer frags.; 3 *bajareque* frags.; 1 figurine frag.; 1 pc. obsidian	Terminal occupation debris (secondary)	Within Strata 2-3
24O/2	75 sherds; 10 pcs. obsidian	Fill	Within Units 1-2

TABLE 3.44

STRUCTURAL/DEPOSITIONAL SUMMARY TIME SPANS: 1-3

Time Span	Construction Stage	Activity	Features	Lots
1	—	Abandonment and burial of Str. 205-261	Strata 2-3, Feat. 1	24O/1
2	Str. 205-261	Construction and use of Str. 205-261	Units 1-2	24O/2
3	—	Preconstruction soil deposition (?)	Stratum 1	—

narrow terraces once covered the full length of Str. 205-261's west face.

The aforementioned basal cobble level (part of Unit 2) consists of horizontally laid small to large cobbles and slabs in an orange clay matrix. There is a general tendency for the cobbles to be stacked into low columns under the exposed terrace stones. Above the level of the fifth terrace the stones slope down to the west. While it is possible that these sloping stones represent a change in the manner of fill deposition, it is more likely that they were dislodged from their original horizontal positions by postoccupation disturbances.

Underlying Unit 2 is a densely compacted orange clay with some charcoal flecks (Unit 1). This fill unit rises to the east, paralleling the rise in the Unit 2 terraces, and reaches a maximum exposed thickness of 0.82 m. The charcoal fragments dispersed through this clay along with some artifacts suggest that Unit 2 originally derived from a cultural deposit.

No plaza pavement is found west of Unit 2, and the ground surface exposed during the use of this structure is not clearly discernible. It seems likely that, at least in the immediate area of Str. 205-261, the plaza was surfaced with tamped earth.

Lot 24O/2 derives from Unit 1 and the stone fill of Unit 2. It is recognized that this collection represents redeposited artifacts with earlier origins elsewhere.

Time Span 1: After this period of construction, the basal levels of Str. 205-261 were buried by Strata 2-3. Stratum 2 is a loosely compacted, orange-brown, sandy clay which slopes down from and buries the two basal terraces of Unit 2. This level varies in thickness between 0.16 and 0.42 m. Stratum 3 caps Stratum 2 and obscures, at least in part, the five preserved terraces of Unit 2. It is a dark brown to black

clay-humus horizon 0.06-0.11 m thick. Also deposited at this time was Feat. 1, a level of tumbled stone architectural debris—unmodified cobbles and slabs—most densely concentrated close to Unit 2 and decreasing in frequency with increasing distance from that terrace system.

Lot 24O/1 was recovered from Strata 2-3. It is very likely, however, that this material originated during the use of Str. 205-261 and was redeposited by erosional forces after abandonment.

STRUCTURE 205-196 (Fig. 47)

Structure 205-196 is a 0.78-m-high structure that closes the northeast side of a small plaza defined by Str. 205-195/197. It was investigated in 1978 by a trench (Op. 24R) 1.5 m east-west by 9.13 m north-south which sectioned the platform from its southwest face to its northeast margin. Excavations penetrated 0.12-0.95 m below ground surface, with the deepest probe located immediately south of Str. 205-196's southern basal wall (see below).

Excavation Lots: Seven lots containing 798 sherds, one censer fragment, one figurine fragment, 201 pieces of obsidian, four pieces of ground stone, and 16 *bajareque* fragments are defined in Op. 24R. Of these lots, three are from terminal occupation contexts (24R/1-3); one is from architectural fill (24R/5); two derive from mixed fill and terminal debris (24R/4 and 6); and one is from a heavily disturbed context (24R/7) (see Table 3.45).

Time Span 3: The first period of activity recognized in Op. 24R involved the deposition of underlying natural soil levels, Strata 1-3, all exposed in the southern portion of the trench. The lowest of these,

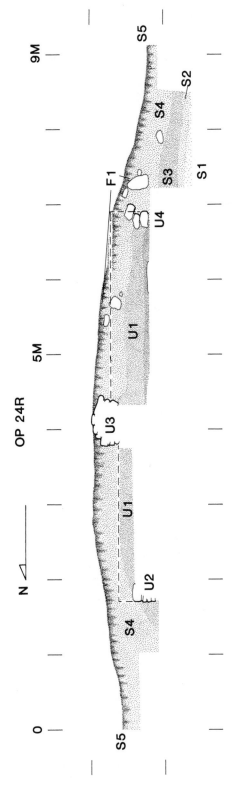

Figure 47.   Str. 205-196, Op 24R, Section.

TABLE 3.45

EXCAVATION SUMMARY

Lot #	Contents	Depositional Significance	Provenience
24R/1	159 sherds; 1 metate frag.	Terminal occupation debris (secondary)	Within Strata 4-5, to 0.14 m below SE corner of Op. 24R, S of Unit 4
24R/2	*	Terminal occupation debris (secondary)	Within Strata 4-5, S of Unit 4 and Feat. 1
24R/3	221 sherds; 14 pcs. obsidian; 1 *bajareque* frag.	Terminal occupation debris (secondary)	Within Stratum 4, mixed with Feat. 1
24R/4	87 sherds; 38 pcs. obsidian	Mixed terminal occupation debris and fill	Within Strata 4-5, between Units 3 and 4, to 0.24 m below ground surface
24R/5	196 sherds; 1 censer frag.; 1 figurine frag.; 127 pcs. obsidian; 3 metate frags.; 4 *bajareque* frags.	Fill	Within Unit 1
24R/6	131 sherds; 11 *bajareque* frags.; 11 pcs. obsidian	Mixed terminal occupation debris and fill	Within Strata 4-5 and Unit 1a, between Units 2-3
24R/7**	4 sherds; 11 pcs. obsidian	Disturbed	Within Strata 4-5, N of Unit 2

*Lots 24R/2 and 3 were mistakenly combined in the lab; the vast majority of the material listed under 24R/3 was originally from 24R/2.

**Ant nests and root activities have so heavily disturbed this portion of Op. 24R that the mixing of materials from different contexts cannot be ruled out.

Stratum 1, is a hard-compacted, gritty yellow clay that slopes gradually from north to south, dropping 0.09 m over a 1.13-m horizontal distance. Stratum 1 is uncovered to a maximum thickness of 0.1 m. The overlying Stratum 2 is a fine-textured, moderately dense, dark brown clay with some included grit. Stratum 3 is a fine-textured tan clay with pebble inclusions, 0.14-0.27 m thick, sloping down from north to south 0.21 m over a 1.28-m distance. In sum, these three naturally deposited levels measure 0.46 m thick at maximum and represent a gradual slope on which Str. 205-196 was built. The top of Stratum 3 is 0.12 m below the base of Str. 205-196 (Unit 4). To the north of Str. 205-196 no clear evidence of any precon-

TABLE 3.46

STRUCTURAL/DEPOSITIONAL SUMMARY TIME SPANS: 1-3

Time Span	Construction Stage	Activity	Features	Lots
1	—	Abandonment and burial of Str. 205-196	Strata 4-5, Feat. 1	24R/1-3
2	Str. 205-196	Construction and use of Str. 205-196	Units 1-4	24R/5
3	—	Preconstruction deposition of natural soil levels	Strata 1-3	—

struction soil horizons was noted, apparently due to disturbance wrought by roots and ant nests.

Time Span 2: The following period saw the construction of Str. 205-196. On its south face is a badly tumbled cobble wall resting just above Stratum 3 and standing to a preserved height of only 0.34 m (Unit 4). This wall is more obvious in the west face of Op. 24R, appearing as a pile of medium to large cobbles, 0.06 by 0.2 to 0.18 by 0.3 m, set in a brown clay matrix (Fig. 47). The lower two superimposed stones are still in position, while the upper courses are in various states of tumble southward from this wall. If we assume these cobbles were included in the original construction of Unit 4, it would have stood to a reconstructed height of 0.52 m. It is clear from the excavated section that this wall is no more than one stone thick, an average of 0.2-0.3 m. Unit 4 in turn retains the clay fill of Unit 1.

The Unit 1 fill is identical in composition to the Stratum 3 clay described above. Throughout its exposed thickness of 0.22-0.48 m, the only change is a gradual darkening in color with increasing depth. The surface of Unit 1 is much higher than Stratum 3; it also stops abruptly at Unit 4 and is not found to continue southward at the same level. These points suggest that the majority of the unit is cultural in origin. It remains possible that an undetermined part of the Unit 1 base incorporates an upward continuation of natural matrix (Stratum 3). Between the preserved top of Unit 1 and the reconstructed surface of Unit 4 a level 0.1-0.31 m thick represents a continuation of Strata 4-5, deposited after Str. 205-196's abandonment (see below). It is likely that Unit 1 once filled this area, but has since eroded. Given the absence of any formal floor in the area between Units 4 and 3 (see below), it is very probable that the Unit 1 surface originally consisted of tamped earth. This would also help account for the erosion that occurred after abandonment.

Unit 3 is 2.51 m north of Unit 4's north face and rests on the preserved surface of Unit 1. This element is a wall 0.36 m high by 0.6 m thick, built of unfaced river cobbles laid in rough horizontal courses, packed with chinking stones and set in a clay matrix. While slumping to the south, Unit 3 was still sufficiently well preserved when uncovered to reveal an orientation of N 15° 30' W. While Unit 3's base is 0.2 m above the preserved top of Unit 4, it is likely that, given the above reconstruction, the basal 0.1 m of Unit 3 was once buried by Unit 1. This would have left at least

0.26 m of Unit 3 projecting above the Unit 1 earthen surface.

Further to the north, Unit 1 continues, underlying Unit 3 and proceeding at this elevation for another 1.22 m before it becomes difficult to discern (due to root and insect disturbances). It is very likely that Unit 1 persisted originally at the same level recognized beneath Unit 3 until it reached its northern structure limit, defined by Unit 2. The earthen fill north of Unit 3 is identical in composition to Unit 1 to the south and undoubtedly represents a continuation of this fill unit. Unit 1 on the north is exposed to a depth of 0.17-0.2 m. The absence of a formal floor in the 2.08 m between Units 3 and 2 indicates that the surface of Unit 1 was left exposed during occupation.

Unit 2, the northern basal wall of Str. 205-196, is preserved to 0.3 m high and constructed of unmodified river cobbles placed in roughly horizontal courses packed with chinking pebbles in a clay matrix. Unit 2 is set 0.08 m below the uncovered base of Unit 4, its southern counterpart. Again, due to disturbance, Unit 2 is preserved only in the center of the trench, and its orientation cannot be obtained. It is likely that it once rose an additional 0.19 m to a full height of 0.49 m. This reconstruction allows for the articulation of Unit 2 with Unit 3 and corresponds to the observed extent of Unit 1, which most likely served as the clay backing to this wall.

Structure 205-196 is, therefore, a 5.19-m-wide platform oriented N 15° 30' W and built primarily of earthen fill faced with basal stone retaining walls. On the north side the structure is faced with a 0.49-m-high cobble wall, which gives way to a level earthen surface that runs back 2.08 m to a medial summit wall or bench (Unit 3) standing at least 0.36 m high and 0.6 m thick. The recovery of 11 *bajareque* fragments from Lot 24R/6 north of Unit 3, although in a mixed context, at least suggests the use of this material in superstructure construction. Further south, the surface of Str. 205-196 is at least 0.1 m higher than it is north of the summit wall. The apparent summit level on both sides, however, remains unpaved, tamped earth. Finally Unit 4, a 0.52-m-high cobble wall, defines the south edge of the structure. The south side of Str. 205-196 probably served as the rear of the structure; most of the artifacts recovered in Op. 24R come from this flank, suggesting that this was a favorite area for jettisoning trash. In addition, the downward slope of the original ground surface to the south would have added to Unit 4's height and made summit access on this side more difficult.

Lot 24R/5 was recovered within the Unit 1 fill. It is realized, however, that this material may well have been deposited earlier elsewhere and redeposited during the construction of Str. 205-196.

Time Span 1: After Str. 205-196 was abandoned it was partially buried by Strata 4-5. Stratum 4 is a fine-textured, loosely compacted orange-brown clay which covers Stratum 3 and all of the Str. 205-196 units save the top of Unit 3. Ranging in thickness from 0.22 to 0.39 m, this element is found over the entire length of Op. 24R. Stratum 5 is a dark brown clay-humus horizon overlying Stratum 4 to a depth of 0.06-0.13 m. Also deposited at this time was Feat. 1, a level of tumbled stones found primarily within Stratum 4 and almost exclusively south of Unit 4, most probably having issued from that construction. These stones are most densely concentrated immediately south of Unit 4 and decrease in density with distance away from it. The relatively few tumbled stones found north of Feat. 1 are also included with this element.

Lots 24R/1-3 were recovered within Strata 4-5 (24R/1), or found mixed with and buried by the stones of Feat. 1 (24R/2-3). It is likely, however, that this material originated during T.S. 2 and was redeposited by natural forces in the postabandonment period.

CHOCO

MAIN GROUP

STRUCTURE 212-4 (Figs. 48 and 49)

Structure 212-4, the large platform separating the north and south courts of the principal group, was investigated by two trenches, Op. 21B and J. The former is an excavation 1.5 m east-west by 8.9 m north-south, designed to remove the overburden from the latest construction surfaces in the approximate center of the south face of this platform. In addition to clearing construction, the trench is dug to a maximum depth of 0.81 m below ground surface in front of the structure and 3.14 m into the fill underlying the upper terraces of the platform (see Fig. 48). The latter operation has been carried down to a maximum depth of 1.82 m below ground level into structural fill. Operation 21J, on the upper north face of the structure in line with Op. 21B, measures 1.4 m north-south by 1.2 m east-west. This trench extends through construction fill to a maximum depth of 2.08 m. The primary goal here was to locate the north side of an early construction encountered in Op. 21B and, if possible, to obtain datable material from fill.

Excavation Lots: Operation 21B is divided into two lots containing a total of 50 sherds, one figurine fragment, six censer fragments, and one piece of obsidian. Lot 21B/1 represents debris associated with the final phase of occupation of Str. 212-4-1st, while 21B/2 contains material associated with the terminal use periods of an earlier construction phase, Str. 212-4-2nd (see Table 3.47). Operation 21J produced no material.

Time Span 5: The earliest evidence of activity uncovered here is associated with the construction of a massive platform, designated Str. 212-4-3rd, incorporating Units 1, 2, 13, and 14. This construction, only the upper portions of which were cleared, has a high, steeply battered central element, c. 9.08 m wide north-south across its base (Units 2 and 14), built atop a series of narrow step-terraces (Units 1 and 13). The steeply inward-sloping construction is preserved to a height of 1.93 m on the south (Unit 2) and 2.91 m on the north (Unit 14) and is built of well-coursed unfaced river cobbles and slabs packed with chinking stones set in a clay matrix (Fig. 49). The cobbles composing this wall measure roughly 0.27 by 0.2 m, while the slabs are somewhat narrower, 0.27 by 0.08 m. The Units 1 and 13 terraces consist of low vertical walls built of large, uncut river cobbles set in rough courses and packed with chinking stones. These low walls are surmounted by a series of flat-laid stone slabs which run under the next higher terrace or, in the case of the highest elements, under Unit 2 or 14. The two most completely exposed terraces, the upper terraces of Units 1 and 13, measure 0.42 and 0.3 m wide, respectively, while the former stands 0.32 m high. How much further these terraces extend below the exposed level is unknown. The orientation of Str. 212-4-3rd is S 82° 30′ E. Access to the summit of this platform must be via an as yet undisclosed formal staircase(s).

No direct stratigraphic links have been found between Units 1 and 2 in Op. 21B and Units 13 and 14 in Op. 21J. The contemporaneity of these elements and their integration into a single structure is suggested by three lines of evidence. First, the method of construction employed on both the north and south is essentially identical and each side mirrors the other in form. Second, the different component units are

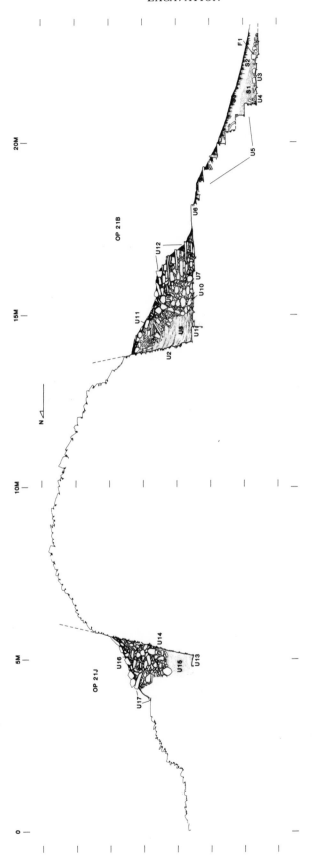

Figure 48.   Str. 212-4, Section.

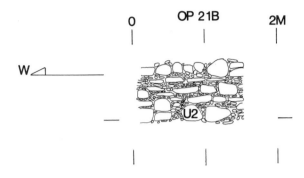

Figure 49.   Str. 212-4, Elevation.

symmetrical in their elevations: Unit 1 is 0.02 m higher than Unit 13. Third, they are both buried by the same general sequence of fill units: Units 8 and 11 in Op. 21B and 15 and 16 in Op. 21J. This latter point indicates that they were all built prior to the construction of Str. 212-4-1st.

Time Span 4: The next construction phase is designated Str. 212-4-2nd and includes Units 3-7, all in Op. 21B. Operation 21J does not extend far enough to the north to encounter traces of this phase of architecture. Time Span 4 saw the burial of Str. 212-4-3rd up to the level of the top of Unit 1 by the construction of the seven step-terraces of Unit 5 (Fig. 48). Similar to Unit 1 of the previous construction phase, these step-terraces consist of vertical walls each 0.16-0.37 m high, built of river cobbles and chinking pebbles surmounted by horizontally set stone slabs. These slabs run 0.35-0.41 m back and under the succeeding low cobble wall. This terrace system ultimately rests on a level of flat-laid slabs (Unit 4), which extend 0.39 m out from and under the basal terraces of Unit 5. These flat slabs, similar to those used to form the terrace treads, probably served as stabilizers for Unit 5. The seven step-terraces of Unit 5 are, in turn, surmounted by a 0.25-m-high cobble and chinking-stone wall

which supports a series of large stone slabs averaging 1.51 m in length (Unit 6). This unit forms a marked break, by virtue of its great width, from the narrow step-terrace pattern of Unit 5. Running back to the north from this unit at the same level is Unit 7, a surface of flat-laid uncut cobbles, only the tops of which have been exposed in excavation. This unit, which ultimately intersects the upper surface of Unit 1, in conjunction with Unit 6, functions as a 3.53-m-wide southern terrace above which rises the still-exposed wall of Unit 2. Surface indications and the results of excavations in Op. 21F (see below) strongly suggest that the eight terraces of this phase (Units 5 and 6) extend the entire length of the south face of Str. 212-4-2nd.

To the south of Unit 4, extending into the south court, is a surface of horizontally laid uncut cobbles in a fine-textured gray clay matrix (Unit 3). The cobbles employed here are fairly large, ranging from 0.27 by 0.4 to 0.18 by 0.18 m. Despite the lack of a direct stratigraphic link between this unit and the units composing Str. 212-4-2nd, it is presumed that the Unit 3 surface dates to this period.

The resulting picture of Str. 212-4-2nd is of a platform with a high, steeply sloping central element fronted on the south by a long, broad terrace, access to which is by means of long, low, narrow step-terraces. The latter construction rests on a series of slab stabilizers, which give way on the south to a paved court floor. The terraces of Units 5 and 6 rise a full 1.98 m over a horizontal distance of c. 2.96 m and are oriented c. S 83° 30′ E.

Lot 21B/2 was found atop the upper terrace of Unit 1, a surface exposed during T.S. 4. The overlying fill, Unit 8, was found to be sterile and seems an unlikely source for this material.

Time Span 3: The final stage of recorded construction activity (Str. 212-4-1st) saw the addition of at least

TABLE 3.47

EXCAVATION SUMMARY

Lot #	Contents	Depositional Significance	Provenience
21B/1	50 sherds; 1 figurine frag.; 5 censer frags.	Terminal occupation debris, Str. 212-4-1st (primary)	On Unit 3, buried by Feat. 1
21B/2	1 censer frag.; 1 pc. obsidian	Terminal occupation debris, Str. 212-4-3rd (primary)	On Unit 1, buried by Unit 8

TABLE 3.48

STRUCTURAL/DEPOSITIONAL SUMMARY TIME SPANS: 1-5

Time Span	Construction Stage	Activity	Features	Lots
1	—	Natural burial of Str. 212-4-1st	Strata 1-2	—
2	—	Abandonment of Str. 212-4-1st	Feat. 1	—
3	Str. 212-4-1st	Construction and use of Str. 212-4-1st	Units 8-12, Units 15-17	21B/1
4	Str. 212-4-2nd	Construction and use of Str. 212-4-2nd	Units 3-7	21B/2
5	Str. 212-4-3rd	Construction and use of Str. 212-4-3rd	Units 1-2, Units 13-14	—

five step-terraces above the level of the Units 6-7 broad terrace on the south side, and the final burial on the north and south of Str. 212-4-3rd (Units 8-12, 15-17). In order of occurrence, a fill block of sterile, fine-textured brown clay streaked with gray (Units 8 and 15) was placed over and against Units 1, 2, 13, 14, and (to a limited extent) 7, on both the south and north sides of the platform. This was soon followed on the south by construction of a fill-retaining wall directly on Unit 7, composed of two parallel lines of river cobbles (Unit 9). These cobbles are 0.2 by 0.33 to 0.26 by 0.14 m. Unit 9 marks the boundary between a fill of densely packed, horizontally set cobbles to the south (Unit 10) and a mixed earthen and smaller-cobble fill to the north (Units 8 and 11). The cobbles composing Unit 11, which override Unit 8 here, are not only smaller than those found in Unit 10, but also more jumbled and generally down-sloping in their orientation. This suggests that they were piled into place from above and allowed to collect against the lower fill-retaining wall of Unit 9. It is also possible that they were disturbed after construction.

The three definite and two putative step-terraces of Unit 12 are built into and over the fill of Unit 10 and rest on the surface of Unit 6. Similar in construction to Unit 5, these terraces consist of vertical walls 0.26-0.29 m high, built up of river cobbles and pebbles, each surmounted by a series of slabs that extend back 0.22-0.26 m to the next higher terrace, under which they run to be ultimately tenoned into the Unit 10 fill. These terraces rise a preserved height of c. 1.12 m over a horizontal extent of 0.86 m. Presumably they

continue to the summit, although extensive postoccupation disturbance makes this interpretation problematic. As with Unit 5, the Unit 12 terraces probably continue the length of the south face of Str. 212-4-1st and are oriented c. S 83° 30' E.

The north side of the platform revealed in Op. 21J is less clear. After the deposition of the lower clay fill (Unit 15), a fill of variable-sized, horizontally laid river cobbles (Unit 16) was set over Unit 15 and against Unit 14. As with Units 11 and 10 on the south, this probably served as a base for now-destroyed construction. Unfortunately, the only hint of this construction is a c. 0.76-m-long horizontal stone slab balanced on its south end by an unfaced river cobble (Unit 17, north edge of trench). This unit has the appearance of a disturbed step-terrace. Slightly further upslope another slab-and-stone combination was noted which might represent a continuation of this step-terrace pattern (included in Unit 17).

Structure 212-4-1st shows major changes from the previous construction phases. First, most of Str. 212-4-3rd is buried; Units 2 and 14 no longer protrude to the same degree as they did in Str. 212-4-2nd. By this time Units 2 and 14 probably function as a stable core supporting the last phase of construction. Second, the once-broad southern terrace of Str. 212-4-2nd is severely truncated by the deposition of Units 8-11 and the construction of the Unit 12 terraces. Despite this activity there is still a marked break in terrace widths here, although Unit 6 is now reduced to only 1.10 m wide. Finally, according to the excavated data, Str. 212-4-1st is faced almost exclusively by step-terraces, a construction style employed in the two earlier phases but never to this extent. In sum, Str. 212-4-1st is a high platform completely faced on the south and, probably, the north by a series of long, low and narrow terraces, broken at several points by broader surfaces, all stepping up in short increments toward the summit.

The inclusion of Units 8-12 and 15-17 in T.S. 3 is based on their similarity in composition and sequence of deposition.

Time Span 2: The penultimate activity is associated with Feat. 1 in Op. 21B; Op. 21J was not carried far enough to the north to uncover evidence relevant to this phase. Feature 1 is a c. 0.12-m-thick level of jumbled cobbles and chinking stones intermixed with a mottled gray clay which overlies Unit 3 by 0.02-0.06 m. It represents collapsed construction material deposited after the abandonment of Str. 212-4-1st. This debris is composed of both stones and, possibly, eroded *bajareque*, as suggested by the orange mottling of the gray clay. The original source of the material is Str. 212-4-1st.

Lot 21B/1 was found directly on Unit 3 and buried by Feat. 1. Given this stratigraphic position, 21B/1 cannot be associated with any time span earlier than the construction and use of Str. 212-4-1st (T.S. 3) or later than the period of its abandonment (T.S. 2). Lot 21B/1, therefore, represents occupation debris from Str. 212-4-1st that was washed down and redeposited in front of that structure after abandonment but before deterioration of the platform (as represented by Feat. 1).

Time Span 1: After the deposition of Feat. 1, Strata 1-3 were laid down. Strata 1 and 2 are both fine-textured gray clays, distinguished by the presence in the former of orange mottling, which increases in intensity toward the base of the layer. Stratum 1 is c. 0.5 m thick immediately adjacent to the basal Unit 5 terrace and extends over the lowest terrace of that unit. Stratum 2 is c. 0.43 m thick over the basal terrace of Unit 5 and overlies the second and third terraces of that unit. Both Strata 1 and 2 slope down to the south away from the structure, thinning to only 0.1 and 0.12 m respectively at the southern edge of Op. 21B. Stratum 3, the uppermost soil level, is a gray-black humus horizon c. 0.06-0.1 m thick. These levels overlie Feat. 1 and Str. 212-4-1st construction. The fine texture of all these strata suggests a riverine origin; they were probably deposited here by periodic floods.

STRUCTURE 212-6 (Fig. 51)

Structure 212-6, closing the west side of the north court, was investigated by a trench 1.5 m north-south by 2.53 m east-west, excavated into the approximate center of its east, court-facing side. Operation 21C extends 1.24 m into Str. 212-6 construction to a maximum depth of c. 1.18 m below ground surface. Excavations were also carried down c. 0.84 m below ground surface in front of revealed construction.

Excavation Lots: Forty sherds and two small, irregular pieces of dark brown *bajareque* were recovered in two excavation lots, 21C/1 and 2. The former derives from the earth outside and over construction and represents terminal occupation debris; Lot 21C/2 is from construction fill (see Table 3.49).

Time Span 3: The first period of activity in this area involved the deposition of Stratum 1, which underlies exposed construction (Units 1 and 2). Stratum 1 consists of yellow-gray, fine-textured clay marked by mottled patches of gritty orange soil. It is exposed to a thickness of 0.02-0.15 m at the base of excavation, and is probably a naturally deposited surface.

Time Span 2: The next period of activity exposed in Op. 21C involved the construction of the terraces of Str. 212-6. First, a fill of densely packed, horizontally laid cobbles in a light orange-brown clay matrix (Unit 1) was deposited. In addition to the horizontal laying of the fill stones, several large cobbles were set in a vertical line under the back of the first low cobble terrace riser. This apparently ensured the stability of the second terrace. After the deposition of Unit 1, a series of five exposed step-terraces (Unit 2) was built into and over this fill. These terraces are constructed of low vertical walls of uncut cobbles forming a single course and packed with chinking stones. The lowest of the walls is surmounted by a series of horizontally set stone slabs, which run under the succeeding higher step and are then tenoned into the fill. Above the basal terrace, slabs are no longer employed in this fashion and are replaced by cobbles, which in the four revealed terraces run under the successively higher risers. The terraces of Unit 2 are 0.14-0.3 m high by 0.12-0.42 m wide and appear, on the surface, to run the length of the structure at an approximate azimuth of S 2° 0′ W. Surface remains further indicate that Unit 2 continues to step up in short increments to the summit beyond excavation limits. No prepared court floor was uncovered east of Unit 2, though it is probable that the interface formed by the junction of Strata 1 and 2 represents an informal court surface used during the occupation of Str. 212-6. This infer-

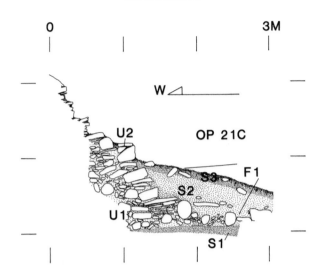

Figure 51.   Str. 212-6, Op 21C, Section.

ence is supported by the fact that tumbled architectural debris (Feat. 1) lies directly on the interface. Lot 21C/2, associated with the deposition of Unit 1, undoubtedly derives from elsewhere.

Time Span 1: After the construction and use of Str. 212-6 there was a period of abandonment and structural collapse marked by the deposition of Feat. 1. The latter is a level c. 0.12-0.16 m thick of tumbled cobbles and small chinking stones extending from the base of Unit 2 eastward to the limits of excavation. Presumably this represents postabandonment structural debris which fell onto an occupation floor, represented by the interface between Strata 1 and 2.

The last phase of activity uncovered in Op. 21C involved the deposition of Strata 2 and 3. Stratum 2 is a yellow-gray, fine-textured clay very similar to Stratum 1, but lacking the orange mottling. Stratum 3 varies in thickness between 0.08 and 0.12 m and is the dark gray, fine-textured humus horizon. Stratum 3 also contains scattered stones (included in Feat. 1)

which probably fell from final-phase Str. 212-6 construction late in the postabandonment period. The fine grain size of both of these levels suggests that they were deposited by particularly high floods of the Rio Encantado. Both Strata 2 and 3 slope down markedly to the east away from Str. 212-6, the lower three terraces of which they bury. Lot 21C/1, found within these soil units, represents occupation debris from the final phase of Str. 212-6's use (T.S. 2), redeposited at the base of construction in T.S. 1.

STRUCTURE 212-1 (Figs. 50 and 52)

Structure 212-1, the large platform closing the southern side of the south court, was investigated by two trenches, Op. 21D and E. Operation 21D is an excavation 1.5 m east-west by 4.4 m north-south, designed to clear the latest construction surfaces in the approximate center of the court (north) side of Str. 212-1. In addition to this, Op. 21D extends 1.2 m

TABLE 3.49

EXCAVATION SUMMARY

Lot #	Contents	Depositional Significance	Provenience
21C/1	35 sherds	Terminal occupation debris (secondary)	Within Strata 2-3
21C/2	5 sherds; 2 *bajareque* frags.	Fill	Within Unit 1

TABLE 3.50

STRUCTURAL/DEPOSITIONAL SUMMARY TIME SPANS: 1-3

Time Span	Construction Stage	Activity	Features	Lots
1	—	Burial and abandonment of Str. 212-6	Strata 2-3, Feat. 1	21C/1
2	Str. 212-6	Occupation and construction of Str. 212-6	Units 1-2, Strata 1/2 interface	21C/2
3	—	Preconstruction soil deposition	Stratum 1	—

(maximum) into fill underlying the four lowest exposed terraces to a maximum depth of 1.46 m below mound surface. The trench also penetrates 0.28-0.74 m below ground surface north of construction. Operation 21E is a trench 1.8 m east-west by 6.1 m north-south, designed to uncover terminal construction levels on the south side of Str. 212-1. This suboperation was excavated c. 1.35 m below ground surface immediately south of construction and to a depth of c. 0.05-0.1 m below the base of that construction. The specific goal here was to locate a trash deposit associated with the final stage of Str. 212-1's occupation to aid in dating that period.

Excavation Lots: Operation 21D produced 23 sherds from three excavation lots (21D/1-3). One of these lots is from fill (Op. 21D/3), while the other two are from terminal debris contexts. Operation 21E produced 157 sherds, two censer fragments, one piece of obsidian, and four small, irregular *bajareque* fragments, all divided into two lots (21E/1-2). Both of the latter represent terminal occupation debris (see Table 3.51).

Time Span 3: The earliest period of activity reflected in either Op. 21D or E involved the deposition of Stratum 3 on the south. This fine-textured gray clay, mottled with orange, extends from c. 0.2 m above the exposed base of the lowest Unit 6 terrace to an undetermined depth below that construction. It is not clearly defined throughout the trench, dipping down and out of the excavation c. 1.6 m south of the aforementioned basal terrace. The stratigraphic relationship between Stratum 1 and the Unit 6 terrace suggests that the former is the soil level into which the uncovered construction was set, and that the interface between Strata 3 and 4 constituted the exposed ground surface during the occupation of Str. 212-1 (see below).

Time Span 2: The next period saw the deposition of Unit 1 in Op. 21D, a fill of densely packed, horizontally laid river cobbles in a matrix of orange and tan mottled soil varying in texture from fine to gritty. Pebbles are employed as a leveling and packing medium behind the slabs and cobbles that make up the terraces of Unit 4. Also, a vertical line of large cobbles is set below the back edge of the stone slab of the third terrace (in Unit 4), adding stability to this step by providing a column of support at its rear.

The deposition of Unit 1 was followed in short order by the setting of Units 3 and 4, as revealed in Op. 21D. Unit 3 is a series of horizontally set stone slabs that extend c. 0.28 m beyond the front of the basal terrace of Unit 4 and run back and under that terrace for c. 0.47 m. When uncovered, these slabs were canted down to the south, presumably as a result of bearing the weight of the overlying terrace system (Unit 4). Unit 3 functions as a stabilizer for Unit 4, which rests directly on Unit 3. Unit 4 is a series of seven step-terraces with vertical risers built of a rough course of uncut cobbles, measuring 0.13 by 0.16 to 0.18 by 0.32 m, laid on a thin level of small pebbles and packed round with small slabs and chinking stones. Capping these low walls are stone slabs that run under the next higher terrace. These step-terraces range in height between 0.26 and 0.39 m and in width between 0.26 and 0.36 m. Surface indications suggest that the terraces run the length of the north face of Str. 212-1 and are oriented c. S 82° 45' E. Topping this series of step-terraces is a 0.38-m-high cobble and chinking-stone wall, similar to Unit 4, surmounted by a 1.1-m-wide slab terrace built of large individual stones. This broad terrace (Unit 5) runs back an undisclosed distance under the next ascend-

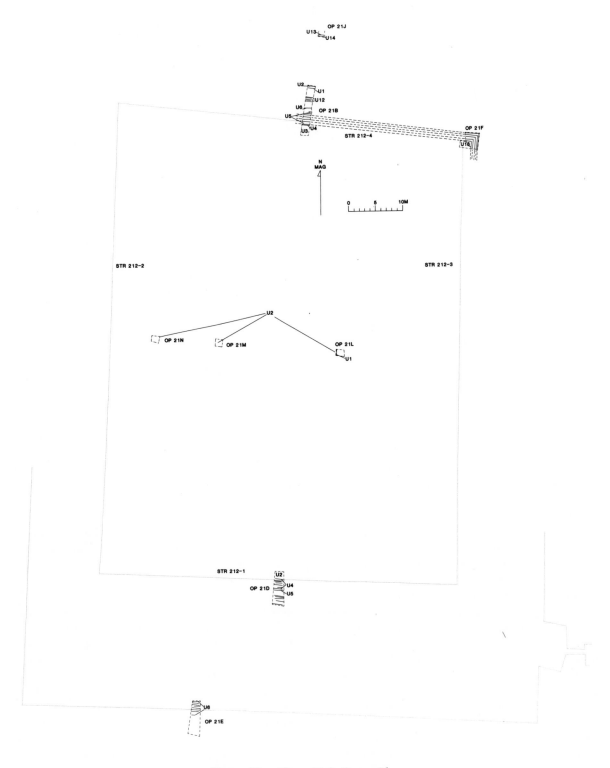

Figure 50.   Choco Main Group Plan.

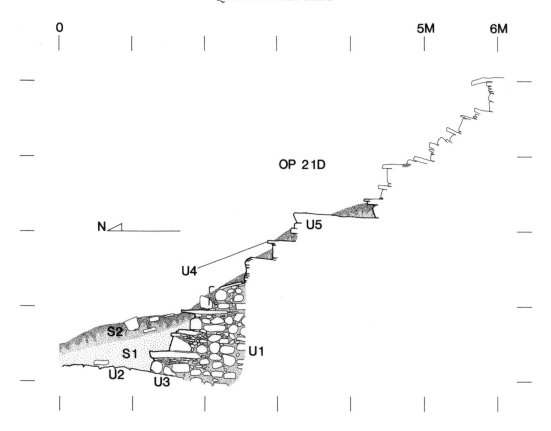

Figure 52.   Str. 212-1, Section.

ing terrace and breaks the otherwise narrow-terrace pattern of lower Unit 4 construction.

Unit 6 represents the terminal phase of construction in Op. 21E, a series of step-terraces very similar to Unit 4 in Op. 21D. The basal terrace of Unit 6 stands to a preserved height of c. 0.82 m and is built of three horizontal courses of large (0.14 by 0.26 to 0.24 by 0.38 m), unfaced river cobbles packed with chinking stones. No stone slabs were noted surmounting this wall. The upper course of cobbles forms the terrace tread and runs under the next low riser. Unfortunately, this basal terrace has fallen to the south and is not preserved across the trench's full width.

The subsequent six step-terraces are similar to those in Unit 4. The terraces are 0.17-0.31 m high by 0.29-0.32 m wide and, on the basis of surface indications, extend the length of the south face of Str. 212-1. Unit 6 is oriented roughly S 82° 30′ E and, together with Units 1, 3, 4, and 5 revealed in Op. 21D, constitutes Str. 212-1. These excavations indicate that the basal width of the platform, north-south, is c. 24.8 m.

Also built at or about the same time was Unit 2 found in Op. 21D, a surface of flat-laid cobbles 0.15 by 0.22 to 0.2 by 0.45 m, set in a fine-textured gray clay matrix and situated at the same level as and immediately north of Unit 3. This cobble surface represents a prepared court floor essentially identical to that uncovered in Op. 21B (Unit 3, at about the same elevation).

Though not excavated, additional terraces rise to the summit of Str. 212-1 beyond the limits of Op. 21D and E. On the north face, seven step-terraces constructed in the same fashion as Unit 4 stand 0.18-0.3 m high and 0.14-0.3 m wide. Above these seven low steps rises a c. 0.44-m-high cobble wall which supports yet another wide terrace similar to Unit 5. While not cleared, this latter terrace is at least 0.5 m wide. Above this the nature of the construction changes somewhat. Stone slabs are no longer in evidence on the surface, and the only stones to be seen are river cobbles and several cut stone blocks. Because of heavy disturbance in this portion of the structure, no indication of how these stones were incorporated into construction has survived (recall that east and west of the centerline,

TABLE 3.51

EXCAVATION SUMMARY

Lot #	Contents	Depositional Significance	Provenience
21D/1	11 sherds	Terminal occupation debris (primary)	Immediately atop Unit 2, sealed by Stratum 1
21D/2	7 sherds	Terminal occupation debris (secondary)	Resting on Unit 5, not well sealed by Stratum 2
21D/3	5 sherds	Fill	Within Unit 1, sealed by Unit 4
21E/1	135 sherds; 2 censer frags.; 1 pc. obsidian; 4 *bajareque* frags.	Terminal occupation debris (secondary)	Within Strata 3-5, above and S of construction, exclusive of area of 21E/2
21E/2	22 sherds	Terminal occupation debris (secondary)	Within Stratum 3, within 0.2 m horizontal distance of basal exposed terrace

above the level of the second major terrace, are found the large cut blocks noted in Chap. 2). In Op. 21E the terraces of Unit 6 continue, according to surface indications, to the summit, broken only by a somewhat broader terrace one-third to one-half of the way up (see Fig. 8). The terraces on the south face of Str. 212-1 are not as clear or as well preserved as those on the north.

The resulting contour of Str. 212-1 is a long high platform formed on both its north and south sides by a series of low terraces stepping up in short increments to the summit and broken at intervals by slightly wider surfaces. The narrow east and west sides above the flanking platforms (see Fig. 8) also show the same mode of construction on the surface, suggesting that in the terminal phase of occupation, this structure was faced on all four flanks by step-terraces.

The identity of building techniques exhibited by Units 4 and 6 suggests that, despite the absence of direct stratigraphic links between them, they form contemporary parts of the same substructure platform.

Unit 2, the exposed portion of the paved south court surface, is included in this time span because it is found at the same level as construction associated with this phase, the stabilizers of Unit 3. This surface must have been exposed and in use at the same time as these units.

The interface between Strata 3 and 4 is also included here because, as the informal ground level

TABLE 3.52

STRUCTURAL/DEPOSITIONAL SUMMARY TIME SPANS: 1-3

Time Span	Construction Stage	Activity	Features	Lots
1	—	Burial and abandonment of Str. 212-1	Strata 1-2, 4-5; Feat. 1	21E/1, 21D/2
2	Str. 212-1	Construction and use of Str. 212-1	Units 1-6, Strata 3/4 interface	21E/2, 21D/1, 21D/3
3	—	Preconstruction soil deposition	Stratum 3	—

TABLE 3.53

EXCAVATION SUMMARY

Lot #	Contents	Depositional Significance	Provenience
21F/1	16 sherds; 1 pc. obsidian	Terminal occupation debris (secondary)	Within Stratum 2
21F/2	63 sherds; 1 figurine frag.; 4 pcs. obsidian	Terminal occupation debris (secondary)	Strata 1/2 interface, and 0.1 m into Stratum 1

exposed during the occupation of Str. 212-1, it was the surface onto which structural debris (Feat. 1) fell after the structure was abandoned.

While artifact Lot 21E/2 derives from within the preterminal construction level (Stratum 3), it is from high up in that layer and may well represent debris scattered and pressed into it during the final period of occupation. Lot 21D/3 presumably represents material accidentally intermixed with the primarily stone fill of Unit 1 and dates to within or before the period of construction. Lot 21D/1 is included here as these artifacts were found directly atop Unit 2, buried by subsequent soil deposition. Most likely, Lot 21D/1 represents *in situ* material associated with Str. 212-1's final use.

Time Span 1: The last phase of activity saw the abandonment and subsequent deterioration of Str. 212-1. During this period Feat. 1, a level of jumbled stone debris resting on Stratum 3, was deposited. This feature is not continuous over the length of the trench and extends c. 2.62 m from the southern basal wall in decreasing density to the south. No comparable evidence of stone collapse was uncovered in Op. 21D. It is probable, however, that the orange mottling found increasingly toward the base of Stratum 1 just above Unit 2 in that trench represents architectural debris; i.e., eroded *bajareque*, redeposited from the summit of Str. 212-1.

Subsequent to this period of structural deterioration, fine clays and silts were deposited, presumably by riverine action, on both the north and south flanks of Str. 212-1. In Op. 21D, Stratum 1, a fine-textured gray clay with increasing orange mottling near its base, overlies Units 2 and 3 and the lower terraces of Unit 4. This stratum varies in thickness between 0.13 and 0.54 m and slopes down markedly to the north. In Op. 21E the comparable level is Stratum 4, a fine-textured brown clay which overlies and extends south of Stratum 3, Feat. 1, and the lower three terraces of

Unit 6, sloping down to the south. Overriding these levels in both operations is a fine-textured brown-black humus horizon c. 0.08-0.21 m thick (designated Stratum 2 in Op. 21D and Stratum 5 in Op. 21E).

Artifact Lot 21E/1 was recovered from Strata 4-5 while 21D/2 derives from Stratum 2. Both probably represent debris deposited originally in the Str. 212-1 area during its period of occupation and redeposited by river floods long after abandonment.

NORTHEAST INTERIOR CORNER OF SOUTH COURT (Figs. 50 and 53)

The northeast corner of the south court, at the junction of Str. 212-3 and -4, was investigated by Op. 21F, a trench 2.7 m north-south by 3.8 m east-west. This operation removed overburden from the surface of the five lowest step-terraces of the terminal construction phase of both platforms and was excavated to c. 1.14 m below ground surface in front of construction (0.24-0.35 m below the base of construction). In addition to the general project goals, Op. 21F was designed to determine how the northeast corner had been closed and, in particular, whether the terraces exposed in Op. 21B (Unit 5) extend to this corner and link up with units from Str. 212-3.

Excavation Lots: The two excavation lots defined here (21F/1 and 2) yielded 79 sherds, five pieces of obsidian, and one figurine fragment. All of this material is associated with the terminal phase of occupation of Str. 212-3 and 212-4 (see Table 3.53).

Time Span 3: The first period of activity recognized in Op. 21F was the deposition of Stratum 1, a fine-textured, homogeneous gray sand which runs under and abuts Str. 212-3 and -4 terminal construction. The top of this stratum is fairly level, although it does slope down gradually to the west, c. 0.1 m over a horizontal distance of c. 2.2 m, and even more gently southward away from construction.

TABLE 3.54

STRUCTURAL/DEPOSITIONAL SUMMARY TIME SPANS: 1-3

Time Span	Construction Stage	Activity	Features	Lots
1	—	Burial and abandonment of Str. 212-3 and -4	Stratum 2	21F/1
2	Str. 212-3 and -4	Construction and use of Str. 212-3 and -4	Unit 18, Strata 1/2 interface	21F/2
3	—	Preterminal construction and soil deposition	Stratum 1	—

Time Span 2: Following the deposition of Stratum 1 was the construction of Unit 18, five exposed step-terraces on both Str. 212-3 and -4 that join at the same level in the northeast corner of the court. The basal terraces of this unit on both structures stand taller than any of the succeeding risers. The basal construction of Str. 212-3 rises to a preserved height of 0.62-0.64 m and has three courses of uncut river cobbles, 0.2 by 0.2 to 0.14 by 0.27 m, packed with small pebbles. A fourth course of thick stone chunks is placed between these cobble courses and the upper stone slab treads that form the c. 0.34-m-wide terrace surface. The basal terrace of Str. 212-4 stands 0.46-0.61 m high and is constructed in the same manner as that of Str. 212-3, although its terrace surface is slightly wider, 0.36-0.38 m. The principal difference between the two terraces is that the base of the Str. 212-4 construction slopes down c. 0.15 m to the east to reach the same level as the base of the Str. 212-3 terrace. Both of these terraces are sunk into Stratum 1, Str. 212-4 by 0.15 m and Str. 212-3 by 0.23 m.

Four step-terraces rise above this base, each consisting of a vertical wall 0.31-0.33 m high, built of a single course of uncut river cobbles surmounted by a level of

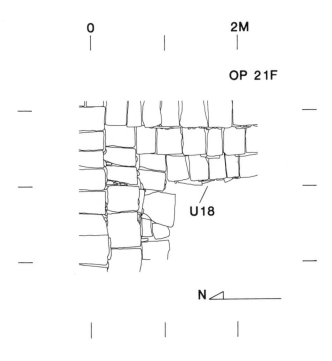

0   2M

OP 21F

U 18

N

Figure 53. Choco Main Court Plan.

flat-laid stone slabs 0.34-0.4 m wide. The orientation of Unit 18 on Str. 212-4 is c. S 83° 30′ E, while on Str. 212-3 it is S 2° 45′ E, deviating somewhat from a right angle at the juncture. According to surface indications, the exposed step-terraces of Str. 212-3 and -4 run the length of their respective platforms. Those on Str. 212-4 line up with the lower terraces (Unit 5) revealed in Op. 21B.

The Unit 18 terraces on both Str. 212-3 and -4 appear to have been constructed at the same time, since they interdigitate at their juncture. The stone slab treads of Str. 212-3 consistently abut those of Str. 212-4, and the same pattern holds for the stones of the terrace risers, except in the basal terraces. Here one of the cobble courses of Str. 212-3's basal construction runs behind its counterpart in Str. 212-4. The cobble coursing in all of the terrace risers is symmetrical; i.e., they meet at the same level in the interior corner. The terraces join to form a series of continuous, level surfaces extending from Str. 212-4 to Str. 212-3. It is certain that the Unit 18 terraces were all exposed and in use during the terminal phase of occupation of both structures and that this corner of the court was closed to access by continuing the step-terraces from one structure to another.

The Stratum 1 surface is interpreted as an occupation floor contemporary with T.S. 2. This surmise is based on the facts that the Strata 1/2 interface is the only soil change near the base of construction, and that its elevation is only 0.33 m lower than the level of the known court surface elsewhere. The recovery of most of the artifactual material found in Op. 21F (Lot 21F/2), and the concentration of possible eroded construction debris (the orange mottling at the base of Stratum 2), at or near this juncture also suggest that this interface represents a surface used during the occupation of Str. 212-3 and -4.

The artifacts of Lot 21F/2 were found on the surface of Stratum 1 and c. 0.1-0.15 m below that level. This material most probably represents debris deposited during the occupation of Str. 212-4 and -3 and therefore corresponds to T.S. 2.

Time Span 1: After this period of construction and use, Stratum 2, a fine-textured gray clay, was deposited over Stratum 1 and the lower three terraces of Unit 18. Orange mottling within Stratum 2 increases in proximity to Stratum 1, indicating the presence of eroded architectural debris (*bajareque*) on and just above this interface. The humus level is poorly represented here and cannot be clearly defined.

The artifacts in Lot 21F/1 were found throughout

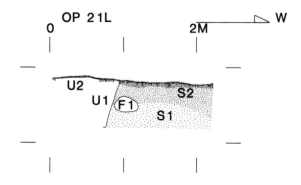

Figure 54.   Choco Main Court Section.

Stratum 1 and were probably deposited by the alluvial forces that created this outwash. It seems probable that these artifacts originated nearby, most likely from Str. 212-3 and -4. While this material was deposited in T.S. 1, it is believed to be terminal occupation debris originally associated with these two platforms.

CENTER OF SOUTH COURT (Figs. 50 and 54)

The south closed court was investigated by three test pits excavated along its east-west centerline (Op. 21L-N). Operation 21L is a pit 1.15 m north-south by 2.06 m east-west in the approximate center of this large court, excavated to locate the east edge of the paved court surface exposed in Op. 21B and D (Units 3 and 2 respectively) but absent in Op. 21F. This was facilitated by the recognition of a drop in surface elevation of 0.2-0.3 m west to east, which formed a north-south line dividing the court into two unequal parts. It was felt that this slight change in elevation might indicate the point where the formal surface of the west gave way to the informal earthen surface found to the east. Accordingly, Op. 21L was placed at this juncture. It involved removing 0.02 m of overburden to uncover the formal court surface and excavating down 0.6 m eastward to define the edge of that surface. Operations 21M and N, measuring 1.3 m square and 1.1 m north-south by 1.4 m east-west respectively, were placed 20 and 31.6 m west of Op. 21L to further define the court surface. In both cases, the work involved the removal of 0.1-0.15 m of overburden.

Excavation Lots: The one defined excavation lot, 21L/1, contains 34 sherds, all probably derived from a single utilitarian jar. This material represents debris deposited during the final phase of court occupation,

TABLE 3.55

EXCAVATION SUMMARY

Lot #	Contents	Depositional Significance	Provenience
21L/1	34 sherds	Terminal occupation debris (primary)	Upper part Stratum 1, buried by Feat. 1, immediately adjacent to Unit 1

buried by postoccupation construction collapse and outwash (see Table 3.55).

Time Span 3: The earliest period recognized in Op. 21L-N involved the natural deposition of Stratum 1, a fine-grained orange sand mottled to gray near its interface with Stratum 2, 0.29-0.46 m below ground surface. This level is found east of, and is intruded into by, Unit 1, and is similar in composition to Stratum 1 exposed in Op. 21F, although different in color. The surfaces of both levels are at almost precisely the same elevation: the Strata 1/2 interface in Op. 21L is 0.02 m higher than the Strata 1/2 interface in Op. 21F.

Time Span 2: Units 1 and 2 were constructed after the deposition of Stratum 1. Unit 1, revealed in Op. 21L, consists of a line of vertically set stone slabs, tilted slightly out to the east when found. These slabs are similar in size and composition to those used to construct the terrace treads revealed in Op. 21B-F. They stand to a preserved height of 0.65 m and form a line oriented N 1° 15′ E. The base of Unit 1 is set 0.3 m into the sand of Stratum 1. Extending to the west from the top of this step-up is Unit 2, a pavement of large, flat-laid stones set in a gray clay matrix. This pavement is encountered in all three court test pits and apparently represents a continuation of the court

surface exposed in Op. 21B and D, given the similarity in construction, composition, and elevation shown by these pavements (differences in elevation among these surfaces never exceed 0.45 m).

East of this pavement and its step-down is a lower informal surface also contemporary with the use of Units 1 and 2, corresponding to the Strata 1/2 interface. This surface is at the same level as the other proposed informal court surface, the Strata 1/2 interface in Op. 21F. In addition, tumbled debris (Feat. 1) was deposited on the surface of Stratum 1 after abandonment, indicating that it was exposed during this period. Finally, this interface is the only one noted in Op. 21L that occurs at a reasonable elevation above the base of Unit 1 to have served as a living surface contemporary with the use of that unit.

The artifacts of Lot 21L/1, 34 sherds apparently from a single vessel, were found just below the Strata 1/2 interface, buried by a stone from the collapse of Units 1-2 (Feat. 1). This stratigraphic position indicates that Lot 21L/1 was deposited on the surface of Stratum 1, possibly as trash swept from the Unit 2 surface, sometime during the period of the main group's use and before abandonment.

Time Span 1: The construction and use of Units 1

TABLE 3.56

STRUCTURAL/DEPOSITIONAL SUMMARY TIME SPANS: 1-3

Time Span	Construction Stage	Activity	Features	Lots
1	—	Burial and abandonment of south court	Stratum 2, Feat. 1	—
2	South court	Construction and use of south court	Units 1-2, Strata 1/2 interface	21L/1
3	—	Preconstruction soil deposition	Stratum 1	—

and 2 was followed by the deposition of Feat. 1, a scattering of jumbled stone found east of Unit 1 resting on the Strata 1/2 interface. This feature represents tumble from construction deposited on the lower informal court surface (Strata 1/2 interface), after the abandonment of the Locus 212 principal group.

This interval of collapse was followed by the natural deposition of Stratum 2, a level of fine-textured gray clay 0.22-0.34 m thick, which covers both Stratum 1 and Units 1 and 2 in the court. The small grain size of this clay suggests that it has a riverine origin and was probably deposited as the result of postabandonment flooding. The humus horizon is poorly defined in all three pits and is no more than a superficial darker gray level 0.02-0.06 m thick.

NONMONUMENTAL STRUCTURES

STRUCTURE 212-22 (Figs. 55 and 56)

Structure 212-22, a low platform c. 252 m southwest of the main group, was investigated by a series of four interlinked trenches, Op. 21G-I and K. The first three of these located and exposed the north and east (Op. 21H), south (Op. 21G-I), and west (Op. 21G) basal platform walls of Str. 212-22 by removing overburden from the platform surfaces and reaching 0.82-0.84 m below ground surface outside construction. Operation 21K was a cut 1 m east-west by 3.42 m north-south through the approximate center of the platform; this trench linked Op. 21I and H and was carried through structural fill below the base of construction.

This series of excavations was undertaken to determine the overall plan and mode of construction of Str. 212-22, a nonmonumental structure within the Choco locus. While the data from the investigation of one structure can hardly be called "representative" of all nonmonumental construction at a site of this size, these excavations provide some balance to the Choco investigations focused primarily on the main group.

Excavation Lots: The Str. 212-22 excavations produced 507 sherds, four figurine and five censer fragments, 36 pieces of obsidian, and nine small *bajareque* fragments. This material is divided into seven excavation lots, all but two of which (21K/1 and 2) contain terminal occupation debris. Lot 21K/1 comes primarily from architectural fill while 21K/2 is from a preconstruction surface (see Table 3.57).

Time Span 4: The first period of activity exposed in the Str. 212-22 area was the apparently natural deposition of Stratum 1. This is a level of loosely compacted, fine-textured brown clay with some gray mottling located between the north and south walls of Unit 1, 0.56-0.6 m below ground surface. Although this level is not apparent to the north and south beyond Unit 1, it seems likely that it continues into this area but cannot be distinguished from Stratum 2.

Lot 21K/2 is assigned to this period because it derives from Stratum 1. While some of these artifacts may have worked their way down into this level from the overlying fill, this seems unlikely. Rather, these materials are thought to represent preconstruction activity on the surface of Stratum 1.

Time Span 3: Set 0.15-0.17 m into Stratum 1 are the basal retaining walls of the Str. 212-22 platform (Unit 1), constructed of uncut river cobbles set in rough horizontal courses, the interstices between stones filled with pebbles, in a fine-textured brown clay matrix. These walls stand to a preserved height of 0.55-0.8 m. The northern and southern walls are the best preserved, while their western and eastern counterparts are in a worse state of repair. The south wall of Unit 1 also has a c. 0.12-m-wide central step-out at its base, formed by a large stone that projects from the basal course of that wall.

In addition to cobbles, stone slabs and a few cut and faced blocks are employed in Unit 1. Four slabs, each c. 0.02 m thick by 0.15-0.2 m long, are placed contiguously in the central part of the southern wall near the preserved top of that facing. The cut blocks are also found primarily in the southern wall, near its base, c. 0.3 m in from the southwest and southeast structure corners. Isolated faced blocks, c. 0.2 by 0.4 m, occur near the bases of the exposed Unit 1 corners. The thicknesses of the north and south basal walls, the two cleared by Op. 21K on both sides, average 0.54 and 0.4 m respectively.

The maximum dimensions of the Str. 212-22 basal platform as defined by Unit 1 are 3.4 m north-south by 4.5 m east-west. While the overall form of the basal platform is quadrilateral, the Unit 1 walls are not precisely aligned with respect to each other (Fig. 56). Platform orientation, therefore, varies between N 3° 0' E and N 2° 45' E on the east and west walls, and between N 82° 0' W and N 77° 0' W on the north and south walls.

The walls of Unit 1 retain the earthen fill of Unit 2. This fill, resting on Stratum 1, is a hard-packed, fine-textured light brown clay containing charcoal

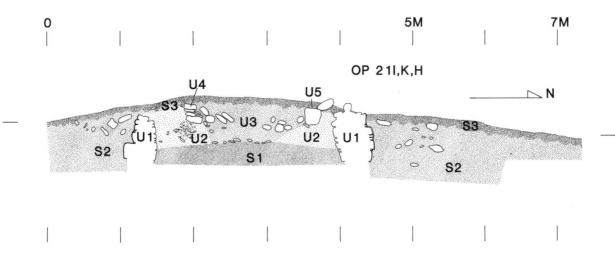

Figure 55.   Str. 212-22, Section.

flecks and a considerable amount of artifactual material (Lot 21K/1).

Surmounting the platform defined by Unit 1 and its fill (Unit 2) are two low cobble walls, Units 4 and 5. The bases of both of these walls, exposed in Op. 21K, rest 0.1-0.18 m below the tops of the southern and northern Unit 1 walls, respectively, and are set as much as 0.2 m into Unit 2. Unit 4 is a cluster of unfaced river cobbles on the south side of the summit of Str. 212-22 and stands to a preserved height of 0.25 m.

On the basis of the direction and current position of the noted stone fall, this unit may originally have consisted of a double stacking of cobbles. Unit 5 on the north side of the Str. 212-22 summit is represented by a single cobble, 0.22 by 0.22 m. Both of these units apparently functioned as stone footings for perishable superstructure walls. The latter were probably constructed of *bajareque*, as fragments of this material were recovered in several excavations (see Table 3.57). The stones of this foundation were also proba-

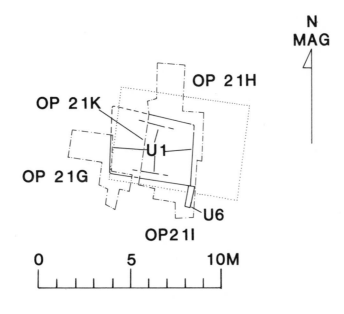

Figure 56.   Str. 212-22, Plan.

151

TABLE 3.57

EXCAVATION SUMMARY

Lot #	Contents	Depositional Significance	Provenience
21G/1	114 sherds; 9 pcs. obsidian; 3 *bajareque* frags.	Terminal occupation debris (secondary)	Within Strata 3-4 W of W wall of Unit 1
21G/2	26 sherds; 1 figurine frag.; 5 pcs. obsidian; 1 *bajareque* frag.	Terminal occupation debris (secondary)	Within Strata 3-4 outside SW corner of Unit 1
21H/1	176 sherds; 3 censer frags.; 2 figurine frags.; 14 pcs. obsidian	Terminal occupation debris (secondary)	Within Strata 3-4 N of N Unit 1 wall
21H/2	35 sherds; 1 pc. obsidian	Terminal occupation debris (secondary)	Within Strata 3-4 outside NE corner of Unit 1
21I/1	43 sherds; 2 censer frags.; 2 pcs. obsidian	Terminal occupation debris (secondary)	Within Strata 3-4 S of Unit 1 wall and Unit 1 SE corner
21K/1	102 sherds; 1 figurine frag.; 5 *bajareque* frags.	Fill	Within Units 2 and 3, primarily from E trench wall below Unit 4; little material came from below and between Units 4 and 5 in center of str.
21K/2	11 sherds; 5 pcs. obsidian	Preconstruction level (secondary)	Within Stratum 1, down to and slightly below base of Unit 1

bly set in a red clay matrix, as suggested by the discovery of this material under the tumbled rocks that define Unit 3. The north-south interior distance between Units 4 and 5 is 1.4 m.

Unit 3 is defined by a concentration of unfaced river cobbles, some of which rest horizontally on top of Stratum 1, while others tilt down from Units 4 and 5 above (Fig. 55). The disposition of these rocks points to the former existence of a V-shaped, flat-bottomed pit dug through Unit 2 to Stratum 1, c. 0.28 m below the base of Units 4 and 5. This pit was subsequently filled in by earth and stones, the latter fallen from the Str. 212-22 superstructure (Units 4 and 5). The pit either was contemporary with the occupation of Str. 212-22 or postdates its abandonment. The lack of any artifacts recovered in Lot 21K/1 dating to a later period, and the absence of clear soil differences between Units 2 and 3, suggest that Unit 3 was dug

TABLE 3.58

STRUCTURAL/DEPOSITIONAL SUMMARY TIME SPANS: 1-4

Time Span	Construction Stage	Activity	Features	Lots
1	—	Abandonment and burial of Str. 212-22	Strata 2 and 3	21G/1, 2, 21H/1,2, 21I/1
2	Str. 212-22	Str. 212-22 modification and continued use	Unit 6	—
3	Str. 212-22	Construction and use of Str. 212-22	Units 1-5	21K/1
4	—	Preconstruction occupation	Stratum 1	21K/2

about the time that Str. 212-22 was occupied. The position of the stones in the pit implies that the filling-in process involved a long period during which the superstructure debris, represented by Units 4 and 5, gradually collapsed inward.

Lot 21K/1 primarily derives from the fill of Unit 2. There is, however, some mixing of material with a few artifacts coming from Unit 3, since this pit was not detected during excavation. These latter items may relate to the use of Unit 3 or could have washed in after abandonment. While this ambiguity makes the interpretation of their significance difficult, the homogeneous content of Lot 21K/1, all sherds deriving from the same time period, strongly suggests that this material originally derived from nearly contemporary deposits.

Time Span 2: After Str. 212-22 was built, it was modified by the addition of Unit 6, a wall c. 0.25 m high by 0.3-0.35 m wide, constructed of small horizontally laid river cobbles packed with chinking stones in a fine-textured brown clay matrix. This wall abuts the southeast corner of Unit 1 and extends c. 1.15 m to the southwest. The base of Unit 6 rests c. 0.1 m above that of Unit 1.

The general form of Str. 212-22 during this final phase of its use was a roughly quadrilateral platform of hard earthen fill (Unit 2) retained by relatively high, vertical cobble facings (Unit 1). Atop this plat-

form was a superstructure presumably built of perishable walls set on a low cobblestone footing (Units 4 and 5). A flat-bottomed, sloping-walled pit (Unit 3) may have taken up most of the floor space of this superstructure. Access to the summit of Str. 212-22 was probably from the south, since the southern wall is somewhat lower than its northern counterpart and is equipped with a narrow step-out at its base. In addition, the masonry in the southern facade is more formalized and this side of the platform faces the plaza formed by Str. 212-22/24. Unit 6 also played a part in the functioning of Str. 212-22, although the nature of this role is unknown.

Time Span 1: After the construction and use of Str. 212-22, the entire area was buried by Stratum 2, except for the very tops of the Unit 1 walls. This soil level consists of a gray-streaked brown, fine-textured clay some 0.58-0.76 m thick. Overlying this stratum and all construction is a darker brown humus which varies in thickness between 0.08 and 0.11 m (Stratum 3). The fine texture of both Strata 2 and 3 suggests that they were deposited by river floods over a period of time after the occupation of Str. 212-22.

Five artifact lots, 21G/1-2, H/1-2, and I/1, derive from Strata 2 and 3. In all likelihood this material originated during Str. 212-22's occupation and was redeposited, probably by river flooding, in T.S. 1.

IV

Data Summary and Analysis

INTRODUCTION

The following chapter presents a summary of the four major data categories dealt with by the LMV Project: artifacts, monuments, architecture, and site planning. The purpose of this section is to provide a concise synthesis of the material patterns revealed by this research. The nature of the data and how they were collected imposes some restrictions on the conclusions derived from them (see Chap. 3, Introduction). Nonetheless, the patterns discussed here provide at least a preliminary model that can be evaluated by future work in the region (see Chap. 9).

ARTIFACTS

The detailed descriptions of the LMV ceramic (pottery, figurine, and miscellaneous industries) and lithic (chipped and ground stone industries) materials are included in QR 6, where they are presented with treatments of all artifacts recovered by the QAP. This chapter, therefore, will include only a brief quantitative summary of the LMV artifacts.

CERAMICS

A total of 15,828 pottery fragments were recovered and examined by the LMV and Nowak projects (only provenienced material from Nowak's work is included here). Of this total, 2529 sherds were discarded without being analyzed because they were either too small or too heavily eroded to permit classification. From the remaining 13,299 sherds that could be fruitfully studied, 1209 were separated as nonvessel fragments; 1161 of these were eventually classified apart as *incensarios*, comprising six form categories and one miscellaneous category (see Table 4.1). The analysis of the remaining 12,090 classifiable sherds dealt with both utilitarian and nonutilitarian vessels. These were divided into eight ceramic groups encompassing 24 type-variety units (see Table 4.2). A complementary form classification employed 22 categories (12 bowl and ten jar forms).

The vast majority of these sherds came from four sources: the three excavated sites of Choco (Locus 212), Playitas (Locus 200), and Las Quebradas (Locus 205), and the surface collection made at Comanche Farm (Locus 210). The material from Playitas includes both the surface-collected and excavated samples gathered by this project in 1979 and the 1555 provenienced sherds (including *incensarios*) recovered by Nowak in his 1974 excavations in Group II.

Forty-six fragments of ceramic figurines were recovered from the LMV, along with one *candelero* (a multiple-hole *incensario*) and one problematic object (both from Las Quebradas). A total of 274 *bajareque* fragments, generally representing the best-preserved examples, were also studied.

LITHICS

The LMV chipped stone inventory includes 1322 items, of which 1254 were analyzed. All but four pieces in the studied collection are obsidian—the exceptions are of chert (one), flint (two), and chalcedony (one). A preliminary analysis identified the following distribution of chipped stones by category: 466 blades, 402 flakes, 66 flake-cores, nine blade-cores, 12 macroblades, and 299 classed as miscellaneous.

Twenty ground stone implements were recovered, including five manos (one whole, four fragments) and 15 metates (all fragments). Vesicular basalt is the most common raw material (two manos, 11 metates), followed by rhyolite (two manos) and unidentified stone (one mano, four metates).

154

TABLE 4.1

SUMMARY OF *INCENSARIO* FORM CATEGORIES

Form Category	Defining Features	Frequency
Effigy Modeled	Vessels of uncertain form with deeply modeled exteriors, sometimes decorated with large incised and/or modeled flanges. Modeled designs are presently unclear though some anthropomorphic features are reconstructible.	40.46%
Ladle Censers	Subhemispherical bowls with everted rims joined to horizontally set, hollow tube handles.	13.17%
Spiked Censers	Outflaring or vertical-walled vessels with flat bases and everted rims decorated on the exterior with appliquéd low conical spikes in undetermined patterns.	24.81%
Pronged Dishes on Pedestal Supports	Large, outflaring-walled vessels associated with low, vertical or slightly flaring pedestal supports; three hollow, cylindrical prongs project upward from the interior of the vessel near the rim.	1.72%
Censer Lids	Shallow, outflaring-walled vessels with burnt interiors; no evidence of scoring or handles.	4.96%
Cruciform-vent	Globular-bodied, flaring-necked vessels decorated with two horizontal, parallel, appliquéd ridges defining the central portion of the vessel which itself is pierced with three cruciform vents; the upper appliquéd ridge supports an undetermined number of outslanting notched flanges. Exterior surfaces may have been covered with an easily eroded red wash.	14.89%

All *incensarios* identified in the LMV are characterized by their coarse orange to tan pastes, unslipped, roughly smoothed surfaces, and thick walls.

The frequencies given here refer to the proportion of all censer fragments that were classified according to form (524 fragments in all) that a category comprises; most recovered censer pieces could not be placed in a particular form category. All *incensario* form taxa are derived from J. Benyo's (1979) study of Quirigua materials, with the exception of the cruciform-vent taxon, which, to date, has not been found at Quirigua or in its immediate periphery.

MONUMENTS

Eight monuments were located and described by the LMV Project in 1977-79. Seven of these large stones were found in the three major groups at Las Quebradas (Locus 205) while the remaining one is from Arapahoe Viejo (Locus 216). All eight monuments share the characteristics of monumental size, lack of carving or decoration, location either singly or in a line of two or three bisecting the center of a monumental court, and, in at least three of the four excavated cases, association with large quantities of censer sherds. All four excavated monuments are also set into pavements made up of small pebbles and earth found on one (Mon. 2 and 4) or both (Mon. 1) of their sides (Mon. 5 was not tested sufficiently to determine this point).

Beyond these similarities, the monuments can be divided into two general and numerically equal categories. The first consists of those stones which were artificially modified from their original forms (Las Quebradas Mon. 1-3 and Arapahoe Viejo Mon. 1). Within this class are three pecked stone spheres of a hard, gray to brown crystalline stone ranging in diameter from 0.34 to 0.51 m (Las Quebradas Mon. 2 and 3, Arapahoe Viejo Mon. 1). There is also one rough column of hard, gray crystalline stone found in the Las Quebradas West Group (Mon. 1) which,

TABLE 4.2

SUMMARY OF IDENTIFYING CHARACTERISTICS OF LMV CERAMIC TYPES

Taxon	Identifying Characteristics	Frequency
Encantado Group		
Encantado Cream: Unslipped Encantado variety	Medium to high-necked jars with soft, cream paste and incised linear and geometric designs on necks.	15.36%
Encantado Cream: Red-washed variety	Same as Encantado var.; decoration includes easily eroded red paint on rims of necked jars and interior or exterior of open bowls; jars frequently have incised decoration on the neck.	1.76%
Encantado Cream: Carved variety	Same as Encantado var., except surfaces are well-burnished and decorated on the exterior with deeply carved, undecipherable designs; forms are open bowls.	0.03%
Bobos Group		
Bobos Orange: Bobos variety	Outslanting-walled bowls, well smoothed, unslipped exterior, orange-slipped interior, hard, tan paste.	3.51%
Bobos Orange: Red-on-orange variety	Same as Bobos var., with the addition of red-painted rim bands and undecipherable red-painted designs on the orange-slipped interior.	0.32%
Bobos Orange: Polychrome variety	Same as Bobos var., with the addition of red- and black-painted designs on orange-slipped interiors and exteriors of hemispherical and vertical-walled bowls.	0.08%
Coroza Group		
Coroza Cream: Coroza variety	Vertical and flaring-walled bowls, slipped on the well-smoothed exterior and, sometimes, interior, decorated with easily eroded red-painted designs over the slip; distinctive soft, salmon, fine paste.	0.32%
Tipon Group		
Tipon Orange: Tipon variety	Burnished flaring and vertical-walled bowls with fine, tan pastes.	9.26%
Chalja Red-on-orange: Chalja variety	Same as Tipon var., with red-painted rim bands and occasional red-painted linear designs on unslipped vessel exteriors.	1.30%
Morja Bichrome: Morja variety	Same as Tipon var., except with red- and white-painted bands on unslipped vessel exteriors; designs appear to be linear but are unclear.	0.01%
Capulin White-painted: Capulin variety	Same as Tipon var., with a dull white-painted band extending from the rim to a variable point down the unslipped vessel exterior.	0.42%
Tarro Incised: Tarro variety	Same as Tipon var., with the addition of linear and geometric incised designs on vessel exteriors.	0.46%
Tasu Fluted: Tasu variety	Same as Tipon var., except that vertical-walled bowls are decorated on the exterior with vertical flutes beginning below the rim.	0.31%
Alsacia Pink: Alsacia variety	Same as Tipon var., with the addition of a pink slip over the exterior; forms unknown.	0.03%
Mariscos Trichrome: Mariscos variety	Same as Tipon var., with the addition of pink- and red-painted, undecipherable designs on vessel exteriors; forms unknown.	0.02%
Tipon Orange: Modeled variety	Same as Tipon var., with the addition of modeled, presently unclear, designs on vessel exteriors; forms unknown.	0.01%

TABLE 4.2 (continued)

SUMMARY OF IDENTIFYING CHARACTERISTICS OF LMV CERAMIC TYPES

Taxon	Identifying Characteristics	Frequency
Mojanal Group		
Mojanal Micaceous: Faceted variety	Large, unslipped, flaring-necked jars with coarse, reddish brown paste; numerous mica inclusions in paste and visible on smoothed vessel surfaces.	39.51%
Mojanal Micaceous: Red-washed variety	Same as Faceted var., with the addition of red-painted rim bands and a red wash on the necks of flaring- and vertical-necked jars. Linear incised designs on jar necks.	2.38%
Mojanal Micaceous: Well-smoothed variety	Medium-textured, gray-brown, micaceous paste; unslipped, well-smoothed interior and exterior surfaces of large outflaring-necked and neckless jars decorated with horizontal grooving (below the rim) and crosshatched incised lines on vessel bodies and neck exteriors.	3.18%
Mojanal Micaceous: Fine-tempered variety	Medium-textured, dull gray-brown paste containing a large number of very fine mica particles. Vessel interiors and exteriors are unslipped and well-smoothed but lack the facets which distinguish Mojanal Micaceous: Faceted variety. Forms consist primarily of large, flaring-necked jars.	3.18%
Mojanal Micaceous: Coarse-tempered variety	Large, unslipped, flaring-necked jars with very coarse, yellowish-brown paste. Inclusions consist primarily of moderately large grit and sand particles; mica flakes, though present, are relatively rare. Vessel interiors and exteriors are smoothed.	0.51%
Switch Molina Group		
Techin Striated: unspecified variety	Unslipped, necked jars with flaring rims, decorated with parallel linear and crosshatched deep striations on the smoother surfaces of jar bodies and shoulders; very coarse, dull brown paste.	15.76%
Vitales Group		
Vitales Thick-walled Vitales variety	Unslipped, necked jars with flaring rims; interior and exterior surfaces are roughly smoothed; very coarse, red to orange paste.	0.29%
San Rafael Group		
San Rafael Red: San Rafael variety	Unslipped, high vertical-necked jars with smoothed surfaces and rim-to-shoulder tube handles, decorated with red-painted rim bands and red paint on handle exteriors and in currently unclear designs on vessel shoulders. Jar necks decorated with linear and geometric, thin, shallow incised designs. Coarse, soft, tan paste.	0.41%

"Identifying characteristics" summarize the predominant features of the types discussed and are not meant to encompass the full range of variation found within these taxa.

"Frequency" refers to the proportion of all analyzed LMV sherds which the members of a particular type represent.

though broken, once stood to a height of c. 2.83 m. The second category consists of all those stones which were not modified (Las Quebradas Mon. 4-7): three white quartz boulders in the west court of the East Group, each 1 m in diameter (Mon. 5-7). Also included here is a large (1.05 by 1.34 m) stone slab (Mon. 4) found in the raised east court of that same group.

Despite this relative diversity of forms, there is no recorded case of monuments of different styles having been included within the same major court. There are no instances of, for example, pecked stone spheres appearing together with shaped columns or unmodified boulders. In fact, when two adjoining major courts contain monuments, e.g., in the Las Quebradas East Group, the stones are distinct morphologically and compositionally. The behavioral significance of these monuments is discussed in Chap. 6.

ARCHITECTURE

The following discussion treats monumental and small structures separately. As noted in Chap. 1, monumental structures are those buildings 1.5 m or more high, at least 10 m long, and incorporated into major architectural groups. Small structures, as their name implies, are below 1.5 m in height and 10 m in length, and/or are part of smaller groups.

Within each category, structures are divided into two components, substructure platforms and superstructures, each with its own set of descriptive dimensions. The dimensions relevant to substructure platforms are masonry, masonry form, facing, fill, contemporary internal construction, superimposed construction, decoration, structure access, and overall platform form. For superstructures, the important dimensions are masonry, flooring, facing, decoration, and overall form. Unfortunately, superstructures have usually been heavily disturbed by either modern agricultural activities or the natural intrusion of tree roots, resulting in considerable loss of information. At the conclusion of this section, plaza and court construction will also be considered; the relevant dimensions here are surfacing, decoration, facing, and access.

MONUMENTAL CONSTRUCTION

SUBSTRUCTURES

Substructure platform masonry consists almost exclusively of uncut and unshaped river cobbles, angular chunks, slabs (mostly of schist), and pebbles used as chinking stones. At the sites of Arapahoe Viejo and Comanche Farm chunks predominate, while cobbles are more common at the other centers. The matrix in which these stones are set is of clay. Cut stone blocks are sporadically used in Str. 212-1 at Choco and Str. 205-41 at Las Quebradas. At Juan de Paz all the smaller structures are built primarily of cobbles and chunks, while their large counterparts are faced with stone blocks. This deviation can be accounted for by the eccentric location of Juan de Paz in the valley, much closer to Quirigua than to any of the other valley centers, and its presumed proximity to sources of easily worked stones, i.e., sandstone (Ashmore 1981b).

The most common masonry form found in the valley is the step-terrace: low, vertical cobble walls surmounted by flat-laid slabs that run under the next ascending terrace. In general, these terraces rise 0.3-0.4 m and are about the same in width. On the basis of both surface and excavation data, these step-terraces extend the full length of the structure. In fact, many of the large closed courts that are a part of so many valley centers are surrounded on all sides by a continuous series of step-terraces running from one structure to another at about the same levels.

Within the general step-terrace masonry form there are two minor variants. The first consists of those structures with a uniform series of step-terraces, from court/plaza to summit. The second consists of structures with narrow step-terraces broken at regular intervals by a wider (c. 1-1.5 m) surface constructed of especially long slabs. This second version of the step-terrace system is generally associated with the highest platforms, e.g., Str. 200-77, 212-1 and -4, and 205-41, while the smaller constructions within the monumental category tend to have the uninterrupted version, e.g., Str. 200-74 and 205-14.

A somewhat greater deviation from the standard step-terrace system involves the absence of stone slabs to form the terrace treads. Instead, the cobbles that form the low risers also function as the terrace surfaces (see Str. 212-6 and -1, south face).

In general, monumental structures tend to possess the same kind of construction on all sides. The result is a platform with continuous step-terraces on all four sides, providing unhindered access to the structure's summit.

There are some variations, however, in this picture of symmetry. The most common exception is a structure with a set of narrow step-terraces on one of its long faces and a system of step-terraces broken by broader surfaces on the other (e.g., Str. 200-23). Less common are structures with step-terraces on one to three of their sides while the remainder are constructed in a different fashion (two excavated examples). In one case (Str. 200-22), two platform facades are built of uncut river cobbles and chinking stones set in a vertical face 0.4-0.58 m high. In the other, a series of 0.56-m-high vertical terraces built of cobbles and chinking stones are used on the side opposite the step-terracing (Str. 205-41). Unfortunately, the non-step-terrace facings have not survived very well, so there is still some question as to how they were constructed. In both of these last two cases, however, an effort was made to maintain symmetry within the courts they enclosed; their step-terraced sides face into courts surrounded by other step-terraced constructions.

Almost all of the monumental substructures visible on the surface use step-terrace masonry, and 14 of the 15 excavated monumental structures conform to this style, at least in their terminal phases. There are still some exceptions, however. Both Str. 205-1-1st and -2nd are faced on the court side by a series of low, narrow cobble steps, with no slab treads, which provide access to an earthen terrace 1.09-1.56 m wide. In Str. 205-1-2nd, the better-preserved of the two, this earthen level was eventually succeeded by a 0.47-m-high vertical terrace wall constructed of cobbles and chinking stones. Behind this wall is another earthen terrace. While the structure is not well preserved, it would appear that the stone steps of Str. 205-1-1st run the length of the structure's court side. This masonry form, in which stone steps provide access to earthen terraces that are also bounded by stone walls, is virtually unknown in the valley outside of Las Quebradas. It does have a counterpart, albeit on a smaller scale, in the nonmonumental structures excavated at Las Quebradas (Str. 205-88, -123, and -196; see below). Structure 205-1-1st also shows asymmetry in construction; the noncourt side is constructed of either a single high vertical cobble wall or a series of somewhat lower vertical cobble terraces.

The second exception is Str. 212-4-3rd, which consists of two symmetrical north-south, inward-sloping facades c. 1.93-2.91 m high, built of river cobbles and pebble spalls, set on a step-terrace system. Undoubtedly, given the height and steepness of these walls, summit access must have been via a staircase not located in excavation.

These exceptions aside, the prevalence of the step-terrace form is undoubtedly due to its stability. Each set of flat-laid slabs served as a stable base for the next higher stone wall which, in its turn, promoted the tread's stability by counterbalancing the slabs. Also, in raising a tall structure by means of a series of low, narrow steps, the original builders reduced the amount of weight any one wall would have to bear. This was an important consideration in the LMV, where the most common building stone was an irregular cobble and the primary binding material was clay. Tall vertical cobble and clay facings would probably not resist erosional forces, especially in an area of high rainfall. In this way the step-terrace, as an interdigitated system of supporting and counterbalancing elements, allowed the stable construction of relatively tall structures. In fact, the greater stability of the step-terrace system can be seen in Str. 205-41, where the step-terraced east face has survived much better than its nonstepped western counterpart.

Structural integrity was also ensured in other ways. Stone slabs are sometimes found at the base of step-terrace systems, set directly into the earth (e.g., Str. 212-1 and -4 and 205-256). These slabs, with their broad surfaces, provide excellent foundations. In some cases, very long stones project from the bases of large substructures, e.g., Str. 200-77 and -78 and 212-7. While these basal slabs may have been intended to increase stability, they seem larger than necessary for that purpose and probably had a decorative function as well. Stability was also increased by setting the basal step-terrace's lower course(s) into the original ground surface.

These masonry forms encase a structural fill that varies from hard-packed earth or clay, to mixed clay and stone, to tightly packed, horizontally laid stones, usually cobbles, set in a clay matrix. In mixed fills, the earth and stone have been deposited as separate units; rarely are large amounts of clay and stone found combined. There is no regularity in the association of fill types with masonry forms or structure heights. There is a tendency, however, when fill stones are used, to cluster them below the inward edge of the slab tread, beneath the point where the next ascending terrace stands. This would have increased the stability of the step-terraces, and decreased the possibility of subsidence. Internal fill-retaining walls are all but absent; one example was noted at Choco (Str. 212-4-1st, Unit 9), though deeper probes of fill might reveal their presence.

Evidence of plaster or facade decoration is absent from almost all of the major valley substructures. The only known example is the use of a gritty white plaster at the largest Playitas structure, Str. 200-77. Interestingly, this was the platform associated with the carved stone tenoned heads described by Berlin (1952). Unfortunately, it is not known which part of the structure was decorated by these heads, as they were found and moved before Berlin saw them. No evidence of other stone carvings, stucco work, or painting of substructures was recorded from the valley.

Monumental structures in the LMV centers range in height from 1.5 to possibly 9 m. As noted earlier, most would have been mounted on all sides by long, narrow step-terraces ascending to the summit in short increments, sometimes broken by broader surfaces. Only two definite examples of superimposed construction were revealed (three stages each in Str. 212-4 and 205-1) along with one possible case at Playitas (Feat. 1, Str. 200-23). Assuredly this partly reflects the restricted probing of the large structures by the LMV investigations. The superimposition of construction is probably more common than this limited sample would indicate.

SUPERSTRUCTURES

The available information on superstructure construction is limited and the following discussion of the relevant dimensions is therefore brief. In three cases, Str. 205-1-1st/2nd and -41, the limits of platform summits are defined on at least one side by a stone-faced step-up. In the last case, this riser is 0.15 m high and roughly constructed of cobbles and chinking stones. In Str. 205-1-1st and -2nd the summit step-ups are 0.77 and 0.45 m high, respectively, and quite substantial, built of horizontally coursed river cobbles and spalls set in a clay matrix.

There is no surface or excavated evidence that the substructure platforms ever supported sizable standing walls of stone masonry. Rather, it appears more likely that the bulk of superstructure construction was of perishable materials, primarily *bajareque*, set onto low, rough cobblestone footings. There are some indications from surface remains that schist slabs may have figured in these constructions (e.g., Str. 210-14 and 212-76), although they are not commonly found on excavated structure summits.

An unusual feature found at several sites is square pillar bases or plinths constructed of tightly packed cobbles, 1-9 m² in area. On the basis of summit excavations on Str. 205-41, these squares apparently supported hardened clay columns or similar constructions. When found, these features were usually regularly spaced in a line down the center of the structure's summit, and must have functioned to support roof beams and, possibly, as room dividers.

The recovered fragments of *bajareque* are very irregular in shape and give little indication of original form or use. Adobe blocks were present at Quirigua, but no trace of this type of construction is found at

other valley sites. Three pieces of stick-impressed *bajareque* were recovered. Thus, while the prevalence of eroded *bajareque* fragments, and the absence of standing stone walls, indicate the importance of *bajareque* in superstructure construction, there is little direct evidence as to how it was employed.

The surfacing or flooring of monumental superstructures shows considerable variation. Within the four superstructures investigated, two are surfaced with a thin level of pebbles set into earthen fill (Str. 200-23 and 205-1-2nd), one possesses a floor of large cobbles set into fill (Str. 205-41), and one has a low step-up of small pebbles above an earthen floor (Str. 205-256). Structure 205-1-1st's summit was apparently surfaced with earth, and both Str. 205-1-2nd and -41 have summits paved only partially in stone, the remainder being exposed earthen fill.

There are no traces of superstructure decoration, unless the tenoned heads described by Berlin (1952) were integrated into Str. 200-77's summit construction. None of the recovered *bajareque* fragments bear remains of paint or plaster.

The overall superstructure form associated with monumental platforms does not appear to have varied considerably. The summits are long and narrow. Superstructures associated with cobble pillar bases were probably long, narrow open rooms that ran the length of the substructures. How these summit rooms were divided, if at all, is not known as no surface or excavated indications of cross-walls were noted. In at least two cases (Str. 205-41 and -256) small stone step-ups 0.19-0.3 m high were found. In the first example this riser runs parallel to the long axis of the structure while in the second it is perpendicular to it. Another superstructure form is recorded at Arapahoe Viejo, where three parallel rectangular depressions have been sunk into the very broad summit of Str. 216-13. These "sunken rooms" range in size from 6 by 10 to 9 by 33 m and cover most of the summit surface. As noted in Chap. 2, these receptacles may have served as storage facilities.

In a general sense, LMV monumental structures most closely resemble the "palace" form of construction defined for the Maya area (G. Andrews 1975). The other usual Classic Maya structure forms—the shrine, ballcourt, funerary mound, and so forth—have few, if any, counterparts in the sampled lower Motagua sites (cf. A. Smith 1950). Several platforms (Str. 216-17, 205-262 and -216), on the basis of height and very small summit areas, may fall within the "temple" class of platforms defined for the Maya zone

(G. Andrews 1975), and Str. 205-26/27 and 205-8/9 have a general ballcourt form. Each major center also has one or more buildings with relatively narrow summits integrated into one of the large court complexes (e.g., Str. 212-4, c. 8.5 m wide). The narrowness of these summits coupled with the absence of any visible superstructure remains implies that they were never meant to support architecture.

Finally, several large structures are linked by constructions, here termed "saddles." To judge by the single excavated example (Str. 200-73/74) and the information gleaned from the surface examination of the rest, these are c. 0.2- to 1-m-high constructions of uncut cobbles and slabs. They appear to have been raised pavements, sometimes with more than one level, which served, in part, to restrict access to the courts they bounded. Several small terraces were also noted, most no more than 1 m high and constructed of river cobbles. Their function appears to have been to level and stabilize the ground around platforms. Low terraces found near the Playitas Group II main court may have been designed to retard erosion. Exceptions to this are the high terraces that define the "open" sides of the two Las Quebradas plazas, and the terracing system noted in Group II of Quebrada Grande (see Chap. 2). In these cases the construction appears to follow the step-terrace approach.

SMALL STRUCTURES

SUBSTRUCTURES

The small-structure basal platforms are built almost exclusively of river cobbles, angular chunks, and pebbles set in a clay matrix. Stone slabs, though occasionally found, are rare and faced masonry blocks are almost entirely absent (exceptions in Str. 212-22). Two general types of smaller platforms can be defined: those faced with relatively high vertical walls, and those constructed using a combination of low cobble walls and earthen terraces. In the former class are Str. 212-22 and 200-16, with basal platforms 0.6-0.8 m high faced on all four sides by horizontally coursed cobbles and small chinking spalls set in a clay matrix. The second style is limited to Las Quebradas and contains Str. 205-88, -123, and -196. In these cases, a low (c. 0.19-0.52 m high) basal stone wall constructed of one or two courses of large cobbles gives way to an earthen terrace 0.51-2.51 m wide. In Str. 205-196 two symmetrical, broad earthen terraces on the north and south provide the base for the

summit construction; in Str. 205-123 the first earthen terrace is succeeded by a *bajareque* wall set on a stone footing, which, in turn, provides access to the second wide earthen terrace. Structure 205-88 yielded few clues to how the earthen terrace resolved above the basal stone wall. It should be noted that structures in the first masonry form class might also have a low frontal earthen terrace (e.g., Str. 200-16).

The fill of all these structures is earth. There is no sign of any fill-retaining walls or superimposed construction. No stairs or other specialized means of access were noted, nor were they expected given the heights of the structures. No evidence of plaster facings or any form of architectural decoration was recovered.

In overall form, Str. 212-22 and 200-16 are quadrilateral platforms 0.6-0.8 m high, and c. 8.1 by 3.5 to 3.4 by 4.5 m on a side. Structures 205-88, -123, and -196 are also quadrilaterals, roughly 6.9 m on a side and 0.43-0.66 m high. As noted above, the latter structures ascend in one or two broad terraces to the summit while the first two rise in a single stage.

SUPERSTRUCTURES

As with the monumental structures, the summits of the humbler constructions are topped by perishable superstructures built, at least in some cases, of *bajareque*. In Str. 212-22 and 205-123 there is evidence of stone footings for *bajareque* walls. Structure 205-88 employs schist slabs in its summit construction, although little else could be discovered of its original form.

The summit of one of the smaller structures, Str. 200-16, is surfaced with a level of uncut stone 0.24-0.31 m thick, while the remaining four excavated examples have earthen summits. No architectural decoration or plastering was noted in association with any superstructures.

Superstructure form was not determined because this use of perishable materials has left little or no trace. In Str. 212-22 evidence was found of a large V-shaped pit which encompassed almost the entire summit area.

PLAZAS/COURTS

There is no vestige of any prepared surfacing of the plazas defined in the small-structure groups. Most probably, these structures enclosed spaces of tamped earth. The monumental courts and plazas display considerably more variation: the majority of these for which information is available (15: 14 excavated and one visible on the surface) are surfaced with earth (nine cases); five are covered, at least in part, by a 0.02- to 0.32-m-thick level of tightly packed pebbles; and one is covered over two-thirds of its extent with large, flat-laid cobbles. The latter surface, found in the Choco south court, is unique within the valley in that it terminates in a north-south line of vertically set stone slabs (the remaining third of the court is surfaced with earth).

There is no strong correlation between the size of the surrounding structures and the nature of the court/plaza surface; the largest structures at a site might face either a tamped-earth level or a paved one. Nor is there a consistent pattern for a particular site or even a major group within that site, since adjoining courts and/or plazas might be surfaced in different ways. No evidence of plaster floors or any form of decoration was noted for any plaza or court surface.

The apparent reluctance to pave an entire court surface in valley centers may have been founded in the need to maintain good drainage. If the amount of rain in the past was equivalent to what the valley currently receives, any attempt to cover a plaza/court surface completely with an impermeable pavement would have resulted in pools of standing water. This would have been an even greater problem in the large courts where all four sides and, quite commonly, all four corners were closed by construction.

An unusual access feature is associated with the main group of Group V at Playitas. Here an earthen ramp, with no surface sign of stone construction, extends 360 m from the southwest corner of that court. The earthen ramp is the only specialized means of court access recorded at any LMV site.

SITE PLANNING

The sites that form the basis of this section are those with high proportions of monumental architecture: Las Quebradas, Playitas, Choco, Comanche Farm, Mojanales, Juyama, Arapahoe Viejo, Bobos, and Quebrada Grande. The important dimensions to be considered are orientation, location, extent, form, and pattern (see Table 4.3).

Five of the monumental sites are on the floodplain of the Rio Motagua or one of its major tributaries, while the remaining four (Las Quebradas, Mojanales, Juyama, and Arapahoe Viejo) are situated along the southern margin of the valley in the foothills of the Espiritu Santo mountains. Four of these sites (Mojanales, Bobos, and the two largest, Playitas and Las Quebradas) are along potentially major routes of communication leading from the LMV across the Espiritu Santo mountains into present-day Honduras. All but two of the monumental sites are on or near good agricultural land and near sources of building stones and water. The exceptions are Comanche Farm, which has no large stone deposits nearby, and Mojanales, which does not seem to have access to good agricultural land. This locational strategy applies to the smaller investigated loci as well, with the exceptions of Los Vitales, Los Limones, and Locus 234, which are not near large expanses of good agricultural land.

All of the major valley sites share a great number of similarities in general form. They all contain a principal architectural focus consisting of a court enclosed on all sides by high, orthogonally arranged structures. Not only are all four sides of the court defined by massive constructions but at least two, and frequently four, of the corners are also sealed by construction. The enclosed courts themselves vary in size from 216 to 5330 m^2 with an average of 1986.35 m^2; open monumental plazas with less restricted access range from 529 to 5320 m^2, averaging 2644.3 m^2. The number of enclosed courts varies (usually) from one to four per monumental site. There is also some variation in complexity within and between sites; court arrangements consist of anywhere from a single example to three adjoining courts/plazas sharing structures between them. In almost every case, however, the same basic pattern is repeated with monotonous regularity. In those cases where two or more courts are joined to make up a single monumental unit, one of the courts tends to be larger than the other(s), and in every site with more than one large court group there is one such unit that dominates the others by the size of its associated structures and its overall extent. At Playitas, the Group I main court complex is larger, contains the highest structures, and is the most complexly organized of all such units at the site. At Quebrada Grande, Group I, with its two adjoining monumental units (one of them raised), fills this role, while the Las Quebradas East Group is clearly the largest such entity at the site. Each group is also dominated by one or two structures that are higher and more massive than the others composing the

TABLE 4.3

SITE MORPHOLOGY

A. *Appearance*—Subcategory
   Orientation
   Location characteristics
   Extent
1. *Orientation*—Characteristic
   a. Percentage of all structures oriented orthogonally
   b. Percentage of all monumental structures oriented orthogonally
2. *Location*—Characteristic
   a. Valley flats
   b. Foothills
   c. Mountain tops
3. *Extent*—Characteristic
   a. Density of structures overall
   b. Existence of clusters
   c. Density within clusters
   d. Distribution of structures by size category
   e. Total site size
B. *Structure Groups*—Subcategory
   Form characteristic
   Nature
1. *Form*—Characteristic
   a. Plaza (structures on two to four sides, at least two corners not obstructed by construction)
   b. Court (structures on four sides, at least three corners closed by construction)
   c. No plazas, structures dispersed
2. *Nature*—Characteristic
   a. Palace-form structures surround the plaza
   b. Temple-form structures surround the plaza
   c. Shrine-form structures surround the plaza
   d. Residential-form* structures surround the plaza
   e. Plaza raised on a prepared platform—may be multilevel
*Residential-form structures are low platforms, with or without superstructures, of small dimensions.
Note: Form and Nature characteristics can be combined to form the following analytical units. It is in terms of
   these combined units that description and comparisons will be carried out.
Form/Nature Combinations
   a. Quadrangle (court fully enclosed on all sides by construction with at least two corners closed. Surround-
      ing structures are monumental: temples, palaces, and/or shrines)
   b. Palace group (plaza surrounded on two to four sides by palace-form structures; at least three open cor-
      ners)
   c. Temple group (same as for palace group except that temples replace palaces around a plaza; at least three
      open corners)
   d. Monumental-structure plaza (mixture of palaces, temples, and/or shrines around a plaza; at least two
      open corners)
   e. Acropolis (plaza of Type b, c, or d atop a prepared platform, often composed of several levels)
   f. Residential group, closed court (small structures surrounding a court on four sides; at least two corners
      closed by construction)
   g. Residential group, plaza (same as Type f but with structures on two to four sides and at least three cor-
      ners not closed by construction)

group (e.g., Str. 200-77 at Playitas Group I; Str. 205-258 and -262 in the Las Quebradas East Group; and Str. 212-1 and -4 at Choco). Major centers, therefore, tend to be dominated by one large court complex which, in turn, is centered around a very large structure(s).

A deviation from this pattern is found at Las Quebradas: attached to the double closed courts of the East and West Groups here are two plazas defined by monumental constructions but devoid of structures on one of their sides. Each of these plazas is a mirror image of the other, though the one in the West Group is smaller; they are located on opposite sides of the site facing each other. It should be noted that while one side of each plaza has been left open, access to this area is not necessarily direct. Both of the plazas are defined on their "open" sides by a drop-off (0.4 m for the West and 6.75-7.3 m for the East Group) artificially faced with stone. Other major open places are found at Arapahoe Viejo and Bobos Group I. Unlike the Las Quebradas examples, there is no reason to believe that access to these enclosed spaces was physically restricted.

Although evidence from excavations is currently inconclusive, it appears that the major courts were closed slowly by accretion, through the lateral expansion of their component buildings. The "unfinished" north end of Str. 200-24 in Group IV at Playitas strongly suggests that the occupants of this complex were in the process of sealing off the one remaining open corner when construction ceased; the amount of trash found in Midden 1 associated with Str. 200-22 is a further sign that the Group was occupied while this construction was going on. The Group as a unit was not constructed in its present form prior to occupation. Rather, the expansion of existing structures was carried out in aggregates that were already occupied. It is *hypothesized*, therefore, that the creation of the closed courts was a gradual process and may not have been an initial goal of the builders.

There is also some variation in the degree to which these courts and plazas are raised above the surrounding terrain. In all, six courts or plazas are set 0.25-2.5 m above ground surface while 17 are even with that level and two are sunk below modern ground level. The west plaza of Group I at Quebrada Grande and the east court of the Las Quebradas East Group are raised c. 4.25 and 4.1 m respectively above ground surface. These units are virtually unique in valley centers outside of Quirigua and represent a considerable investment of labor in their construction.

Surrounding the major groups are the smaller structures, sometimes found singly, though usually in groups of three to six. The forms taken by these small-structure aggregations vary considerably more than those of their monumental counterparts. Many are merely irregular collections of platforms surrounding a central open space and showing no common orientation. Others, however, are orthoganally arranged around three or four sides of a central plaza. In general, the larger the structures involved and the flatter the surrounding terrain, the more orthogonal the organization of the group. Rarely is more than one corner of these plazas closed by construction and, quite frequently, all are left open. As with the monumental-structure groups, one or two structures dominate each group by virtue of their size. These general trends hold for the small-structure groups in large site zones as well as for those found independently of such zones, e.g., La Coroza and Los Limones.

The densities of the small structures tend to be highest in the immediate vicinity of the large courts and to decrease rapidly away from them. The largest of the humble structures are also found most commonly close by the monumental groups.

The resultant site plan consists of a major court or courts surrounded by a fairly dense clustering of small structures with increasingly dispersed and more diminutive constructions found at increasing distances from these courts. This clustering leads to difficulties in defining individual structure groups near the main groups. This idealized picture is not strictly applicable to all the valley centers, however. At Playitas, Group IV's main group is not the focus of a small-structure concentration as are Groups I, II, and V. Rather, small platforms are dispersed fairly evenly around the court complex in clearly recognizable individual groups. Similarly, no structure clustering was noted around the main groups of Arapahoe Viejo and Bobos. The sites of Comanche Farm and Quebrada Grande generally lack smaller structures, though this may be attributable to their burial by river silts in these floodplain locations. Even within this variation, however, a pattern emerges. The smaller the main group in a site zone, the fewer small structures associated with it and the less marked their nucleation around that focal point. This pattern is borne out in Table 4.4, where the numbers of structures of the different groups focused on a major court at Playitas and Las Quebradas are compared; the largest courts are marked with an asterisk. Even within one site some of the smaller courts attract fewer additional structures

TABLE 4.4

NUMBER OF STRUCTURES ASSOCIATED WITH MONUMENTAL COURT GROUPS AT THE SITES OF PLAYITAS AND LAS QUEBRADAS (INCLUDES MONUMENTAL AND SMALL STRUCTURES)

Playitas

*Group I	78 structures	2 rock concentrations
Group II*	22 structures	5 rock concentrations
Group IV	51 structures	5 rock concentrations
Group V	56 structures	30 rock concentrations

Las Quebradas

*East Group	124 structures	8 rock concentrations
West Group	112 structures	1 rock concentration
Northwest Group	41 structures	1 rock concentration

*Playitas Group II is not contemporary with Groups I, IV, and V (see Chap. 5 on chronology).

and have a much less nucleated pattern than the larger courts (cf. the Northwest Group at Las Quebradas as compared to the East and West Groups at that site). Both temporal and functional factors could be used to explain this pattern. Such an explanation must be deferred, however, to Chap. 6, where site planning and other lines of evidence will be brought to bear on the question of the intrasite organization of behavior at valley centers.

At no site do all of the structures share precisely the same orientation. There is some variation between sites, however, in how closely this idealized pattern is approached.

Turning to site extent, the areas covered by each of the major investigated sites for which these data are available are given in Table 4.5. The numbers of the

structures recorded at each of these sites are also given in the table. In general there is a considerable gap between the two largest monumental sites, Las Quebradas and Playitas, and the remainder of the known centers. This discrepancy may be somewhat exaggerated by differential alluvial burial: sites with large courts, such as Quebrada Grande and Comanche Farm, are located in floodplains, where such burial might account for their low structure numbers.

As noted earlier, most of the nonmonumental sites visited replicate the patterns seen in the aggregations of small structures at major sites. Oneida and Juan de Paz, however, each have one or two open plazas surrounded by high structures around which the remaining, generally smaller structures are distributed. These relatively large sites (Juan de Paz has 81

TABLE 4.5

AREAS COVERED BY THE RECORDED MONUMENTAL SITES AND THE NUMBERS OF STRUCTURES FOUND AT EACH

Playitas	212 structures	42 rock concentrations	3.18 km^2
Las Quebradas	285 structures	10 rock concentrations	2.0 km^2
Quebrada Grande	49 structures	0 rock concentrations	? km^2
Choco	84 structures	0 rock concentrations	0.35+ km^2
Comanche Farm	23 structures	0 rock concentrations	1.10 km^2
Juyama	110 structures	0 rock concentrations	0.21+ km^2
Bobos	36 structures	0 rock concentrations	? km^2
Mojanales	7 structures	0 rock concentrations	? km^2
Arapahoe Viejo	23 structures	0 rock concentrations	0.05 km^2

recorded structures) mirror on a smaller scale their larger, monumental counterparts in this very general way. As with the larger sites, there is some variation in the degree of structure dispersal: Juan de Paz is much more nucleated than Oneida. This may be due to topographic conditions; Juan de Paz is on a restricted bluff above the Rio Motagua while Oneida is on a more extensive terrace. The brief survey of the sites of Cruce de Morales, Monterey, Finca America, and Puente Virginia indicates that they are more dis-

persed than Juan de Paz and, hence, more closely resemble Oneida.

In reference to Table 4.3, the Form/Nature combination that best approximates the monumental courts is the quadrangle, either single, double, or triple, surrounded by "palace" structures. Palace and temple groups were not recognized in the LMV and the four recorded plazas are best classed as "monumental-structure open plazas." All of the smaller structure aggregations are classed as "residential groups, plazas."

V

Chronology

INTRODUCTION

The purpose of this section is twofold: first, to place the investigated LMV sites within a relative temporal sequence, and then, primarily through the use of ceramic cross-ties, to relate that sequence to the broader southern Mesoamerican chronology. All artifacts recovered by excavation at the sites of Playitas, Choco, and Las Quebradas have been examined for variations that might indicate temporal differences. Pottery and *incensarios* prove to be the most useful artifact classes in chronologically ordering deposits. No temporal distinctions are found in the figurine, ground stone, or chipped stone collections. Monuments, architecture, and site plans have also been examined with an eye to their chronological utility. While structural organization and architecture may have some temporal significance, monuments are too restricted in their distribution to be of much use in this endeavor.

After establishing the chronological sequence, we have dated the Project's surface collections and placed their associated sites, at least tentatively, in the sequence. Those sites which yielded little to nothing in

the way of surface finds are assigned a general chronological position according to their site plans or locations.

The external reference sites used to establish cross-ties have been chosen on the basis of their proximity to the LMV and their sharing the greatest number of ceramic similarities. The most detailed comparisons are made with the site of Quirigua, because of its location in the LMV, its many ceramic similarities with valley sites, and the ceramic sequence already established there (Bullard and Sharer n.d.). In fact, the Quirigua sequence has helped define and refine the basic ceramic sequence for the valley. In addition, Copan, c. 50 km to the southwest, and sites in the Naco valley, c. 45 km to the southeast, both in Honduras, provide important specific cross-ties for the valley occupation sequence. In all of these cases, ceramic and *incensario* comparisons have been carried out through the author's visual inspection of the collections, both in the field and at ceramic conferences in the United States (Willey et al. 1980).

INTERNAL ORDERING: EXCAVATED EVIDENCE

POTTERY

No good stratified artifact deposits were uncovered by either Nowak or the LMV Project. Any changes in ceramic types and varieties through time would thus have to be inferred through a comparison of the pottery collections from different excavation units. At first the percentages of the different types and varieties found in each excavation lot were computed, compared, and examined for any evidence of change following the assumptions and procedures of seriation (e.g., Ford 1962). In this and all subsequent analyses, *incensario* sherds were excluded from the lot totals, while unclassified sherds were included. Attention focused on percentage changes in the four major valley types (Mojanal Micaceous: Faceted variety; En-

cantado Cream: Encantado variety; Techin Striated: unsp. variety; and Tipon Orange: Tipon variety) in arranging the associated excavation units into a sequence. These types were found in most of the recovered lots and varied sufficiently in their percentages to suggest their potential use in temporal ordering. But this initial effort did not produce a coherent chronological pattern, largely because of the small size of most of the lots and consequently broad variation in the type percentages.

To circumvent the problem of small sample size, the units of comparison were expanded to individual structures. All lots recovered from the excavation of a particular structure were assigned to one of three categories: terminal debris (including primary, secondary, and midden contexts), construction fill, and preconstruction debris. This allowed the creation of larger samples comprising all the items within a particular context from a single structure. All lots from mixed contexts were excluded. Monument excavations were also excluded as their consistently high percentages of Mojanal Micaceous: Faceted variety sherds might well have been attributable to functional rather than temporal factors; i.e., the inclusion of *incensario* fragments with a Mojanal paste due to the difficulty in distinguishing between small fragments of Mojanal Faceted vessels and *incensarios*. This procedure succeeded in reducing the radical variations noted in the individual lot comparisons, although a consistent chronological pattern still failed to appear. No matter how the contexts of the different structures were arranged, the type percentages did not show a pattern of increasing or decreasing frequencies that consistently put the preconstruction material of a structure prior to its terminal debris.

A final effort to overcome this difficulty involved the combination of material from a single context associated with a group of contemporary structures. The major quadrangles found at the three excavated sites are examples of such groups. The criterion of contemporaneity was structural arrangement; the organization of a set of structures into a coherently planned group was assumed to indicate that these platforms would have all been occupied at the same time. As it could not be assumed that they were all built simultaneously, fill and preconstruction material were not considered and the terminal debris formed the focus of study. Once again, this effort failed to yield a consistent pattern of changes in type frequencies.

While the detailed study of ceramic percentages has produced no clear evidence of chronological change in the excavated valley materials, certain gross patterns of ceramic variation are noted. There is a marked difference in the presence/absence of certain types between the excavated assemblages from Las Quebradas, Choco, and Playitas Groups I and IV on the one hand and those securely known to come from Playitas Group II on the other (Op. B, C, and E of Nowak). The former assemblages are characterized by their sharing of the major taxa—Mojanal Micaceous: Faceted variety, Encantado Cream: Encantado variety, Techin Striated: unsp. variety, and Tipon Orange: Tipon variety—as well as other minority categories (see Table 5.1).

These four primary types comprise a sizable percentage of the ceramics recovered from each of the above sites and/or groups (see Table 5.2). The material recovered from Playitas Group II contains a different configuration of types; Mojanal Micaceous: Faceted variety and Techin Striated: unsp. variety percentages fall to the lower portion of the range defined for the other excavated LMV collections, while Encantado Cream: Encantado variety, Mojanal Micaceous: Red-washed and Well-smoothed varieties, Chalja, Capulin, Tarro Incised, Tasu Fluted, Vitales Thick-walled, Coroza Cream, and San Rafael Red are totally absent (see Table 5.1). The Playitas Group II excavated assemblage also includes two types not found elsewhere in the valley, Mojanal Micaceous: Coarse-tempered variety and Riachuelo Buff: Riachuelo variety.

In interpreting these differences, several explanations could be advanced. First, the Tipon Orange: Tipon variety sherds from Playitas Group II are heavily eroded, so that types within the Tipon Group with similar pastes but different surface treatments (distinct types) cannot be distinguished. This still leaves marked differences between the two collections that cannot be accounted for by erosion. Variations in collection size could explain these differences. The Playitas Group II assemblage is considerably smaller than the sample excavated from the other centers. The Playitas Group II assemblage might not be expected, then, to exhibit the range of variation of its larger counterparts. This would still not account for the total absence in the Group II collection of types prevalent elsewhere in the valley (e.g., Encantado Cream: Encantado variety), or the exceptionally small percentages of others (Techin Striated: unsp. variety), or the presence of types not found in the larger collections (Mojanal Micaceous: Coarse-tempered variety and Riachuelo Buff: Riachuelo variety).

A more plausible interpretation would posit functional differences between Playitas Group II and the other major valley centers. In this view, the activities carried out at Group II required pottery not needed in the other excavated groups, where these activities were absent. There is, however, no further support for this position. First, the organization of structures, or the setting for the activities carried out at Group II, is not different from those at the other excavated groups. The monumental quadrangle enclosing a court and surrounded by smaller constructions is a common site plan in all investigated valley centers, including Playitas Group II. Second, the general nature of the Group II and other pottery collections is very similar; they are all dominated by utilitarian types. This would imply that Group II, like its architec-

TABLE 5.1

CHOCO, LAS QUEBRADAS, AND PLAYITAS GROUPS I AND IV

Type	Number of Contexts Found In	Percentage range	Average Percentage and Standard Deviation		Type Key
Mojanal: Faceted	44/95.65%	8.99-100.00%	×50.91%	±25.77%	1
Mojanal: Well-smoothed	21/45.65%	0.21-23.80%	×4.82%	±5.35%	2
Mojanal: Fine-tempered	16/34.78%	0.07-28.00%	×11.18%	±8.82%	3
Mojanal: Coarse-tempered	0	0	0		4
Riachuelo Buff	0	0	0		5
Encantado: Encantado	33/71.74%	2.86-63.60%	×22.27%	±16.01%	6
Encantado: Red	14/30.44%	0.14-34.44	×4.64%	±8.51%	7
Techin Striated	30/65.22%	1.43-38.11%	×14.78%	±8.52%	8
Tipon Orange: Tipon	28/60.87%	1.06-40.00%	×11.27%	±12.42	9
Chalja Red	15/32.61%	0.21-12.68%	×3.08%	±3.06	10
Capulin White	9/19.57%	0.17-9.01%	×2.72%	±3.27	11
Tarro Incised	6/13.04%	0.154-0.71%	×0.36%	±0.19	12
Tipon Grooved	4/8.70%	0.43-2.69%	×1.48%	±1.49	13
Bobos Orange: Bobos	27/58.70%	0.71-50.00%	×7.30%	±9.53	14
Bobos Red-on-orange	5/10.87%	0.30-4.4%	×2.32%	±1.72	15
Vitales Thick-walled	3/6.52%	0.27-1.18%	×0.62%	±0.40	16
San Rafael Red	3/6.52%	0.18-23.60%	×9.53%	±10.13	17
Coroza Cream	8/17.39%	0.14-50.00%	×9.07%	±15.84	18
Playitas Group II					
Mojanal: Faceted	4/80.00%	8.33-37.50%	×21.85%	±11.18	1
Mojanal: Red-washed	0	0	0		2
Mojanal: Well-smoothed	0	0	0		3
Mojanal: Coarse-tempered	3/60.00%	1.79-4.96%	×3.84%	±1.45	4
Riachuelo Buff	2/40.00%	68.02-69.85%	×68.94%		5
Encantado: Encantado	0	0	0		6
Encantado: Red	0	0	0		7
Techin Striated	2/40.00%	0.53-0.76%	×0.65%		8
Tipon Orange: Tipon	4/80.00%	4.20-77.78%	×45.94%	±26.49	9
Chalja Red	0	0	0		10
Capulin White	0	0	0		11
Tarro Incised	0	0	0		12
Tipon Grooved	0	0	0		13
Bobos Orange: Bobos	3/60.00%	2.78-16.67%	×7.67%	±6.37	14
Bobos Red-on-orange	1/20.00%	1.53%	1.53%		15
Vitales Thick-walled	0	0	0		16
San Rafael Red	0	0	0		17
Coroza Cream	0	0	0		18

tural counterparts in other parts of the valley, was the focus of domestic activities (see Chap. 6), and not the center of some specific set of distinct functions. In addition, at both Las Quebradas and Playitas, where more than one major structural group was excavated, the associated artifact assemblages do not differ markedly from each other in overall composition. This indicates that major functional differentiation among

TABLE 5.2

PERCENTAGES OF THE FOUR MAJOR VALLEY CERAMIC TYPES BY SITE/GROUP

Playitas Groups I and IV

Mojanal Micaceous: Faceted variety	32.92%
Encantado Cream: Encantado variety	17.67%
Techin Striated: unsp. variety	15.81%
Tipon Orange: Tipon variety	6.61%
	73.01%

Las Quebradas

Mojanal Micaceous: Faceted variety	37.84%
Encantado Cream: Encantado variety	17.90%
Techin Striated: unsp. variety	19.54%
Tipon Orange: Tipon variety	12.84%
	88.12%

Choco

Mojanal Micaceous: Faceted variety	44.18%
Encantado Cream: Encantado variety	24.48%
Techin Striated: unsp. variety	11.19%
Tipon Orange: Tipon variety	1.34%
	81.19%

Playitas Group II

Mojanal Micaceous: Faceted variety	22.28%
Encantado Cream: Encantado variety	0.00%
Techin Striated: unsp. variety	0.51%
Tipon Orange: Tipon variety	10.78%
	33.57%

groups within a site is not a common valley pattern (see Chap. 6). It is unlikely, therefore, that the differences in the ceramic assemblages between Playitas Group II and the other excavated valley Groups can be attributed solely to differences in the activities performed there.

The most likely explanation for these variations is that they represent temporal differences between the occupation of Playitas Group II and the valley's other excavated major structural foci. Group II would, therefore, have been occupied in a period when Encantado Cream: Encantado variety was absent, Techin Striated: unsp. variety found only in low frequencies, and Mojanal Micaceous: Faceted variety only a relatively small proportion of the overall assemblage. The other excavated valley groups, in turn, were occupied when Mojanal Micaceous: Coarse-tempered variety and Riachuelo Buff: Riachuelo variety were not part of the valley potters' repertoire. The presence in both valley and Group II assemblages of

common types, i.e., Tipon Orange: Tipon variety and Mojanal Micaceous: Faceted variety, indicates, however, that the interval between the occupations of Group II and the other valley centers was short.

INCENSARIOS:

In general, the *incensario* sherds are very similar in paste and surface treatment in all of the excavated collections, including Playitas Group II. But censer forms are not equally represented in all of the excavated centers. In a gross presence/absence measure of difference, Playitas Group II has no ladle, pronged, or lid censer fragments, forms found in variable percentages at the other excavated valley Groups, including Playitas Groups I and IV. Playitas Group II, in addition, possesses a form—the cruciform-vent—not recorded in the other excavations. The Playitas Group II collection also contains a relatively high percentage (14.29%) of modeled cacao-pod effigies, a form recorded from only one other excavated valley site outside of Quirigua, Choco (one sherd).

The distinctiveness of the *incensario* forms found at Playitas Group II cannot be attributable to differences in sample size, since the censer sample from Group II is approximately equivalent to the samples recovered from other excavated valley sites. Therefore, functional or temporal factors must explain the divergence. The functional argument is the weaker of the two, for the same reasons cited earlier in the discussion of pottery. The differences in censer form between Group II and the other valley collections support the chronological argument advanced earlier based on pottery evidence. Once more, however, the existence of some shared form types between the two collections indicates a relatively short time difference between them.

ARTIFACTS

The other artifact categories, i.e., ground and chipped stone and figurines, either are too poorly represented to be useful in determining temporal change, or show no clear evidence of change through time.

MONUMENTS

Monuments are so limited in number (eight) and restricted in their distribution (Las Quebradas and Arapahoe Viejo) that their chronological significance cannot be determined.

ARCHITECTURE

The architecture characteristic of the valley sites exclusive of Playitas Group II is remarkably uniform in both the materials employed and overall structure forms. In the two cases where superimposed construction was revealed, some change in architectural style could be seen—from a high, steep-sided platform in Str. 212-4-3rd to a step-terrace construction in Str. 212-4-1st; and from a low, stone-faced platform in Str. 205-1-3rd to an earth-and-stone stepped structure in Str. 205-1-2nd and -1st. The only generalization suggested by these limited examples of architectural change is that the step-terrace form of construction was preferred for monumental structures during the valley centers' final phase of occupation. The Playitas Group II architecture does not appear markedly different from that uncovered elsewhere, although this point is not certain given the limited nature of Nowak's excavations (see App. I).

SITE PLANS

As noted above, the site plans of all the investigated monumental centers are very similar. There is no reason to believe, at present, that any of the examined major site plans date to a markedly different time period than the others. There is some variation, however, in the location of sites, between those centers found on the floodplain and those situated in the foothills. While there is a general tendency within Mesoamerica for later sites, especially those in the Postclassic (c. AD 1000-1500), to be located on higher, more defensible ground than their Classic (c. AD 250-1000) counterparts (e.g., Shook and Proskouriakoff 1956), there is no evidence that differences in topographic location can be used to define temporal shifts in the LMV.

The only exception to this point is, once more, Playitas Group II. Here the question is not so much how the structures are arranged but their position relative to the other groups in the site. At other multi-group sites (Las Quebradas, Quebrada Grande, and Juyama) the distances between the major quadrangles never exceed 0.41 km (average 0.3 km) and the intervening areas are often filled with smaller constructions. At Playitas, Groups I, IV, and V conform to this generalization, while Group II is c. 1 km from the nearest quadrangle (Group V). Despite two seasons of investigation at Playitas (1977 and 1979) no intervening smaller constructions were recorded over this rather long distance. The isolated position of Group II, unique among known valley centers, suggests that it dates to a different time period from Playitas Groups I, IV, and V, as well as from the other excavated valley centers.

RESULTS

The chronological model constructed from the above observations proposes that all of the excavated valley Groups outside of Playitas Group II share a consistent, albeit restricted, ceramic repertoire with some limited variation in the type percentages by structure and context, and hence date to the same period (see Table 5.1). The results of the analysis of *incensarios* point to the same conclusion. Furthermore, a variety of evidence suggests that these excavated sites were all occupied for only a short period of time—the absence of stratified deposits; the shallowness of uncovered middens; the apparent absence of temporal depth associated with sequent construction; the lack of significant differences in the composition of material from terminal debris, fill, and preconstruction contexts; and the paucity of preconstruction material in general. Playitas Group II, on the basis of the same lines of evidence, dates to a slightly different period, a view supported by its physical isolation. Is Playitas Group II earlier or later than its valley counterparts, and in what time span do all the valley sites fall? Internal evidence alone cannot provide answers to these questions. After placing the unexcavated sites in a chronological framework, we will consider these issues by examining the evidence from ceramic cross-ties.

INTERNAL ORDERING: SURFACE EVIDENCE

The unexcavated loci divide into two types based on the nature of the data used to place them chronologically: those with surface collections and those without. Placement of the latter set is very tentative and depends primarily on the use of the less time-specific indicator of site plan.

Fifteen sites yielded surface collections (see Table 5.3). Comanche Farm and Playitas Group V produced collections in excess of 250 sherds, 269 and 338 respectively, while the remainder averaged only 25 sherds per site. The Comanche Farm and Playitas Group V samples, for which the type percentages were computed, are very similar to all the excavated valley site collections (other than Playitas Group II) in terms of both the types represented and their relative frequencies (cf. Tables 5.1 and 5.3). As a result, these can be confidently placed within the same time span as the valley centers exclusive of Playitas Group II. The remaining 13 collections are so small that any percentage computations would be meaningless. They and their associated loci are placed within a time period based solely on the presence/absence of certain types. This procedure results in very tentative temporal assignments. As an examination of Table 5.3 indicates, in nine cases the presence of Encantado Cream: Encantado variety and/or Techin Striated: unsp. variety, both important types in the non-Group II valley assemblages, along with Mojanal Micaceous: Faceted variety, suggests that the loci are contemporary with the excavated sites of Choco, Las Quebradas, and Playitas Groups I and IV. The absence of such Playitas Group II-related diagnostics as Mojanal Micaceous: Coarse-tempered variety, Riachuelo Buff: Riachuelo variety, cruciform-vent censers, and cacao-pod effigy censers from these collections also indicates that none should be placed in the same time period as this Group.

These findings are supported by evidence from site plans. Seven of the surface-collected loci possess monumental architecture, and these share very similar plans with the excavated Groups, including Playitas Group II. Insofar as the canons governing the arrangement of structures may change through time, this similarity in site morphology indicates that the seven centers under discussion are broadly contemporary with the excavated sites of Las Quebradas, Choco, and Playitas. Similarities in site form, however, for reasons discussed below, can indicate only a general degree of contemporaneity among loci, as was suggested by the contrast between similar site plans and different pottery/*incensario* collections of Playitas Group II and the other excavated Groups.

The ten remaining sites produced no surface collections. Nine of these lack monumental architecture, although they vary considerably in size (see, for example, Los Limones and Oneida). Because none of these sites was excavated, or, if they were, the contexts of the material are unknown (e.g., Puente Virginia; Nowak 1975), pottery could not be used in dating them. Further, because they were not major centers, their structural arrangements could not be compared with those at the excavated monumental sites in order to place them within a temporal period. A possible indication of the broad temporal placement of the larger nonmonumental sites, Oneida, Cruce de Morales, Monterey, Finca America, and Puente Virginia, is obtained by comparing their general site plans with that known from Juan de Paz, which did produce a surface collection (40 sherds). All of these sites share a basic pattern of structure organization—a set of somewhat larger structures arranged orthogonally around a plaza and surrounded by irregularly oriented smaller structures. On the basis of this very general similarity, it may be hypothesized that these sites date to the same period as Juan de Paz; in other words, that they are equivalent in date to the occupation of the excavated valley centers outside of Playitas Group II. Further, the three small sites of Los Limones, Los Vitales, and Locus 234, because of their location on a probable communication route originating at Playitas, probably also date to the period when at least one of the Playitas groups was occupied.

Mojanales is the only major center with no surface collection. Its unique location within a high, restricted

TABLE 5.3

DISTRIBUTION OF TYPE/VARIETY UNITS FROM SURFACE COLLECTION.

(Relative Type Percentages are Given for the Three Largest Collections: Comanche Farm, Playitas Group V and Las Quebradas West Group. Otherwise an "X" Indicates a Type's Presence and a "0" its Absence. Size of the Sample is Given Following the Type Counts)

Site	Mojanal Faceted	Mojanal Red	Mojanal Fine	Encantado Encantado	Encantado Red	Techin Striated	Tipon Tipon	Chaljn	Capulin	Tarro	Grooved	Tipon Misc.	Bobos Bobos	Bobos Red on Orange	Bobos Polychrome	Vitales	Corosa Polychrom	Specials	Usulutan	Total
Comanche Farm	21.2%	.74%	12.3%	20.3%	19.7%	8.6%	3.7%	.74%	1.1%	.74%	.4%	1.5%	3.4%	.4%	—	—	—	5.2%	—	269
Playitas Grp. V	29.6%	.3%	7.4%	20.1%	—	27.5%	4.7%	1.8%	2.1%	—	—	—	4.7%	—	.3%	.3%	—	1.2%	—	338
L. Q. West Grp.	26.8%	.4%	—	11.5%	1.9%	45.0%	4.1%	.4%	.4%	—	—	—	1.1%	—	—	—	3.7%	4.8%	—	269
L. Q. East Grp.	X	X	0	0	0	X	X	0	0	0	0	0	0	0	0	0	0	0	0	14
L. Q. South Grp.	X	0	0	0	0	X	X	X	X	0	0	0	0	X	0	0	0	0	0	37
Quebrada Grande	X	0	0	X	0	X	X	0	0	0	0	0	0	0	0	0	0	0	0	11
Piedras de Sangre	X	0	0	X	0	0	0	0	0	0	0	0	0	0	0	0	0	0	0	3
Juan de Paz	X	X	0	X	0	X	X	0	0	0	0	0	X	0	0	0	0	X	0	40
Zaculeu C.6 Cable 2	X	0	0	X	X	X	X	X	X	0	0	X	0	0	0	0	0	X	X	105
Arapahoe Nuevo	X	0	0	0	0	0	0	0	0	0	0	0	0	0	0	0	0	X	0	5
Bobos	X	0	0	X	0	0	0	0	0	0	0	0	X	X	0	0	0	X	0	9
Lankin	X	0	0	0	0	X	0	X	X	X	0	X	X	0	0	0	0	0	0	18
Zaculeu Z-2 Cable 2	X	X	0	0	0	0	0	0	0	0	0	0	0	0	0	0	0	X	0	11
Juyama	X	0	0	X	X	0	0	0	0	0	0	0	0	0	0	0	0	X	0	26
Arapahoe E-8 Cable 2	X	0	0	X	X	X	X	0	0	0	0	0	0	0	0	0	0	0	0	19
Coroza Viejo	X	0	0	X	X	X	0	0	X	0	X	0	0	0	0	0	0	0	0	25

173

valley also precludes any expectation of detailed similarities in site form to other investigated centers. The latter all enjoy access to larger areas for building, hence the canons developed in such a situation could not be easily replicated in a more restricted zone. Despite this problem, however, Mojanales Str. 233-1/3 form a small plaza group with narrowly defined open corners, using the adjacent hill to close off the northeast side. This arrangement generally resembles the quadrangle form. Structures 233-4/7, while partially obscured by vegetation, also seem to take on this form. The available evidence on monumental structure arrangements at Mojanales, therefore, suggests that it was contemporary with the occupation of the other major valley centers including Playitas Group II. The location of Mojanales on a probable prehistoric communication route emanating from Playitas also supports this view.

This brief survey of the chronological placement of unexcavated sites leaves a residue of five loci, all apparently without visible architecture, reported by Nowak, but which we were unable to relocate precisely. Four of these loci—Arapahoe Nuevo; Lankin Seccion E2, Cable 2; Piedras de Sangre; and Zaculeu Seccion E8, Cable 2—produced small and undistinguished collections which permit only a very tentative temporal placement. Zaculeu Seccion C6, Cable 2, on the other hand, yielded a relatively large (105 sherds) and mixed collection. Techin Striated: unsp. variety, Mojanal Micaceous: Faceted variety, Encantado Cream: Encantado and Red-washed varieties, and Tipon Group sherds are represented here, pointing clearly to occupation contemporary with the major excavated centers exclusive of Playitas Group II. Also recovered, however, were 28 Usulutan-decorated sherds, a type with negative-painted designs not found in any of the excavated valley collections. As will be noted in the following section, it is very likely that the remains from two different occupations have been mixed here, probably a consequence of collections derived from the backdirt of a deep BANDEGUA canal.

GENERAL CHRONOLOGICAL PLACEMENT

The placement of the LMV sites within a broader, dated temporal sequence relies on the establishment of cross-ties to existing archaeological sequences. The apparent utility of ceramics and *incensarios* and, to a lesser extent, site plans in the internal temporal ordering of the valley collections suggests that any inter-areal comparisons for dating purposes should focus on these data categories. Material suitable for radiometric dating was rarely recovered by the Project.

INTERREGIONAL COMPARISON

POTTERY

The site of Quirigua, for the reasons cited earlier, offered the basic referent for valley ceramics (Bullard and Sharer n.d.). Because of the way the valley pottery was originally ordered, comparisons with Quirigua are made according to the presence/absence of specific pottery types and do not involve the computation and comparison of type percentages.

The examination of Quirigua and valley pottery both in the field and in later analysis strongly suggests that the latter material most closely corresponds to the final two phases of Quirigua's occupation, the Hewett and Morley Ceramic Complexes (c. AD 700-1000) (cf. Tables 5.1 and 5.4). This conclusion is based on both type and form inventories. In particular, the prevalence of Techin Striated: unsp. variety, a member of the Switch Molina Group, points to the Hewett Complex, while the high percentage of Mojanal Group sherds in valley collections indicates a slightly later Morley Complex association. Tipon Group sherds were associated with both of these complexes at Quirigua. The restriction of certain ceramic groups to collections from either the valley, e.g., Encantado and Bobos, or Quirigua, e.g., Chinok and Quequexque, probably reflects intraregional variation rather than temporal differences. The fact that so many ceramic similarities do exist within the LMV makes any significant temporal discontinuity between the valley centers and Quirigua very unlikely.

Turning to vessel forms, the vast majority of recovered valley bowl sherds are Bullard and Sharer's A form (57.06% of all form-classified bowl sherds) while 2.44% and 3.24% are from B and B-1 bowls respectively. This fits well with characteristic forms of the Quirigua collection in the Hewett Complex (Table 5.4). The D-1 jar form, also diagnostic of the Hewett Complex, is, however, absent from the valley collec-

TABLE 5.4

PRELIMINARY QUIRIGUA PROJECT CERAMIC ANALYSIS

Diagnostic Types of Quirigua's Early Development (c. AD 450-700)
    Dartmouth Ceramic Group (orange ware)
      Forms: Bowls, A-2, A-3, Delicias Red-on-orange
      (Minor types include orange monochrome and red- and black-painted polychrome)
    Cementerio Ceramic Group (domestic jars)
      Mapache Grooved: Guaya variety
      Chilmecate Incised
Diagnostic Types of Quirigua's Major Building Phase (c. AD 700-800)
    Tipon Ceramic Group (orange ware)
      Forms: Bowls, A, B, B-1, Tipon Orange
      Chalja Red
      Capulin Cream
      Alsacia Pink
      (Minor types are decorated by combination of colors and/or with incising, fluting, carving, etc.)
    Chinok Ceramic Group (coarser orange ware; includes 'cache boxes')
      Chinok Orange
      Biafra Red-on-orange
    Switch Molina Ceramic Group (domestic jars)
      Switch Molina Striated
      (Variations include red-painting and appliqués)
    Masica Ceramic Group (domestic jars)
      Tipante Incised
      (Variations include red-painting)
Diagnostic Types of Quirigua's Late Occupation (c. AD 800-?)
    Panama Ceramic Group (hematite red bowls)
      Forms: Bowls, G-1, Panama Red
    Mojanal Ceramic Group (domestic jars)
      Mojanal Micaceous
      Yuma Unslipped

Note: Adapted from Bullard and Sharer n.d.

tions. The G-1 bowl and A-1 jar forms, diagnostic of the succeeding Morley Complex at Quirigua, are also found in valley assemblages, albeit in low percentages (0.88% and 0.61% respectively). The C bowl, diagnostic of both the Hewett and Morley Complexes, was also recovered from valley centers (5.59%). Unfortunately, few base fragments are associated with this form, so the temporally significant question of the presence/absence of supports cannot be answered (see Table 5.5). The Playitas Group II material produced only 24 form-classified rims (17 jars, seven bowls). While this sample follows the general pattern noted in the valley excavations, it is too small for any meaningful comparison. Bowl forms diagnostic of

other Quirigua Complexes are also found in the valley collections, i.e., E bowls (2.94%), D bowls (0.59%), and G bowls (0.29%). Their small percentages, however, indicate their relative unimportance in these assemblages.

In sum, the comparison of valley pottery types and forms with their Quirigua counterparts indicates a placement equivalent to the Hewett and Morley Complexes of that Maya site. This applies to all valley centers, including Playitas Group II. To further test and refine this general temporal placement, a search has been made for external analogues to LMV types (see Table 5.5). San Rafael Red, Tipon Group taxa, Bobos Polychrome, and Copador Polychrome are the most useful types for this comparison. San Rafael Red, a minority type in the valley collections (0.41% of the classified ceramics), is almost identical in surface finish, decoration, and form to Reina Inciso sherds from Copan (Viel 1983: 522). The latter type has been dated at Copan to the Coner Phase or c. AD 700-850 (ibid.: 538). One vessel of this type was also recovered from a substela cache at Copan (beneath Stela J; Longyear 1952: fig.113b) and could be dated by association with that monument to 9.13.10.0.0 in the Maya Long Count (AD 704). San Rafael is also generally similar to the incised-necked jars (Masica Incised) recovered from Los Naranjos in western Honduras and dated to the Late Classic period (Yojoa Phase, AD 550-950; Baudez and Becquelin 1973: 296-299). The Tipon Group has a long history at both Copan and Quirigua, especially the undecorated Tipon type (Acbi II to Coner Phase at Copan, c. AD 550-850) (Willey et al. 1980). The painted types of Tipon, however (e.g., Chalja and Capulin) appear to be restricted to the later phases at both sites (Hewett at Quirigua and Coner at Copan, c. AD 700-850).

The distribution of Copador in the LMV is less clear. It has been found, to date, outside of Quirigua only in two of Nowak's Playitas suboperations for which provenience and contextual data are absent (Op. 9D and F). Judging from the overall type percentages represented in the lots associated with Copador (Lots 9D/1-3 and F/4), we surmise that they were recovered from the Playitas Group II test pits. In particular, the absence of Encantado Cream: Encantado variety in these collections, the relatively low percentages of Techin Striated: unsp. variety, and the presence of Mojanal Micaceous: Coarse-tempered variety and Riachuelo Buff: Riachuelo variety all support this conclusion. The suboperations designated 9D and F also match the known Group II sequence of excavations, 9B, C, and E. If, as seems likely, Copador sherds were associated with the Playitas Group II occupation at some point, then they can be tentatively used for dating purposes. Copador has been securely dated at Copan, by virtue of its clear association with dated monuments, to c. AD 740-750 (Leventhal 1986). Viel has recently (1983: 520-522) argued that Copador dates to the Coner Phase at Copan, c. AD 700-850.

Finally, Bobos Polychrome, again known only from a single excavated context, presumably at Playitas Group II (Lot 9F/4), has its closest analogue in Chamelecon Polychrome recovered from the Naco valley of Honduras, c. 45 km to the southeast (Urban 1986b: 120-128). Unfortunately, Chamelecon Poly-

chrome has a long span of use, c. AD 400-950, and while this does not contradict the evidence for the dating of Group II's occupation, it does not help to pin it down more precisely. Though not listed in Table 5.5, members of the Bobos Ceramic Group found at all excavated valley sites bear a general similarity to members of the Chamelecon Group in the Naco valley (ibid.) in their surface finishes and decoration, an orange slip sometimes with a red band along the rim (La Champa Orange: Plain and Bichrome varieties; ibid.), and share the same basic form, gently convexly curving walled bowls. The Naco examples date to c. AD 300-1000, consistent with the Classic date for the occupation of the excavated valley loci.

The foregoing ceramic evidence points to a Late Classic date of c. AD 700-1000 for all of the dated valley centers. More specifically, there is some ceramic evidence pointing to a slightly earlier date within this broad period for the occupation of Playitas Group II. First, the Group II collections contain lower percentages of Mojanal Group sherds than do those from the other valley centers. Insofar as Mojanal is a diagnostic of the later Morley Phase at Quirigua, its relative paucity here may suggest an earlier, pre-Morley date. Second, it has been argued convincingly elsewhere that Copan and Quirigua severed their political ties c. AD 738, after which relations and, presumably, their material manifestations were greatly attenuated (e.g., Jones and Sharer 1986; Riese 1986, Sharer 1990). If this sequence of events is applicable to the valley as a whole, the ceramic collections from Choco, Las Quebradas, and Playitas Groups I and IV would appear to reflect a period after contacts were broken off (San Rafael Red being the only indication of a possible Copan connection). The Playitas Group II assemblage, despite its much smaller size, manifests close connections with Copan (in the form of Copador Polychrome). This suggestion of more intense Copan connections manifest in the Group II collections is further substantiated by a study of the *incensarios*.

INCENSARIOS:

The excavated *incensario* sample from the valley centers outside of Playitas Group II is characterized by a variety of forms (see Table 4.1). The composition of this collection fits well with that defined for Construction Stages 2-1 at Quirigua (Hewett through early Morley equivalent, c. AD 700-850; Benyo 1979: 41). In particular, this period at Quirigua is characterized by ladle censers, a relative increase in the importance of

TABLE 5.5

INTERREGIONAL CERAMIC AND *INCENSARIO* CROSS-TIES

Type	Valley Location	Analogue	Analogue Location	Dates	Reference
San Rafael red painted	Playitas Group IV, Str. 200-22 (midden) Playitas Group I, Str. 200-77 (terminal debris, secondary) Choco, Str. 212-22 (fill)	Masica Incised: Reina Var.	Copan (Coner Phase)	700-800 AD	Visual inspection of Copan material; (Longyear 1952; Fig. 113b; Baudez and Becquelin 1973)
Bobos Polychrome	Playitas Group V (surface) Playitas Group II, Lot 9F/4	Chamelecon Polychrome	Naco Valley	400-800 AD	J. Henderson pers. comm. and visual comparison
Tipon Group Types	Associated with all Strs. save: Strs. 205-1-3rd, 205-56, 212-1	Tipon Group	Copan (Acbi II-Coner Phases)	550-800 AD	Willey et al. 1980; visual inspection
Copador Polychrome	Playitas Group II, Lots 9D/1-3 and 9F/4	Copador Polychrome	Copan (Coner Phase)	730-800 AD	Leventhal 1980
Usulutan	Zaculeu Seccion C. 6, Cable 2; La Coroza area (reported)	Usulutan vars.	SE Maya area generally; Late Preclassic-Early Classic	400 B.C.-250 AD	Demarest and Sharer (1982)
Modeled cacao pod censers	Playitas Group II, Lots 9D/1-2	Cacao pod modeled effigy censers and cache pots	Copan (Classic)	590-810 AD	Longyear 1952; Figs. 105b, 109f, 112n-q, 114a; visual inspection

modeled censers, and a peaking in the diversity of censer forms. All of this corresponds to the moderate to high percentages of ladle and modeled censer forms at the excavated valley centers exclusive of Playitas Group II, and the representation of all forms save the cruciform-vent at these loci. Prior to Construction Stage 2 at Quirigua (c. AD 700) both ladle and modeled forms were very rare (ibid.: 40-41). The Playitas Group II censer collection has a different configuration which supports the somewhat earlier date already attributed to this Group. First, there is an absence of pronged and lid forms here, a curious fact given their continued popularity throughout the Quirigua sequence (ibid.). More important is the complete absence of the ladle form in the Group II collection. Given the large size of the Group II *incensario* sample and the proximity of this locus to Group IV, where ladle censers were found, it is hard to account for this lack except on a temporal basis; i.e., that Group II was abandoned before ladle censers became prevalent. The large percentage of modeled censers from Group II, however, by analogy with Quirigua, also indicates that it still shares some similarities with Construction Stage 2-1 assemblages. Modeled censers at Quirigua, however, cover a relatively long time span. The cruciform-vent form found at Playitas Group II has no Quirigua analogues.

If we consider the Playitas Group II censers in more

detail, the cacao-pod effigies included within the modeled category are very similar to examples recovered from Copan and dated there to the Full Classic by Longyear (c. AD 590-810; Longyear 1952: figs. 105b, 112n-q, 109f, 114a). Several of these censers were found in caches beneath Copan Stelae P and M, dated at 9.9.10.0.0 and 9.16.5.0.0 respectively (AD 625 and 758; ibid.: 52-53). It is interesting that, once again, another close Copan linkage is found at Playitas Group II and virtually absent at the other valley centers. Modeled cacao-pod effigies are found only sporadically at Quirigua and Choco. As noted above, if the argument for the cessation of ties with Copan made for Quirigua is applicable to the valley as a whole, then this would place Group II's occupation in the pre-AD 738 period when contact was still maintained. The paucity of Copan-inspired forms in the censers from the other valley centers supports the view of their occupation as coming after contact was severed in AD 738.

In sum, the general chronological conclusions derived from the analysis of the ceramics are supported by the study of the *incensarios*. All the valley centers possess a full Late Classic *incensario* assemblage. More specifically, Playitas Group II, because of its lack of ladle censers and its evidence of Copan ties, may date to the first 40 to 50 years of this period, while its more parochial counterparts possessing ladle censers were occupied slightly later.

SITE PLANS

The general monumental site plan characteristic of the valley, with its central quadrangle and surrounding dispersed smaller structures, was also characteristic of Quirigua by at least the Hewett Phase. The Acropolis had by this time the general form of a valley quadrangle: a small raised court enclosed by monumental structures with restricted access (Sharer et al. 1983). Adjoining this central, private architectural focus was a large open plaza also bounded by monu-

mental structures (the Great Plaza). Such a juxtaposition of plazas and courts is replicated in the West and East Groups at Las Quebradas. Further, the location of the impressive Quirigua monuments in this spacious area may indicate that its openness was a modification of the quadrangle pattern to encourage viewing the sculptures (see Chap. 7). Around these two monumental units is a scattering of smaller structures, especially dense to the north and east, similar in their overall form to the distribution of smaller structures noted in other valley centers (Ashmore 1981b).

As was noted earlier, it is still questionable how sensitive to change site plans are. Since structures are the physical facilities for the performance of activities, modifications in site morphology must be understood in functional as well as temporal terms. The unique functional position of Quirigua within the LMV must hence be borne in mind in comparing valley and Quirigua site plans (see Chap. 7). Quirigua's location on, and orientation toward, the Rio Motagua may also have influenced its final form. Nevertheless, it is likely that within a particular region traditions of the "proper" use of space existed, at least partly independent of the more pragmatic requirements of activities. Changes in site morphology, therefore, can be helpful in constructing and testing local chronologies. This is especially true where the functions performed at the different sites were at least roughly similar. As will be argued later, this seems to have been the case for Quirigua and other valley centers (Chap. 7). The considerable amount of effort required to reorganize a site, especially when dealing with monumental construction, would also ensure that such changes through time would be very slow. Similarities in site organization between Late Classic Quirigua and the known valley centers, including Playitas Group II, therefore support a general contemporaneity between them as already indicated from the pottery and *incensario* comparisons.

CONCLUSIONS

On the basis of artifact comparisons and, to a lesser extent, the analysis of site plans, the following chronological model is proposed. Within the Late Classic of the LMV there were two phases of occupation, both involving monumental construction. The first corresponds to the early part of the Hewett Complex at Quirigua, c. AD 700-740, and is represented by the

construction and occupation of Playitas Group II. Excavations here revealed a restricted ceramic assemblage composed primarily of Mojanal and Tipon Group types on the one hand and modeled, cruciform-vent, and spiked censers on the other. Evidence provided by the presence of Copador Polychrome, Bobos Polychrome sherds, and modeled cacao-pod effigy censers indicates close, if limited, ties with areas outside the valley, primarily with Copan. In the next period, equivalent to the late Hewett and Morley Complexes at Quirigua (c. AD 740-850), certain earlier types disappear (Riachuelo Buff: Riachuelo variety and Mojanal Micaceous: Coarse-tempered variety) and a new ceramic group is introduced (Encantado), as are ladle censers. The types Techin Striated: unsp. variety and Mojanal Micaceous: Faceted variety increase in relative percentages and Mojanal Micaceous: Red-washed and Well-smoothed varieties, Coroza Cream, and Vitales Thick-walled appear for the first time in limited numbers. In general, the noted changes in the assemblages are not major and there is, therefore, no inferable hiatus in occupation or construction within the LMV. The later collections are more varied than before and more parochial, with only the San Rafael Red type clearly indicating continued tenuous links with Copan and the general area of western Honduras (e.g., Masica Incised at Los Naranjos; Baudez and Becquelin 1973: 296-299). Throughout both periods, connections with Quirigua are close, as manifested especially in the importance of the Mojanal, Switch Molina (represented in the valley by Techin Striated: unsp. variety), and Tipon Groups in valley pottery collections and modeled and spiked censers in the *incensario* samples. Site plans remain unchanged throughout the Late Classic within the valley, including Quirigua, as does monumental and small architecture. The absence of clear Postclassic diagnostics, e.g., Plumbate, along with other "late" Quirigua diagnostics, e.g., Panama Red, indicates cessation of occupation at these major valley centers early in this period, arbitrarily set at AD 850.

The absence of diagnostic Playitas Group II types from preconstruction levels at other valley sites indicates that there was a horizontal movement of population after AD 700-740 and the later sites were built and occupied for a relatively short time span (c. 100 years). This was certainly the case at Playitas, where the later occupation—represented by Groups I, IV, and V—is c. 1 km farther out onto the floodplain north of Group II. Such a movement may partially account for our inability to locate deep stratified deposits at any excavated valley site.

All 12 surveyed valley sites that produced surface collections were contemporary with the occupation of Choco, Las Quebradas, and Playitas Groups I and IV, i.e., fall within the AD 740-850 time span. Eight sites, including one monumental example, Mojanales, are placed in the c. AD 700-850 period on the basis of nonceramic data alone. So far only Playitas Group II can be assigned to the AD 700-740 span. This pattern suggests a rapid increase in the pace of site occupation and monumental construction at the conclusion of the Late Classic in the LMV.

The Late Classic is, therefore, the major recognized period of occupation within the valley. All known monumental construction dates to this time span. The ceramics recovered from Zaculeu Seccion C6, Cable 2 and reported from the La Coroza area, however, point to the existence of an earlier occupation. Usulutan-decorated sherds, probably pertaining to the Late Preclassic or Early Classic period, have come from these areas, along with a large mammiform tetrapod bowl with negative-painted Usulutan decoration. Further, Nowak's excavation at Juyama revealed at c. 1.6 m below ground level an artifact-rich deposit with diagnostic Early Classic material (c. AD 250-600; Nowak 1975: 18; App. I). Late Preclassic-type figurines were also recovered from the same area though their precise provenience is unknown (ibid.). The Zaculeu and Juyama materials were apparently originally exposed in deep canal cuts made into the floodplain of the Rio Motagua and its tributaries by BANDEGUA. This suggests that much of the earlier, pre-Late Classic valley occupation, roughly equivalent to the poorly known Catherwood Complex at Quirigua, AD ?-400, may lie deeply buried beneath the valley alluvium. Occupation assignable to this period therefore might have been more extensive than surface indications suggest. This was certainly the case at Quirigua, where a thick covering of river-deposited silts effectively hid all evidence of Quirigua's pre-Late Classic occupation (Ashmore 1981b). That some evidence of this earlier occupation may be found above the floodplain in the surrounding foothills is suggested by the reported La Coroza pieces. This supposition, however, could not be substantiated by the Project in 1979 (see Chap. 2). In sum, while the Catherwood occupation in the valley may have been quite extensive, involving both floodplain and foothill settlement, it is only poorly understood.

VI

Intrasite Activity Distribution

INTRODUCTION

This chapter identifies the range and spatial distribution of the ancient activities performed at LMV monumental centers. The inductive bases for this reconstruction are the patterns noted in the excavated artifact samples recovered from Choco, Las Quebradas, and Playitas (including Group II); in the three large surface collections from Comanche Farm, Playitas Group V, and the Las Quebradas West Group; and in the data on architecture, monuments, and site planning gathered at all of the investigated major valley centers. Because the three excavated sites are the best known they provide the bulk of the information on which the following functional model is constructed.

The reconstruction of activities carried out at the wider valley centers began with the identification of a set of expected activities based on work at major lowland Classic Maya sites. After these "possible activities" had been defined, their material correlates were enumerated. These correlates were used to recognize their associated activities in the LMV data. The possible activities and their physical manifestations are summarized briefly in Table 6.1. A fuller justification for their use is presented in App. II. In Table 6.1 the evidence associated with each activity is divided into five categories where applicable: artifacts used in, or resulting from, that activity; the nature of the architectural setting in which it was carried out or the type of architecture that resulted from it; the general arrangement of structures the activity might require (site morphology); the nature of any monuments associated with that activity; and the general effect on site placement it might exercise (site location). The definitions of the proposed activities are given at the end of this introductory section and repeated in App. II. It should be understood that not every activity type listed or every piece of material evidence cited was found in the LMV. The actual number of activities that could be inferred from the 1977-79 work in the valley is only a segment of this potential list.

The resultant picture of intrasite activity distributions presented here must be treated as a *preliminary* model, since the data on which it is based are limited. Placement of excavations did not follow a probabilistic sampling design, hence their results cannot be assumed to offer a representative picture of activity distributions. Similarly, only a small proportion of the buildings at these large sites could be tested, so it cannot be asserted that evidence for the full range of ancient activities has been recovered. Despite these difficulties, however, certain gross statements on the kind and distribution of behaviors characteristic of the larger valley centers can be made based on the general patterns noted in the data. These statements form the framework of a general activity distribution model, the propositions of which can be refined and tested as further work is carried out (see Chap. 9 for a summary of this model and suggestions for testing it). The following activities were defined:

DOMESTIC

All those tasks which contribute to the daily physical maintenance of an individual household, including water and food acquisition and storage, food preparation and cooking, cleaning, and the provision of facilities for sleeping.

MANUFACTURE

The production of goods for consumption. *Household Level*—Manufacture for the use of the resident group where production was performed. *Local Level*—Manufacture for a market beyond the household but still restricted to the residents of a site and its immediate hinterland. *Export Level*—Production in considerable quantities for a broad market accessible through regional or interregional trading networks.

CEREMONIAL

Those activities which involve the propitiation, manipulation, or placation of a supernatural force. *Private-*

180

—Ceremonies carried out by individuals for their own good or that of their immediate households. *Public*—Ceremonies carried out for the general good of a supra-household unit by its members or specialized representatives.

ADMINISTRATION

Activities involving the organization and control of the political and social lives of a population by a segment of that population. The activities of this governing segment ensure the integration of a number of residential units into a single coherent society. *Local*—Restriction of the governing segment's administrative power to a site and its immediate hinterland.

Regional—Control by the governing segment over several large sites (i.e., those with monumental construction) and their respective hinterlands.

MARKETING

Those activities associated with the exchange of goods. *Local*—Activities that facilitate the movement of goods within the restricted area of the site and its immediate hinterland. *Regional*—Activities that facilitate the movement of goods through a wider trade area, usually defined by a single cultural or physiographic region. *Interregional*—Activities that facilitate the movement of goods over long distances between two or more different physiographic zones.

DOMESTIC ACTIVITIES

The data categories of ceramics, chipped and ground stone, and site planning all strongly indicate the performance of domestic activities at all of the investigated structures at Choco, Las Quebradas, and Playitas (including Group II).

The ceramics from terminal debris contexts at these three centers are primarily from the Mojanal and Encantado Groups and Techin Striated within the Switch Molina Group (see Tables 6.2, 6.3). All of these taxa are simply decorated or plain utilitarian vessels, primarily large jars. The specific functions performed by these containers are not securely known. It seems likely, given their large size, forms, and ubiquity, that they were used in a number of common domestic maintenance tasks such as storage and carrying (see below). Another component of these primarily utilitarian assemblages is the Bobos Group, represented, albeit in low frequencies, by orange-slipped, wide-mouthed bowl forms. Once more, the simplicity of decoration—with only an occasional red rim band to break the monotony of the overall orange slip—and the vessel form imply the use of these bowls in daily household activities. No evidence of hearths or vessels showing signs of having been used in cooking were recovered.

In general, the same utilitarian ceramic types/varieties were found in the terminal debris contexts of all contemporary excavated structures, large or small. This finding supports the view that all investigated constructions were the foci of domestic activities, based on the assumed linkage between the presence of utilitarian ceramics and domestic labor. This assertion, however, can be made somewhat stronger. If

domestic tasks composed an important segment of the total range of behaviors carried out in or near a structure, then we would expect that the utilitarian ceramic taxa outlined in Table 6.2 should make up a large percentage of the ceramic assemblage recovered from the terminal debris of that structure. On the basis of the figures presented in Tables 6.3-5, it appears that domestic activities were important in the functioning of all but perhaps one of the investigated groups. Of the 13 relevant excavation contexts measured, all but two contain 75-97.1% utilitarian ceramics in their terminal debris collections. The exceptions are Str. 205-123 in the Las Quebradas Northwest Group, a small construction with 42.9% utilitarian sherds, and the Playitas Group II monumental court with 9.97% utilitarian ceramics. The low utilitarian percentage at Playitas Group II is due to the recovery of sizable quantities of censer sherds near the base of Str. 200-193 (193 sherds; 60.13%).

This pattern is supported by an analysis of utilitarian vessel forms from terminal debris contexts (see Table 6.5). Generally, of those rims which can be identified as to form, jars make up the vast majority of the excavated collections (72.9% overall) and bowls constitute a much smaller proportion (27.1%). Looking more closely at the terminal debris collections containing form-classified rims, we can see that certain shapes (A, A-2, B, and E jars; A and B-2 bowls) have an almost universal distribution, being found at both large and small structures. These forms, together, also represent 75.18% of all form-classified sherds from these collections. The A and A-2 jars, because of their wide necks, would probably have

TABLE 6.1

MATERIAL CORRELATES OF THE FIVE POSSIBLE ACTIVITY TYPES AND THEIR SUBTYPES

Activity: Domestic
　Evidence: Artifacts
　Utilitarian ceramic types with simple, little, or no decoration
　Ceramic vessel forms: large jars and widemouthed bowls
　Large, relatively thick obsidian blades
　Manos and metates
　Jars and bowls with evidence of burning
　Architecture
　Size: variable, larger examples include multiroom (palaces)
　Architectural features: benches, windows, curtain-holders, hearths, subfloor burials
　Site Morphology
　Domestic structures generally arranged into plaza groups
　Located and organized so as to ensure privacy
Activity: Manufacturing (General)
　Evidence: Artifacts
　Manufacturing debris in quantity
　Tools used in production
　Recovery of a variety of forms of the finished product, and/or rejected, unfinished examples of that product
Activity: Household Manufacturing
　Evidence: Artifacts
　Limited amounts of manufacturing debris widely distributed through a site
Activity: Local Manufacturing
　Evidence: Artifacts
　Moderate amounts of manufacturing debris found at a restricted number of locations at a site
　Skill involved in manufacture requires at least part-time specialization
Activity: Export Manufacturing
　Evidence: Artifacts
　Large amounts of manufacturing debris found at only a few locations
　Skill involved in manufacture requires at least part-time specialization
　The specific correlates of a commonly recognized Maya-area manufacturing activity, obsidian-tool production, are detailed in App. II.
Activity: Ceremonial (General)
　Evidence: Artifacts
　Pottery censers
　Caches
　Elaborate tombs
　Architecture
　Special religious structures: temples, shrines, ballcourts, altar/ceremonial platforms, mortuary structures
　Site Morphology
　Temple groups
Activity: Private Ceremonialism
　Evidence: Artifacts
　Small amounts of *incensario* debris widely distributed at a site
　Some admixture with artifacts used in other, primarily domestic, behaviors
　Censer forms: three-pronged, censer lids, and spiked censers
　Architecture
　Censers associated with domestic structure groups; variable sizes

TABLE 6.1 (continued)

MATERIAL CORRELATES OF THE FIVE POSSIBLE ACTIVITY TYPES AND THEIR SUBTYPES

Activity: Public Ceremonialism
  Evidence: Artifacts
  Sizable concentrations of censer material at a few restricted locales
  Little admixture with artifacts used in other activities
  Censer form: effigy modeled censers
  Architecture
  Censers associated with special religious structures, i.e., temples, ballcourts
  Site Morphology
  Temple groups
Activity: Administration (General)
  Evidence: Artifacts
  Concentrations of finely crafted stone artifacts in the same restricted sectors as the above ceramics
  Presence of quantities of imported goods at a site
  Architecture
  Large-scale building projects resulting in a hierarchy of structures and structure groups at a site
  Use of nonlocal and/or difficult-to-work materials in monumental constructions; and their absence in other
    constructions
  Elaborate decoration of monumental structures; little decoration on others
  Presence of large-scale public works projects
  Monuments
  Presence of carved monuments with inscriptions relating dynastic histories and figures bearing symbols of
    authority
  Site Morphology
  Coherent organization of a site according to a reconstructible overall plan
Activity: Local and Regional Administration
  Evidence: Artifacts
  Greater amounts and variety of imported goods at regional centers than at local ones
  Architecture
  Greater numbers of monumental structures at regional centers than at local ones; those at regional centers
    tend to be larger
  Monumental structures at regional centers that are more elaborately decorated than those at their local
    counterparts
  Site Morphology
  Regional centers that are much larger than their local counterparts
  Regional centers that are more complexly organized than local ones
Activity: Marketing (General)
  Evidence: Artifacts
  Some evidence of goods derived from the marketing area of the site identified on stylistic or compositional
    grounds
  Architecture
  If identifiable, small ephemeral stalls associated with traded goods
  Site Morphology
  An easily accessible, open space where trading takes place

TABLE 6.1 (continued)

MATERIAL CORRELATES OF THE FIVE POSSIBLE ACTIVITY TYPES AND THEIR SUBTYPES

Activity: Local Marketing
  Evidence: Artifacts
  Only locally available items appear at investigated sites
  Architecture
  Same as for general case
  Site Morphology
  Same as for general case
Activity: Regional Marketing
  Evidence: Artifacts
  Presence of a moderate amount of goods not found in the immediate vicinity of the site
  Architecture
  Same as general case
  Site Morphology
  Same as general case
  Site Location
  Located along an inferred route of communication within the region
Activity: Interregional Marketing
  Evidence: Artifacts
  Large amounts of goods from several distant sources recovered from a site
  Architecture
  Location of structures designed to facilitate trade; in particular, large storage facilities situated in an inaccessible portion of the site
  Site Morphology
  Long-distance trading may take place in inaccessible portions of a site to ensure security; such goods would, then, not be expected in the open areas where local and regional trading were carried out
  Site Location
  Situated along an inferred route of communication out of the region

been unsuitable for carrying food or water and may have functioned primarily as stationary storage containers. B jars, with their very low, wide necks, might also have been used for storing or processing foodstuffs. E jars, on the other hand, have relatively high vertical necks which would have made better carrying vessels. E jars, in fact, bear a general resemblance to *tinajas*, modern Mesoamerican water-carrying vessels. The two bowl forms, primarily because of their wide diameters (0.19-0.21 m average for A bowls and 0.23-0.25 m for the B-2 form) and the absence of any charring pointing to their use in cooking, may have been used as serving vessels. The wide distribution of these bowl and jar forms suggests that the domestic activities of food/water storage and serving were carried out at both large and small structures.

The evidence provided by the analysis of chipped stone tools provides another avenue of testing for the presence of domestic activities and their distribution within valley centers (Table 6.6). It must be borne in mind that obsidian artifacts were used in other contexts beside the domestic in Mesoamerica—i.e., in rituals requiring bloodletting (e.g., Thompson 1966; Schele and Miller 1986: 125). In general, however, it is expected that obsidian tools used in such ceremonies would be thinner and show less use-wear than those employed in more prosaic pursuits. While the analysis of the wider-valley obsidian is still in progress, basically all of the obsidian was sufficiently large and worn to indicate its functioning in domestic tasks. Given that relatively large and sturdy obsidian prismatic blades and flakes were used in such mundane

TABLE 6.2

LIST OF LMV UTILITARIAN DOMESTIC CERAMIC TYPES

Mojanal Group
  Mojanal Micaceous: Faceted variety
  Mojanal Micaceous: Red-washed variety
  Mojanal Micaceous: Well-smoothed variety
  Mojanal Micaceous: Coarse-tempered variety
  Riachuelo Buff: Riachuelo variety
Encantado Group
  Encantado Cream: Encantado variety
  Encantado Cream: Red-washed variety
Switch Molina Group
  Techin Striated: unsp. variety
Bobos Group
  Bobos Orange: Bobos variety
  Bobos Orange: Red-on-orange variety
Vitales Group
  Vitales Thick-walled: Vitales variety

endeavors as meat and hide cutting and woodworking (e.g., Lewenstein 1981), their distribution within a site should provide a rough idea of where these activities were carried out. At Playitas, Choco, and the Las Quebradas West Group, both obsidian blades and flakes were found in terminal debris contexts of small and large structures. In the Las Quebradas East and Northwest Groups blades and flakes were recovered from the terminal debris lots of the excavated small structures, Str. 205-196 and -123 respectively, but were only rarely associated with monumental structures. In general, therefore, those tasks requiring the use of obsidian cutting implements were apparently carried out at both large and small structures except in the Las Quebradas East and Northwest Groups, where they *may* have been restricted to the smaller structures. The very small size of the terminal debris obsidian sample from both of the latter groups (15 and 13 pieces respectively) makes such a statement very tentative.

While ground stone artifacts were not common, their distribution is still of some interest in reconstructing the presence and nature of domestic activities at the excavated centers (see Table 6.7). At those sites where manos and metates were found in excavated contexts (Playitas and Las Quebradas), they were recovered from the terminal debris of both monumental (Str. 205-41 and 200-21/23) and small (Str. 200-17, 205-123 and -196) constructions. These tools were employed in the grinding of food, primarily maize, prior to cooking, and their distribution suggests that this activity was pursued at structures of varying size within the valley.

The organization of almost all of the structures within the LMV sites also indicates that at least one of their functions was to serve as the locus of domestic activities. The smaller structures were generally arranged in either orthogonal plaza groups or irregular aggregations, a form known from archaeological, ethnohistoric, and ethnographic accounts to be a common one for residences in the Maya area (e.g., Ashmore and Wilk 1988; Wisdom 1940; Wauchope 1938; Miles 1957). Similarly, the larger monumental structures were generally organized so as to ensure the privacy of their occupants. The massive, high substructures arranged into quadrangles commonly enclosed almost completely a small interior court and would, therefore, have effectively restricted access to both these courts and their surrounding structures. This pattern of monumental construction has been associated with large-scale residences within the Maya area archaeologically (Harrison 1970: 251-253, 302-303; Hammond 1975; G. Andrews 1975: 63-66). Unfortunately, architectural details from superstructures, such as benches, curtain-holders, and the like, which might have further substantiated the domestic/residential functions of both large and small buildings, were not recovered.

TABLE 6.3

PERCENTAGES OF CERAMIC TYPES FROM TERMINAL DEBRIS (PRIMARY AND SECONDARY) CONTEXTS FOR ASSOCIATED STRUCTURE TYPE (MONUMENTAL OR SMALL), GROUP, AND SITE

Context	Mojanal Faceted %	Mojanal Red-washed%	Mojanal Well-smoothed %	Mojanal Coarse-tempered %	Riachuelo Buff %
(A) Playitas Group IV main court	23.3	3.2	6.9	0	0
(B) Playitas Group I main court	16.5	0.3	9.8	0	0
(C) Playitas Group IV small structures	42.1	5.2	2.6	0	0
(D) Las Quebradas W Group main court	35.13	1.0	0.1	0	0
(E) Las Quebradas NW Group main court	85.7	5.7	0	0	0
(F) Las Quebradas E Group main court	69.5	0	0	0	0
(G) Las Quebradas W Group small structures	37.8	0	0	0	0
(H) Las Quebradas NW Group small structure	27.7	3.6	0	0	0
(I) Las Quebradas E Group small structure	42.9	11.2	3.7	0	0
(J) Las Quebradas W Group Mon.	42.8	1.0	0	0	0
(K) Las Quebradas NW Group Mon.	4.7	0	0	0	0
(L) Las Quebradas E Group Mon.	56.2	1.5	2.6	0	0
(M) Choco main court	56.0	0.6	7.1	0	0
(N) Choco small structure	35.8	0.3	4.0	0	0
(O) Playitas Group II main court	8.4	0	0	0.3	0
(P) Playitas Group II small structure	24.4	0	0	4.4	62.3
(Q) Playitas Group V surface	—	—	—	—	—
(R) Comanche Farm surface	—	—	—	—	—

In general, therefore, it appears on the basis of artifactual and site-planning criteria that domestic/maintenance activities were carried out in both large and small structures at all three excavated centers. In fact, it seems likely that *all* of the excavated structures and quite probably the vast majority of all extant constructions housed these behaviors.

In addition to this general pattern of activity distribution, there is some slight evidence that the same domestic activities may not have been practiced in

TABLE 6.3 (continued)

PERCENTAGES OF CERAMIC TYPES FROM TERMINAL DEBRIS (PRIMARY AND SECONDARY) CONTEXTS FOR ASSOCIATED STRUCTURE TYPE (MONUMENTAL OR SMALL), GROUP, AND SITE

Context	Encantado Cream %	Encantado Red-washed %	Techin Striated %	Tipon Tipon %	Capulin White %	Chalja Red %
A	22.8	2.8	15.8	2.9	0.4	2.9
B	35.6	6.5	15.5	3.7	0.7	1.5
C	5.4	1.7	14.6	5.7	0.7	1.6
D	19.9	0.5	17.3	14.6	0.2	0.2
E	2.9	0	1.4	2.9	0	0
F	1.1	0	0	1.1	0	0
G	23.4	0	17.1	14.4	0.9	1.8
H	7.1	0	4.5	55.4	0	0
I	11.5	0	23.5	2.2	0	3.7
J	3.7	0.2	9.4	0.5	0.9	1.8
K	1.1	0	3.6	11.8	0	0
L	1.9	0	9.0	1.1	1.5	0
M	25.7	0.3	3.5	1.6	0	0
N	17.6	0.3	18.2	4.3	0	0
O	0	0	0	26.5	0	0
P	0	0	0.5	0	0	0

Context	Tipon Incised/Carved %	Alsacia Pink %	Tasu Fluted %	Tipon Grooved %	Tipon Modeled %	Coroza Cream %
A	0.2	0.3	0	0	0	2.2
B	0	0	0	0	0	0
C	1.2	0	2.6	0	0	0.1
D	0.2	0	0	0.4	0	0.3
E	0	0	0	0	0	0
F	0	0	0	0	0	0
G	0	0	0	0	0	0
H	0	0	0	0	0	0
I	0	0	0	0	0	0
J	0	0	0	0	0	0
K	0	0	0	0	0	0
L	0	0	0	0	0	0
M	0	0	0	0	0	0
N	0	0	0	0	0	0
O	0	0	0	0	0	0
P	0	0	0	0	0	0

every structure group at a site or even at every structure in a group. Once again, the evidence is primarily artifactual (ceramic and chipped stone distributions) and architectural.

If it is assumed that vessels in the different ceramic groups performed somewhat different, if possibly overlapping, functions, then the frequencies of these ceramic groups in the terminal debris utilitarian

TABLE 6.3 (continued)

PERCENTAGES OF CERAMIC TYPES FROM TERMINAL DEBRIS (PRIMARY AND SECONDARY) CONTEXTS FOR ASSOCIATED STRUCTURE TYPE (MONUMENTAL OR SMALL), GROUP, AND SITE

Context	Bobos Orange %	Bobos Red-on-orange %	San Rafael Red %	Censers %	Figurines %	Specials %
A	1.2	0	0.1	10.8	0.5	3.5
B	3.7	0	4.7	0.2	0	1.5
C	3.7	0.3	0	4.3	0.7	7.8
D	4.4	0.3	0	3.1	0.4	2.2
E	1.4	0	0	0	0	0
F	5.3	0	0	23.2	0	0
G	3.6	0	0	0	0.9	0
H	0	0	0	0.9	0.9	0
I	1.9	0	0	0	0	0
J	0.3	0	0	40.0	0	0
K	0	0	0	78.9	0	0
L	0.4	0	0	25.8	0	0
M	3.2	0	0	2.3	0.6	0
N	3.0	0	0	3.6	1.0	11.9
O	1.3	0	0	60.1	0	3.4
P	0	0	0	8.4	0	0

Note: Percentages of total figures are for all terminal debris sherds recovered by structure type in a given group at a site.

collections from different structure aggregations should indicate whether these activities were homogeneously distributed over a locus or tended to cluster in specific areas. While it is not currently possible to specify precisely what these functions might have been, their percentage distributions should at least provide some hint of differential domestic activity clustering, which can be pursued in more detail in the future. An examination of Table 6.8 suggests the existence of two and possibly four patterns of utilitarian ceramic group frequencies. The first is represented by the excavated monumental structures of Playitas Groups I and IV and the Las Quebradas West Group along with Str. 205-88 and 212-22, both small platforms. This pattern is characterized by moderately high frequencies of Mojanal Group sherds (30-51%), slightly lower percentages of the Encantado Group (22-48%) and Techin Striated (17-23%) representatives, and low percentages of Bobos Group sherds (1-5%).

The second pattern was recognized at Str. 200-16 and -17 and 205-196, all small structures. Here the frequency of Mojanal is somewhat higher (60-66%) and Encantado considerably lower (9-13%). Techin Striated and Bobos Group percentages are much the same as in the first pattern (19-25% and 2-6% respectively). A potential third pattern, noted to date only from the Choco main group, is similar to the second but with a much lower percentage of Techin Striated (3.7%).

These patterns of utilitarian ceramic percentages indicate that domestic maintenance activities may not have been equally distributed throughout the valley centers. The fact that structures of both monumental and small sizes are found within Pattern I also implies that there is no consistent association between the percentages of utilitarian ceramic groups and structure sizes.

A more detailed examination of Table 6.5 indicates that some subtle difference may exist in the percentages of the different vessel forms found in these collections. Here we will focus on the three largest collections: Playitas Group IV monumental constructions (59 sherds); Playitas Group IV small structures

TABLE 6.4

PERCENTAGE OF *TOTAL* TERMINAL DEBRIS CERAMIC ASSEMBLAGES MADE UP BY THE FOUR PRINCIPAL UTILITARIAN CERAMIC GROUPS: MOJANAL, ENCANTADO, BOBOS (EXCLUDING POLYCHROME VARIETY), AND SWITCH MOLINA

Context	Utilitarian Ceramic Percentage
Playitas, Group IV main court	76.0
Playitas, Group I main court	87.9
Playitas, Group IV small structures	75.6
Las Quebradas, W Group main court	78.3
Las Quebradas, NW Group main court	97.1
Las Quebradas, E Group main court	75.9
Las Quebradas, W Group small structures	81.9
Las Quebradas, NW Group small structures	42.9
Las Quebradas, E Group small structures	94.7
Choco, main court	96.4
Choco, small structures	79.2
Playitas, Group II main court	9.97
Playitas, Group II small structures	91.6
Playitas, Group V surface	89.7
Comanche Farm, surface	86.8

(60 sherds); and the Las Quebradas monumental platforms (179 sherds). Two tentative patterns emerge here based on differences in the four major jar-form percentages. The first includes monumental structures from both Playitas Group IV and the Las Quebradas West Group and is characterized by moderately high percentages of A jars (30-37% of all form-classified rims), somewhat lower frequencies of the A-2 jar (14-15%), and low proportions of the B jar (3-4%). The E jar is found at Las Quebradas (4.47%) while the closely related E-2 form is known from Playitas (1.70%). The percentages of A and B-2 bowls differ markedly at these two sites (see Table 6.5).

The second pattern is represented by the small excavated structures in Playitas Group IV. Here A jars make up a slightly higher proportion (45%) of the total terminal debris collection, A-2 jars are much less frequent (3.33%), and E jars are more common (15%). The B jar frequency (6.67%) is only slightly larger than in the first pattern. The overall percentage of bowls is slightly smaller here than in the previous two cases (25% vs. 31-32%). It is interesting to note that the patterning noted in Table 6.5 parallels that seen in Table 6.8. Both Playitas Group IV and Las Quebradas

West Group monumental structures fall within utilitarian type Pattern I in the latter table, while the small structures of Playitas Group IV follow Pattern II. This parallelism reinforces the general contention that domestic activities may have been differentially distributed among structures within sites.

An examination of Table 6.6 also indicates that there might have been some differences in the use of obsidian cutting tools between monumental and small structures. Specifically, 54% of all blades and flakes from Playitas terminal debris contexts (Groups I and IV) were recovered from the small-structure excavations in Group IV. At Choco, 72.09% of this material comes from the excavation of Str. 212-22, a small construction. As was noted above, in the Las Quebradas Northwest and East Groups all but one of the recovered obsidian blades and flakes in terminal debris contexts are from smaller structures. Only in the West Group of this site is there an exception to this pattern. Here, 88% of all recovered blades and flakes associated with architecture come from monumental constructions. The general trend, however, is for a slightly greater concentration of the tasks that em-

TABLE 6.5

DISTRIBUTION OF CERAMIC FORMS FROM TERMINAL DEBRIS (PRIMARY AND SECONDARY) CONTEXTS PRESENTED BY ASSOCIATED STRUCTURE TYPE (MONUMENTAL OR SMALL), GROUP, AND SITE

Context	A	A-1	C	A-2	A-3	B	D	D-1	E	E-2	F	N/% Jars
A	33.9	1.7	0	15.3	1.7	3.4	6.8	5.1	0	1.7	0	41/67.9
B	37.9	0	0	41.4	0	10.4	0	0	0	0	3.5	27/93.1
C	45.0	1.7	0	3.3	0	6.7	3.3	0	15.0	0	0	45/75.0
D	37.4	0	0.6	14.5	0	3.9	7.3	0	4.5	0	0	122/68.2
H	33.3	0	0	66.7	0	0	0	0	0	0	0	3/100.0
I	57.1	0	0	4.8	0	0	0	0	9.5	0	19.1	19/90.5
M	27.3	9.1	0	27.3	0	9.1	0	0	9.1	0	0	9/81.8
N	70.0	0	0	10.0	0	10.0	0	0	10.0	0	0	10/100.0
O and P	100.0	0	0	0	0	0	0	0	0	0	0	13/92.9
Q	14.3	0	0	14.3	0	7.1	0	0	14.3	0	0	7/50.0
R	35.7	0	0	21.4	0	0	0	0	0	0	0	8/57.1

Context	A	B	B-1	B-2	C	D	D-1	E	G	G-1	K	N/% Bowls
A	15.3	1.7	0	1.7	0	1.7	0	0	0	1.7	8.5	18/32.0
B	0	0	0	6.9	0	0	0	0	0	0	0	2/6.9
C	3.3	1.7	0	15.0	1.7	0	1.7	0	0	0	1.7	15/25.0
D	1.7	1.7	0.6	20.1	0.6	0.6	1.1	3.9	0.6	0.6	1.1	57/31.8
G	66.7	0	0	33.3	0	0	0	0	0	0	0	3/100.0
I	9.5	0	0	0	0	0	0	0	0	0	0	2/9.5
M	18.18	0	0	0	0	0	0	0	0	0	0	2/18.18
O and P	0	0	0	0	7.1	0	0	0	0	0	0	1/7.1
Q	0	0	0	35.7	0	0	0	0	0	0	14.3	7/50.0
R	14.3	14.3	0	14.3	0	0	0	0	0	0	0	6/42.9

Only groups with form-classified sherds are included; monument excavations are excluded. Percentages are for all form-classified sherds within the given context, including bowls and jars (context designations are given in Table 6.3).

ployed obsidian tools to be associated with the peripheries of the major quadrangles.

While architectural details are usually not sufficiently well preserved to aid in this reconstruction, they do provide some indications that different structures within a single group might have served different purposes. At Choco, for example, Str. 212-22 appears to have had a deep, V-shaped depression dug into its summit (see Chap. 3). Given the size and depth of this pit, it is doubtful that Str. 212-22 could have functioned as a residence, although it might have served as a storage structure for the Str. 212-22/24 group. This view is based on the platform's relatively small size and restricted access to the interior pit.

Other constructions within the group might then have functioned as sleeping quarters, kitchens, and so forth (e.g., Wisdom 1940). Arapahoe Viejo Str. 216-13, with its three parallel sunken rooms, may have also been used for storage, although on a larger scale (see Chap. 7). Playitas Str. 200-16, given its association with obsidian-blade manufacturing debris (see below), may have been used primarily as a locus for cutting-tool production. This meager evidence suggests that internal variation in domestic activities was commonplace.

In sum, the available evidence points to domestic activities associated with all of the investigated structures. Food and water storage and serving, cutting, and grinding were apparently carried out at most of

TABLE 6.6

DISTRIBUTION OF CHIPPED STONE ARTIFACTS (OBSIDIAN) FROM TERMINAL DEBRIS (PRIMARY AND SECONDARY) CONTEXTS PRESENTED BY GROUP AND SITE

Context	Blades %	Macro-blades %	Blade-Cores %	Flakes %	Flake-Cores %
A	70	0	0	30	0
B	81	0	0	19	0
C	88	0	4	8	0
D	72.2	3.2	0.6	21.5	1.9*
E	0	0	0	0	0
F	7.1	0	0	89.3	3.6
G	61.9	0	4.8	33.3	0
H	76.9	15.4	0	7.7	0
I	28.6	0	7.1	28.6	35.7
J	15.7	0	0	75	8.3
K	100	0	0	0	0
L	4.8	0	0	90.5**	2.4
M	41.6	0	0	58.3	0
N	93.5	0	0	6.5	0

* One chipped stone (chert?) point was found, 0.6% of the assemblage.
** Includes one flake of unidentified stone.
Percentages refer to the proportion of the terminal debris chipped stone assemblage that a given category composes in a particular context (context designations given in Table 6.3).

these constructions, regardless of size. At the same time, the data suggest that there were some differences in either the kinds of domestic activities performed, or their intensities, both between and within individual groups.

The unexcavated monumental centers, on the evidence of their site plans and the available surface collections (see Table 5.3), fit generally into the above reconstruction. The smaller, nonmonumental sites, also according to their structure organization and

TABLE 6.7

DISTRIBUTION OF GROUND STONE ARTIFACTS FROM TERMINAL CONTEXTS (PRIMARY AND SECONDARY) BY STRUCTURE TYPE (MONUMENTAL OR SMALL), GROUP, AND SITE

Context	Manos	Metates
Playitas, Group IV main court	0	2
Playitas, Group IV small structures	1	0
Las Quebradas, W Group main court	1	3
Las Quebradas, NW Group small structures	2	1
Las Quebradas, E Group small structures	0	1
N	4	7

TABLE 6.8

PERCENTAGES OF *UTILITARIAN* CERAMIC TAXA FROM TERMINAL DEBRIS (PRIMARY AND SECONDARY) CONTEXTS PRESENTED BY ASSOCIATED STRUCTURE TYPE (MONUMENTAL OR SMALL), GROUP, AND SITE

Context	Mojanal Group %	Encantado Group %	Techin Striated %	Bobos Group %	Vitales Thick-walled %	N
A	44.2	33.5	20.7	1.5	0	787
B	30.3	47.9	17.6	4.2	0	528
C	65.8	9.7	19.2	5.3	0.3	926
D	45.9	25.9	22.0	5.9	0.3	2506
E	94.1	2.9	1.5	1.5	0	68
F	91.7	1.4	0	6.9	0	72
G	46.2	28.6	20.9	4.4	0	91
H	72.9	16.7	10.4	0	0	48
I	60.9	12.2	25.0	2.0	0	304
M	65.7	27.3	3.7	3.4	0	297
N	50.6	22.6	23.0	3.8	0	239
O	87.5	0	0	12.5	0	32
P	99.5	0	0.5	0	0	566

Monument excavations are excluded. Only utilitarian ceramic totals are used to compute percentages (context designations are given in Table 6.3).

associated ceramics, were probably used primarily for domestic activities as well. The two largest surface ceramic collections from unexcavated loci, Playitas Group V and Comanche Farm (Table 5.3), are dominated by utilitarian types (86-90% of the entire collection; see Table 6.4). This suggests that both centers were loci of domestic activities. The vessel forms found in these two collections (see Table 6.5) are mostly A, A-2, B, and E jars and A, B, and B-2 bowls—forms correlated with daily maintenance tasks.

MANUFACTURING

The only traces of manufacturing activities recovered from wider-valley centers relate to obsidian-blade and -flake production. At both Playitas and Las Quebradas there is some evidence for the production of obsidian tools in both the blade-core and flake traditions (see Table 6.6). Playitas Group IV Str. 200-16 produced two polyhedral core fragments from terminal debris contexts. In the Las Quebradas West Group, six blade-cores and macroblades are associated with monumental construction, composing 3.8% of the chipped stone recovered from the terminal debris of these structures. One blade-core fragment was recovered from the terminal debris of Str. 205-88, the small excavated West Group platform, 4.8% of the chipped stone artifacts from that context and structure. Two macroblades were also found in the Northwest Group (Str. 205-123, 15.4%) and one blade-core was recovered from a terminal debris context at Str. 205-196 in the East Group (7.1%). Flake-cores and/or obsidian cobbles were also recovered from the terminal debris of West Group monumental structures (three pieces, 1.9% of the terminal debris collection) and their East Group counterparts (one piece, 100%) at Las Quebradas. Structure 205-196 also produced five flake-cores and/or cobbles, 35.7% of its terminal debris collection.

Several conclusions can be drawn from this distribution. First, while the manufacture of both flakes and prismatic blades was carried out in and around small and monumental structures, there was a slight tendency for these activities to be concentrated near the humbler constructions. Second, the manufacture of blades and that of flakes were not mutually exclusive: the same structure might show evidence of both activities (e.g., Str. 205-196; cf. Sheets 1983). Finally, although the sample is limited, there is no evidence of obsidian-tool production on an export scale. The recovery of several polyhedral core fragments from Str. 200-16 tentatively suggests that some structures may have served as the foci for local-level production; i.e., beyond the needs of a single household, but still limited to the site and its hinterland. Furthermore, the skill and, hence, training an artisan required to produce obsidian prismatic blades, one intuitively presumes, would not have been available to every household. Some low-level specialization in blade

production for local distribution is thus implied by the data.

No evidence of obsidian-blade production was noted at Choco. This could be the result of limited excavations here (11 suboperations), an unperceived bias in the excavated structures (i.e., chance selection of those associated with nonmanufacturing activities), or the actual absence of blade/flake production at this site. Only further, more representative excavations at Choco can provide a basis for choosing among these alternatives. The recovery of one polyhedral blade-core from the surface at Quebrada Grande may indicate that some blade production was carried out there. Surface collections from the other valley sites lack any evidence of manufacturing activities.

CEREMONIAL ACTIVITIES

The distribution of *incensario* fragments in terminal debris contexts is shown in Table 6.3. As can be seen, *incensario* pieces constitute 0-23.2% of total monumental-structure and 0-4.3% of total small-structure terminal debris ceramic collections. The one exception is the Playitas Group II monumental court, which will be discussed separately below. Eight of these 12 collections contain 0.2-10.8% identifiable *incensario* sherds and only three contain no censer material. This distribution suggests that ceremonial activities were associated with both large and small platforms. The low frequency of these material correlates, however, suggests that ritual activities were not intensively practiced at most buildings. The low *incensario* percentages from excavated platforms, in fact, point to the performance of small-scale private ceremonies.

The distribution of *incensarios* from the terminal debris around monuments shows a completely different pattern. The range of *incensario* percentages from the four monuments excavated at Las Quebradas (Mon. 1, 2, 4, and 5) is 8.3-78.9%, including one broken but cached censer (Cache 1) associated with Mon. 2. Monuments 1, 2, and 4 have high percentages of associated censers, 29.4-78.9%, while Mon. 5, which was incompletely excavated, has the lowest, 8.3%. These relatively high frequencies of censer debris indicate that the monuments were important foci of religious ceremonies. The relatively low percentages of utilitarian ceramic types in these contexts further imply that these stones were used almost exclusively for ritual. It should be recalled that the high percentage of Mojanal Micaceous: Faceted variety sherds

found at Mon. 1, 4, and 5 may be the result of the inclusion of small *incensario* fragments in this taxon. The similarity in paste and wall thickness between censers and the Mojanal Group makes such accidental inclusions almost inevitable, especially when the fragments are small and otherwise undistinguished. The relatively low frequencies of utilitarian chipped stone artifacts found in the terminal debris of monuments also point to the absence of domestic or manufacturing activities in their vicinity. The one exception is, again, Mon. 5, where, despite the shallowness of the probe (Op. 24Q), 39 flakes, two blades, and one flake-core were recovered (90.7%, 66.6%, and 14.3% of the members of these chipped stone categories for the East Group as a whole). The significance of this concentration is unclear, although, given its density, it may also have been a ceremonial offering (cf. the use of chipped stone in Classic Maya ceremonial deposits; e.g., Coe 1965).

The density of censers around monuments, the relative unimportance of artifacts associated with other, primarily domestic, activities, and the nature of the monuments themselves—large, centrally located stones associated with prepared pavements—all suggest that they were the foci of ceremonial activities. Whether the ceremonies carried out here were public or private is the next question to address. The high percentage of *incensario* fragments relative to other ceramic types points to public rituals. Yet all monuments at the Motagua valley sites are within the very private monumental courts. Access to these purportedly public rituals would have been either difficult or

TABLE 6.9

PERCENTAGE DISTRIBUTION OF CENSER FORMS FROM TERMINAL CONTEXTS BY ASSOCIATED STRUCTURE TYPES AND MONUMENTS

Context	Effigy Modeled	Pronged	Lids	Spiked	Ladles	Cruciform-vent	*N*
Monumental structures (excluding Playitas Group II)	35.58	1.23	3.68	22.7	36.8	0	163
Small structures	16.67	16.67	37.5	16.67	12.5	0	24
Monuments	78.4	0.8	0	18.4	2.4	0	125
Monumental structures (including Playitas Group II)	24.0	0.8	2.4	18.5	23.6	30.7	256

controlled by the residents of the court. To resolve this issue we must consider the percentage distribution of form-classified censers in terminal debris contexts (Table 6.9).

By analogy with Quirigua (see App. II), effigy modeled censers are associated primarily with public rituals, while the other forms (lids, pronged, spiked, and ladle censers) probably functioned in more private observances. When considered together, monumental structures from Las Quebradas, Choco, and Playitas, excluding Str. 200-193 in Group II, yielded a moderately low percentage of modeled censers (35.58%). The small structures at these three sites produced an even lower proportion of this form (16.67%). However, a full 78.4% of the 125 form-classified censers recovered from terminal debris contexts around the monuments are modeled. If the analogy with Quirigua is valid, this distribution suggests that the rituals performed around monuments were different from those associated with structures, and may have been public in nature. The other censer forms correlated with private rituals at Quirigua make up very low percentages of monument-related debris, 0-19% (see Table 6.9). The secluded location of the monuments would, then, imply either that public attendance at the rituals was strictly controlled or that, while the rituals may have been performed for the common benefit, many members of the local community were not in attendance. In either case, the residents of the monumental quadrangle surrounding a monument(s) may have been the sponsors or masters of ceremonies.

A closer examination of Table 6.9 indicates other gross patterns. While the overall percentage distribution of censer sherds suggests that private rituals were performed at both monumental and small structures, the distribution of forms points to a more complex picture. Monumental structures, in general, have higher percentages of modeled, spiked, and ladle censer forms than do small platforms, where lids are the dominant form. The sample size for both construction types is too small to postulate specific functional distinctions. Indeed, this may be simply a case of different forms being employed for the same purposes. The pattern is, nonetheless, intriguing and warrants further investigation.

We have some indications that the monuments were not the only foci of intensive ritual activities. There is a faint possibility at Las Quebradas that some of the structures defining the courts in which monuments were set may have been used for ritual to a greater degree than their counterparts elsewhere. The terminal debris on the west side of Str. 215-1-1st, which faces Mon. 1, contained 18.52% censer sherds, much higher than the proportions of censers obtained from most other monumental structures. Only one of these fragments is of the modeled category and the rest of the form-classified sample are from spiked censers. Ritual activity here, therefore, appears to have been primarily private, although possibly related in some way to the activities performed around Mon. 1. The debris on the east, nonmonument-facing side of the structure did not contain censer material. Structure 205-56 produced 28.5% censer material (three modeled and one unidentified as to form), all from the north side of the platform facing Mon. 4. The small size of this last sample (14 total sherds) urges caution in any interpretation. Nonetheless, the distribution does imply that the rituals associated with monuments were also performed on or near some of the surrounding structures. Whether they were public or private rites remains unknown. Not all structures facing monuments share this pattern. The excavation of Str. 205-118 in the Northwest Group, bounding the south side of the court containing Mon. 2-3, produced no censer fragments.

In the Playitas Group IV main court, Str. 200-23 had a high proportion of censers in its terminal debris (33.82%, 46 sherds). Of the form-classified sherds, 100% are effigy modeled, possibly from a single broken censer left atop the structure. This percentage raises the possibility that in sites without preserved monuments some structures may have served as foci for public ritual. That this was not the function of the entire Group IV court complex is suggested by the low proportion (8.54%) of censers in the terminal debris of Str. 200-22, directly opposite Str. 200-23 to the north. Most (92%) of the Str. 200-22 form-classified censers are of the ladle type, generally associated with private rites at Quirigua. In none of these cases is there any evidence, such as the absence of utilitarian ceramic types, that Str. 205-1-1st, -256, and 200-23 functioned exclusively as religious centers.

At Playitas Group II, Nowak's excavations into the south, court-facing side of Str. 200-193 produced a sizable amount of *incensario* fragments (77.51% of the terminal debris ceramic collection, 193 sherds). This is a percentage that approaches the upper limits of even the Las Quebradas monument excavations for censer frequency. Of the form-classified censers in this collection 85.71% come from one reconstructible vessel of the cruciform-vent type. It is unknown whether this vessel form, which had apparently been cached in front of Str. 200-193 (Nowak 1975b), was associated with either public or private rituals. Nowak's Op. 9D, presumably in the Group II area (precise provenience and context unknown), also produced a high proportion of censers (83.56%, 894 sherds). The majority of these fragments derive from Lots 9D/1-2 (822 sherds), of which modeled censers make up 45.68% of the form-classified sherds and spiked censers the remainder. The high censer concentration within these lots, and the especially high proportion of modeled examples, suggest that Op. 9D sampled another center of ceremonial activity in Playitas Group II.

Few valley structures have the form attributes used to identify special religious/ceremonial structures in the Maya lowlands. Structure 205-16 in the Las Quebradas West Group, Str. 205-262 in the East Group, and Str. 216-17 at Arapahoe Viejo, because of

their pyramidal form, narrow summits, and steep sides, may have served a specialized ceremonial purpose. Structures 205-279/280 in the Las Quebradas Southeast Group and Str. 209-1/2 at Bobos may have carried out similar functions, to judge by their similar form.

Two possible ballcourts were recorded at Las Quebradas, Str. 205-26/27 and -8/9, although neither set clearly represents this form category. The most striking examples of possible ceremonially oriented spaces are two large plazas, one each in the Las Quebradas East and West Groups. These plazas are defined on three sides by monumental constructions, with the south sides bounded by high structures with narrow limits which may have served exclusively ceremonial functions (Str. 205-262 and -16 respectively). The open sides are defined by steep terraces. Activities in these plazas could, conceivably, have been visible from the surrounding structures, although access to them was not totally unobstructed. The distinctive form of these plazas, plus their association with possible ritual structures, hints at their use as arenas for public rites. Unfortunately, the very limited excavations carried out in these plazas (Op. 24H and O) did not confirm this supposition. The large plaza at Arapahoe Viejo, also associated with a possible ritual structure, Str. 216-17, could have been designed for public ceremonial purposes as well. This space is defined by only two monumental structures, and access to it is much less restricted than at Las Quebradas. As will be noted in the succeeding chapter, the functions of this site, while tantalizing, are far from clear.

In sum, we conclude that private ceremonies were carried out at both large and small constructions at the LMV sites. The differential distribution of censer forms between large and small platforms in the period AD 740-850 suggests that some differences existed in the rituals performed at these structure types. The Quirigua model supports our contention that public ceremonies were carried out primarily around monuments and, possibly, in and around some adjacent monumental structures. Architectural form implies that a few structures might have been devoted largely to the performance of these rites. The association of public-ritual evidence with monumental platforms indicates that the residents of these structures may have controlled the ceremonial life of their respective settlements to some extent. In general, however, ritual facilities are relatively sparse at the excavated valley sites, especially when compared with the situation in the nearby Lowland Maya zone.

The monument at Arapahoe Viejo (Mon. 1), by analogy with Las Quebradas, may have served as a focus of public ritual. Private rituals were probably performed in the other wider-valley sites, at both monumental and small structures, although this has not been established by excavation. The recovery of censer fragments from the two largest surface collections, Playitas Group V and Comanche Farm (3.7 and 0.74% of these collections respectively), is good evidence for the practice of ceremonial activities at these two areas.

ADMINISTRATIVE ACTIVITIES

The first step toward inferring administrative activities at the three excavated sites was a comparison of the percentages of elite-style ceramics in the terminal debris collections of both large and small structures. Tipon Group vessels, because of their fine pastes, care in manufacture, and varied decorations, are assumed to be associated with elite activities. Coroza Cream and Bobos Polychrome, primarily because of their complex painted decorations, are also considered elite-related types.

After making these comparisons (exclusive of Playitas Group II), we find no difference between the terminal debris ceramic collections of excavated monumental and small structures in the percentages of these taxa (see Tables 6.3 and 6.4). If anything, there is a slight tendency for these so-called elite ceramics to be more frequently associated with small structures. At Playitas Group II (c. AD 700-739), the monumental court excavations produced examples of Tipon Orange pottery from terminal debris contexts (26.5%), along with some eroded polychromes (3.12%). The small excavated platform in the group (Str. 200-180) had only utilitarian sherds in its terminal debris lots. This either indicates a trend toward decreasing differentiation in ceramic assemblages through time or, much more likely, is the result of a small analyzed sample. Regardless, it seems clear that by c. AD 740 elite-type ceramics were fairly evenly distributed throughout at least three wider-valley centers, but we have no evidence for a spatially distinct elite administrative group at these sites. The few clearly imported ceramics are so rare that their distribution cannot be used to identify elite occupation.

No special forms of chipped stone artifacts, such as eccentric flints, that might indicate the presence of an elite group were noted in the wider-valley collections. The presence of quantities of obsidian at the three excavated sites, most of it not locally available, does imply the existence of an upper social stratum capable of organizing and funding this material's acquisition from distant sources. Once acquired, it would appear to have been evenly distributed throughout each site, with its manufacture into tools, perhaps, concentrated in the smaller structures around the principal groups (see Manufacturing, this chapter). The absence of large quantities of other imported items, especially those (such as jade) usually associated with high-status social leaders may indicate the limited economic, organizational, and investment abilities of the LMV elites.

The best evidence for the existence of an administrative elite is found in architecture and site planning. Architecturally, the marked differences in size between structures forming monumental quadrangles and the surrounding smaller platforms strongly point to the presence of an administrative authority capable of calling up, organizing, and supporting the labor forces required to construct them. The fact that both large and small structures had primarily domestic functions (see Domestic, this chapter) indicates that the residents of the monumental quadrangles summoned this labor force for their personal use. One of the hallmarks of an elite presence is differential control of labor based on its abilities to mobilize large networks of social obligations. The resources involved in monumental construction in the LMV, the need to carefully select specific construction materials, along with the planning required to raise such massive structures, further imply the existence of an elite with some engineering expertise.

In considering the broader topic of site planning, we can trace several lines of evidence pointing to the existence of a social hierarchy within the LMV monumental centers, headed by an administrative elite group. First, the overall arrangement of monumental platforms into coherent, largely orthogonal complexes implies the existence of a planning agency capable of seeing its organizational schemes carried out. Second, those sites with more than one contemporary monumental court complex (Playitas and Las Quebradas) show a ranked distribution of total structure area, component structure size, and architectural complexity. The East Group monumental complex at Las Quebradas is much larger (17,429 m²) than its

West Group counterpart (14,436 m²), and both of these are more complex and larger than the single Northwest Group quadrangle (4745 m²). Group I at Playitas dominates that site in both size (covering 17,088 m²) and complexity (three interlinked courts). Group V is much smaller (6318 m²) and has only one quadrangle, while Group IV's main group is smaller and simpler still (2610 m²). Once more, given the assumption that the size and complexity of a structural group reflect the power and prestige of its residents, then this ranking of main groups is a manifestation of social ranking within the upper class at these two sites (see also Michels 1979). Note that in addition to having the largest structures at Playitas, Group I has the only structure with plaster and stone sculptural decorations at that center (Str. 200-77). This implies that its residents were able to call on skilled artisans in addition to large numbers of unskilled laborers.

There is also variation in size and complexity within the class of small-structure groups, perhaps reflecting some social differentiation among the nonelite segment of LMV society. As with the larger quadrangles, this proposition is based on the presumption that the investigated groups are contemporary and all were used in essentially the same domestic functions.

An interesting pattern is discernible at Las Quebradas and Playitas involving the size and density of the structures surrounding monumental quadrangles. This relationship may be stated as follows: the larger the monumental court complex, the larger and the more densely packed the surrounding "smaller" structures. This phenomenon might be explained if the largest complexes are the oldest and, thus, would have attracted more surrounding residents through time than their younger counterparts. These structures would therefore be larger simply because they had more time to grow by accretion than those in the environs of younger quadrangles. Alternatively, the largest platforms might be the residences of the most powerful and prestigious elite, who attracted more people to share in any advantages that may have accrued through association with the powerful. The nucleation of adherents might also have facilitated their control by local leaders (e.g., Montmollin 1989). The status of these attracted individuals may have been relatively high as well and is reflected in the somewhat larger satellite constructions. Conversely, the less powerful elite in correspondingly smaller quadrangles attracted and controlled fewer immediate retainers of lower status.

Both of these alternatives could be correct. In fact, as a postulate for further testing, it is proposed that the degree of structure clustering around monumental quadrangles and the size of their surrounding smaller constructions are directly related to the length of occupation *and* the relative power/prestige of the quadrangle's residents. Both of these factors would be reflected in the size and complexity of the central court complex. At present, some slight evidence exists that the larger quadrangles may have housed the most powerful elite at the site; see, for example, the special attention provided such structures as Str. 200-77 in Playitas Group I (above). Similarly, there is some indication that the smaller platforms were occupied over shorter intervals: Str. 200-24 of Playitas Group IV's main court, the smallest complex at the site, was still being constructed when the court was abandoned.

Unfortunately, while the existence of an administrative elite can be inferred at Choco, Playitas, and Las Quebradas, we can presently make very few statements about its specific activities. Its members certainly controlled labor for monumental construction and oversaw the acquisition of nonlocal resources, such as obsidian, eventually redistributing it to their supporters. Given the location of public ritual foci in or near areas of monumental construction, the elite almost certainly discharged religious leadership functions as well. Beyond these statements, few indications of elite administrative services were discerned, and it seems probable that the LMV elite operated at only a local level of administrative control. In fact, based on site-plan data, we may conjecture that the administrative effectiveness of the valley rulers was very limited. The multi-quadrangle sites of Las Quebradas and Playitas have a very disjointed appearance since each is composed of three separate contemporary monumental court complexes, surrounded by smaller constructions that decrease in frequency away from the focal courts. Thus, each quadrangle is the center of its own, spatially distinct, collection of structures. While there is the aforementioned ranking of courts and attendant structures, it still appears that the largest centers were collections of semi-autonomous elite residential groups surrounded by their immediate dependents. This interpretation of the organization of the largest valley sites is speculative, but fits with other lines of evidence suggesting that the effective authority exercised by the wider-valley elite was restricted. The facts that Las Quebradas and Playitas contain only three contemporary monumental quadrangles and that nowhere in the valley are more than four found in any one site zone also imply that there may have been a limit to the integration of the valley's elite within a single center. Moreover, the short time span during which these centers were occupied (c. 100 years) would put an effective limit on their size. It has recently been argued that Late Classic Lowland Maya polities were organized along segmentary principles (e.g., Demarest 1989; Fash 1988; cf. Southall 1970). Lower Motagua societies may reflect this same trend.

The monumental quadrangles at the unexcavated valley centers, judged by visible architecture and site plan, fit this pattern, and thus probably served as seats of limited administrative activities (see Chap. 4). At the larger nonmonumental sites, such as Juan de Paz, Oneida, Cruce de Morales, Finca America, Piedras de Sangre, and Puente de Virginia, there are usually one or more dominant groups composed of larger, more regularly arranged structures. At Juan de Paz, several of these structures (Str. 207-32 and -32a) contain cut sandstone blocks, while another major construction (Str. 207-3) has large schist and sandstone slabs protruding from its north face. The other buildings at this site seem to have been built primarily of river cobbles and irregular stone chunks. The size of structures such as Str. 207-32, their arrangement into well-planned groups and association, as at Juan de Paz, with distinct architectural features, all point to their functioning as small administrative complexes. The absence of known quadrangle groups in the vicinity of these sites suggests that they may have been administrative centers either independent, or under the loose control, of the larger valley centers to the south and east (see Chap. 7).

MARKETING ACTIVITIES

No direct evidence has yet been uncovered for the presence of markets at any scale in the excavated LMV centers. The only structurally defined plazas in the excavated sample—the East and West Group monumental plazas at Las Quebradas—that might have been of sufficient size to house a market produced no artifactual evidence of this function. Neither of these plazas is fully open in that one side is defined by a relatively steep terrace. In general, the presence of obviously imported items such as obsidian, ground stone, and several ceramic types indicates that the LMV centers were integrated into a long-distance trading network. The relative paucity of all these remains, save the obsidian, suggests a low level of participation in such exchange. The only possible evidence for large-scale storage facilities is in Str. 216-13 at Arapahoe Viejo, where three large rooms are sunk into the platform's summit. Similar features have been identified as storage facilities in other parts of the world (e.g., Morris and Thompson 1974; Keatinge 1974) and, to a lesser extent, in the Maya area (Sabloff and Freidel 1975: 397-404). Further excavations are required to answer this question of function (see also Chap. 7).

The largest LMV centers, Las Quebradas and Playitas, are, however, strategically located to control long-distance commerce passing along the Rios Bobos and Chinamito. In the case of the pass cut by the Rio Chinamito and one of its tributaries, there are four sites, one with monumental architecture, along the communication route. A recently discovered monumental center, Tepemechines, is also situated on the Chinamito pass (Nakamura 1988). The location of these loci in very small and strictly bounded valley pockets indicates that access to major trade routes was the determining factor for ancient settlement. Possibly, Playitas and Las Quebradas were in a position to control the disbursement of goods coming into the valley by these routes, thereby placing less strategically located sites in an economically dependent status (see Chap. 7).

While it is possible, therefore, that the LMV centers served as economic foci at the local, regional, or interregional level, the evidence supporting such contentions is weak and inferential for all known valley sites. The only possible exceptions are Playitas and Las Quebradas, whose locations suggest a relatively greater concern with interregional commerce.

SUMMARY

The model of activity distribution developed for LMV centers dated to c. AD 700-850 sees them primarily as foci of domestic functions. Their residents were dominated by a ranked authority structure reflected in the architectural and site-plan data. The administrative elite at each center resided in monumental quadrangles, built for them by a local labor force, and were internally ranked (as seen in differential quadrangle size and complexity). The occupants of the smaller structures surrounding each monumental complex were probably the resident elite's primary retainers. It is possible that, given the differing sizes of monumental constructions within each site, all of the center's nonelite residents owed ultimate allegiance to the occupants of the largest quadrangle complex. Some social ranking may have existed among nonelite residents as well, and is manifest in differences in small-group sizes and complexity. In general, based on structure sizes, it could be reasonably argued that the nonelite population allied to the residents of the larger quadrangles had more social power and prestige than those clustered around the smaller quadrangles. The extent of the power wielded by the elite at each site is uncertain. At present, it seems to have been restricted to organizing the import of some necessary resources, the planning and carrying out of large-scale building projects, and the control of public rituals.

In addition to public ceremonies, evidence for private rites is associated with both monumental and small structures. At Las Quebradas, several quadrangle courts are the settings for plain stone monuments. It is important to reiterate here that in no case does a court contain more than one compositional or stylistic monument type (see Chap. 4). This may suggest that each of these ceremonial foci was associated exclusively with the elite residents of the enclosing monumental platforms, and, by extension, with the larger network of their retainers. These distinct monuments may have been used to symbolize or identify different social units at Las Quebradas and, possibly, Arapahoe Viejo.

Manufacturing was limited in both scope (only obsidian recognized to date) and scale (local level). Marketing activities, while they may have existed, were not clearly recognized archaeologically at any of the centers. Undoubtedly long-distance trade was pursued to bring in goods such as obsidian, but beyond this, little can be said for the present.

In sum, all the available evidence points to the basic repetition of the same set of limited activities at all of the wider-valley monumental centers.

VII

Regional Interaction

INTRODUCTION

The purpose of this section is to add two components to the model introduced in the previous chapter. The first is a synchronic reconstruction of interactions among the residents of the known LMV monumental centers, including Quirigua and the adjacent Wider Periphery sites such as Morja, Jubuco, and Chapulco. The time period dealt with is equivalent to the Hewett and Morley Ceramic Complexes, the era of greatest building activity at Quirigua and occupation at all the wider-valley centers. The reconstruction of intercenter interaction is, of course, based on the inferred nature and scale of activities carried out within the sites involved. These inferred activities for the wider-valley centers were presented in Chap. 6. To complete the task, the same activity categories

(domestic, manufacturing, ceremonial, administrative, and marketing) will be briefly presented for Quirigua and its three adjacent Wider Periphery sites. As this falls within the scope of other Project investigations, unless otherwise noted the following discussion is based on QR 4 (for the Floodplain and Wider Peripheries) and QR 5 (for the site core).

The second component of the model is a diachronic reconstruction aimed at understanding the rapid increase in building activity throughout the wider valley c. AD 740 and the cessation of that activity not long thereafter. As with all other aspects of this model, this chapter provides a preliminary formulation of relationships requiring future testing and refinement (see Chap. 9).

QUIRIGUA

DOMESTIC ACTIVITIES

Evidence for domestic activities is ample at Quirigua, both within the site core and in the broader floodplain settlement. Its architectural focus, the Acropolis, is interpreted as an elite residential complex (Sharer 1978: 60; 1990; Jones et al. 1983). This view is based primarily on constituent architecture and the privacy afforded by its raised construction (ibid.; Jones 1977: 6; Ashmore 1977: 11). All but one of the ultimate-phase masonry Acropolis structures (Str. 1B-2/5) are multiroom buildings containing benches, windows, and curtain-holders, features generally associated with elite residences (palaces) at other Lowland Maya sites (Sharer 1978: 60; Jones et al. 1983). Although associated artifactual debris was cleared from these buildings long before the QAP investigations, the excavation of Str. 1B-18, an adobe-block building on the east side of the Acropolis, revealed fragments of kitchen/storage ceramic vessels sealed *in situ* by the collapse of construction (Sharer 1978: 60). In the Floodplain Periphery, beyond the limits of the current park, Ashmore has identified a range of smaller residential

structures, using—where possible—artifact, ecofact, and feature correlates of domestic activity (QR 4) along with criteria of structure size and abundance. In all, 49 groups, 50 structures, 12 pavements, 21 disturbed features, three wells, and one pit are tentatively assigned domestic functions, most during Periphery Time Spans (P.T.S.) 3 and 2 (Hewett and Morley Ceramic Complex equivalents). The estimated average population density for P.T.S. 3/2 on the floodplain was 500 to 550 people/km² with a total "Greater Quirigua" resident population of c. 1500-2000 people (QR 4).

MANUFACTURING

Good archaeological evidence exists at Quirigua for the manufacture of commodities from three resources, obsidian, clay, and fibers (probably cotton) (Ashmore 1988). Less direct evidence suggests processing of a fourth, cacao (Ashmore 1977: 7; Sharer 1990). Obsidian-blade production was recognized at a total of 16 Floodplain Periphery loci in P.T.S. 3/2, ceramic production at five locations in the same time span, and textile manufacture at five loci. In addition, a large amount of debris from an apparent obsidian blade-core workshop was found redeposited on the floor of Str. 1B-Sub3 in the Acropolis (Special Deposit 10; Sheets 1983). Ashmore has postulated the association of these manufacturing loci with residential groups, based on their dispersal throughout the Floodplain Periphery; and from the co-occurrence of evidence for the production of several items at one spot, she argues that these crafts were geared to a local or—at the most—limited regional market (within 15 km of Quirigua). Neither textile, ceramic, nor obsidian production required full-time specialists in P.T.S. 3/2 and each seems to have been part of common household maintenance tasks.

Ashmore (1980) also notes a possible cacao-processing center (Str. 3C-5) in the Quirigua P.T.S. 3/2 settlement. The size of the proposed processing facility, the inferred extent of the supply area (the farms), and the presumed importance of cacao in long-distance trade all point to production on the export scale. It must be noted, however, that the inference of cacao production remains tentative.

Other manufacturing tasks, presumably requiring specialists, are inferred for Quirigua on the basis of indirect evidence and would have been executed by sculptors, architects, masons, and possibly jade, copper, and stucco workers. Production in these areas may well have been limited to the local level, perhaps involving individual commissions.

CEREMONIAL ACTIVITIES

Benyo (1979: 52-55), in her analysis of the censers recovered from Quirigua, notes a roughly complementary distribution of the effigy modeled and the three-pronged, lid, and spiked censer forms. The former type, because of its elaborate form, the amount of time and care required in its manufacture, and its association with open, public spaces (i.e., the Great Plaza), is interpreted as having functioned in public rituals (ibid.). The last three form classes are assigned roles in private, domestic rites based on their simple forms and broad spatial and temporal distributions (ibid.). This research, therefore, indicates that Quirigua was probably the focus of both public and private rituals, with the Great Plaza as a center of public ceremonies and the Acropolis as a locus of private/domestic ceremonies.

Ashmore (1981b), in her more recent work on this topic, supports Benyo's thesis and expands it somewhat by incorporating more detailed information

from the Floodplain Periphery. She sees at least three possible loci for public ceremonies in the floodplain settlement: the Great and Ballcourt Plazas in the site core and the large plaza surrounding the earlier but still visible Str. 3C-14, bounded on the east by Str. 3C-5 and -7 (ibid.; pers. comm. 1981). A great many of the small domestic structures in the Floodplain Periphery also show some evidence for the performance of private rituals. An elite focus for such private, presumably ancestral, rites has been proposed for Str. 1B-6 in the Acropolis (Becker 1972; Sharer 1978). Other evidence of ritual activity at Quirigua is found in the caches associated with buildings and monuments.

While it is difficult to gauge the scale of ceremonial activities, three lines of evidence point to Quirigua as the focus of a sizable ritual community. First, there is the very great size of the proposed ritual plazas, capable of accommodating large audiences. Second, there is the apparent increased concentration of censer use at Quirigua at the same time this activity diminishes in the Wider Periphery (Benyo 1979: 61). Finally, there is the location of public ritual arenas within Quirigua in association with architectural and sculptural indicators of wealth and power. All of these points suggest a centralization and control of public ceremonialism at Quirigua by at least AD 740, and the dependence on this site, for these activities, of a sizable population beyond the immediate floodplain settlement. The relative importance of ceremonialism at Quirigua is also suggested by the provision of facilities specifically for that purpose, including two sequent ballcourts (Sharer 1979: 12), a monumental temple pyramid (Str. 1A-11; ibid.), and two possible Acropolis temples that once faced the Ballcourt Plaza (Str. 1B-Sub3, -Sub4; Jones et al. 1983). The precise limits of Quirigua's ceremonial hinterland are not known, but may have been coterminous with its administrative zone (see below).

ADMINISTRATION

The presence of a ruling elite is clearly indicated at Quirigua by the monumentality of construction, which in turn reflects control over a sizable labor force; the recovery of artifacts associated with elite usage in the Maya lowlands (i.e., eccentric flints, pyrite mirrors, jade, and hematite); and, most directly, the large carved monuments with portraits of rulers and glyphic inscriptions detailing dynastic histories. The physical focus of these administrative activities was the Acropolis, an impressive architectural complex where the rulers must have resided (e.g., Sharer 1978: 60). The presence of elite administrators in this complex is indicated by the amount of labor invested in raising the residential complex, the degree of architectural elaboration and decoration lavished here in the form of carvings, painting, and stucco work, the seclusion afforded by the enclosed court, and the fineness of the cut-block masonry. All this is evidence for control of both skilled and unskilled labor by the Acropolis residents.

The extent of the administrative elite's power is difficult to judge. The fact that the Acropolis is so much larger than any other plausible elite residential complex within the site implies that Quirigua's rulers were sufficiently powerful to monopolize the local labor force. This view is further substantiated by the dynastic records deciphered from the inscriptions, which indicate the continuing presence of a well-organized and powerful ruling elite.

One innovative proposal has been that the range of Quirigua's administrative control might be coterminous with the area from which it obtained its raw materials for building (Ashmore 1977). The range of these materials used in the site core expanded through time to include ever more distant sources, beginning with locally available cobbles and silt and finally, in Quirigua's ultimate stage, incorporating marble, the closest source of which is c. 7 km to the southeast up the Morja river (Peter Muller, pers. comm. 1977). If this expansion of utilized raw materials reflects a concomitant increase in Quirigua's area of administrative control, then its greatest extent would have encompassed an area of roughly 161.30 km^2 (including the Morja site area, see below). This is also the territory that corresponds to the Quirigua ceramic assemblage, an assemblage different in certain ways from that found farther east and west in the wider valley. Unfortunately, it is difficult to correlate the distribution of material items and styles with administrative boundaries (e.g., Hodder 1978b). At the very least, the evidence points to a complex and well-organized administrative elite at Quirigua capable of controlling sizable populations and of challenging and defeating the much larger site of Copan to the southwest (Sharer 1978: 66-67; Jones and Sharer 1986).

MARKETING

The identification of marketing facilities, such as storage rooms and marketplaces, has so far proven difficult at Quirigua. The southern portion of the Great Plaza, because of its large size, accessible location, and associated utilitarian artifacts, has been interpreted as a focus for a local market, as well as for ceremonial activities (e.g., Ashmore and Sharer 1978). The large northern plaza, fronted by Str. 3C-5 and -7, for the same reasons, also may have functioned as a local marketplace (Ashmore, pers. comm. 1981).

Evidence also exists to support Quirigua's function as an important node in interregional trade. First, the center is strategically located to control commerce flowing along the Rio Motagua between the Guatemalan highlands and the Caribbean coast. This passage has long been a route of considerable importance in colonial and modern Guatemala and would, presumably, have been equally important prehistorically (e.g., QR 4; Hammond 1972; Sharer 1978, 1990; Thompson 1970). In addition, in the 19th century, the route from Lake Izabal to the Motagua valley intersected the Quirigua periphery (Stephens 1841). Any trade passing north-south from Lake Izabal and ultimately the central Maya lowlands to western Honduras and Copan might well, therefore, have passed close by Quirigua and have been within its control. This would be the case if north-south trade followed the most direct route through the Espiritu Santo mountains along the Rio Morja pass. The northern end of this pass is c. 4 km southeast of Quirigua. This possibility is strongly suggested by the use of the Morja pass today and the number and size of Late Classic centers found on both the Guatemalan and Honduran sides of the route—the Morja and El Paraiso sites respectively (Yde 1938; Vlcek and Fash 1986). Other north-south passes do exist through the Espiritu Santo mountains, however, and at least two were apparently controlled by wider-valley centers: the Rio Bobos by Las Quebradas and the Rio Chinamito by Playitas (see below).

Because of this crossroads location, Quirigua was positioned at a very convenient "break-bulk" point in both north-south and east-west trading systems. Break-bulk stations are those centers where traded goods are repacked either for shipment along routes other than those on which they arrived or because the mode of conveyance is to be changed (Burghardt 1971). Quirigua's situation, near the limits of effective navigation on the Rio Motagua (Schortman 1976), might also have contributed to the break-bulk appeal of its location; goods coming from the west or east could have been transferred to canoes or carriers at this point. Centers favorably located at break-bulk points along several routes connecting ecologically different zones have been called "Gateway Cities" in the economic geography literature and have been recognized elsewhere prehistorically (Burghardt 1971; Hirth

1978). The ecological zones potentially linked through Quirigua were the highlands of Guatemala to the west, the tropical lowlands to the north and east, and the valleys at intermediate elevation to the south in Honduras.

In addition to location, the large numbers of imported obsidian and basalt tools recovered from Quirigua, along with smaller amounts of jade, flint, hematite, pyrite, and a few foreign ceramics, suggest the site's participation in diverse long-distance exchange networks. In his review of Quirigua obsidian, Sheets (1983) notes that the knappers producing prismatic blades at this center were not miserly in their use of this material. The CE/M ratio of these blades, a measure of the relationship between the length of a blade's cutting edge and its mass, is 3-5 cm/g. This is a measurement consonant with a powerful Maya elite center at an intermediate distance from blade-core source material (ibid.). Sheets's study reinforces the view that Quirigua had the managerial expertise and resources to procure sizable quantities of high-quality obsidian through long-distance trade. The fact that most of Quirigua's tested obsidian derives from the Ixtepeque source c. 155 km to the southwest also reinforces this interpretation (ibid.; Sharer et al. 1983). The tentatively proposed processing of cacao for export would further illustrate Quirigua's complex and extensive trading ties.

Finally, adding to the evidence is Quirigua's specific location immediately adjacent to the Late Classic course of the Rio Motagua and the construction of a special docking facility immediately west of Str. 1A-11 in the site core (Ashmore et al. 1983). The latter facility was a stone jetty extending into an embayment that probably once connected to the Motagua. The embayment may itself have been constructed to provide a quiet harbor for canoe docking (ibid.). The location of the river along the west side of the Great Plaza, its open flank, further suggests that this large open space served some commercial purpose.

WIDER PERIPHERY MONUMENTAL SITES

Five loci containing at least some monumental architecture and dated to AD 700-850 are located in the Quirigua Wider Periphery on the south side of the Rio Motagua: Morja, Jubuco, Chapulco, Finca La Marina, and Finca Nueva. Other than Quirigua Groups A and C, only one monumental site, Vega Grande, is found north of that river. Another monumental center, now destroyed, may have been located in Quirigua Town, although this may simply represent a continuation of the floodplain settlement onto the higher terraces (Ashmore, pers. comm. 1981). Four Wider Periphery sites were excavated in 1977-78—Morja, Jubuco, and Groups A and C—while the rest are known from surface remains alone.

DOMESTIC ACTIVITIES

Two of these centers, Jubuco and Chapulco, contain monumental quadrangles. The privacy provided by their enclosed courts and the utilitarian ceramics found in the Jubuco excavations led us to assign domestic functions to the platforms in both loci. One of the excavated Jubuco quadrangle structures, Str. 089-2, also has an L-shaped bench on its summit, an architectural feature commonly associated with elite Lowland Maya residences (Jones et al. 1983). The Morja site contains no extant quadrangles comparable to those noted at the other two loci, although some privacy was still obtained by structural arrangements. To judge by surface remains, Jubuco and Chapulco did not house a large, nonelite population; the Morja site's population is difficult to assess because of alluvial burial or loss to cutting by the Rio Morja (Ashmore, pers. comm. 1981). Small-house remains at Jubuco, Chapulco, and Morja have probably suffered greatly from modern land-use practices as well. The profusion of modest structures found at Vega Grande suggests the presence of residential/domestic structures at this site (ibid.). The remaining sites, all in Ashmore's QP 5, 4, and 7 patterns, could have had domestic functions, though this is not certain.

MANUFACTURING

The only manufacturing locus uncovered at a far-periphery monumental site is an obsidian blade-core workshop at Morja (Sheets 1983). The scale of production may have been local.

CEREMONIAL ACTIVITIES

On the basis of censer form types and their distributions, it appears that the Morja and Jubuco sites were the foci of both public and private rituals (Benyo 1979:

58). Excavations in the closed court of the Jubuco quadrangle uncovered a large number of pronged, lid, and spiked censers, all indicative of private/domestic ritual activity (ibid.). At Morja, pronged, lid, ladle, and vented cylinders were the only forms recognized (Ashmore 1980: notes), once more indicating the performance of private rituals. The existence of some public ceremonies at the Wider Periphery sites is implied by the presence of large plazas surrounded by monumental constructions. As at Quirigua, such open areas could have provided suitable arenas for public rites. At the Morja and Finca Nueva sites the identification of public ritual activity is further supported by the presence of probable ballcourts, while the recovery of some effigy modeled censer fragments from Jubuco's quadrangle implies similar activities at this site as well. The public ceremonies performed at these centers may have served only the residents of the individual site and its immediate hinterland—in any case they must have been carried out on a lesser scale than at Quirigua, as the facilities provided for them are smaller and less diverse.

ADMINISTRATION

The architectural elaboration of the Wider Periphery sites, seen in both structure size and quality of construction, implies the existence of an administrative elite capable of calling up and directing a sizable force of skilled and unskilled laborers. The quadrangles at Jubuco and Chapulco, closely paralleling in form the Quirigua Acropolis, also point to the presence of an administrative elite group. The regular spacing of the Morja, Jubuco, and Chapulco sites across the Chapulco plain, c. 2.5-3 km apart, further implies the division of this fertile area into three uniform administrative districts (Schortman 1976).

The scope of this administrative activity was much less than that inferred for Quirigua. There are no stone monuments at periphery loci recounting the dynastic histories of the rulers, the structures are smaller and less elaborately decorated than those at Quirigua, and no elite-related artifacts were recovered that would indicate the ability of the local notables to use their position to acquire these goods. The raw materials employed in large-scale constructions also seem limited to those locally available, pointing to a more restricted range of areal control than that noted for Quirigua. In fact, all of the P.T.S. 3/2 monumental sites in the Wider Periphery have been interpreted as politically, socially, economically, and possibly ritually subordinate to Quirigua (Benyo

1979: 61; QR 4; Sharer 1979; Sheets 1983). Presumably, these monumental sites would have administered segments of the Quirigua realm. The specific administrative tasks carried out at these centers are unknown, though it has been hypothesized that Jubuco and Chapulco functioned as control and collection points within the broader Quirigua cacao-farm system (QR 4).

MARKETING

The public spaces at all Wider Periphery monumental centers could have served as local marketplaces, just as portions of the Great Plaza may have filled this role at Quirigua. No other trade-related facilities were clearly recognized at far-periphery centers. Immediately north of the Chapulco quadrangle the remnants of a massive stone platform suitable for storing large quantities of traded goods were noted (Ashmore 1981b; see also Sabloff and Freidel 1975: 397-404). Unfortunately, the feature was so disturbed by recent activities that this proposition could not be tested.

The presence of imported materials, in particular obsidian and basalt, at Morja and Jubuco implies that these loci participated in long-distance trading networks, although imports may have been acquired from the nearby site of Quirigua. The low CE/M ratio of obsidian blades found at Morja (8.3 cm/g), along with the evidence for frequent polyhedral-core rejuvenation there (Sheets 1983), suggests that knappers at this center had to be more parsimonious with their materials than their Quirigua peers. This observation would be in line with a system in which Quirigua was the center of a network that imported and subsequently redistributed obsidian and other resources to smaller sites.

None of the Wider Periphery monumental centers is as strategically located on as many potential trade routes as Quirigua. Morja is situated at the point where the Rios Morja, Jubuco, and Motagua join, a potentially important point for monitoring traffic south into Honduras and toward Copan. Vega Grande is located along a modern trail that leads over the Sierra de las Minas toward Lake Izabal to the north. Thus neither Morja nor Vega Grande controlled more than one potential trade route. It could be argued that one of their roles involved monitoring trade entering the valley on Quirigua's behalf. The other monumental centers are not located on equally obvious communication routes.

QUIRIGUA/LMV SITE COMPARISONS

SIMILARITIES

The models of activity distribution developed for the LMV monumental centers and Quirigua are very similar. All of these loci, regardless of size, functioned in part as elite residential/administrative units as well as centers of nonelite residences. It is interesting to note that their elite residential/administrative cores were most commonly quadrangles. The private space obtained by this grouping dominates sites as diverse as Quirigua (where the Acropolis is quadrangular), Jubuco, Comanche Farm, and Las Quebradas. The general identity of form and function embodied in the quadrangle implies that it represents a valley-wide conception of the proper organization of space for a specific set of functions, primarily associated with elite residential and administrative activities.

The general organization of structures within monumental sites is also similar throughout the known valley, each focused on a quadrangle surrounded by smaller platforms arranged in irregular and orthogonally oriented groups. The manufacture of obsidian blades is recorded at four of the six excavated centers: Quirigua, Morja, Las Quebradas, and Playitas. At Quirigua, Las Quebradas, and Playitas evidence points to the smaller structures around the monumental courts for the production of blades for a local or, at most, limited regional market (see Ashmore 1988 for Quirigua). At the Morja site blade production is associated with monumental structures, a phenomenon not totally unknown elsewhere in the valley (e.g., Str. 205-41, Las Quebradas).

Ceremonial activities, both public and private, are attested for all of the excavated centers using essentially the same censer forms. The use of similar censer forms in similar contexts may imply a sharing of ceremonial patterns. Interestingly, in more specific terms, Ashmore (1981b) has postulated a marked correlation between the Quirigua carved monuments and the use of effigy modeled censers. This closely parallels the association of the modeled form with the Las Quebradas uncarved monuments. Such a correlation suggests that in addition to their roles in public rites throughout the valley, monuments carved and uncarved may have been the foci of ceremonies expressing a more specific regional tradition. It is also likely that the LMV and Quirigua elite played a large role in conducting public rituals.

The location of the largest LMV centers, Playitas and Las Quebradas, was guided by the same economic concern, the control of trade, that appears to have dictated the location of Quirigua. Whereas Quirigua dominated the important east-west and at least one of the north-south routes, the former two centers were each situated so as to control movement along the Chinamito and Bobos passes southward into Honduras. This location implies similar interests in trade/contacts outside the valley at all three centers.

Finally, there are great similarities in the ceramic and *incensario* assemblages throughout the valley. While differences do exist (see Chap. 5), the resemblances are sufficiently strong to indicate the presence of a valley-wide general ceramic tradition c. AD 700-850. The forms of the chipped and ground stone artifacts found at all investigated valley centers are also very similar.

In sum, current evidence points to several broad valley patterns in ceramics, stone tools, *incensarios*, the distribution of manufacturing loci, and the organization of space for differing functions. A social hierarchy is inferred for all of the monumental valley centers consisting, minimally, of an elite administrative group resident in the large quadrangles, and a surrounding nonelite population that contributed to the building and support of these complexes. The extent of these similarities leads to the conclusion that the residents of all Late Classic valley monumental centers shared a certain number of common traditions, implying the existence of interaction and communication networks.

DIFFERENCES

Despite these similarities, there are certain distinctions between Quirigua and the LMV centers. These are mostly differences in the scale at which certain activities were carried out. Additional areas of divergence, especially those relevant to the definition of Lowland Classic Maya "culture," will be discussed in Chap. 8. Here, the divergent activity types to be considered are: manufacturing, ceremonies, administration, and marketing.

Excavations at Quirigua have revealed a greater variety of manufacturing and processing activities than could be inferred for the wider-valley centers. Three production activities are securely identified, one is less securely postulated (cacao processing), and six more crafts are indirectly inferred at Quirigua. Only obsidian-blade and -flake production could be inferred at the wider-valley sites. Part of this discrepancy is surely due to differences in the intensity of excavation at Quirigua and the other valley sites. Undoubtedly, crafts producing generally needed goods such as pottery and textiles were also practiced throughout the wider valley, if only because their products have such a high breakage/wear rate and need constant replacement.

Quirigua is the only investigated site that possesses tentative evidence of production above the local level—the processing of cacao for export. Unlike most obsidian and ceramic products, cacao was traditionally reserved for specific functions usually associated with the elite in Lowland Maya society. As a result, it would probably not have required as elaborate an installation as that proposed at Quirigua if its products were meant for local use alone. Quirigua might, therefore, have produced cacao *primarily* for export, a fact that would then tie in with its postulated role in interregional trade. While it is possible that other valley centers were involved in similar export production, no data to support this contention have yet come to light.

The specialists resident at Quirigua, jade and copper workers, masons, and sculptors, differ from those postulated for the wider-valley centers, not so much in scale as in type. All of these inferred crafts were oriented to a sophisticated and specialized elite market. Their presence at Quirigua and virtual absence in the wider valley implies the absence of similar demand in the latter area. Not that a social/political elite was absent from such centers as Playitas, but this elite group either was not powerful enough to secure the appropriate raw materials or craftspeople, or did not possess the same artistic canons reflected by these specialized trades. It should be noted that the limited sculptural and plaster work noted at Playitas (Str. 200-77) and the faced masonry at Choco (Str. 212-1 and -22) could have been commissioned from individual specialists resident elsewhere, perhaps at Quirigua. There is simply not enough evidence for these specialized activities to infer the presence of such artisans within the wider valley.

The large size of Quirigua's Great Plaza dwarfs all similar public spaces at other valley centers. This implies the participation of a larger audience for ceremonial and other activities than at other sites. It is also important to note that the formally defined public spaces at Quirigua are more accessible than similar areas at the LMV centers. In general, efforts in these valley sites were devoted primarily to the construction of large enclosed spaces, the quadrangles, and not to the building of plazas. It is possible that the public

rites performed in the quadrangle courts did not require large numbers of participants. In sum, whereas facilities for large-scale public events were provided at Quirigua and adjacent peripheral centers, they were largely absent in the other valley sites. This may reflect differences in both audience size and the activities conducted within these settings.

Another indication of the greater investment in ceremonial activities at Quirigua than in other valley sites is the presence of specialized ritual facilities at Quirigua, including ballcourts, a temple pyramid, and Acropolis temples. Several possible pyramidal substructures that might have supported ceremonial structures were noted at Las Quebradas, Arapahoe Viejo, and Bobos. There is a small ballcourt at Morja, a larger one at Finca Nueva, and two possible ballcourts at Las Quebradas (see Chaps. 2 and 3). Ritual facilities at Quirigua are more diverse and represent a greater investment of labor than at any other individual valley center. It is assumed, therefore, that Quirigua provided more ritual services at a larger scale than its valley counterparts.

In a broader sense, however, none of the known valley monumental sites, including Quirigua, were as strongly devoted to the performance of esoteric ceremonies as were most of their Late Classic counterparts in the Maya lowlands. The latter sites are often dominated by massive funerary temples and contain a wide array of ritual artifacts and deposits, which are only poorly represented even at Quirigua (see Chap. 8). In fact, the wider-valley sites all have a "secular" feel to them, since most of their labor was used to construct massive quadrangular elite administrative/ residential complexes.

As we have seen, Quirigua has all the hallmarks of a powerful administrative elite center capable of controlling a relatively large area. This ability is not apparent in the other investigated valley centers. This may be due, in part, to the absence of locally available materials comparable to those worked by Quirigua craftspeople (see Chap. 8). However, the fact remains that the other valley centers have very few of the criteria by which pre-Hispanic elite wealth and power are traditionally measured in Mesoamerica. It seems, therefore, that the social systems integrated through these valley monumental centers were less complex than that inferred for Quirigua.

This proposition is supported by the fact that the other valley centers are composed of essentially redundant structure forms, the single, double, and triple quadrangles surrounded by groups of smaller structures. Structures are the physical facilities for activities; as the latter vary the facilities that house them will also diversify. In light of this assumption, the other valley centers appear to have been used for a limited range of activities (see also Flannery and Marcus 1976: 206, 220-221; Sanders 1974: 98, 109; Spencer 1982: 13). This association of activities and structure forms would be especially close when activities are highly specialized and important in the functioning of the society at large. In such cases, the physical requirements of the activities would be equally specific, leading to a diversification of structure forms built with the labor of the society in which they functioned. With increasing complexity in the social system, specialized and diverse activities performed on a large scale will also increase, along with more varied physical facilities designed to accommodate them. The proliferation of different structure forms and groupings at such large Lowland Maya sites as Tikal and Copan (cf. G. Andrews 1975; A. Smith 1950; and Chap. 8) may be at least partly accounted for by this relationship. While Quirigua is not as structurally complex as some Maya centers, it does possess a greater variety of structure forms and groupings than the wider-valley centers. This supports the view that the Quirigua social system was more complex than its wider-valley counterparts.

In sum, the Quirigua elite appear to have directed a more complex social system, and had a greater administrative control over their dependents, than the scions of other valley centers (see Chap. 8). The Quirigua rulers were also capable of monopolizing labor within the site for their own benefit, concentrating it at the Acropolis and restricting its availability to lesser notables, such as the residents of Group 3C-5. At the largest other valley centers, such as Las Quebradas, a number of elite households had access to the local population to construct their residential quadrangles. The result is a series of court complexes covering a broad range in size from the largest and most complex to increasingly smaller and simpler ones. At Quirigua, no residential complex even approaches the Acropolis in size. This monopoly of labor at Quirigua implies that the ruling dynasty centralized power and wealth in their own hands as well. The other valley rulers apparently did not possess this ability to an equal degree.

The strategic "break-bulk" location of Quirigua, controlling several important trade routes, indicates the important role played by interregional trade in the functioning of this center. The existence of a possible cacao-farming and -processing system at Quirigua, oriented toward the export market, adds further weight to this supposition, as does the recovery of large-scale trade-related facilities, such as the apparent stone jetty and river embayment. To date, obsidian for prismatic-blade production and basalt manos and metates are the most numerous archaeologically recovered imported goods at Quirigua. Jade, hematite, flint, and some few sherds of nonlocal polychrome vessels are found in much lower numbers. A greater variety of foreign items representing the different areas trading through Quirigua might be expected if this site served as a "Gateway City." It is likely, however, that many of the traded goods were perishable, while some were deposited in special ceremonial offerings (caches and tombs) which have yet to found. Also, if Quirigua was an especially efficient, commercially oriented economic center, most of the exchanged goods would have been kept in circulation and not "wasted" through investment in such noncommercial offerings (Sabloff and Rathje 1975: 13-14).

The other valley centers do not possess similar strategic locations. Morja, Playitas, Mojanales, and Las Quebradas are situated along potentially important north-south routes through the Sierra de Espiritu Santo range. None is in a position, however, to control the important east-west traffic. Comanche Farm and Bobos may have been located near the Rio Motagua prehistorically, but, given their position downriver from Quirigua, it is doubtful that they could have monopolized the east-west flow of goods. The latter two sites are also located where the valley is very wide and could have been easily bypassed even by water-borne commerce (following the parallel course of the Rio San Francisco), thereby reducing their potential middleman status. Quirigua, on the other hand, situated at the head of the floodplain with its large outliers at Groups A and C, could not have been easily avoided by east-west traffic, thereby assuring its brokerage position. In addition, many other valley centers were not located on potential extravalley trade routes. Trade facilities are rare to nonexistent at the known valley centers, with the possible exception of the sunken rooms at Arapahoe Viejo and Chapulco's postulated platform (see above). Imported items found in valley centers are more limited in variety and quantity than those recovered from Quirigua.

Thus, Quirigua seems to have been more fully involved in long-distance trade than any of its Late Classic valley neighbors. As has been suggested elsewhere (Ashmore et al. 1983), Quirigua's involvement in this trade possibly extended back to c. AD 400 or earlier, and may have influenced the site's original foundation on the Motagua floodplain.

No differences in local marketing functions can be inferred among the different valley sites, including Quirigua. It might be argued that the large Quirigua plazas, such as the Great Plaza, indicate the presence of equally sizable local markets at this site and their absence at other centers. The dimensions of these plazas, however, might well have been determined by their use in other contexts, e.g., public ceremonies, monument display, interregional commerce, and so forth, and cannot be attributed solely to local market activities.

In summary, Quirigua differs from the other valley centers in its more extensive participation in long-distance trade; its wealthier, more powerful, and complexly organized administrative elite; and its possible production of exportable items, such as cacao. The public rituals performed at Quirigua also seem to have been larger in scale and somewhat different from those performed elsewhere in the valley.

VALLEY INTERACTION

SYNCHRONIC

The synchronic interaction of the known valley sites can be modeled for the period c. AD 700-850 by arranging them into a hierarchy based on size and postulated function. Site size is measured by both structure numbers and the total area covered by monumental courts and plaza units. The use of this latter measure is based on the assumptions that these large complexes were built with community labor and that their number and size hence reflect the administrative power of the resident elite. A ranking of sites by the extent of such construction, therefore, should also reflect the relative power of those rulers.

The hierarchy is headed by one Class I site, Quirigua, with a total size in P.T.S. 3/2 (Hewett and Morley Complexes) of at least 189 structures and a monumental plaza/court area in the site core of 107,792 m². Quirigua's paramount position within the LMV site hierarchy is due in large part to the scale of the activities carried out there. As we have seen, Quirigua may well have been the conduit through which a great many imported items initially entered the valley, especially obsidian and basalt. The two largest known, aboriginally important obsidian sources, Ixtepeque and El Chayal, are located in the Guatemalan highlands and it is likely that Quirigua, with its control of east-west trade and the highland route, would have been an important intermediary for this trade within the valley. This role has been suggested previously, especially with respect to obsidian from the Ixtepeque source (Hammond 1972). The majority of the obsidian blades analyzed as to source from Quirigua's site core and near and far periphery are from Ixtepeque (Sheets 1983). Preliminary investigations conducted at the large obsidian flows of La Esperanza in south-central Honduras indicate that this source may have provided an alternative to highland Guatemalan obsidian for the Classic-era LMV residents (Hirth 1988). While the major valley centers may have been dependent on Quirigua for their imported obsidian, the possibility thus remains that they could have supplemented or even replaced the Guatemalan highland material with obsidian independently secured from Honduras. Nevertheless, the proximity of Quirigua to the wider-valley loci and the presence of sizable amounts of obsidian at the former site suggest that the Quirigua rulers played an important role in distributing obsidian throughout the Late Classic valley. The recovery of blade-manufacturing debris from excavations at three wider-valley centers indicates that polyhedral cores were distributed, probably from Quirigua, to the larger sites, where they were used to manufacture finished products. The general paucity of blade-production debris from within the Quirigua realm outside of the site core suggests that this center and, to a lesser extent, the Morja site supplied finished tools to its population (Sheets 1983). Obsidian tools produced by the flake-core technique, relying on a locally available, dispersed resource—cobbles found in the bed of the Rio Motagua—were probably made throughout the Quirigua realm and may have even replaced blades in some common tasks (ibid.).

Failure to find debris from the production of grinding tools, manos, and metates at any valley center suggests that these tools arrived in finished form at Quirigua and were then redistributed throughout the LMV. Quirigua may also have provided certain esoteric services, e.g., plaster work and stone masonry, to other valley centers, e.g., Str. 200-77 at Playitas.

The economic preeminence attributed to Quirigua

implies the mutual exchange of goods among all LMV centers. To date, there is no clear evidence as to what may have passed from wider-valley polities to Quirigua. It has been suggested that the other valley sites were control points for an extensive cacao-production system centered at Quirigua (Sharer 1979). The latter center would have functioned as a collection and processing center for cacao, e.g., at Str. 3C-5, for export (Ashmore 1981b). Bergmann (1969: 94), based on his study of Aztec tribute lists, reports cacao production in the general area of the LMV, in "... the Izabal Lowland, particularly lands bordering the Rio Polochic," and along the Rio Cahabon, a tributary of the Polochic. A functioning cacao grove was noted in 1978 close by the site of Choco on the Motagua floodplain. It is possible, therefore, that this perishable product was "capital" exchanged by the valley centers to obtain imported goods from Quirigua. Other crops, including surpluses of basic subsistence items such as maize, might also have been cultivated in the fertile valley for shipment to Quirigua. In order to take full advantage of its strategic position controlling interregional communication networks, Quirigua may well have required large amounts of a valued export commodity and cacao is at least a plausible candidate for this role (see below).

Administratively, Quirigua seems to have controlled an area of c. 161.3 km², and presumably provided adjudicative services to the population of this zone. It would have been from this hinterland that the resident dynasty drew its labor force and other tribute payments. Ceremonial services might also have been provided to this same zone at regular intervals. There is no evidence that Quirigua provided administrative or ritual services to the valley at large.

The next level in the hierarchy, Class II centers, includes the sites of Las Quebradas, Playitas, and possibly Morja. The first two centers contained 190-285 extant structures in the period AD 740-850 and possessed three contemporary monumental court/plaza units covering an area between 26,016 m² and 36,610 m². The extensive destruction wrought by the Morja river has rendered the hierarchic placement of this center a difficult task (see Ashmore 1981b). The size of its extant structures and the large areas over which they are found suggest that it probably should be included at this level.

The principal feature that distinguishes these three sites from the next lowest order (Class III) is their location adjacent to routes leading out of the valley along which trade might have been carried out. The goods that passed along the proposed routes remain unknown. That contact was maintained between the residents of Class II LMV sites and populations east of the sierra is strongly suggested, however, by recent discoveries in the La Entrada and Tras Cerros valleys (Nakamura 1985, 1987, 1988; Nakamura et al. 1986). Research on the Honduran side of the posited Rio Chinamito and Bobos routes has produced a pattern of regularly spaced (c. 6-7 km apart) Late Classic monumental centers that continues the distribution first noted on the Guatemalan side of the border. The existence of such sizable centers along the postulated communication channels suggests the importance of the contacts maintained along them. Furthermore, the two recovered loci closest to the current Guatemalan/Honduran border, Techin on the Chinamito and Tras Cerros on the Bobos, exhibit marked similarities in site plan and ceramics to Playitas and Las Quebradas. All the evidence accumulated since the completion of LMV research in 1979 serves to confirm the original hypothesis of strong interregional connections linking Class II centers with societies across the sierra in Honduras (see Schortman 1984: 642-643). As at Quirigua, although on a smaller scale, the hinterlands dependent on Class II sites for imported items were probably far larger than those dependent on them for other services, such as administration. Class II and III centers were essentially equal in the level of local economic, administrative, and public ceremonial services offered. Because of their location away from obvious external trade routes, the Class III centers, and all lower levels of the hierarchy, would have had to depend to some degree on the Class II sites for imported goods.

Assuming that each center competed with others for a suitably sized area to support its trade in imported goods, and each was supplying a redundant set of items, we can reconstruct a hypothetical trade, local exchange, or redistribution area for each by drawing Thiessen polygons around Class II sites (Haggett 1975: 431-432). The current channel of the Rio Motagua is the arbitrary northern boundary of these zones and the 100-m contour, above which the Espiritu Santo mountains rise quite steeply, is the southern limit. For the purposes of this reconstruction, it is assumed that another Class II site will be found at the Rio Negro, north of Las Quebradas, as this is the next river to cut a pass through the mountains into Honduras (preliminary research has recovered evidence for such a site, Las Animas, though its full size remains unknown [Nakamura 1988]). The resultant trade-zone sizes are: Playitas 119.3 km^2; Las Quebradas 110.8 km^2; and Morja 63.89 km^2.

Nevertheless, present evidence suggests that the east-west route along the Motagua may have been economically more important in the Terminal Classic than the north-south channels outlined above. Consequently, all valley sites, including Class II centers, depended on Quirigua for the bulk of their imported goods. Quirigua's hinterland for imported items, then, encompassed the known valley while the economic hinterland of each Class II site was a segment of it.

The Class III sites are Choco and Quebrada Grande, the former with one and the latter with four monumental courts covering an area of 14,222 m^2 and 23,098 m^2 respectively (excluding the heavily overgrown quadrangle at Quebrada Grande). They possess 84 and 49 structures respectively. Because the monumental court at Choco is so large, much larger than any of those at the Class IV level, this site is tentatively included in Class III even though it is smaller than Quebrada Grande.

On a local economic level, Class II and III sites show no evidence of production for export. If we assume ancient cultivation of cacao or other crops, then they may have served as collection points for such harvests before the latter were forwarded to Quirigua or, possibly, to Class II sites for subsequent export. The recovery of good evidence for obsidian-blade production at all three excavated Class II sites and the polyhedral core surface-collected from Quebrada Grande imply that both site classes could have served as nodes for the disbursement of obsidian blades to their hinterlands. Class II and III sites might also have served as redistribution points within their hinterlands for imported goods, obtained either from other valley centers or through their own trading connections.

If the comparably sized Class II and III centers were equally powerful administratively, they were competitors for supporting hinterlands. To measure these postulated administrative zones, Thiessen polygons can also be drawn around each Class II/III site. The resultant areas administratively controlled by Playitas and Las Quebradas, the two sites bounded by Class II or III sites on either side, are c. 50.7 km^2 and 52.9 km^2 respectively. If the Morja site shared the intervening territory equally with Quirigua, its administrative hinterland would have been 59.3 km^2. It has been argued earlier in this chapter, however, that larger and more powerful Quirigua actually exercised

political control over this center and, hence, its hinterland would have fallen within Quirigua's realm. The dependent hinterland of Quebrada Grande would have been 57.9 km^2 if, as proposed earlier, another Class II site was situated on the Rio Negro to the north. The size of the Choco hinterland is roughly 68.6 km^2.

The regular spacing of known Class I-III sites, averaging 5.88 km apart, also suggests active ancient competition among them for supporting hinterlands (Morrill 1974; Haggett 1965). If Quirigua, as has been suggested elsewhere (Sharer 1979), exercised political dominion over these remote portions of the valley, one might expect that the sites in its regional hinterland would show some evidence of this dominion. In two New World examples of centralized control of regional settlement (Classic-period Teotihuacan in Mexico and Chimu-period Chan Chan in coastal Peru), the elite residential/administrative complexes subordinate to the major center are very much smaller and closely resemble functionally similar architectural complexes at the dominant center (Keatinge 1974, 1975; Keatinge and Day 1973 for Chan Chan; Parsons 1974; Sanders et al. 1979 for Teotihuacan; see also Flannery and Marcus 1976: 217-219; Spencer 1982: 12-13). Las Quebradas, Playitas, and Quebrada Grande are very close to Quirigua in size and, while similar in overall plan to that site, are in no way precise replicas of any part of it. It seems unlikely, if Quirigua politically dominated the valley, that it would have relaxed its monopoly of labor and, presumably, tribute obligations to the extent reflected by the large structures at the Class II/III sites. Quirigua's rulers certainly did not exhibit such generosity within its own hinterland, where sites under its control are significantly smaller than the political capital. Administratively, Class II and III centers appear to have been the centers of politically autonomous units, with Morja the only possible exception.

As noted in Chap. 6, the available data point to a relatively weak administrative structure in Class II and III centers. Certainly, we see less centralization of power here than at Quirigua. It is questionable, therefore, how strictly the resident valley administrators could control their dependent populations and how much they could demand from them in tribute and labor payments. The range of adjudicative/administrative services provided to their dependent zones may have been correspondingly limited.

Class II/III centers most likely served as foci of public ceremonial activities carried out for the residents of their administrative zones. The large amounts of censer material recovered from the environs of Las Quebradas monuments and several monumental structures at Playitas, along with the large size of the area that may have functioned as an arena for public rites at Morja (see Ashmore 1981b), suggest this interpretation. Also, given the close association of secular/administrative and ceremonial duties within Mesoamerican polities in general (e.g., Thompson 1966; Harrison 1970) and the possible control of public rituals by the valley elite in particular, it is possible that the area politically subordinate to a center also constituted its maximum ritual community. The aforementioned (Chap. 6) paucity of public ritual facilities at these sites, however, suggests that public rituals were not an important factor in their daily functioning.

The next level in the hierarchy (Class IV) consists of those sites with a single quadrangle or monumental plaza unit or two adjoining ones encompassing an area between 3922 and 11,250 m^2 and containing 21 to 110 visible structures. The members of this class are Comanche Farm, Juyama, Jubuco, Chapulco, and Playitas Group II. Because they possess considerable monumental construction formally comparable to that found in Class II/III sites (quadrangles), they are presumed to have served as foci of local elite residence and interaction, albeit on a smaller scale than Class II/III sites.

Administratively, their smaller size implies a smaller dependent population obligated to provide labor. Administrative zones for Class IV sites, therefore, probably constituted a segment of the larger Class I, II, or III site hinterlands. By extension, it is argued that their resident elite were less politically powerful than those at the Class I-III sites and were, therefore, subordinate to the closest of these centers. Jubuco and Chapulco would have been subordinate to Quirigua, possibly along with Morja; Comanche Farm was probably dependent on Choco; while the case of Juyama is not clear (see below). Playitas Group II, because of its postulated earlier date of occupation and abandonment, was not subordinate to any known valley center.

A tentative delineation of the Class IV-dependent administrative zones assumes that Class I-III sites provided some limited set of administrative services to their total dependent zones and may have acted to legitimize the local authority of the subordinate elites resident in the Class IV quadrangles. On a daily basis, however, commonly required administrative functions would have to have been performed by the elite in all Class I-IV centers. Problems requiring immedi-

ate action and a detailed knowledge of local conditions are most efficiently dealt with through a dispersal of administrative authority through a number of centers. Therefore, while Class I-III centers offered a restricted range of high-threshold services, all Class I-IV sites would have provided a greater array of low-level services, each to its own immediate hinterland (high threshold services refer to those which require dense concentrations of people and/or elevated demand levels to support. Low threshold services can exist in the context of dispersed populations and/or restricted demands.). This supposition follows the basic tenets of central-place theory (e.g., Morrill 1974: 72-82; Haggett 1965: 121-122). If this position is valid then the sizes of these low-level administrative zones of Class I-IV centers can be estimated by drawing Thiessen polygons around the loci for which sufficient data are available. The hinterlands of these centers range from 14.6 to 22.3 km^2 with an average of 17.8 km^2. Juyama is the one exception (see below).

Because Class IV sites did not control major points of egress from the valley, they were probably dependent on the closest larger center for imported goods to be distributed to their dependent populations. Regularly required, low-threshold products such as utilitarian ceramics were probably manufactured at each Class I-IV center, if only because a regular high demand for them would be assured. The slight macroscopic differences in paste noted between representatives of the same ceramic type at Choco, Playitas, and Las Quebradas suggest that each site was exploiting a slightly different clay source to fuel its production of pottery vessels. It is also possible that the areas dependent on Class IV centers were too small to maintain specialized artisans, e.g., obsidian-blade knappers. To date, no Class IV center has produced evidence of this activity and they may have been dependent on the Class I-III sites for these products. Local markets may have been carried out at all Class I-IV centers to facilitate the distribution of goods within the immediate areas of these sites.

According to earlier arguments, each Class IV center probably served as a focus of public rituals attended by the residents of its administrative zone. As with economic and administrative functions, these sites probably also met the ritual needs of their local populations on a regular basis.

Juyama is an anomalous Class IV site partly because of its large size, a minimum of 110 structures covering an area of roughly .21 km^2, but also because of its location. An examination of Fig. 1 shows it to be situated almost midway between two Class II/III sites, Morja and Choco. It is possible, however, that Juyama was sufficiently far from both of these centers to resist direct control by either of them. Its location on the proposed boundary of two administrative zones and its massiveness, including substantial monumental constructions, suggest this view. If Juyama does represent an independent Class III site, its presence would require a redefinition of the Choco and Morja hinterlands. Until more work has been carried out at this major center, including a comprehensive mapping, we cannot determine its classification with any certainty. For the moment, it is placed in Class IV on the basis of a subjective impression that it is smaller than other Class III sites.

The next site category (Class V) consists of those centers with two small monumental quadrangles or one quadrangle and one monumental plaza unit. Members of this class are Mojanales, Bobos, and Arapahoe Viejo, consisting of between seven and 36 structures. Their monumental plazas/courts cover between c. 3790 (low estimate for Mojanales) and 11,185 m². Each of these sites is in some way unique. They all contain one small monumental quadrangle, or quadranglelike unit, 1710-5245 m² in area, which points to the presence of an administrative elite group resident at the site. The small size of these centers, however, indicates an equally restricted control of labor and, most probably, political subordination to the nearest Class II/III entity—Mojanales subordinate to Playitas, Bobos to Las Quebradas, while Arapahoe Viejo's allegiance remains unclear (see below).

Mojanales is unique, among valley sites with monumental construction recorded by the LMV Project, for its location high in the Espiritu Santo mountains along a possible trade route leading southward from Playitas. This position implies that its residents were involved in monitoring or controlling commercial traffic through this pass. In fact, it seems plausible that Mojanales was founded with this goal in mind. Given its eccentric location within a restricted pocket valley away from extensive tracts of arable land, we propose that Mojanales was a commercial outpost of Playitas devoted to controlling trade on behalf of that site. Ceremonially and administratively it was dependent on Playitas; economically, it may have relied on Playitas for access to goods not obtainable from the Chinamito trade.

Arapahoe Viejo is noteworthy because of both its location, high in the foothills of the Espiritu Santo mountains, and its possession of a large plaza defined on two sides by unusual constructions. One is a high, steep pyramidal substructure with a very narrow summit (Str. 216-17) whose form alone reveals that it probably was not residential and may have been a ritual structure. On the west side of the plaza is a massive platform with three sunken "rooms" in its summit (Str. 216-13). The location of the site, well away from known population concentrations, may have made it attractive as ensuring the safety of imported goods which could have been stored in Str. 216-13. (Cf. Sabloff and Freidel 1975 for a similar concern with protecting stored goods on Cozumel.) The adjacent plaza may then have functioned as a marketplace for interregional trade. Long-distance commerce need not be handled in public places and, indeed, might be carried out in isolation from such areas (e.g., Hill 1971: 310-315). On the other hand, if Str. 216-17 did serve as a ceremonial focus, Arapahoe Viejo could have been a specially segregated ritual site, the "storerooms" receptacles for ceremonial regalia, and the plaza the area in which the rites were performed or witnessed. At present both interpretations are equally plausible and excavation is required to resolve the issue.

The Class II/III center with which Arapahoe Viejo is associated is equally unclear. It is closest to Choco, c. 3 km to the north, but its enclosed court contains a pecked stone sphere (A.V. Mon. 1) nearly identical in appearance, location, and size to Las Quebradas Mon. 2 and 3 from the Northwest Group court. No such stones are recorded elsewhere in the valley. This might indicate some sort of tie with Las Quebradas, especially given the possible use of monuments as social identity markers discussed earlier (Chap. 6). If so, why is this site situated so far from Las Quebradas and closer to the Class II center of Playitas and the Class III site of Choco? One intriguing possibility is that Arapahoe Viejo was allied to Playitas, Choco, and Las Quebradas and performed special ritual and/or economic functions for all of them. Arapahoe Viejo may, then, have been politically neutral because the activities performed there were of great importance to these major centers.

Bobos' administrative position appears to be clearer—it is c. 5.8 km northwest of Las Quebradas and directly connected to that site via the Rio Bobos. No Class IV center has yet been found in the Las Quebradas administrative zone and Bobos, while small (5245 m² covered by monumental construction), may have functioned in this capacity. If so, it would have commanded a subsidiary economic, ceremonial, and administrative zone of roughly 17.2 km². Bobos' location, very close to the present junction of the Rios Motagua and Bobos, suggests it may have served as a meeting place for trade passing east-west along the Motagua and north-south through Las Quebradas from the Honduran side of the sierra. Given Las Quebradas' location in the foothills of the Espiritu Santo mountains, c. 6 km from the current course of the Rio Motagua, it might have been convenient for the elite of this site to maintain a presence closer to the latter river. This would facilitate both sending goods to Quirigua and acquiring items in return from that site. The plaza defined by the long, low substructures of Str. 209-4/8, because of its large size and accessibility, may have been the locus of these commercial transactions. At present, this interpretation is conjectural. What does seem clear is that Bobos was probably administratively and ceremonially subservient to Las Quebradas. Economically, it may have performed certain trade-related services for that site under the control of the elite resident in its small quadrangle (Str. 209-10/15). In this regard, it would have been functionally similar to Mojanales.

Class VI sites consist of loci with no large court complexes but with monumental structures arranged in one or more small plaza groups. These groups are, in turn, surrounded by variously oriented smaller structures, singly or in groups. Members of this class are Juan de Paz, Oneida, Vega Grande, and—less securely—Cruce de Morales, Finca America, Puente Virginia, and Monterey. Structure numbers for the first three named sites range between 20 and 81 visible constructions. None of these sites were excavated, and their relation to the larger Class I-III centers remains unknown. The presence of some relatively small, regularly arranged monumental structures indicates a degree of control of local labor possibly exercised by a resident elite. These loci, therefore, may have fulfilled some limited administrative functions. To date, most are known from the north side of the Rio Motagua, averaging c. 8.8 km from the nearest Class I-III center. They may have been subordinate to these larger sites or, possibly, autonomous, occupying zones of little interest to the elite of the larger centers. Nothing can be said at present about their ceremonial roles.

Since only Juan de Paz and, possibly, Vega Grande were located along potential major trade routes, these Class VI centers had to depend on Class I/II sites for imported materials. Juan de Paz probably had direct access to goods flowing east-west along the Motagua

valley and Vega Grande may have been able to acquire goods directly from the north via the trail to Lake Izabal, which still passes close by the site. Both of these sites, however, would have had to rely on major centers, probably Quirigua, to supply them with items accessible only from other routes.

The final category (Class VII) consists of small sites with no more than one large structure. Total structure numbers range from two to 11. Members of this class are Los Cerritos, La Coroza, Los Limones, Los Vitales, Locus 234, Cristina, and various small loci in the Quirigua Wider Periphery (see Sharer et al. 1979: fig. 1). The paucity or absence of monumental construction implies that they were primarily nonelite residential hamlets dependent for public ceremonies, administrative services, and imported manufactured goods on the nearest Class I-V site. Relatively little is known about this level of the settlement hierarchy, and it is presumed that they represent the residences of those who, together with the nonelite occupants of the Class I-IV centers, contributed to the support of these sites. Undoubtedly they are more numerous than is recorded here, being underrepresented because of vulnerability to transformational processes and the focus of this project on sites with monumental architecture (see Chap. 1).

SYNCHRONIC SUMMARY

From the foregoing it is hypothesized that in the period AD 700-850 the valley was divided into a number of competing administrative zones, at least five of which are recognized here: one dominated by Quirigua, and four respectively focused on Las Quebradas, Playitas, Quebrada Grande, and Choco. The political status of Morja remains unclear. These five Class I-III centers provided high-level administrative and ceremonial services to the populations of their respective zones and three of them, Playitas, Las Quebradas, and Quirigua, acted as conduits through which imported goods reached the valley. Among these top-level sites Quirigua was economically preeminent, controlling the important Motagua trade route and, quite possibly, the north-south passage along the Rio Morja to Copan. Quirigua may have engaged more intensively in interregional trade than its contemporaries and provided at least some of their needs for imported goods, e.g., obsidian and basalt. In return, the Class II and III centers exchanged with Quirigua some locally available goods (e.g., cacao) and/or, in the case of Class II sites, some items available to them through their southward connections beyond the valley. Quirigua's service area for imported goods, therefore, may well have extended over the known portions of the LMV. The dependent areas of the Class II sites were somewhat smaller. Administratively and ceremonially Quirigua may have been more sophisticated and complexly organized than its valley counterparts. There is no evidence at present, however, to suggest that Quirigua dominated any Class II or III center politically or ritually, with the possible exception, once again, of Morja.

Class IV sites were smaller versions of Class I-III centers and served as intermediates that facilitated the control of local populations and the distribution of economic, ceremonial, and administrative services to them. They housed a local elite administrative group in their monumental quadrangles, but were politically subordinate to the closest Class I-III site. Each Class I-IV locus provided commonly needed services to its own immediate population. This supposition conforms to the available data—i.e., there is no clear evidence of Class I-IV special-purpose sites designed to perform only a restricted range of high-level functions. Each lower-order center appears to have been a smaller replica, in terms of the activities performed and general form, of the higher-order sites. The data suggest that the same general kinds of services were performed at each, although at different levels.

Class V centers were also occupied by an elite administrative group resident in small quadrangles or quadranglelike groups. They may also have served other, more specialized purposes. Two of these centers, Mojanales and Bobos, on the basis of location and certain aspects of site planning, apparently monitored trade for Playitas and Las Quebradas respectively. Arapahoe Viejo, again for location and site-planning reasons, might have carried out specialized ceremonial and/or economic functions for a region larger than that dependent on any one Class II/III site. Each of these three sites probably also exercised limited administrative control over its own immediate hinterland, and provided certain low-level economic and ceremonial services to that area as well. Class V centers appear similar in function, if not form, to special-purpose monumental sites in the Quirigua periphery, such as Group A (see Ashmore 1981b).

Class VI and VII sites were primarily nonelite residential loci, although the presence of some large-scale construction at the former suggests the limited performance of restricted administrative and/or ceremonial services here as well. While their relationship to the major sites remains unclear, it is probable that they represent the small agricultural settlements dependent on the major Class I-V sites.

The synchronic system reconstructed here generally conforms to the "dispersed cities" model developed in economic geography (Morrill 1974: 82; Haggett 1965: 130-132). In areas where population density is low and/or transportation difficult, there is insufficient support to allow one primate center to provide services to all residents of a region. As a result, the standard central-place hierarchy is simplified and economic, administrative, and ceremonial services are distributed through a number of smaller, dispersed centers. Because the hinterland of each of these "cities" is smaller than that which a regional primate center could command, the level of services it can offer is correspondingly lower. Medium-level administrative, economic, and ceremonial services are thereby brought closer to the population rather than requiring the population to travel long distances to a single primate city. It is still possible that one center may provide a limited range of services to the entire region, services that require a large population to support. This would have been the case in the LMV c. AD 700-850, when administrative and ceremonial behaviors were dispersed through a number of centers, but Quirigua and, to a lesser extent, Playitas and Las Quebradas acted as importers of goods ultimately distributed throughout the valley.

DIACHRONIC

One of the most remarkable facts revealed by this research is the relatively short period of time in which the major valley centers outside of Quirigua were constructed and occupied. No monumental valley center is known to date prior to c. AD 700. From AD 700-740 only one Class IV monumental locus, Playitas Group II, has been found. After that time, c. AD 740-850, the remaining monumental sites were constructed. This phenomenon poses a two-fold question: what factors lay behind the rapid development and then the cessation of monumental construction? Some insight into this problem may be provided by an examination of the developmental sequence at Quirigua.

Quirigua had apparently been a node in interregional exchange since the Early to Middle Classic, at which time its first carved dynastic monuments were raised (Mon. 26, 21, and 20; see Jones 1983; Sharer 1990). Shortly thereafter the elite residential/administrative structures of the Acropolis were begun (Ashmore 1981b). After initial close links with the Peten lowlands during this time, Quirigua seems to have been politically dominated by Copan (Fash 1988; Sharer 1987, 1990). Epigraphic evidence indicates that in AD 738, however, ties with Copan were dramatically severed and thereafter building and monument carving at Quirigua increased in intensity and elaboration (Sharer 1978, 1990; Jones and Sharer 1980). Building activity also underwent a dramatic rise in the Wider Periphery, and the excavated sites of Jubuco and Morja were occupied and possibly built during this interval (Jones et al. 1983; Ashmore 1981b).

Quirigua's longstanding role in long-distance trade and the correlation between the break with Copan and increased investment in site aggrandizement suggest the following reconstruction. Quirigua may well have functioned as a transshipment point for Copan prior to AD 738, acting as an outpost through which the latter could tap into and control trade flowing along the Motagua (Sharer 1979, 1990). Also, Copan is located c. 135 km from the Caribbean, direct distance. Quirigua is both closer to and more accessible from this coast, and might have provided Copan with easier connections to the coastal trade as well. In this regard, the situation would have been generally similar to a "trading-post empire" model proposed for precolonial West Africa (Curtin 1975: 59-64). Here, a major center politically and economically controls a number of subsidiary sites that function largely to direct the flow of goods back to the home base. By AD 738 Cauac Sky, ruler of Quirigua, gained sufficient power to break free from this domination and, probably aided by the relatively long overland distance from Copan, gained both political and economic independence. All the goods previously directed to Copan could now remain at Quirigua for later reshipment or distribution through the valley. This may have introduced two new factors into the regional situation: greater wealth for the Quirigua elite now free of the Copan monopoly of profits, and a greater need than before to generate tradable commodities to maintain their newfound strategic economic position. Formerly, the prestige of Copan along with the commodities it exchanged might have made Quirigua an attractive place for merchants to congregate. Indeed, Quirigua's strategic break-bulk location would have given it a "natural" middleman status in a passive sense—i.e., allowed it to profit from monitoring and controlling exchanges taking place within its boundaries (see Schortman 1978; also Sabloff and Rathje 1975). But once on its own, more profits could

be obtained, and continued commerce through it ensured, if Quirigua had some high-value good to offer and became, in short, an active middleman. As the name implies, active middlemen not only control the economic transactions of traders who congregate at their centers but also take part in the trading themselves (see Schortman 1978). They could do this, possibly, by organizing long-distance caravans to acquire goods for exchange or through their control of a valuable local resource marketable through interregional exchange networks (see also Fagan 1972; Lamphear 1970; Miracle 1960; Roberts 1970). Prior to Quirigua's independence, Copan may have either provided the goods for exchange or acted to suppress any active middleman aspirations of the local Quirigua elite. Afterward, it is proposed, Quirigua's rulers intensified control of their administrative zone, as represented by the building of the Class IV Jubuco and Chapulco centers, and domination of the Class II Morja site, as a step to intensifying the local production of some valued commodity, presumably cacao (Ashmore 1981b). This would have provided Quirigua with its local tradable resource.

At the same time, the demand for increasing quantities of cacao, or some other valued product, filtered down the valley and led to the development of good agricultural land capable of producing this or some other important crop. The consequence was the rapid growth of large Class II/III centers. The extent of this intensification of production may be reflected in the position of the Class III sites of Choco and Quebrada Grande. Their large size and location away from major extravalley trade routes suggest that their growth was dependent solely on access to good agricultural lands and, presumably, on the "boom" period of cacao or other cultivated crops.

The social hierarchy reflected in sites such as Las Quebradas and Playitas may have been built on a local, ranked base, although evidence for this earlier social system has not yet been found. The demands placed on their interaction partners within the LMV by Quirigua's rulers would have required some form of adaptation to facilitate increased surplus production and/or the efficient movement of traded goods. One likely reaction to this stress would have been the development of local social hierarchies (Johnson 1978, 1983; Schortman and Urban 1987). Similarly, as wider-valley Class II/III centers strove to increase, say, cacao production the new social leaders would have received, in turn, access to more imported goods, especially from Quirigua. This differential access to highly valued imports would have allowed the emerging elites to accumulate wealth and, by extension, power and prestige (Flannery 1968; Schortman and Urban 1987). The importance of control over imports in the process of political centralization and hierarchy development has been ably explored by several recent authors (e.g., Earle 1987; Freidel 1986b; Spencer 1982). Simply put, I would hypothesize that exclusive elite access to goods derived from outside the wider-valley social systems, and so outside local kin-based requirements to share, would have put these leaders in a position to monopolize an important resource. These goods could then have been distributed to local populations in the context of gift-giving or feasts, and so serve to cement and expand intrasocietal alliances—along which lines surplus production traveled up the social hierarchy. Similarly, elites could increase surplus production or labor contributed to public work projects by introducing more of these imports or "political currency" into the system (e.g., Freidel 1986b; Spencer 1982: 42-47). The elites' increased power was then reflected in the large amounts of labor they could command for large-scale building projects. In this model, growing trade demands emanating from Quirigua both posed stresses to which LMV societies adapted, and provided the means by which local social hierarchies developed to meet those demands.

Social complexity, however, despite the rapid physical growth of elite centers, remained relatively low in LMV sites, with the only major social distinction being between commoners and elite. The latter group, while performing some administrative, ceremonial, and economic services for fairly large areas, was not internally specialized and the services it offered may have been only infrequently performed. That is, there is no evidence for the diversification of structure forms and groupings which might indicate a concomitant increase in the importance of, and specialization in, certain high-level activities. All of the administrative, economic, and ceremonial functions at these sites were probably carried out by the elite in and around their residential complexes, the quadrangles. That some social and activity differentiation was beginning to occur is suggested by the aforementioned ranking of quadrangles within a site by size, complexity, and architectural elaboration, along with the marked differences in the size and extent of monumental sites, e.g., Class II sites vs. Class V examples. Both facts

suggest the development of differential access to local labor and, hence, a hierarchy of control over dependent populations. The Class V sites and the few presumably nondomestic structures noted at the larger centers also point to the rudimentary development of specialization in elite-level activity performance. None of the wider-valley centers approach Quirigua on these points. This is probably due to both Quirigua's longer history of *in situ* development as an elite center and the ties of its rulers to the socially complex Maya lowlands (Sharer 1978, 1990; also Chap. 8).

This growth process did not continue indefinitely, for by AD 850 major construction at all known LMV centers stopped. The cessation of building activity was abrupt, as evidenced by unfinished structures at Playitas (Str. 200-24) and Quirigua. Quirigua may have been occupied beyond this date, but it had apparently suffered a great loss of power and wealth. If the rapid rise in LMV settlement complexity is attributable to trade, then the reasons for its decline might also be found there. It is possible that with the increased sophistication in deep-water navigation technology that presumably took place in the Postclassic period (AD 900-1500) in Mesoamerica (Sabloff and Rathje 1975; Sharer 1979: 28-29), Quirigua, relatively far from the coast, lost out to new competitors closer to the Caribbean (Sharer 1978, 1979). Certainly, it might still have controlled commerce along the Motagua, though even this route could have been bypassed in importance by the Lake Izabal-Polochic connection to the sea. With depopulation in the central Maya lowlands, overland travel along the north-south passes decreased in importance, causing additional problems for Quirigua and the Class II sites that depended on these external contacts for imports. The valley's production of cacao might have come under the control of a seaport center, possibly Nito (reported by Cortes near Lake Izabal [ibid.]), or been usurped in importance by the groves along the Rio Polochic to the north, which appear in the Aztec tribute lists (Bergman 1969: 94). Whatever the case, elites at Quirigua and other valley centers, who had developed in response to the pressures of interregional commerce and by means of control of that commerce, could not withstand a rapid decrease in trade volume (see Schortman and Urban 1987). Unable to rationalize their superordinate positions on the grounds of the organization of trade or to monopolize control of imported "political currency," social leaders lost their local legitimacy and preeminence. The result was a return to a simpler social system, resident in small, as yet undiscovered sites. The rapidity in the growth and demise of the valley polities may be reflected in the apparently truncated settlement pattern. The currently known Late Classic system is "top-heavy" with a relatively large number of Class II/III centers and few of their presumed subordinates, the Class IV and V loci. It is possible that the latter were still developing at the time when the "boom" collapsed.

The above models, synchronic and diachronic, are offered as propositions to be tested and further refined. The manner in which this might be done is outlined in Chap. 9.

VIII

Interregional Interaction

The purpose of this chapter is to use the data and reconstructions presented earlier in this report to phrase hypotheses concerning the processes of interregional interaction that linked the residents of the LMV, including those at Quirigua, with contemporary populations in neighboring zones. In particular, I will focus on reconstructing the nature, intensity, and directions of these contacts as well as on their effects on local processes of sociopolitical change.

We will begin by addressing a very basic question: Why did the hallmarks of "Maya culture" (listed in Table 8.1), so well represented at Quirigua, fail to diffuse to the investigated portions of the contemporary LMV? The flat floodplain of the Motagua certainly presented no physical obstacles to the spread of these traits, nor were the major Class II/III centers in question located at considerable distances from Quirigua. The answer, therefore, must be sought in the operation of other variables, including the environments occupied by the primary LMV interactors, the natures of their societies, and the circumstances of the interactions themselves. We will begin by examining the nature and significance of the Maya material pattern as represented at Quirigua.

THE MAYA

In an earlier work (1984: 668-672) I have presented in some detail the arguments for Quirigua's status as a Maya center. Suffice it to say here that Quirigua has long been recognized as falling into the "Maya" category because of its possession of a majority of the definitive traits enumerated in Table 8.1. This simple categorization does not take us very far, however, in understanding the behavioral significance of these traits or toward providing an answer to our initial question. In order to interpret the distribution of Maya cultural items within the Late Classic LMV and determine what information they can provide us on patterns of interaction, we must attempt to place these traits in their behavioral contexts (see Hodder 1978c: 102, 104, 110; Lange 1976: 180). Until the cultural roles of artifacts can be inferred, little behavioral information will be derived from plotting their distributions (e.g., Ball 1983; Binford 1962; R. Haaland 1977: 1-3; Hodder 1978a: 24; 1986). The principal weakness of the trait-list approach is that it combines the products of a number of different behavioral spheres into a single monolithic entity, an archaeological culture, whose spatial distribution is frequently seen as coterminous with the existence of an equally monolithic and culturally homogeneous prehistoric population (see Shennan 1978: 114-118, 135).

The first step in our reconstruction of ancient interaction patterns is, therefore, to specify the behavioral significance of the Maya traits under study (see Table 8.2). In order to achieve this end I suggest the following behavioral subdivisions: technological, social, ideological, and proxemic (see Schortman 1986, 1989; Schortman and Urban 1987). The technological class consists of those material traits which reflect a society's methods of construction, production, and consumption. The dissemination of these elements depends primarily on the recipient's mastery of a set of mechanical skills and access to appropriate raw materials. As a result, the distribution of technological traits is controlled primarily by environmental factors.

The proxemic category includes those elements which reflect a society's conceptions of the proper use of space (e.g., Donley 1982; Hall 1973; Rapoport 1982). In Table 8.2, the fact that temple groups are associated with plazas, while palace and quadrangle groups are not, suggests that the activities carried out within the first configuration were public while those linked to the last were private. The ideological realm includes features that reflect something of the belief structure of the group, both religious views and underlying rationalizations for the sociopolitical system. Maya glyphic inscriptions fit well in this class as they had extensive relationships with both cosmological (calendrics) and political (dynastic histories) aspects of elite Maya life. Religious structures and signs of ritual performance also fall into this category as do

TABLE 8.1

CHARACTERISTICS OF MAJOR LOWLAND CLASSIC MAYA SITES

Architecture
    Substructure Platforms
        Cut-block masonry
        Plaster
        Broad staircases, usually only one on a structure
    Superstructures
        Cut-block masonry
        Plaster
        Temple, Palace, and Shrine Forms
        Decoration in stucco or stone with frequent use of paint
        Roof combs
        Stone vault
        Burials and caches within construction, including residences
    Special Structures
        Ballcourts and Ballcourts markers
        Terraces
    Special Features
        Superimposed construction
Monuments
    Characteristics
        Carved stelae and associated altars, often with glyphs
        Associated with dedicatory caches
    Location
        In plazas
Artifacts
    Ceramics
        Decorated polychromes with "traditional Maya" designs
    Obsidian
        Polyhedral cores with their associated prismatic blades
Site Morphology
    Appearance
        Orthogonal site plans
    Structure Groups
        Temple groups
        Palace groups
        Acropoleis
        Quadrangles

References: G. Andrews 1975:1-78; Coe 1965; Hardoy 1973:203-209, 222, 229, 233; Longyear 1947; Marquina 1964:506-516; Pollock 1965; Proskouriakoff 1963:xi-xii, xv-xvii; Ruz 1965; Smith 1950; Thompson 1966:60-65, 68, 70-71, 73, 77-80; 1970.

interment practices, insofar as these last activities reflect concepts of the afterlife and the relationship of the living to the dead. Within the social category are items suggesting the range of activities carried out at a site in order to articulate individuals within a coherent, interacting group. The importance of these activities and the extent to which they require special physical facilities for their performance are also in-

TABLE 8.2

Characteristics of Major Classic Lowland Maya Sites Arranged by Behavioral Categories

Technological
  Architecture
  Substructure Platforms
  Cut-block masonry
  Plaster
  Broad staircases, usually only one on a structure
  Superstructures
  Cut-block masonry
  Plaster
  Decoration in stucco or stone with frequent use of
    paint
  Roof combs
  Stone vault
  Special Features
  Superimposed construction
  Artifacts
  Ceramics
  Decorated polychromes with "traditional Maya"
    designs
  Obsidian
  Polyhedral cores with their associated prismatic
    blades
Proxemic
  Special Structures
    Terraces
  Site Morphology
  Appearance
    Orthogonal Site Plans
  Structure Groupings
    Temple groups
    Palace groups
    Acropoleis
    Quadrangles
  Monuments
  Location
  In plazas

Ideological
  Architecture
  Superstructures
  Temple and shrine forms
  Burials and caches associated with construction;
    burials also found beneath the floors of residen-
    tial structures
  Special Structures
  Ballcourts and ballcourt markers
  Monuments
  Characteristics
  Carved stelae and associated altars, often with
    glyphs
  Associated with dedicatory caches
  Location
  In plazas
Social
  Architecture
  Superstructures
  Temple, palace, and shrine forms
  Site Morphology
  Temple groups
  Palace groups
  Acropoleis
  Quadrangles

cluded. As noted in Chap. 6, it is assumed here that the larger and more complexly organized a society is, the more diversified and specialized will be the activities carried out to integrate all of its segments. This relationship should find material expression in the size of public architecture, its diversity of form and groupings, and the sizes and numbers of residences built to house the governing social segment (see also

Flannery and Marcus 1976: 206, 220-221; Sanders 1974: 98, 109; Spencer 1982: 13). Maya structure forms and groups are included in this class. Social and political factors controlled the dissemination of elements functioning in the last three categories with the physical environment playing a less significant role.

The list presented in Table 8.2 is undoubtedly incomplete. More detailed study of Maya monumental centers would surely reveal other material similarities that could be related to the four behavioral categories. There is also some overlap among the defined subdivisions. Elements included in one class might well be found in others as well. This is because behavioral typologies arbitrarily divide the continuum of a culture into smaller units for analysis. In reality, any one material item or pattern is formed by a number of different factors and its final configuration reflects the operation of these factors to some degree. Taking the temple group as an example, the arrangement of these massive pyramidal platforms owes something to the Maya conception of the proper use of space (proxemics) and to their system of beliefs (ideology), and reflects the complex nature of the society that built them and was integrated through the activities pursued in and around these constructions (social). Nevertheless, the proposed classification provides an initial basis for understanding the factors that may have controlled the distribution of Maya traits within the LMV in particular and southern Mesoamerica in general. It does this by requiring that we explain any trait distribution in terms of factors relevant to the behavioral realm in which a trait originally functioned (Binford 1962; Cohen 1978: 383).

Having made this subdivision of the Maya trait list, I will go on to postulate that the rulers of Late Classic Quirigua were part of an extensive interregional interaction network, which linked the social leaders of distinct polities throughout the Maya lowlands. This elite interaction system included those individuals who shared a wide range of basic assumptions, values, and standards for evaluating proper behavior in all of the defined behavioral realms. These assumptions, standards, and values were manifest materially in the extensive distribution throughout the southern lowlands of the co-occurring traits listed in Table 8.2. As I have argued elsewhere (1986, 1989; Urban and Schortman 1987), the sharing of such an extensive set of material similarities strongly suggests that the Late Classic Lowland Maya, including the rulers of Quirigua, shared a single social identity that set them apart both from their subjects, who retained regionally distinctive behavioral and material patterns, and from other southern Mesoamerican elites.

The sharing of this identity and the symbols signifying membership in it had significant effects on the structure and functioning of Lowland Maya polities. First, the holding in common of a single affiliation among widely dispersed elites would have greatly facilitated communication over long distances. By sharing a wide range of basic assumptions the members of this elite identity system could easily communicate with and trust one another, a situation that is often difficult to achieve across social and political boundaries (Schortman 1989; Freidel 1979; 1986b: 419-420; Rathje 1972). This phenomenon can be seen operating in a number of different ethnographic and historical cases where spatially dispersed populations maintained close contact with one another, despite conditions of poor transportation, by sharing a common identity in terms of which interaction was carried out. Examples include the trading diasporas discussed by Curtin (1975, 1984) and Cohen (1969) as well as the European aristocracy of the Middle Ages (Anderson 1971).

Social identities such as those cited above and reconstructed for the Maya are generally employed as parts of strategies by individuals to accomplish a particular set of goals. The ethnographic literature suggests that one such goal is the control of interregional trade (e.g., Cohen 1969; Curtin 1975, 1984). I would argue here that the traits listed in Table 8.2 symbolized and reflected the existence of a supralocal elite identity network used by its members to secure the efficient and safe passage of exchanged goods over large parts of the Maya lowlands (see also Freidel 1979, 1981). Accompanying these exchanges and reinforcing the personal connections on which they were based were ceremonial (R. Adams 1971) and social interchanges, e.g., marriage alliances (Molloy and Rathje 1974).

Not only did the sharing of a common identity facilitate interregional trade across the Maya lowlands, but it ensured that the members of the elite identity network could effectively monopolize these exchanges. The case has been made before that intersocietal trade in the Late Classic Maya lowlands was an elite monopoly (e.g., Rathje 1972). One way to guarantee that monopoly was by limiting access to interregional exchanges to those who prominently displayed the symbols of membership in the pan-lowland identity system and gave evidence of knowing the appropriate behaviors associated with them (see Cohen 1981; Kipp and Schortman 1989; Wobst 1977). This use of identity membership and its symbols to restrict access to interregional trade is commonly attested in the operation of ethnographically and historically documented trading diasporas such as the Swahili (Donley 1982), Hausa (Cohen 1969), and Jahaanke Mori (Curtin 1975) of Africa. By drawing symbolic boundaries around participation in long-

distance trade, ruling elites could effectively monopolize the acquisition and distribution of nonlocal resources and so enhance their own local power and
prestige (see Kipp and Schortman 1989). Imports
thus obtained from interregional trade could then be
used by local rulers as markers of their preeminent
status within their societies and as gifts and rewards to
their dependents to cement intrasocietal alliances and
ensure continued surplus production (Freidel 1986b;
Spencer 1982; Earle 1987).

The sharing of a pan-Maya identity among the
dispersed ruling elite of the southern Mesoamerican
lowlands would have both facilitated trade and ensured that the control of the imports resulting from
those exchanges remained firmly in elite hands. The
"Maya identity" was, therefore, used strategically by
spatially dispersed social leaders to maintain and
enhance their local positions of power and prestige.
The Maya were certainly not alone in recognizing the
utility of such extensive identity systems, as these
affiliations have been noted in a number of different
areas around the world and seem to represent a
common adaptation to the problems of carrying out
and monopolizing trade among distinct complex societies (e.g., Hopewell [Brose and Greber 1979; Braun
1986], Mississippian [Brown 1975, 1976], Bell-Beaker
[Shennan 1982, 1986], Chavin [Patterson 1971]; see
also Earle 1987; Freidel 1981, 1986b; Schortman
1989; Schortman and Urban 1987).

It should be noted that sharing an identity does not
preclude the possibility of conflict, even warfare,
among its holders. Such intra-identity hostilities have
been attested for the Maya themselves (e.g., Freidel
1986a) as well as within other identity systems (e.g.,
the Mississippian of North America [Brown 1975], the
aristocracy of medieval Europe [Anderson 1971]).
While research on these competitive relations remains

scant, it does not appear that such skirmishing precludes continued contact (e.g., ibid.: 104). In fact,
those armed conflicts may be carried out in accordance with rules subject to the standards of behavior
dictated by the common identity (e.g., Renfrew 1986:
9-10; Schele and Freidel 1990).

In sum, I hypothesize that the demands of interregional trade in the Late Classic lowlands of southern
Mesoamerica required the development of strong
personal bonds that would effectively unite the primary traders, the elite, in dispersed, politically autonomous societies. These ties took the form of a pan-
Lowland Maya social identity whose holders shared a
wide array of assumptions, values, and standards for
evaluating behavior. Participation in this system was
symbolized by and reflected in the traits listed in Table
8.2. Once established, this identity network facilitated
the exchange of goods over long distances and was
used by local elites to monopolize control of imports
by restricting access to interregional exchanges to
those who possessed the appropriate identity symbols
and knowledge of their use. The rulers of Quirigua,
therefore, were part of this interaction network, as
were their compatriots to the south at Copan. It may
well be that some of the unusual features of Copan
and Quirigua, especially the size and elaborateness of
their carved monuments and the location of these
stones in highly visible areas, are explained by the
position of these sites on the southern margins of the
Maya identity network. Situated so far from the
network core, rulers may have felt compelled to
"overstate" their Maya affiliations to prove that their
identity remained undiluted by distance (Urban and
Schortman 1988). Their self-image as well as economic well-being may have depended on their success
in making this case.

THE MAYA IN THE LOWER MOTAGUA VALLEY

Having made the argument concerning the behavioral significance of the Maya identity system and
Quirigua's place within it, we can now return to our
initial question of why the other LMV elite did not
participate in this system. This question is especially
significant as much of the developing literature on the
spread of social identities is concerned with why new
groups acculturate to these affiliations and not with
the factors underlying resistance to or exclusion from
participation (cf. Urban and Schortman 1988). The
reasons advanced here for the exclusion of the wider-

valley elite from the Maya identity system fall into
three categories: differences in the environments occupied, the natures of the societies in contact, and
interactions between Quirigua's elite and other LMV
rulers.

The presence of elements in the Maya technological
sphere at Quirigua and their absence from other
monumental LMV sites may reflect no more than the
differential distribution of necessary raw materials. It
is obvious from even a casual examination that river
cobbles, the most common building material in the

research area, are abundant near wider-valley centers. Similarly, easily worked sandstone and rhyolite are found close by Quirigua (P. Muller, pers. comm. 1979). While detailed geological surveys have not been carried out within the wider valley, no sandstone or rhyolite outcrops were located during the survey. The distribution of Maya technological traits within the valley would seem to owe a lot to such prosaic concerns as ready access to appropriate resources.

Interestingly, turning to the proxemic realm we find a close similarity between Quirigua and its other valley contemporaries in the presence of a structure grouping, the quadrangle, used in both areas for the same purpose, elite residence and administration. In general, proxemic patterns do not spread easily from one society to another, as they are learned "out of awareness" and hence form assumptions that are crucial to daily life and rarely questioned (Hall 1973: 162-185). The prominence of the quadrangle in both Quirigua and other valley centers' site plans, therefore, implies the existence of a set of proxemic assumptions shared among their residents. This distribution may be due to the existence of an ancient valley-wide practice of structure arrangement predating the Late Classic. Alternatively, the ubiquity of this form may stem from its having been borrowed wholesale from the residents of Quirigua by the newly developing wider-valley elite. If the absence of pre-Late Classic monumental construction is not merely the result of sampling error and alluvial burial, then it would appear that the local elites did not have a long tradition of hierarchic social organization and the construction of facilities associated with its activities. Consequently, there may have been no model for such large-scale constructions other than that provided by Quirigua's rulers. The borrowing of this set of innovations would not have conflicted with any preexisting set of proxemic assumptions within wider-valley societies concerning the organization of "elite space." Only more work in the valley will help determine which of these alternative interpretations is correct.

The differences between Quirigua and the massive Class II/III centers in the social and ideological realms can be explained, in part, by reference to cultural and social factors. A considerable part of this variation may be accounted for by the different levels of social complexity represented in these two segments of the LMV (see Chaps. 6 and 7). It is probable that the societies integrated through Class II and III sites were neither sufficiently large nor complexly enough segmented to warrant the investment of labor

in the construction of elaborate physical facilities for diverse elite activities. The result is that the varied Maya structure forms and groupings associated with the integration of large, complex lowland societies could not readily spread throughout the research area. The level of complexity of wider-valley polities did not warrant the acceptance of these traits and the sociopolitical systems they represented. Similarly, ideological elements of the Maya system, such as glyphic inscriptions with their ties to both Maya religion (calendrics) and political legitimization (dynastic histories), could not easily be transferred to areas where these complex sociopolitical conditions did not exist (see Hodder 1977: 247). Coupled with this restriction was the tremendous body of esoteric knowledge the recipient group would have to master before they could read or write in the hieroglyphic script. The result is the absence of inscriptions in the simpler social systems of the wider valley. Further, what we can surmise of wider-valley religious practices, with their ceremonial foci hidden away in inaccessible parts of sites, conflicts with what we know of these practices in the Late Classic Maya lowlands. In the latter area at least some rites were performed for large audiences in plazas associated with temple groups. If these religious differences were significant and widespread then there may have been little incentive, and perhaps much reluctance, among wider-valley populations to adopt elite Maya religious practices and their material manifestations.

While cultural and environmental differences may well have played significant roles in determining the distribution of Maya behavioral patterns and their material correlates throughout the research area, other significant factors pertain to the nature of the interactions between Maya and non-Maya. As noted earlier, participation in the Maya elite identity, reflected in the distribution of traits in Table 8.2, allowed its members to effectively monopolize trade within the Classic-period southern Maya lowlands. Consequently, the Maya rulers of Quirigua may have consciously sought to restrict access to the symbols of their identity and, thereby, exclude other valley notables from direct participation in that trade. If the wider-valley rulers had been able to acquire these symbols they would have been in a better position to compete with Quirigua's dynasts for the control of commerce. It may also have been important to the self-image of the Quirigua elite to retain exclusive control over symbols of elite Maya identity membership within the valley. This would especially be the case if, as seems likely, Quirigua's rulers were an intrusive element within the valley (Kelley 1962; Morley 1935; Sharer 1978). In this case, the self-esteem of the Quirigua elite may have rested, in part, on their continued distinctiveness as a nonlocal group whose ties lay toward "high-prestige" zones in the Peten.

These points still do not answer the basic question of why the wider-valley elite were not incorporated to some extent within the Maya elite identity network. If the reconstruction of intense intravalley interaction during the Late Classic advanced in Chap. 7 is correct, it seems that these close contacts should have led to the sharing of the same identity to facilitate contact and communication. One significant factor here may have been competition between Quirigua and its LMV contemporaries, a competition so profound and pervasive that it precluded the spread of the Maya identity. Ethnographic (e.g., Barth 1969a; Cohen 1978: 396-397; Collins 1975: 70-72; Despres 1975; Fishman 1977: 26-27; Hodder 1977; Knutsson 1969: 90-95, 99) and archaeological (e.g., Brose 1979; Hodder 1979) research indicates that one element contributing to the exclusive distribution of material-culture patterns among two or more adjoining societies is competition for the same set of resources. Under this condition, material and nonmaterial cultural features that distinguish one group from another are emphasized as symbols of the corporate will to compete (Shibutani and Kwan 1965: 220, 465) or to ensure the rapid and accurate identification of affiliations among the interactants (e.g., Rapoport 1982). The latter identification facilitates assigning rights of access to available resources where competition is resolved through granting such rights to the holders of particular identities (e.g., Barth 1969b: 25-26; Brose 1979; G. Haaland 1969: 71; Shibutani and Kwan 1965: 577). Competition, active or resolved, places a premium on the participant's ability to clearly assign each individual encountered to a particular identity. This results in the proliferation of social symbols (proxemic, social, and ideological domains) that "overstate" affiliations and so avoid errors in recognizing group affiliation (Rapoport 1982).

Within the Late Classic LMV, competition among the residents of monumental sites, including Quirigua, may have been over both local resources and external trade routes. As noted earlier, Class II/III centers are located so as to control large expanses of good agricultural land, possibly used for cacao production (Chap. 7). There could well have been intravalley rivalry over

land suitable for growing this crop. Equally important may have been competition for control of extravalley trade. Quirigua and the largest Class II settlements are all located so as to control potential routes of egress from the region. This distribution suggests the importance to their residents of participation in inter-regional commerce, and there may well have been some contesting for its control. The significance of this commerce to the wider-valley elite is reflected in the reported distribution of large centers strung out along the Chinamito and Bobos routes on the Honduran side of the sierra (Nakamura 1985, 1987, 1988; Nakamura et al. 1986). The close similarity in details of site plans and ceramics among monumental centers on both sides of the sierra along these routes (see Techin, Piladeros, and Tras Cerros in Nakamura 1987) further suggests that elites in Class II centers were involved in a distinct identity system that stretched south and away from areas controlled by the Maya. This involvement would have motivated the wider-valley elite to maintain their distinct material patterns to symbolize membership in this developing transmontane interaction system. Adoption of behavioral and material innovations from Quirigua by Class II elites would have threatened their participation in this non-Maya system. The limited attested extent of this southern non-Maya network could be the result of the short time period in which it developed and spread (apparently limited to the Late Classic) and/or to our still-limited knowledge of material patterns in southeastern Mesoamerica (see Urban and Schortman 1988). Whatever the case, the distribution of monumental sites along the Chinamito and Bobos routes, and the possible development of a dispersed identity network linking their elites, support the argument that competition for control over interregional trade played a large part in conditioning Late Classic interactions and material distributions within the Late Classic LMV.

It should be remembered that while the large Class II valley centers, Playitas and Las Quebradas, share a considerable number of material similarities they are not identical. Specifically, Las Quebradas has two large plazas as well as monuments, while Playitas lacks both features but possesses stone tenoned-head sculpture not found at its northern contemporary. These features are related to the proxemic and ideological realms of behavior and may hint at significant differences in the nonmaterial value orientations of both polities. This suggests that competition was not limited within the valley to two monolithic entities of

"Maya" and "non-Maya" but was found among wider-valley societies as well. As research proceeds under the aegis of the La Entrada Archaeological Project at centers such as Piladeros and Techin, it will be interesting to note whether these behavioral and material distinctions also characterize sites along the Bobos and Chinamito routes. The results of this work will help us understand to what extent these large sites were participating in different, competitive, interaction systems.

Intersocietal competition need not preclude regular interactions among societies (e.g., Barth 1969b: 10; Hodder 1977, 1979). In fact, research in the specific area of ethnic identities has shown that these affiliations exist only in opposing pairs at the same level of generalization (e.g., Barth 1969b; Cohen 1978; Royce 1982). Not only is opposition between identities an important element in their maintenance, but it is frequently in terms of these affiliations that interpersonal interaction is structured. Individuals organize their behaviors according to their expectations of other people's actions based on their proclaimed affiliation (ibid.). The contrasting elite identity systems operating within the Late Classic LMV thus need not have seriously hampered intraregional interaction. The great similarities in the ceramics of Quirigua and its wider-valley neighbors certainly argue for intense interaction throughout the period. Similarly, if the reconstruction of intraregional exchange patterns proposed in Chap. 7 is valid, then Quirigua's residents would have been the principal middlemen for the valley's supply of imports and so some persistent intersocietal commerce would have been essential.

SUMMARY

This chapter has argued that a variety of factors, acting together, determined the distribution of Maya material traits within the Late Classic LMV. These factors fall within three categories: the physical environments of the interacting groups, differences in their respective social and cultural contents, and the circumstances of interelite interactions. It is possible, of course, that other as yet unnamed variables played significant roles in determining the observed distributions. Needless to say, as with all of the hypotheses advanced in this report, these views must be tested by further work both within the LMV and in neighboring regions, including detailed examinations of Maya material patterns themselves, to determine how well the notion of a Maya elite identity system fits the available data. Nevertheless, this effort has suggested that there is considerable information to be gleaned from the study of material traits and their distribution.

IX

Conclusions

This chapter summarizes the interpretations discussed in Chaps. 5-8, based on the LMV data presented in Chaps. 2-4 and App. I, stated as a series of untested hypotheses. Each hypothesis is followed by a brief summary of the evidence on which it is based. These hypotheses are grouped into the major interpretive categories to which they apply, i.e., chronology, intrasite activity patterning, regional interaction, and interregional interaction, arranged in order from those for which the supporting data are most secure to those for which support is least secure.

These summary hypotheses have been derived from the data collected by the LMV program, and are intended to act as the starting point for the next phase of investigation in the region. To facilitate the future testing of these propositions, the concluding section of this chapter details a series of suggestions as to how future work might be carried out in the valley.

SUMMARY OF HYPOTHESES

A. CHRONOLOGY

A-1)

The LMV sites, monumental and nonmonumental, recorded during this survey date to the Terminal Late Classic period (c. AD 700-850).

Evidence

a) Ceramics: The LMV ceramic types and forms correspond very closely to those dated to AD 700-850 at Quirigua. Beyond Quirigua, certain LMV pottery types closely match dated ceramic taxa in western Honduras that fall within the period AD 550-810 (see Table 5.5). If we assume that similar ceramic taxa were used at about the same time, the construction and occupation of the three excavated wider-valley centers of Las Quebradas, Playitas, and Choco fall within the Terminal Late Classic. Those sites which were not excavated but did produce surface collections (see Table 5.3) are tentatively dated to the same period.

b) Incensarios: Censer forms from the LMV sites fit well with those defined by Benyo (1979: 41) as characteristic of Construction Stages 2-1 at Quirigua (c. AD 700-850).

c) Site planning: The general plan characteristic of monumental LMV sites, with its central quadrangle and surrounding smaller structures, was also found at Quirigua in its final stages of construction (c. AD 700-900). While there is some question as to how sensitive site plans are to change (see Chap. 5), it is

suggestive that the site-plan data support the chronological placement based on ceramic and *incensario* analyses. Those unexcavated sites not producing surface collections are assigned a tentative Terminal Late Classic date based on the similarity of their site organization to other LMV sites and Quirigua.

d) Other lines of evidence: The reconstructed period of primary wider-valley construction at excavated sites encompasses only c. 150 years. The relative brevity of this span is supported by absence of stratified deposits; shallowness of middens; lack of evidence for temporal depth associated with sequent construction; lack of significant differences in artifacts from terminal debris, fill, and preconstruction contexts; and general paucity of preconstruction debris. All of this evidence suggests that the centers of Playitas, Las Quebradas, and Choco were the products of relatively short occupations. The available surface collections support this view for the other, unexcavated sites as they all contain the same limited range of ceramic types that characterize the excavated assemblages. Obviously, the dating of all wider-valley sites must ultimately be based on an extensive and systematic excavation program.

A-2)

While the Terminal Late Classic is the major recognized period of occupation, there are earlier, nonmonumental LMV settlements dating back to the Late Preclassic and/or Early Classic period.

Evidence

Ceramics: The evidence for earlier occupation in the LMV is scattered and derives mostly from beneath the river alluvium. Some diagnostic Early Classic/Late Preclassic ceramic types, in particular Usulutan-decorated taxa, and figurines have been recovered from the backdirt and faces of BANDEGUA drainage canals on the Motagua floodplain. When found *in situ*, this material usually comes from deep within the canals with no visible evidence of its presence on the surface. Some scattered fragments of pre-Late Classic ceramics have also been found in local private collections, although nowhere are they plentiful. As no clear architectural remains of this period have yet been recovered, it is presumed that the sites involved are relatively small.

B. INTRASITE ACTIVITY PATTERNING: DOMESTIC ACTIVITIES

B-1)

The majority of the large and small structures at all wider-valley centers served, in part, as the loci of domestic activities.

Evidence

a) Ceramics: The ceramics found at all of the excavated structures are primarily utilitarian types (see Table 6.3) as identified by their limited form inventory (widemouthed bowls and jars), lack of decoration, and general crudeness of manufacture. This distribution (13 of 15 excavated groups had over 75.6% utilitarian ceramics in terminal debris contexts) suggests that domestic activities involving these ceramics were carried out on all of the investigated structures.

b) Lithics: Both obsidian blade and flake tools were found in the terminal debris of most large and small structures (nine of 11 excavated structures contained *both* blade and flake tools). This suggests that the domestic tasks in which they were used (e.g., Lewenstein 1981) were widely distributed among most of the excavated structures (Table 6.6).

c) Site planning: The arrangement of structures at all recorded sites also suggests that most had domestic functions. Small, nonmonumental constructions are generally clustered into either orthogonal plaza groups or irregular aggregations, consistent with ethnohistoric and ethnographic descriptions of Maya residential patterning (e.g., Ashmore and Wilk 1988; Wisdom 1940; Wauchope 1938; Miles 1957). Similarly, the larger monumental structures are, by and large,

organized into orthogonal quadrangles built, apparently, to ensure the privacy of their occupants. These massive, high substructures commonly enclose a small interior court and access to both the courts and their surrounding structures is effectively restricted. This pattern of monumental construction has been associated archaeologically with residences within the Maya area (e.g., Harrison 1970: 251-253, 302-303; Hammond 1975; G. Andrews 1975: 63-66).

d) It should be noted that this hypothesis is based on two assumptions. First, that the recovery of an artifact in the terminal debris of a structure indicates that the activity in which that artifact functioned was performed on or near the investigated building. Given an absence of major postoccupation disturbance at the investigated platforms, this assumption appears to be valid. Future excavations will, hopefully, provide evidence in primary, use-related contexts to test this hypothesis. Second, it is assumed that evidence from investigated structures can be extended to all unexcavated architecture recorded by this project. While this assumption is supported by the site-plan data described above, and the recovered surface collections that contain predominantly utilitarian ceramics, it can be fully evaluated only by further excavation.

B-2)

Domestic maintenance activities were performed with variable intensity at the different structure groups within the monumental wider-valley sites, and there may have been some variation in the domestic activities performed among different structures in one group. Specific domestic tasks were not associated exclusively with large or small structures.

Evidence

a) Ceramics: Ceramic group percentages among utilitarian pottery collections from terminal debris vary between structure groups. This suggests that the domestic functions associated with each were not performed with equal intensity at each structure aggregation (see Table 6.8), if we assume that vessels in different ceramic groups served different, possibly overlapping, purposes. This hypothesis is further supported by differences in utilitarian vessel-form frequencies between structure groups (Table 6.5). Assuming that different vessel forms presumably were designed for different functions, these functions were variably distributed within the excavated sites.

b) Lithics: There is a slight tendency for obsidian tools to be concentrated in the environs of the small structures surrounding the monumental quadrangles as opposed to the terminal debris of those massive court complexes (Table 6.6). This suggests a slightly greater concentration of the tasks employing obsidian tools in the peripheries of the quadrangles.

c) Architecture: Among the excavated structures, several appear to have had certain specialized domestic functions within their particular groups. Structure 212-22 at Choco has a deep, V-shaped pit dug into its summit that might have been used for storage. This interpretation is based on the structure's small size and the restricted access to the interior pit from the top of the construction. Other structures within the group might then have functioned as sleeping quarters, kitchens, and so forth, according to ethnographic analogy (e.g., Ashmore and Wilk 1988; Wisdom 1940). Similarly, Str. 200-16 at Playitas, because of its small size and association with obsidian blade-production debris, may have acted as a platform for manufacturing activities within the larger structural group. This meager evidence, combined with the general observation that structures within groups of all sizes vary in height and basal dimensions, implies that internal variation in the performance of domestic activities is a strong possibility.

d) Ceramics and lithics: While there is some variation in the percentages of ceramic groups and forms and stone tools between structure groups, all excavated groups with large artifact samples from terminal debris contain all of the known utilitarian ceramic groups and stone tools. This suggests that while the intensity of performance of different activities varied between structure groups, basically the same domestic tasks were carried out at all of the investigated examples.

C. INTRASITE ACTIVITY PATTERNING: MANUFACTURE

C-1)

Class II and III centers served as loci for the production of obsidian blade and flake tools.

Evidence

Lithic debris: The debris marking the location of obsidian-tool manufacture consists of either polyhedral cores and macroblades for the blade-core industry, or flake-cores for the flake-core industry (Sheets 1983). At both Las Quebradas and Playitas, excavations uncovered evidence of blade- and flake-tool production from the terminal debris of several struc-

tures (see Table 6.6). At Quebrada Grande a polyhedral core was found in a surface collection. Choco produced no evidence of stone-tool manufacture (see Table 6.6), but this could be due to the small size of the excavated sample. No evidence of lithic-tool manufacture was recovered in surface collections from the unexcavated Class IV-VII sites. At present, this implies that obsidian-tool manufacture was not pursued at the latter sites. Further excavation, of course, must be conducted to establish this point.

C-2)

The manufacturing loci of blade and flake tools are distributed among the large and small structures at Class II and III centers and are not mutually exclusive; i.e., both blade and flake tools were manufactured at the same location. There is some tendency, however, for blade production to cluster in certain small-structure groups around the main quadrangles.

Evidence

Lithic debris: Obsidian tool-production debris was found in terminal deposits of both monumental and small structures at Playitas and Las Quebradas. Slightly over half of the total of this debris came from the smaller constructions (see Table 6.6).

Several structures and groups at Las Quebradas produced evidence of both obsidian blade- and flake-tool production (Las Quebradas West Group and Str. 205-196 in the East Group).

C-3)

Obsidian-tool production, whether in the blade or flake tradition, never exceeded levels required for local consumption. Obsidian-blade production involved some part-time specialization, while the manufacture of obsidian flake tools did not. The latter were probably made within individual households as needed.

Evidence

Lithic debris: The low volume of obsidian-tool production is suggested by the relative paucity of obsidian manufacturing debris found by excavation. The postulation of part-time specialists in blade production is based on research by Sheets (1983) concerning the skill and knowledge needed to strike prismatic blades from a core, and the assumption that such skill would not have been available to every household. Some low-level specialization in blade production for local-level redistribution is therefore likely, and is supported by the recovery of two polyhedral core fragments from the terminal debris of Str. 200-16 at Playitas. The recovery of two cores in close proximity suggests production of blade tools above the needs of the immediate household but, still, on a relatively small scale. The argument against specialization in flake-tool production is founded on the small amounts of flake-manufacturing detritus and the relative ease with which flakes can be struck from obsidian flake-cores (ibid.).

D. INTRASITE ACTIVITY PATTERNING: CEREMONIAL ACTIVITIES

D-1)

The vast majority of all wider-valley structures served, in part, as the loci for the performance of small-scale private rituals carried out for the benefit of the immediate residential unit.

Evidence

Incensario distribution: Seven of the 16 ceramic collections from the terminal debris of excavated individual structures contain 0.2-10.8% identifiable *incensario* pieces (only three contain none). If we assume that the presence of *incensario* fragments in the terminal debris of a structure reflects the performance of religious rites, this distribution indicates that ceremonial activities were carried out at both large and small structures. The relatively low percentages of the material correlates of ritual activities within terminal debris ceramic collections indicate that religious observances involving the use of *incensarios* were not intensively practiced at these structures.

That the rites performed were private is suggested by the low frequencies of *incensarios* from the investigated structures. This interpretation is further supported by the censer forms found in the relevant collections that have been associated at Quirigua with private religious observances (Benyo 1979). These compose the majority of the form-types found on and around large and small wider-valley constructions (see Table 6.9).

D-2)

The types of private rituals performed differed between the large and small structures.

Evidence

Incensario distribution: Monumental structures, in general, have higher percentages of modeled, spiked, and ladle censer forms than do the smaller structures, where lids are dominant. While the sample sizes for all structure types are small, the current evidence suggests that somewhat different rites were being performed in the large quadrangles than in the small constructions. I have assumed that there is at least a rough correlation between censer form and the specific type of ritual performed and that the pattern seen in the excavated data applies to unexcavated structures as well. The last assumption can be tested only with further excavation.

D-3)

The large monuments found at several wider-valley centers and a few monumental structures served as foci of public rituals carried out for the benefit of the larger social unit, i.e., the residents of the site and its sustaining hinterland.

Evidence: Monuments

a) Incensario density: Terminal debris ceramic collections associated with the four excavated Las Quebradas monuments (Mon. 1, 2, 4, and 5) contain very high percentages (8.3-78.9%) of identifiable *incensario* fragments, much higher than those noted from terminal debris contexts around structures (Table 6.9). These relatively high frequencies of censer debris strongly suggest that the monuments were important foci of public religious rituals using large numbers of *incensarios*. The relatively low percentages of utilitarian ceramic types in these contexts further indicate that the activities carried out around the monuments were restricted to ritual performances.

b) Incensario forms: At Quirigua, effigy modeled censers were found to be associated with public rituals (Benyo 1979). In the case of the four excavated wider-valley monuments, 78.4% of the 125 form-classified censers recovered from terminal debris contexts are of the effigy modeled type. If the analogy with Quirigua is valid, then this distribution suggests that the rituals carried out around the monuments were also public in nature.

c) Monuments: The monuments themselves are large, centrally located within quadrangle courts, and associated with prepared stone pavements, further suggesting their importance as religious foci.

Evidence: Structures

a) Incensario density: Two LMV monumental structures produced high percentages of censer fragments from their terminal debris—Str. 200-23 and -193 at

Playitas. These high *incensario* frequencies (33.82-77.51%) imply that some monumental platforms served as centers of public ritual performance. That this was not necessarily their only function is indicated at Str. 200-23, where utilitarian ceramics are also numerous.

b) Incensario forms: All of the *incensario* sherds recovered from Str. 200-23 are of the effigy modeled type associated with public rites at Quirigua. At Str. 200-193 the cruciform-vent form made up the majority of the censer fragments. At present, this form has not been linked to either public or private religious observances.

c) Structure forms: Several very large, unexcavated monumental platforms at Las Quebradas, Arapahoe Viejo, and Bobos may have served primarily ritual purposes. This surmise is based on their large size, steep flanks, and very narrow summits, all of which mitigate against their having served as loci of domestic activities. That they acted as ritual structures is also suggested by their formal similarity with pyramidal Maya temples. In addition, two possible ballcourts were noted at Las Quebradas. Ballcourts are generally associated with ritual activities in the Maya area (e.g., Hammond 1975).

The most striking examples of possibly ceremonial-oriented spaces in the LMV are the two massive plazas at Las Quebradas. These spaces are defined on three sides by monumental constructions; the south sides in particular are bounded by high pyramidal structures that could have had ceremonial functions. The open sides are delimited by relatively steep terraces. The distinctive form of these plazas, plus their association with possible ritual structures, suggests that they were the focus of religious activity, perhaps of a public nature. The limited excavations carried out in the bordering structures produced no supporting evidence for this contention. The monumental plaza at Arapahoe Viejo is also bounded by a high pyramidal structure, and may have served as a religious focus as well. Lacking a steep bordering terrace, however, the Arapahoe Viejo plaza was much more accessible than the Las Quebradas examples.

D-4)

Public rituals were performed by the resident elite (the occupants of the large, high, monumental quadrangles).

Evidence

Site planning: All foci of inferred public ritual activity are bounded by, or incorporated into, the monumental structures that served as elite residences (see Hypothesis E-1 immediately below). By virtue of this close association, it is proposed that the wider-valley elites resident in these large structures performed the public rituals.

E. INTRASITE ACTIVITY PATTERNING: ADMINISTRATION

E-1)

Ancient LMV societies were divided into two hierarchically arranged segments: the residents of the large/high monumental quadrangles (termed the *elite*) and the residents of the small, low, nonmonumental structures (termed the *nonelite*).

Evidence

a) Lithics: The presence of quantities of obsidian, most of it not locally available, at the three excavated LMV monumental centers implies the existence of an elite group with the managerial expertise to organize and fund the acquisition of this stone from distant sources.

b) Architecture: The marked differences in size between structures composing monumental courts and the surrounding smaller platforms strongly point to the existence of differential control of labor: an administrative elite capable of calling up, organizing, and supporting the labor forces required to construct the court complexes. The bulk of the population probably organized their own construction on a household level. The fact that both large and small structures were primarily domestic indicates that the inhabitants of the quadrangles were able to summon this labor for their own personal use. Differential control of labor is one of the hallmarks of an elite presence, based as it is on differential abilities to mobilize large networks of social obligations.

c) Site planning: The overall arrangement of the monumental courts into coherent, largely orthogonal, complexes implies the existence of a powerful planning agency capable of seeing its organizational schemes carried out.

E-2)

Beyond this basic division of society into two ranked segments, further ranked social distinctions existed within both the elite and nonelite populations.

Evidence

a) Site planning: At those centers with more than one contemporary quadrangle group (Las Quebradas, Playitas, and possibly Quebrada Grande), these court complexes could be ranked by total areas covered, size of component structures, and complexity (see Chap. 6). If we assume that the size and complexity of a structure group reflect the power and prestige of its occupants, then the ranking of court-group sizes seen at these site zones is a manifestation of social ranking within the elite groups.

The class of small, nonmonumental constructions also displays some variation in the size and complexity of structure groups (see Chap. 6). If the above assumption is correct, there probably was some social differentiation within the nonelite segment of the society as well. As with monumental quadrangles, this proposition is based on the further assumptions that the groups compared at a site are contemporary and that all performed essentially the same domestic functions; i.e., that differences in group sizes/complexity reflect social distinctions and not functional or temporal differences.

Finally, there is a direct relationship at the multi-court sites of Las Quebradas and Playitas between the size of a quadrangle and the number and density of the small structures that surround it. While the significance of this pattern cannot be firmly established at present it may also reflect the power and prestige of the residents of the largest courts. That is, the highest-ranked elite would attract more people to reside near them to share in the advantages that accrue through such association than would the lower-ranked elites resident in the smaller court complexes.

b) Architecture: A correlation may exist between the size of a court complex at a multi-court site and the degree of architectural decoration on its structures. This is clearest at Playitas, where the largest structure in the largest group (Str. 200-77 in Playitas Group I) is unique in having plaster and stone sculptural decorations. This implies that the residents of Group I were capable of calling on large amounts of both skilled and unskilled labor. Unfortunately, this relationship was not noted at Las Quebradas. The reason for this may be the small size of excavations at Las Quebradas. Should the correlation hold, however, it would suggest that the most powerful elite (in the largest courts) controlled more skilled labor reserves than did their less powerful contemporaries.

E-3)

The administrative power of the wider-valley elite was limited; they operated only on a local administrative level, and the amount of labor they could call on and wealth they could amass was not great. While they undoubtedly performed services for their respective dependent societies, the range of these services was small.

Evidence

a) Artifacts: Wealth is here defined as the accumulation of imported luxury goods such as jade, elaborate polychrome pottery, and similar exotic items. None of these objects were found within the wider-valley centers, in either excavation or surface collections. While the small scale of excavations warrants caution, it appears at this time that the wider-valley elite did not accumulate wealth to any great degree. The absence of luxury items may well indicate a limit on the elite's economic, organizational, and investment abilities.

b) Site planning: The site-plan data reflect the amount of labor the wider-valley elite could control. The largest excavated wider-valley centers, the multi-quadrangle sites, have a very fragmented spatial organization. Each is composed of three separate contemporary foci, the monumental court complexes, surrounded by smaller constructions that decrease in density as one moves away from the focal courts. Each quadrangle, then, is the center of its own spatially distinct collection of structures. This gives the appearance of a group of semi-autonomous elites residing at the largest centers, each surrounded by their own dependents and supporters. If this is the case, a proposition which must be further tested, it strongly suggests that even the highest-ranking LMV elite did not monopolize all of the available labor for their own use, did not organize the largest centers into a coherent whole, and did not severely impinge on the autonomy of the other elites resident at these sites.

c) Administrative activities: On the basis of architecture and site planning we surmise that the wider-valley elite controlled labor for monumental construction and monument placement; on the basis of lithic debris we surmise that they organized the acquisition and distribution of obsidian blades; on the basis of the location of public ritual foci we surmise that they served in a religious capacity for their dependent societies. Beyond these few statements little can be said about elite administrative roles. Unfortunately the material correlates of administrative activities

231

(hearing disputes, distributing land, and so forth) are notoriously hard to recognize archaeologically. The absence of specialized structures clearly related to the duties of administration, however, permits us to argue that the wider-valley rulers performed relatively few high-level services for their dependent societies. This opinion rests on the assumption that the more services the elite performed, the greater the need would have been for some special physical facilities to house these activities (e.g., Flannery and Marcus 1976; Sanders 1974). In the absence of these specialized structures, we presume that the administrative functions of the wider-valley elite were discharged at their places of residence. This association of residential and administrative activities has some precedent in the ethnohistoric literature for the Maya area (e.g., Harrison 1970: 251-253, 302-303).

d) The above hypothesis and supporting evidence are largely derived from the three excavated valley sites, but are meant to apply to all wider-valley centers with monumental constructions (Class II-V sites). Here the same differences in architectural size and pattern of structure arrangement are noted as were seen at the three more thoroughly investigated loci.

F. INTRASITE ACTIVITY PATTERNING: MARKETING

F-1)

Marketing did not play a major role in the functioning of the LMV monumental centers (Class II-V sites). "Marketing activities" here refers to the distribution of goods through a marketplace.

Evidence

a) Site planning: No surface or excavation data have been recovered that suggest the presence of market facilities at any of the investigated Class II-V centers. It is presumed that marketing facilities should be large and provide easy access to their interiors: i.e., large plazas. Such structure arrangements are found at only three of the recorded sites, Las Quebradas, Arapahoe Viejo, and Bobos, but the accessibility of the Quebradas monumental plazas is not complete since their unobstructed sides are faced with steep terraces. It is possible, of course, that markets were held outside of any formalized plaza area, but this has yet to be established within the valley.

G. REGIONAL INTERACTION: TRADE

G-1)

Class II centers served as nodes in interregional exchange networks extending south and southeastward (into present-day Honduras).

Evidence

a) Site location: The strongest evidence for this hypothesis is found in the location of the two Class II sites. Both Las Quebradas and Playitas are situated along potentially important routes of communication leading south-southeast into Honduras. Las Quebradas sits on the Guatemalan side of the pass cut by the Rio Bobos through the Sierra de Espiritu Santo, while Playitas is in an analogous position on the pass cut by the Rio Chinamito through the same high mountain range. Such passes are relatively rare in this portion of the valley, so that by their location alone Las Quebradas and Playitas would have been in a good position to monitor and profit from any commerce flowing along these routes.

b) Artifacts: Both Class II sites yielded evidence of obsidian blade-tool production. According to the argument that polyhedral cores were imported to the valley (Sheets 1983), it seems most likely that the cores would be found at sites from which the finished tools were distributed. This view is consonant with the earlier observation that blade-tool manufacture was attested only for Class II and III centers.

Finally, a minority of the ceramics at Class II sites appear to have been directly imported from areas in Honduras (Reina Inciso and Copador Polychrome) or to have been influenced by Honduran styles (Bobos Group sherds resemble those of the Chamelecon La Champa Groups from the Naco valley, Honduras; Los Vitales vessels closely resemble containers found more commonly in the northern La Florida valley, Honduras). Presumably such a flow of goods and stylistic influence presupposes a certain amount of communication and trade between Class II centers and areas to the south-southeast.

c) Data from relevant portions of Honduras: The reality of these potential communication routes is suggested by recent work conducted at monumental centers in the Tras Cerros and La Entrada valleys (Nakamura 1985, 1987; Nakamura et al. 1986). Here, large sites such as Techin and Tras Cerros, situated on the Honduran side of the Chinamito and Bobos passes respectively, share patterns of site organization and ceramics with Playitas and Las Quebradas that set them apart from other monumental loci in neighboring portions of Honduras. These material similarities suggest the existence of strong ties of communication and exchange across the sierra.

G-2)

The imported goods that arrived in the Class II centers were distributed to other sites by means of elite-controlled exchange.

Evidence

a) Site location: Class II centers are the only LMV sites situated on potential routes leading out of the valley. As a result, any goods entering the valley via these routes would, presumably, first pass through the hands of the trade managers resident there before arriving at other sites.

b) Site planning: The question of how these imports were distributed to other wider-valley sites can be addressed, at present, only through appeals to negative evidence. In particular, the absence of recognized, formalized installations for markets within the investigated LMV sites (see Hypothesis F-1), suggests that centralized markets were not the means of redistributing imported goods. The inference of the elite control of imports, then, rests in part on the absence of evidence of market activities. It is also based on reconstructed patterns of Late Classic Maya interregional trade, which is currently seen as having been elite-controlled (e.g., Rathje 1972).

H. REGIONAL INTERACTION: SOCIOPOLITICAL UNITS

H-1)

The LMV was divided ceremonially, economically, and administratively among a series of Class II and III centers. Each of these sites was the locus of large-scale ceremonial, administrative, and economic services performed by the resident elite for its dependent hinterland.

Evidence

a) The evidence for the performance of ceremonial, economic, and administrative services by the elite at the Class II and III centers has been discussed above. The principal question yet to be addressed is the evidence for the Class II/III sites' having been centers of independent sociopolitical units.

b) Site planning: The Class II and III sites are the largest centers discovered within the valley, as measured by their numbers of monumental constructions, especially quadrangles. If there is a direct relationship between the size of a structure and the power and prestige of its residents, then the largest sites (Class II/III centers) should also be the centers of the most powerful elites. Any site subordinate to another will not be able to control the same amount of labor as the dominant locus and, as a result, will be smaller and less complex. Equality in size, therefore, strongly implies equality in control of labor and, hence, equality of power and independence. Because all four Class II/III loci are comparable in size and complexity, we presume that they were equally powerful and, hence, independent.

c) Site location: Class II and III centers are spaced, on average, 5.88 km apart, and controlled roughly equivalent zones (50.7-68.6 km²). This distribution is what would be expected of equally powerful, independent centers distributed over the landscape at roughly equal distances as a result of competition for sufficiently large supporting hinterlands.

H-2)

Below the level of the Class II and III centers were the Class IV-VII sites, in which the population subordinate to the major centers lived. The Class IV sites were loci of elite occupation and functioned, in part, to provide lower-level administrative, economic, and ritual services to the populations in their hinterlands. Class II/III centers also provided these low-level services to the populations resident in their immediate vicinities.

Evidence

a) Site planning: The recovery of monumental quadrangle construction at Class IV sites points to the presence of a resident elite with some control over local labor, if one accepts the argument, elaborated earlier, that the quadrangle form had the same functions of elite residence and administration at excavated and unexcavated sites. This view is supported by investigation at Choco, Playitas, Las Quebradas, and Quirigua, where the quadrangle (at Quirigua, the Acropolis) is believed to have served elite residential and administrative purposes. The small size of these loci relative to Class II/III centers suggests that their residents' control of labor was less than that exercised by the elites at Class II/III centers. We therefore contend that the Class IV elites were less powerful than, and subordinate to, Class II/III elites. This conclusion is tentative, however, and requires further testing.

b) Theoretical considerations: The argument for the performance of low-threshold services at Class II-IV centers is based on the assumption that there were a set of administrative functions that the elite performed for the population residing at these sites and in their immediate hinterlands. These services would have dealt with problems that required immediate action and an intimate knowledge of the local situation to resolve, such as the adjudication of disputes and the redistribution of land. This is in addition to the larger-scale economic, administrative, and religious services that the rulers of Class II/III sites performed for their entire dependent societies. This hypothesis is in keeping with the essential tenets of classic central-place theory as developed in economic geography (e.g., Morrill 1974: 282) and subsequently modified and used in archaeology (e.g., Hodder and Orton 1976).

H-3)

Although Class V sites functioned, in part, like Class IV centers, they also served special purposes. Mojanales and Bobos were trade-monitoring sites for Playitas and Las Quebradas respectively, while Arapahoe Viejo was a commercial and/or economic focus for allied Choco, Las Quebradas, and Playitas.

Evidence

a) General: site planning: The presence of monumental quadrangle construction at Bobos and Arapahoe Viejo and its possible existence at Mojanales indicate a resident elite group at these sites performing some administrative, economic, and ceremonial services for their dependent populations. The relatively small sizes of the sites in general, and their monumental constructions in particular, point to their subordination to the larger Class II/III centers as argued above.

b) Mojanales: location: Mojanales' setting, high in the Sierra de Espiritu Santo in a small pocket valley along the Rio Chinamito pass leading toward Honduras, is the strongest argument for its trade-monitoring function. This seemingly eccentric position, away from good agricultural land and along a major potential route of communication, strongly suggests its role in monitoring commerce. That it performed this role for Playitas is suggested by the latter's position on the Guatemalan side of the route and the likelihood that

the residents of Playitas would not have permitted an independent competitor to prosper along this pass. At present, therefore, it seems probable that Mojanales was a commercial subordinate of Playitas. As noted earlier, further south along this channel are a string of large centers, including Techin, whose close material similarities with Playitas suggest intense Late Classic interaction, probably including trade.

c) Bobos: location and site planning: Bobos, very close to the present junction of the Rios Bobos and Motagua, would have been strategically situated to handle goods moving north to south along the Rio Motagua to and from Las Quebradas.

The Bobos plaza, surrounded by relatively low structures, might—given its large size and accessibility—have served as a locus for commercial transactions. Obviously, excavations at Bobos should be directed to testing this proposition.

d) Arapahoe Viejo: location, site planning, and monuments: The position of Arapahoe Viejo, high in the foothills of the Sierra de Espiritu Santo, away from good agricultural land, population concentrations, and any apparent trade routes, suggests that the role it played in intravalley interactions was different from that of other LMV sites.

In addition to a small monumental quadrangle, Arapahoe Viejo has a large, accessible plaza bounded by two unusual monumental structures. One of these, Str. 216-17, is possibly a ritual platform, and the other, Str. 216-13, may have had a storage function. The site's distance from known population concentrations also hints at an economic role: i.e., the storage and trading of valued imports. The adjacent plaza may then have functioned as a marketplace for interregional trade. On the other hand, if Str. 216-17's function was religious, Arapahoe Viejo could have been a specially segregated ritual site, with storerooms for ceremonial regalia and a plaza for ritual performances and/or viewing. At present both interpretations are equally plausible and require further testing.

The pecked stone sphere in the monumental court (A.V. Mon. 1) is nearly identical in appearance, location, and size to Las Quebradas Mon. 2 in the Northwest Group court. Otherwise such stones are not known from the LMV. The presence of this monument at Arapahoe Viejo points to some connection between the Arapahoe Viejo and Las Quebradas elites.

In summary, its location, the presence of a monument similar to those found at Las Quebradas, and its situation c. 3 km from Choco and 7.1 km from Playitas all point to ties between Arapahoe Viejo and these three major centers. The unusual types of structures found here imply the performance of large-scale ritual and/or economic services for these allied centers.

H-4)

Class VI sites performed some minor administrative, ceremonial, and/or economic functions for their immediate populations although, like Class VII loci, they were primarily nonelite residential foci.

Evidence

a) Architecture and site planning: The existence of few monumental structures at Class VI sites, organized into plaza groups, indicates the presence of an elite group capable of organizing a modicum of labor for construction purposes. The fact that at one of these sites (Juan de Paz), several of the large constructions received special architectural treatment (facings of cut sandstone blocks and large schist slabs), lends further support to this conclusion.

The paucity of sizable constructions, their relatively small dimensions when compared with examples from the Class II-V sites, and the absence of the quadrangle form strongly suggest that the power of these elites was very limited. Presumably, the range of services they offered was equally restricted.

By far the majority of the structures at Class VI and VII sites are low, small constructions found singly or arranged into groups. This points to a primarily nonelite residential function.

b) Location: Presumably, the residents of these sites owed allegiance to the closest Class II/III center. The occupants of the latter overshadowed their Class VI and VII counterparts in their power and prestige manifest in the size of their monumental residences. How close these ties were is currently unknown, but those Class VI/VII sites north of the Rio Motagua are at considerable distances from known Class II/III centers and may well have been independent of or only nominally subservient to Class II/III overlords.

H-5)

Ultimately both power and imported goods derived from the Class II/III centers and flowed down the site hierarchy while allegiance, labor, and, presumably, tribute flowed in the opposite direction.

Evidence

This proposition is supported solely by logic and not by any archaeological evidence. It has been ar-

gued that the Class II/III sites served as the residences of the most powerful LMV elite. Each successively lower level in the site hierarchy contains sites with ever-decreasing amounts of monumental construction, which, in turn, reflect ever-decreasing control of nonelite labor and loyalties. At the bottom are the Class VII sites, where all construction is nonmonumental and labor seems to have been organized solely at the household level to meet household needs. It has been further argued, based in part on general principles of central-place theory, that in return for labor and loyalty, elites provided some services (the ceremonial, economic, and administrative categories discussed earlier). Again, as one moves down the hierarchy, the elite-provided services become increasingly localized for an increasingly limited dependent population.

I. REGIONAL INTERACTION: WIDER VALLEY AND QUIRIGUA

I-1)

Quirigua (the only Class I site in the LMV) differs from other known valley monumental centers by possessing evidence for a greater variety of manufacturing and processing activities; more extensive participation in long-distance trade and the scale of its export production for that trade; a wealthier and more powerful ruling elite; larger-scale, more elaborate and diverse ritual facilities; and a more complexly organized social system. The rituals performed at Quirigua may have been somewhat different from those carried out at the other valley centers.

Evidence

a) Economic variables: Excavations at Quirigua have revealed a greater variety of manufacturing and processing activities than can currently be inferred for any wider-valley center (QR 4). Three production activities were securely identified, one (cacao processing) was less securely postulated, and six more crafts were indirectly inferred at Quirigua (ibid.). Out of this list, only obsidian-blade and -flake production could be inferred from the wider-valley sites.

Quirigua is the sole investigated valley site that yielded tentative evidence of production above the local level—the cacao produced for export at Str. 3C-5 (ibid.). Quirigua is also the only valley center to furnish evidence of specifically trade-related constructions: i.e., the stone jetty and river embayment (ibid.; Ashmore et al. 1983). No similar evidence was recovered from the wider-valley centers. The location of Quirigua athwart two major communication routes—the east-west route along the Rio Motagua connecting the Atlantic coast and the highlands, and a north-south channel including the pass cut by the Rio Morja toward Copan—also suggests that long-distance trade played an important role in the functioning of this site.

b) Elite power and wealth: While not found in great quantities, such hallmarks of Maya elite wealth as jade, pyrite, and copper were found at Quirigua and not at other wider-valley centers. Further, it has been hypothesized that the demand for these products at Quirigua was sufficient to support the existence of full-time specialist artisans in these and related fields, e.g., masons, sculptors, plasterers (QR 4). No evidence for the existence of such resident craft workers was found within the contemporary wider valley.

Quirigua possessed all the hallmarks of a powerful administrative elite center controlling a relatively large area: monuments recording dynastic histories; large skilled and unskilled labor forces; and the ability to ensure access to a variety of distant construction materials. The Quirigua ruling elite also monopolized labor within the site for their own benefit, concentrating it on the construction of the Acropolis and Great Plaza, and restricting its availability to lesser notables. This paramount elite monopoly of labor at Quirigua implies that they were in a position to reduce competition for other resources as well, e.g., power and wealth, and ensure their right of first access to them. The wider-valley social leaders were incapable of monopolizing labor to this degree; the largest sites have a fragmented organization as discussed earlier. Further, there are no recorded dynastic histories at wider-valley centers and the raw materials used in construction are limited to local resources. In sum, the power of the Quirigua elite seems greater than that possessed by their wider-valley contemporaries.

c) Ritual facilities: Temples, shrines, ceremonial caches, ballcourts, and large plazas have all been attested at Quirigua. None of these ritual deposits or facilities have been clearly recognized at wider-valley centers to date. On the basis of current evidence, then, there appears to have been a greater investment of labor in the construction of ritual facilities at Quirigua than at other LMV centers.

d) Public rituals: Wider-valley public ritual foci were largely enclosed by, or incorporated into, the massive quadrangles. The actual space for ritual performance and/or observation by an audience was therefore restricted. At Quirigua, large plazas that were easily accessible and could have held large numbers of participants/observers were the loci of at least some public rites. This implies that public ceremonies at Quirigua were meant to be attended/observed by larger numbers of people than were the ceremonies in the wider valley. By extension, the nature of the rituals performed may have differed.

e) Social complexity: It is assumed that the more complex a social system is, the greater the number of specialized parts it is divided into, and the more specialized and diverse are the activities performed on a large scale to integrate all of the elements of that society (e.g., Flannery and Marcus 1976). Following from this, and the presumption that these activities will require physical facilities to house their performance, the more complex the society, the greater the diversity of structure forms. While Late Classic Quirigua is not as structurally complex as some Lowland Maya centers, it possesses a greater variety of structure forms and groupings than the other valley centers. In the latter case redundant monumental architectural forms, the single, double, and triple quadrangle, characterize all Class II/III sites. This redundancy implies that the wider-valley centers were the foci of a limited range of large-scale activities, which acted to integrate the societies focused on them. As a result, the Quirigua social system appears to have been more complex than its wider-valley counterparts.

I-2)

Despite their differences, Quirigua and the LMV Class II-V centers partook of a common valley-wide tradition involving a series of shared understandings reinforced by constant and intensive interactions.

Evidence

These shared understandings are manifest in the common use of the quadrangle structure group to house the administrative elite; the sharing of very similar ceramic, *incensario*, and lithic assemblages; the use of the effigy modeled censer in public rites, especially those connected with monuments, and the lid, spiked, pronged, and ladle forms in private ones; and a tendency to distribute obsidian manufacturing among small structures. These similarities fall within the proxemic and ideological realms of behavior defined in Chap. 8. This range of shared understandings implies the existence of constant and intensive interactions among all monumental valley centers (Class I-V sites).

I-3)

Quirigua was the ultimate source of most imported goods in the LMV, especially obsidian and basalt tools. Despite its more complex and sophisticated administrative and ceremonial systems it did not politically or ritually dominate the major valley centers, with the possible exception of Morja, during the Late Classic. In return for imported items, the LMV centers provided locally produced goods to Quirigua. These latter items may have included cacao or other valued crops, which were then processed and traded out of the valley from Quirigua.

Evidence

a) Quirigua's trade position: Quirigua's preeminent role as the valley's importer and exporter is based on its location astride two major trade routes (see Hypothesis I-1), and the recovery at Quirigua of a greater variety and quantity of imported items than were found at other valley centers. That obsidian and basalt tools may have come into the valley via Quirigua is suggested by the location of major sources of these objects in the highlands of Guatemala, to which the Rio Motagua provides easy access. It has been argued elsewhere that Quirigua was a major node in interregional trade in Ixtepeque obsidian (Hammond 1972). Reinforcing this interpretation are Quirigua's ties with areas outside the valley documented by recent excavations (dating to at least as early as the Early/Middle Classic period) (QR 4). That the LMV centers exchanged some goods for the items they received through Quirigua seems logical, but their identity is currently unknown. Cacao has been offered as one possibility because of both the fertility of the valley soils and the presence of a possible cacao-processing facility at Quirigua (ibid.).

b) Quirigua's control: At present there is no evidence that Quirigua furnished political or ceremonial services to the other valley polities. If Quirigua exercised dominion over the surveyed portion of the wider valley, one might expect that the sites here would show some evidence of this control such as being appreciably smaller; but the Class II/III centers are about equivalent in size to Late Classic Quirigua. This implies that each Class II/III center exercised independent control over its own labor pool. Morja is a possible exception to this observation, primarily because of its proximity to Quirigua.

J. WIDER-VALLEY DEVELOPMENT

J-1)

Increases in social and architectural complexity occurred very rapidly in the wider valley within the final Late Classic century and were related to developments at Quirigua. Quirigua broke free of Copan's domination in AD 738, at which time it established itself as an independent trading entity and consequently increased its demand for local products (such as cacao) that could be used in interregional commerce. Other societies within the LMV had to adapt to these new measures in order to maintain their independent positions within the developing trade network. This adaptation took the form of the development of local social hierarchies to facilitate the organization of increased levels of production and goods transfer. Reinforcing this trend was the increasing flow of imports. By controlling access to those foreign goods, wider-valley social leaders could effectively enhance their prestige and power over other members of society. Participation in interregional commerce, initiated by Quirigua's actions in AD 738, therefore, both encouraged and made possible the rapid development of sociopolitical complexity witnessed in the Late Classic LMV.

Evidence

There is only sparse evidence to support this hypothesis. It can be tentatively established at present that the LMV monumental centers did develop in a very short interval (c. AD 700-850), and that this coincides with the period after Quirigua severed its ties with Copan (AD 738; supported by epigraphic evidence, e.g., Sharer 1978; Riese 1986). Further, there is a close correlation between this last date and the initiation of a rapid increase in building activity at Quirigua itself, documented by extensive excavations at that site (Jones et al. 1983; Jones and Sharer 1986). As has been discussed at some length earlier, it is also arguable that Quirigua had long occupied a strategic position along interregional trade routes. Based on these data, the above hypothesis was constructed to present only one possible interpretation of how these developments were related. It posits trade, production, and the pressures of information transfer as the foremost causal forces in the development of the LMV social systems in the Terminal Late Classic (e.g., Johnson 1978, 1983). This does not imply that alternative hypotheses are invalid.

J-2)

As overland trade declined in importance with the advent of advances in deep-sea navigation techniques (e.g., Sabloff and Rathje 1975), the trading "boom" in the lower valley collapsed along with Quirigua and the developing LMV societies that depended on it.

Evidence

Direct evidence to support this interpretation is lacking. It has been established that occupation of the LMV centers ceased c. AD 850 and that Quirigua was abandoned soon thereafter (Sharer 1978, 1990). If the prosperity of these societies did depend on long-distance trading as hypothesized above, then it is logical to assume that their collapse can also be attributed to these economic factors. It is generally established that deep-sea navigation had improved by the end of the Late Classic to the point where sea routes may have begun to eclipse land-based passages in importance (e.g., Sabloff and Rathje 1975). Once again, if interregional trade was central to the prosperity of the Late Classic wider-valley centers, then their inland locations would have placed them at a disadvantage in competing for participation in that trade as the routes shifted seaward. An assessment of the applicability of this view to the LMV awaits, in large part, the testing of Hypothesis J-1 and systematic investigations along the Caribbean coast of Guatemala.

K. INTERREGIONAL INTERACTION

The following hypotheses are based on the assumption that the material remains of human activity can be divided into four behavioral categories, the technological, proxemic, social, and ideological (see Chap. 8).

K-1)

The similarities in material traits among sites traditionally defined as Classic Lowland Maya, including Quirigua, are accounted for by the existence of a Maya elite identity system (Freidel 1979, 1981; Sabloff 1986) that linked the rulers of different social units throughout the area. This identity network consisted of shared technological, ideological, social, and proxemic elements and was quite comprehensive in the range of shared understandings involved. Membership in this system was used by local elites to facilitate long-distance trade and maintain a monopolistic control over imports. Ties within the Maya identity network were reinforced by constant religious and social (e.g.,

marriage) exchanges and were important in defining the social status of its members.

Evidence

a) Definition: To be sure, the determination of social identities from the archaeological record is not often easy or secure. Nonetheless, I would argue that if material items which functioned in the proxemic, social, and ideological behavioral systems show a consistent association over wide areas, then they represent a dispersed social affiliation. This assertion is based on the assumption that embedded in these categories are those core beliefs which determine how a group perceives itself, the social and physical world around it, and the propriety of individual behaviors. Variation in the technological realm may be somewhat less significant in defining social identities, for the distribution of these traits may be controlled, in part, by noncultural, environmental forces.

b) Application of the social-identity concept to the Late Classic Lowland Maya: Archaeological work over the past century or so at Late Classic Lowland Maya centers, including Quirigua, has revealed a number of shared material traits that arguably functioned within the four behavioral categories (see Table 8.2). Lowland Maya monumental sites have generally been seen as centers of elite residence, administration, and large-scale ritual performance (e.g., Ashmore 1981a; Thompson 1966). It is argued that the elite at these Late Classic sites were participants in a large-scale interacting ethnic network. This system seems to have involved only the elite; there is no evidence at present that the nonelites participated in the network. It seems probable that the Maya identity connected a series of rulers each resident within his/her own distinct social and political unit.

c) Maintenance of the network: The evidence for the perpetuation of the Late Classic Maya affiliation is drawn solely from the work of others. Ties among dispersed Maya elites have long been hypothesized to have been based on economic (e.g., Freidel 1979; Rathje 1972), ceremonial (R. Adams 1971), and social (Molloy and Rathje 1974) exchanges. It is these lines of communication that would have been necessary to the maintenance of a distinct, widely dispersed, self-conscious social identity. The strategic use of this identity system to control long-distance trade is also based on investigations by Maya scholars who have convincingly argued this case (e.g., Freidel 1979, 1981; Sabloff 1986) and the comparison of the Maya case with analogous patterns of elite interregional interaction identified elsewhere in the world (e.g.,

Brown 1975, 1976; Renfrew 1982, 1986; Renfrew and Cherry 1986; Shennan 1982; see Schortman 1989).

K-2)

The LMV monumental centers, despite some underlying similarities to the Maya site of Quirigua, share a distinct material pattern that reflects an equally distinctive and shared ideological, proxemic, social, and technological system. Many of the Maya behavioral innovations and their material correlates found at Quirigua could not be accepted into the other LMV societies because of the limitations of the local environment or because their acceptance would have necessitated basic changes in the structure of valley social systems.

Evidence

a) Technological realm: The wider-valley elite did not have access to the necessary raw materials, in particular easily cut stone, to adopt many Maya technological traits. These resources were, however, within easy reach of the residents of Quirigua. This argument is based on the detailed geological surveys that have been carried out around Quirigua (P. Mueller, pers. comm. 1979) and personal observations within the wider-valley environment. The latter observations are not systematic and should be amplified by more careful surveys in the future.

b) Social realm: The diverse Maya structure forms enumerated in Table 8.2 are, by and large, not found in wider-valley centers. From the arguments detailed in Chap. 6 and summarized above, it has been hypothesized that the LMV social systems were relatively simple, certainly not as complex as those reconstructed for Late Classic Lowland Maya polities. It has also been argued that there is a direct relationship between the complexity of a society, the diversity of the services performed to integrate all of its segments, and the variety of the monumental forms built to house those services. According to these assumptions, it appears that the LMV societies were much simpler than their Maya counterparts and there would have been no place within the former for the diverse services and associated structures of the latter.

c) Ideological realm: Just as the Maya's architectural groupings and types did not easily spread to societies where the level of complexity did not require them, elements associated with their ideological system were similarly limited in their distribution. This contention rests on two premises. First, that the simpler LMV societies did not require the complex systems of social justification for elite rule employed by the Maya and

manifest in their elaborate glyphic inscriptions. Second, that there were basic differences between LMV and Late Classic Maya religious practices that would have militated against the adoption of those Maya material traits which functioned in the ritual sphere. In particular, the performance of rites within the confines of massive quadrangles is in direct opposition to the large open spaces (plazas) provided for ritual activity among the Maya.

I therefore postulate that differences on the ideological level between wider-valley and Maya elites played a role in restricting the distribution of Maya traits and practices to Quirigua within the lower valley.

d) Proxemic realm: In contrast to these differences in material traits between the Maya and wider-valley societies, there is relatively close similarity on the proxemic level. In particular, both the wider-valley Class II-V centers and the Maya elite at Quirigua shared a common structure group, the quadrangle, which housed the same set of functions, elite residence and administration. The quadrangle form is found quite commonly at monumental Maya centers in general (e.g., G. Andrews 1975). Several explanations for such a detailed similarity on the proxemic level are possible. It may be that this sharing of the quadrangle form represents a commonly held tradition of the proper use of space among the Maya and LMV elites. It is also possible, however, that it reflects the wholesale borrowing of a Maya structure form to fill a new need in the Late Classic LMV—the housing of an administrative elite. The latter view is based on the observation that monumental construction developed rapidly in the LMV, and if this correlated with a rapid rise in the power of local elites, there may have been no local precedent for the construction of elite residential/administrative facilities. The local rulers then simply modeled their constructions on the Acropolis at Quirigua, the closest available paradigm. Only further investigations within the valley will allow a choice between these alternatives.

e) Summary: There is some inferential evidence that, in addition to environmental variation, basic sociocultural differences between the LMV and the Maya elite resident at Quirigua were partly responsible for the failure of the other valley societies to participate in the Maya elite's interaction system and adopt many of its material manifestations.

K-3)

The second set of factors controlling the distribution of Maya elite traits within the Late Classic LMV

239

was embedded in the nature of the interactions between the Maya at Quirigua and the LMV elite. In particular, competition over interregional trade and local resources, a desire for secrecy on the part of the Maya elite to maintain their own prestige and self-image—and their monopoly over long-distance trade with other Maya centers—led to a restriction of most Maya traits to Quirigua and its immediate hinterland. Some minor differences in material culture among LMV Class II/III centers may also be attributable to competition between them for local resources and trade. Despite this proposed intersite competition, constant, intensive contact was maintained among the valley centers.

Evidence

a) Competition: theory: This hypothesis is based on findings from ethnography (e.g., Barth 1969a; Hodder 1977) and archaeology (Brose 1979; Hodder 1979) that strongly point to intergroup competition as a potent force in encouraging the development and maintenance of material differences between neighboring societies. This view holds that under conditions of stress where two or more groups are in competition for the same resources, all those features which act to separate the groups involved, material and nonmaterial, will be emphasized to reinforce group solidarity and the corporate will to compete, facilitate the identification of group members, and provide an unambiguous means of assigning rights of access to the available resources (e.g., Barth 1969b: 25-26; G. Haaland 1969: 71; Shibutani and Kwan 1965: 220, 465). There appears, therefore, to be a direct correlation in the anthropological and archaeological literature between the degree of intergroup competition and the distinctiveness of the material cultural patterns of the groups involved. This observed correlation implies that competition among the Late Classic valley societies, including Quirigua, may account in part for the differences in material patterns observed within the valley.

b) Competition: evidence: At present there is no unequivocal evidence of active competition between lower-valley monumental sites; for example, no defensive walls have been found. Competition, however, need not always express itself through warfare, and the absence of defensive works is not definitive evidence against the presence of intersocietal rivalry. The extant evidence for intersite competition is totally inferential. First, the Maya elite, as an intrusive element in the LMV (e.g., Morley 1935; Sharer 1978, 1990), could be expected to maintain their self-esteem

through their distinctiveness as a nonlocal group with ties to other, high-prestige zones, e.g., the Maya lowlands. Second, if, as argued elsewhere, interregional trade was largely an elite-controlled phenomenon (e.g., Freidel 1986b; Rathje 1972; Sabloff 1986) in the Late Classic Maya lowlands, then it may have been to Quirigua's advantage to maintain its exclusive (within the Late Classic lower valley) participation within the Maya identity system. If the symbols (reflected in material traits) of membership in this network and the knowledge of their use were allowed to spread throughout the valley, the other valley elites might have been in a better position to compete with Quirigua for control of that trade. Third, competition between the largest Late Classic lower-valley centers (Class I-III sites) may have been over both productive land and trade routes out of the valley, according, in part, to the economic model presented earlier, which outlined the factors that gave rise to the rapid appearance of the Class II/III centers. If much of the lower valley's prosperity, reflected in the large increase in monumental construction, was founded on the production of goods for export and trade, then it is likely that this generated some local contention over the control of that trade and production. Further, evidence from the Honduran portions of these postulated routes suggests that communication along the Chinamito and Bobos passes was both intense and important (Chap. 8). So close are the currently attested material similarities from large centers on *both* sides of the sierra that the Class II notables may well have been in the process of forging their own elite interaction network in the Late Classic in competition with the Maya at Quirigua. The restriction of Maya material traits to Quirigua would, therefore, be partly the result of intravalley competition. At the same time slight material differences between wider-valley centers can also be attributed to this competition: i.e., the presence of monumental plazas and monuments at Las Quebradas and their absence at Playitas, Choco, and Quebrada Grande. It should be very clear, however, that testing is required before this hypothesis can be accepted as an adequate interpretation.

c) Quirigua-wider-valley contacts: Competition need not lead to the total cessation of all intercourse (Barth 1969: 10; Hodder 1977). As noted earlier in Hypothesis I-2, residents of the wider-valley centers and Quirigua shared a number of assumptions manifest in their similar ceramic, *incensario*, and lithic assemblages, the use of the quadrangle group, and so forth.

Also, if as has been argued earlier Quirigua was a major conduit for imported goods entering the valley, then communication between the wider valley and that Class I center would have been essential.

d) In sum, it is argued that both intrinsic sociocul-tural differences between the Late Classic elite at the LMV centers and the Maya rulers of Quirigua, and the nature of their interaction account for the restriction of characteristic Maya elite traits to Quirigua and its immediate hinterland.

SUGGESTIONS FOR FURTHER RESEARCH

In order to test these hypotheses the following work would be necessary. First, a more detailed reconnaissance and survey designed to locate all signs of Precolumbian occupation should be carried out within the entire wider valley. This survey universe should include the floodplains of the Rio Motagua and its tributaries, the surrounding hills, and those side valleys and passes which might have provided egress from the valley. Special attention should be paid on the floodplain to the examination of the commercial BANDEGUA ditches, which might reveal traces of buried deposits of Late Classic date and any evidence of previous occupation. Subsequently, the investigated settlements could be arranged into a hierarchy based on their size, complexity, presence/absence and extent of monumental construction, and the range of inferred activities carried out at them. Those that can be dated from surface collections should be separated into their respective time periods prior to hierarchic classification. The seven site classes offered here could serve as a basis for this initial division, although it will probably require further refinements as work progresses.

This initial research having been accomplished, a random sample of sites from each of the hierarchic categories should be drawn for excavation, according to a sampling procedure to be determined in the field. Stratification of each site class by topographic location would be desirable, e.g., separating those sites on the floodplain from those in the foothills, to help ensure the representativeness of the sample.

In the larger sites chosen for excavation (Class II-VI) it would probably be wise to stratify the component structure groups and then draw a random sample for excavation from within each class. Given the possibility of functional variation among structures in any one group, these aggregates and not the individual structure should probably be the unit of study at this level. Group classes can be defined on the basis of components' sizes and extent, the nature of their organization, and the presence/absence of special features. In sites composed of more than one quadrangle and surrounding smaller structures, each structure cluster should be treated as a separate testing universe and samples drawn from each independently. In this way propositions, such as those concerning the functional redundancy of monumental court groups in one site zone, can be tested.

Once the excavation sample has been chosen, both horizontal and vertical operations should be carried out. Questions of chronology and the location of ritual deposits in construction require deep cuts into structures and artifact deposits. For this work, the largest structures within a group would be the best choices. The work carried out by this project indicates that at least some of the more sizable platforms were built up over time through superimposed construction and, hence, might prove the most fruitful in reconstructing the full sequence of occupation within a group.

The answering of functional questions requires extensive clearing of entire groups (e.g., Webster and Gonlin 1988). In this way, sizable artifact samples from the terminal debris contexts of different structures can be obtained and more secure functional inferences made. As always, artifacts from primary, use-related terminal contexts are especially to be sought and horizontal excavations would be the best way to ensure encountering them. Soil samples should also be drawn from good contexts, e.g., sealed primary deposits and middens, for later flotation processing. In addition to clearing all structures in a group, a grid set up away from these constructions and in the plazas/courts they surround could be used to excavate a stratified random sample of these "empty" spaces. The criterion for defining these strata would be location. The planned program would test for the presence of activity areas not directly associated with structures and buried construction. Of course, divergence from the random sampling program would allow testing of special features as they are encountered.

Obviously, the proposed project would involve a staggering amount of work. The LMV is very large, c. 2000 km², and given the diversity and density of sites found in the segment studied here, the remainder may have been densely populated prehistorically. Difficulties of access and in locating small sites on the floodplain, where they may be buried by alluvial deposits, pose substantial problems. In addition, the use of cobble and earthen construction in monumental structures makes deep probes difficult and expensive. These logistical concerns do not preclude the accomplishment of the work outlined above, but they do suggest that it might be undertaken in segments, perhaps within one postulated administrative zone at a time.

This proposed field research would provide data that would permit the testing and refinement of the hypotheses proposed by the research reported here, once precise test implications have been stated. Addi-

tional research in the Classic Maya lowlands is also necessary to evaluate and, hopefully, refine the concept of the Maya elite interaction system. The goal of this research would be to define more precisely the Classic Lowland Maya elite identity network, and how it varied in time and space. It is only after this more detailed analysis has been completed that precise behavioral inferences can be made from the distribution of Maya elite traits.

In sum, the investigations carried out in the LMV in 1977-79 have defined a set of hypotheses that only more detailed work can refine and test, and have contributed a framework that—in the meantime—should be useful for better understanding an important area of Maya research.

Appendix I

In 1974 T. Nowak conducted excavations at at least two major valley sites, Playitas and Juyama. The full extent of these excavations remains unknown. Information on this work is presented over two and a half pages, accompanied by four section drawings, in one of Nowak's unpublished reports (1975: 16-18, figs. 2-5). It is on this report that I have based the following excavation descriptions.

PLAYITAS

GROUP II

In February 1974 Nowak conducted excavations in the area of the large southern quadrangle designated here as Group II (Nowak's Group B). Of the excavations initiated at this time, the locations of three could be reconstructed (Subop. B, C, and E). Sherds assignable to these test trenches were located in Nowak's collections in the Quirigua Project laboratory after he had left the Project and were analyzed by the author and Patricia Urban (see Chap. 5). We infer that Subop. D and F, for which sherds were also found, were also dug in the area of Group II, simply because they fit within the sequence of suboperations for this Group. Unfortunately, their precise proveniences remain unknown and no drawings or descriptions of them are extant.

The goal of Nowak's work in Group II was to uncover artifacts in primary contexts to aid in dating the period of occupation. Presumably, some evidence of construction details was also sought.

STRUCTURE 200-193 (Fig. 57)

Structure 200-193 is a c. 3.75-m-high substructure that bounds the north side of the large Group II court. This construction was investigated in 1974 by one known test pit, Subop. B, in the approximate center of the structure's south, court-facing side. It is uncertain, but it appears that Subop. B was also placed just south of the break in slope from the court's surface to the structure's southern flank. Suboperation B measured c. 2 m on a side and reached a maximum depth of 2.02 m below court surface. It does not appear to have penetrated construction. The extant drawing of this pit (Fig. 57 here) shows its north face, where presumably it would have been immediately adjacent to Str. 200-193.

Excavation Lots: One hundred twenty-seven sherds, 198 censer fragments (78 of which are from one broken but recognizable vessel), one reported "cache" of obsidian blades (Cache 1), and three pieces of *bajareque* were recovered from the Str. 200-193 excavations. No ground stone tools were found. This could be due either to a complete absence of these items, or to their having been bagged separately and not refound during our analysis. Nowak's excavation lots were arbitrarily defined at 0.2-m intervals from the surface, resulting in a reconstructed figure of ten lots,

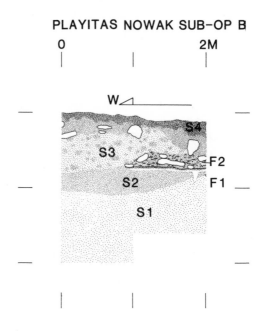

Figure 57.   Str. 200-193, Section (Nowak).

243

only four of which contain artifacts (B/2-5). Of the latter, three are from terminal occupation contexts (B/2-4) and one (B/5) is from an apparently preconstruction level.

Time Span 4: The first period of activity recognized in Subop. B involved the deposition of Stratum 1, a "relatively sterile mottled buff-gray *telpetate*" (Nowak 1975: fig. 5; Fig. 57 here). The upper surface of this earth level is concave, dipping down toward the center of the pit and rising slightly toward its east and west margins. This level is exposed to a maximum depth of 1 m, though its base was never encountered. At present, there is no reason to believe that Stratum 1 had anything but a natural origin. Stratum 2, found immediately atop Stratum 1, consists of a "mottled buff-red *telpetate*" (ibid.), which varies in thickness between 0.24 and 0.38 m. Its upper surface is fairly level. Unlike Stratum 1, Stratum 2 does contain cultural material, including one obsidian-blade cache (Cache 1). At present, there is no reason to interpret Stratum 2 as anything but a naturally deposited soil level.

The stratigraphic position of Strata 1 and 2, underlying the elements associated with T.S. 3, allows the definition of T.S. 4. Lot B/5 is also included in T.S. 4 as the artifacts were found in Stratum 2 and, hence, were probably deposited over the same time interval as this level. The one exception to this is Cache 1, found at a depth of 0.9 m below the pit's northwest corner in Stratum 2. This deposit may well have been intruded into the earth layer in an activity associated with the use of Str. 200-193. Unfortunately, this interpretation cannot be established by the available data.

Time Span 3: Time Span 3 is represented by the deposition of Feat. 1, a "burned clay floor" (ibid.) 0.04-0.06 m thick over most of its extent. It is relatively flat and not continuous through the drawn portion of the excavation, running for only 1.16 m from east to west. Nowak views this unit as a purposefully laid construction element, as suggested by its flat surface and distinctiveness from the surrounding earth levels. It is also possible, however, that it represents a level of debris which washed out from construction early in the process of its deterioration. This view would help explain its discontinuous distribution. Feature 1's association with construction remains uncertain. Its stratigraphic position atop Stratum 2 with portions intruding into Strata 1 and 2 suggests that it was deposited after the earth levels. It is therefore included in T.S. 3. Whether Feat. 1 repre-

sents a prepared floor or construction debris, it is likely that its location marks the surface of the original Group II court. No artifacts are recorded as having come exclusively from this feature. It is possible, though, that some of the material in Lot B/4 derives from this area.

Time Span 2: Feature 1 is overlain by Feat. 2, a "mottled brown-buff *telpetate* with concentrations of ceramics and carbon" (ibid.). It is 0.04-0.2 m thick and is restricted in its horizontal distribution in the north trench wall to the area above Feat. 1. In addition to containing sherds and carbon, it is marked by a fairly dense concentration of jumbled stones, mostly river cobbles and slabs. Nowak seems to view this feature as construction fill (1975: 17). On the basis of my experience with similar deposits elsewhere in the valley and the absence of any recorded construction that might have faced this fill, I see Feat. 2 as artifactual and construction debris washing out from Str. 200-193. The apparent lack of order among the included stones also supports this view. Its association with Str. 200-193 is somewhat conjectural and based solely on the close proximity of that construction.

The stratigraphic position of Feat. 2, capping Feat. 1, clearly indicates that it was deposited after this element. If Feat. 1 represents debris outwash, then it is likely that both features were deposited within a brief period and may actually belong in the same time span. No artifacts can be exclusively associated with Feat. 2, though it is likely that a good number of those in Lot B/4 came from this area.

Time Span 1: After Feat. 2's deposition, Stratum 3 was laid down over it and Stratum 2. Stratum 3 is a "mottled brown-buff *telpetate*" (ibid.) 0.49 m thick at its maximum and lensing out on the east over Feat. 2. It contains, in addition to a sizable artifact collection, jumbled river cobbles and stone slabs. Once more, Nowak interprets this as construction fill. However, the absence of any facing construction, the presence of jumbled stones, and the similarity of its composition to that of the underlying natural levels (Strata 1 and 2) suggest that it represents a naturally deposited stratum containing some outwashed debris from Str. 200-193. Also included in this period is Stratum 4, the humus horizon. This uppermost level varies in thickness between 0.11 and 0.49 m.

The stratigraphic situation of these strata, overlying Feat. 2 and Stratum 2, points to their deposition in the latest recognized time span, T.S. 1. Lots B/2-4 are included here as they were found within these two strata and, therefore, were probably deposited at the same time. Most of the material probably originally derived from nearby Str. 200-193, to judge by both the large number of sherds found here and their proximity to that construction. One broken but recognizable censer was recovered in Lot B/3. Whether this represents a cache is not certain (cf. Nowak 1975: 17); its broken condition suggests that it was part of the large quantity of *incensario* debris that fell from Str. 200-193 after its abandonment.

In sum, little can be said át present about the construction and general appearance of Str. 200-193. The presence of cobbles and slabs in outwashed debris contexts (Feat. 2, Strata 3 and 4) indicates that construction here may have been in the step-terrace mode so common elsewhere in LMV monumental constructions. Unfortunately, this cannot be established by the available data. In general, the failure to find a clear, prepared court surface, outside of a possible earth level, accords well with the picture obtained from other court excavations, e.g., the Playitas Group IV quadrangle investigations (Chap. 3).

MAIN COURT (Fig. 58)

The court of the Group II quadrangle was tested by a 2-m-square pit (Subop. C) placed directly in the center of the court (Nowak 1975: 17). Suboperation C was carried down to a maximum depth of 1.4 m below current court level as measured from the northwest excavation corner. The one extant section drawing of this pit (ibid: fig. 3; Fig. 58 here) is of its west wall.

Excavation Lots: One hundred seventy-nine sherds and one *bajareque* fragment, all from terminal debris contexts, were recovered from Subop. C. No obsidian or ground stone tools were found in our analysis of Nowak's material from this pit. Apparently, excavation lots were arbitrarily defined at 0.2-m intervals. Only Lots C/3 and 4 contain artifacts; those above and below are sterile (seven reconstructed lots in all).

Time Span 3: Time Span 3 is represented by the earliest recorded event recognized in Subop. C, the deposition of Stratum 1. This level is a "mottled buff-gray *telpetate* level" (ibid.: fig. 3; Fig. 58 here) exposed to a depth of 0.5-0.7 m, though its base was never reached, and it was apparently devoid of cultural materials. There is no reason at present to believe that Stratum 1 was artificially introduced and it was probably deposited naturally. It appears to correspond in composition, color, sterility, and *possibly* elevation to the naturally introduced Stratum 1 exposed in Subop. B. It is possible that both levels were

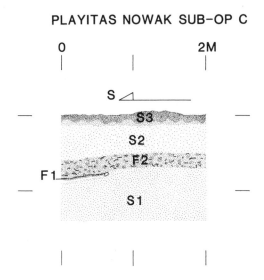

PLAYITAS NOWAK SUB-OP C

Figure 58.   Playitas Group II Main Court Section (Nowak).

part of the same depositional episode. Stratum 1's placement in T.S. 1 is based on its stratigraphic position.

Time Span 2: Feature 1, a "gray, sandy-clay floor" (ibid.) overlies Stratum 1 at a depth of 0.84 m below ground surface from the southwest trench corner. It is limited in its horizontal extent to the southwestern portion of the pit and extends to the north only 0.66 m from the southwest trench corner. It is 0.04-0.06 m thick and slopes up slightly from south to north. The significance of this feature is unclear. Nowak calls it a "floor," presumably because it differs in color and texture from the surrounding soil levels, which are primarily "buff-gray *telpetate*." It is equally possible that Feat. 1 is a debris line deposited after the abandonment of either one of the major surrounding structures or some other, closer and smaller buried construction. No sherds come exclusively from this feature, though it is possible that some from Lot C/4 originally derived from this area. Its stratigraphic position atop Stratum 1 but buried by Feat. 2 has led to Feat. 1's placement in the intermediate T.S. 2.

Also within this time span is Feat. 2, a level 0.18-0.24 m thick composed of "mottled buff-gray *telpetate* with heavy concentration of ceramics, carbon and burned adobe" (ibid.). This level is continuous in its north-south extent through the pit, slopes up slightly from south to north, and caps both Feat. 1 and Stratum 1. Given the concentration of cultural material found here, Feat. 2 might well represent refuse deposited on or near the original court surface (upper portion of Stratum 1) after abandonment. It is similar in color and composition, minus the stones, to Feat. 2 in Subop. B, also interpreted here as postabandonment debris. Alternatively, Feat. 2 may be construction fill for the court surface. The absence of any preserved remnants of this surface in Subop. C, however, makes this doubtful.

Since both Feat. 1 and 2 potentially represent construction debris, they are considered sequential collapse events within the same episode of structural deterioration. In this interpretation, the time elapsed between their depositions would have been slight. Lots C/3 and 4 are placed in this period (T.S. 2) despite the fact that they are not limited to either Feat. 1 or 3. The recorded density of cultural material in Feat. 2 makes it probable that at least the majority of the artifacts found in these lots originally derived from Feat. 2.

Time Span 1: The final period of recognized activity was the postabandonment burial of the Group II court's surface, represented by Strata 2 and 3. Stratum 2 is a "mottled buff-gray *telpetate*" (ibid.), 0.36-0.46 m thick, which completely buries Feat. 2. This level is similar in apparent composition and color to the lower Stratum 1 and may represent the continuation of the natural soil deposition in the area, which

was interrupted by the construction of the monumental court. Stratum 2 is also roughly similar to Stratum 3, which overlies evidence of structural collapse (Feat. 2) in Subop. B. The highest recognized soil level is Stratum 3, the humus horizon, which is 0.12-0.2 m thick and caps Stratum 2. Both strata appear to have been naturally deposited. The stratigraphic situation of Strata 2 and 3 has led to their inclusion in the final time span of this sequence.

In general, the lack of a prepared court surface recognized in Subop. B is confirmed here. Most likely, this court had a tamped-earth surface, e.g., the Stratum 1/Feat. 1/2 interface.

STRUCTURE 200-180 (Fig. 59)

Structure 200-180 is a c. 0.44-m-high structure located c. 32 m north of the Group II main court complex. The known excavation carried out here, Subop. E, was oriented east-west and placed against and into the eastern face of the structure. It was 4.04 m long (width unknown), extended 1.42 m into the fill of Str. 200-180, and was carried down to a depth of 0.74 m (maximum) into that fill below ground surface and to 2 m below ground surface immediately outside (east) of construction. The south face of the trench

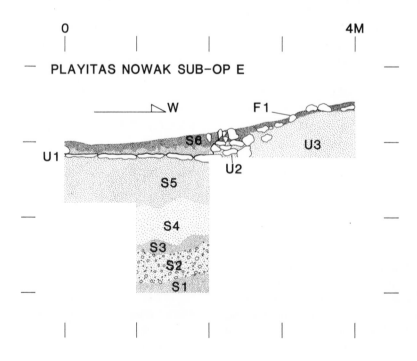

Figure 59.   Str. 200-180, Section (Nowak).

was drawn and forms the basis of this description (Fig. 59).

Excavation Lots: Nine hundred thirty-eight sherds and 75 censer fragments were recovered from Subop. E excavations along with 17 fragments of *bajareque*. Ground and chipped stone artifacts were not found in our analysis of Nowak's materials. Of Nowak's four artifact-containing lots from this excavation (E/1-4), one is most likely from a terminal debris context (E/2), while the rest are from uncertain contexts, either construction fill or preconstruction levels.

Time Span 4: This period is represented by the natural deposition of five soil levels, Strata 1-5. Stratum 1 is the lowest of these and consists of a "brown clayey-sand" (ibid.: fig. 4) exposed to a depth of 0.15-0.27 m at the base of Subop. E's deep probe. Immediately above and capping it is Stratum 2, a "brown sandy-clay and gravel" (ibid.) ranging between 0.38 and 0.44 m thick. Stratum 3, which covers Stratum 2, is 0.04-0.2 m thick and consists of a "brown clayey sand" (ibid.) apparently identical to Stratum 1 in color and composition. Stratum 4 overlies 3 and is a "buff clay with red and gray ferric oxide mottling" (ibid.), c. 0.44-0.64 m thick. Capping this sequence is Stratum 5, a "mottled gray-buff clay with carbon flecks" (ibid.) 0.5-0.66 m thick. All of these levels are generally horizontal, although the lowest, Strata 1-3, show a slight tendency to slope up toward the west. There is little reason (at present) to believe that any of these levels were artificially introduced. In fact, the alternation of sands and gravels in the Strata 1-3 sequence may represent changes in the nature of the depositing medium through time, e.g., proximity and type of load of the nearby Rio Chinamito. Nowak seems to interpret Stratum 5 as construction fill of a large platform on which Str. 200-180 rests (ibid.: 17). While the carbon flecks in Stratum 5 point to its cultural origin, this is far from certain, so it is designated here as the last in a sequence of naturally deposited soil levels. The total exposed depth of this sequence is 1.83 m. The stratigraphic position of Strata 1-5 indicates that they were all deposited prior to the initiation of Str. 200-180 construction.

Time Span 3: Following the deposition of Strata 1-5, Str. 200-180 and the adjoining stone surface (Units 1-3) were built. Unit 1 is a paved surface of flat-laid, uncut stone slabs extending eastward from the east face of Str. 200-180 and running under its basal eastern wall for 0.16 m. This pavement is 0.04-0.1 m thick (one stone's thickness) and rests on top of Stratum 5.

Unit 2 is the east basal retaining wall of Str. 200-180, composed of "river cobbles" apparently set in a "brown clay" matrix, c. 0.58 m thick, and preserved to a height of 0.38 m. On its eastern edge it rests on the westernmost exposed slab of Unit 1; further west the level it was set into is unclear. This wall encloses Unit 3, a "brown clay construction fill" (ibid.: fig. 4) ranging in thickness from 0.33 to 0.62 m. Given that Unit 1 partially runs under Unit 2, which in turn contains Unit 3, it would appear that these construction units were laid down in a sequence: first Unit 1, then Unit 2, and finally Unit 3. Given the close interdigitation of these elements, however, it is also likely that the time interval in which they were all constructed was very short.

Lot E/2 is included here on the supposition that this sizable collection represents the "great amount of ceramics [found] lying directly on top of the floor [Unit 1]" (ibid.: 17). Lot E/2 is the largest of Nowak's Subop. E collections and, presumably, represents this material. *If* Lot E/2 was found immediately atop Unit 1 and buried by Stratum 6 (see below), then it is likely that it represents debris deposited during the use of Str. 200-180 and not cleaned away prior to its abandonment. As such, it would be a primary deposit.

Time Span 2: The collapse of Str. 200-180 is represented by the jumbled stones (Feat. 1) found resting on the earthen fill of Unit 3 and protruding up into Stratum 6 (see below). Nowak's drawing (ibid.: fig. 4) shows this as not a concentrated deposit of rocks but, rather, a more dispersed jumble of construction stones. Feature 1 seems not to have extended any further east than the line of Unit 2.

Feature 1's location, above Str. 200-180 construction (Units 2 and 3), indicates that it was deposited after this construction had been abandoned and allowed to deteriorate.

Time Span 1: The burial of Str. 200-180 is represented by Stratum 6, the humus horizon 0.06-0.28 m thick overlying all exposed construction, and the last element deposited in the Subop. E sequence. It was probably laid down by natural means.

In sum, Str. 200-180 stood to a minimum height of 0.6 m—on the basis of preserved fill depth—and was fronted on the east by a low, thick cobble wall and a paved slab surface. The nature of superstructure construction is unknown, though the recovery of *bajareque* from the Subop. E lots implies the use of this material to some extent.

JUYAMA (Figs. 60-61)

Nowak carried out at least one excavation in the far northeastern portion of Juyama (ibid.: 17-18, figs. 5 and 6). There, on the east bank of the Rio Juyama, he noted a considerable number of sherds, including quantities of Protoclassic mammiform supports, coming from a canal cut near a group of four large constructions. A 10-m section of the canal was subsequently cut back (Subop. B) in June and July of 1974 and drawn (ibid.: fig. 5; see Fig. 61 here). This cut was generally 2 m deep except in one 1-m-wide area, where it was carried down to 3.1 m below ground surface.

Excavation Lots: Because of time limitations and uncertainty as to the precise original provenience of the material, the artifacts from Nowak's Juyuma excavations were not examined in detail, but only briefly reviewed. This cursory study confirmed two of Nowak's original statements: that the amount of sherds found here was great and that they probably dated to a pre-Late Classic occupation of the valley. The latter point is considered further in Chap. 5.

Time Span 3: Time Span 3 involved the deposition of eight natural soil levels (Strata 1-8) making up a total exposed depth of 1.25 m. Strata 1 and 3 are both composed of "dark reddish-brown sand and pebbles" (ibid.: fig. 5) separated by a c. 0.05-m-thick level of "black sand and pebbles." Stratum 3 is 0.15-0.2 m thick. Stratum 4 is a level of "fine red-buff sand" (ibid.) 0.2-0.25 m thick, which overlies Stratum 3. Next is Stratum 5, a "gravel" level overlying Stratum 4 to a depth of 0.2-0.25 m. Capping this sequence of culturally sterile levels is Stratum 6, composed of "dark brown sandy-clay with pebbles and very small ceramic fragments" (ibid.). This earth layer is roughly 0.5 m thick and extends from west to east in the cut for 7.1 m, at which point it was apparently truncated by the deposition of Stratum 14 (see below). The presence of small sherds in Stratum 6 seems to have led Nowak to the conclusion that it was "construction fill" (ibid.: 18). Apparently no evidence of facing construction was found to support this conclusion. As a result, I see no reason to view Stratum 6 as anything but a natural soil level carrying redeposited artifacts as part of its load. Within Stratum 6 is a culturally sterile lens of "reddish sandy-clay" (ibid.: fig. 5) 0.05-0.1 m thick (Stratum 7). It is found only in the eastern portion of Stratum 6,

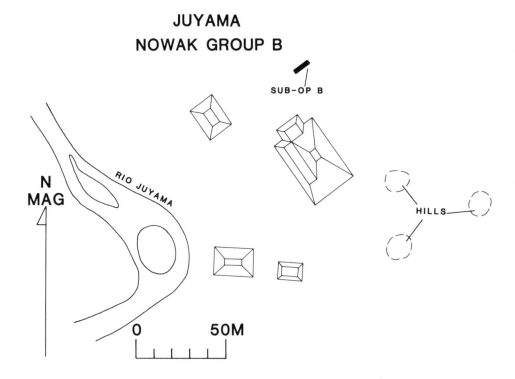

Figure 60.   Juyama Group B Plan (Nowak).

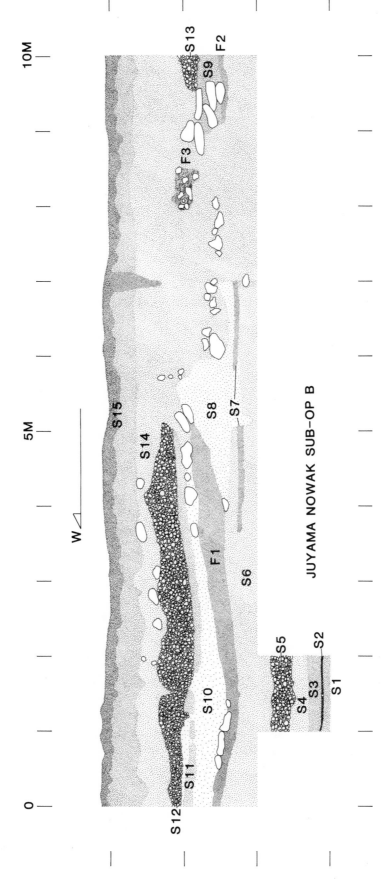

Figure 61. Juyama Op B Section (Nowak).

where it extends for a preserved distance of 3.4 m, and is cut at several points in the middle by Stratum 8. The latter is a "light sandy-clay with very few ceramics" (ibid.) and varies in thickness from 0.1 to 0.85 m. This irregularly shaped lens is found only at the center of Subop. B, where it covers a horizontal distance of 3 m.

While the depositional picture here is complex, it appears that these levels were more or less sequentially deposited by natural means, probably by the nearby Rio Juyama. As Strata 1-7 are all located beneath the elements associated with T.S. 2, they were probably deposited before them and are placed in T.S. 3. Stratum 8 poses a more difficult problem: because it intrudes into Strata 6 and 7, it must have been laid down after they were deposited. Still, because Feat. 1 (see below), deposited in T.S. 2, *seems* to slope up and into Stratum 8, it is at least probable that the latter was deposited prior to Feat. 1. As a result of its seemingly intermediate position, Stratum 8 is tentatively interpreted as the last deposit in T.S. 3. The presence of some ceramics in the uppermost of these strata (Strata 6 and 8) indicates human occupation somewhere in the area of the cut during this interval.

Time Span 2: Time Span 2 is represented by two discontinuous features, Feat. 1 and 2. Feature 1 is a level of "heavy cultural material with carbon, pebbles and dark sandy-clay" (ibid.) c. 0.15-0.3 m thick. It was from this level that Nowak recovered quantities of large ceramic fragments (ibid.: 17-18). Feature 1 rests atop Strata 6 and 8 and dips down in the middle, rising on both its eastern and western ends. It covers a horizontal distance of 5.15 m, continuing into the west wall of the cut, but is truncated on the east by the deposition of Stratum 14. Feature 2 is 0.05-0.1 m thick and extends out from the east wall of the Subop. B cut for 1 m. Nowak apparently thought that Feat. 1 and 2 were originally part of the same deposit, which had been cut by the force that deposited Stratum 14. This interpretation appears likely on two grounds: first, their similar composition, and second, their approximately equal elevations. Something apparently truncated the underlying Stratum 6 and may also have severed the original link between Feat. 1 and 2. The only problem with this view is explaining why Feat. 2, as shown in Fig. 61, is underlain by Stratum 14 and not by a continuation of Stratum 6, which is found beneath Feat. 1. If Stratum 14 was deposited by an event which also cut Feat. 1 and 2, then how did Feat. 2 come to rest on the former level? This inconsistency may be due to the very similar compositions of Strata

14 and 6 and the resultant failure of the excavator to recognize the continuation of Stratum 6 beneath Feat. 2.

Nowak interprets Feat. 1 and 2 as a primary-context midden derived from a nearby structure. Given the dense concentration and large size of the included sherds, this view appears reasonable. The location of Feat. 1, above and resting on strata built up in T.S. 3, indicates that it was deposited after these levels were laid down. Feature 2, although spatially separated from these strata, is seen here as contemporary with Feat. 1 because of their similar composition and elevation.

Time Span 1: Time Span 1 encompasses a rather complex period of riverine deposition of soil levels that buried and disturbed to some degree the earlier evidence of occupation. The depth of this mantle is 1.2-1.65 m. The first of these deposits was Stratum 10, a layer 0.1-0.3 m thick of "light buff silt with some ceramics" (ibid.: fig. 5) that buries Feat. 1 but is not found further east in Subop. B. On the east, Feat. 2 is covered by Stratum 9, 0.3-0.35 m thick, whose east-west horizontal extent is limited to the area above Feat. 2. This is a "reddish-brown sand lens (sterile)" (ibid.) containing some jumbled stones. A very similar deposit, Stratum 11, was found above Stratum 10 in the west portion of Subop. B, where it is 0.05-0.15 m thick and runs for c. 5 m east to west. It is possible that Strata 9 and 11 were once part of the same deposit, as Nowak appears to believe, and that their observed separation is a result of the event that laid down Stratum 14. The same may have been the case for Strata 12 and 13, found in the west and east portions of the trench respectively. They are described as "gravel (sterile)" (ibid.) levels; Stratum 12 is 0.15-0.5 m thick and 5.1 m long west to east, and Stratum 13 is 0.15-0.2 m thick and only 0.45 m long east to west. Once more, Stratum 14 intervened, and it is possible that these two similar levels, Strata 12 and 13, were deposited as part of the same event. Stratum 14 itself is a "dark buff sandy-clay" level "with stones and cultural material" (ibid.). It extends throughout the east-west extent of the cut, ranging from 0.1 to 1.7 m in exposed thickness. Because of the marked drop it takes in the eastern portion of Subop. B and the existence on its east and west sides of levels that might have originally been joined, Stratum 14 is interpreted as an intrusive element deposited by or after an event that truncated the previously deposited strata. There is no available evidence to support Nowak's contention that this represents construction fill (ibid.: 18, fig. 5). A natural origin cannot be ruled out.

Contained within Stratum 14 is Feat. 3, a small pocket, 0.2-0.35 m thick by 0.7 m long (east-west), of black carbon-stained soil with burned stones and one sherd. Nowak views this as a "hearth," and this may well be the case. Feature 3 is 0.85 m below ground surface. Capping this sequence is Stratum 15, a horizontal level 0.45-0.6 m thick of "dark buff silt (sterile)" (ibid.), which extends the full east-west length of the exposed cut.

There is no reason to believe that Strata 9-15 were artificially introduced into the area as construction fill. It seems more likely, in the light of current evidence, that they were naturally deposited here. In fact, the alternation of sands and gravels revealed in this sequence suggests that the depositing medium may have been the close-by Rio Juyama, which, in the course of its meanderings, deposited different types of load as its distance from the cut shifted. It may, in fact, have been this river that created the cut later filled by Stratum 14. The Rio Juyama in 1974 was c. 103 m northwest of the exposed face, where it was restricted by an apparently artificial levee.

The location of Strata 9-13 above Feat. 1 and 2 suggests that they were sequentially deposited after these cultural deposits had been laid down. The fact that Stratum 14 runs over these layers as well as fills in the area between them suggests that it was deposited after the aforementioned levels had been laid down and then cut. Feature 3, within Stratum 14, undoubtedly was deposited when the latter was being laid down. Finally, Stratum 15, which caps all levels, must have been the last of these elements to be deposited. The period during which Strata 9-15 and Feat. 3 were laid down was probably quite long. As was noted earlier, however, there is no reason to believe that the essential, natural mechanisms of deposition changed appreciably during the period. This, of course, does not mean that the area went unoccupied in this interval. The large number of structures at the site of Juyama apparently date to a period later than that represented in Feat. 1 and 2 (see Chap. 5); the cultural materials in Strata 10 and 14, and the presence of Feat. 3 also confirm the existence of human occupation in the area.

While no evidence of construction was reported from the cut, Feat. 1 and 2 clearly point to an early, now deeply buried, period of occupation. The significance of the ceramics recovered in Feat. 1 and 2 is discussed in Chap. 5. It should be noted that the depth of these deposits precludes their association with platforms now visible at the site.

NOWAK SURVEY SITES

In addition to those loci noted by Nowak and relocated by this project, there were three I did not visit: Zaculeu Seccions C6 and E8, Cable 2; Arapahoe Nuevo; and Lankin Seccion E2, Cable 2. None of these loci were even briefly described in Nowak's preliminary reports and their existence was revealed only when artifacts collected from them were found amidst the material Nowak turned over to the QAP in 1976. The documentation associated with these artifacts suggests that they were recovered from either the banks or backdirt of BANDEGUA drainage canals on the modern company *fincas* of Zaculeu, Arapahoe Nuevo, and Lankin. There is no indication that any architecture was visible at the collection points. If this interpretation is correct, it is likely that commercial excavations at these sites had uncovered small-scale, nonmonumental loci of prehistoric occupation now buried by deposits of river alluvium. This situation would be similar to the discoveries of pre-Hispanic occupation made in the course of ditch excavations near Quirigua and Aztec Farm on BANDEGUA lands (Ashmore 1981b). All of these loci are on the broad floodplain of the Rio Motagua and its major tributaries. Finca Zaculeu is located roughly 3 km northwest of Choco and 3.5 km north of Arapahoe Viejo, Finca Lankin is c. 3.5 km north of Choco, and Finca Arapahoe Nuevo is found roughly 3 km northwest of Arapahoe Viejo. All three are given locus numbers, 220, 218, and 235 respectively, but are not located on the valley map (Fig. 1) because of the uncertainty of their actual positions.

Appendix II

The purpose of this appendix is to briefly outline the theoretical considerations that underlie the behavioral expectations presented in Chap. 6. In constructing the functional model of activity types and their distributions at wider-valley centers, we considered five potential activity types based on previous work in the Lowland Maya area of the Classic period: domestic, manufacturing, ceremonial, administration, and marketing. In the following discussion these activity types are defined and their anticipated material correlates detailed.

Domestic: Domestic activities are all those tasks which contribute to the daily physical maintenance of an individual household. They include water and food storage, food preparation, cleaning, and cooking as well as the provision of facilities for sleeping. The material manifestations of these activities within the Lowland Maya area are usually hearths, utilitarian ceramics (especially large jars and bowls suitable for storage), jars and bowls showing evidence of having been used in cooking (e.g., exterior or interior burning), manos and metates for food grinding, and obsidian and/or flint blades and flakes used in cutting food (Harrison 1970: 231, 238; Lewenstein 1981). Architecturally, domestic structures vary considerably in size and the quality of their masonry within the lowlands. The larger and more elaborate residences are long, rectangular structures on low platforms (palaces) containing several rooms commonly arranged in two parallel interconnecting rows. Special features are sometimes found in the more elaborate residences, such as secluded benches for sleeping, windows, and curtain-holders, which once functioned as parts of screens providing some rooms with privacy (G. Andrews 1975: 43-50; Pollock 1965: 381; Harrison 1970: 251-253, 302-303). Small domestic structures are usually incorporated into groups of similar constructions surrounding a patio (G. Andrews 1975: 47-50; Ashmore and Wilk 1988; Pollock 1965: 381). Monumental domestic constructions also follow this arrangement, albeit on a larger scale, and are situated to ensure their privacy, i.e., either located in the less accessible portions of the site (Hammond 1975) or organized so as to reduce traffic in their area and access to their interiors (Harrison 1970: 251-253, 302-303; G. Andrews 1975: 59-66). It must be kept in mind, however, that not all of the structures within a single group housed precisely the same domestic functions. Separate buildings might be devoted to cooking, storage, household rituals, and sleeping (e.g., Ashmore and Wilk 1988; Webster and Gonlin 1988; Wisdom 1940).

Manufacture: Manufacturing involves the production of goods for consumption and is divided here into three levels depending on the scale of that production. Household-level manufacture is for the use of the resident group where the production is carried out. Local-level manufacture is for a market beyond the household but still restricted to the residents of a site and its immediate hinterland, while the export level involves production of considerable quantities for a broad market accessible through regional and/or interregional trading networks. The differences among these three levels are defined primarily by the amount of material produced and the distribution of the workshops associated with each. Household-level workshops produce only limited amounts of manufacturing-related debris that is found generally distributed among most if not all of the structure groups at a site. Local-level workshops produce correspondingly more debris and the areas of manufacture are more restricted, as each household is not producing all that it needs of this item. Export-level workshops are larger still and are even more restricted in their distribution to very specific areas of a site (e.g., Tosi 1984). Each of these levels, of course, incorporates elements of the lower ones: i.e., at the export level, producers may still be manufacturing the exported items for their own use and that of the consumers within the site as well as for the broader market. It is also likely that at any one center certain material classes will be produced on a household level, obsidian blades on a local, and fine-ware ceramics on the export level. Local and export workshops are also generally associated with the production of items requiring skill beyond that which one would intuitively expect to be available to every household. They are therefore usually associated with part- or full-time specialists.

Workshops themselves are usually recognized in the Maya area by reference to the following set of criteria: the location of quantities of debris associated with the manufacture of the item in question; the association with this debris of tools inferred to have been used in the manufacturing process; and the location at the workshop of a variety of forms of the finished product or imperfect, discarded examples of the product (Feinman 1985; Rice 1987; Stark 1985). The last criterion suggests that the locale served as a workshop and not an area in which the object was used in some other activity (Becker 1973: 398-400). The latter situation would, presumably, imply the presence of a restricted range of artifact forms manufactured from a particular raw material adapted to the performance of the task in question (ibid.).

Of all manufacturing activities recognized among the Classic Maya, the one to receive the most attention in recent years is obsidian production. Within the Maya area there are two recognized traditions of obsidian-tool production: the blade- and flake-core approaches (Sheets 1983), both of which are represented at the excavated LMV centers (Chap. 6). The hallmarks of the former tradition are long, thin, sharp prismatic blades—the end products—polyhedral cores, core spalls (produced during the rejuvenation of the core), core-preparation flakes, and macroblades manufactured during an early period of core shaping (Sheets 1972, 1974, 1975, 1983; Hester, Jack, and Heizer 1971). The recovery of cores, spalls, preparation flakes, and macroblades is generally taken to indicate the existence of a prismatic blade-manufacturing locus somewhere in the area (e.g., Sheets 1983). The care and skill required to produce tools in this tradition has generally led to its association with both specialized artisans and access to long-distance trading networks to acquire obsidian of sufficient quality to meet its demanding specifications (ibid.). The flake-core technology is much simpler, involving the percussive removal of flakes from natural, river-borne (in this area) cobbles (Sheets 1974, 1983). Its hallmarks are flake-cores with evidence of flake removal, river cobbles, and flakes usually with evidence of cortex on their dorsal (exterior) sides (ibid.). Because of the ease with which these cobbles can be obtained and worked, the flake-core tradition is commonly associated with largely untutored producers operating on a part-time basis at best (ibid.). Flake-core technology is usually associated with local, dispersed "cottage industry" tool

production (Sheets 1983). In Chap. 6, only those items diagnostic of chipped stone tool production are taken as evidence for that activity, i.e., flake- and polyhedral cores, polyhedral platform spalls, core-preparation flakes, and macroblades. The presence of the tools themselves, the blades and flakes, may reflect the location of tasks using those implements and not their area of manufacture. As a result, they cannot be employed in identifying obsidian workshops.

In addition to production areas for flint and/or obsidian tools, other manufacturing/processing activities at least tentatively recognized archaeologically in the Lowland Maya and Southeast Periphery zones are: pottery making, woodworking, dental work, stucco and stone working, ground stone tool production, monument carving, and cacao production (Becker 1973; Haviland 1974; Ashmore 1981b; Bruhns in press; Rice 1987; Sheets 1974; Stark 1985; Webster and Gonlin 1988).

Ceremonial: Ceremonial activities are those which involve the propitiation, manipulation, or placation of a supernatural force, which may be a deity, ancestor, or similar figure. Ceremonial activities are usually divided into two subtypes, public and private. Public ceremonies are those rituals carried out for the general good of a supra-household organizational unit by its members and/or their representatives (specialists). Private ceremonies are carried out by individuals for their own good or that of their immediate households.

Ceremonial activities, no matter which type, are associated in the Maya area with the use of pottery incense burners (Sabloff and Freidel 1975: 381-383). In general, private rituals are associated with small amounts of *incensario* debris, though this is widely distributed at a site, being found in low frequencies at a number of domestic groups. Public ceremonies tend to involve the use of more censers and, hence, the locus of their performance is marked by a greater concentration of this material. There should also tend to be less admixture of other ceramic types in public-ritual debris: public ceremonies involve the intensive practice of one particular kind of activity with a resultant restriction in the variety of ceramics, and other artifacts for that matter, associated with it. The locus of public ceremonies would be more specific in that they would habitually be performed at only one or several particular spots. This area(s) would be associated with some features of community significance either human-made (e.g., a temple) or natural (e.g., a cave). Recently, Benyo (1979: 53-62) has also suggested that different censer forms found at

Quirigua may be correlated with differences between public and private rituals. Three-pronged censers, censer lids, and spiked censers, because of their broad spatial and temporal distribution at Quirigua and their association with the primarily residential structures of the Acropolis, are argued to have functioned in private ceremonies (ibid.: 53-54). Effigy modeled censers, because of their elaborate forms, the time and care required for their manufacture, and their association with the publicly oriented Great Plaza, functioned primarily in public ceremonies (ibid.: 55). Censer forms, at least in the LMV, may therefore provide an indication of the public or private nature of the associated ceremonies.

Ceremonial foci are identified in the Maya area and the Southeast Periphery by the presence of purposefully placed deposits associated with the dedication or destruction of structures (i.e., caches, certain burials and tombs, termination deposits), elaborate preparations for interments (i.e., tombs), and the construction of special structures with presumed religious functions (i.e., temples, shrines, altar/ceremonial platforms, ballcourts, and mortuary structures). Temples, commonly noted at major Lowland Maya centers, are small buildings, usually with no more than one to three diminutive rooms each, situated atop high, steep pyramidal substructures (G. Andrews 1975: 39-42; Pollock 1965: 409). Temples are commonly found organized into "temple groups" of two or three structures arrayed around two or three sides of a plaza with the largest construction facing the unobstructed plaza side (G. Andrews 1975: 46; A. Smith 1950: 73; Pollock 1965: 417). Altars and ceremonial platforms are low, flat-topped structures located in central places within plazas or courts. They did not support a superstructure (G. Andrews 1975: 46; Pollock 1965: 411). The only clear archaeologically observable criterion distinguishing the two is their size: altars are smaller than ceremonial platforms (ibid.). Mortuary structures are relatively rare, though they are noted in both the Maya region (A. Smith 1950: 73; Pollock 1965: 411) and northern Central America (Baudez and Becquelin 1973). They are simply platforms containing large numbers of burials. Ballcourts, comprising two relatively low, parallel structures facing each other across a narrow alley, with or without closed end-zones, have also been ascribed a ceremonial function (e.g., Blom 1932). Temples and ballcourts are associated with public ceremonies, while shrines and altars/ceremonial platforms may have served in public or private rituals depending on their

location. The public or private ritual significance of mortuary structures remains unclear.

Administration: Administrative activities, the fourth category, involve the organization and control of the social and political lives of a population by a segment of that population. They are, in essence, those activities ensuring the integration of a number of residential units or households into a single coherent society. The governing "segment" referred to is an elite group that monopolizes the right to organize secular and, possibly, ceremonial supra-household activities. This activity category is divided into two types depending on the spatial extent of the power exercised by this elite: the local and regional levels. The former defines the situation where the elite's administrative power is restricted to a site and its immediate hinterland. In the case of regional administrative power, the elite resident at a monumental center exercise political and social control over several other large sites and their associated hinterlands. The size and degree of elaboration of the administrative bureaucracy in the latter case would also be greater than in the former.

Of all the aspects of activity thought to be applicable to the Lowland Maya area, administration has received the least amount of explicit attention. Consequently, the material correlates of administrative activities are still poorly understood for this region. There are several reasons for this problem. First, secular authority tends to leave little physical trace in the archaeological record at the locale where it is exercised. Political or social authority may well take the form of a social contract between a set of regularly interacting individuals underlain and delimited by a system of traditional social statuses and roles. To be effective, it may require merely an activation of those social obligations and, especially in relatively simple social systems, little in the way of material correlates. Second, the locus of administration in the Maya area cannot be assumed to have been physically separated from that of other activity areas, in particular those in the domestic sphere (Harrison 1970: 257-259). Residences in which private rituals were carried out might also have been the centers of administrative functions (ibid.). Despite these problems, some material correlates of administrative activities can be enumerated.

Given the association between the presence of an elite group and the performance of administrative services, material vestige of such a group is one line of evidence that can be used to infer the existence of administrative activities. In ceramics, therefore, one would expect to see a differential distribution of types throughout a site with the finer, perhaps imported, examples restricted in numbers and location to a very few sectors. Stone artifacts should parallel this distribution with imported and/or especially fine examples located in the same areas where finely made ceramics are found. Both of these artifact distributions would reflect the differential access to wealth and resources that characterizes social hierarchies (e.g., Fried 1967: 185-226). The presence of large quantities of imported materials within a site, no matter what their distribution, would also suggest the existence of an administrative elite with the organizational ability and power to fund the trading enterprises that obtained the exotics (e.g., Rathje 1972).

Because one aspect of administrative authority is the ability of the elite to control labor above the household level, the presence of this authority should be manifest architecturally. Large-scale building projects, whether elite residences or community constructions, such as temples and defensive walls, imply the presence of an authority capable of planning, calling up, supporting, and organizing sizable labor forces (Sabloff and Freidel 1975: 379, 381-383). The presence of an administrative elite, therefore, can be inferred from the existence of a hierarchy of structure sizes at a site. Further, the use of nonlocal and/or difficult-to-work materials and the care with which they are fashioned in these monumental constructions are other indications of the elite's ability to command not only large labor forces but corps of skilled artisans as well. Elite authority is also manifest in the organization of the largest structures at a site into some coherent plan. In the Maya area, elaborately carved monuments bear glyphic inscriptions detailing dynastic histories and display figures with symbols of authority, e.g., scepters and bars, also strongly indicate the existence of an administrative elite at the sites where they are found (e.g., Proskouriakoff 1963; Schele and Freidel 1990). In essence, then, evidence of differential access to resources, whether labor or imported items, is a strong indication of the presence of an administrative hierarchy.

The differences between local and regional levels of administration are more of degree than of kind. Regional centers housed larger, more complexly organized and powerful elite bureaucracies than local-level sites. They therefore have correspondingly larger and more numerous monumental structures, drawing on a larger dependent population for their construction, and more complexly organized site plans (Sabloff and Freidel 1975: 389-394). They also possess larger

amounts and varieties of imported goods with, perhaps, even more restricted distributions within a site corresponding to a rigid distinction between elite and nonelite statuses. In cases of particularly powerful regional elites, settlement in areas under their control may be affected in both site location and form (e.g., Keatinge 1974, 1975 for the Chimu state of Chan Chan; and Parsons 1974 and Sanders, Parsons, and Santley 1979 for the Teotihuacan state). This latter situation appears to have been rare among the Late Classic Lowland Maya.

Marketing: Finally, marketing activities are those associated with the sale and/or transshipment of goods and are divided into three levels: the local, regional, and interregional. The local level concerns the movement of goods among individuals within the restricted area of the site and its immediate hinterland. The regional level incorporates a larger area in its marketing sphere, while the interregional level connotes the movement of goods over considerable distances between two or more physiographic zones (see Reina and Hill 1978: 207; Renfrew 1975). The latter type of marketing also involves well-organized trading expeditions funded and overseen by local elites through professional merchants.

Evidence for marketing activities is of two types, imported items and economic facilities. Local-level exchange by definition excludes imported goods. The facilities required for this level of marketing are limited, perhaps consisting of no more than an open space for a market. Any structures associated with marketing would be small and ephemeral, leaving little trace in the archaeological record (Bunzel 1967: 30-31, 74; McBryde 1933: 112). Large-scale storage facilities would be unnecessary, as those goods not sold on any day would merely return home with the vendor. The location of the market itself should be in an easily accessible portion of the site, possibly in the same area as the monumental structures (Hammond 1975: 84). This location would be partly an expression of elite control over commerce and partly an attempt to take advantage of the number of individuals attracted to these constructions for other purposes (ibid.).

The regional level would be characterized by many of the same features except that nonlocal goods should now be found at the sites under study. The recognition of a diversity of origins for traded commodities can be based on either stylistic or compositional grounds or both (Bishop et al. 1986). Material correlates of the interregional level of marketing at a site are somewhat different. First, sizable quantities of the goods native to the zones trading through the center should be recognized by either stylistic or compositional criteria. Of course, a site that functioned as a conduit for the movement of foreign goods would probably not serve as the ultimate repository of those items (Sabloff and Rathje 1975: 13-14). Nevertheless, some of the traded items should have been incorporated within the archaeological record of the site.

The question of facilities is a more difficult one. Large-scale interregional trade may well be carried on outside of a formal marketplace, may indeed take place in the more secluded portions of a site, where transactions can be strictly controlled and protected (e.g., Hill 1971: 310-315). This would be especially true of commodities with high social or ideological value whose distribution may have been restricted to an elite class (ibid.). These facilities, then, might be no more than a room or two in the houses of resident traders/entrepreneurs and could be recognized by the large amounts of demonstrably foreign goods recovered from them. Artifacts associated with domestic activities would be expected in these deposits as well. Another requirement of long-distance commerce that might be preserved archaeologically is storage facilities. Unlike local and regional exchange, cycles of production and shipment of high-value items are not necessarily well integrated, so there may be some lag time between the arrival of goods at a trading center and their eventual resale. Any center that facilitated the movement of goods through an extensive interregional trading network would have to provide secure areas where goods could be stored awaiting later shipment and sale (e.g., Sabloff and Freidel 1975: 397-404). These facilities would take different forms depending on the nature and requirements of the goods stored—whether they had to be kept dry, out of

the sun, and so forth. The specification of their form *a priori* thus is not possible. They would, however, have to be located in a relatively inaccessible portion of the site to ensure the safety of the objects they contained and, given that this trade was probably elite-controlled, would most likely be found in or adjacent to areas of monumental construction (Sabloff and Freidel 1975: 397-409; see also Morris and Thompson 1974; Keatinge 1974).

Both regional and interregional marketing centers should also be located along inferred routes of communication. At the regional level, these routes should connect the center with other points within the same cultural and/or physiographic zone. A focal point of interregional commerce should be situated on an avenue leading out of the local region. The development of at least several major Maya centers may have owed a great deal to their strategic location along routes of interregional commerce (e.g., Rathje 1972; Jones 1980; see also Hirth 1978).

The marketing levels are not mutually exclusive and it is very likely that at a major site evidence of several levels can be found. A monumental center could have served as the focus of a local and regional market as well as a node in an interregional exchange system. It would not be surprising, then, to encounter the material correlates of several levels at one site.

It is not claimed here that this general set of five activity types encompasses all that will eventually be recognized within the Maya and Southeast Periphery areas. Nor are the material correlates of each considered to exhaust all possible archaeological manifestations of each type. The list does provide, however, a basic set of concepts out of which a general description of the activities performed at a Maya or Southeast Periphery locus can be fashioned.

Appendix III

TABLE III.1

PLAYITAS STRUCTURE HEIGHTS

Structure	North	South	East	West	All Sides
1					1.33 m
2					1.56 m
3					0.69 m
4					0.20 m*
5					0.99 m
6			1.09 m	1.33 m	
7					0.22 m
8				(plowed)	0.00 m
9					0.35 m
10					0.46 m
11					1.19 m
12					0.25 m
13					1.00 m
14					0.21 m
15					1.57 m
16					0.60 m
17					0.84 m
18					0.18 m
19	0.64 m	0.32 m			
20					0.42 m
21					2.35 m
22					1.13 m
23					1.77 m
24					1.81 m
25			0.69 m	0.84 m	
26					0.30 m
27					0.11 m*
28					0.42 m
29					0.55 m
30					0.73 m
31					0.89 m
32					0.21 m
33					0.51 m
34					1.12 m
35					0.41 m
36					0.63 m

TABLE III.1 (continued)

PLAYITAS STRUCTURE HEIGHTS

Structure	North	South	East	West	All Sides
37					0.19 m
38					0.91 m
39					1.07 m
40					0.50 m
41					0.60 m
42					1.30 m
43					0.19 m
44					0.30 m
45					0.45 m
46					0.60 m
47					0.14 m
48					0.40 m
49					0.91 m
50					0.77 m
51					0.94 m
52					0.20 m
53					1.37 m
54					1.60 m
55					1.19 m
56					0.72 m
57					0.20 m
58			0.72 m	0.48 m	
59	0.81 m	0.65 m			
60			0.45 m	0.72 m	
61					0.61 m
62					0.18 m
63					0.69 m
64					0.10 m
65					2.31 m
66					0.45 m
67	0.25 m	0.67 m			
68	0.15 m	0.00 m			
69	0.32 m	0.14 m			
70					0.14 m
71					0.26 m
72	1.99 m*	1.06 m*			
73			1.99 m	1.06 m	
74			2.00 m*	1.10 m*	
75	1.10 *	2.00 m*			
76					5.50 m*
77					7.50 m*
78					6.50 m
79					5.50 m*
80			3.00 m*	3.50 m*	

TABLE III.1 (continued)

PLAYITAS STRUCTURE HEIGHTS

Structure	North	South	East	West	All Sides
81	3.50 m*	3.00 m*			
82			3.50 m*	3.00 m*	
83					2.41 m
84					0.65 m*
85	1.50 m	0.50 m			
86					0.90 m*
87					1.47 m
88					1.30 m
89					1.07 m
90					1.69 m
91					0.82 m
92					0.50 m
93					1.13 m
94					0.27 m
95					0.65 m
96					0.60 m*
97					0.65 m
98					0.64 m
99					1.07 m
100					0.77 m
101					0.95 m
102					0.43 m
103					0.41 m
104					1.83 m
105					1.98 m
106			0.51 m	0.06 m	
107					1.58 m
108					2.34 m
109					1.61 m
110					1.30 m
111					0.54 m
112					0.80 m
113					0.34 m
114					1.04 m
115					2.14 m
116					1.90 m
117					1.44 m
118					0.85 m
119					1.05 m
120					0.11 m
121					0.60 m
122					0.92 m
123					1.68 m
124					0.50 m*
125					1.20 m

TABLE III.1 (continued)

PLAYITAS STRUCTURE HEIGHTS

Structure	North	South	East	West	All Sides
126					0.35 m
127					0.30 m
128					0.26 m
129					0.38 m
130					0.28 m
131					0.22 m
132					0.18 m
133					0.47 m
134					0.80 m
135					0.17 m
136					0.63 m
137					0.55 m
138					0.13 m
139					0.27 m
140					0.31 m
141					0.20 m
142					0.42 m
143					0.17 m
144					0.41 m
145					0.34 m
146					0.18 m
147					0.20 m
148					0.25 m
149	0.51 m	0.37 m			
150	0.55 m	0.22 m			
151	0.17 m	0.38 m			
152					0.39 m
153	0.62 m	0.86 m			
154					0.28 m
155					0.15 m
156					0.98 m
157			0.20 m*	0.00 m	
158					0.86 m
159			1.65 m	1.08 m	
160					0.30 m
161					0.39 m
162					0.13 m
163					0.30 m*
164			1.22 m	1.60 m	
165	1.33 m	0.81 m			
166			0.78 m	1.80 m	
167			0.96 m	1.95 m	
168					0.40 m
169			0.46 m	0.60 m	
170					0.25 m

TABLE III.1 (continued)

PLAYITAS STRUCTURE HEIGHTS

Structure	North	South	East	West	All Sides
171					0.13 m
172					0.20 m
173					0.30 m
174					0.16 m
175					0.30 m
176					0.30 m*
177					1.50 m*
178					0.75 m*
179					0.30 m*
180					0.44 m
181					0.30 m*
182					0.75 m*
183					0.75 m*
184					1.00 m*
185					1.00 m*
186					0.50 m*
187					0.50 m*
188					1.00 m*
189					0.75 m*
190					3.25 m*
191					3.50 m*
192					4.00 m*
193					3.75 m*
194	0.75 m*	1.25 m*			
195					0.75 m*
196					0.50 m*
197					2.25 m*
198					0.45 m
199					0.70 m*
200					0.10 m*
201					1.44 m
202					0.32 m
203					1.35 m
204					1.09 m
205					0.68 m
206					0.80 m*
207					0.75 m**
208					2.00 m**
209					1.00 m**
210					0.75 m**
211					1.00 m**

* Structure heights marked with a single asterisk were estimated and not measured.

** Structure heights marked with a double asterisk refer to structures in Group III and do not appear in Figure 2. These structure heights were also estimated by eye in the field.

TABLE III.2

LAS QUEBRADAS STRUCTURE HEIGHTS

Structure	North	South	East	West	All Sides
1			2.52 m	1.90 m	
2	2.50 m	1.25 m			
3			2.45 m	1.69 m	
4	4.36 m	3.30 m			
5			3.04 m	1.72 m	
6			2.79 m	3.17 m	
7					6.00 m*
8					0.54 m
9					0.67 m
10					0.19 m
11	1.36 m	0.56 m			
12					3.08 m
13					3.95 m
14					4.00 m
15	1.00 m*	1.00 m*			0.00 m
16	3.83 m	4.31 m			
17	0.49 m	0.03 m			
18					0.45 m
19					0.15 m
20					0.43 m
21					1.90 m
22					0.40 m
23					1.47 m
24					1.12 m
25					1.64 m
26					1.98 m
27	3.32 m	2.09 m			
28	0.94 m	0.48 m			
29					1.70 m
30					0.79 m Avg.
31					1.24 m
32					0.60 m
33					0.74 m
34	0.50 m*	0.30 m*			
35					0.50 m
36					1.06 m
37					1.60 m
38					0.66 m
39			1.22 m	2.05 m	
40					0.98 m
41					3.52 m
42			(above platform)		0.56 m
43					3.46 m
44					1.20 m*
45					0.39 m
46					1.10 m

TABLE III.2 (continued)

LAS QUEBRADAS STRUCTURE HEIGHTS

Structure	North	South	East	West	All Sides
47					0.64 m
48	1.05 m	0.44 m			
49			0.26 m	1.40 m	
50			0.43 m	1.35 m	
51			0.71 m	1.32 m	
52			0.66 m	1.824 m	
53			0.14 m	0.66 m	
54			0.78 m	1.50 m	
55			0.61 m	1.54 m	
56			0.43 m	1.04 m	
57			2.55 m	2.73 m	
58					1.60 m
59					1.10 m
60	0.46 m	0.67 m			
61			0.89 m	1.04 m	
62	0.70 m	1.05 m			
63			0.70 m	1.00 m	
64					0.90 m
65					0.41 m
66			0.30 m	1.00 m	
67	1.00 m	0.54 m			
68					0.80 m
69					1.03 m
70					0.96 m
71					1.01 m
72					1.40 m
73					0.50 m
74					0.87 m
75					1.02 m
76					0.42 m
77					0.63 m
78					0.35 m
79					4.00 m*
80					0.96 m
81					1.20 m
82					0.28 m
83					0.33 m
84					0.83 m
85					0.25 m
86					0.82 m
87			0.84 m	0.37 m	
88					0.58 m
89					0.15 m*
90					0.81 m
91					0.56 m

TABLE III.2 (continued)

LAS QUEBRADAS STRUCTURE HEIGHTS

Structure	North	South	East	West	All Sides
92					0.62 m
93					0.81 m
94	0.00 m	0.40 m*			
95					0.46 m
96					0.62 m
97					1.30 m*
98					0.25 m*
99					0.80 m*
100	0.00 m	0.40 m			
101	0.00 m	0.34 m			
102					0.30 m*
103					0.22 m
104					1.05 m
105					0.46 m
106	0.00 m	0.24 m			
107					0.40 m
108	0.35 m	1.00 m			
109	0.57 m	1.29 m			
110					0.50 m*
111					0.65 m*
112					1.25 m*
113					1.14 m
114					0.77 m
115	0.76 m	2.18 m			
116			1.20 m*	2.80 m*	
117					1.00 m
118	3.90 m	7.28 m			
119			1.40 m*	2.00 m*	
120	0.47 m	1.03 m			
121					0.29 m
122					0.56 m
123					0.43 m
124					0.30 m
125					0.32 m
126					1.00 m*
127					0.75 m*
128					1.20 m*
129					1.60 m*
130					0.60 m*
131	0.20 m*	0.60 m*			
132					1.00 m*
133					0.80 m*
134					1.10 m*
135					1.20 m*
136	0.60 m*	0.25 m*			

TABLE III.2 (continued)

LAS QUEBRADAS STRUCTURE HEIGHTS

Structure	North	South	East	West	All Sides
137					0.25 m*
138					0.15 m*
139					0.30 m*
140			0.00 m	0.30 m*	
141					0.80 m*
142					0.40 m*
143					0.90 m*
144					0.25 m*
145					0.25 m*
146	0.50 m*	1.15 m*			
147					0.40 m*
148					0.60 m*
149					0.75 m*
150					0.80 m*
151			0.50 m*	0.75 m*	
152					0.50 m*
153					1.00 m*
154					2.02 m
155					1.40 m*
156	0.88 m	1.40 m			
157	2.00 m*	1.50 m*			
158	0.08 m	0.70 m			
159	0.10 m	0.33 m			
160					1.30 m
161	0.10 m	0.47 m			
162					0.39 m
163			0.64 m	1.12 m	
164	0.44 m	0.60 m			
165					0.71 m
166					1.29 m
167	3.12 m	4.24 m			
168			1.75 m	2.05 m	
169					1.20 m
170	0.60 m*	1.50 m*			
171	0.60 m*	1.40 m*			
172					1.52 m
173			0.00 m	0.40 m*	
174					0.70 m
175	0.00 m	0.35 m*			
176					0.44 m
177	0.24 m	0.47 m			
178					0.20 m*
179	0.60 m*	0.90 m*			
180	0.60 m*	1.25 m*			
181	0.90 m*	1.25 m*			

TABLE III.2 (continued)

LAS QUEBRADAS STRUCTURE HEIGHTS

Structure	North	South	East	West	All Sides
182					0.90 m
183	0.70 m	1.64 m			
184	1.75 m*	1.00 m*			
185	1.10 m*	2.50 m*			
186					2.45 m
187	1.20 m	2.50 m			
188					1.70 m*
189					2.00 m*
190					1.40 m*
191			0.74 m	1.67 m	
192			0.64 m	2.39 m	
193					1.15 m*
194					0.53 m
195					0.33 m
196					0.66 m
197					0.27 m
198					0.51 m
199					5.00 m
200	1.09 m	1.41 m			
201					0.72 m
202					0.36 m
203					0.00 m
204					1.79 m
205					5.00 m*
206					1.38 m
207	0.59 m	1.00 m			
208	0.99 m	1.53 m			
209	1.86 m	2.43 m			
210					0.54 m
211					0.40 m*
212	0.14 m	0.43 m			
213					0.68 m
214					0.25 m
215					0.57 m
216					0.56 m
217					0.50 m
218					0.46 m
219					0.46 m
220			2.14 m	0.86 m	
221					1.14 m
222					0.48 m
223					0.54 m
224					0.45 m
225					0.13 m
226					0.25 m

TABLE III.2 (continued)

LAS QUEBRADAS STRUCTURE HEIGHTS

Structure	North	South	East	West	All Sides
227					1.60 m*
228					1.40 m*
229					0.99 m
230					3.85 m
231					0.58 m
232					1.56 m
233	2.20 m*	5.50 m*			
234			1.71 m	3.51 m	
235	0.98 m	6.12 m			
236	2.40 m*	1.00 m*			
237					0.75 m
238					0.83 m
239					0.60 m
240					0.20 m
241					0.20 m
242					0.60 m
243					0.50 m*
244					1.20 m*
245					0.90 m*
246	1.83 m	1.12 m			
247			1.70 m	2.77 m	
248					0.35 m
249					0.31 m
250					0.59 m
251					1.71 m
252					0.50 m*
253	2.83 m*	3.50 m*			
254					6.30 m
255	4.50 m*	5.00 m*			
256			1.00 m	4.00 m*	
257	5.50 m*	2.50 m*			
258			8.00 m*	3.90 m*	
259	2.50 m*	4.50 m*			
260	1.89 m	1.39 m			
261					6.50 m*
262					7.50 m*
263			1.00 m	4.25 m	
264	6.75 m	7.30 m			
265					1.50 m*
266					0.20 m
267					0.26 m
268					0.20 m*
269					0.30 m*
270					0.00 m
271					3.00 m*

TABLE III.2 (continued)

LAS QUEBRADAS STRUCTURE HEIGHTS

Structure	North	South	East	West	All Sides
272					2.50 m*
273					1.75 m*
274					1.20 m*
275					0.00 m
276					0.00 m
277					2.00 m
278					0.40 m*
279					2.50 m*
280					3.25 m*
281					0.30 m
282					0.37 m
283					0.40 m*

* An asterisk beside a figure indicates that the altitude of that structures was estimated by eye and not measured.
Note: Structures 273-280 are located in the Southeast Group of Las Quebradas and are not shown on the overall map of that site. They appear on a separate sheet as they were sketch-mapped in the field.

TABLE III.3

HEIGHTS OF MAPPED QUEBRADA GRANDE STRUCTURES

Structure	North	South	East	West	All Sides
1					2.00 m
2	7.00 m	1.00 m			
3	7.00 m	1.00 m			
4					6.50 m
5					1.00 m
6	4.00 m	8.00 m			
7			6.00 m	1.50 m	
8					2.00 m
9					4.00 m
10					3.00 m
11					3.50 m
12					1.75 m
13					4.50 m
14					4.50 m
15	7.00 m	3.50 m			
16			5.00 m	1.00 m	
17			5.50 m	5.00 m	
18			5.50 m	1.30 m	
19					2.50 m
20					2.75 m

TABLE III.3 (continued)

HEIGHTS OF MAPPED QUEBRADA GRANDE STRUCTURES

Structure	North	South	East	West	All Sides
21			5.00 m	5.50 m	
22	3.50 m	0.50 m			
Plat. 1					5.50 m
Plat. 2	3.50 m	3.00 m			
Plat. 3	3.00 m	3.50 m			

Note: All Quebrada Grande structure heights were estimated by eye; none were measured with an instrument.

TABLE III.4

CHOCO STRUCTURE HEIGHTS

Structure	North	South	East	West	All Sides
1	5.96 m	6.71 m			
2			1.69 m	2.53 m	
3			2.96 m	1.99 m	
4	5.51 m	6.00 m			
5			4.00 m*	3.10 m*	
6			2.58 m	3.08 m	
7	2.65 m	1.66 m			
8					0.53 m
9					0.75 m
10	2.76 m	2.55 m			
11					0.23 m
12					0.32 m
13					1.15 m
14					0.18 m
15					0.50 m*
16					0.50 m*
16 Terrace	0.53 m	0.00 m			
17					0.72 m
18					0.84 m
19					1.00 m*
20					1.88 m*
21					1.47 m
22					0.43 m
23					0.31 m
24					0.32 m
25					0.78 m
26					1.55 m
27					0.74 m
28					0.13 m
29					0.90 m*

TABLE III.4 (continued)

CHOCO STRUCTURE HEIGHTS

Structure	North	South	East	West	All Sides
30					0.80 m
31					0.75 m*
32					0.25 m
33	1.29 m	1.60 m			
34					0.37 m
35					0.49 m
36					0.25 m
37					1.00 m
38					0.60 m*
39					2.20 m
40					2.30 m
41					1.34 m
42					0.86 m
43	1.37 m	1.06 m			
44					1.62 m
45					1.10 m
46					0.20 m*
47					0.50 m*
48					4.00 m*
49					0.64 m
50					0.74 m
51					0.50 m*
52					2.20 m*
53					0.52 m
54					1.22 m
55					2.24 m
56					0.82 m
57					0.32 m
58					0.38 m
59					0.80 m
60					0.58 m
61					0.51 m
62					0.69 m
63					0.61 m
64					1.32 m
65					0.61 m
66					1.50 m*
67					1.25 m*
68					0.75 m*
69					0.75 m*
70					2.00 m*
71					0.75 m*
72					1.75 m*
73					0.80 m*
74					0.80 m*

TABLE III.4 (continued)

CHOCO STRUCTURE HEIGHTS

Structure	North	South	East	West	All Sides
75					2.50 m*
76					1.75 m*

Note: All structure heights are based on transit measurements, except those marked with an asterisk (*), which were estimated by eye. Only those structures actually mapped are included here.

TABLE III.5

COMANCHE FARM STRUCTURE HEIGHTS

Structure	North	South	East	West	All Sides
1					2.25 m
2					1.00 m
3					0.60 m
4					0.60 m
5	0.75 m	1.10 m			
6			0.75 m	1.00 m	
7	?	0.40 m			
8			0.60 m	0.40 m	
9	1.00 m	1.50 m			
10			5.00 m	4.50 m	
11	1.50 m	2.00 m			
12			2.75 m	2.25 m	
13			1.50 m	2.00 m	
14	?	3.00 m			
15			3.00 m	2.50 m	
16					5.50 m

Note: ? indicates that the side in question has been destroyed and was not measurable in 1977.

TABLE III.6

JUYAMA STRUCTURE HEIGHTS

Structure	North	South	East	West	All Sides
1					1.20 m
2					0.10 m
3			0.40 m	1.00 m	
4			0.50 m	1.00 m	
5					1.00 m
6					1.75 m
7	1.90 m				1.70 m
8	2.40 m	1.70 m			
9					0.75 m
10					0.30 m

TABLE III.7

BOBOS STRUCTURE HEIGHTS

Structure	North	South	East	West	All Sides
1					2.00 m
2					2.00 m
3					2.50 m
4			1.50 m	1.00 m	
5	1.00 m	0.75 m			
6	1.00 m	0.75 m			
7			1.00 m	1.50 m	
8					0.50 m
9					0.75 m
10					2.50 m
11					2.00 m
12					1.75 m
13					1.00 m
14					1.50 m
15					1.00 m

TABLE III.8

MOJANALES STRUCTURE HEIGHTS

Structure	Northeast	Southeast	Northwest	Southwest	All Sides
1					2.75 m
2	0.50 m			1.25 m	
3	1.00 m			2.50 m	
4					4.00 m
5					5.00 m
6					1.40 m
7					2.20 m

TABLE III.9

ARAPAHOE VIEJO STRUCTURE HEIGHTS

Structure	North	South	East	West	All Sides
1	0.30 m	0.10 m			
2	0.75 m	0.50 m			
3	0.70 m	0.50 m			
4	1.00 m	0.80 m			
5	1.10 m				
6	2.20 m	1.90 m			
7	0.55 m	0.40 m			
8					1.50 m

TABLE III.9 (continued)

ARAPAHOE VIEJO STRUCTURE HEIGHTS

Structure	North	South	East	West	All Sides
9			2.50 m	4.00 m	
10	2.50 m	1.00 m			
11					2.50 m
12					3.00 m
13	3.00 m	1.00 m			
14	1.00 m	0.75 m			
15	0.50 m	0.00 m			
16	0.50 m	1.50 m			
17					5.50 m

TABLE III.10

JUAN DE PAZ STRUCTURE HEIGHTS

Structure	North	South	East	West	All Sides
1					0.65 m
2			1.21 m	0.89 m	
3	4.60 m	4.20 m			
4					0.48 m
5					0.22 m
6					0.13 m
7a	0.49 m	0.94 m			
7b					1.23 m
8					0.77 m
9a					0.47 m
9b	0.26 m	0.96 m			
10a					0.88 m
10b	0.34 m	1.51 m			
11					0.68 m
12	0.53 m	2.67 m			
13					0.64 m
14	0.11 m	0.59 m			
15					0.30 m
16	2.40 m	1.23 m			
17	0.10 m	0.70 m			
18	0.94 m	1.67 m			
19	0.10 m	0.60 m			
20					0.66 m
21	0.31 m	0.78 m			
22					1.44 m
23					0.84 m
24			0.41 m	1.31 m	
25					0.98 m

TABLE III.10 (continued)

JUAN DE PAZ STRUCTURE HEIGHTS

Structure	North	South	East	West	All Sides
26a					0.56 m
26b	0.45 m	1.48 m			
27	0.10 m	0.42 m			
28	0.16 m	1.01 m			
29a	0.96 m	1.61 m			
29b					2.36 m
30					0.64 m
31					3.16 m
32a					2.51 m*
32b	2.42 m	3.62 m			
33					1.81 m
34	0.96 m	0.04 m			
35	1.63 m	0.39 m			
36	0.59 m	2.14 m			
37a	0.37 m	1.04 m			
37b					1.69 m
38	0.15 m	0.76 m			
39	0.10 m	0.51 m			
40	0.48 m	1.67 m			
41	2.80 m	4.05 m			
42	0.20 m	0.84 m			
43	0.30 m	0.81 m			
44	0.20 m	1.10 m			
45a			0.98 m	0.12 m	
45b					0.88 m
45c					0.98 m
46					0.85 m
47	0.33 m	0.56 m			
48a	?	0.68 m			
48b					0.68 m
49a					0.89 m
49b					0.55 m
50					?
51					0.55 m
52b					0.20 m
52c					1.05 m
53					0.42 m
54a					0.50 m
54b					0.51 m
55					0.35 m
56					0.43 m
57					?
58	0.24 m	1.45 m			
59	0.11 m	0.83 m			
60	0.17 m	0.99 m			

TABLE III.10 (continued)

JUAN DE PAZ STRUCTURE HEIGHTS

Structure	North	South	East	West	All Sides
61	0.08 m	0.56 m			
62	0.46 m	1.35 m			
63	0.16 m	1.31 m			
64	0.55 m	3.15 m			
65					0.10 m
66					0.70 m
67	0.18 m	0.90 m			
68					0.36 m
69	0.32 m	1.74 m			
70					?
71					?
72	1.21 m	0.98 m			
73	0.36 m	1.22 m			
74	3.47 m	4.45 m			
75	0.38 m	0.83 m			
76					0.13 m
77					0.25 m
78					0.12 m
79	0.30 m	0.78 m			

Note: The projection from Str. 32a is 1.67 m high.

TABLE III.11

LOS CERRITOS STRUCTURE HEIGHTS

Structure	North	South	East	West	All Sides
1					1.00 m
2					2.25 m
3					0.60 m
4					0.60 m
5					1.20 m
6	1.50 m	2.20 m			
7	1.25 m	1.50 m			
8	—	0.50 m			

Bibliography

Adams, F.
    1914   *The Conquest of the Tropics*. New York: Doubleday.

Adams, R.
    1970   Suggested Classic Period Occupational Specialization in the Southern Maya Lowlands. Pp. 487-502 in *Monographs and Papers in Maya Archaeology*, ed. W. Bullard. Papers of the Peabody Museum, Vol. 61. Cambridge, Mass.: Harvard University.
    1971   *The Ceramics of Altar de Sacrificios*. Papers of the Peabody Museum, Vol. 63, No. 1. Cambridge, Mass.: Harvard University.
    1981   Settlement Patterns of the Central Yucatan and Southern Campeche Regions. Pp. 211-258 in *Maya Lowland Settlement Patterns*, ed. W. Ashmore. Albuquerque: University of New Mexico Press.

Agurcia, F. R.
    1980   Late Classic Settlements in the Comayagua Valley. Paper presented at the 45th Annual Meeting of the Society for American Archaeology, Philadelphia.

Anderson, R.
    1971   *Traditional Europe: A Study in Anthropology and History*. Belmont, Mass.: Wadsworth.

Andrews, E. W., V
    1976   *The Archaeology of Quelepa, El Salvador*. Middle American Research Institute, Publication 42. New Orleans: Tulane University.

Andrews, G. F.
    1975   *Maya Cities: Placemaking and Urbanization*. Norman: University of Oklahoma Press.

Ashmore, W.
    1977   The Quirigua Project: The Site Periphery Program. Paper presented at the 42nd Annual Meeting of the Society for American Archaeology, New Orleans.
    1980   The Classic Maya Settlement at Quirigua, Guatemala. Paper presented at the 45th Annual Meeting of the Society for American Archaeology, Philadelphia.
    1981a   (ed.) *Lowland Maya Settlement Patterns*. School of American Research Advanced Seminar. Albuquerque: University of New Mexico Press.
    1981b   Settlement at Quirigua, Guatemala: A Functional Definition of the Site and a Taxonomy of Maya Settlement Units. PhD dissertation, Department of Anthropology, University of Pennsylvania.
    1984   Quirigua Archaeology and History Revisited. *Journal of Field Archaeology* 11: 365-380.
    1988   Household and Community at Classic Quirigua. Pp. 153-169 in *Household and Community in the Mesoamerican Past*, ed. R. Wilk and W. Ashmore. Albuquerque: University of New Mexico Press.

Ashmore, W., E. Schortman, and R. Sharer
    1983   The Quirigua Project: 1979 Season. Pp. 55-78 in *Quirigua Reports*, Vol. 2, ed. E. Schortman and P. Urban. UMM 49. Philadelphia: University Museum.

Ashmore, W., and R. Sharer
    1978   Excavations at Quirigua, Guatemala: The Ascent of an Elite Maya Center. *Archaeology* 31: 10-19.

Ashmore, W., and R. Wilk
    1988   Household and Community in the Mesoamerican Past. Pp. 1-27 in *Household and Community in the Mesoamericcan Past*, ed. R. Wilk and W. Ashmore. Albuquerque: University of New Mexico.

Ball, J.
    1983   Teotihuacan, the Maya, and Ceramic Interchange: A Contextual Perspective. Pp. 125-145 in
            Highland-Lowland Interaction in Mesoamerica: Interdisciplinary Approaches, ed. A. Miller. Washington,
            D.C.: Dumbarton Oaks.

Barth, F.
    1969a   (ed.) *Ethnic Groups and Boundaries: The Social Organization of Culture Difference*. Boston: Little, Brown
            and Co.
    1969b   Introduction. Pp. 9-38 in *Ethnic Groups and Boundaries: The Social Organization of Culture Difference*, ed.
            F. Barth. Boston: Little, Brown and Co.

Baudez, C.
    1970   *Central America*. Geneva: Nagel.
    1983   (ed.) *Introducción a la Arqueología de Copán, Honduras*. 2 vols. and maps. Tegucigalpa: SECTUR
            (Secretaria de Estado en el Despacho de Cultura y Turismo).

Baudez, C., and P. Becquelin
    1973   *Archéologie de Los Naranjos, Honduras*. Mission Archéologique et Ethnologique Française au Mexique,
            Vol. 2. Mexico City: Etudes Américaines.

Becker, M.
    1971   The Identification of a Second Plaza Plan at Tikal, Guatemala, and Its Implications for Ancient Maya
            Social Complexity. PhD dissertation, Department of Anthropology, University of Pennsylvania.
    1972   Plaza Plans at Quirigua, Guatemala. *Katunob* 8: 47-62.
    1973   Archaeological Evidence for Occupational Specialization Among the Classic Period Maya at Tikal,
            Guatemala. *American Antiquity* 38: 396-406.

Benyo, J.
    1979   The Pottery Censers of Quirigua, Izabal, Guatemala. MA thesis, Department of Anthropology, State
            University of New York, Albany.

Bergman, J.
    1969   The Distribution of Cacao Cultivation in Precolumbian America. *Annals of the Association of American
            Geographers* 59: 85-96.

Berlin, H.
    1952   Novedades Arqueológicas. *Antropología e Historia de Guatemala*, Publicación No. 2: 41-46.

Bevan, B., and R. Sharer
    1983   Quirigua and the Earthquake of February 4, 1976. Pp. 110-117 in *Quirigua Reports*, Vol. 2, ed. E.
            Schortman and P. Urban. UMM 49. Philadelphia: University Museum.

Binford, L.
    1962   Archaeology as Anthropology. *American Antiquity* 28: 217-225.
    1967   Smudge Pits and Hide Smoking: The Use of Analogy in Archaeological Reasoning. *American Antiquity*
            32: 1-12.
    1968   Archaeological Perspectives. Pp. 5-32 in *New Perspectives in Archaeology*, ed. L. Binford and S. Binford.
            Chicago: Aldine Publishing Co.

Bishop, R., M. Beaudry, R. Leventhal, and R. Sharer
    1986   Compositional Analysis of Copador and Related Pottery in the Southeast Maya Area. Pp. 143-167 in
            The Southeast Maya Periphery, ed. P. Urban and E. Schortman. Austin: University of Texas Press.

Blom, F.
    1932   *The Maya Ball Game Pok-Ta-Pok (Called Tlachtli by the Aztecs)*. Middle American Research Institute,
            Publication 4. New Orleans: Tulane University.

Boggs, S.
1944   Excavations in Central and Western El Salvador. Appendix C in *Archaeological Investigations in El Salvador*, by J. Longyear, III. Memoirs of the Peabody Museum, Vol. 9, No. 2. Cambridge, Mass: Harvard University.

Bordaz, J.
1970   *Tools of the Old and New Stone Age*. Garden City, N.Y.: Natural History Press.

Braun, D.
1986   Midwestern Hopewellian Exchange and Supralocal Integration. Pp. 117-126 in *Peer Polity Interaction and Socio-Political Change*, ed. C. Renfrew and J. Cherry. Cambridge: Cambridge University Press.

Brose, D.
1979   A Speculative Model for the Role of Exchange in the Prehistory of the Eastern Woodlands. Pp. 3-8 in *Hopewell Archaeology: The Chillicothe Conference*, ed. D. Brose and N. Greber. Kent, Ohio: Kent State University Press.

Brose, D., and N. Greber, eds.
1979   *Hopewell Archaeology: The Chillicothe Conference*. Kent, Ohio: Kent State University Press.

Brown, J.
1975   Spiro Art and Its Mortuary Contexts. Pp. 1-32 in *Death and the Afterlife in Pre-Columbian America*, ed. E. Benson. Washington, D.C.: Dumbarton Oaks.
1976   The Southern Cult Reconsidered. *Mid-Continental Journal of Archaeology* 1: 115-135.

Bruhns, K.
1986   The Role of Commercial Agriculture in Early Postclassic Developments in Central El Salvador: The Rise and Fall of Cihuatan. Pp. 296-312 in *The Southeast Maya Periphery*, ed. E. Schortman and P. Urban. Austin: University of Texas Press.

Bullard, M., and R. Sharer
n.d.   Ceramics and Artifacts of Quirigua, Guatemala. In preparation for QR 6. Philadelphia: University Museum.

Bullard, W., Jr.
1960   Maya Settlement Pattern in Northwest Peten, Guatemala. *American Antiquity* 25: 355-372.

Bunzel, R.
1967   *Chichicastenango: A Guatemalan Village*. Seattle: University of Washington Press (first publ. 1952).

Burghardt, A.
1971   A Hypothesis about Gateway Cities. *Annals of the Association of American Geographers* 61: 269-285.

Caldwell, J.
1970   Interaction Spheres in Prehistory. Pp. 133-143 in *Hopewellian Studies*, ed. J. Caldwell and R. Hall. Scientific Paper No. 12. Springfield: Illinois State Museum (first publ. 1964).

Carr, R., and J. Hazard
1961   *Map of the Ruins of Tikal, Guatemala*. Tikal Reports, No. 11. Philadelphia: University Museum.

Coe, W.
1965   Caches and Offertory Practices of the Maya Lowlands. Pp. 441-461 in *Handbook of Middle American Indians*, Vol. 2, ed. R. Wauchope and G. Willey. Austin: University of Texas Press.
1970   *Tikal, A Handbook of the Ancient Maya Ruins*, 3rd ed. Philadelphia: University Museum.

Cohen, A.
1969   *Custom and Politics in Urban Africa: A Study of Hausa Migrants in Yoruba Towns*. Berkeley: University of California Press.

Cohen, R.
    1978   Ethnicity: Problem and Focus in Anthropology. Pp. 379-403 in *Annual Review of Anthropology*, Vol. 7, ed. B. Siegel, A. Beals, and S. Tyler. Palo Alto, Cal.: Annual Reviews, Inc.
    1981   *The Politics of Elite Culture*. Berkeley: University of California Press.

Collins, T.
    1975   Behavioral Change and Ethnic Maintenance Among the Northern Ute: Some Political Considerations. Pp. 59-74 in *The New Ethnicity: Perspectives from Ethnology*, ed. J. Bennett. New York: West Publishing Co.

Curtin, P.
    1975   *Economic Change in Pre-Colonial Africa: Senegambia in the Era of the Slave Trade*. Madison: University of Wisconsin Press.
    1984   *Cross-Cultural Trade in World Prehistory*. Cambridge: Cambridge University Press.

Day, K.
    1972   Urban Planning at Chanchan, Peru. Pp. 927-930 in *Man, Settlement, and Urbanism*, ed. P. Ucko, R. Tringham, and G. Dimbleby. London: Duckworth and Co.

Demarest, A., and R. Sharer
    1982   The Origins and Evolution of Usulutan Ceramics. *American Antiquity* 47: 810-822.

Despres, L.
    1975   Ethnicity and Ethnic Group Relations in Guyana. Pp. 127-147 in *The New Ethnicity: Perspectives from Ethnology*, ed. J. Bennett. New York: West Publishing Co.

Dimick, J.
    1941   *Notes on Excavations at Campana San Andres, El Salvador*. Carnegie Institution of Washington Yearbook. Washington, D.C.: Carnegie Institution.

Donley, L.
    1982   House Power: Swahili Space and Symbolic Markers. Pp. 63-73 in *Symbolic and Structural Archaeology*, ed. I. Hodder. Cambridge: Cambridge University Press.

Earle, T.
    1987   Chiefdoms in Archaeological and Ethnohistorical Perspective. Pp. 279-308 in *Annual Review of Anthropology*, Vol. 16, ed. B. Siegel, A. Beals, and S. Tyler. Palo Alto, Cal.: Annual Reviews, Inc.

Edmonson, M.
    1960   Nativism, Syncretism, and Anthropological Science. Pp. 181-204 in Middle American Research Institute, Publication 19. New Orleans: Tulane University.

Escoto, J.
    1964   Weather and Climate of Mexico and Central America. Pp. 187-215 in *Handbook of Middle American Indians*, Vol. 1, ed. R. West. Austin: University of Texas Press.

Fagan, B.
    1972   *Ingombe Ilede: Early Trade in South Central Africa*. Module 19. Reading, Mass.: Addison-Wesley Modular Publications.

Fash, W. L., Jr.
    1983   Maya State Formation: A Case Study and Its Implications. PhD dissertation, Department of Anthropology, Harvard University.
    1988   A New Look at Maya Statecraft from Copán, Honduras. *Antiquity* 62: 157-169.

Feinman, G.
    1985   Changes in the Organization of Ceramic Production in Pre-Hispanic Oaxaca, Mexico. Pp. 195-223 in *Decoding Prehistoric Ceramics*, ed. B. Nelson. Carbondale: Southern Illinois University Press.

Fishman, J.
1977   Language and Ethnicity. Pp. 15-57 in *Language, Ethnicity and Intergroup Relations*, ed. H. Giles. New York: Academic Press.

Flannery, K.
1968   The Olmec and the Valley of Oaxaca: A Model for Inter-Regional Interaction in Formative Times. Pp. 79-110 in *Dumbarton Oaks Conference on the Olmec*, ed. E. Benson. Washington, D.C.: Dumbarton Oaks.

Flannery, K., and J. Marcus
1976   Evolution of the Public Building in Formative Oaxaca. Pp. 205-221 in *Cultural Change and Continuity: Essays in Honor of James Bennett Griffin*, ed. C. Cleland. New York: Academic Press.

Ford, J.
1962   *A Quantitative Method for Deriving Cultural Chronology*. Pan-American Union, Technical Manual 1. Washington, D.C.: Organization of American States, Technical Publications and Documents.

Freidel, D.
1979   Culture Areas and Interaction Spheres: Contrasting Approaches to the Emergence of Civilization in the Maya Lowlands. *American Antiquity* 44: 36-54.
1981   Civilization as a State of Mind: The Cultural Evolution of the Lowland Maya. Pp. 188-227 in *The Transition to Statehood in the New World*, ed. G. Jones and R. Kautz. Cambridge: Cambridge University Press.
1986a   Maya Warfare: An Example of Peer Polity Interaction. Pp. 93-108 in *Peer Polity Interaction and Socio-Political Change*, ed. C. Renfrew and J. Cherry. Cambridge: Cambridge University Press.
1986b   Terminal Classic Lowland Maya: Successes, Failures and Aftermaths. Pp. 409-430 in *Late Lowland Maya Civilization*, ed. J. Sabloff and E. W. Andrews, V. Albuquerque: University of New Mexico Press.

Fried, M.
1967   *The Evolution of Political Society*. New York: Random House.

Gordon, G.
1896   *The Prehistoric Ruins of Copan, Honduras*. Memoirs of the Peabody Museum, Vol. 1, No. 1. Cambridge, Mass.: Harvard University.

Haaland, G.
1969   Economic Determinants in Ethnic Processes. Pp. 58-73 in *Ethnic Groups and Boundaries: The Social Organization of Cultural Difference*, ed. F. Barth. Boston: Little, Brown and Co.

Haaland, R.
1977   Archaeological Classification and Ethnic Groups: A Case Study from Sudanese Nubia. *Norwegian Archaeological Review* 10: 1-31.

Haggett, P.
1965   *Locational Analysis in Human Geography*. London: Edward Arnold, Ltd.
1975   *Geography, A Modern Synthesis*, 2nd ed. New York: Harper and Row.

Hall, E.
1973   *The Silent Language*. Garden City, N.Y.: Doubleday, Inc.

Hammond, N.
1972   Obsidian Trade Routes in the Mayan Area. *Science* 178: 1092-1093.
1975   *Lubaantun, A Classic Mayan Realm*. Monographs of the Peabody Museum, No. 2. Cambridge, Mass.: Harvard University.

Hardoy, J.
1973   *Pre-Columbian Cities*. New York: Walker and Co.

Harrison, P.
1970   The Central Acropolis, Tikal, Guatemala: A Preliminary Study of Its Structural Components During the Late Classic Period. PhD dissertation, Department of Anthropology, University of Pennsylvania.

Hatch, M.
    1975   A Study of Hieroglyphic Texts at the Classic Maya Site of Quirigua, Guatemala. PhD dissertation, Department of Anthropology, University of California, Berkeley.

Haviland, W.
    1966   Maya Settlement Patterns: A Critical Review. Pp. 21-47 in Middle American Research Institute, Publication 26. New Orleans: Tulane University.
    1974   Occupational Specialization at Tikal, Guatemala: Stoneworking, Monument Carving. *American Antiquity* 39: 494-496.

Hempel, C.
    1966   *Philosophy of Natural Science*. Englewood Cliffs, N.J.: Prentice-Hall, Inc.

Henderson, J.
    1975   Pre-Columbian Trade Networks in Northwestern Honduras. Paper presented at the 74th Annual Meetings of the American Anthropological Association, New Orleans.

Henderson, J., I. Sterns, A. Wonderley, and P. Urban
    1979   Archaeological Investigations in the Valle de Naco, Northwestern Honduras: A Preliminary Report. *Journal of Field Archaeology* 6: 169-192.

Hester, T., R. Heizer, and R. Jack
    1971   Technology and Geologic Sources of Obsidian Artifacts from Cerro de las Minas, Veracruz, Mexico with Observations on Olmec Trade. *Contributions of the University of California Archaeological Research Facility* 13: 133-141.

Hester, T., R. Jack, and R. Heizer
    1971   The Obsidian of Tres Zapotes, Veracruz, Mexico. *Contributions of the University of California Archaeological Research Facility* 13: 64-131.

Hewett, E.
    1911   Two Seasons' Work in Guatemala. *Bulletin of the Archaeological Institute of America* 2: 117-134.
    1912   The Excavations at Quirigua in 1912. *Bulletin of the Archaeological Institute of America* 3: 163-171.
    1916   Latest Work of the School of American Archaeology at Quirigua. Pp. 57-162 in *Holmes Anniversary Volume Anthropological Essays*, ed. F. Hodge. Washington, D.C.

Hill, P.
    1971   Two Types of West African House Trade. Pp. 303-318 in *The Development of Indigenous Trade and Markets in West Africa*, ed. C. Meillassoux. International African Institute. Oxford: Oxford University Press.

Hirth, K.
    1978   Interregional Trade and the Formation of Gateway Communities. *American Antiquity* 43: 35-45.
    1988   Beyond the Maya Frontier: Cultural Interaction and Syncretism along the Central Honduran corridor. Pp. 297-334 in *The Southeast Classic Maya Zone*, ed. E. Boone and G. Willey. Washington, D.C.: Dumbarton Oaks.

Hirth, K., P. Urban, G. Hasemann, and V. Veliz R.
    1980   Regional Settlement Patterns in the Cajon Region, Department of Comayagua, Honduras. Paper presented at the 79th Annual Meetings of the American Anthropological Association, Washington, D.C.

Hodder, I.
    1977   The Distribution of Material Culture Items in the Baringo District, Western Kenya. *Man* 12: 239-269.
    1978a   Simple Correlations Between Material Culture and Society: A Review. Pp. 3-24 in *The Spatial Organization of Culture*, ed. I. Hodder. Pittsburgh: University of Pittsburgh Press.
    1978b   (ed.) *The Spatial Organization of Culture*. Pittsburgh: University of Pittsburgh Press.

1978c The Spatial Structures of Material 'Cultures': A Review of Some of the Evidence. Pp. 93-111 in *The Spatial Organization of Culture*, ed. I. Hodder. Pittsburgh: University of Pittsburgh Press.

1979 Economic and Social Stress and Material Culture Patterning. *American Antiquity* 44: 446-454.

Hodder, I., and C. Orton

1976 *Spatial Analysis in Archaeology*. Cambridge: Cambridge University Press.

Johnson, G.

1978 Information Sources and the Development of Decision-Making Organizations. Pp. 87-112 in *Social Archaeology: Beyond Subsistence and Dating*, ed. C. Redman et al. New York: Academic Press.

1983 Organizational Structure and Scalar Stress. Pp. 389-421 in *Theory and Explanation in Archaeology: The Southampton Conference*, ed. C. Renfrew, M. Rowlands, and B. Segreaves. New York: Academic Press.

Jones, C.

1977 Research at Quirigua: The Site-Core Program. Paper presented at the 42nd Annual Meeting of the Society for American Archaeology, New Orleans.

1980 Tikal as a Trading Center: Why It Rose and Fell. Paper presented at the International Congress of Americanists, Vancouver.

1983 Monument 26, Quirigua, Guatemala. Pp. 118-128 in *Quirigua Reports*, Vol. 2, ed. E. Schortman and P. Urban. UMM 49. Philadelphia: University Museum.

Jones, C., W. Ashmore, and R. Sharer

1983 The Quirigua Project: 1977 Season. Pp. 1-38 in *Quirigua Reports*, Vol. 2, ed. E. Schortman and P. Urban. UMM 49. Philadelphia: The University Museum.

Jones, C., and R. Sharer

1980 Archaeological Investigations in the Site-Core of Quirigua. *Expedition* 23: 11-19.

1986 Archaeological Investigations in the Site Core of Quirigua, Guatemala. Pp. 27-34 in *The Southeast Maya Periphery*, ed. P. Urban and E. Schortman. Austin: University of Texas Press.

Keatinge, R.

1974 Chimu Rural Administrative Centers in the Moche Valley, Peru. *World Archaeology* 6: 66-82.

1975 Urban Settlement Systems and Rural Sustaining Communities: An Example from Chanchan's Hinterland. *Journal of Field Archaeology* 2: 215-227.

Keatinge, R., and K. Day

1973 Socio-Economic Organization of the Moche Valley, Peru, During the Chimu Occupation of Chanchan. *Journal of Anthropological Research* 29: 275-295.

Kelley, D.

1962 Glyphic Evidence for a Dynastic Sequence at Quirigua, Guatemala. *American Antiquity* 27: 323-335.

Kidder, A.

1935 *Notes on the Ruins of San Agustin Acasaguastlan, Guatemala*. Carnegie Contributions 3. Washington, D.C.: Carnegie Institution.

Kipp, R., and E. Schortman

1989 The Political Impact of Trade in Chiefdoms. *American Anthropologist* 91: 370-385.

Knutsson, K. E.

1969 Dichotomization and Integration: Aspects of Inter-Ethnic Relations in Southern Ethiopia. Pp. 86-100 in *Ethnic Groups and Boundaries: The Social Organization of Culture Difference*, ed. F. Barth. Boston: Little, Brown and Co.

Lamphear, J.

1970 The Kamba and the Northern Mrima Coast. Pp. 75-101 in *Pre-Colonial African Trade: Essays on Trade in Central and Eastern Africa before 1900*, ed. R. Gray and R. Birmingham. London: Oxford University Press.

Lange, F.
  1976   The Northern Central American Buffer: A Current Perspective. *Latin American Research Review* 11: 177-183.

Leventhal, R.
  1980   A Reexamination of Stela Caches at Copan: New Dates for Copador. Paper presented at the 45th Annual Meeting of the Society for American Archaeology, Philadelphia.
  1986   A Reexamination of Stela Caches at Copan: New Dates for Copador. Pp. 138-142 in *The Southeast Maya Periphery*, ed. P. Urban and E. Schortman. Austin: University of Texas Press.

Leventhal, R., A. Demarest, and G. Willey
  1987   The Cultural and Social Components of Copan. Pp. 179-205 in *Polities and Partitions: Human Boundaries and the Growth of Complex Societies*, ed. K. M. Trinkaus. Anthropological Research Papers, No. 37. Tempe: Arizona State University.

Lewenstein, S.
  1981   Mesoamerican Obsidian Blades: An Experimental Approach to Function. *Journal of Field Archaeology* 8: 175-188.

Longyear, J., III
  1944   *Archaeological Investigations in El Salvador*. Memoirs of the Peabody Museum, Vol. 9, No. 2. Cambridge, Mass.: Harvard University.
  1947   *Cultures and Peoples of the Southeastern Maya Frontier*. Theoretical Approaches to Problems, 3. Washington, D.C.: Carnegie Institution.
  1952   *Copan Ceramics: A Study of Southeastern Maya Pottery*. Publication No. 597. Washington, D.C.: Carnegie Institution.

Lothrop, S.
  1939   The Southeastern Frontier of the Maya. *American Anthropologist* 41: 42-54.

McBryde, W.
  1933   *Solola: A Guatemalan Town and Cakchiquel Market-Center*. Middle American Research Institute, Publication 5. New Orleans: Tulane University.

Marcus, J.
  1976   *Emblem and State in the Classic Maya Lowlands*. Washington, D.C.: Dumbarton Oaks.

Marquina, I.
  1964   *Arquitectura Prehispánica*. Memorias del INAH, Segunda Edición. Mexico City: Instituto Nacional de Antropología e Historia.

Michels, J.
  1979   *The Kaminaljuyu Chiefdom*. College Park: Pennsylvania State University Press.

Miles, S.
  1957   The Sixteenth-Century Pokom-Maya: A Documentary Analysis of Social Structure and Archaeological Setting. *Transactions of the American Philosophical Society* 47: 731-781.

Miller, A.
  1980   Art Historical Implication of Quirigua Sculpture. Paper presented at the 45th Annual Meeting of the Society for American Archaeology, Philadelphia.

Miracle, M.
  1960   Plateau Tonga Entrepreneurs in Historical Inter-Regional Trade. *Rhodes-Livingstone Journal* 26: 34-50.

Molloy, J., and W. Rathje
  1974   Sexploitation Among the Late Classic Maya. Pp. 431-444 in *Mesoamerican Archaeology: New Approaches*, ed. N. Hammond. Austin: University of Texas Press.

Montmollin, O. de
  1989   *The Archaeology of Political Structure*. Cambridge: Cambridge University Press.

Morley, S.

1920   *The Inscriptions at Copan*. Publication No. 219. Washington, D.C.: Carnegie Institution.

1935   *Guide Book to the Ruins of Quirigua*. Publication No. 437. Washington, D.C.: Carnegie Institution.

1937-38 *The Inscriptions of Peten*. Publication No. 437. Washington, D.C.: Carnegie Institution.

Morrill, R.

1974   *The Spatial Organization of Society*. North Scituate, Mass.: Duxbury Press.

Morris, C., and D. Thompson

1974   Huanco Viejo: An Inca Administrative Center. Pp. 191-208 in *The Rise and Fall of Civilizations*, ed. J. Sabloff and C. Lamberg-Karlovsky. Menlo Park, Cal.: Cummings Publications Co.

Nakamura, S.

1985   Informe de Actividades del Proyecto Arqueológico La Entrada: Abril a Junio, 1985. Ms. on file in the archives of the Proyecto Arqueológico La Entrada and Instituto Hondureno de Antropología e Historia, Tegucigalpa.

1987   Archaeological Investigations in the La Entrada Region, Honduras: Preliminary Results and Interregional Interaction. Pp. 129-141 in *Interaction on the Southeast Mesoamerican Frontier: Prehistoric and Historic Honduras and El Salvador*, ed. E. Robinson. Oxford: British Archaeological Reports.

1988   Reconocimiento Arqueológico en el Valle Inferior del Montagua, Izabal, Guatemala. Unpublished ms. in the archives of the Instituto Nacional de Antropología e Historia de Guatemala, Guatemala City.

Nakamura, S., K. Aoyama, and E. Oratsuji, eds.

1991   *Investigaciones Arqueológicas en la Región de La Entrade*. 3 vols. San Pedro Sula: Instituto Hondureño de Antropología e Historia, Servicio de Voluntarios Japoneses para la Cooperación con el Extranjero.

Nakamura, S., M. Kinoshita, M. Mikami, R. Takaichi, E. Sato, K. Ayoama, and M. Abe

1986   Informe de Actividades del Proyecto Arqueológico La Entrada, No. 5. Ms. on file in the archives of the Proyecto Arqueológico La Entrada and Instituto Hondureno de Antropología e Historia, Tegucigalpa.

Nowak, T.

1973a   The Lower Motagua Valley Survey Project: First Preliminary Report. Ms., Department of Anthropology, Harvard University.

1973b   Mercantilism and Colonization: A Study of Prehistoric Regional Community Patterning and Cultural Change in the Lower Motagua Valley, Guatemala. Ms., Peabody Museum, Harvard University.

1975   Prehistoric Settlement and Interaction Networks in the Lower Motagua Valley, Guatemala: A Regional Analysis. Ms., Peabody Museum, Harvard University.

Parsons, J.

1974   The Development of a Prehistoric Complex Society: A Regional Perspective for the Valley of Mexico. *Journal of Field Archaeology* 1: 81-108.

Patterson, T.

1971   Chavín: An Interpretation of Its Spread and Influence. Pp. 29-48 in *The Dumbarton Oaks Conference on Chavín*, ed. E. Benson. Washington, D.C.: Dumbarton Oaks.

Pollock, H.

1965   Architecture of the Maya Lowlands. Pp. 378-440 in *Handbook of Middle American Indians*, Vol. 2, ed. R. Wauchope and G. Willey. Austin: University of Texas Press.

Proskouriakoff, T.

1963   *An Album of Maya Architecture*. Norman: University of Oklahoma Press.

1973   The Hand-Grasping-Fish and Associated Glyphs on Classic Maya Monuments. Pp. 165-178 in *Mesoamerican Writing Systems*, ed. E. Benson. Washington, D.C.: Dumbarton Oaks.

Rapoport, A.

1982   *The Meaning of the Built Environment: A Nonverbal Communication Approach*. Beverly Hills, Cal.: Sage.

Rathje, W.
1972   Praise the Gods and Pass the Metates: A Hypothesis for the Development of Lowland Rainforest Civilizations in Mesoamerica. Pp. 365-392 in *Contemporary Archaeology: A Guide to Theory and Contributions*, ed. M. Leone. Carbondale: Southern Illinois University Press.

Reina, R., and R. Hill, II
1978   *The Traditional Pottery of Guatemala*. Austin: University of Texas Press.

Renfrew, C.
1975   Trade as Action at a Distance: Questions of Integration and Communication. Pp. 3-59 in *Ancient Civilization and Trade*, ed. J. Sabloff and C. Lamberg-Karlovsky. Albuquerque: University of New Mexico Press.
1982   Polity and Power: Interaction, Intensification, and Exploitation. Pp. 264-290 in *An Island Polity: The Archaeology of Exploitation in Melos*, ed. C. Renfrew and M. Wagstaff. Cambridge: Cambridge University Press.
1986   Introduction: Peer Polity Interaction and Socio-Political Change. Pp. 1-18 in *Peer Polity Interaction and Socio-Political Change*, ed C. Renfrew and J. Cherry. Cambridge: Cambridge University Press.

Renfrew, C., and J. Cherry, eds.
1986   *Peer Polity Interaction and Socio-Political Change*. Cambridge: Cambridge University Press.

Rice, P.
1987   Economic Change in the Lowland Maya Late Classic Period. Pp. 76-85 in *Specicalization, Exchange, and Complex Societies*, ed. E. Brumfiel and T. Earle. Cambridge: Cambridge University Press.

Ricketson, O.
1935   Maya Pottery Well from Quirigua Farm, Guatemala. *Maya Research* 2: 103-105.

Ricketson, O., and F. Blom
1940   Index of Ruins in the Maya Area. Ms., Peabody Museum, Harvard University.

Riese, B.
1986   Late Classic Relationship between Copan and Quirigua: Some Epigraphic Evidence. Pp. 94-101 in *The Southeast Maya Periphery*, ed. P. Urban and E. Schortman. Austin: University of Texas Press.

Roberts, A.
1970   Nyamwezi Trade. Pp. 39-74 in *Pre-Colonial African Trade: Essays on Trade in Central and Eastern Africa before 1900*, ed. R. Gray and R. Birmingham. London: Oxford University Press.

Robinson, E.
1980   Site Typology of the Prehistoric Settlement of the Eastern Alluvial Fans, Sula Valley, Honduras: Comparison to Maya Settlement Forms. Paper presented at the 45th Annual Meeting of the Society for American Archaeology, Philadelphia.

Royce, A.
1982   *Ethnic Identity: Strategies of Diversity*. Bloomington: Indiana University Press.

Ruz, L.
1965   Tombs and Funerary Practices in the Maya Lowlands. Pp. 441-461 in *Handbook of Middle American Indians*, Vol. 2, ed. R. Wauchope and G. Willey. Austin: University of Texas Press.

Sabloff, J.
1986   Interaction among Classic Maya Polities: A Preliminary Examination. Pp. 109-116 in *Peer Polity Interaction and Socio-Political Change*, ed. C. Renfrew and J. Cherry. Cambridge: Cambridge University Press.

Sabloff, J., and D. Freidel
1975   A Model of a Pre-Columbian Trading Center. Pp. 369-408 in *Ancient Civilization and Trade*, ed. J. Sabloff and C. Lamberg-Karlovsky. Albuquerque: University of New Mexico Press.

Sabloff, J., and W. Rathje, eds.

1975   *A Study of Changing Pre-Columbian Commercial Systems*. Monographs of the Peabody Museum, No. 3. Cambridge, Mass.: Harvard University.

Sanders, W.

1973   The Cultural Ecology of the Lowland Maya: A Reevaluation. Pp. 325-366 in *The Classic Maya Collapse*, ed. T. Culbert. Albuquerque: University of New Mexico Press.

1974   Chiefdom to State: Political Evolution at Kaminaljuyu, Guatemala. Pp. 97-121 in *Reconstructing Complex Societies*, ed. C. Moore. Supplement to *Bulletin of the American Schools of Oriental Research*, No. 20. Cambridge, Mass.: American Schools of Oriental Research.

1986   (ed.) *Excavaciones en el Area Urbana de Copán*, Vol. 1. Tegucigalpa: Secretaria de Cultura y Turismo, Instituto Hondureno de Antropología e Historia.

Sanders, W., J. Parsons, and R. Santley

1979   *The Basin of Mexico: Ecological Processes in the Evolution of a Civilization*. New York: Academic Press.

Sanders, W., and B. Price

1968   *Mesoamerica: Evolution of a Civilization*. New York: Random House.

Sanders, W., and D. Webster, comps.

1983   Reports on the Progress of the Proyecto Arqueológico Copán, Second Phase. Ms. on file in the archives of the Proyecto Arqueológico Copán and Instituto Hondureno de Antropología e Historia, Tegucigalpa.

Sapper, K.

1895   *Altinindianische Ansiedlungen in Guatemala und Chiapas*. Veröffentlichungen aus den Königlichen Museum zur Volkerkund, Bd. IV, Heft 1. Berlin: Kgl. Museum.

1897   *Das nördliche Mittel America nebst einem Ausflug nach dem Hochland von Anahuac*. Berlin: Brunswick.

Schele, L., and D. Freidel

1990   *A Forest of Kings*. New York: William Morrow.

Schele, L., and M. Miller

1986   *The Blood of Kings: Dynasty and Ritual in Maya Art*. Fort Worth, Tex.: Kimball Art Museum.

Schortman, E.

1976   The Application of Geographic Models to the Study of Prehistoric Quirigua and the Lower Motagua Valley, Izabal, Guatemala. Ms., Department of Anthropology, University of Pennsylvania.

1978   Models of Trade and Communication Derived from Pre-Colonial Africa. Ms., Department of Anthropology, University of Pennsylvania.

1984   Archaeological Investigations in the Lower Motagua Valley, Izabal, Guatemala: A Study in Monumental Site Function and Interaction. PhD dissertation, Department of Anthropology, University of Pennsylvania. University Microfilms, Ann Arbor.

1986   Maya/Non-Maya Interaction along the Classic Southeast Maya Periphery: The View from the Lower Motagua Valley. Pp. 114-137 in *The Southeast Maya Periphery*, ed. P. Urban and E. Schortman. Austin: University of Texas Press.

1989   Interregional Interaction in Prehistory: The Need for a New Perspective. *American Antiquity* 54: 52-65.

Schortman, E., and P. Urban

1983   (eds.) *Quirigua Reports*, Vol. 2. UMM 49. Philadelphia: University Museum.

1987   Modeling Interregional Interaction in Prehistory. Pp. 37-95 in *Advances in Archaeological Method and Theory*, Vol. 11, ed. M. Schiffer. Orlando, Fla.: Academic Press.

Sharer, R.

1978   Archaeology and History at Quirigua, Guatemala. *Journal of Field Archaeology* 5: 51-70.

1979   Classic Maya Elite Occupation in the Lower Motagua Valley, Guatemala: A Preliminary Formulation. Paper presented at the Ethnohistory Workshop, University of Pennsylvania.

1988   Quirigua as a Classic Maya Center. Pp. 31-65 in *The Southeast Classic Maya Zone*, ed. E. Boone and G. Willey. Washington, D.C.: Dumbarton Oaks.

1990   *Quirigua: A Classic Maya Center and Its Sculpture*. Durham: Carolina Academic Press.

Sharer, R., W. Ashmore, E. Schortman, P. Urban, J. Seidel, and D. Sedat

1983   The Quirigua Project: 1978 Season. Pp. 39-54 in *Quirigua Reports*, Vol. 2, ed. E. Schortman and P. Urban. UMM 49. Philadelphia: University Museum.

Sharer, R., C. Jones, W. Ashmore, and E. Schortman

1979   The Quirigua Project: 1976 Season. Pp. 45-64 in *Quirigua Reports*, Vol. 1, ed. W. Ashmore. UMM 37. Philadelphia: University Museum.

Sheets, P.

1972   A Model of Mesoamerican Obsidian Technology Based on Ceramic Workshop Debris in El Salvador. *Cerámica de Cultura Maya* 8: 17-33.

1974   Differential Change Among the Precolumbian Artifacts of Chalchuapa, El Salvador. PhD dissertation, Department of Anthropology, University of Pennsylvania.

1975   Behavioral Analysis and the Structure of a Prehistoric Industry. *Current Anthropology* 16: 369-391.

1978   The Artifacts. Pp. 2-107 in *The Prehistory of Chalchuapa, El Salvador*, Vol. 2, ed. R. Sharer. Philadelphia: University of Pennsylvania Press.

1983   Guatemalan Obsidian: A Preliminary Study of Sources and Quirigua Artifacts. Pp. 87-101 in *Quirigua Reports*, Vol. 2, ed. E. Schortman and P. Urban. UMM 49. Philadelphia: University Museum.

Shennan, S.

1978   Archaeological 'Cultures': An Empirical Investigation. Pp. 113-139 in *The Spatial Organization of Culture*, ed. I. Hodder. Pittsburgh: University of Pittsburgh Press.

1982   Ideology, Change, and the European Early Bronze Age. Pp. 155-161 in *Symbolic and Structural Archaeology*, ed. I. Hodder. Cambridge: Cambridge University Press.

1986   Interaction and Change in Third Millennium BC Western and Central Europe. Pp. 137-148 in *Peer Polity Interaction and Socio-Political Change*, ed. C. Renfrew and J. Cherry. Cambridge: Cambridge University Press.

Shibutani, T., and K. Kwan

1965   *Ethnic Stratification: A Comparative Approach*. New York: Macmillan Co.

Shook, E., and T. Proskouriakoff

1956   Settlement Patterns in Meso-America and the Sequence in the Guatemalan Highlands. Pp. 93-100 in *Prehistoric Settlement Patterns in the New World*, ed. G. Willey. Viking Fund Publications in Anthropology, No. 23. Washington, D.C.:

Smith, A.

1950   *Uaxactun, Guatemala, Excavations of 1931-1937*. Publication No. 588. Washington, D.C.: Carnegie Institution.

Smith, A., and A. Kidder

1943   *Explorations in the Motagua Valley, Guatemala*. Carnegie Contributions 8. Washington, D.C.: Carnegie Institution.

Smith, R., G. Willey, and J. Gifford

1960   The Type-Variety Concept as a Basis for the Analysis of Maya Pottery. *American Antiquity* 25: 330-340.

Southall, A.

1956   *Alur Society: A Study in Processes and Types of Domination*. Cambridge: Heffer.

Spencer, C.

1982   *The Cuicatlán de Cañada and Monte Albán: A Study of Primary State Formation*. New York: Academic Press.

Stark, B.

1985   Archaeological Identification of Pottery Production Locations: Ethnoarchaeological and Archaeological Data in Mesoamerica. Pp. 155-194 in *Decoding Prehistoric Ceramics*, ed. B. Nelson. Carbondale: Southern Illinois University Press.

Stephens, J.

1841   *Incidents of Travel in Central America, Chiapas, and Yucatan*. 2 vols. New York: Harper and Bros.

Stevens, R.

1964   The Soils of Middle America and Their Relations to the Indian Peoples and Cultures. Pp. 265-315 in *Handbook of Middle American Indians*, Vol. 1, ed. R. Wauchope and R. West. Austin: University of Texas Press.

Stone, D.

1941   *Archaeology of the North Coast of Honduras*. Memoirs of the Peabody Museum, Vol. 9, No. 1. Cambridge, Mass.: Harvard University.

1957   *The Archaeology of Central and Southern Honduras*. Papers of the Peabody Museum, Vol. 49, No. 3. Cambridge, Mass.: Harvard University.

1972   *Pre-Columbian Man Finds Central America: The Archaeological Bridge*. Cambridge, Mass.: Peabody Museum Press.

Streuver, S., and G. Houart

1972   An Analysis of the Hopewell Interaction Sphere. Pp. 47-79 in *Social Exchange and Interaction*, ed. E. Wilmsen. Anthropological Papers, No. 46. Ann Arbor: Museum of Anthropology, University of Michigan.

Strömsvik, G.

1936   The Ruins of the 'Comanche Farm' in the Motagua Valley. *Maya Research* 3: 107-109.

Tamayo, J., and R. West

1964   The Hydrography of Middle America. Pp. 84-121 in *Handbook of Middle American Indians*, Vol. I, ed. R. Wauchope and R. West. Austin: University of Texas Press.

Thompson, J.

1966   *The Rise and Fall of Maya Civilization*. Norman: University of Oklahoma Press.

1970   *Maya History and Religion*. Norman: University of Oklahoma Press.

Tosi, M.

1984   The Notion of Craft Specialization and Its Representation in the Archaeological Record of Early States in the Turanian Basin. Pp. 22-52 in *Marxist Perspectives in Archaeology*, ed. M. Spriggs. Cambridge: Cambridge Universtiy Press.

Trik, A.

1939   Temple XXII at Copan. Pp. 81-103 in *Carnegie Contributions* 5. Publication No. 509. Washington, D.C.: Carnegie Institution.

Urban, P.

1978   A Brief Summary of the Naco Valley Survey Project, 1978 Season. Ms., Department of Anthropology, University of Pennsylvania.

1980   Precolumbian Settlement in the Naco Valley, Honduras. Paper presented at the 45th Annual Meeting of the Society for American Archaeology, Philadelphia.

1986a   Precolumbian Settlement in the Naco Valley, Northwestern Honduras. Pp. 275-295 in *The Southeast Maya Periphery*, ed. P. Urban and E. Schortman. Austin: University of Texas Press.

1986b   Systems of Settlement in the Precolumbian Naco Valley, Northwestern Honduras. PhD dissertation, Department of Anthropology, University of Pennsylvania. University Microfilms, Ann Arbor.

Urban, P., and E. Schortman

1987   Copan and Its Neighbors: Patterns of Interaction Reflected in Classic Period Western Honduran Pottery. Pp. 341-395 in *Maya Ceramics: Papers from the 1985 Maya Ceramics Conference*, ed. P. Rice and R. Sharer. Oxford: British Archaeological Reports.

1988   The Southeast Zone Viewed from the East: Lower Motagua-Naco Valleys. Pp. 223-267 in *The Southeast Classic Maya Zone*, ed. E. Boone and G. Willey. Washington, D.C.: Dumbarton Oaks.

Urban, P., E. Schortman, L. Neff, C. Siders, V. Clark, L. True, M. Ausec, L. Aldrete, E. Bell, S. Buchmueller, L. Collins, J. Douglass, H. Henderson, K. Miller, N. Ross, and S. Yates

1990   The 1990 Season of the Naco Valley Archaeological Project: Preliminary Field Report. Unpublished ms. on file in the archives of the Instituto de Antropología e Historia, Tegucigalpa, and Kenyon College, Gambier.

Urban, P., E. Schortman, S. Smith, J. Miller, L. Neff, L. True, M. Ausec, S. Kane, H. Mahan, M. Dall, C. Eaton, D. Schafer, L. Collins, P. Reed, P. Whooley, N. Condon, and R. Goebels

1988   Sociopolitical Developments in Northwestern Honduras: The 1988 Season of the Naco Valley Archaeological Project. Unpublished ms. on file in the archives of the Instituto de Antropología e Historia, Tegucigalpa, and Kenyon College, Gambier.

Viel, R.

1983   Evolución de la Cerámica en Copán: Resultados Preliminares. Pp. 473-543 in *Introducción a la Arqueología de Copán, Honduras*, ed. C. Baudez. Tegucigalpa, SECTUR (Secretaria de Estado en el Despacho de Cultura y Turismo).

Vivo Escoto, J.

1964   Weather and Climate in Mexico and Central America. Pp. 187-215 in *Handbook of Middle American Indians*, Vol. 1, ed. R. Wauchope and R. West. Austin: University of Texas Press.

Vlcek, D., and W. Fash

1980   Survey in the Outlying Regions, and the Copan-Quirigua 'Connection'. Paper presented at the 45th Annual Meeting of the Society for American Archaeology, Philadelphia.

1986   Surveying in the Outlying Areas of the Copan Region, and the Copan-Quirigua 'Connection'. Pp. 102-113 in *The Southeast Maya Periphery*, ed. P. Urban and E. Schortman. Austin: University of Texas Press.

Vogt, E.

1961   Some Aspects of Zinacantan Settlement Patterns and Ceremonial Organization. *Estudios de Cultura Maya* 1: 131-146.

Voorhies, B.

1969   San Felipe, A Prehistoric Settlement in Eastern Guatemala. PhD dissertation, Department of Anthropology, Yale University.

Wagner, P.

1964   Natural Vegetation of Middle America. Pp. 216-264 in *Handbook of Middle American Indians*, Vol. 1, ed. R. Wauchope and R. West. Austin: University of Texas Press.

Walters, G.

1980   *The San Agustin Acasaguastlan Archaeological Project, 1979 Field Season*. Museum Brief 25. Columbia: Museum of Anthropology, University of Missouri.

Wauchope, R.

1938   *Modern Maya Houses: A Study of Their Archaeological Significance*. Publication No. 502. Washington, D.C.: Carnegie Institution.

Webster, D.

1975   Warfare and the Evolution of the State: A Reconsideration. *American Antiquity* 40: 464-470.

Webster, D. and N. Gonlin
   1988   Household Remains of the Humblest Maya. *Journal of Field Archaeology* 15: 169-190.

West, R.
   1964a   The Natural Regions of Middle America. Pp. 363-383 in *Handbook of Middle American Indians*, Vol. 1, ed. R. Wauchope and R. West. Austin: University of Texas Press.
   1964b   Surface Configuration and Associated Geology of Middle America. Pp. 33-83 in *Handbook of Middle American Indians*, Vol. 1, ed. R. Wauchope and R. West. Austin: University of Texas Press.

West, R., and J. Augelli
   1976   *Middle America: Its Lands and Peoples*, 2nd ed. Englewood Cliffs, N.J.: Prentice-Hall, Inc.

Whetten, N.
   1974   *Guatemala: The Land and the People*. Westport, Conn.: Greenwood Press.

Willey, G.
   1981   Maya Lowland Settlement Patterns: A Summary Review. Pp. 385-415 in *Lowland Maya Settlement Patterns*, ed. W. Ashmore. Albuquerque: University of New Mexico Press.

Willey, G., and R. Leventhal
   1979   Prehistoric Settlement at Copan. Pp. 75-102 in *Maya Archaeology and Ethnohistory*, ed. N. Hammond and G. Willey. Austin: University of Texas Press.

Willey, G., R. Sharer, R. Viel, A. Demarest, R. Leventhal, and E. Schortman
   1980   A Study of Ceramic Interaction in the Southeastern Maya Periphery. Paper presented at the 45th Annual Meeting of the Society for American Archaeology, Philadelphia.

Wisdom, C.
   1940   *The Chorti Indians of Guatemala*. Chicago: University of Chicago Press.

Wobst, H.
   1977   Stylistic Behavior and Information Exchange. Pp. 317-342 in *For the Director: Research Essays in Honor of James B. Griffin*, ed. C. Cleland. Anthropological Papers, No. 61. Ann Arbor: Museum of Anthropology, University of Michigan.

Wolters, O.
   1967   *Early Indonesian Commerce: A Study of the Origins of Srivijaya*. Ithaca: Cornell University Press.

Yde, J.
   1938   *An Archaeological Reconnaissance of Northwestern Honduras*. Middle American Research Institute, Publication 9. New Orleans: Tulane University.

Index